Vintage Base Ball

Vintage Base Ball

Recapturing the National Pastime

JAMES R. TOOTLE

McFarland & Company, Inc., Publishers
Jefferson, North Carolina, and London

LIBRARY OF CONGRESS CATALOGUING-IN-PUBLICATION DATA

Tootle, James R.
Vintage base ball : recapturing the national pastime / James R. Tootle.
 p.   cm.
Includes bibliographical references and index.

ISBN 978-0-7864-3599-9
softcover : 50# alkaline paper ∞

1. Baseball.
2. Baseball — History.
I. Title.
GV867.T56 2011   796.357 — dc22   2011014272

BRITISH LIBRARY CATALOGUING DATA ARE AVAILABLE

©2011 James R. Tootle. All rights reserved

No part of this book may be reproduced or transmitted in any form or by any means, electronic or mechanical, including photocopying or recording, or by any information storage and retrieval system, without permission in writing from the publisher.

Front cover: In 1859, the Knickerbockers and Excelsiors lined up for a photograph that is often published in books on baseball history. In 2004, the Champion City Reapers (Springfield, Ohio) and Ohio Village Muffins re-created the scene with each player assuming the pose of his counterpart in the famous photo. The 1859 photograph provides evidence that early clubs lined up together before the game, as is the custom in vintage base ball; the lemon peel design of the ball with a one-piece leather cover was common in the early days of base ball (from the author's collection)

Manufactured in the United States of America

McFarland & Company, Inc., Publishers
Box 611, Jefferson, North Carolina 28640
www.mcfarlandpub.com

Acknowledgments

Since vintage base ball has great visual interest, a book on the sport benefits from informative images that illustrate how the game is played and presented to the public. Joel Moore, a teammate for many years and a talented sports photographer, has provided a number of his excellent action photos to enhance this book. Another long-time teammate, Tracy Martin, was generous in sharing the wonders of his magnificent base ball memorabilia collection. A talented artist and designer, Lee Oldfield of InForm Studio worked her magic in combining the 1858 image of the Knickerbockers and Excelsiors with the re-creation of that photo by the Muffins and Champion City Reapers. Thanks also go to Andy Shuman (another long-time teammate) and museum professional Dr. Connie Bodner for allowing their writings to be quoted.

Sincere appreciation goes to my fellow members of the Ohio Historical Society's vintage base ball program. Over the past twenty seasons, they have been players, umpires, scorers, interpreters, and friends. As they read this book, many will hear echoes of the conversations we have had about the vintage game. Thanks also go to the members of other vintage clubs who are such wonderful colleagues in the "base ball fraternity." It has been a pleasure to visit their sites, host them at Ohio Village, and talk with many of them over the years about how we can make our great game even better. Some of their good ideas and best practices are presented as models for others to consider.

The book would not have been possible without the indispensible contributions of my wife, Barbie Tootle. In addition to providing endless encouragement, advice, inspiration, and support, she has contributed countless hours of her Hall of Fame–level professional talents to the tasks of organizing topics, taking and selecting photos, and editing the text. Since she has attended hundreds of matches, many in period dress as an interpreter, she knows the vintage game well and provided many insightful suggestions along the way. Because of her invaluable contributions, she is the unanimous MVP of the project.

Table of Contents

Acknowledgments v
Introduction: Stepping Back in Time 1

1. Origins and Growth of Vintage Base Ball 7
2. The Appeal of Vintage Base Ball 24
3. The Value of a Vintage Base Ball Program 37
4. Choosing an Era to Portray 49
5. The Gentlemen of the Clubs: Expectations and Responsibilities 65
6. Club Organization and Administration 75
7. Club Operation and Leadership 94
8. Women in Vintage Base Ball: A History of Involvement 111
9. Period Uniforms 124
10. Vintage Equipment 143
11. The Field of Play 157
12. The Umpire 174
13. The Scorer 188
14. Interpreters: Enhancing the Game Experience 201
15. Points of Play: Infield and Outfield 221
16. Points of Play: Catching and Pitching 233
17. Pitching: Slow or Swift? 249
18. Points of Play: Batting and Base Running 263
19. Base Running Interpretations: Leadoffs, Sliding, and Stealing 281
20. Game Day: Preparation and Pre-Game Activities 296
21. Game Day: Playing the Match 313
22. Game Day: The Ninth Inning and Post-Game Activities 326
23. Authenticity, Accuracy, Accommodations, and Opportunities 339
24. Vintage Base Ball's Relevance on the Contemporary Sports Landscape 358
25. Huzzah for the National Game! 375

Bibliography 379
Index 383

Introduction: Stepping Back in Time

As the game begins, the batter with a thick-handled wooden bat in hand steps up to the round, white iron disk that serves as home plate. He is wearing long, dark trousers, a wide belt, and a loose-fitting white shirt accented by a neat bow tie at the collar. The shield on the front of his uniform shirt is emblazoned with the gothic monogram of his base ball club. He straightens his cap and, after offering a word of greeting to the catcher and the umpire, takes his proper stance at the white chalk line that runs through home plate.

Off to the side of the plate, fifteen feet or so down the first-base line in foul territory, stands the umpire in a frock coat, woolen trousers, vest, necktie, and top hat. In the friendly spirit of the day, he has been chatting amiably with the spectators along the baseline prior to the start of the match. Now he peers intently at the home plate area, ready to render a decision if his impartial judgment is needed on a play.

Forty-five feet in front of the batter, the pitcher has taken his position at the pitcher's point, a white iron disk set flush with the ground. With an underhand motion, he pitches the handmade brown leather ball in an arc toward the plate. The batter swings at the pitch and strikes the ball sharply to the left side of the infield. The shortstop glides quickly to his right, and before the ball can go into left field, grabs it barehanded on the first bound off the grass. The batter, "showing his ginger," sprints a few steps down the first-base line before seeing he has been put out on a one-bound catch. With a gentlemanly tip of his cap to the shortstop, who has made an excellent play to retire him, the batter heads back to his club's bench.

Most of the ladies and gentlemen who have come to watch the match are supporters of the batter's club. Appreciative of good play by either side, they offer their applause and a hearty "huzzah" for the fine, manly catch made by the fielder. On this sunny day, the colorful banners of the two clubs fly in the summer breeze and a horse-drawn farm wagon rumbles along the dusty lane that borders the outfield as the second batter steps to the plate and sends a fly ball down the left-field line. The left fielder sprints to his right, judging the flight of the ball. He reaches out and catches the ball barehanded while on the run. Once again the spectators cheer the batter for hitting the ball well and the fielder for making a very fine play to put him out.

The third batter steps to the plate and strikes the ball solidly to the middle of the outfield. The center fielder reaches the ball on the second bound. The batter runs to first base and holds there with a safe hit as the center fielder tosses the ball to the second baseman.

With his teammate on first, the fourth batter approaches the plate and swings at the first pitch. He tips the ball, sending it sharply into foul territory behind the plate. The ball hits the ground once, but the catcher quickly reaches down and grabs it before it hits the ground for the second time. The batter is out, ending the inning. As the third out is recorded by the scorer sitting at a table near the playing field, the two nines change sides and quickly prepare for another fast-paced inning.

Is this an account of a mid-nineteenth-century base ball match? It could be. Actually, it describes the way base ball is played in the twenty-first century by teams on grassy playing fields across the country as they (and the spectators) enjoy an afternoon of vintage base ball.

Vintage base ball (two words in the nineteenth century) refers to the colorful and enjoyable sport of playing America's national pastime according to the rules of the game as they existed at an earlier period. Vintage base ball is a participant and spectator sport that is growing rapidly because of its wide appeal. It is a unique combination of an athletic contest, a colorfully packaged history class, a time-travel experience, an outdoor summer theatre performance, and a model of good sportsmanship. It is, most of all, baseball.

The sport of vintage base ball is a lively and vibrant version of the national pastime that combines re-creation and recreation. Blending historical authenticity, serious research, healthy exercise, gentlemanly behavior, and the pure fun of playing base ball, the vintage game has developed into a picturesque, educational, and enjoyable enterprise that has spread throughout North America in recent years.

Vintage base ball can be appreciated on several levels. Baseball scholars and knowledgeable fans value and enjoy the opportunity to learn more about the history of the game and the era in the nineteenth century when the sport emerged as the national pastime. Casual baseball fans are attracted to the vintage game because of its fast-paced action, historical charm, and emphasis on honorable, gentlemanly behavior.

Most of the teams playing vintage base ball today pursue the goal of re-creating the game as it was played around 1860, on the eve of the Civil War. Other programs have chosen to represent earlier or later time periods with considerable success. In addition to playing by the rules of the era being portrayed, vintage clubs also use the equipment of that time: wooden bats and leather base balls. Vintage teams wear uniforms that are modeled after those portrayed in photographs and illustrations from the period being presented on the field. Umpires, scorekeepers, and interpreters also wear period dress. Players on the many teams portraying the game as it was played around 1860 catch the ball barehanded since gloves did not come into common use until the 1870s and 1880s. Vintage teams representing the latter decades of the nineteenth century wear fielder's gloves, but they are quite small and seem primitive compared to modern gloves.

Those who are involved in the vintage game employ the language, manners, and customs of the time. One basic principle of vintage base ball representing the 1860 era is its emphasis on the good sportsmanship associated with the social norms of the nineteenth century. Like wearing old-style uniforms and using wooden bats, good manners and gentlemanly decorum set vintage base ball apart from the modern version of the national pastime. The result is an engaging and educational sporting event that enables participants and onlookers to step back in time and relive base ball as it was played in its early years.

This book will consider the origins, spread, and nature of the sport of vintage base ball, examining the reasons for its appeal and, along the way, highlighting several of the many excellent programs that have developed as the game has grown and matured. As vintage base ball seeks to recapture and preserve the history of the game's early years, it has forged an interesting identity and history of its own.

It is a goal of this book to also serve as a helpful "how-to" guide, describing the best practices of established programs while providing suggestions and strategies for creating and growing a successful program and effectively staging the games. Established vintage base ball programs have, helped new clubs form by sharing their knowledge, insights, and experiences. One aim of this book is to contribute to that collegial spirit. This book should be helpful to museums, historical societies, and communities starting a vintage base ball program; individuals who are interested in becoming involved in vintage base ball; and clubs already active in the sport that wish to improve and expand their programs with fresh approaches that have proven successful elsewhere.

Any discussion of vintage base ball naturally leads to questions about the early development of the game in America in the mid-nineteenth century. This book is not a history of the game of baseball. That fascinating and complex topic is addressed in a growing number of excellent scholarly works produced by the members of an outstanding community of baseball historians doing research on the game's early years. Nonetheless, since vintage base ball participants need to know what they are trying to re-create in a historically accurate manner when they take the field to play the game, this book does include material about the origins of the national pastime with attention to how the historical aspects of the game provide the structure for a vintage match. Attempting to play the game as it was played in 1845, 1860, 1869, 1886, or whatever era a given program chooses to portray requires knowledge of the state of the game at that time in its evolutionary development and a commitment to doing things as accurately and authentically as possible.

This relationship between researching the early history of base ball and putting the resulting findings into practice on the playing field is one of the interesting aspects of vintage base ball. New information and fresh interpretations are continually emerging regarding rules, customs, playing practices, and the contributions of the game's pioneers. Vintage base ball itself is an important part of these scholarly endeavors, serving as an impetus and inspiration for further research and as a living laboratory for testing theories on how the game was played. This interplay between what we know of the early history of base ball and the vintage game's attempts to replicate and present it to the public form another theme in this book.

Throughout the following pages, it is my hope that the reader will benefit from a sampling of the author's experiences as a participant in the sport of vintage base ball. It was my good fortune to discover vintage base ball in 1991 and to become affiliated with the Ohio Village Muffins program that is part of the Education and Interpretation Division of the Ohio Historical Society in my hometown of Columbus, Ohio. I have had the opportunity to take part in some 500 games since becoming a volunteer member of this excellent program. The home games of the Muffins are played at their "grounds" (as base ball fields were often called in former times), known as Muffin Meadow in the nineteenth-century setting of the Ohio Village at the Ohio Historical Center in Columbus. In the words of the Society, Ohio Village was designed to recreate the appearance of a "typical county-seat town in Ohio during the mid-nineteenth century, about the time of the Civil War" and, therefore, provides a historically authentic and aesthetically pleasing setting for vintage games.

The Muffins have played away games at the home fields of many vintage teams at museums and historical societies, as well as at a variety of city parks, village greens, farm meadows, lawns of historic homes, and modern baseball and softball diamonds around Ohio, the Midwest, and beyond. On special occasions, members of the Muffins have played in vintage base ball games at a variety of out-of-state venues, from New York to California and from Minnesota to Florida. All of these games, both at home and on the road, have provided the opportunity to play at some truly memorable venues; meet bright, energetic, dedicated men and women who are active in vintage base ball throughout the country; and gather ideas on how to continually improve the vintage game. As Yogi Berra famously said, "You can observe a lot just by watching." Having had the opportunity to travel widely in connection with vintage base ball and to observe many games in many different settings, another goal of this book will be to share not simply how the Muffins approach the game, but how our colleagues around the country operate fine programs.

Over the years, many people have asked me how I happened to become involved in vintage base ball. The story is one that I hope will encourage others to get involved and will remind the reader that opportunities to expand our horizons and enhance our lives can emerge unexpectedly. For me, a serendipitous occurrence developed into a long-term, life-enriching experience. It began with a book, one that I would strongly recommend to anyone thinking about becoming involved in the vintage game.

In March 1991, I had just finished reading Darryl Brock's masterful historical novel *If I Never Get Back*, a truly remarkable work. The book had been recommended to me by my wife, Barbie, an enthusiastic and knowledgeable fan of the national pastime who, among her many talents, keeps a neat and accurate box score whenever we go to any type of baseball game. She happened to discover *If I Never Get Back* first and, recognizing Brock's wonderful story-telling ability, his in-depth knowledge of his subject, and his original approach to covering an era in baseball history that neither one of us knew much about, insisted that I read it as soon as she was finished.

Brock's book proved to be everything she said and more. *If I Never Get Back* tells the story of a modern-day time-traveler, Sam Fowler, who, after striking his head in a fall, is transported back to the year 1869. Fowler awakens on the wooden platform of an old-time railroad station just as a nineteenth century-style train pulls up. A bit dazed and confused, Fowler steps aboard the train, which happens to be carrying the legendary Cincinnati Red Stockings Base Ball Club. In the novel's plot, Fowler joins the ball club's traveling party and thereby becomes an observer and a participant in that notable and celebrated season in 1869 in which the Red Stockings went undefeated against the best teams in the country while breaking historic ground as the first openly all-professional team. Brock's book immediately earned a place on my list of all-time favorites and, understandably, *If I Never Get Back* has enjoyed great popularity among vintage base ball participants throughout the country.

Soon after my total immersion in Brock's thoroughly researched tale of the 1869 Cincinnati Red Stockings, my own opportunity for time travel materialized. A colleague in the Colleges of the Arts and Sciences at Ohio State University stopped by my desk one day and alerted me to a newspaper ad announcing that the Ohio Historical Society was seeking players for its 1860s-era vintage base ball program, the Ohio Village Muffins. "Did you see this item?" she asked. "Since you like American history and baseball, you might look into this." A telephone call to the Historical Society led to an application and an interview to become a volunteer player on the team. The fact that a place on the team was to be gained through a written application and an interview rather than a try out suggested that this would be a baseball experience different from any I had encountered.

While it seemed like this would be a good fit for my interests, I had some reservations. Since I was into my forties when this prospect arose, I was concerned that the rough-and-tumble play of the 1869 Red Stockings and their opponents described in Brock's book, with games featuring fast pitching and a very combative environment, would be better suited to skilled players in their late teens and twenties with recent high school and college playing experience. My concerns were put to rest in my early conversations with OHS staff member Nick Herold, the team manager at that time. He informed me that the gentlemanly style of play favored by the amateur clubs in the 1850s and early 1860s, as replicated by the Muffin program at OHS, was much more player-friendly than the more aggressive style of play of an elite professional club, such as the Red Stockings of 1869. Herold assured me that I, along with a number of other new volunteers of various ages who had also responded to the ads OHS had placed in the local newspaper, would all be welcome additions to the program.

In April 1991, I took part in a series of training sessions held in the Historical Society's classrooms on rules and practices, followed by several outdoor field practices. The first order of business was attempting to master the art and science of catching a base ball barehanded. By early May, I was wearing the team uniform and playing in my first game according to nineteenth-century rules. By the end of that month, and after only a handful of games, I found myself traveling on my first extensive road trip with my new teammates to Cooperstown, New York, for a weekend of games with the local vintage team, the Leatherstocking Base Ball Club. The games were played on the grounds of the Farmers' Museum and at Doubleday Field, just down Main Street from the National Baseball Hall of Fame and Museum. Surveying my surroundings as I stepped upon the playing field wearing my nineteenth-century uniform, I concluded that I must have boarded that train with Sam Fowler and traveled back in time. It was very much as if Darryl Brock's novel had come to life.

Every vintage player has an interesting story of how he or she got involved in the sport. I am sharing my tale not because it is unique, but because it is so typical of many others. It includes the basic elements that help a vintage base ball program succeed — a museum or community organization that has a solid program (or an institution that is eager to build one); a well-organized, energetic, and welcoming staff member (Nick Herold at that time) who knows how to run a program and is committed to doing things the right way; and some well-placed publicity that calls attention to the program and attracts a wide variety of potential volunteers.

Every year since 1991, as the Muffins have worked their way through an ambitious annual schedule of 30 to 50 games, my teammates and I continue to find it extraordinary that we have the opportunity to take that step back in time and play 1860s-style base ball almost every weekend from April through October. We continually remind each other how lucky we are to take part of this exciting and growing version of the national pastime.

Playing vintage base ball has been great fun, as the game of base ball was most assuredly intended to be from the very beginning. If this book encourages and inspires others to become involved in vintage base ball and enables them to form and operate successful vintage base ball programs that provide the kind of enjoyable experiences that my wife and I have had over the years, it will have fulfilled its purpose.

A note to the reader on style and usage: Since the national pastime was usually spelled as "base ball," two words in the nineteenth century, and as "baseball," one word beginning around the turn of the twentieth century, that distinction will be preserved by using "base ball" when referring to the nineteenth-century game and to the vintage game that seeks to portray that era. "Baseball" (one word) will be used in reference to the modern game. As to recreation and re-creation, following the form of *Merriam-Webster's New Collegiate Dictionary*, the non-hyphenated word "recreation" will refer to the sport of base ball as a "refreshment of strength and spirits after work; a means of refreshment or diversion." The earliest clubs played for recreation and exercise 150 years ago as do the vintage teams of today. The hyphenated "re-creation" and "re-create" will be used to mean "to create again; especially to form anew in the imagination," something vintage players do when they take the field for a game representing the way the national pastime was played in the nineteenth century.

Welcome to the sport of vintage base ball. Have fun.

1
Origins and Growth of Vintage Base Ball

Definition of Vintage Base Ball

Each weekend from spring until fall, dozens of vintage base ball teams across the country take a giant step back in time by playing base ball as the games were conducted in the national pastime's early years. *The New Dickson Baseball Dictionary* defines "vintage base ball" as "presenting the game of baseball as it was played during its formative years in the mid-nineteenth century in accordance with the rules, equipment, uniforms, field specifications, customs, practices, language, and behavioral norms of the period." Dickson closes the definition by citing the synonyms historic baseball; period baseball. The language of the Dickson definition is based on the mission statement of the Vintage Base Ball Association (VBBA), an organization formed by thirteen clubs from five states in 1996 to "preserve, perpetuate, and promote base ball as it was played in its formative years in the nineteenth century and other historic eras."

Many individuals and historical organizations have found vintage base ball to be an enjoyable, engaging, and appealing activity. The sport of vintage base ball is growing rapidly in popularity and, in the past decade or so, has spread from coast to coast. According to the best available estimates, there are about 200 vintage base ball clubs operating in the United States and Canada, with more clubs being organized and taking the field every year.

The number of games or "matches" played by active teams varies considerably. Most clubs play in the neighborhood of ten to twelve games per season. The Ohio Village Muffins program, based at the Ohio Historical Society in Columbus, has a very active schedule, playing some fifty games a year. The several teams that comprise the Old Bethpage program on Long Island together play a combined total of about sixty games a year. At the other end of the spectrum, some teams may play only once or twice a season at an annual event, such as a Fourth of July celebration or a community festival.

The number of active players in a club varies, influenced by the number of years the team has been in existence and the number of games on its schedule. A club needs at least a dozen to fifteen dedicated players to be able to play an average schedule throughout a season. Although all the players may be committed to the program and enjoy playing, everyone on the roster will inevitably not be available for every game due to work or family obligations. And, of course, there are the occasional sprained ankles and pulled hamstrings that may render a player unable to take the field. Some of the larger established programs may have more than thirty active players. In addition to the players, most vintage base ball clubs have several non-playing members who attend games in period dress and serve as umpires, scorers,

Vintage base ball is a research-based endeavor that re-creates the game as it was played in its early years.

and interpreters. Some of the more established programs will have at least two or three and as many as eight to ten non-playing participants in period dress (men and women), adding greatly to the ambiance of the vintage match.

The Character of the Game

In its earliest days, the principal reasons to play base ball was recreation and exercise. The first rule in the 1845 Rules of the Knickerbocker Club of New York City states that "Members must strictly observe the time agreed upon for exercise, and be punctual in their attendance." Rule two (regarding the appointment of the umpire) begins with the phrase, "When assembled for exercise," and Rule six explains what to do, "If there should not be a sufficient number of members of the Club present at the time agreed upon to commence exercise." From these references, it is clear that the 1845 game is to be played for the purposes of exercise and recreation, and for most vintage teams this continues to be the case (although few players would choose exactly those words to describe the main reason they participate on weekends).

Make no mistake — vintage base ball teams play to win. Players typically give an all-out effort to enable their club to emerge victorious. This is "real" baseball in every way, requiring the unique blend of quick thinking and athletic skill that has made the game so attractive to players and spectators through the decades. Vintage players keep their heads in the game and compete to the best of their ability.

On offense, strikers try their best to hit the ball hard, get on base, move their teammates

In re-creating base ball as it was played in its early days, vintage clubs use bats and balls authentic to the period being represented on the field.

around the bases, and come around to score a run (also known as an "ace") for their club. When the ball is hit, the striker runs toward first base with the same effort (if perhaps not at the same speed) as any professional player. Runners move around the bases with intelligence and verve, always looking to take an additional base when possible. Since there are no base coaches, it is the runner's responsibility to keep the game situation in mind and make quick and smart decisions on his own as to whether to hold or advance.

On defense, infielders are on their toes with the pitch, ready to scoop up hard-hit grounders or handle rapidly spinning pop-ups without the benefit of gloves. Outfielders must judge fly balls correctly and make difficult barehanded catches of well-hit drives, sometimes while on the run. Catchers must be alert for the tricky backspin that characterizes many foul tips and swinging bunts. It is the role of the pitcher to deliver the ball "to the bat," but his job entails much more than lobbing the ball over the plate. Pitchers need to snare smashes up the middle, field dribblers in front of the plate, handle high pop flies, and cover first on ground balls to the right side of the infield. Players at every defensive position have opportunities to make some truly brilliant plays that would legitimately qualify as "web gems" if they were playing in the ESPN era. In fact, occasional barehanded plays by today's major leaguers almost always make the ESPN highlights.

But for all their skill and hustle and their interest in winning the game, vintage players seldom lose sight of the fact that in the era they are representing, base ball was played for recreation and exercise. Games are conducted in the manner of the day, according to a gentlemanly code of behavior and with a considerable amount of sportsmanship and good will among all participants. If ever a sport could be said to exemplify the noble spirit of the phrase "friendly competition," it would be mid-nineteenth century base ball and, therefore, vintage base ball.

Origins and Geographic Scope of the Vintage Game

The origins of the national pastime continue to be researched and debated by a host of knowledgeable and talented historians. Similarly, the origins of vintage base ball are difficult to assign to any exact day or place. Just as no one person "invented" the game of baseball, the emergence of vintage base ball is also a matter of evolution rather than invention.

The modern vintage base ball movement seems to have begun independently and at about the same time at two sites: the Ohio Historical Society's Ohio Village in Columbus and the Old Bethpage Village Restoration on Long Island, New York, around 1980–81. In 2005, Dean Thilgen of the St. Croix Base Ball Club of Stillwater, Minnesota, a widely respected citizen of the vintage base ball community for many years, researched the development of vintage base ball and compiled the following chronology of the early years of the sport:

1979 — A Civil War reenactment group visiting Old Bethpage Village plays a ball game.
1980 — Based on the success of the earlier reenactment game, more experimental ball games are played at Old Bethpage Village Restoration.
1981 — The Ohio Village Muffins program begins at Ohio Village, Columbus.
1983 — The Old Time Base Ball program formally begins at Old Bethpage Village Restoration with two 1860s teams, Hempstead Eurekas and Mineola Washingtons. They play approx. four games during the summer months for eight seasons.
1984–1985 — The Leatherstockings town ball club is established at Farmers' Museum, Cooperstown, New York.

Thilgen's report continues with 100 entries listing the founding dates for many clubs throughout the country and information on other events important to the development of vintage base ball.

The programs at Old Bethpage and Ohio Village developed into strong and viable entities over the years, but were generally unaware of each other's existence until the mid–1990s. Gradually, these two groups, along with the Cooperstown program, gained a degree of notoriety through newspaper stories, occasional spots on radio and television news programs, traveling to play games beyond their home grounds, and word of mouth. Eventually, other museums and historical societies learned about the existence of vintage base ball and took steps to form their own teams.

While the pioneering programs in Ohio and New York have been successful and important cornerstones of the sport of vintage base ball, their good work since the early 1980s does not represent the first time attempts have been made to re-create the early days of the national pastime. There are documented examples of earlier, albeit singular efforts to re-create base ball as it was played in an earlier time.

1959: Amherst, Massachusetts

In 2006, baseball historian John Thorn, widely respected author and researcher who is continually sharing his discoveries, alerted colleagues to a *New York Times* article of May

16, 1959, describing a vintage game planned as part of the festivities marking the centennial of the first college game, played July 1, 1859, between Amherst and Williams. "Tomorrow will be dedicated to the past," wrote reporter Howard M. Tuckner. "Two teams of thirteen players each, elected by the students of each school, will meet at Amherst in box hats, black trousers, striped dress shirts and suspenders for a limited replay of the first college baseball game in history." The centennial game was played by Massachusetts Rules, the rules used in the original 1859 contest played at Pittsfield, Massachusetts, which was won by Williams, 73–32.

History was repeated on May 3, 2009, when the varsity teams from Williams and Amherst met again in Pittsfield to mark the sesquicentennial of the first college game, an event that was nationally televised by ESPN. Prior to the modern game between Amherst and Williams, alumni from the two institutions, dressed in period shirts and hats, played a match using the original 1859 rules. According to an announcement of the vintage game on the Amherst College website, "As with the first game in 1859, there will be a chess tournament played simultaneously on the sidelines!"

1939: Cooperstown, New York

At the dedication of the National Baseball Hall of Fame and Museum in Cooperstown, New York, two games were held that could be described as vintage matches. Under the heading "The Cavalcade of Baseball," the printed program of the day lists the following events held at Doubleday Field, beginning at 3:00 P.M. on June 12, 1939:

A game of Town Ball as played 100 years ago
 Enacted by the boys of Cooperstown High School
 Directed by Lester G. Bursey
A game of the eighteen fifties between the first two adult teams to wear regular uniforms......"
The Knickerbockers and Excelsiors"
 Enacted by U.S. Army soldiers of the 16th
 Infantry from Fort Jay, Governor's Island, New York\
 Directed by Walter B. Brown, Director of Fort Jay Y.M.C.A.

Following the two vintage games, the celebration continued with a big league all-star game (American League vs. National League) billed as follows:

Modern Day Baseball. Played by stars from the 16 teams of the Major Leagues
 Managers — Honus Wagner and Eddie Collins

The planners of the dedicatory proceedings certainly had a good sense of history and an interest in educating the audience by staging not one, but two games in which teams "enacted" the game as it was played according to the rules of former times.

The year 1939 was chosen for the opening of the Baseball Hall of Fame because it was the centennial of the year Abner Doubleday allegedly "invented" baseball in Cooperstown. Those involved in vintage base ball need to know that the "Doubleday myth" (still widely accepted by many current baseball fans) is now generally considered by baseball historians to have no basis in fact. The actual beginnings of baseball are complicated and open to discussion but are often traced to the set of rules written and adopted by the Knickerbocker Base Ball Club of Manhattan in 1845. While it is generally accepted that Doubleday had no role in the creation of baseball, historians continue to research the contributions of Alexander Cartwright (the person often credited with drawing up the "Knickerbocker

Rules") and other pioneering members of the Knickerbockers, along with the histories of other stick-and-ball games, in an ongoing effort to arrive at an accurate understanding of how baseball began.

1887: Elmira, New York

Other examples of vintage base ball predate the Cooperstown event in 1939. A very early vintage game was played in the time of Grover Cleveland's first administration, more than fifty years before the Baseball Hall of Fame dedication. An website devoted to providing information about the life and career of Mark Twain (www.twainquotes.com) includes a humorous but revealing article from the *Elmira Daily Advertiser* of July 2, 1887, which gives an account of this event:

> A number of distinguished people will be on hand to-day to see the old-fashioned game of base ball at which Mark Twain will be one of the umpires, between the Alerts and Unions. These two clubs were the leaders in the sport in southern New York twenty one years ago, and were reorganized for this one game. The players are all prominent business and professional men. Mark Twain, who is at his summer home at Quarry Farm, consented to be one of the umpires on condition that a chair, a fan, an umbrella and a pitcher of ice water be furnished him. Colonel D. C. Robinson assured him that they would be supplied and the engagement was made.

The humorous tone of Twain's "demands" is in keeping with the light-hearted nature of the contest, with entertainment and good fun emphasized over competitiveness and winning. "The game to-day will begin at 4 P.M., and five innings only will be played. Permissions will be given the players to carry umbrellas into the field for protection from the sun if they see fit. The rumor that messenger boys will be employed to carry the ball is emphatically denied. Tricycles will also be barred out." Admission was to be charged "for gentlemen" at the rate of twenty-five cents for "reserved seats in the lower part of the grand stand" and "in the up-part ten cents." Special rules for the match included the provision that "Any boy who 'Haw-haws' at a muff by his parent may be disciplined behind the grand stand, but not in it." Another rule stated that "players will not be allowed to receive flowers while running the bases."

As it turned out, Twain did not umpire the game. The *Washington Post* of July 3, 1887, reports that the humorist excused himself from officiating on the grounds that "he could not make a martyr of himself, not withstanding the fact that he would be glad to perish in a good cause, and took a seat with Mr. Beecher in the grandstand." (Reverend Thomas K. Beecher of the Park Church in Elmira was the brother of Harriet Beecher Stowe and Henry Ward Beecher; he was also invited to serve as an umpire but declined.) The *Post* reported Twain "used a big fan in a vigorous manner and said he would encourage the players with his presence, but he must refuse to go out in the sun."

While this 1887 game was staged in a humorous way, it does, in fact, seem to have been a true vintage game in that the participants re-created the way base ball had been played by local clubs in earlier days. An account of the match appeared in the February 1981 issue of the *Mark Twain Society Bulletin*, "paraphrased with quotes" from the July 3, 1887, edition of the *Elmira Sunday Telegram*:

> The rules followed were the rules of 1866 when the two teams were first organized right after the Civil War. "Base ball was then in its infancy, so to speak, and only the fundamental principles are now displayed. Pitched balls were the rule, bound catches were considered out, there was no calling of strikes and balls, and all the modern features of the game were unknown." The Unions beat the Alerts in the old timer's contest 23 to 10.

The term "pitched balls" refers to the pitcher delivering the ball with an underhand motion, as was specified by the old rules. Overhand throwing by the pitcher was the established norm by 1887. The mention of "bound catches" refers to the fact that, according to the rules of the early 1860s, any fair or foul ball that was caught on the fly or the first bound was an out. Despite the informality and fun that was the spirit of the day in Elmira, this contest seems to have been one that could be defined as a vintage game — two clubs met, a score was kept, and the match was played by a set of rules of a bygone era.

Post–Civil War: A Sampling of Vintage Games Around the Country

The idea of playing a base ball game according to the rules of an earlier time seems to have occurred to a number of people in various locales. In "The Jolly Old Knickerbockers, 1845–1856," a chapter in *Baseball's First Inning,* William Ryczek discusses several early members of the Knickerbocker Base Ball Club, including James Whyte Davis, who, having joined in 1850, "played with the Knicks into the mid–1860s and took an active part in the club's affairs for a long time after that." Ryczek then cites an early example of what appears to have been a vintage game. "In 1880, the club commemorated the thirtieth anniversary of his first match and Davis and a number of his old mates took part in an old-time game."

"The Old Settlers' Jubilee," a lengthy article in the *Mauston Star* of June 28, 1888, lists the events comprising a festival held in that Wisconsin community to celebrate its pioneer heritage. Along with a foot race for men over fifty years old, a "scrub race" for old horses, the building of a log cabin, picnics, dances, story telling by older citizens, and other activities highlighting the town's early days, the *Star* reported, "There was an old-fashioned base ball game, but only for practice as only one side was on the ground." In the 1886 edition of *The Chronicles of Cooperstown* by S.M. Shaw, there is an account of a vintage game played in 1877 attended by a substantial crowd. "A famous game of base ball was played here in August — Judge Sturgis heading the 'Reds' and Judge Edick the 'Blues'—16 on a side. The victory was with the 'Blues.' It called together a large concourse of people."

In his article, "A Reconstruction of Philadelphia Town Ball," in *Base Ball: A Journal of the Early Game*, Richard Hershberger observes that after the Civil War, the term "old-fashioned base ball" was used to describe a number of "local variants" of base ball played before the war. Therefore, while the 1880 commemorative game for James Whyte Davis was probably played by the Knickerbocker Rules of 1850, the "old fashioned" games held in Cooperstown, New York, in 1877 and Mauston, Wisconsin, in 1888 may have been conducted according to even earlier rules in which the field was laid out in a rectangle rather than a diamond, the bases were stakes, and runners were put out by being hit with a thrown ball.

The Reintroduction of Vintage Base Ball

While the programs at Bethpage and Ohio Village did not "invent" the idea of playing vintage base ball, both reintroduced it at about the same time and then developed the concept by creating successful programs that have become established institutions. One important difference from the vintage games of 1959, 1939, and the nineteenth-century examples is that rather than putting together two teams to play a single game for a special event, these two ground-breaking programs established permanent teams that played a full schedule of games throughout the season, year after year. These stable, enduring teams became models and the inspiration for many of the vintage base ball programs that have followed.

The Ohio Historical Society

Vickie Tabor Branson, a museum professional at the Ohio Historical Society, was a founding force for the program in Columbus and served as the first manager of the Ohio Village Muffins, the men's team that began playing at Ohio Village in the spring of 1981. Recalling the series of events that led to vintage base ball at the Ohio Historical Society, she credits Dr. Amos Loveday, the chief curator of the Society at the time, for his key role in the decision to begin playing nineteenth-century base ball at the Village.

"It was Amos's idea. At that point ... I was at the Village ... working in the school house, and during the winter ... the staff that was there full-time were given research projects to do. One of the two projects I was given that year ... was to do research for baseball." The vintage base ball program came about "because Amos said we had all kinds of things being interpreted at the Village, but we had no recreation activities. So there was nothing people could look at. [They could say] we see the daily work life, we see the daily [tasks of] how you cook and clean, but there were no recreation activities being shown." In the first year, games were played by the shopkeepers, artisans, and other museum staff members, along with "volunteers who were already active in the Village. They were invited to join the team. Many of them were great contributors of equipment and expertise."

The new team took on the whimsical name of the Muffins as a result of Branson coming across the term in her research on nineteenth-century base ball. A muffin, for those unfamiliar with the term, is defined in *The New Dickson Baseball Dictionary* as an "unskilled or ineffective player; the equivalent of golf's 'duffer.'" The phrase comes from the nineteenth-century custom of calling a misplay a muff; a "muffin" being a player who frequently "muffs" the ball. "I loved that the slang of sport started even in the beginning," Branson recalled. "I had to convince others that this would be a good way to introduce the slang of the time and sport to visitors. Surprisingly, I was never beaten up by the players for naming them 'Muffins.' They all took it with a wonderful sense of humor."

Uniforms, based on the Currier and Ives 1866 illustration *The American National Game of Base Ball*, were acquired for the players. Branson reports that the Ohio Village team began playing a modest schedule of games in 1981. "For the early years [when there were no other organized vintage teams to play], we looked for groups already playing baseball or softball or historical groups like other historical sites or outdoor dramas." As for uniformed opponents in those early years, "the only people that we costumed were the historical sites like Slate Run Farm [a living history 1880-era farm in the Columbus Metro Parks system], who played in their historic costumes or the cast of *Tecumseh!* [an outdoor drama in Chillicothe, Ohio], who played as pioneers and American Indians. The teams that played us that were already-formed baseball teams played in their own uniforms. Though not ideal, it allowed for interpretation about how uniforms have changed through the years."

In the decade of the 1990s, the program continued to grow, attracting more volunteer participants as players, umpires, scorekeepers, and interpreters. The Muffins were able to build and maintain a roster of thirty to forty active players. This enabled the program to present an exhibition of vintage base ball in the form of a club match (intra-squad game) at Ohio Village on special occasions when there was a good crowd on hand, such as the

Uniforms reminiscent of the nineteenth century help spectators and players such as Duane Koons of the Ohio Village Muffins (Columbus) travel back in time to the era of gentlemanly play.

Fourth of July, or to put two separate teams on the field on the same day — one nine playing at a community event out of town and another nine playing a home game with another vintage team at Ohio Village. The training program for new members was expanded into a series of winter meetings for both new and veteran players.

The Muffins often helped new programs get started by traveling to various museum sites for games during the playing season. In the offseason, the Muffins sent representatives (typically the team manager, an umpire, scorekeeper, and several veteran players) around the state and beyond to share their knowledge and experience with local museum professionals and prospective volunteers.

Local, regional, and national publicity helped raise the awareness of vintage base ball. The Muffins were featured in an article in *Sports Illustrated* in 1987, on the front page of *The Wall Street Journal* in 1992, in a cover story in the Southwest Airlines *Spirit* magazine in 1993, and again in *Sports Illustrated* in 1994.

From 1991 through 2006, the Muffin program produced a regular newsletter, *The Muffin Tin*, which was edited and published by dedicated volunteers John and Mardi Wells. Since it contained informative articles and "how-to" advice that would benefit a wider audience, it was mailed to other programs throughout the vintage base ball community. Since 2006, communications have been via website, e-mail, and other social media. In 1992, Ohio Village was the site of the first Ohio Cup tournament, involving four teams. This event has grown into the annual Ohio Cup Vintage Base Ball Festival, typically involving 25 to 30 clubs from six or seven states.

A ground-breaking achievement for the Ohio Historical Society program was the establishment of the first women's vintage base ball club, the Diamonds, in 1994. Also in the mid–1990s, a Muffins/Diamonds Advisory Board was created to provide a means of regular communication between the OHS administration and the many volunteers in the vintage base ball program. A total of eight representatives are elected from the ranks of the volunteers to meet on a monthly basis with the museum administrator in charge of the program to discuss scheduling, recruiting, event planning, travel, training, finances, uniforms, historical standards, and similar issues so that management of the program is done in a cooperative and coordinated manner, enabling the club to continue to operate on a strong footing.

Old Bethpage Village Restoration

Although the Old Bethpage Village Restoration is located just off the busy Long Island Expressway, about 35 miles from Times Square, participants and spectators can step back into the quieter atmosphere of the mid-nineteenth century. The OBVR website states that

> from spring through December, Old Bethpage recreates the atmosphere of a pre–Civil War Long Island Village, illustrating agricultural, domestic and commercial activities through the actual practice of crafts and skills. On some 200 acres of rolling hills, more than 55 historic buildings—all original structures saved from destruction and moved to the site—provide the setting for costumed interpreters to portray farmers, teachers, storekeepers, blacksmiths, civic leaders, and the others who made up a community of the mid–1800s.

The vintage base ball program is one of the main attractions at Old Bethpage. In the Winter 2005 issue of *The Base Ball Player's Chronicle: A Quarterly Publication of the Vintage Base Ball Association*, Tom Fesolowich, a veteran member of the program, provided a thoughtful look at the beginning of vintage base ball on Long Island. Fesolowich attributed much of the program's success to Ken Balcom, who served as "director of the Old Bethpage Village for 32 years until his retirement this year. Ken along with a handful of others are responsible for starting vintage base ball at Old Bethpage Village in 1979 with a Civil War reenactment game played between the soldiers. The next year vintage base ball became a staple at the village with the formation of two teams, the Hempstead Eurekas and the Mineola Washingtons." Fesolowich praises Balcom as being "responsible for bringing Vintage Base Ball to the forefront of American Society, starting with numerous newspaper articles to a small article in *American Way* magazine to the *Smithsonian Magazine* and more recently the *Conan O'Brien Show* and *This Week in Baseball*, just to name a few." The late Al "Old Dutch" Dieckmann, an active player, a fine and thorough researcher, and a person of great vision, was another guiding spirit behind the growth of vintage base ball on Long Island.

Drawing on local history, the teams at Old Bethpage adopted the names and uniform styles of actual teams that played in the Long Island area in the nineteenth century. Four teams played in a league under 1864 rules (underhand pitching): the Knickerbockers, Mineola Washingtons, Hempstead Eurekas, and Brooklyn Excelsiors. Four other teams were in another league that is governed by 1887 rules (overhand pitching): the Glenhead Zig Zags, Hicksville Ozones, Bellmore Seminoles and the Seacliff Idlewilds. The teams typically play their games on their extraordinarily scenic playing fields in the midst of quaint nineteenth-century buildings, rail fences, and farm fields bordered by wooded areas. The grounds of the farm provide a superb setting for vintage base ball. The OBVR website points out that the pioneering Long Island-based program "has its own traveling squad, the Mutuals, which represent Bethpage at various tournaments and whenever other traveling teams come to town."

While the Old Bethpage program enjoys a quiet agrarian setting for its games, its proximity to New York City provides excellent media access and visibility, and that exposure has increased public awareness of vintage base ball. As Fesolowich observes, the *Smithsonian* cover story [October 1998] "is often pointed to by ballists as the reason they started in vintage base ball." In 2004, Old Bethpage hosted a visit by television personality Conan O'Brien, whose comedic experiences playing nineteenth-century base ball were prominently featured in a lengthy segment on his *Late Night with Conan O'Brien* program on NBC. "A rising tide lifts all the boats" certainly applies to the growth and increasing popularity of vintage base ball. This large-market media coverage of New York-area teams — including the Gothams, who play their games in Central Park — benefits programs in all regions of the country.

The Vintage Base Ball Association

From its beginnings at the Ohio Historical Society and Old Bethpage Village Restoration, vintage base ball has spread. Teams representing different time periods and styles of play were formed along the East Coast and throughout the Midwest. Soon clubs had formed across the country, including Colorado, Florida, and California. However, communication among these widely scattered programs was informal and irregular.

Throughout the early 1990s, the Ohio Historical Society's program was holding annual winter meetings to educate and prepare participants to take the field in the spring. These meetings included sessions on all phases of playing vintage base ball and presenting the game to the public. In addition to discussions of base ball history, presentations were made by museum professionals and volunteers on the social, economic, and political issues of the time as well as the customs and manners of the 1860s. The material covered in these meetings was reported though the club newsletter and sent to other known clubs.

When the existence of these helpful and informative meetings became known throughout the vintage base ball community, staff members from other museums, especially those interested in starting vintage base ball teams, asked about sending representatives to attend the classroom sessions to learn more about organizing and operating a successful program. The Ohio Historical Society welcomed these visitors and provided information, assistance, and encouragement to all who were interested in vintage base ball. In addition to those who attended some of the sessions, others began calling and writing for information on the organization and operation of vintage teams.

As a result, the vintage base ball program at the Ohio Historical Society began functioning as an informal clearinghouse for the growing vintage base ball community. Brochures and kits were prepared to help new programs get started, and the winter meetings became a place where information was exchanged and program leaders got acquainted. The steady stream of inquiries coming into the OHS offices along with the growing discussion on the history and rules of the early game indicated a need for a type of umbrella organization that would assume some of the functions that had fallen, de facto, to the vintage base ball program at the Ohio Historical Society.

Accordingly, OHS invited all interested parties to attend a meeting in 1995 for the purpose of discussing the creation of an association of all clubs playing various versions of nineteenth century base ball. Doug Smith, a talented and knowledgeable staff member of the Ohio Historical Society and team manger for the Muffins and Diamonds program, was chosen to preside over the organizational phase. Smith, well known in the vintage base ball community for the assistance and encouragement he had given to many programs, was the right person in the right spot to organize what became known as the Vintage Base Ball Association.

During the 1995 vintage base ball season, work progressed on a mission statement and constitution. Another meeting of interested parties was held over Labor Day weekend when, as usual, a large number of clubs converged on Ohio Village in Columbus to participate in the Ohio Cup Vintage Base Ball Festival. This setting provided a good opportunity to discuss progress on the mission statement. The work of drafting a constitution continued as club leaders agreed to meet again at OHS in Columbus during the coming off season.

Representatives from all clubs known to exist at that time were invited to meet at the Ohio Historical Society in Columbus in the winter of 1996 for the purpose of establishing a formal association of vintage clubs. The organizational meeting of delegates from thirteen vintage clubs was held on February 11, 1996, and resulted in the formation of an association to help new teams get started and enable members to share information and research on rules, customs, uniforms, and equipment.

In selecting a name for the organization, the term "vintage" was agreed upon as the best descriptor of the practice of playing by earlier rules and customs (rather than "historic" base ball or "old-time" base ball). The term "national" was discussed as part of the organization's title, but was rejected on the grounds that the existence of the Woodstock Actives (a club in southern Ontario) and the possible formation of other clubs outside of the United States made "national" too narrow and restrictive. It was agreed that the nineteenth-century spelling of "base ball" as two words should be retained. After considerable discussion, the Vintage Base Ball Association (VBBA) was approved as the organization's official name.

The Muffins and most other clubs involved in founding the VBBA played according to the rules used around 1860. However, the VBBA decided to open membership to all teams that were engaged in portraying baseball as it was played in any historic period. This included teams playing town ball, the Massachusetts game, or any other variant of base ball that preceded the creation of the original Knickerbocker Rules in 1845 to those playing according to the rules of the early twentieth century. The most modern team at that time was an Ohio-based club known as the 1922 Giants. After some discussion, it was determined that while late nineteenth-century and early twentieth-century teams would be playing a far different game than those who portrayed the 1860 era, the VBBA would not exclude any group that was interested in the history of the national pastime. The guiding principle was to be welcoming and inclusive to all who are portraying various periods of the history of the national pastime. The existence of this one short-lived twentieth-century team should not cloud the fact that the great majority of the founding members of the VBBA played according to rules and customs of the 1860 era. In opening membership to clubs of later eras, the stipulation was made that these clubs should agree to conduct their interactions with the other member clubs in the gentlemanly, sportsmanlike manner that was more characteristic of the earlier eras. These terms were agreeable to all parties.

At this organizational meeting conducted by interim president Doug Smith, officers were chosen. John Husman, president of the Great Black Swamp Frogs Base Ball Club based in the Toledo suburb of Sylvania, Ohio, was the first president elected under the terms of the new VBBA constitution. A respected player, organizer, researcher, and historian of the early game, Husman was an excellent choice to get the new organization up and running.

When he took the podium to assume his new role, Husman astutely remarked how much the process of creating the VBBA paralleled the process by which the National Association of Base Ball Players was established in 1857. In both cases, clubs sensed that some consistency in rules and practices was needed. In both cases, a pioneering club, the Knickerbockers in 1857 and the Muffins in 1996, had taken the initiative to call a general meeting for the purpose of creating an organization to bring about better communication and understanding between all clubs. And in both cases many of the leading clubs of the day came together at a special meeting and in a very cooperative and congenial spirit successfully established a framework for further interaction and the playing of matches.

The essence and character of the game is spelled out in the mission of statement of the Vintage Base Ball Association.

Vintage Base Ball Association Mission Statement

The mission and purpose of the Vintage Base Ball Association shall be to preserve, perpetuate, and promote the game of base ball as it was played during its formative years in the mid-nineteenth century and other historic eras. This worthy objective shall be accomplished by the following activities and endeavors:

- Presenting the game of base ball as it was actually played in accordance with the rules, equipment, uniforms, field specifications, customs, practices, language, and behavioral norms of the period.
- Supporting the formation and strengthening of vintage base ball clubs by sharing vintage base ball information, setting standards of historical accuracy and participation, and providing a means to recognize and communicate with other vintage base ball clubs.
- Encouraging research and disseminating information in order to recreate the game in keeping with the highest levels of accuracy and authenticity.
- Educating the public regarding the character, history, and growth of the game with attention to the historical context in which it originated and developed.
- In order to achieve its goals and sustain the traditions and values which it seeks to honor and emulate, the Association and all of its members will conduct all matches, meetings, and other activities — both on and off the field — according to the highest standards of sportsmanship, gentlemanly behavior, courtesy, and respect for others which characterized the Knickerbockers Base Ball Club, established, September 23, 1845.

The principled language of the VBBA mission statement does not represent a departure, but rather a continuation, of the foundation on which the sport had prospered and grown to that time. It reflects the way people had been relating to each other and the manner in which games were being conducted throughout the vintage base ball community. Three important themes run through the carefully chosen wording of the mission statement: a commitment to historical authenticity; the formal establishment of a friendly, congenial, and cooperative atmosphere among vintage clubs and players; and a strong emphasis on good sportsmanship and gentlemanly behavior. All teams, but especially those closely associated with a museum or historical society, would also find support in the mission statement to emphasize education and historical interpretation instead of the overly competitive atmosphere and the "win at all costs" mentality that has come to pervade many modern baseball and softball leagues.

As a member of the committees that drafted the mission statement and the constitution, I can report that setting high standards for the physical components of the game (appropriate uniforms and equipment) and establishing high standards for sportsmanship (in keeping with the norms of the 1860 era) were what the founders had in mind at the organizational meetings of the VBBA in 1995 and 1996 when crafting these documents.

Over the years, the worthy goal of playing by the rules of the 1860 period has proven more difficult than it first appeared. The rules of 1860 and other nineteenth-century vintage base ball eras were few in number, brief in wording, and sometimes lacking in clarity. Time has shown that the rules can be interpreted differently by vintage programs in different parts of the country, depending on such variables as safety, skill level of the players, interpretations favored by neighboring programs, local history, the mission and goals of the sponsoring museum, and other factors. The VBBA facilitates communication on such matters and encourages research. But, recognizing the game was played differently by the various clubs that were active in the 1860s, the VBBA does not require every program to play the game exactly the same way. The VBBA holds an annual meeting, generally in the offseason. The conference attracts people intending to form a program while also reuniting. Speakers, workshops, and vendor displays advance the knowledge of the game. Points of play are discussed, best practices shared, and even some matches are scheduled for the coming season. In its programs and activities, the conference reflects the spirit of the early days of the game.

The most current listing of active clubs can be found on the website of the Vintage Base Ball Association at www.vbba.org. This site also contains general information on the vintage game, the rules of play, links to member clubs, and numerous photographs (sometimes referred to as "tintypes" by devotees of the nineteenth-century game).

The listing of clubs is incomplete and should not be taken as a comprehensive roster of all the teams playing nineteenth-century base ball around the country. Some new teams and others that have been in existence for several seasons have, for various reasons, not taken the step of formally joining the VBBA. Some have not kept their membership current and are therefore not included in the listing of active clubs. This is regrettable and makes it difficult to determine where and how many teams and individuals are playing vintage base ball. Teams that have not joined the VBBA or have let their membership lapse are always welcome to join and are encouraged to become an official part of the "base ball fraternity" (as it was often called in the nineteenth century). Membership in the VBBA strengthens the organization, supports the member clubs, increases the visibility of the game, contributes to sharing knowledge, and enables established programs to help new clubs get started.

Resurrecting the name of base ball pioneer Henry Chadwick's 1860s publication, the Vintage Base Ball Association produces an informative newsletter, *The Base Ball Players' Chronicle*, which includes articles on base ball history and reports on various tournaments and festivals, VBBA Board actions, the formation of new clubs, and similar items. The VBBA also maintains a very busy and active listserv, which was begun under the leadership of Dean Thilgen, a member of the St. Croix Base Ball Club and a staff member of the Minnesota Historical Society who served as chair of the VBBA Education and Interpretation Committee. This listserv often contains enlightening discussions on various points relevant to the game that are of great value to the members of the vintage base ball community.

Who Do You Play?

A common question asked of vintage base ball participants is, "Who do you play?" The answer to this question provides insight into the early history of the national pastime and the growth and popularity of vintage base ball. The answer is that vintage clubs can play several types of opponents, with each type of game providing an enjoyable but different experience.

One of the reasons for the growth of vintage base ball is that clubs like the Rochester (Michigan) Grangers enjoy re-creating the customs of a bygone era such as giving the opposing club three cheers at the end of the match.

Club Matches

As was the case in the game's early years, vintage teams often play club matches, or what we might think of in modern terms as intra-squad games. It is important to keep in mind that the earliest base ball organizations in the 1840s and 1850s were actual clubs, with a constitution, by-laws, officers, dues, meetings, and the general organizational characteristics and trappings of a fraternal or social club. Club members met at a convenient playing field once or twice a week, usually in the late afternoon or on Saturdays. Two designated captains divided the available players into two teams that played a game for recreation, exercise, and the social enjoyment of being together for friendly competition. Vintage clubs that have enough players for two teams follow this practice and hold club matches throughout the season, just as their forbearers did a century and a half ago.

Matches with Other Vintage Clubs

Where time and travel allow, vintage teams play matches with other vintage teams. The Midwest and the East Coast are the two areas with the highest concentration of active teams, and many clubs are fortunate enough to have ten or more other clubs within a drive of an hour or two. Matches are typically arranged in the offseason so that by spring each club can publish its schedule of matches for the year. This practice also reflects the early history of base ball when the secretary of one club would send a letter to the secretary of another club proposing a match. Until the 1870s, there were no "leagues," as that term is used today where each member club plays the same number of games and meets the other clubs a predetermined number of times (as is the case in modern baseball). In the 1860s and earlier, games were arranged one at a time by the clubs, and this practice is followed by most teams today.

Vintage clubs usually play nearby teams often while getting to know each other's players well and establishing a friendly relationship over the seasons. In addition to these matches, some clubs also schedule a few overnight road trips per season. It is not unusual for well-established teams from such divergent locales as Ohio, Minnesota, Colorado, and New York to travel by cars, vans, and occasionally a team bus to each other's sites for games.

Vintage Leagues

Some vintage programs are organized on the league model. For example, the programs at the Genesee Country Village and Museum in Mumford, New York and at Old Bethpage on Long Island have created leagues in which their teams play each other in a predetermined schedule of games. This format has proven to be a convenient way for a program to create a full season of games, especially if that program is somewhat geographically isolated and playing games with other teams would involve extensive travel. Teams that play a regular schedule in a league format may also arrange to play other teams outside their league.

Tournaments and Festivals

In addition to single matches with other teams, vintage clubs often get together for multi-team tournaments and festivals. The number of teams involved in these events can range from three or four up to more than twenty, with games being played all day on several fields over a weekend. These events maximize the rewards for the expense of travel by offering multiple matches with different opponents. Festivals are good events for publicizing vintage base ball and are often attended by those starting a program in order learn from others.

Civil War Reenactor Games

A match between a vintage club and a group of Civil War reenactors is another type of vintage game opportunity. Museums or communities hosting Civil War reenactments or encampments sometimes invite a vintage base ball team to take part in the festivities. Vintage clubs that portray the game as it was played in the 1860s are a natural fit since these are the rules that would have been familiar to the soldiers who played base ball for recreation during their free time in camp during the war. Visiting a Civil War-era event is an interesting experience for vintage base ball participants and adds breadth and depth to their knowledge of the period.

A Civil War reenactment can also be a lot of fun and provide a surprise or two. At a Muffin game that was part of a reenactment in Keokuk, Iowa, an excellent Abraham Lincoln impersonator stopped by the ball diamond as the match was about to begin, delivered a few remarks, and took a turn at bat — a memorable occurrence for the large group of spectators and everyone on the field that day. On several other occasions, a President Lincoln has thrown out the ceremonial first pitch to begin the match.

Historical precedent does exist for a game between an established base ball club and a military unit. Historian Frank Ceresi has done extensive research on many base ball topics, including the National Base Ball Club of Washington, D.C. According to the article "Early Baseball in Washington, D.C.: How the Washington Nationals Helped Develop America's Game," by Frank Ceresi and Carol McMains, which can be found in the "National Treasures" section of his website at www.fcassociates.com, "one of the Nationals' biggest games of 1861 was played on July 2 against the 71st New York Regiment," one of the many units stationed in the Washington, D.C., area. "In August of 1862 the Nationals again played against New York's 71st Regiment in Tenleytown, Maryland (now part of the District of Columbia)." After commenting on various games played during the war by the Nationals against other local clubs, Ceresi observes, "The Nationals continued to test their skills against Union soldiers right up until the very end of the war. For example, on May 17, 1865, the team battled the 133rd Regiment of New York in a game played at Fort Meigs in Maryland as the Union troops were mustering out of the military."

Matches with Community Teams

In addition to matches within the club, games with other vintage teams, and contests with other reenactors, a vintage club may schedule a game at a community celebration with a group of players assembled specifically for that event serving as the opposing team. These matches often occur at a special observance in the host community, such as a sesquicentennial or bicentennial, heritage days celebration, park dedication, annual community festival, or local fair. The Ohio Village Muffins program at the Ohio Historical Society has been especially active in this area, traveling around Ohio and beyond while demonstrating early base ball and providing an afternoon of educational entertainment for the host community. These are particularly enjoyable occasions for vintage team families. Sometimes a game with a community team has been so successful that the participants have decided to form their own permanent vintage team and become part of the vintage base ball movement.

Vintage base ball, which adapted to a variety of venues and formats, is enjoying continued growth in both the number of teams and visibility. The VBBA and the cordial and cooperative relationships that exist among the member clubs have woven a strong fabric of support and interest in the vintage game. Whether traveling 30 miles to play a game at a community festival with a team of prominent local citizens that includes the mayor, a former major league player, and an Olympic medalist or 400 miles to another state to play a game with a new vintage team started by a transplanted former teammate, vintage base ball participants and their families enjoy a remarkable array of memorable experiences. As more clubs are formed and the game continues to spread throughout the country, the opportunity to create more base ball memories continues to grow.

2

The Appeal of Vintage Base Ball

The basic appeal of vintage base ball is simple, direct, and related to the appeal of all forms of baseball—it is fun to play and fun to watch. It is an enjoyable, lively, content-rich and positive experience. Matches are fast moving, colorful, and educational. Vintage base ball programs encourage spectator involvement and promote sportsmanship, good manners, civility, and historical education.

Most Americans have some experience playing and/or watching the national pastime and therefore have some familiarity with the basics of the game. This makes vintage base ball very attractive to spectators. They ask good questions about the similarities and differences with modern baseball. Some make plans to return for subsequent matches and even investigate ways to get involved in the program as players, umpires, scorekeepers, or interpreters. In addition to the nearly universal appeal of baseball, several other factors explain their interest in vintage base ball.

Vintage Base Ball as a Family Activity

Many correctly see involvement in vintage base ball as an activity that can be enjoyed by the whole family. Vintage base ball provides special opportunities for a father and son, father-in-law and son-in-law, and brothers to play together on the same team. All of these combinations currently exist in the vintage base ball community. Younger children can serve as mascots and often enjoy the chance to dress in period clothing for the games.

The Pace of the Game

Vintage games are fast-paced, overcoming a common criticism of modern baseball. The continuous action and relatively short length of a match contribute to the appeal of vintage base ball and reflect the original appeal of the game as it was played in its formative years. Writing in 1866, Charles A. Peverelly included this observation in *The Book of American Pastimes* (p. 15): "The game of Base Ball has now become beyond question the leading feature of the out-door sports of the United States, and to account for its truly proud position, there are many and sufficient factors. It is a game which is peculiarly suited to the American temperament and disposition; the nine innings are played in the brief space of two and one-half hours or less." The typical 1860-era nine-inning vintage game is played in less than two hours.

American spectators "cannot be kept in one locality for two or three hours without being offered something above the ordinary run of excitement and attraction," wrote Peverelly, who found base ball exceptionally compatible with the American character. "From the moment the first striker takes his position, and poises his bat, it has an excitement and *vim* about it, until the last hand is put out in the ninth innings." The pace of a base ball game played by the earlier rules appeals to spectators, states Peverelly, because it "caters to their inclinations and desires to a nicety; in short the pastime suits the people, and the people suit the pastime." The slow pace and extended length of modern professional baseball games are frequent areas for complaints; pace and length are positive features of vintage base ball.

Player-Friendly and Playable

Played by the one-bound rule and slower-pitch practices of the 1860 era, vintage base ball has grown and prospered in recent years because it is playable by people of both exceptional and moderate athletic ability. While millions enjoy following the pennant races and watching professional baseball in person or on television, only a tiny fraction of the public possesses the requisite skill to play the game in its present form, including 90-mile-per-hour fastball pitching.

The 1860 rules are sufficiently challenging for the many highly skilled and relatively young, athletic players who participate in this type of vintage base ball. Some are former high school and college athletes who are excellent ballplayers. However, the rules are also sufficiently player-friendly to accommodate older players and those of more modest abilities. The 1860 rules allow players of a wide range of ages and ability levels to hold their own in a game, make genuine contributions to their team's success, and have a wonderful time playing (without being plagued by excessive worry over getting injured). Under 1860 rules, it is common for fathers and sons to treasure the experience of playing together and for age barriers to disappear as high school-age players and AARP cardholders are often teammates on the same club.

In response to an inquiry in 2005 from a VBBA Board member regarding the average age of the players participating on vintage clubs, Anthony Prasatek, a member of the Rochester Grangers of Rochester Hills, Michigan, captured the spirit that prevails throughout the vintage base ball community in his reply:

> We pride ourselves on the fact we have a diverse array of players. We have one gent who had his 70th birthday this year [and] a few near his age. Frankly, I'd have to say the average age is about 45–47, [with] myself one of the younger at 35. I'd like to think we are very able-bodied and capable team. Some of the older fellows know their limitations and admit this and play effectively and happily within their means. We have never thought of having a young team or a team of ringers. We do this for the love of the game. We win, we lose, but we do it with pride for the greatest game and to have fun with other teams.

Upon reading Prasatek's comment about the Grangers being "able-bodied and capable," veteran player Paul Hunkele of the Regular Club of Mt. Clemens, Michigan, observed, "I'd say that is understatement—being the only club I know of to just about finish an entire season undefeated; 22–1 with the only loss being the last game." Indeed, diversity of ages does not prevent the Grangers (and other clubs) from playing the game well.

Responding to the same inquiry, Jerry Wasserman, a member of the Spiegel Grove Squires, a club based at the Rutherford B. Hayes Presidential Center in Fremont, Ohio, also commented on the positive aspects of the wide age range of vintage players on his club:

> I am 50 years old and I enjoy this great game and the fact I can still play. I enjoy traveling to

Vintage base ball is an active game that is fast paced and entertaining to play and watch as evidenced by the effort of this St. Louis Perfecto player (courtesy Joel Moore).

different places in Ohio, Michigan, and Canada and playing with and meeting some great people. I have the privilege of playing on the same team as my 17-year-old son, David "Smooth" Wasserman.... My first grandson, Braden "Buster" Estep, was born 9 weeks ago. It is now my goal to play at least one season with myself, Smooth, and Buster on the field at the same time. I have already asked our scorebook keeper, Jim "Tallyman" Miranda, to pencil us all in the lineup for the 2020 season. To me, there is nothing better than playing this great game at the same time as your own younger generations.

Sportsmanship

A big part of the appeal of vintage base ball is its emphasis on sportsmanship and gentlemanly behavior. Conducting oneself as a gentleman while playing base ball is historically authentic. In *The Book of American Pastimes* (1866), Charles Peverelly describes the Knickerbocker Club as being composed "mostly of those whose sedentary habits required recreation,

Muffin Tom Della Flora (center) and his sons Evan (left) and Michael get ready for a match with the Cincinnati Red Stockings at Fort Ancient.

and its respectability has never been undoubted. The same standard still exists, and no person can obtain admission in the club merely for his capacity as a player; he must also have the reputation of a gentleman" (pp. 340–341).

Although the reference is to the Knickerbocker Club of long ago, this passage applies to vintage base ball clubs as well. Like the Knickerbockers and their contemporaries, many of today's vintage players have sedentary jobs and look forward to the opportunity for exercise on the ball field once or twice a week. And, to be successful and contribute to the overall objectives of a vintage base ball program, an individual must also conduct himself in the spirit of the times as a gentleman.

Good sportsmanship was a recurring theme in the writings of the "Father of Base Ball," Henry Chadwick. In the August 15, 1863, issue of the *New York Clipper*, Chadwick emphasized the importance of sportsmanlike behavior by players and spectators, reminding his readers that

> a creditable victory abides only with that party who, in winning the match, have marked their play as much by their courtesy of demeanor, liberality of action, and display of good humor, as by their [playing] skill ... and this rule applies with equal force to the losing party, for the nine who gracefully and honorably submit to a fair defeat, get rid of half its sting, besides meriting as much credit for their moral victory as their opponents for the physical one.

Spectators are quick to pick up on the gentlemanly nature of vintage base ball. It is not only the skills of the players that cause people to come to watch the games. Spectators enjoy vintage base ball because it is set apart from the modern game by the emphasis on sportsmanship and good manners. Because of its gentlemanly nature, vintage base ball contributes to the wholesome family experience for participants and spectators. When presenting the culture of an earlier time, there is no improper language, arguing, and temper tantrums, such as throwing down a bat or cap if one makes an out. There will not be any kind of language or behavior during a vintage game that would be inappropriate for a elementary school-age child to hear or see. The only "parental guidance" that should be needed at a vintage game is for parents to help their children notice and understand all the positive things that are happening before, during, and after the match.

Reverse Appeal

Unfortunately, one reason the popularity of vintage base ball has been growing is that fans have been turned off by the negative aspects of modern major league baseball and other professional sports. To them, the vintage game represents a sharp and welcome contrast.

In the August 17, 1992, issue of *The New Yorker*, Roger Angell gave an account of his visit to a minor league game in Oneonta, New York, "a hundred and sixty-odd hilly miles to the north and west of Yankee Stadium." He reports that he journeyed to the quaint Class A ballpark "in full flight from Diamond-Vision commercials, four-hour games, ill-tempered crowds, skulking tabloid sports tales, slump-haunted millionaire players, owner-commissioner squabbles, another major-league drug suspension, another overpriced Mets team apparently gone sour (so soon!), another vapid evening of game-to-game channel-switching," and other ills of the modern game. He makes it clear that he "wasn't running away from baseball ... only from modern major-league ball and the wearying distractions that accrue at the top of the sport ... as we fans try to keep alive our old hopes and affiliations, and to hold on to joys that once seemed closer at hand." (p. 75).

Angell's perceptive article goes on to tell how he found a more pure and basic version of base ball in the peaceful setting of that small-town minor league park in upstate New York. Spectators at vintage games often express similar sentiments as they see base ball being played by amateurs in its original form.

Those attending vintage games often express both surprise and approval when they see the players on one team applaud a fine defensive play by an opponent. Spectators are often amazed at the sight of a runner calling himself out if he knew the umpire had erred in calling him safe. One facet of the appeal of vintage base ball is, regrettably, its contrast to the boorish behavior and fighting too often seen in modern professional sports. The vintage game represents a set of values and behaviors that many participants and spectators find more in keeping with their personal principles and standards.

Some major league ballparks have set aside family seating areas that are removed from negative crowd behavior as a way to draw youngsters and their parents to the games. Vintage base ball spectators need not worry about bringing children to a match where the members of the crowd pick up on the tone of the game and generally adopt the civility and courteous behavior of the players.

There has been little enthusiasm or inclination within the vintage community to exploit major league baseball's weaknesses and shortcomings in order to promote the vintage game. Most vintage base ball participants are genuinely troubled and saddened by the negative points of professional sports, especially the unsportsmanlike behavior, selfishness, self-promotion, substance abuse, and the on-field and off-field violence by some players. Many vintage players are thoughtful and intelligent fans of professional baseball that tend to see

With its emphasis on sportsmanship, vintage base ball is a family activity where youngsters can get close to the action. Parents can be sure the experience will be appropriate for young children.

themselves, along with ball players from youth leagues to the majors, as fellow members of the base ball fraternity and feel a special bond with others who enjoy the national pastime.

Connecting Generations

The National Baseball Hall of Fame and Museum in Cooperstown has adopted a wonderfully brief but expressive statement that captures its mission: "Preserving History, Honoring Excellence, Connecting Generations." These words also reflect the goals of the many fine vintage base ball programs across the country.

In regard to preserving history, the vintage base ball community presents the game as it was played in the nineteenth century. This enables the public to learn about the game's development and its place on the greater stage of American history. Many individual vintage programs honor excellence by recognizing those people who have contributed their time, talent, and treasure — on and off the field — to further the mission of the sponsoring organization and help the vintage game grow and prosper.

In the important area of connecting generations, vintage base ball is right in step with the mission of the Baseball Hall of Fame. Spectators at a vintage game are of all ages, from T-ball players who are just learning the basics of the game to seniors telling stories of seeing Mickey Mantle play fifty seasons ago. Watching a vintage game together encourages conversations between children, parents, and grandparents. Recollections and stories are shared

The umpire often chats with the crowd as they arrive for the game. Vintage base ball is enjoyed by spectators of all ages and encourages inter-generational conversations among families attending the game.

as spectators talk about the game, past and present. People of every age have a baseball story. Vintage base ball helps put baseball's many eras in historical perspective and provides a sense of the game's stature as an American cultural institution that has been played, watched, and enjoyed in many forms for a long, long time.

Kinship with Other Re-Creators and Reenactors

Beyond the appeal of our national pastime, the growth of vintage base ball is part of the widespread interest in an array of historical re-creating and reenacting activities. The English writer C.C. Colton (1780–1832) continues to be remembered for his aphorisms, one of which helps explain the appeal of such activities: "To look back to antiquity is one thing, to go back to it is another."

Civil War reenactors and reenactments immediately come to mind as the largest and perhaps most well-established form of re-creating history. R. Lee Hadden writes knowledgeably in *Reliving the Civil War: A Reenactor's Handbook* (p. 4):

> Civil War reenacting was done almost from the beginning of the war, as soldiers demonstrated to family and friends their actions during the war, in camp, in drill, and in battle. Veterans organizations recreated camp life to show their children and others how they lived and to reproduce the camaraderie of shared experience with their fellow veterans.

He points out "large reenactments were done as military training exercises on the battlefield, such as the U.S. army field maneuvers on the Manassas battlefield in September 1904." He reports that reenacting became even more popular during the centennial of the Civil War, when the North-South Skirmish Association (NSSA) was founded. "These individuals began competitive shooting with original and reproduction black powder firearms (including cannons) and produced a lucrative market for equipment and uniforms that sparked the modern reenactment hobby." Citing the nation's bicentennial in 1976 as having an enormous impact on historical reenacting, Hadden states that "the quest for accuracy in uniforms boosted the authenticity movement in Civil War reenactment tremendously. Research began on uniforms and equipment, and manufacturing of good reproductions was started." By the time the 125th anniversary of the start of the Civil War arrived, Hadden reports that "*Time* magazine estimated that in 1986 there were more than 50,000 reenactors of all sorts in America" (pp. 4–6).

Historical reenacting is by no means limited to the Civil War. There are many enthusiasts who are involved in Revolutionary War-era reenacting on an ongoing basis. One notable example from this period of American history is the annual December reenactment of the crossing of the Delaware River by George Washington and his troops. Rowing wooden boats that are replicas of those used by Washington's army, the reenactors in period dress make their way across the Delaware to commemorate the daring nighttime maneuver that enabled Washington to surprise the Hessians on Christmas morning 1776 at the battle of Trenton.

Under the headline "Hamilton-Burr duel re-enactment stays in the family," an article in the July 12, 2004, issue of *USA Today* (with the appropriate dateline of Weehawken, New Jersey) began, "The bitter grudge between their ancestors has long faded, but on Sunday descendents of Alexander Hamilton and Aaron Burr marked their paces with pistols in hand. Antonio Burr, a descendant of Burr's, arrived by rowboat in period costume and fired a replica of the .54-caliber pistol that mortally wounded Hamilton 200 years ago in the July 11, 2004, duel. Douglas Hamilton, a fifth-great-grandson of Hamilton, feigned the historic hip wound, dropping to one knee and then falling to the ground in sitting position." The article reported that "more than 1,000 attended the re-enactment near the Hudson River" across from New York City, near the spot of the original event.

The State of New York celebrated its quadricentennial in 2009, marking the voyages of discovery of Henry Hudson and Samuel de Champlain. Visitors sailed the river on a replica of Hudson's ship, the *Half Moon*, according to the Hudson River Maritime Museum. With its "cabins and decks furnished authentically with sea chests, weapons, tools, navigational instruments, and trade goods," the ship had the appearance of the 1609 voyage.

In 2007 an elaborate reenactment project commemorated the 400th anniversary of the founding of Jamestown, in 1607, with replicas of the ships that brought the colonists to Virginia, the *Godspeed*, the *Susan Constant*, and the *Discovery*, visiting Jamestown and several major East Coast cities.

Re-creating daily life in the colonial era was the subject of the noted 2004 PBS series *Colonial House*, in which a large television audience watched "two dozen time travelers find out the hard way what early American colonial life was really like" as they grappled with the hardships of living without modern conveniences. Set in New England in 1628 and described on the PBS website as "hands-on history," the program required the colonists to use "only the tools and technology of the era." Historical expertise for the project was provided by Plimoth Plantation, "the living history museum of the Plymouth colony" where visitors are offered "a chance to share the Colonial House experience through a new exhibit and a series of workshops, events, and activities that will let visitors roll up their sleeves and dive into 17th century life, as seen on *Colonial House*." Re-creating the settling of the West was presented on a similar PBS program, *Frontier House*, in 2002. Three families lived the lifestyle of homesteaders in Montana in 1883. As was the case with *Colonial House*, the *Frontier House* series drew a large audience and considerable media attention.

The American Mountain Men were described in the November 25, 2003, issue of *USA Today* as a "35-year-old coast-to-coast brotherhood of 600 devotees" who celebrate "a window of time—1800 to 1840—when fur trappers lived by their wits in the Rocky Mountains." An accompanying photo pictured a reenactor in period dress "suited up, neck to toe, in deerskin hides stitched with animal sinew." According to the organization's website, these hardy modern-day mountain men are "dedicated to the preservation of the traditions and ways of our nation's greatest, most daring explorers and pioneers, the Mountain Men; to the actual conservation of our nation's remaining natural wilderness and wildlife; and to the ability of our members to survive alone, under any circumstances, using only what nature has to offer."

The *Arizona Republic* of January 3, 2003, reported, "More than 100 teenagers have been pulling large carts through the desert this week as part of an exercise designed to re-enact the hardships endured by Mormons in the mid–1800s." The girls "wore prairie dresses, bonnets, and aprons, while the boys donned wool trousers, suspenders, and flannel shirts" as they participated in this "exercise designed to re-enact the mass migration of 3,000 Mormon immigrants who came from Europe and trekked 1,000 miles to Salt Lake City from 1856–60<in> (the same years base ball was establishing itself as the national game). The teens (ages 14 to 19) pushed "handcarts loaded with 400 to 500 pounds of food, bedding, clothing and cooking utensils" and "learned to churn butter, cook in a Dutch oven, and pluck and cook chickens over an open fire for the event."

The annual Newport Vintage Dance Week, sponsored by the Commonwealth Vintage Dancers, is described by that organization as "a week-long extravaganza of dance and amusements in and around the mansions of Newport, Rhode Island" with participants being invited to "travel back in time to the summer playground of the Gilded Age" in order to "perfect your dancing skills with classes taught be leading experts." Similar to the approach taken by vintage base ball programs, the Commonwealth Vintage Dancers combine "exquisite costuming with a fine sense of period manners, style and customs" as they "bring to life the most popular dances of their day." "Evening Hours; Newport Nostalgia," an article on the Commonwealth Dancers and the Newport event in the August 9, 2009, edition of the *New York Times*, explains that "the group's members share an interest in the dances and clothing of the period between the Civil War and the Jazz Age. Each of the five nights is devoted to a ball or dance of a particular time." Evidence that the Commonwealth Dancers are successful in their re-creation endeavors appeared in the January 3, 2010, edition of the *New York Times*, which included Newport Vintage Dance Week on its list of "Memorable Parties of 2009."

Some reenactments come with a sense of humor. The Bonnie & Clyde Festival is held annually in Gibsland, Louisiana, "on the weekend closest to the May 23, 1934, anniversary of the ambush" of the notorious couple, Bonnie Parker and Clyde Barrow. The website for this unique event encourages visitors to "bring family and friends and join us each year" for activities, including "fun festivities, great food, music and authentic reenactments." The weekend includes a Jambalaya dinner, guest speakers, parade, and a pancake breakfast. "The festival winds down around 4:30 P.M. when everyone drives out to the actual ambush site for a reenactment of the fateful day when Bonnie & Clyde were gunned down by the law."

Caitlin Evans in the May 5–7, 2006, issue of *USA Weekend* points out that "people continue to gather to relive the couple's final moments during a stirring re-enactment that takes place on the exact spot where they died." With a large crowd on hand, "the 'couple' drives by, often in the same car used in the [1967] movie. Six men portraying the law officers, all dressed in 1930s garb, shoot well over a hundred blanks in the car's direction, while the two re-enactors inside squeeze fake blood out of tubes." Clearly, there is no limit to the imagination of communities in staging historical reenactment activities.

Reenacting activities are not confined to themes in American history. The plot of the December 6, 2005, episode of the popular CBS television series *CSI* involved a group of Sherlock Holmes reenactors who, dressed in period English clothing authentic to the Victorian Era, held monthly meetings to discuss, over tea, the characters, settings, and plots of the Arthur Conan Doyle books. There are, in fact, numerous groups of these literary fans who refer to themselves as "Sherlockians" and seek to re-create the life and times of the noted detective.

The literary works of another more recent British author, J. K. Rowling, have also inspired reenacting. Krista Henneck, writing in the June 8, 2009, edition of the Ohio State University student newspaper, *The Lantern*, describes the campus Quidditch League. Colleges and universities around the country "follow the guidelines set by Middlebury College students, who created an official handbook for the 'muggle,' or non-magical version of the game." As they re-create the game played by Harry Potter and his classmates at Hogwarts, the students (without the power to fly) must make some accommodations in the rules, but have fun bringing the "sport" to life.

The thousands of people who run marathons every year can be considered to be reenactors since every marathon is, in essence, a reenactment of the heroic feat of the messenger Phidippides, who ran as swiftly as he could from Marathon to Athens in 490 B.C. to announce the news of the victory of the Greeks over the Persian Army at Marathon and to warn Athens of a forthcoming naval attack by the Persians. The standard distance of 26.2 miles for all marathons (officially established at the 1908 Olympic Games in London) re-creates the approximate distance covered by Phidippides on his legendary run.

The September 17, 2006, issue of *The Columbus Dispatch* carried the headline "Niagara festival to include largest kite in the world" and described a festival to be held in Niagara Falls, New York, in early October that would attract kite-flying enthusiasts from around the world. Going back in time to commemorate an event contemporaneous with the days of the Knickerbockers, organizers announced that the centerpiece of the festival was to be "a re-enactment of an 1848 kite contest" that originally "was held to get a string across the Niagara Gorge as a prelude to building a suspension bridge."

In "Saving a Mayan Game of Sacrifice" the December 10, 2004, issue of *The Chronicle of Higher Education* reports, "In a remote corner of northwestern Mexico, six men in leather loin cloths volley a heavy rubber ball across a dirt court using only their hips." The men "are reviving the game of *ulama de cadera*, or hip *ulama*" described as "how extreme sport probably looked in 1500 B.C." Manuel Aguilar, an assistant professor of art history at UCLA who is behind the effort to save the traditional game, described it as "central to the cultures of the Maya and Aztecs." It was "once as popular throughout Mesoamerica and Mexico as soccer is today."

The mission statement of the Society of Hickory Golfers includes the phrase "To promote the experience of golf in a manner consistent with how the 'royal and ancient game' was played in the hickory era," an objective similar to the Vintage Base Ball Association's objective of conducting matches in a manner consistent with how the national pastime was played in the Knickerbocker era. Organizing hickory golf tournaments in which participants use wood-shafted clubs and wear period clothing, the SoHG seeks "to assist members and others in discovering the playing characteristics of wood shaft golf clubs" and "to develop and maintain equipment standards for hickory play."

Since the early 1990s, there has been a resurgence of interest in old-time skiing in the Sierra Nevada Mountains, where a group of enthusiasts has revived the sport of longboard skiing as it existed in the days following the California Gold Rush. According to the Plumas Ski Club, skis "were first introduced to the mining camps in 1853. Due to the remoteness of the Plumas and Sierra county camps, skis were the perfect vehicle for winter transportation." The term "longboards" comes from the fact that "traveling skis were generally eight to ten feet long, while the racing skis were a minimum of ten feet and might reach an unwieldy length of fifteen feet!" The area's skiing heritage includes the first organized downhill race, held in 1867.

"Longboard revival sign of the good ol' days," in the March 17, 2008, issue of the *Denver Post*, describes the reproduction skis used by today's longboarders as "built more or less the same as the originals, constructed of tight, vertically grained Douglas fir, with a steering groove cut out of the bottom and tips bent up by a long steaming process. Bindings consist only of two pieces of leather attached to the sides and laced tight over leather boots, with a small block of wood attached to hold heels in place."

Modern-day longboard skiers enjoy re-creating the races of the early miners. As with vintage base ball players, longboard skiers wear period dress. The Plumas Ski Club specifies that when competing in longboard races held at the Plumas-Eureka Ski Bowl in Johnsville, California, participants "must be dressed in period-style clothing and only dope [the nineteenth-century term for wax] from authentic recipes and ingredients may be used on the skis."

Period clothing is highlighted in "Revisionist Skiing," an article in the December 12, 2008, issue of *Forbes*:

> Racer Scott Lawson [director of the Plumas County Museum], striving for authenticity, wore a red flannel shirt emblazoned with a white star on the chest — a replica of shirts worn by the Altruas Snowshoe Club, one of the earliest sponsors of the race. Women compete wearing pantaloons and long dresses, which they carefully pin down, hoping to prevent a wardrobe malfunction. Sometimes despite their efforts, "The skirts blow up in their faces," says Lawson.
> "They end up showing everyone their bloomers." Worse, they can't see where they are going.

On the theme of historical authenticity, the *Forbes* article observes, "Goggles and helmets — which the ancients did not use — are disallowed. Flasks of whiskey are not."

Another re-creation of a winter sport was described in an article in *Sports Illustrated* by Michael Cannell: "Return of the Blade Runners" (March 10, 1997). Under the intriguing headline "Victorian ice yachts, which once ruled the Hudson, are out of hibernation," Cannel wrote that "During the Hudson River's Victorian heyday, each winter grand ice yachts commanded the frozen river," especially along "Millionaires' Belt," an area north of New York City and south of Albany. The article described the work of a modern-day group known as the Hudson River Ice Yacht Club, "a fraternity of some 75 antiquarian ice boaters" that was praised for its dedicated efforts to re-create the past by "gradually reclaiming yachts abandoned in barns and outbuildings," restoring them, and putting them back on the ice.

There are several conflicting explanations regarding the origins of the annual Iditarod Dogsled Race (not unlike the various myths, interpretations, and viewpoints regarding the origins of baseball). One explanation is that the race re-creates the Anchorage to Nome "serum run" of 1925 in which a relay of dog sled teams delivered a shipment of diphtheria serum that was needed to save the lives of the children of Nome during an outbreak of the deadly disease. The last leg of the 658-mile dog sled run was made by a team led by a heroic and indefatigable Siberian husky named Balto. The legendary canine is immortalized by a statue in Manhattan's Central Park, not far from the route taken each fall by the thousands of runners in the annual New York City Marathon. As the runners, who have trained diligently to re-create the heroic achievement of Phidippides, pass near the Balto memorial and head for the finish near the Tavern on the Green, they are probably not thinking of the Iditarod. But in Alaska and elsewhere at that very moment, teams of mushers and their sled dogs are training diligently to re-create the heroic achievement of Balto.

These are but a few examples of re-creating and reenacting history that show how these activities can take many forms. While the time period, setting, clothing, and equipment may vary from one activity to another, the people engaged in these activities have much in common. As is the case with the vintage base ball community, these reenactors and re-creators are passionate about what they are doing and possess an admirable interest in connecting with the past by actively reliving it as authentically as possible. They seek to gain a better appreciation of their heritage by having the same experiences as past generations. Far from being a quaint and isolated activity, vintage base ball is part of a much larger general movement that seeks to understand the past by authentically re-creating activities associated with former times and then publicly presenting these activities for the enjoyment and edification of others who are curious about history and wish to learn more.

Turning Research into Action and Action into Research

Vintage base ball has a special appeal for those interested in historical research. Vintage base ball and base ball research go hand in hand, with the sport driving further investigation into the early years of the national pastime. The efforts of vintage base ball programs to re-create the nineteenth-century game turn action into research as program volunteers and museum professionals seek evidence of how base ball was once played. Old newspapers provide interesting accounts and box scores of games played 150 years ago. Researchers analyze these findings in the context of the rule books of the appropriate period. Letters, diaries, and other primary sources are explored for base ball references. City directories provide information on the ages and occupations of the members of the early ball clubs. Locating old photographs is extremely beneficial in that these images provide important information on uniforms and equipment.

Vintage base ball also functions as a living laboratory by providing the opportunity to test theories of how the game was played, turning research into action. The language of the old rule books is often vague and subject to various interpretations. It is sometimes difficult to understand the meaning and intent of some of the rules just by reading the book. However, by trying out different interpretations in game situations, it is possible to gain new insight on how a given rule might have been implemented in the nineteenth century.

Many vintage base ball club members enjoy research activities that make base ball a year-round sport. One can have fun playing, officiating, and watching games in the summer and then can get involved in fascinating research projects when autumn comes and the weather drives participants inside. The "offseason" becomes more of an "indoor base ball season" as members of the vintage community do the reading and research that will add to our knowledge of the era being re-created and may improve the way the game is played when spring rolls around again.

Vintage base ball has great appeal on many levels — as a family-friendly activity; as a fast-paced participant and spectator sport; as a lesson in sportsmanship; as an alternative to the shortcomings of modern professional sports; as a vehicle for encouraging inter-generational family conversations; as a historical re-creation experience that provides time travel to other eras; and as an inspiration for reading and research. All of these characteristics add to the game's appeal and are factors in its continued growth.

3

The Value of a Vintage Base Ball Program

A vintage base ball program is a splendid fit for a sponsoring museum or historical society whose mission includes education. Consistent with the themes of most such organizations, vintage base ball educates through a colorful and engaging activity; provides a means for visitors to connect with the broader scope of American history; generates publicity and visibility for the museum; enables the institution to develop a cadre of volunteers to support its other programs; and creates a program that is complementary to and supportive of the institution's other activities.

An Educational Activity on Your Field of Dreams

Teams that play nineteenth-century base ball are often affiliated with museums and historical societies interested in the educational benefits of demonstrating the history of the game. Watching the old-time game encourages awareness and understanding of the true beginnings of the national pastime and of the times in which the sport developed as a significant part of American culture.

Vintage base ball has come to be viewed by many museums and historical societies throughout the country as an effective way of connecting with visitors and providing a history-based experience that is both educational and entertaining. Visitors of all ages know baseball at least in general terms and like it. Vintage base ball can be a natural magnet for attracting and holding the interest and attention of visitors.

History, literature, and especially film have given baseball a nostalgic feel. Visitors at a museum or historical society are quick to associate the game with American history. As James Earl Jones so eloquently expressed in his memorable speech in the closing moments of the 1989 movie *Field of Dreams*, based on W.P. Kinsella's novel *Shoeless Joe*,

> the one constant through all the years, Ray, has been baseball. America has rolled by like an army of steamrollers. It has been erased like a blackboard, rebuilt, and erased again. But baseball has marked the time. This field, this game — it's a part of our past. It reminds us of all that once was good and it could be again.

The reason this speech is remembered by moviegoers more than twenty years after it was first delivered is that it captured the feelings so many people have toward the national pastime. The frequently quoted passage from Alexander Pope's 1711 poem "An Essay on Criticism" comes to mind: "What oft was thought but ne'er so well expressed." Although they may be hazy on the details of the game's origins and early history, most Americans have the general sense that the game has been a part of American society for generations. They have memories of their parents and grandparents talking about playing baseball and going to baseball games when they were young. They know baseball as a cultural institution. What better vehicle to arouse the curiosity of museum visitors and stimulate questions and comments about earlier time periods than a ball game?

Matches conducted by the rules of the 1860s are especially effective history lessons because the Civil War period is a familiar and interesting era to many.

A Truly Interactive Experience

When the game is well presented to the public, visitors learn about baseball and the historical period being represented on the field. This, in turn, leads to consideration of how sports and other leisure activities have changed over the years, and the ways in which the broader American society has changed or remained the same. Vintage base ball encourages this kind of thoughtful reflection.

Some things in baseball have remained the same since the 1860s — nine players on a team, 90 feet between the four bases, nine innings in a game, three outs in an inning, three strikes and you're out. But some things are different in the modern game. For example, a ball caught on one bounce is no longer an out, the players are now playing with gloves, and we don't see players wearing neckties. Today, home plate is five-sided rather than round, and there is no longer a single umpire standing off to the side of the plate. This educational experience comes packaged in a most entertaining, interactive, and enjoyable way: sitting outside at a ball game on a pleasant afternoon, thinking about the present and the past, chatting with the umpire and the players, and perhaps even taking a turn at bat.

As the match begins, the questions start coming: When did players start wearing gloves? How does the ball being used in this game compare to a modern baseball? Were the players in 1860 paid to play ball? Where and when was baseball "invented"? Did that runner actually just call himself out on that close play at first base?

In the past, permanent static exhibits utilizing traditional display cases, framed wall hangings, and mannequins were staples of many museums' efforts to preserve and present the past. However, faced with declining attendance (a nationwide trend at even some of the most well-respected institutions), severe budget cuts, and increasing competition from other forms of education and entertainment, museum leaders are seeking creative ways to stimulate public interest, visitorship, memberships, and financial support. Museums and historical societies everywhere are searching for ways to reach the public.

An article by Judy Keen in the August 11, 2008, issue of *USA Today* with the headline, "Museums pinched by higher costs, fewer visitors," summarized the situation. "Many museums across the USA are experiencing declining attendance and budget crises they blame on rising gas prices, a drop in school field trips and shrinking interest in history and art," writes Keen. She supports the point with an observation from Timothy Walch, director of the Herbert Hoover Presidential Library & Museum in West Branch, Iowa (which had 16 percent fewer visitors in 2005 than 2004): "The overall trend is moving down." Keen cites several smaller museums that closed in recent years, but points out that "big attractions such as Virginia's Colonial Williamsburg and venerable ones such as the Maryland Historical Society have had problems. Williamsburg's annual attendance is down from 1.2 million in the mid–1980s to just more than 700,000 last year." The response of museums has been to "try new exhibits and programming to draw visitors." The article concludes with the following observation from another knowledgeable museum professional, Bruce Teeple: "History is more than a quilt [or] a stick of furniture. It's time to use history to understand and appreciate the role of change in our lives."

Cultural institutions of all types are expanding programming to reach new audiences. Special events, such as festivals, fairs, and traveling exhibits, can be public relations bonanzas in the short term. Capitalizing on the magical nocturnal happenings in the hit movie *A Night at the Museum*, scout troops and other groups of young guests are invited to sleepovers and flashlight tours. In 2009, this idea was adopted by the National Baseball Hall of Fame and Museum in Cooperstown, which offered an "Extra Innings Overnight Program" for children nine or older, giving them "the opportunity to sleep in the Hall of Fame Plaque Gallery and explore the entire Museum after hours."

Seeking more hands-on activities for visitors, many museums offer opportunities to touch and hold objects, try on clothes and hats, take photographs of themselves in historical settings, write a caption for a photograph, carve a pumpkin, or make a craft project to take home. Taking full advantage of the recent, remarkable, and rapid advances in computer technology, museums have adopted electronic devices and adapted them to the history setting, creating exhibits that offer games, simulations, and tailored experiences to engage visitors of all ages with historical events.

The challenge of coming up with new programming led to the establishment of vintage base ball at Fort Vancouver, Washington. An article by Brett Oppegaard in the August 19, 2005, edition of *The Columbian* (Clark County, Washington) reported that five years earlier, park ranger Doug Halsey and his colleagues were "trying to come up with another popular interpretive event for the Vancouver National Historic Reserve" when, while combing through stacks of historic photos and looking for "something sports-related," they found "a single frame in which one could spot an empty baseball diamond in the background." Subsequent research revealed that base ball "started becoming popular in the Northwest in the Civil War era." This led to the creation of a new event called "An Evening of 1860s Base Ball" at which two teams took the field on the fort's Parade Ground: the Vancouver Occidentals (based on a local nineteenth-century club) and a military reenactor group, the 1st Oregon Volunteer Infantry. Halsey was pleasantly surprised when a "crowd of a couple hundred spectators gathered along each foul line for the first game in 2001." He reports that event has drawn "consistently larger crowds" each year. "The high interest was totally unexpected," recalled Halsey of the positive public reaction. "The first year we played we had radio stations calling for interviews from all across the country." In addition to an item on the Associated Press wire service, "there was a brief article in *The Wall Street Journal*." The successful venture continues today with the two teams meeting twice a season with large crowds in attendance.

In searching for fresh ways to present history, vintage base ball emerges as an activity that is truly active. Unlike a modern baseball game, where fans are passive spectators who sit, watch, and have little opportunity to interact with the players, vintage players and umpires mingle with the audience. A player will leave the bench and sit in the middle of the spectator area, talking about the game and giving everyone in the stands a chance to handle a nineteenth century-style wooden bat and leather ball. The onlookers become part of the event, with good-natured banter the norm during the match. Vintage game participants engage visitors in conversations before, during, and after the game.

For those attending a game, sportsmanship is not a lecture but an entertaining demon-

A vintage base ball club such as the Ohio Village Muffins can bring a historic site to life.

stration. Crowds are asked to cheer for good plays by both their favorite team and the opponent. The fans learn that players respected the umpire's decision and did not argue if a call went against them, accepting a negative ruling as part of the game.

Spectators can get actively involved in helping the umpire make the correct call. He may ask them what they saw if they had a better view of the play than he did. Spectators also pick up some period language, learning to shout "Huzzah!" when cheering a player's performance. They learn that the players on the field in the 1860s would have no knowledge of the song "Take Me Out to the Ball Game" since it was not written until 1908.

Male and female interpreters in period dress circulate among the crowd, seeking support for a social or political issue of the day. The interpreter may be a proponent of women's suffrage asking for signatures on a petition supporting voting rights for women. On another occasion, the spectators might be asked by a member of the temperance movement to sign the pledge against using alcohol. Later, someone might make a short speech between innings, asking the audience to support a certain political candidate.

In short, a vintage base ball game is a platform for a wide range of educational experiences. All these activities transport audience members to another era, actively encouraging them to consider how they might have felt about the important political, economic, and social issues of that time, many of which remain topics for discussion in the twenty-first century.

Young spectators are often invited to come onto the field at the conclusion of the game to take a turn at bat and run the bases. For those institutions seeking a history-related "hands-on" experience for their visitors, offering the chance for the youngsters to step to the plate and swing at a pitch with an old-style wooden bat and catch a ball barehanded is about as "hands-on" as it can get.

And, of course, the experience need not end when the day at the museum is over. Families who have attended a vintage game can continue learning when they get home, playing ball together in the backyard and experimenting with some of the rules, techniques (no gloves), behavioral norms, and language they learned during their museum visit. The vintage base ball experience may lead to reading about the history of the national pastime (and history in general), and can initiate some substantive conversations on such topics as umpiring and sportsmanship the next time the family attends a modern baseball game.

Public and Governmental Relations: Visibility and Goodwill

A vintage base ball program can greatly enhance the visibility of the historical society or museum. Many clubs carry a large banner on their travels and display it at a prominent place near the field so that spectators are aware of the affiliated historical organization. The Muffins have carried the Ohio Historical Society's name to the Cleveland Indians' Jacobs Field on its opening day, Cincinnati's traditional Findlay Market Opening Day Parade, and dozens of large and small communities in between. Most teams hand out a printed program that contains information about the nineteenth-century game. This publication also makes the spectators aware that the base ball team is a program of a particular museum, historical society, or other sponsoring organization.

Efforts to attract the media to vintage games are often successful. Vintage base ball, with the players in old-fashioned uniforms and interpreters in period dress, is photogenic and captures the attention of the media. Local media often feature photographs of vintage games. Local newspapers run stories several days in advance of the game to publicize the event and encourage attendance. Local television stations frequently send a crew to shoot game action and conduct interviews with players and the umpire for the evening news. The photogenic character of vintage base ball gives the game a visual attractiveness that can be an excellent fit for both print and electronic media looking for a colorful feature.

At a match held in conjunction with a baseball-related exhibit at the University of Dayton library, the Clodbuster Base Ball Club invited two Dayton-area sportscasters to put on uniforms and try their hand at playing in a nineteenth-century-style match. In 2003, the Lah-de-Dah Club had Hall-of-Fame broadcaster Ernie Harwell do play-by-play for a couple of innings at Greenfield Village. The Muffins have several extra uniforms on hand in various sizes to accommodate a guest player from the media. Enjoyable experiences of this type have short-term and long-term benefits. If a sportscaster plays in a game, the station often airs the game action that evening, resulting in some immediate favorable publicity for the team, vintage base ball, and the historical organization. Positive experiences of this type also build a good relationship with the media outlet that can be leveraged to get coverage of the institution's other events, exhibits, and programs. When Ken Burns' landmark documentary *Baseball* aired on PBS, the Columbus affiliate, WOSU-TV, produced a documentary on the Ohio Village Muffins, which was shown along with the Burns program and rebroadcast many times since.

A vintage program can provide a fresh angle on America's interest in baseball and can earn national publicity for the team and its affiliated historical organization. Vintage base ball programs have been featured in *The Sporting News, Sports Illustrated, The Wall Street*

The Muffins represent the Ohio Historical Society at many community events, including the parade celebrating the 2009 grand opening of Huntington Park, new home of the Triple-A Columbus Clippers.

Journal, Inside Sports, Smithsonian, and several airline magazines. Regional magazines featuring articles on vintage base ball have included *Midwest Living, Home & Away* (the Ohio AAA publication), and *Ohio Magazine.* Articles in some of these publications specifically encourage travel and tourism.

Vintage teams are goodwill ambassadors for their affiliated organizations and sponsors. By providing a wholesome family-oriented game of old-time base ball that is enjoyed and appreciated by the local audience, the team generates publicity for the sponsor. For any program, inviting elected officials to participate in games in their communities can be valuable when seeking public funding for historic sites and organizations. On several occasions the Muffins have played a match on the Ohio Statehouse grounds in downtown Columbus with the opposing team composed of state legislators and their aides and staffers. Held in the late afternoon as thousands of downtown workers are coming out of their office buildings at the end of the day, the game has typically drawn a crowd of curious onlookers while helping to build a good relationship between the state government and the state historical society.

The positive exposure created by a vintage base ball team that travels throughout the state is especially important in difficult economic times when museums, libraries, and other cultural arts organizations face serious budget cuts. People who may not have visited a particular museum recently feel reconnected to that museum when its base ball team comes to their town to play in the local bicentennial, heritage days, or other community festival.

The Value of a Vintage Base Ball Program 43

Top: A billboard near Interstate 70 promoting the National Road Celebration of Morristown, Ohio, July 29, 2006, features the Ohio Village Muffins, providing great visibility for the Ohio Historical Society. *Bottom:* The late Thomas Moyer (left), then chief justice of the Ohio Supreme Court, discusses plans to throw out the first pitch at the Fourth of July vintage game at Ohio Village with museum professional Mark Holbrook (center) and umpire Richard Schuricht.

Base Ball Cards and Other Merchandise

Another form of visibility and public relations for base ball clubs and the organizations they represent is the production of a set of base ball cards as a "takeaway." Several organizations, such as the Rochester (Minnesota) Roosters, the Rochester (Michigan) Grangers, the clubs in the Colorado Vintage Base Ball Association, the New York Mutuals, and the Muffins, have had cards printed. The cards are either handed out at games or sold in sets at a nominal price.

In his book *Base Ball Cartes: The First Baseball Cards*, Mark Rucker, a noted authority on early base ball photographs, points out that "the invention of photography and the advent of the game of baseball" came along at approximately the same time, calling this one of "the most wonderful coincidences of modern times" (p. 3). Images of base ball from the 1840s and 1850s are rare. "But it was with the mass marketing of photographs through the introduction of the Carte-de-Visite (CdV) that baseball images began to appear in significant numbers" (p. 3). A CdV is a paper photoprint glued to a card mount, approximately 2½ inches by 4 inches. They appeared in the late 1850s in France, England, and the U.S. but came to be known by the French phrase that translates as "visiting card."

In discussing the early history of base ball cards, Rucker, the president of Transcendental Graphics and an experienced vintage player, states that by 1860, "the CdV was catching on fast" and was becoming "**the** handy and inexpensive mode of sharing pictures. It was the perfect size for giveaway use by individuals, organizations, and businesses alike" (p. 3). Providing additional valuable information about these early cards, Rucker comments that "baseball cartes depicted individual players, entire teams, game scenes, and accoutrements. These CdVs were not usually made for commercial purposes, but as pictures for family and friends" (p. 4). This information is important for any program considering having cards printed in that it verifies that such cards are authentic to the period.

Baseball Cartes contains more than fifty pages of nineteenth-century base ball images. These photographs are a remarkable record of the early years of the game. For a club planning to have cards printed, these images are a guide to poses authentic to the period, adding to the look and feel of the photo. The superb period photographs in Rucker's book also provide excellent examples of borders, layout, print fonts, and other details that can make the cards of a vintage team resemble the cards from the nineteenth century. The photos are particularly useful for vintage teams that are getting started since there are dozens of images of uniforms styles and equipment.

In addition to *Baseball Cartes*, another outstanding source of early baseball cards is in the "American Memory" section of the Library of Congress website. The on-line exhibit "Baseball Cards 1877–1914" contains hundreds of cards from a later era. These images will be especially helpful to clubs recreating baseball in the last quarter of the nineteenth or early twentieth century, but can also be enjoyed by 1860-era teams interested in tracing the evolution of the uniform or learning more about teams that actually played in the vintage club's geographic area. These cards also provide examples of typical nineteenth-century poses.

Base ball cards designed and printed in the style of the CdVs of the 1860s are an excellent item for a vintage team to hand out to spectators — especially children. The cards enable them to learn the players' names and make the whole experience of going to a vintage game more participatory and personal. Cards enable the spectators to make a connection with those who are on the field in period dress. Players are, of course, quite pleased to comply when youngsters ask them for their card or for their autograph on the card. Distributing different cards at each home match can drive attendance as youngsters become collectors.

In addition to a photograph of a player or the team on the front, the reverse can contain educational information about the history of the national pastime, the sport of vintage base ball, or the team. It can provide information about other programs and events of the sponsoring organization, and it can drive spectators to the team's website to learn more about the history of the game and view other cards. Players enjoy chatting with the spectators as they pass out the cards at both home and away games. Even when not at the ball field on game day, vintage participants enjoy giving cards to family members, friends, and business associates. The Roosters and Hens teams at the History Center of Olmsted County, Minnesota, distribute some 30,000 baseball card schedules each year at schools, senior centers, and service clubs.

Vintage programs often have base ball-related merchandise available for purchase. Joanna Shearer, who heads the Deep River Grinders in Hobart, Indiana, was one of the first to see the potential in marketing a line of base ball-themed items at the site where vintage games are played throughout the summer. She has the park's gift shop well-stocked with pennants, posters, books, and toys related to the national pastime. The gift shop at Greenfield Village also carries a number of baseball items. The program at the Fort Vancouver National Historic Site in Washington sells an 1860-style leather base ball attractively packaged in a collectible tin, a vintage base ball booklet, and postcards featuring team photos. Many clubs, including the Grinders, Roosters, Lah-de-Dahs, Akron Black Stockings, Muffins, and many others, have T-shirts, sweatshirts, balls, hats, greeting cards, books, and other wares available for purchase by the public online or at the site's gift shop, general store, or sales table next to the ball diamond. This merchandise generates revenue, extends the visibility of the program and its sponsoring organization, and adds to the general experience.

Creating a Cadre of Volunteers

Vintage base ball participants are a valued part of the volunteer corps of the affiliated museum or historical organization. Team members may be history buffs who play ball or ballplayers with an interest in history. In either case, they may have no prior volunteer experience with a historical organization and should participate in general volunteer orientation and training sessions before representing the organization in a public way. They will need to be informed of the high professional standards of historical interpretation in the institution's public programs. This includes historical accuracy in uniforms, equipment, language, and behavior by the players and other on-field participants. This emphasis on education and historical accuracy makes this experience different from playing on a modern softball and baseball team.

Although participants are unpaid volunteers, spectators often assume that everyone on the field is a staff member who works at the institution. It is not uncommon for some regular staff members to play on the institution's vintage team or to serve as umpires, scorekeepers, or interpreters. While the participants on the field know who is a staff member and who is a volunteer, the spectators have no way to make this distinction since everyone wearing a team uniform or other type of period dress appears to be an official representative of the host museum. Volunteers will need to be coached on museum protocols and policies beyond the rules of playing the game. Tips on how to interact with the public in answering questions, giving directions, and, of course, handling emergencies are essential.

While staff time and energy will need to be invested in these training activities, the payoff for the museum or historical organization is enormous. Participants in the institution's vintage base ball program develop a sense of pride in being part of a well-established, high-quality program or in being part of starting and building a new program into a successful operation. They are honored to represent a prestigious organization such as a state historical society, local museum, or historic farm. Their service as volunteers in the base ball program often develops loyalty and commitment to the institution that provides the administrative home and the home field for the team.

Volunteers often contribute to the life and vitality of the institution in many ways other than base ball. They often become dues-paying members of the institution, volunteers at other activities, and supporters and frequent attendees of the institution's programs and events. A first baseman may become Father Christmas at the holiday season and an outfielder may be Ichabod Crane at Halloween. Ballplayers become advocates and ambassadors for the institution, speaking positively to their friends and colleagues at work and in the community about their volunteer experiences. They encourage others to attend events and recruit family members and friends to become volunteers.

Another advantage of having a vintage base ball program for the sponsoring institution is that the team is largely composed of men. Throughout the cultural arts community—historical societies, art museums, literary groups (including book clubs and organizations supporting the homes of notable authors)—the majority of the volunteers, guides, docents, and event attendees are women and, often, senior citizens. Administrators are aware of the gender imbalance and actively explore ways to recruit more men, especially men in their late teens through their forties who are significantly underrepresented in the volunteer corps of many cultural arts institutions. A vintage base ball team is an excellent way to attract a group of able, energetic male volunteers who are a significant asset to a museum or historical society often beyond base ball. Initially drawn to the institution through the opportunity to participate on the base ball team, members can be recruited to volunteer along with their families for a wide range of programs and activities.

Base Ball as a Complement to Other Programs

A vintage base ball match supports and enhances other programs and events taking place on the grounds of a museum. A base ball game can be held before or after a featured musical event with a nineteenth-century flavor, such as a concert by a brass band or vocal group that performs period music. Having a music group play nineteenth-century tunes on the fiddle, guitar, banjo, and dulcimer between innings works well with a vintage game and helps the spectators feel they have traveled to another time.

Baseball is linked to Fourth of July celebrations in many ways, from Little Leaguers in parades to softball tournaments. A museum, historical society, or community can give the holiday a nineteenth-century character by planning a day of activities that includes a parade of costumed interpreters and Civil War reenactors, musical performances typical of the period, orations that focus on the social and political issues of the era, picnic fare that includes food that would have been common in earlier times, games and contests representative of bygone days, and a vintage base ball match. Vintage base ball can help capture the look and character of the way Independence Day would have been celebrated 150 years ago.

A vintage base ball game can be a good partner for other museum-sponsored special events, such as a garden plant and herb sale in the spring, an "old-fashioned" ice cream social in the summer, or an apple butter, apple cider, or harvest festival in the fall. Pairing a Civil War reenactment or encampment with an 1860s base ball game is another example of complementary programming. Because of its near-universal appeal, vintage base ball can be a lively, colorful, and enjoyable event in itself as well as an accompaniment to almost any activity with a nineteenth-century theme, adding to the attractiveness and family-friendly appeal of a visit to the museum.

Vintage Base Ball and Historical Organizations: A Great Team

For museums seeking ways to maintain and increase attendance, vintage base ball provides an opportunity to tap into the national pastime's potential and pull in visitors who already possess an attachment to the game. After reminding us of baseball's long association with the broad sweep of American history, James Earl Jones concludes his *Field of Dreams* speech with the following predictions and observations:

> People will come, Ray. They'll come to Iowa for reasons they can't even fathom. They'll turn up your driveway not knowing for sure why they're doing it. They'll arrive at your door as innocent as children, longing for the past. Of course, we won't mind if you look around, you'll say. It's only twenty dollars per person. They'll pass over the money without even thinking about it. For it is money they have, and peace they lack. And they'll walk out to the bleachers, sit in shirt-sleeves on a perfect afternoon. They'll find they have reserved seats somewhere along one of the baselines where they sat when they were children and cheered their heroes. And they'll watch the game and it'll be as if they dipped themselves in magic waters. The memories will be so thick they'll have to brush them away from their faces.... People will come, Ray. People most definitely will come.

It would be a stretch to promise that the creation of a vintage base ball program by a museum will suddenly generate the long lines of cars that miraculously appeared in the final scene of *Field of Dreams*. After all, those spectators were coming to see the ball diamond in the Iowa cornfield where the ghosts of "Shoeless" Joe Jackson and his contemporaries had materialized. In contrast to these supernatural superstars, the players on a vintage team are everyday people with regular occupations who simply enjoy playing and presenting a ball game as it would have been done in the past. However, there are some truths in author W. P. Kinsella's lyric prose that resonate with potential museum visitors. Many visitors may well be "longing for the past," at least for an escape to the past where they can "sit in shirt-sleeves on a perfect afternoon" and take in a ball game from another era.

While a vintage base ball program cannot guarantee everyone will feel as if they have been "dipped in magic waters," spectators do express similar sentiments about having a transforming and uplifting experience when attending a vintage game. No living person could have any personal recollections of nineteenth-century base ball. But the vintage game, characterized by its old-time sights and sounds and its near-magical aura of simplicity, purity, and fun, does cause many spectators to reach back as far as they can to bring forth their own wonderful memories (some perhaps "so thick they'll have to brush them away from their faces," as Kinsella suggests) of playing catch at age eight with a parent in the backyard, choosing up sides for pick-up games with childhood pals at the school yard, listening to games on the radio on summer evenings long ago, and attending ball games — perhaps with parents and grandparents no longer living — played in ballparks no longer standing.

Muffin Meadow at Ohio Village has been a "field of dreams" for vintage base ball since 1981. Since a skin infield, outfield fence, and backstop are not needed, almost any open area can be used for vintage games.

After watching several innings of a Muffin game recently, one spectator who had never been to a vintage game made it a point to tell the players, "You know, I would rather watch this game than a big league game." Observations of this type reinforce the idea that the vintage game may, in fact, possess a measure of those mystical qualities that James Earl Jones articulates in the movie and raises the possibility that any grassy diamond where vintage base ball is played can be a "field of dreams"—a place where reality can be suspended for a few hours on a summer afternoon and participants and spectators can be transported to another time. That is the true and incalculable value of a vintage base ball program.

4

Choosing an Era to Portray

Considerations in Selecting an Era

The first consideration when starting a vintage base ball program is: What era will we re-create? That question is more complicated than it seems. While decision makers may not want to become baseball historians, some study is necessary for success. When starting a vintage base ball team, it is important to do some thoughtful reading and research on the early history of the game before deciding what set of rules and practices you are going to adopt.

How is an era chosen? Local history is a factor. Some organizations may be inclined to present an era of base ball that is in keeping with the year or era represented by the historic farm, village, homestead, or museum that sponsors the team. Others choose the date of the community's founding, the date of a historical event associated with that state such as admission to the Union, a significant Civil War battle, a famous trial, the establishment of a college, a notable election campaign, or the heyday of a local canal, turnpike, or railroad. Another strategy is to find out when early base ball clubs from that area played their first games and select the rules of that year. Many communities have a signature event that is celebrated every year with a parade or festival. Establishing a base ball club that represents the era of that occasion can be a good choice in that it presents opportunities for the team to be identified with an already popular event. Yet another approach would be to choose a "favorite son" (or daughter), such as a political figure, inventor, author, ball player, or other notable citizen, from that area and re-create the game as he or she would have played it or watched it as a child growing up in the nineteenth century. It may be strategic to choose to play by rules and practices that are followed by other clubs in the area and/or widely used throughout the vintage base ball community (such as the 1860 rules).

Vintage Eras

The nineteenth century was a time of enormous growth and change in the national game. In the context of the times, there was little standardization across the country. Communication was slow, especially in the early decades of the game. Base ball evolved at a different pace and in different ways across the country. There was no magic day when everyone suddenly dropped the old rules and practices and began playing by new rules. There was considerable overlap of different versions of base ball being played in various cities and towns and even variations of the rules in the same area.

In *But Didn't We Have Fun? An Informal History of Baseball's Pioneer Era, 1843–1870*, author Peter Morris provides several important observations about the 1830s and 1840s in the chapter "Before the Knickerbockers" that are important in selecting a year or era.

> The desirability of centralized legal and governmental systems was still a hotly debated topic, so the idea of a national pastime would have seemed bizarre. And even if Americans had perceived a national sport as a desirable concept, the notion would have been hopelessly impractical in a vast country with primitive transportation and communication. Just getting the staples of life and essential news from town to town was an ordeal; trying to disseminate the rules of a game would have seemed absurd [p. 12].

Morris points out that the various regions of the country "developed their own bat-and-ball games, some of which had generally agreed-upon practices while others were so fluid that their rules and even their names changed constantly." In describing some of the bat-and-ball games played in the pre–Knickerbocker era, Morris reminds us that this was a time of "continued reliance on oral communication. Word-of-mouth transmission creates imprecision in any endeavor and this is especially true in the case of an ephemeral activity such as a game" [pp. 12–13].

As museum professionals and members of vintage programs revisit the nineteenth century in order to decide on a period to represent on the ball field, it is important to understand that the labels on these eras are imprecise. Five general areas are briefly presented here along with their implications for effectively re-creating base ball. The geographic diversity of bat-and-ball games and the primitive state of communications are two important factors that provide perspective in looking at these five general eras in the development of base ball.

The Pre-Civil War Era: Town Ball and the Massachusetts Game

Some museums and historic sites that are set in the pre–Civil War period of the 1830s through the early 1860s may choose to play games according to the rules of an early form of base ball often known as "town ball." Because of similarities in rules and the configuration of the playing field, town ball shares many characteristics with the "Massachusetts Game" and the two terms are often used interchangeably in the vintage base ball community.

In *Baseball (1845–1881) from the Newspaper Accounts*, Preston D. Orem states that "the principal difference in the Massachusetts Game from town ball was the distance of sixty feet between the bases, instead of forty." Noting their similarities, Orem states, "Both were played upon a square, not a diamond-shaped field" (p. 5). According to the rules of the Massachusetts Game, "the bases shall be wooden stakes, projecting four feet from the ground." The "thrower" stood approximately in the middle of the square formed by the bases and delivered the ball from a distance of 35 feet from the striker who stood "inside of a space of four feet in diameter, at equal distance between the first and fourth bases." The rules provide for the striker to be put out if he should swing and miss three times or hit a ball that is "caught flying." If he reaches base and becomes a runner, he can then be put out by the practice of "plugging" or "soaking"—the fielder throwing the ball at the runner and successfully hitting him while he is attempting to advance around the bases. Section 14 in the 1860 Rules and Regulations for the Massachusetts Game states that "If a player, while running Bases, be hit with the Ball thrown by one of the opposite side...while off a Base, he shall be considered out." A player successfully running around the four bases "shall be entitled to one tally."

Town ball was preceded by several other bat-and-ball games that were played in Europe and America before the game recognizable as modern baseball eventually emerged. Fortunately, interest in the early game has heightened and several researchers have added immeasurably to the vintage base ball community's understanding of town ball and its predecessors. In his award-winning 2005 book *Baseball Before We Knew It: A Search for the Roots of the Game*, David Block provides an enlightening and well-researched examination of baseball's antecedents and is a "must read" for anyone interested in gaining a better understanding of the origins of the game. "Base Ball Discovered," a 2009 documentary on the origins of the game described by reviewer Mark Newman as "a detailed exploration of the many generational theories about the origins of America's national pastime," features Block's travels to Surrey County in England to investigate a report of the existence of a 1755 diary with a reference to "base ball." Members of the vintage base ball community will be interested in noting the similarities and differences between base ball and other bat-and-ball games from the segments of the film that provide demonstrations of stool ball, rounders, cricket, and bat and trap (a game still popular in English pubs).

Seymour and Mills's classic 1960 work, *Baseball: The Early Years*, remains a valuable resource in understanding the nature of town ball's development. Following their description of informal forerunner games such as stool ball and old cat, which were often played by small groups of children, they write, "For yet larger numbers of players, games variously known as 'town ball,' 'round-ball,' and later the 'Massachusetts' or 'New England' game... were devised" (p. 7).

In *But Didn't We Have Fun? An Informal History of Baseball's Pioneer Era*, Peter Morris discusses the bat-and-ball games that were popular before the Civil War. He states that "the game known as town ball sprang up in a number of large cities without following any obvious pattern. The Olympic Ball Club [of Philadelphia] was formed in 1833 from the remnants of two groups of town ball players and lasted long enough to celebrate its golden anniversary in 1883 (although it had switched from town ball to baseball in 1860) (p. 18). Morris concludes that it is "quite conceivable that 'town ball' varied so much from one locale to another that 'town ball' itself was effectively a catchall term" (p. 21).

Like cricket, town ball and the Massachusetts Game use all 360 degrees of the playing field with no foul territory. In these games, the pitcher and the batter are in the middle of the field, surrounded by the fielders. Therefore, these early versions of base ball have the disadvantage of placing the spectators a considerable distance from the center of the action. They require a larger playing area than the later versions of base ball played on a diamond-shaped field where the foul territory along the first- and third-base lines provides good viewing areas for the audience.

The practice of "plugging" or "soaking" the runner with a thrown ball is a sobering one for museum professionals, to say nothing of prospective volunteer players. There are, however, some museums that have had success in re-creating the Massachusetts Game and town ball by using a soft ball that would not cause injuries. Especially noteworthy is the pioneering town ball program based for many years at the Farmers' Museum in Cooperstown, New York. When the Muffins visited Cooperstown and played a town ball game with the Leatherstocking Club, the playing area was modified to a 180-degree configuration by orienting the field so that the catcher stood with his back to the wall of a large barn and the batter stood at home base, about 15 or 20 feet in front of the wall. This compromise arrangement worked reasonably well in that it gave players and spectators a good general idea of how town ball was played (wooden stakes for bases, plugging the runner with the ball, etc.) while creating spectator viewing areas.

For museums interested in creating a town ball team of the 1830s through the 1860s, ample evidence exists of adult men playing the game. The Society for American Baseball

Research's Protoball Project reports there were two clubs in New York City in 1832 and states that "Both of these clubs played in the old-fashioned way of throwing the ball and striking the runner, in order to put him out." Orem reports that "Six senior clubs called a meeting in Dedham, May 13, 1858, at which a code of rules was adopted, also a constitution and by-laws for the "Massachusetts Association of Base Ball Players." By 1860 (when the name was changed from "Massachusetts"' to "New England"), the Association had 32 member clubs, "mostly located in Boston and the vicinity" (p. 5).

Good sportsmanship is documented as a characteristic of town ball. In regard to the Olympic Club of Philadelphia, Morris quotes a contemporary source who states, "There were no quarrels or disputes among the players, who always found the principles of good-fellowship and gentlemanly intercourse a sufficient rule for their guidance" (p. 19). An interesting item in the 1837 constitution of the Olympics (published in *Early Innings: A Documentary History of Baseball: 1825–1908*, compiled and edited by Dean A. Sullivan) states that the club officer, known as the Recorder, "shall have charge of the pattern uniform owned by the Club," thus establishing the fact that uniforms were worn (p. 6).

These four factors — the historical evidence of the existence of men's clubs going back to the 1820s and 1830s; the availability of the rules adopted by the Dedham meeting in 1858; the practice of wearing uniforms; and an environment of good sportsmanship — combine to form a constellation of traits that would enable a museum to create a program using the rules and customs of town ball. For a time in the 1840s and 1850s, the Massachusetts Game and the New York Game coexisted. A contest that is usually considered to be the first college game, a victory for Amherst over Williams by the score of 73–32, held in Pittsfield, Massachusetts, on July 1, 1859, was played by the rules of the Massachusetts Game, long after the Knickerbockers adopted the rules that became widely known as the New York Game. Gradually, the New York Game came to dominate, and the Massachusetts Game declined markedly in popularity. However, for several decades, the version of base ball known as town ball or the Massachusetts Game was widely played in the East and Midwest. Orem reports that "after the Civil War, there was little or no interest in the 'Massachusetts' or 'New England' game of base ball" (p. 5).

The Pre–Civil War Era: The New York Game

If the setting for the museum or historical site hosting the vintage base ball program is 1845 or later, the decision could be made to play the games according to the original Knickerbocker Rules or the variations of those rules that occurred as they evolved over time. The authorship of these rules has been traditionally attributed to Knickerbocker club member Alexander J. Cartwright, who was elected to the Baseball Hall of Fame in 1938. Cartwright left New York for the California Gold Rush in 1849 when base ball was still in its infancy, spent most of his adult life in Hawaii, and never returned to New York. As a result, the nature and scope of his actual contributions have been the subject of recent inquiry and research. Monica Nucciarone's 2009 biography, *Alexander Cartwright: The Life Behind the Baseball Legend*, examines the relevant issues in detail and provides a balanced interpretation of the role of Cartwright and his contemporaries, adding to the vintage base ball community's understanding of how base ball began.

According to Charles Peverelly's 1866 work, *The Book of American Pastimes*, "During the years 1842 and '43, a number of gentlemen fond of the game" casually assembled "on a plot of ground in Twenty-seventh street" in lower Manhattan, "bringing with them their

Vintage teams, like the Hoover Sweepers of North Canton, Ohio (left), and the Greensboro (North Carolina) Patriots, wear colorful uniforms that add to the visual appeal of the game. Uniform style should be carefully considered when choosing the period that the program will portray (courtesy Joel Moore).

bats, balls, etc." By 1845 vacant lots in Manhattan had become scarce. The members of this group started taking the short ferry boat ride across the Hudson River in order to play their ball games at the Elysian Fields in Hoboken, New Jersey. On September 23, 1845, this group, which included Cartwright, established the formal organization to be known as the Knickerbocker Base Ball Club and adopted a new set of written rules for playing base ball (pp. 339–340).

These rules, which came to be known as the "New York Game," eliminated the practice of plugging or soaking the runner. Instead of a 360-degree field, the playing area was based on a diamond configuration containing a 90-degree area of fair territory with foul territory outside the lines running from home to first base and home to third base. The existence of foul territory behind home plate and along the base lines allowed the spectators to be closer to the action.

While the Knickerbockers are often given credit for establishing the distance between the bases at 90 feet, that is not entirely accurate. The Knickerbockers' Rule No. 4 actually states that "The bases shall be from home to second, forty-two paces; from first to third base, forty-two paces, equidistant." If we use three feet as the definition of a "pace," the distance from home to second is 126 feet, which establishes the distance from home to first as 89.1, not 90 feet. Some historians, citing military marching manuals from that era, have made a case that a "pace" should be defined as 2.5 feet, which would make the distance from home to second only 105 feet and the distance from home to first only 74.246 feet.

The original Knickerbocker Game of 1845 includes Rule No. 12 that states, "If a ball be struck, or tipped, and caught, either flying or on the first bound, it is a hand out." This establishes a fundamental tenet of the original Knickerbockers' version game: any ball, fair or foul, which is caught on the fly or the first bounce, is an out. Rule No. 9 states that "The ball must be pitched, and not thrown, for the bat," thereby establishing another fundamental part of the game — underhand pitching. Both of these points make the game playable by re-creators of both moderate and expert skill and indicate that the original New York Game was played in a gentlemanly atmosphere.

Under the original 1845 Knickerbocker Rules, the winner of the match was the first team to score 21 "counts, or aces." It was not until May 1857 that this rule was changed so that a match would be determined by the score after nine innings rather than the first team to score 21 runs. Though not specified in the rules, bag-type bases replaced stakes. The Knickerbocker Rules are generally considered to be the basis of modern base ball.

Program leaders seeking to represent an early time period will find that, in comparison to town ball, the game created by the Knickerbocker Rules of 1845 or after — played on a diamond with bags for bases and no "plugging" permitted — looks more like modern base ball. Players of various skill levels can hit a ball pitched underhand and catch a ball on the bound for an out. Of the bat-and-ball games of the pre-Civil War era, the Knickerbockers' Game of the 1840s and 1850s is very well suited to a re-creation effort. The next iteration, the 1860 rules, also adapts well to a vintage base ball program.

The Middle Era circa 1860

Most vintage clubs play by the rules of the late 1850s or early 1860s. This form of base ball, developed from the original 1845 Knickerbocker Rules, continued to be known as the New York Game. Many vintage clubs have found that the rules and practices of the late 1850s and early 1860s provide an enjoyable and entertaining game for both participants and spectators.

The 1860 rules are readily available in print and on the Internet. In addition to the rules, the 1860 publication *Beadle's Dime Base-Ball Player* contains commentary by Henry Chadwick, the foremost rules expert of the nineteenth century. Chadwick provides valuable information on how the rules and associated practices should be interpreted and how the game was to be played at that time. The 1860 rules are widely used because vintage programs have access not only to the rules, but also to Chadwick's commentary, which clears up some (but not all) of the questions regarding how the game was played. These rules can be interpreted to include slower underhand pitching, making the game enjoyable for players representing a wide range of ages and skill levels.

The rules of this 1860 era, when base ball was played by the Knickerbockers and other gentlemen's clubs in the greater New York area, while similar to the rules of modern baseball, include important differences. Any ball (fair or foul) caught on the first bound is an out. A runner must return to his base immediately on a foul ball by the batter or he can be put out if the ball reaches the base before he gets back. A ball struck by the batter is judged fair or foul by where it touches the ground first; the ball does not have to pass first or third base as a fair ball as in modern baseball. Therefore, a struck ball that hits the ground in front of the plate and then bounces or rolls into foul territory is considered fair, with the batter trying to make it safely to first and all runners eligible to advance. Most other rules are similar to the modern game—nine players on a side, ninety feet between the bases, three outs to an inning, nine innings to a game,.

These similarities provide a feeling of familiarity and continuity that is easily grasped by the player who is new to the vintage game and by the spectator who watches a few innings. The variations from the modern game are just different enough to be a source of interest and give the vintage game a unique appeal and a personality all its own. At a vintage game set in the 1860 period, spectators will immediately notice that base ball gloves are not worn. They will take note that a batter can be put out if the ball he hits is caught on the fly or first bound. Many will recall informal games of "first bounce or fly" as kids and will quickly relate to the concept.

Under these rules, a full nine-inning game usually can be played in about 90 minutes, with even high-scoring games wrapping up in under two hours. In addition to the relatively short time needed to take in a game, spectators will also appreciate the emphasis placed on good manners, sportsmanship, and gentlemanly decorum, all traits of the game that are in keeping with the way a base ball game was conducted at that time.

If electing to adopt the 1860 rules as a framework for a vintage program, there are still decisions to be made regarding slow pitching or fast pitching. While most vintage programs prefer the practice of slow pitching that was the norm through the 1850s, some have chosen to interpret the 1860 rules and practices to include faster pitching that was beginning to appear about that time, at least among the elite clubs of the East. Adopting "swift pitching," as it was called, changes the nature of the game significantly, making it more difficult to play.

Both pitching styles are historically accurate, but a program considering the adoption of the practice of swift pitching rather than the traditional pattern of slow pitching should realize that this step carries with it a number of significant implications. These include: the length of a game; expenses relating to equipment and the playing field (a backstop to protect visitors and to keep the game moving); recruitment and retention of qualified players; spectator appeal; opportunities to play matches with community teams; maintaining an atmosphere of good sportsmanship; compatibility with the mission of the organization sponsoring the team; and the safety of players and spectators. A more complete discussion comparing and contrasting slow pitching and swift pitching is found in Chapter 17.

The rules of 1860, if based on the traditional practice of slow pitching, create a competitive yet sportsmanlike game that provides an excellent look at how modern baseball developed. Comparisons and contrasts are quickly grasped by the spectator, especially when pointed out by the umpire, scorer, and interpreters in period dress, and by the players as they interact with the crowd before and during the match. Since it works so well in actual practice, it is the era most commonly portrayed throughout the vintage community.

The Post–Civil War Era

Some vintage base ball programs have elected to portray the era after the Civil War, conducting their games according to the rules and practices in use from the mid–1860s through the mid–1880s. In the post–Civil War era, the fly game replaced the bound game in the rule book, swift pitching became more common, and professional players gradually took over the game as it was played at the highest level.

The fly game became part of the rules (at least for the elite clubs) for the 1865 season.

Up to this time, the rules called for a batter to be put out if he hit a ball (fair or foul) that was caught on the fly or the first bound. In *A Game of Inches: The Game on the Field*, Peter Morris provides an explanation of how this came about, citing games in the late 1850s in which the Knickerbockers and the Excelsiors began experimenting with requiring the ball to be caught on the fly. "Pleased with the results" of these experimental games, "the Knickerbockers led a campaign to permit an out only for catching a ball on the fly. The issue was heatedly debated for the next few years and was brought up at the annual convention of the National Association of Base Ball Players no fewer the six times." At the NABBP meeting in December 1864, "they finally carried their point, and fielders were required to catch fair balls on the fly, although foul balls could still be caught on the first bounce until the 1880s" (pp. 39–40).

Another major change involved the speed of the pitching. Beginning with the legendary Jim Creighton, who was regarded as the most outstanding player in the game in the early 1860s, most researchers agree that faster pitching was becoming a part of games played by some of the established elite clubs in the East. Some observers believed that Creighton may have been breaking the existing rules, which required that "the ball must be pitched, not jerked or thrown, to the bat." Despite the stipulation that the ball was to be pitched (delivered with an underhand motion), Creighton was able to get away with delivering the ball with considerable swiftness (in the language of the time), perhaps in the manner of a modern fast-pitch softball pitcher or submarine-style baseball pitcher. Since Creighton was so effective, faster underhand pitching seems to have crept into the game as an acceptable practice, at least among the clubs familiar with Creighton's style.

At about this same time, professionalism entered the game as some of the established clubs began to employ more highly skilled players in order to increase the club's prospects of winning its matches against other clubs. Skilled batters were needed to keep pace with the swifter pitching that was more difficult to hit. As playing to win became more important than playing for exercise and recreation, amateur players began to be replaced by paid professionals.

While NABBP rules prohibited paying players, compensation for playing became increasingly common in the form of under-the-table payments or "jobs" that required little or no actual work other than playing base ball for the club. Since payments were often made in secret, it is difficult to document the advent or frequency of paid players. These under-the-table arrangements continued from about 1860 through the latter part of the decade when the 1869 Cincinnati Red Stockings emerged as the first openly all-professional team. For the first time, it was acknowledged that each player on the club received a salary for the season, thereby ushering in a new era of professionalism.

In the post–Civil War era, the nature of base ball changed rapidly, producing a game played by more skilled professional players that was significantly different — faster underhand or sidearm pitching, base stealing, sliding, and a rougher, more aggressive style of play — than the play of the amateur era by gentlemen's clubs from the mid–1840s through the early 1860s. These developments had a profound effect on the game. As winning became more important, play became rougher in nature. Playing by the rules and practices of the post–Civil War period is more suited to programs with younger, more highly skilled, more athletic players: basically those who are already quite proficient and experienced in competitive baseball or fast-pitch softball and have the ability to hit faster pitching. Cognizant of the fact that introducing the fly game, fast pitching, and unrestricted stealing makes the game more difficult to play, some program leaders, players, and clubs still prefer this "faster"

Commemorating an important event in local baseball history, the Cincinnati Red Stockings and Ohio Village Muffins hold the coin toss prior to a match at Columbus' Schiller Park, where the Washington Nationals played during their famous western tour in 1867. Harry Wright, captain of the original Red Stockings and future member of the Hall of Fame, umpired that game.

version of nineteenth-century base ball, which, they point out, reflects the changing nature of the game as it moved from the amateur era to the professional era. Teams playing by the rules and practices that came into being in 1864, 1865, and after have been successful and include the programs at Greenfield Village and Old Bethpage, along with a number of newer clubs from Maryland to Massachusetts.

Some players enjoy the added challenge of playing in this manner. However, museum professionals and club leaders should keep in mind that this more aggressive version of the vintage game has implications for equipment expense, spectator and participant safety, and the general tone of the game. Spectators watching the earlier versions of the game often remark on how refreshing it is to get away from the overly competitive behavior exhibited by the players in modern baseball. The line between competitive and aggressive is a fine one, requiring effective program leadership.

The Era of Overhand Pitching: 1884 and After

Beginning in 1884, the pitching rules no longer made any attempt to regulate the angle of delivery, thus permitting overhand pitching. Therefore, those groups playing by the 1886 and 1887 rules listed on the VBBA website (or by the rules of any year from the mid–1880s on) can employ fast, overhand pitching. While wearing the quaint uniforms of the 1880s or 1890s makes the players of later eras resemble the players of the 1860s at first glance, the game itself becomes much different and, like modern baseball, is characterized by a duel between the pitcher and the batter, with fewer balls being put in play by the batter. Since the umpire is now calling balls and strikes, there are both strikeouts and walks.

Batters face the serious challenge of hitting fastballs and sharp-breaking curveballs, just as in modern baseball. A club or program that portrays this era will need to recruit mostly young, athletic, experienced, and highly skilled players who are able to hit overhand fast pitching with some degree of success.

A program based on overhand pitching of the mid–1880s and later will definitely need to construct a backstop since there will be more fast pitches that get through the catcher (wild pitches and passed balls in modern terminology). The program will require catcher's equipment — an added expense. Reproduction catcher's equipment may be hard to find and expensive, and may not provide the protection of modern gear. Original equipment would probably be too rare and expensive to use in vintage play. Modern catcher's equipment is sturdy and readily available, but its use would compromise the authentic look of a nineteenth-century game. Faster pitching will also result in broken bats, which is another safety concern and expense.

Vintage base ball games based on overhand pitching may be well suited for a modern baseball diamond at a local high school field or public park that has a skin infield and a backstop to protect spectators from sharply hit foul balls. If the games are played on the museum grounds, program administrators will need to think about dedicating an area for the field since a backstop is needed. Thought also should be given to placing spectator seating areas farther from the field and perhaps screening off some areas to prevent hard-hit foul balls from going into the stands.

The more competitive nature of this faster, more aggressive type of nineteenth-century base ball appeals to some players and spectators. Replicating the later era can definitely be done, as evidenced by the successful programs playing by the late-nineteenth century rules, but it should be kept in mind that 1880s or 1890s base ball is much closer to the modern game of the twenty-first century than it is to the gentlemanly game played by the amateur clubs just twenty or thirty years earlier. Independent teams, perhaps composed of players who also enjoy the competitive nature of adult fast-pitch baseball leagues, may like to play by the rules of the 1880s and 1890s. However, fast-pitch games (underhand or overhand) can take on an unpleasant edge that is usually not seen in the pre–Civil War version of vintage base ball. An edgy, combative atmosphere was undoubtedly authentic to base ball as it was actually played in this later era. Overhand pitching and the more aggressive style of play that goes with it can produce a game that is colorful and interesting to watch. However, by the 1880s and 1890s, the game was characterized by arguments with the umpire and less-than-cordial relations between the competing teams, which museum visitors can see at any professional ballpark or on television.

One successful enterprise representing the latter part of the nineteenth century is the Bay Area Vintage Base Ball program in northern California, which makes a conscious effort to retain the gentlemanly character of the earlier eras. The website reports that the program operates as a league that is "dedicated to preserving the style of play that was in effect in 1886" where the game is played "the way it was before $50M contracts, shoe sponsorships, and 25 man rosters." The league includes twelve clubs, "which play 12 games a season in a fun, relaxed atmosphere." While the 1880s and 1890s were an era of extreme competitiveness,

Programs adopting overhand or swift underhand pitching need to consider constructing a backstop similar to this excellent wood and wire example at Old Bethpage Restoration on Long Island, N.Y.

the program attempts to retain the gentlemanly aspects of the earlier eras, describing its brand of vintage base ball as a place where "true grit is displayed and sportsmanship is the holy grail." In regard to uniforms and equipment, "Each team is outfitted in reproduction uniforms from the 1880s, and the equipment consists of reproduction balls, gloves, bases, etc., that are made to look, feel, and perform as they did when the game was still home-grown."

The Providence Grays in Rhode Island are another very successful club that portrays the later years of the nineteenth century. Their website reports that "inspired by similar historical teams in New York," the club was created "to form a tribute to the 1884 Grays," a reference to Providence's membership in the National League and the pennant won by the original team in 1884. As evidenced by the material on the website, the club has demonstrated admirable attention to detail in re-creating everything from an authentic belt for the team uniforms to an authentic nineteenth-century mask for the umpire.

These successful programs show that re-creating base ball as it was played in the 1880s and 1890s can be done, but program leaders should keep in mind that it presents some extra challenges. Depending on the sponsoring institution's mission, club organizers will need to carefully consider if this type of competitive fast-pitch base ball is a good fit for visitor demographics, the characteristics of the area available for a playing field, and program goals.

Decision Points

Each of these five eras has successful vintage programs playing by the rules and practices appropriate for that period. The colorful uniforms and interesting equipment of the nineteenth century give the vintage game of any era great visual appeal. The sponsoring institution should keep in mind that while various eras of vintage base ball may look similar at first glance, the playing styles are considerably different once the game starts, with each era having a unique character that may call for different types of players. Each era has a definite tone and distinctive ambiance, with the earlier versions of the game emphasizing gentlemanly behavior and sportsmanship and the later eras known more for a more aggressive, faster game played by more highly skilled players.

Also, there are differences in uniform styles for the various eras, and it is important to give careful thought to the era to be portrayed before placing orders. As the organizer of one vintage club advised other new clubs on the Vintage Base Ball Association listserv, "Be sure to pick an era first. I made the mistake of not being quite thorough enough in the beginning with my research, and purchased uniforms based on a later era than we play. Not much later I found out that base ball had very early beginnings in our town, and we really could have based our styles on more of an 1865–1868 look. Research should always be the first point of action. That way you don't have to talk people into accepting changes, and breaking bad habits." This is superb advice from someone who has been there.

The style of play needs to be carefully weighed when selecting an era. Choosing the 1860 era as characterized by slow pitching and restrictions on base stealing produces a sportsmanlike, gentlemanly game that provides an educational and interesting experience for visitors. It can also be well played and competitive in the best sense of the word. There is a smaller likelihood of injuries, and it is less expensive to present than later eras. It is more inclusive and is most often consistent with the values and philosophy of the affiliated institution. That is why this style of play has been adopted by so many successful programs. Some may find the more aggressive style of play with faster pitching, unrestricted stealing, and a more combative atmosphere more exciting. However, it would be wise for representatives from a museum or historical organization to visit several sites representing this style of play so that they can observe actual games and talk to the leaders and players on some of the established teams. It is always a good idea to consult those who have programs up and running before making a commitment to a specific time period.

Merging Local History with an Appropriate Set of Rules

The VBBA website, under the heading "Rules Commonly Played in Vintage Base Ball," contains the texts of the Knickerbocker Rules for 1845; the rules adopted by the National Association of Base Ball Players for 1858, 1860, 1861, 1862, 1864, 1867, 1869, and 1873; and the rules adopted by the National Association of Professional Base Ball Players for 1886 and 1887. This is a valuable resource for all vintage clubs and a good place to start when attempting to become familiar with the rules from different years.

Logic suggests that the time period of the historic site or community signature event should correspond to the published rules of base ball in that year. Yet, oftentimes that decision is not as easy as it seems. Different eras of vintage base ball may be more or less suitable for an organization depending on the size and location of the area available for the playing field, the age and skill level of the ball players, safety concerns, the overall type of programming the institution endeavors to provide, and the values, goals, mission, and philosophy of the sponsoring institution.

Regional differences are another consideration. It is well documented that by the mid–

1860s, the Eastern clubs were dealing with the issues of paid professional players, an increased emphasis on winning, and the growth of gambling on games along with the associated unpleasant reality of ball games being fixed and thrown for bribes. At the same time, new clubs forming in the Midwest were playing a much more recreational version of base ball with clubs composed of amateur players (similar to the style of base ball played by the Knickerbockers and the other gentlemen's clubs of the East in the 1840s and 1850s). Post–Civil War base ball in the Midwest was characterized by groups of social friends and business associates who formed clubs, elected officers, and got together to choose up sides to play informal games for recreation and exercise in city parks and other areas used for leisure and sporting activities.

It is instructive to compare the well-developed game in the East with the much less formal version of base ball played in other parts of the country in the year after the Civil War ended. Research on the beginnings of base ball in the typical Midwestern city of Columbus, Ohio, reveals a game more like earlier base ball in New York City. The first three base ball clubs to exist in Columbus—the Buckeye, Capital, and Excelsior—all formed in the spring of 1866, the first year that many young men were back from the army where they may have been introduced to base ball. The clubs began holding their organizational meetings and conducting "field exercise" sessions (what we might call intra-squad games). James Comly, the editor-publisher of the leading local newspaper, *The Ohio State Journal*, and first president of the Capital Club, ran frequent articles and notices urging folks to come out and watch the new game of base ball as played by all three of the newly formed amateur clubs.

The initial game of the Capital Club on April 14, 1866 (exactly one year after the assassination of President Lincoln), was played not before a large throng of spectators at a well-established sporting venue such as Hoboken's Elysian Fields, but at the rear of the downtown-area residence of William Platt, the president of the local gas company and brother-in-law of future U.S. President Rutherford B. Hayes. The *Journal* article reported, "Quite an interest was manifested in the first game played by the Capital Base Ball Club on Saturday afternoon, and in spite of the threatening state of the weather, quite a number of ladies and gentlemen were present as spectators. The scorer reports not a very good game but a 'jolly good time.'"

An account of a game played in Columbus on April 24, 1866, relates, "The Capital Club met for field exercise on their grounds at the South End yesterday afternoon, and had a very pleasant game. The high wind interfered somewhat with the smooth progress of affairs, but it was considered an inconvenience rather than a difficulty to be overcome. There were many visitors present, who seemed to find much enjoyment in the game as non-participants."

The account in Chapter 1 of the early "vintage" game played in Elmira, New York, in 1887 also reinforces the point that the game was played differently in different locales. The newspaper description of the Elmira game states that the game was played by "the rules of 1866 when the two teams were first organized right after the Civil War. ... Pitched balls were the rule, bound catches were considered out, there was no calling of strikes and balls, and all the modern features of the game were unknown." The rule requiring balls to be caught on the fly rather than the first bound was changed in the NABBP rule book for 1865. However, it is clear from this account that the Elmira clubs were playing the bound game, not the fly game, when the city's first clubs were formed in 1866. One logical explanation for not playing the fly game after it had been formally adopted in 1865 might be that the rules the young men of Elmira learned while serving in the army provided for outs on bound catches and those were the rules they brought home from the war. They may not have known the rule had been changed, or they may have been aware of the new rule and knew that the fly game was being played by the New York City clubs 230 miles away, but simply preferred playing the one-bound rule. In any case, they were not observing the most current rules formulated and published in New York City. Some clubs had begun to experiment with the fly game before the rule was changed for the 1865 season and other clubs probably continued to play the bound game long afterward.

The point is that geography matters. Base ball as it was played at the "Championship Match" at the Elysian Fields in Hoboken in 1866 by the well-established clubs of the greater New York City area and base ball as it was played by a newly formed club in the Midwest in the backyard of a leading citizen or at a city park in 1866 would likely have been two quite different games. Re-creating base ball as it was played in the same year in the 1860s in New York City or Elmira or Columbus suggests different presentations. Given the state of communications and absence of a truly national structure, the fact that a certain rule was passed by the NABBP and published in a guide book does not necessarily mean that it was immediately and universally observed by all clubs throughout the land. Since base ball was played differently in various parts of the country in a given year, program organizers who prefer to re-create the gentlemanly style of play have some latitude in choosing to present games according to a set of rules and customs consistent with that choice.

"Friendly Games"

While the tone and atmosphere of base ball was beginning to change among some of the established clubs in the New York City area, other veteran clubs continued to emphasize gentlemanly play. The Knickerbockers did not play any matches with other clubs in 1861 or 1862. When they resumed playing in 1863, Charles Peverelly, in *The Book of American Pastimes*, speaks of "friendly" games being arranged by the Knickerbockers with their only opponent over the next three seasons being the Excelsior Club. While it might be surmised that the Knickerbockers' suspension of play against other clubs in 1861 and 1862 was largely due to the upheaval caused by the start of the Civil War with many able-bodied ballplayers going off to military service, the lack of matches might also be traced to the changing nature of the game of base ball at this time, as less-gentlemanly play and the use of paid players began creeping into the game.

According to Peverelly's accounts, the other New York-area clubs that the Knickerbockers had been playing in the 1850s did not cease playing games when the war broke out, nor did they suspend operations as the hostilities continued. The Gothams played three games in 1861, seven in 1862, five in 1863 (including a match on July 1, the first day of the Battle of Gettysburg), and ten in 1864. Similarly, the Eagle, Empire, and Excelsior clubs all continued to play matches during the war.

This reference to the Knickerbockers playing only "friendly games" may have been a product of some of the other clubs not playing in a friendly, sportsmanlike manner. The Knickerbockers seem to have been striving to maintain the tradition of recreational and gentlemanly play that had characterized base ball to that point. By cutting back on the number of games with other clubs and by specifying that matches with their old colleagues, the Excelsiors, were being played as "friendly games," they may have been differentiating their games from the way base ball was being played by other clubs.

What are the implications of the introduction of the term "friendly games" in the 1860s for the sport of vintage base ball and the way vintage games should be conducted? Peverelly says that by maintaining their traditional standards that required each member to be a gentleman (rather than recruiting skilled players solely on their base ball talents), the Knickerbockers were no longer a competitive club.

From uniforms and equipment to the ambiance of a match, selecting an era is the important first step in creating a vintage base ball program. Since the tone and manner of vintage games played by the rules and practices of the later eras can result in a less-sportsmanlike presentation, museum professionals should consider the pattern of what actually happened as the decade of the 1860s unfolded. They may decide to adopt a gentlemanly model for the game, but they also need to set and reinforce player standards and expectations so that the sportsmanlike character of the program does not gradually drift into a more aggressive version of vintage base ball that may not fit the institution's public programming goals.

In "Prologue: Reliving the Past" in *Baseball's First Inning*, William Ryczek addresses this point as he tells of his experiences playing vintage base ball. He observes that "the vintage game has wide appeal, providing exercise and entertainment for athletes, former athletes, historians, the curious, and any combination thereof." He also points out that "one can read about the rules of baseball as they were in the nineteenth century, but the way to gain an appreciation of the nuances of the game is to play it" (p. 9). Ryczek then draws on his vintage base ball experience to discuss how his team "unintentionally followed the path forged in the nineteenth century." The vintage game, he observes, "has emulated the early days of baseball in more than just the rules" (p. 11).

As a member of the Mansfield Club of Middletown, Connecticut, when it was founded in 1996, Ryczek recalls the team, which "consisted of local attorneys, teachers, professors, members of the historical society and the like" at first enjoyed the general experience of playing nineteenth-century base ball. When they lost to a more skilled club, "we took our overwhelming defeat with grace, applauded the good plays of our opponents and socialized with them after the game," just as things would have been done in the late 1850s or 1860. But after losing subsequent games to teams with more talented players, the Mansfields "were no longer content to be the hapless victims of our opponents." The result was that "in one game, our pitcher, enraged by the call of the umpire, slammed the ball to the ground in disgust and shouted an obscenity." Ryczek correctly points out, "This was clearly not the game of the 1850s when players never, ever disputed the call of the umpire, no matter how erroneous or ill-informed it might be." He states that "the rest of the team apologized profusely but a sea change had taken place. The 1850s were over. It was 1860. We wanted to win" (p. 12).

Ryczek reports that the emphasis on winning brought about a further transformation in his team. "Over the next two years, the membership of the Mansfields began to change. The older, respectable, but less talented members of the team, the lawyers, historical society members, and professors, began to yield to younger players who didn't know much about vintage baseball or the history of the game but had a little bit of playing experience and the springy legs and strong arms that enabled them to make a better showing. Misplays on the field led to grumbling on the bench, and the respectable gentlemen who remained were sometimes the object of resentment when their muffs led to a series of runs." Comparing the course his team was taking to what happened in the game's early days, Ryczek observed, "We were in the early 1860s when the Knickerbockers, Excelsiors and Gothams yielded to the Atlantics, Mutuals and Eckfords" (p. 12).

The pattern continued. Describing the Mansfield Club's participation in the Capital City Cup in Hartford, Connecticut, Ryczek cites the similarities between the increasing combativeness in the vintage game and the flow of events in the 1860s and early 1870s. "At the Capital City tourney there was a near-brawl, after which some players threatened to call the police." Such ill-will "would have been unheard of" in the Mansfield's founding year of 1996, and "a string of emotional emails followed the altercation." Ryczek observes that some of these correspondents "called for a return to the pristine, gentlemanly play of the mid–1990s" just as early ballplayers of the mid–1860s "were longing for the halcyon days of the 1850s when gentlemen played the game for enjoyment and the idea of disputing an umpire's decision or using foul language was reprehensible" (p. 13). "Unknowingly," writes Ryczek, "the practitioners of vintage base ball in the twenty-first century have emulated their nineteenth-century predecessors, not just in playing the game, but in the evolution of the sport, shedding light on the reasons why baseball developed as it did" (p. 13).

It is not inevitable, of course, that a vintage base ball club will always adopt a rougher, less-gentlemanly style of play. In fact, the VBBA mission statement guards against this very development by affirming that "all of its members will conduct all matches, meetings, and other activities — both on and off the field — according to the highest standards of sportsmanship, gentlemanly behavior, courtesy, and respect for others which characterized the Knickerbocker Base Ball Club, established, September 23, 1845."

Many vintage clubs have followed these principles and have continued to play the game in a gentlemanly manner over many seasons. Ryczek's perceptive account of his experiences in vintage base ball can serve as a cautionary tale, however, as to what can happen. Aware of the possibility of a program drifting toward an overly competitive approach, effective leaders can set standards for how the game is to be presented and played that will maintain its sportsmanlike and gentlemanly character.

5

The Gentlemen of the Clubs: Expectations and Responsibilities

The members of the vintage base ball fraternity have in common a love for the game. Whether they come to the vintage diamond directly from years of playing baseball and softball or have not picked up a bat since Little League, once they are on the vintage team they share a responsibility to the sponsoring organization, to one another, and to the history of the game.

Being a person who reenacts or re-creates history is a particular responsibility. In *Reliving the Civil War*, Lee Hadden defines reenactment as "a re-creation of an actual historical event that is both representative and historically correct" (p. 14). Presenting vintage base ball differs from Civil War and other military reenactments in that the outcomes are not certain. The teams do not "act out" known games, following a script or box score. Instead, the framework of rules and customs is respected and matches follow their own course. In this circumstance, it is even more important for each vintage player to understand the players and the culture of the era portrayed so that they can make decisions during a match that are "representative and historically accurate."

Vintage base ball participants usually find that being affiliated with a museum-based program is a positive experience. Vintage team participants should understand that the sponsoring institution understandably puts a high priority on its primary goals of historical interpretation and education, not necessarily winning every game by as large a margin as possible. This can be a remarkable revelation for players who grew up approaching sports with a "winning is everything" orientation. Scoring more runs than the opposing team is fine, and everyone would rather win than lose. But what really counts is providing a first-rate (and safe) educational experience for the players and visitors.

This approach to the game is historically authentic, in keeping with the way base ball was played in the earliest years of the game. As Henry Chadwick recommended in Haney's *Base Ball Book of Reference: The Revised Rules of the Game for 1867*, "Play earnestly at all times whether in an ordinary practice game or in a match. Get in the habit of doing your best on all occasions." But if things go badly in a game, the player is advised to "control yourself and take it smilingly." The message from Chadwick is clearly to play hard, but also to keep winning and losing in perspective. "Next to seeing a man field well, the most attractive is to see a player who takes things easy and good naturedly," Chadwick reminds us. "Remember that the winning of the trophy is [only] one of the main objects in view, and ... it is not the most important thing in life to win it or a very great disaster to lose it" (pp 134–135).

A Contemporary Description of the Gentlemanly Knickerbockers

To develop the mindset of a gentleman of a nineteenth-century base ball club, it is helpful to look back at accounts of the ways of the gentlemen of that era. In his *The Book of American Pastimes*, Charles A. Peverelly describes the participants in these early informal contests played in lower Manhattan in the 1840s as "a number of gentlemen, fond of the game" (p. 339). Peverelly goes on to explain how these gentlemanly players formed the Knickerbocker Base Ball Club, an organization he describes as one whose "respectability has ever been undoubted" (pp. 340–341).

Those who took the field as players on the base ball clubs of the 1840s and 1850s were, in socio-economic terms, much like the vintage base ball players of today. In the 1960 groundbreaking work in sports history, *Baseball: The Early Years*, Seymour and Mills reported on the occupations of the Knickerbockers. "Among some fifty-odd names on their roster from 1845 to 1860 were 17 merchants, 12 clerks, 5 brokers, 4 professional men, 2 insurance men, a bank teller, a 'Segar Dealer,' one hatter, a cooperage owner, a stationer, and a United States Marshal, and several 'gentlemen'" (p. 16). Seymour and Mills comment, "Mere skill in playing was not the only requisite for admission; a certain standing in the community was necessary as well," but this remark should not be interpreted as suggesting the Knickerbockers were elitist. The occupational breakdown indicates that many members held a variety of regular jobs but were not wealthy. These were men who went to work every day in their offices, shops, and stores to earn a living.

In 1860, gentlemanly decorum even extended to politics. In "Election Day 1860," in *Smithsonian* magazine (November 2008), Harold Holzer provides a memorable vignette of the societal and political norms of the time. As the election approached, "Lincoln had done next to nothing publicly, and precious little privately, to advance his own cause. Prevailing political tradition called for silence from presidential candidates." Holzer reports that on election day, Lincoln voted the straight Republican ticket, but only "after first cutting his own name, and those of the electors pledged to him, from the top of his preprinted ballot so that he could vote for other Republicans without immodestly voting for himself."

For some players, this emphasis on gentlemanly behavior that is representative of earlier times is a new approach to playing sports. Some who have been accustomed to playing baseball, softball, and other sports with a "win-at-all-costs" attitude may find the concepts and definitions of a gentleman very "old fashioned." Exactly. This transition into playing base ball in a more sportsmanlike manner may be difficult for some. One museum professional commented that although the official position of the museum's vintage base ball program was to emphasize education and interpretation rather than won-lost records, there were always some players who could not let go of their twenty-first century mindset that the team's won-lost record and even individual statistics were of primary importance.

Examples of developing a more mature and gentlemanly approach to winning and losing come from many sources. In an April 2007 post on the *Prairie Home Companion* website, a father asked program host and author Garrison Keillor how to help his nine-year-old son get through the disappointment of submitting a story to a writing contest that did not win the prize the boy had hoped for. In his reply to this request for help in getting the son to "pick up his pencil and keep writing," Keillor provided an answer that should strike a chord with vintage base ball participants: "A writing contest is a game and you play it for fun. It's the same as in baseball: you'll play better if you love playing the game itself, and if you love the game, you'll accept losing. The game is the beautiful thing, and you'd rather be in the game, and losing, than be in the bleachers watching."

Modern Misunderstandings: What Is a Gentleman?

Today, people seem confused about what qualities define a gentleman. The term "gentlemen" is too often used indiscriminately, having been diluted to include virtually any adult male. Entertainers, politicians, public address announcers, and others who have the opportunity to speak to large audiences routinely use the phrase "ladies and gentlemen," even though they may have little idea of the character of the persons being addressed. While it can be argued that it may be polite to assume the best about audience members, overuse and misuse of the term "gentlemen" pervade modern culture.

Listen to the evening news. You may hear a police officer describe a bank robbery by saying that "two gentlemen" wearing ski masks entered the door with guns drawn, threatened the lives of the tellers and customers, then fled with the money. In describing a stalker who got past security systems and entered a movie star's home, a reporter may say that "the gentleman" was apprehended by police and charged with breaking and entering. A feature on CBS *Sunday Morning* included an interview with a museum director who held up a glass jar containing a mass of human tissue and identified the contents as the brain of Charles Guiteau, "the gentlemen" who shot President Garfield. In mentioning the notorious Bernie Madoff, convicted of swindling billions of dollars from his closest friends and several charitable groups, David Lettermen, in his opening monologue one night, referred to Madoff as being at age 72 "an older gentleman." To the vintage base ball community, as with the nineteenth-century players, the word "gentleman" is a more meaningful term.

The Vintage Base Ball Gentleman

Dictionary definitions of a gentleman include the words kindness, courtesy, and honor; high ideals and thoughtful actions — "a man whose conduct conforms to a high standard of propriety or correct behavior," according to Webster. The term "gentleman" is applicable to those who were members of the early base ball clubs and those who play vintage base ball today. The slim but enlightening book *How to Be a Gentleman: A Contemporary Guide to Common Courtesy* by John Bridges was published in 1998 but provides insight on the traditional good manners of much earlier times. In the introduction, Bridges points out that "The truth of the matter is, being a gentleman is not rocket science. Being a gentleman requires a little logic, a little forethought, and a great deal of consideration for others. It is not about complicated rules and convoluted instructions. Instead it is about honestly and sincerely being a nice guy" (p. ix). This insight, in turn, helps us comprehend how people approached playing base ball in its early years and provides some useful guidelines as to how vintage players should approach the game today.

Bridges explains, with specific examples and suggestions, how a gentleman handles various situations, offering such advice as, "A gentleman always offers to share an umbrella" and "A gentleman always glances behind him when he walks through a door. He never slams a door in another person's face. It does not matter whether the other person is a man or a woman ... [he] makes the world a little easier for the person after him. That is, after all, why gentlemen exist" (p. 22, 11).

There is no specific chapter titled "How a Gentleman Plays Baseball," but most vintage players could help Bridges write one that is in keeping with the tone and spirit of his guide book on gentlemanly behavior. Along with providing advice on proper behavior at such formal occasions as weddings and funerals and in such everyday situations as going through the grocery store checkout line, Bridges does offer this advice to a gentleman attending a sporting event: "He does not begrudge the other team its victory. If his own team is the victor, he does not taunt the opposition" (p. 18). Bridges' comments on winning with class and losing with grace are very much in keeping with the gentlemanly mindset of players of the Knickerbocker era as well as modern vintage base ball players.

In mid-nineteenth-century America, a gentleman was a person of good character who was honest and upright in his professional and business dealings, never taking unfair advantage of anyone. Where the rules of base ball are imprecise or do not cover specific situations that may arise in a game, it is wise to consider how a gentlemanly player would have handled that situation and proceed accordingly.

Most vintage base ball players have a lot of fun acting the part of a nineteenth-century gentleman before, during, and after the game. For example, players on the home team will greet the opposing team warmly when they arrive for the match and will congratulate an opponent who makes an especially fine fielding play. These are small gestures that reinforce the tone of the match. Being a gentleman and a good sport (in both victory and defeat) are characteristics of vintage base ball and set the nineteenth-century game apart from modern base ball and softball — a difference not lost on the spectators at a vintage match.

Disputing an umpire's call, knocking down an opposing player with a hard slide, throwing down a bat in anger over making an out, gloating over a mistake by someone on the other team, or using inappropriate language might be tolerated in a modern softball league, but such behavior would be totally out of place at a vintage game. The vintage base ball player is not just representing himself; he is representing his team and often a sponsoring organization that expects the highest standards of personal conduct from anyone playing on the club.

Teams that are not under the direct guidance of a museum professional (independent teams and those with loose affiliations with institutions) need to set and maintain high standards of historical interpretation. This is especially important if they play a match on museum property or at a community festival where value is placed on the goal of education rather than winning the game. All vintage clubs should remember that when they are invited to play a match on another club's grounds, they should respect the team and institutional guidelines, such as arriving at the site of the game in full uniform and not bringing plastic coolers to the bench area.

The Clodbuster Base Ball Club of Dayton, Ohio, developed the following statement, and sent it out in advance to visiting clubs for games played on the grounds of an historic farm.

> Watches, jewelry, (necklaces and earrings), and sunglasses, are **greatly** discouraged. Carriage Hill MetroPark is a living history museum representative of 1880s life. Unless you are under orders of a doctor, we do ask that you respect the farm and not wear any non-period items while on the field.

Statements of this type, which share the home program's very reasonable guidelines with visiting clubs, are helpful in setting expectations and establishing the tone of the game. Even veteran players may need a reminder occasionally and newer players who have not thought about some of these things may inadvertently walk on the field wearing modern sunglasses or carrying a plastic water bottle.

When two vintage clubs arrange a match, they should think of themselves as partners (not opponents) as they present a vintage game to the public. The captain of the visiting team (perhaps jointly with the host club's captain or the umpire) should review the host's protocols with his team before the game. If there are any questions or problems in complying with the home club's expectations, these matters should be settled by the visiting captain so that the host institution is not put in the awkward position of having to speak to a visiting player about his appearance, equipment, or behavior. All teams playing on museum grounds should understand that part of being a gentlemanly player is to respect the standards and policies of the host club's home grounds, including regulations in regard to alcohol possession and consumption, having pets on the grounds, or other matters.

The Association for Living History, Farm and Agricultural Museums (ALHFAM) provides direction on the importance of accurate attire in the article "How Important Is Accurate Reproduction Clothing?" Carol Hall, associate director of interpretation and education at Old Salem in Massachusetts, states, "We have observed that visitors are much more knowledgeable about inaccurate clothing than they used to be. They may not know what is right, but many notice what is wrong, such as modern glasses, make up, jewelry, and the style of shoes." In the same article, Thomas Shaw, assistant site manager at Fort Snelling in Minnesota, observes that in matters of clothing and accessories, "Museums have a public responsibility to be as accurate as current scholarship allows. Since museums form public perception, they are obliged to do the best they can." Therefore, while playing at the home institution or as guests at another museum property, vintage base ball program participants need to help the museum meet its professional standards for accuracy. Any personal inclination to wear non-period items needs to be subservient to the institution's goals of maintaining the program's standards in the areas of authenticity and safety.

Clubs and "The Base Ball Fraternity"

When listening to an interview with a modern-day baseball manager you will often hear him use the phrases "the ball club" or "the club" rather than "the team." In football, basketball, and other sports, the dressing area for the players is commonly called the locker room. But baseball insiders and knowledgeable media professionals always refer to the dressing area for baseball players as the "clubhouse." This use of the term "club" is no accident, but rather a reflection of the game's origins.

"The earliest baseball organizations were genuine social clubs, in which baseball playing was an important but far from the only activity," writes historian Warren Goldstein in *Playing for Keeps: A History of Early Baseball*. "Baseball clubs had much in common with other male fraternal organizations in antebellum America. They were governed by constitutions, by-laws, and officers. Members paid dues and met regularly, either at their 'club rooms' (usually located in a hotel or tavern) or on the playing field. Membership ranged from a dozen to more than two hundred." In order to provide insight regarding the nature of these early clubs, Goldstein cites the constitution of one as representative of the norms of the time: "The objects of the Club shall be to 'improve, foster and perpetuate the American game of Base Ball,' and advance morally, socially, and physically, the interests of its members" (p. 17).

In *Sports in American History: From Colonization to Globalization*, authors Gerald Gems,

Linda Borish, and Gertrud Pfister discuss the formation of nineteenth-century sports clubs. The authors cite the work of such reformers as Thomas Wentworth Higginson, who, in addition to campaigning "for causes including education reform, abolitionism, women's rights, and temperance," worked "to establish a populace made up of strong, vital, and moral citizens...in order to advance the young democratic nation" (p. 64). Higginson and his fellow antebellum reformers "promoted the value of robust health and the benefit of sport in articles published in popular magazines and books."

These reformers advocated participation in sports that were "deemed appropriate for respectable, disciplined, and hard-working" individuals, who formed "voluntary associations for organizing appropriate sporting activity and rational recreation." Base ball clubs were a prime example of this movement. "The rise of sport during the mid-nineteenth century (1840–1870) was apparent in the number of sporting clubs organized for men and boys and the spectators they attracted to their competitions" (p. 122).

As Goldstein points out, the antebellum era was a period of growth for fraternal organizations. It is not a coincidence that many Greek-letter college fraternities were founded in the same years that saw the advent and growth of base ball clubs. Beginning with the founding of the Kappa Alpha Society in 1825, *Baird's Manual of American College Fraternities* notes that five additional fraternities were established in the late 1820s and early 1830s, then lists seventeen others formed in the East and Midwest between 1839 and 1858. This is the same period that the first base ball clubs were being established and the sport of base ball was developing into the national game with the founding of the Knickerbocker Club in 1845 and the formation of the National Association of Base Ball Players in 1857. As might be expected, the founding of college fraternities was curtailed with the start of the Civil War, but as the conflict drew to a close, this movement resumed with more fraternities being founded in the post-war era at the same time that a large number of new base ball clubs were formed.

Fraternal organizations for adult men (sometimes called "lodges") also were founded in this era that saw the establishment of many base ball clubs, reflecting the ongoing movement toward forming organizations with high ideals. The Red Men were established in 1847, followed by the Odd Fellows in 1851. The YMCA, which originated in England in 1844, arrived in North America (Montreal and Boston) in 1851. The Knights of Pythias were founded in 1864, followed by the Elks in 1868. The Masons trace their origins to the Middle Ages and became well established in America in the eighteenth century (George Washington, Benjamin Franklin and other founding fathers were members), but grew to become an extremely large and influential organization during the 1840s and 1850s when the other lodges came into being. The fraternal movement continued with the Knights of Columbus coming along in 1881 and the Moose in 1889.

As Goldstein points out, the base ball organizations were "genuine social clubs," products of the era. Peverelly's description of the formation of the Knickerbocker Base Ball Club provides a wonderful window on base ball's early days and is entirely in keeping with the spirit and tone of Goldstein's comments on the nature of the early clubs.

> In the spring of 1845 Mr. Alex. J. Cartwright, who had become an enthusiast of the game, one day upon the field proposed a regular organization, promising to obtain several recruits. His proposal was acceded to, and Messers. W. R. Wheaton, Cartwright, D. F. Curry, E. R. Dupignac, Jr., and W. H. Tucker formed themselves into a board of recruiting officers, and soon obtained names enough to make a respectable show. At a preliminary meeting, it was suggested that as it was apparent they would soon be driven from Murray Hill [an open space in Manhat-

tan where the group had been playing its games] some suitable place should be obtained in New Jersey where their stay could be permanent; accordingly a day or two afterwards, enough to make a game assembled at Barclay street ferry, crossed over, marched up the road, prospecting for ground on each side until they reached the Elysian Fields, where they "settled." Thus it occurred that a party of gentlemen formed an organization, combining together health, recreation, and social enjoyment, which was the nucleus of the now great American game of Base Ball, so popular in all parts of the United States, than which there is none more manly or more health-giving.

The parent Knickerbockers claim for themselves the original organization, from which the succeeding clubs derive their rules of playing....The organization bears the date the 23rd of September, 1845 [pp. 340–341].

In choosing and admitting members, the Knickerbockers and other early clubs were interested in men of the middle class who could be counted upon to fulfill the reasonable expectations of membership: meeting the modest financial responsibilities of belonging ("Annual dues were five dollars, and the initiation fee was two dollars," according to Seymour and Mills [page 17].); attending the games and social activities of the club; playing in a gentlemanly, sportsmanlike manner on the field; and conducting themselves off the field in an honorable manner that would bring credit rather than discredit to the organization and its members. These common-sense expectations are in keeping with what modern vintage base ball clubs (and most other civic organizations, social clubs, and fraternal groups) ask of their members.

The early base ball clubs were composed of amateurs, not professional players who were paid to play base ball. By the late 1850s and early 1860s, however, the paying of skilled players by some clubs was becoming an issue. The gentlemanly clubs resisted the concept of paid players, endeavoring to maintain the amateur character of the game. This high regard for the concept of amateurism that was so valued by the early gentlemen's clubs is revealed in the writings of Walter Camp (1859–1925), who is remembered today as "The Father of American Football," but wrote on other sports, including baseball and golf. Growing up in the 1860s, he reaffirmed the values of that era in *Walter Camp's Book of College Sports*, published in 1893. "A gentleman never competes for money, directly or indirectly," Camp cautioned more than a century ago. "Make no mistake about this. No matter how winding the road may be that eventually brings the sovereign into the pocket, it is the price of what should be dearer to you than anything else — your honor. It is quite the fashion to say 'sentimental bosh' to any one who preaches such an old-fashioned thing as honor; but among true gentlemen, my boy, it is just as real an article as ever, and it is one of the few things that never ring false" (p. 3).

The Decline of the Gentlemanly Amateur Era

The game of base ball, at least as it was played at its highest level among the elite clubs of the East, was starting to move away from its gentlemanly origins and ideals as early as 1860. Incidents that occurred that year at the last of three matches between the Atlantic Club and the Excelsior Club illustrate the changing nature of the game when there emerged an increased emphasis on winning, swift pitching, gambling, and a general decline in gentlemanly behavior among players and spectators. In recounting the events of the 1860 season, Preston Orem reports that when the two teams met on July 19 "no admission was charged," with the expenses of putting on the game having been met by the "dues paying members" of the two clubs. "Theoretically, at least, the game was still conducted upon a strictly amateur basis." The Excelsiors won the first match, 23–4. Twelve thousand spectators were on hand for the second contest on August 9, "the greatest crowd ever up to that time to witness a base ball game." The Excelsiors got off to a good start and held a big lead until pitcher Creighton "who was ill, weakened and was replaced" in the eighth inning, allowing the Atlantics "to win after an uphill battle," 15–14, in a game that was "not decided until the last man was out" (pp. 30–32).

The third match on August 23, 1860, drew a crowd "variously estimated at from 15,000 to 20,0000." Orem reports that "for several days before the game, statements were openly made by the 'roughs' among the Atlantic supporters that they would not permit the Excelsiors to win in a close contest." When the Excelsior Club took a lead, "the gang of toughs who backed the Atlantics were unruly from the outset but increased their clamor in the 5th inning, as they voiced their disapproval of the decisions by the umpire." Although Orem reports that the decisions of the umpire were "perfectly fair," the toughs exhibited "violence" in demanding his removal and in their "hootings against the Excelsiors." This hostile environment at the game was clearly a departure from the traditional atmosphere of gentlemanly behavior that had characterized base ball in the 1850s. With the assistance of the police, "a temporary lull was secured," but Excelsior captain Joe Leggett "stated that he would withdraw his club if the tumult was renewed." With the Excelsiors ahead, 8–6, "the hooting was once more started with increased vigor," and the Excelsiors left the field. As they left, they "were followed by a crowd of toughs" and the umpire declared the match a draw. After this bad experience, "the Excelsior stated they would not play the Atlantics again except in an enclosed park, where the game would take place in comparative privacy, but in an orderly manner." However, "no further games were ever played between the two clubs" (pp. 32–34).

This type of unruly activity by a group of spectators, identified by Orem as part of "the betting fraternity," signals a gradual decline in the courteous behavioral norms and good sportsmanship that had been associated with the conduct of base ball games between amateur clubs up to this time. Henry Chadwick and the more gentlemanly clubs continued to take the high road, condemning abuse of umpires, lamenting any instances of ill-will between clubs, and calling for a continuation of the gentlemanly style of play. Most vintage base ball clubs that play according to the rules and customs of the 1850s and early 1860s also take the high road and endeavor to present their games in an environment of good will and good sportsmanship as promoted by Chadwick and represented by the Knickerbockers.

The mission statement of the Vintage Base Ball Association, which speaks of conducting matches "according to the highest standards of sportsmanship, gentlemanly behavior, courtesy, and respect for others," provides the guiding principles for all vintage base ball programs. When the VBBA was established in 1996, these words were carefully crafted and thoughtfully adopted as representing the high ideals of the founding clubs, and they continue to serve as the standard for playing and presenting games and interacting with member clubs. Those who find it difficult to follow these principles and prefer to play base ball in an aggressive manner while conducting themselves in a manner that is not in keeping with the concepts of "courtesy and respect for others" may be happier gravitating toward other forms of baseball and softball, where sportsmanship and gentlemanly behavior are not so important.

Lessons from Other Sports

The manners and customs of golf provide an instructive model to adapt to playing vintage base ball. Golfers are unfailingly courteous and respectful toward their opponents.

Golf etiquette requires players never to distract another player while he is in the process of making his shot. Golfers call penalties on themselves and keep their own scorecards.

There are also behavioral lessons to be learned from the sport of distance running. Noted marathoner and author Jeff Galloway, in his regular column in *Runners World* magazine (October 2004), provided insight regarding a healthy approach to sport and recreation. When a reader asked, "For my first marathon, what should my goal be?" Galloway provided interesting advice. Instead of responding with some specific goal, such as "under four hours" or "under nine minutes per mile" (as the reader no doubt expected), Galloway provided a blueprint for success that went far beyond any numbers that might appear on the runner's stopwatch at the end of the 26.2-mile distance. Galloway's wise answer was as follows: "Goal 1: To enjoy the whole race from start to finish. Take in the scenery, talk to the runners around you, thank the crowd, and take part in the post-marathon party. If you only accomplish this goal your experience will be positive."

Brothers Tom (left) and Ed Shuman (seated) of the Fulton Mules (Canal Fulton, Ohio) and Andy Shuman of the Ohio Village Muffins enjoy friendly competition when their clubs meet.

This philosophy is directly applicable to vintage base ball. Just as the runner is advised to enjoy the entire experience of being at the race, vintage players, umpires, scorekeepers, and interpreters should make sure to enjoy the experience of being at the ball field and taking part in the day's activities. If all the participants in period dress are enjoying the match, the spectators will also have a wonderful time. Everyone likes to win, but whether leading or trailing on the scoreboard, participants should enjoy the setting and appreciate each turn at bat, each fielding play, and each opportunity to run the bases.

Players should by all means follow Galloway's advice to "take in the scenery." There is something aesthetically pleasing, often to the point of exhilarating, about being outdoors on the green grass of a base ball diamond on a warm, sunny day while re-creating the early days of the national pastime at home or on the road.

Galloway's "talk to the other runners" translates directly as "talk to the other players." Players should get to know their teammates. They may come in all ages, shapes, sizes, and skill levels, and represent a wide range of occupations, but they all share a common interest in base ball. Veteran players should welcome the newcomers to the team and make them feel comfortable and confident. New players should visit with veteran club members, who always have great stories about their experiences in the vintage game. Vintage players also enjoy getting to know the members of the other clubs. In the early days of base ball, the various clubs did not view each other as opponents or enemies but as fellow members of "the base ball fraternity."

Prepositions are usually small and easily overlooked words but they can be very important and revealing in our daily discourse. It is enlightening to note that vintage clubs usually speak of having a game *with* a certain club rather than *against* that club. The vintage base ball community understands that it is important to revive and retain this concept of "the base ball fraternity" and to treat the opposing team with the old-fashioned courtesy that would have been part of a match 150 years ago.

During the match itself, friendly conversation is the norm. Players who are previously acquainted often ask about each other's families, recap recent games, report on road trips, introduce new teammates, share recent research findings, and discuss uniforms and equipment. This mature, friendly approach to the game has its counterparts in modern professional baseball. Consider Sean Casey, known in his playing days for conversing with everyone, from teammates to opponents to umpires to groundskeepers to fans. Anytime the television camera showed the base runner being held on first by Casey, there seemed to be a good-natured conversation in progress. Throughout his major league career, Casey was an accomplished hitter with a lifetime average over .300 who made the All-Star team three times. No one would ever question his dedication or his desire to win the game. Yet, he was a master of the art of going about his business with a greeting and a good word for everyone on the field. Casey provides an excellent model for a vintage player to emulate when thinking about how he should conduct himself during a re-creation of a nineteenth-century game. Vintage base ball is not a game to be played with clenched teeth. Like Casey, players should treat everyone in a friendly and respectful manner.

Galloway's reminder to marathoners to "thank the crowd" holds true for vintage base ball. A game is more fun when there is a crowd on hand, and spectators should be made to feel that their presence is appreciated. In the formal announcements made at the end of the match, most vintage clubs include a sentence or two thanking the crowd for attending. But informal opportunities to acknowledge and thank the spectators arise throughout the game, since they often sit close to the playing area. Interaction with players encourages interest in vintage base ball and increases the chances that spectators will return to future games. When the spectators are folding up their chairs and gathering children and belongings after the game, they should be talking about how friendly and sportsmanlike the players on both teams were and asking how soon the visiting team will be coming back for another game like the one they just saw. Among the reasons that many vintage players enjoy the game is that it allows them to serve as ambassadors for their team, the organization it represents, and the growing sport of vintage base ball.

Galloway's fourth bit of advice — "take part in the post-marathon party" — also applies to vintage base ball. The host team often provides post-game refreshments. Whether it is a quick round of lemonade or watermelon slices, an informal lunch, or a full "sit-down" potluck with a program or entertainment, members of both teams should make the most of these opportunities to socialize. If invited to stay for something to eat or drink, the traveling party of the visiting club should by all means sit down with the host club and enjoy some conversation, especially if it is clear that the players and families of the host club have gone to some effort to provide a "collation" (as it was often called in nineteenth-century accounts) for their guests. Events of this type are an opportunity to share knowledge and experiences and get better acquainted with the other club's players and their families.

6
Club Organization and Administration

Getting Started: Museum Affiliation

Many existing vintage base ball clubs were created by museums, historical societies, parks, or historic homes and farms that view them as an excellent complement to their mission. Some vintage teams have been organized by individuals who later established an association with a sponsoring organization. In other instances, teams have been formed by members of a local chapter of the Society for American Baseball Research (SABR). A few teams are completely independent of any affiliation with a museum or historical society. These independent teams may not have a home field or they may play at a site administered by the local parks and recreation department rather than on museum grounds.

The VBBA website points out that "participating in an open-air museum program has its perks, such as well-made uniforms, added attention to correct equipment reproductions, a permanent playing field and a full summer schedule of games in front of big museum crowds." In addition to a historical setting for the games, museums also provide facilities for meetings and events, guidance and training on historical accuracy issues, promotional support and publicity for games, financial support, and liability insurance. The time, expert guidance, and thoughtful supervision of the museum professional with responsibility for the institution's base ball program should not be underestimated; in fact, it is a major strength of a museum-based team.

In answering the question "how can I start a club?" the VBBA website points out that in addition to those programs based in open-air museums, "another common arrangement is for clubs to have a relationship with some other group, such as an historical society, SABR chapter or county park. Because these teams are stand-alone programs, they usually have a degree of autonomy not found at the larger open-air museums but usually not as much direct support. The resources offered by the park, historical society or SABR chapter make it easier to recruit, raise funds, etc." In regard to clubs that are totally independent, the VBBA website observes, "Independent clubs are usually in it 'all-for-fun' and do it all themselves. This allows complete freedom. For most of these clubs, the old rules are the focus. They don't expect to teach visitors or impress with perfect uniforms."

The organizational model that is strongly recommended is the one in which the vintage base ball team is part of a museum, usually an "open-air" museum, such as a historic village or farm where there is space for a base ball field. In weighing the value of a relationship with a museum, a new club or an established club considering a change in affiliation would do well to consider the following four points.

Museum professional Mark Heppner, long-time captain of the Akron Black Stockings, introduces "President Lincoln" at the club's home grounds on the lawn at Stan Hywet Hall.

Liability: Being affiliated with a historical society or museum can take care of liability issues since the institution's insurance usually covers volunteers who are engaged in activities on behalf of the institution. The independent team means the ball club will need to arrange for its own liability insurance for participant and spectator safety. A player can get hurt in a collision, a spectator can be injured by a batted or thrown ball, or someone can have an accident traveling to a game. One of the most attractive features of vintage base ball is that the spectators often sit close to the field. That arrangement puts them in jeopardy of getting struck by a ball or bat or stepped on by a player going after a ball. Insurance is available, but for independent teams the cost involved would be borne by the team's players or treasury. Insurance may prove expensive, but is essential in team formation.

Accountability: Associated with the liability issue is accountability. An independent team needs some kind of formal legal leadership structure. An individual or an official board or committee needs to be authorized to take responsibility for signing contacts and agreements to play games and to receive and spend funds. There needs to be a bank account and an accounting of all money received and spent. Setting up the ball club as a separate entity involves considerable thought and organization. Members will need to act as officers and take official responsibility for the club's activities and business. In addition to the liability question involving possible injuries, there could be problems, such as a team agreeing to play a game at some event for a specific amount of money and then failing to come up with nine players on game day. The host organization that arranged for the team to come and play could become upset and demand their money back or even sue for failing to appear as the agreement specified. To protect individual team members' assets, a legal entity may need to be established to represent the program and be accountable for it. To the extent that it is possible, creating a 501(c)3 non-profit organization will be an advantage when soliciting donations.

Credibility: One major advantage of being part of a historical society or museum is that the host institution already has a positive reputation in the community. This "good name" is transferred to the ball club, enabling it to have immediate credibility as a legitimate historical and educational organization. Also, the historical society or museum usually has a public relations strategy and staff that helps promote the games. An independent club needs to do all of its own promotions and public relations.

Teams associated with museums and historical societies receive guidance and often support to present the game in an authentic manner. A high standard is set for uniforms, equipment, period language, bench appearance, and more. With little or no leadership and direction from a historical organization, authenticity standards can slip, and independent clubs sometimes drift into less-accurate portrayals of the game, such as wearing incomplete uniforms, wearing sunglasses, using modern bats, and having cell phones and plastic bottles on the bench. Where an independent team usually relies on word-of-mouth and on-the-job learning about historical re-creation, a museum-based program offers orientation and training programs and publishes policy guidelines to address these issues (along with information on how to educate and interact with spectators). There is an expectation among everyone associated with the program that the players will be familiar with the museum's policies so that they know what they are doing before going onto the field.

Continuity: Ball clubs associated with an institution have a built-in continuity that enables programs to prosper over time. Independent clubs often have one or two strong individual leaders who establish the team. Problems arise when a leader moves away, has a heath problem, or takes on more family or work responsibilities, thereby spending less time and energy on the ball club. Clubs based on one strong leader can fall apart if there is no succession plan. Ball clubs affiliated with a host organization have a framework of leadership and support that can withstand the departure of a key staff member or volunteer leader. Historical organizations have active recruitment programs to attract new volunteers. Some independent teams do not have plans to replenish their ranks, and when the original members get a little older, sustain some injuries, or move away, the club falters. The solutions for some of these areas of potential concern will vary from program to program, but these are topics that any club must consider.

Organizing a program within the structure of a museum brings with it many benefits:

Pride: Participants in the vintage base ball program are usually considered not only players, but official members of the volunteer corps of the museum. Most vintage base ball players take pride in representing a museum that is held in high regard and has established a long-standing reputation for high-quality historical exhibits, interpretation, and programming.

Support and Encouragement: The museum typically provides many resources and administrative services that contribute significantly to the successful operation of a vintage club. Some museums and historical societies assign a staff member to coordinate the vintage base ball program as part of his or her job description. This staff member often makes decisions regarding the team, including financing, scheduling, and historic standards. Museum staff members often write and edit educational and promotional materials, maintain communication with other programs, conduct and coordinate the research needed to ensure historical accuracy in the presentation of the games, and provide the professional leadership needed to coordinate the base ball team's activities with the overall goals and mission of the institution. In an established program, these duties are typically undertaken in collaboration with experienced program members. In times of financial challenge, an increasing number of these responsibilities may be delegated by the museum or historical society to these very capable volunteers who often contribute their time and talents related to their professions and hobbies — marketing, public relations, accounting, historical research, website management, graphic arts, printing, photography, bat and ball making, woodworking, tailoring and sewing, food service, and general "handyman" skills. A good organizer and "detail person" can take over scheduling matches and making all the necessary arrangements for tournaments and festivals. The owner of a dry-cleaning establishment can perform the valuable service of keeping uniforms laundered. Some club members may have valuable contacts through their employers that can result in grants, gifts-in-kind, and other forms of financial support for the program.

Museums provide leadership and direction throughout the year. Indeed, many projects, such as game scheduling, recruitment and training activities, designing and ordering uniforms, preparing brochures, and other behind-the-scenes activities, need to occur in the off season so that everything is well planned and ready to go when the team takes the field for the opening game.

In addition to administrative and financial support, the sponsoring organization offers important intangibles — encouragement, moral support, and words of appreciation — that contribute to morale, member retention, and spirit. Museum members, donors, and other volunteers can provide a receptive audience, accelerating the start-up process and generating community interest.

In lean times, of course, staff support for the base ball program can be down-sized or dropped. But a strong volunteer organization in partnership with the museum leadership can not only protect the program but allow it to grow when other activities are being cut or scaled back.

Historic Environment: Museum affiliation often results in a regular, established place to play — often a nineteenth-century setting. Playing in the environment of a historic site helps participants and spectators feel as if they have stepped back in time. Playing on the grounds of a respected museum or a well-known historic site also means the public knows where it is, parking is available, and it is likely that crowds will be on hand to watch the games.

A major drawback to not being closely affiliated with a museum or historical society is that independent teams have difficulty maintaining the high standards in uniforms, equipment, and gentlemanly behavior that are hallmarks of clubs that are affiliated with an institution. Even for those independent programs attempting to preserve some measure of accuracy in their games, the absence of ways to monitor historical standards often diminishes the effectiveness of the team in presenting the game to the public. Players on independent teams often have not had any type of orientation or training, and therefore have only a passing acquaintance with the rules and behavioral norms of the period. In such a climate, standards erode. Players begin showing up for games without hats or belts and wearing shoes that bear the modern logos. Players engage in non-period behavior, such as celebrating with high-fives and fist-bumps. Car keys, iPods, and sports drink containers are scattered around the bench area as they would be at a softball game. Once standards start to slip, it is difficult to reestablish them.

Vintage base ball relies on everyone being proud to do his or her part to contribute to an accurate presentation of the game. When that norm is lost, either through ignorance of how the game was played long ago or disregard for doing things correctly, it is difficult to run a cohesive and successful program. Teams that are overtly casual about authenticity in

Club Organization and Administration

The vintage base ball teams that play at the scenic, rural setting of Old Bethpage Restoration on Long Island, New York, have adopted the league format.

uniforms and equipment should not expect to be invited to play on the grounds of open-air museums where historical accuracy is valued, to play before large crowds at commemorative games, or to be recommended for participation in any special events, such as marching in parades or playing demonstration games at major league parks. Teams that place primary importance on the competitive aspects of playing the game tend to lose the sense of the higher purpose and the educational mission that comes from being part of a museum. Modern softball league norms take over, sportsmanship and historical accuracy go by the wayside, and these loosely organized teams often fall apart after a few seasons.

While some independent teams have been around for a while, it is most often the teams with close affiliations to museums and historical societies that have the resources and continuity required for a stable and enduring program. An affiliation with a museum, historic village, historic farm, or some other organization can be the key to success and beneficial for everyone involved.

Forming Vintage Base Ball Teams

When a museum, historical society, or independent group of players is considering involvement in vintage base ball, one of the first questions to be addressed is whether to form one team or more than one. The proximity of vintage teams is one important consideration. If there are a number of other vintage teams nearby, forming one club may be sufficient. However, if geographically isolated from existing teams, a program will need to organize enough players for two or more teams in order to play even a modest schedule of matches.

Some organizations, such as the programs in Denver, the San Francisco Bay area, Old Bethpage, and the Genesee Country Village and Museum, have approached the problem of geographic isolation by forming a league of four to six teams that play each other in a series of regularly scheduled games throughout the season. In some instances, several clubs in the same geographic area have formed a league. Seven clubs in New Jersey, Delaware, Maryland, and Virginia announced the formation of the Mid-Atlantic Vintage Base Ball League for the 2009 season and invited other clubs from those four states plus Pennsylvania and the District of Columbia to consider joining in the future. The association, known as the New England Vintage Base Ball League, includes thirteen 1880s teams arranged in two divisions that play in a format in which won-lost records and standings are posted. NEVBBL also includes nine Civil War-era clubs.

Regardless of whether other clubs are located nearby, it is useful for any club to have enough players for two teams. A set of caps or neckties of a different color or a reversible shield will differentiate the two nines. Having enough players for two teams enables a program to put on a club match at a special event at the affiliated institution or stage a demonstration match at a professional ballpark. As a result, the program will have a big enough roster to field a full team for scheduled matches all season.

Program organizers should keep in mind that matches involving members of the same club (what we would think of as intra-squad games) were common in the 1840s though the 1860s. Rule No. 3 in the Knickerbocker Base Ball Club's original rules of 1845 outlined the process for conducting this type of match:

> The presiding officer shall designate two members as Captains, who shall retire and make the match to be played, observing at the same time that the players opposite to each other should

be as nearly equal as possible; the choice of sides to be then tossed for, and the first in hand [turn at bat] to be decided in like manner.

An authentic model for holding games is to have all the players meet on the field where the two captains can organize them into two teams for that day's match. The two captains choose up sides. The selecting should be done privately so that the players are not aware of the order in which they were chosen. No player should ever be embarrassed in front of his teammates by publicly being one of the last to be chosen.

Another method is to divide the players according to some prearranged criteria, as was often done in the game's early days. Nineteenth-century clubs sometimes divided up according to "Married vs. Single" or "Fats vs. Leans." Therefore, a vintage club might have the married men play the single men. Next week the teams might divide up according to the veteran players in the program versus the newer players or the older players versus the younger ones. Also, players may be asked to draw numbered slips of paper out of a hat — those that draw even numbers are on one team and those drawing the odd numbers are on the other. The point is that if the players are scrambled every week, a given player's teammates will vary from game to game. This prevents any unhealthy, long-tern rivalries from developing and allows everyone to get to know all the other players in the program. These kinds of games are characterized by a good-natured atmosphere where lop-sided scores are usually avoided and competitiveness is kept in bounds.

Choosing a Name and Identity

Selecting a name for a vintage team requires thought and planning. The name becomes a brand for the team and must stand the test of time and change.

One common practice in vintage base ball is for a new team to select the name of a team that actually existed in that community in the nineteenth century. According to information provided by the program at Greenfield Village (part of the Henry Ford Museum in Dearborn, Michigan), the name Lah-de-Dahs was chosen because it was used by "an actual amateur base ball club which played in Waterford, Michigan, in the 1880s." When the vintage team in Grand Rapids, Michigan, was formed in 1991, Gordon Olsen, team founder and city historian, identified an early local team as the Kent Base Ball Club, and that name was adopted. Furthermore, the new Kent team adopted uniforms based on those worn by the original team — blue pants, blue neckties, and white shirts trimmed in blue with the letters KBBC in blue on the uniform shield.

The vintage teams that play in the Old Bethpage program have taken the names of local nineteenth-century teams from nearby Long Island communities. The program at Old Bethpage is also the home of the New York Mutuals, described on the VBBA website as a vintage team established in 1999 to "recreate the 1870 National Champion Club" from New York City. Dressed in the white uniforms with green trim of the original club, the Mutuals "travel to all parts of the country demonstrating the roots of our national pastime." Similarly, the Brooklyn Atlantics, New York Gothams, and Brooklyn Stars have taken their names and identities from actual early clubs in the New York City area whose histories go back to the pre–Civil War era when they were contemporaries of the Knickerbockers. In Rhode Island, the Providence Grays pattern themselves after the local club that won the championship of the National League in 1884. On the banks of the Ohio River, the 1869 Cincinnati Red Stockings and Cincinnati Buckeyes authentically re-create two teams that once played in the "Queen City of the West." There are many more similar examples throughout vintage base ball.

In regard to club names, Warren Goldstein in *Playing for Keeps: A History of Early Baseball* points to the relationship between some of the early base ball clubs and the volunteer fire companies to which their members belonged, noting that the New York Mutuals, "one of baseball's leading clubs into the 1870s, were founded in 1857 by the Mutual Hook and Ladder Company No. 1." Goldstein's observations on club names should provide ideas and inspiration to organizations looking for a suitable name. He points out that the names of the fire companies and, by extension, some of the early base ball clubs "tended to cluster around place names (Buckeye, Missouri, Knickerbocker, Atlantic [Avenue]); Indian names (in New England); patriotic names (Washington, Franklin, Liberty, Union, Lafayette); names referring to water (Neptune, Oceana, Cascade); and names suggesting admirable qualities (Invincible, Perseverance, Alert, Friendship, Good Intent)." Goldstein indicates that "water references naturally held less attraction for base ball clubs, which compensated by reaching to the heavens (Star, Constellation, Meteor) and into the classical past (Olympic, Minerva, Neptune, Sparta). Ballplayers chose Indian names more frequently (Powhattan, Pocahontas, Mohawk), and occasionally named their clubs after their trades or workplaces (Typographical, Eckford, Henry Eckford [Henry Eckford was a Brooklyn-based shipbuilder.], Fulton Market, Chestnut Street Theatre)" (pp. 28–29).

Many additional examples of club names of the period are found in Marshall D. Wright's *The National Association of Base Ball Players, 1857–1870*, which contains the records of member clubs and reflects the categories mentioned by Goldstein: place names (Gotham, Metropolitan, Harlem, Hoboken); patriotic and historical references (Eagle, Columbia, Jefferson, Hamilton, Charter Oak); and admirable qualities (Athletic, Resolute). Other terms signified energy and high aspirations (Excelsior, Enterprise, Empire, Continental), and others were indicative of America's growing role in world commerce (Baltic, Oriental).

In *But Didn't We Have Fun? An Informal History of Baseball's Pioneer Era, 1843–1870*, Peter Morris offers the following reminder in the area of semantics that should be helpful to clubs in the process of selecting a name. "Club names during the era were generally rendered with the nickname preceding the city name; e.g. the Eckford Base Ball Club of Brooklyn, or, for simplicity, the Eckfords of Brooklyn. Only as the era was ending did the order begin to be reversed" (pp. 10–11). With this in mind, it would be historically authentic to select a club name that represents a positive, abstract term (rather than a fearsome animal or person) that will stand alone in singular form, and pair the club name with the name of the city. This pattern is exemplified in names from the 1850s, such as the Union Club of Morrisania and the National Club of Washington. In these examples, the plural forms (Unions and Nationals) can also be used to refer to the club.

Vintage team organizers will note the absence of the common tendency in modern sports to use plural nicknames based on animals known for their ferocity (Bears, Lions, Panthers, Tigers, Wildcats, Bulldogs, Sharks) and humans with menacing and criminal connotations (Pirates, Buccaneers, Raiders, Marauders, Bandits). In that more gentlemanly time, base ball clubs consistently chose names that were noble, inspirational, and uplifting rather than threatening and intimidating. It would be inappropriate to model a vintage club's name on the modern template that has produced such team names as the Nashville Predators and the New Jersey Devils.

As an alternative to adopting the name of an actual nineteenth-century club, some programs have created a team name based on a connection with the history of the local area. The Leatherstocking Base Ball Club in Cooperstown, New York, has drawn on the community's literary heritage. Known widely as the home of the National Baseball Hall of Fame and Museum, Cooperstown is also the home of James Fenimore Cooper (1798–1851), author of the Leatherstocking Tales, some of which are set in the environs of Cooperstown and scenic Lake Otsego.

Toledo is located in northwestern Ohio on the western shore of Lake Erie, an area that was once known as "the Great Black Swamp." Toledo's nickname was once "Frog Town" because of the large number of amphibians that lived in the swampy area. Based on the natural history of their region, John Husman, Craig Stough, and other founding members of the vintage team based in the Toledo suburb of Sylvania came up with a colorful name, the Sylvania Great Black Swamp Frogs, and that has served the club well through the years.

The central attraction at Deep River Park near Hobart, Indiana, is a historic water-powered grist mill originally constructed in 1838. When the park decided to start a vintage base ball team, the historic mill led them to choose the name Grinders. The town of Canal Fulton, Ohio, is located on the old Ohio and Erie Canal. Therefore, when Ed Shuman and his compatriots of the local Heritage Society decided to start a vintage base ball team, they chose the name Fulton Mules in tribute to the sturdy draft animals that once contributed so much to the nation's economy and folklore by pulling the boats along the canal's towpaths. Springfield, Ohio, was known historically as "the Champion City" because the Champion Reaper, a piece of farm machinery important to the agricultural development of the country, was manufactured locally, dating back to the 1850s. Noting this part of the area's heritage, organizer Mark Miller and his colleagues adopted the name Champion City Reapers when forming their vintage club.

Other teams have taken the approach of choosing more generic names based on nineteenth-century terms. The name for the Ohio Village Muffins came from the historically accurate term for mediocre players — those of modest skills who tend to "muff" the ball. If there were no teams in the local area, if no photo or description of the early team exists, or if the decision is made to create a team that is not based on any one specific club of the past, a name based on nineteenth-century terminology or one of the early nineteenth-century clubs in the New York area (Knickerbocker, Excelsior, Empire, etc.) may be a good choice.

The club name and its backstory will influence uniform design. While uniforms are discussed in detail in Chapter 9, club organizers should keep in mind that the name and uniform are powerful symbols and will become known in the club's home community and throughout the vintage base ball world. A good reputation and identity are part of a successful brand. It is costly (financially and in terms of both time and image) to select a name and then have to go back and choose another name or uniform that is more accurate or appealing. Programs should take time to get the name right at the time of founding. The museum or historical society affiliated with the team should consider registering the club name and logo in order to maintain control of its use.

Who Plays This Game? Profiles of Men's Teams

Adult men who are attracted to a vintage base ball program typically have some experience in modern baseball or softball. Some may currently be softball players or participants in adult baseball leagues, but others have not played much since high school or their youth league days. The common thread seems to be that all have retained an interest in the game

The Grinders Base Ball Club takes its name from the grist mill at their home grounds at Deep River Park in Hobart, Indiana.

and are eager for the opportunity to connect with the national pastime. Many participants also have an interest in American history in general and the history and lore of the national pastime in particular.

Players come from many occupations, backgrounds, ages, and skill levels. This diversity is one of the strengths of the game. While players need some degree of playing skill and a working knowledge of the rules and customs of the game in order to play vintage base ball, it is by no means necessary for a person to have been a superior player at the high school or college level or to be an exceptionally strong and agile twenty-something in his athletic prime. Year after year, the membership of the Muffins has ranged from high school and college students to a handful of players over sixty, and every age group in between. This age range is common throughout vintage base ball as many teams (at least those that play by rules that feature slower underhand pitching) include players of all ages.

In keeping with its inclusive tradition, most vintage teams welcome all prospective players who agree to observe the basic tenets of the vintage game, including playing according to the rules and customs of the period being represented, dressing accordingly, using appropriate period equipment, conducting themselves in a sportsmanlike manner consistent with the era, and endeavoring to meet the expectations and standards of the historical society or museum sponsoring the team.

Program leaders are encouraged to look beyond playing skills and athleticism when organizing a team. Participants often bring a variety of talents to the program and contribute to success in many ways. In addition to or instead of playing, some of the most valuable

Vintage base ball has many fathers and sons who are teammates on the same club. Veteran Muffin player Don Andersen (center) has enjoyed playing with his sons Steve (left) and Craig for many seasons.

members of a club are those who strengthen the program by filling the important roles of umpire, scorer, and interpreter.

Participants in vintage base ball often contribute on game day beyond playing. A person with a theater or teaching background may be excellent at engaging the crowd. A baseball memorabilia collector may volunteer to set up an attractive and educational display of antique equipment, uniforms, and photos in a tent on the sidelines. It is great to have a club member who can play the guitar, banjo, or fiddle and provide period music on the sidelines or accompany the other players as they perform the club song. (Yes, there were club songs in the nineteenth century and some vintage teams continue that tradition.) In addition to these special skills, players typically possess a spirit of helpfulness and will volunteer to come early and set up the field, bring food and refreshments for the post-game picnics, and stay late to put the equipment away and clean up the field after the game has ended. It takes a great deal more than nine players with excellent playing skills to have a successful program. People who love the game of base ball and are willing to give their time and talents to the success of the program are valuable assets regardless of the level of their playing skills.

Another point that deserves consideration is the lower age limit for a "men's" team. To be historically authentic in representing the men's base ball clubs of the nineteenth century, the team should be composed of adult men. That said, teams generally tend to welcome the sons of current players who understand the game and are eager for the opportunity to play alongside their fathers on the vintage club. The Muffins have set the lower age limit at sixteen. Boys of that age are able to hold their own in a men's game by being sufficiently physically mature to hit and field successfully. They are usually big enough so that they do not detract from the look of the game, causing spectators to wonder why children are playing in what was advertised to be a representation of nineteenth-century base ball played by men's clubs. If the teenagers have been attending vintage games for several years and have absorbed the behavioral norms of the game, they seem to be emotionally mature enough to understand the importance of playing in a sportsmanlike manner and conducting themselves on the field with a sense of decorum.

In addition to playing on the men's team, another possible way to get youngsters involved in vintage base ball is through the creation of a junior club composed of teenage boys. Junior clubs did exist in the nineteenth century, so this is an approach that would be historically accurate. In the 1990s, the Muffins made a good effort to establish a junior club, but the results were not very productive. Teenage boys who are interested in playing baseball have many opportunities to do so through various well-organized youth leagues in their communities. Consequently, while starting a junior club is a good premise and a worthy goal, it may prove difficult in reality to implement.

Setting policies relating to teenagers who want to play vintage base ball should involve the sponsoring organization, which may have policies in place regarding age requirements for volunteers in its programs. The participation of minors may have implications for liability coverage as well, and may require a parental consent form. From time to time, when a men's team finds itself short-handed, it is not unusual to have a young fellow familiar with the rules and practices of vintage base ball — usually related to a club member — take a spot in the lineup. As a general practice, however, in order to maintain the historical accuracy and integrity of the presentation of nineteenth-century base ball, the team should be composed of adults.

Recruitment and Training

Recruiting players, umpires, scorers, and interpreters is a continual process, but the ideal time to add new participants to an existing program is during the off season so that those new to the game can participate in training meetings, acquire a uniform, and engage in practice sessions before taking the field for the first game of the season. Vintage base ball employs rules and practices that are, in some respects, substantially different from modern baseball and softball. There is much to learn, such as how to wear the uniform correctly, norms of conduct for a nineteenth-century gentleman, and more. Vintage clubs should have an orientation and training process for new players (and an ongoing base ball educational program for the full club), as well as a few practice before the season. Just as a new member of a community brass band, singing group, or theatre company would expect to take part in some training and rehearsal sessions before giving a public performance, new (and returning) vintage base ball players should expect to take part in some kind of training and behind-the-scenes preparation before stepping up to bat in an actual game with spectators present.

When forming a new team, players can be recruited in a variety of ways. The best way is to start close to home, seeking players from the ranks of the staff and volunteers who are already associated with a museum or historical organization. Seek out members of an existing softball team who might be interested in becoming a vintage team. Introducing vintage base ball as a recreational and educational activity to the members of a civic or community group is another approach. One notable instance of this latter model occurred when members of the local Masonic lodge in Worthington, Ohio, became interested in vintage base ball as an activity for their organization and approached the Muffins for advice and assistance in starting a team. Preliminary research by the group's leaders revealed that Masonic lodges frequently had base ball teams in the nineteenth century, so they felt that creating a vintage team would be thoroughly in keeping with the group's heritage. A number of lodge members immediately volunteered to serve as players, umpires, and scorers, and others expressed their willingness to support the team as spectators. The Muffins assisted them in learning the rules of the game and provided guidance on acquiring uniforms and equipment. Before many weeks had passed, the Masonic Lodge's Blue Ashlar Club was able to put a team on the field and played several games. Vintage base ball teams have also formed from members of Civil War reenactor groups who see playing ball by the rules of the 1860s as a natural complement to their reenacting activities.

In addition to forming teams from existing groups, both new teams and established teams should continually recruit individuals. Ads and articles in the media indicating that a museum is looking for players for the institution's vintage team will often result in interested parties coming forward to ask about joining. Fine players can be added through the team's participation in festivals and celebrations. After playing for the local community nine against the visiting vintage club, a player on the team formed for the special occasion may become an enthusiast of the game and inquire about joining the established vintage club. Word-of-mouth recruiting is also effective, with current players often "recruiting" other players from among their family, co-workers, and friends. Feature stories on television and in newspapers encourage attendance at matches and prospective players to contact the museum.

A team should always be prepared to respond to anyone who expresses an interest in playing or officiating. Sometimes a prospective player may be interested in getting involved, only to assume that the club already has enough players and be a little shy about making an inquiry. In other cases, a prospective player among the spectators might think the game looks interesting but might not know who to contact. Let the public know that new players are always welcome. In this day of on-line communication and pervasive social media, vintage clubs would be wise to have a web presence to communicate within the club, attract spectators, and recruit new team members.

While recruiting new members during the offseason is ideal, it is also a good idea to keep an "open door" policy throughout the year. Because of the visual appeal of a well-presented vintage game, it is not uncommon for a baseball-minded spectator to come out of the viewing gallery and approach a team member on the spot to ask about getting involved. Also, a current player may have a softball teammate or friend from work who comes to see a match, gets "hooked" on the game, and asks about joining during the season.

It is helpful for the vintage club to have a fact sheet or brochure—both printed and electronic—that can be distributed. It should cover the frequently-asked questions of prospective players, media, and sponsors. These materials might include the club's mission, museum affiliation, schedule of games, expectations and opportunities for team members, and contact information for the person in charge of recruitment and training (that is, the museum professional with responsibility for the operation of the team or the membership chair from among the volunteer officers). A mid-season recruit should attend several games as a spectator to learn the rules, practices, and customs of vintage base ball. This provides an opportunity to see how the game is presented and to ask questions about the rules of the game as it unfolds, and it can be an effective way to prepare a new player to take the field.

When getting organized, new clubs often ask representatives of established clubs to come and conduct a training/recruitment session or two for their members. Veteran members of well-established clubs are pleased to be asked to share their organizational and historical knowledge and on-field experience while presenting a training program of this type. To help a new team get started and then watch that team proudly take the field in their new uniforms and join the base ball fraternity is one of the most rewarding experiences that can come from being part of vintage base ball. Helpful information on starting a new team appears on the Vintage Base Ball Association website.

Scheduling Games

Scheduling games was far different in the mid-nineteenth century than in modern baseball and softball. In an earlier time, the secretary of one base ball club would write a letter to the secretary of another club proposing a match at a certain date, time, and place. The letter, written in the courteous language of the day, would specify whether the game was to be played between the first nines, second nines, or muffin nines of the two clubs. The secretary of the club receiving the offer of a match would then write a formal letter of reply, usually accepting the proposed arrangements, but perhaps suggesting an alternative date if his club had a conflict.

Since transportation difficulties in those days made a trip of five or ten miles to play another club an all-day project, games with other teams were relatively few in number. According to the season records published in *The National Association of Base Ball Players, 1857–1870* by Marshall Wright, the member clubs played only a handful of matches with other clubs each year, averaging 5.4 games in 1857, 5.3 in 1858, 6.6 in 1859, and 8.3 in 1860—about one game a month from spring to fall (pp. 14, 27, 39, 52). In vintage base ball, while club secretaries no longer write formal letters to propose matches (pens and stationery having been replaced by cell phones and email), the basic principle remains the same for most vintage clubs—the person in charge of scheduling for one team contacts his counterpart on another team and proposes a game for a specific date, usually inviting the other team to come to his club's home grounds. Many games are scheduled in this manner during the offseason and others are scheduled as the season rolls on.

In an area where there are multiple teams, an off-season meeting of scheduling representatives from several clubs may be held. To minimize travel and increase playing opportunities, arrangements can be made for two teams to travel to the home field of a third, playing the host club and each other on the same afternoon in a round-robin format. The annual meeting of the VBBA is also an opportunity to make scheduling contacts, although many clubs may have their schedules for the upcoming season set by the time of the VBBA meeting in the early spring. Making contacts at the VBBA meeting is especially valuable for newly formed clubs. A club may also attend one of the several well-established tournaments and festivals that provide a chance to play many clubs and make scheduling contacts at that event.

Before filling out a schedule, club organizers should survey team members as to their availability and preferences for matches. A conservative schedule in the first season or two will help define what level of activity can be sustained by the current membership.

The League Model: Pros and Cons

Spectators interested in knowing how many teams are playing this type of base ball may ask how many teams are in the league. The inquiry provides the opportunity to explain that there is a national "association" (a good nineteenth-century term) of vintage clubs and that there are more than 200 clubs coast-to-coast playing base ball by nineteenth-century rules. An answer might also mention how many vintage clubs are located in the state or within an hour's travel from the site of that day's game or the spectator's home. The goal is to let spectators know that there are a significant number of clubs involved in vintage base ball.

Another answer to the spectator's question is that in most cases vintage clubs do not play in a league; that is, if "league" is defined according to the modern model whereby several teams have formed an organization, play each other a specific number of times during the season, schedule their games in advance, and compete for a championship at the end of the season. Since a league format generally exists in most forms of modern baseball or softball, from youth leagues to the majors, it is a logical question but one that points to how base ball was different 150 years ago.

While spectators may assume that the team plays in a league, such an arrangement is not needed if a new program is starting up in an area where there are a number of other teams nearby that can serve as playing partners. Geographic isolation, however, may lead a program to compromise on the question of historical authenticity and form several teams that would share a common home field at the museum site and play in a league.

While it may seem natural for a new vintage base ball program to arrange itself in the manner of a modern baseball or softball league, organizers should exercise caution before this format is selected as it can lead to unforeseen problems and complications. One consideration is that a league format would not be historically authentic if the program is representing an era prior to the mid–1870s. At the VBBA meeting hosted by the Rochester Grangers of Rochester Hills, Michigan, in 2003, Professor Carl Osthaus, chair of the history department at Oakland University, gave a presentation on the "themes, attitudes, lifestyles, and paradoxes" of the Civil War era and the Gilded Age. He pointed out that leagues were not feasible until post–Civil War advances in passenger train travel made it possible for teams to move economically and quickly between the member cities of the league.

Another consideration in forming a league is the possibility of teams becoming overly competitive. Caution needs to be observed if a program is forming a group of teams that will play each other on a regular basis with the goal of determining a champion. While it might seem that the quick and obvious answer to geographic isolation is to form two rival teams or several teams that will play in a league, that situation may not work well if the players are permanently assigned to one specific team. Overly competitive play and some disregard for the culture of the era may creep into matches.

When setting up multiple teams, it is important to keep the skill levels of the teams as equal as possible. This may prove to be difficult. Most vintage teams and players are mature enough to understand that educational objectives are of primary importance to most museums and winning the match at hand is not the most important goal. Of course, no one wants to get beaten by a lopsided score every game. If this happens, interest in the program will wane. Relations between the two teams may suffer if the games are consistently too one-sided. After losing several games, a team might start to recruit a few highly skilled softball players solely for their playing ability and not for any interest these new players have in the proper presentation or history of the nineteenth-century game. The introduction of "ringers" may result in players taking the field who have not gone through any kind of training program and who may not understand the mission and values of the sponsoring museum.

Spectator interest is another factor to keep in mind. If games are too one-sided, spectator involvement declines. If a game becomes a rout, the spectators will tend to lose interest and drift away from the match to find something more interesting to watch. Opportunities for history lessons and educational experiences planned for the day will be lost if most of the spectators depart and few are watching the game after the fourth or fifth inning.

Another problem area that could develop in a league is an over-emphasis on winning the league championship. As Henry Chadwick wisely observed on the subject of championships: "They lead to the alienation of clubs from one another that were once fast friends; they create a feeling of rivalry that leads to endless disputes." Games played to win a championship can lead to arguments with the umpire over close calls and other forms of combativeness and ill-will that can detract from a vintage game. Historically, this is what happened in the 1860s. The increased importance placed on winning resulted in an increased pressure on the umpire. Henry Chadwick commented in the 1860 *Beadle's Dime Base-Ball Player* on the umpire's role as follows: "The Umpire should be a player familiar with every point of the game. The position of an Umpire is an honorable one, but its duties are any thing but agreeable, as it is next to an impossibility to give entire satisfaction to all parties concerned in a match." This telling passage indicates that the umpire was no longer being treated with the same degree of respect as in the recent past. This growing tendency to dispute calls (which would get worse instead of better as time went on) created an unfortunate state of affairs that vintage programs should try to prevent. Instead, they should work hard to maintain the gentlemanly nature of the game in which the umpire's decisions are accepted without argument.

Henry Chadwick would no doubt heartily approve of the organizational approach taken by the Colorado Vintage Base Ball Association. In answer to an email inquiry about the organization of the successful program in the Denver area, a representative responded, "I want to be clear here about what goes on in Colorado. We are not a 'League' so much as an association. Most of the regular teams in Colorado…are under the umbrella of the CVBBA…We play monthly matches against each other — 2 or three games in a day — and always at a different home field (Denver and Central City share a home field; Berthoud, Greeley, Littleton each have their own). The rest of the season is spent playing against local community teams for festivals or events, as well as traveling to exotic places like Kansas, Nebraska and Wyoming." The message concludes with sound advice on an organizational model: "We are not set up as a league — no standings or trophy at the end. While we always try to be competitive on the field, we don't feel that standings and a league format is as conducive to a friendly environment."

In the twenty-first century, we have become conditioned to accepting an ultra-competitive environment as the norm in the popular team sports. In major league baseball, there is the post-season playoff process that leads to the crowning of a World Series champion. In college baseball, there are conference championships and conference tournaments to decide which teams get invited to regionals, super-regionals, and, ultimately, qualify for the College World Series, where one team will win the national championship. In professional football there is the playoff structure, culminating in the Super Bowl. In college football, national rankings are talked about throughout the season as teams vie for spots in the important and lucrative BCS bowl games at the end of the season. Competitive as this system already is, many are critical that it is not competitive enough and that the five BCS games should be reorganized into a tournament that would produce a more definitive national champion (leaving the others that came close but did not win with an empty feeling at the conclusion of an otherwise outstanding season). The NBA has several rounds of playoffs with a championship series at the end. College basketball is characterized by conference championships, conference tournaments, and the "bracketology" of "March Madness," with a field of 68 teams (67 of which will finish their season with a disappointing loss) battling for the national championship.

This array of championship formats creates a number of very important games which, in turn, produce a vast amount of exciting television programming and revenue. These contests can be dramatic and entertaining, but the importance now placed on these contests represents a recent development in the evolution of sports, long after the era of the amateur base ball clubs of the mid-nineteenth century. In this context, it is easy for vintage base ball programs to fall into the modern pattern of focusing on winning and programs organizing themselves around the modern goal of crowning a champion. Mid-nineteenth-century base ball, as played by the amateur men's clubs of that era, had different perspectives and priorities. These amateur ideals eroded over time, replaced by an overly competitive style of play that developed into the way professional baseball and other modern team sports are now played.

Vintage base ball leaders must think carefully about the structure and character of their programs and the need to take their models for competition from the past rather than the present. Resisting the tendency to copy the modern formats (and the ultra-competitive attitudes that go with them), club organizers strive to ensure that their programs reflect the spirit of the clubs of a century and a half ago rather than being patterned after the way team sports are conducted today.

Festivals and Tournaments

Many museums and historical societies hold an annual tournament or festival, inviting several teams from near and far for an exciting and colorful day or weekend of vintage base ball. Some of these events involve three or four clubs, but the larger tournaments and festivals can attract more than twenty teams, with games being played on several diamonds simultaneously. Participating in a festival or tournament is an excellent way for a new club to learn through observation and to get acquainted with existing teams.

These special events draw the local media, as radio and television stations often send reporters and camera crews to cover the event. Stories and photos of the festival often appear in the newspaper. These articles are sometimes in the sports pages but, owing to the wide appeal of vintage base ball, they are just as likely carried in the lifestyle, travel, or arts and entertainment section, or possibly the weekend magazine.

Logistics and arrangements are a major responsibility for a museum or historical society that is hosting a tournament or festival. The invitations should be sent and confirmations received several months in advance of the event. Driving directions and maps need to be mailed to all participants along with any rules or expectations relevant to matches at the host institution. Parking areas and parking permits need to be made available. Meals, accommodations, tickets and passes for family members, field preparation, and social events require considerable planning. The payoff is worth the effort and energy that goes into the preparations.

The host team and the host institution planning an event should give careful thought to the format. Some of these gatherings follow the tournament model, with teams playing their way through brackets and the two most successful teams meeting in a championship match at the end. Tournaments can be very suspenseful and exciting as teams vie for the championship. However, a tournament can also have drawbacks, causing some programs to consider and adopt other formats.

The most popular alternative to a tournament is the festival setting where the schedule of matches is drawn up in advance and the games are conducted in a round-robin arrangement. While there may be too many clubs involved for every team to play every other team (a true round-robin), the scheduler tries to have all the teams play as many different clubs as possible, with special attention to arranging games involving teams that have traveled many miles to attend and would not otherwise get to play each other.

An example of one major event that switched from a tournament to a festival format is the Ohio Cup Vintage Base Ball Festival, which has been held annually since 1992 at the Ohio Historical Society. It takes place each year over Labor Day weekend and is billed as the largest gathering of vintage base ball clubs in the country, drawing 25 to 30 teams from six to eight states, with games being played on three or four fields simultaneously.

In order to maximize the opportunities for each team to play as many other teams as possible, Ohio Cup Festival games have a time limit. Matches start on the hour. At ten minutes before the next hour, the teams involved in the games do not begin a new inning. At the completion of the inning in progress, a winner is declared. The teams then move on and play a new game with a different opponent. This changing of opponents every hour enables each team to play many other teams, and allows everyone at the festival to get better acquainted. The reasons for adopting these arrangements are discussed in this excerpt from "The Festival Format," an article that appeared in the 2009 Ohio Cup program:

> The Ohio Cup matches are played as a two-day festival rather than a tournament. The emphasis is on celebrating the wonderful game of vintage base ball and the joy of playing the 1860s-era version of the national pastime. Matches are limited to one hour (rather than the customary nine innings) so that teams have the opportunity to play a number of opponents, some of which have traveled a great distance.
>
> In its early years, the Ohio Cup was played as a tournament. But in the traditional bracket format, Ohio teams that had already played each other several times during the summer often played each other again, thereby missing out on the opportunity to get acquainted with our out-of-state guests. The bracket format also made it difficult for visiting teams to make travel plans since they did not know in advance what times their games would be played. Most important, it was felt that playing for a tournament championship placed too much emphasis on winning at the expense of the general spirit of good sportsmanship and camaraderie that characterizes vintage base ball and the Ohio Cup.
>
> The festival format has proved to be a great success, creating a colorful, educational, and sportsmanlike setting for Ohio Cup participants and spectators to step back in time and experience base ball as it was meant to be played.

Just as an over-emphasis on winning a trophy or title may have a negative influence on the tone and character of a vintage base ball event, it also was a source of concern in the 1860s. Writing in the August 15, 1863, *New York Clipper* of a game between the Mutuals and Atlantics, Henry Chadwick offered definite advice on crowning champions. "The discreditable scenes that took place toward the close of the game lead us to sincerely hope that this will be the last season that any of these championship games are played. It is unquestionably for the best interests of the game that matches for the championship, together with the title of champion, be entirely done away with, and the sooner the leading men of the fraternity frown this class of matches down the better."

Some clubs continue to stage an annual tournament, and this type of event can work well. Program leaders who are contemplating accepting an invitation to play at an event or establishing their own event should weigh all the factors involved. While both the tournament format and the festival format can be successful, such factors as game scheduling, travel considerations, and the potential for teams becoming overly competitive should be kept in mind in making decisions that will provide the best experience for the participants and the spectators.

7

Club Operation and Leadership

A successful vintage base ball program is not built only on the field. It requires a well-planned schedule of social, educational, and informational activities that promote camaraderie and elevate competence. When the team takes the field for the first time, everyone should know how to wear the uniform, how to play by the rules of the era being portrayed on the field, how to conduct oneself in the wide variety of situations that may arise during the game, and how to relate to the spectators.

Administration and Governance

Responsibility for setting policies, making operational decisions, and managing and leading a vintage club follows a number of different patterns. If oversight of the vintage base ball program is the responsibility of an administrator of the sponsoring organization, that person is usually the one to direct the program with players and other volunteers following guidelines set by the institution. At the other end of the spectrum are unaffiliated independent teams, where all the decisions are made by the players, or perhaps by one individual who has organized the team and is recognized as the leader of the club.

A very workable middle ground that is more the norm throughout vintage base ball is for the museum professional and the club members to work together for the general welfare of the program. The museum professional often needs to make final decisions on matters such as historical authenticity standards, safety and security issues, and financial expenditures. The volunteers can manage rosters, produce internal communications, and plan club programming. In times of diminished resources, volunteers may need to take on more responsibilities. Good decisions regarding both general policies and day-to-day operational matters will result if the museum administration and the volunteer group are working together in an environment of cordiality, cooperation, and communication.

One model for collaborating successfully is to establish a formal advisory group from the volunteer ranks to work with the administration of the sponsoring organization and guide the activities of the vintage club. At the Ohio Historical Society, an eight-member advisory board was created in 1996 to provide recommendations to the museum professional in charge of the program while also taking on some of the administrative work, such as scheduling matches, organizing the hospitality efforts for visiting teams, and ordering uniforms and equipment. The board meets on a monthly basis with the museum administrator in charge of the program to discuss scheduling, recruiting, event planning, travel, training, finances, uniforms, historical standards, and the general business of running the program.

All members of the program are invited to attend the monthly meetings and participate in the discussions.

The advisory board model is designed to keep everyone involved and informed. The museum administration receives valuable input from the board members and the volunteers receive a continuous flow of information from the administrator. This relationship ensures that the vintage base ball program and the museum are working as a team toward common goals.

Training Seminars

Vintage base ball players do not need to wait for warm weather for the season to start. There is always more to learn about the history of the game and how to present it successfully to the public. Clubs can meet in January and February to prepare for the upcoming matches in the spring. For a number of years, the Ohio Historical Society has been conducting a series of seminars in the winter months. While the sessions are conducted in a classroom setting, they are generally light in tone and members find them enjoyable. They are also content-rich, with a good blend of fun and substance represented in the agenda.

An off-season social is recommended to kick off the seminar series. It reconnects members and their families and provides a venue for introducing new teammates. The administrator for the program can preview the schedule, highlighting any special trips and events. This generates enthusiasm and allows families to begin planning vacations around the team calendar. Family-friendly games like bingo can be adapted to include nineteenth-century base ball terms (instead of letters and numbers) to fill out the cards. Door prizes (a way to liquidate old T-shirts) and giveaways generate loyalty and add to the fun. The goal is to get everyone back together some time around Groundhog Day when the coming of spring is on everyone's mind, major league spring training is in the news, and people start thinking of baseball.

Two or three subsequent seminars on Saturday mornings in February and March focus on content. Volunteers learn more about the early history of the game and the community, the rules of early base ball, nineteenth-century uniforms and equipment, and other topics related to a successful season. Seminar presenters can be volunteers in the program, historical society staff, or leaders from other vintage clubs. Asking team members to make a presentation encourages research and engages interest.

Presentation Topics

While rules and practices of play are always reviewed and discussed, the content of the seminars goes beyond how the game is played on the field. Volunteers hear presentations on the clothing styles, language, and manners of the 1860s so that they can effectively and accurately represent people from that era. Volunteers also are briefed on customer service, from giving directions to restrooms to handling emergencies. They are informed about the sponsoring organization, its personnel, policies, and procedures. One of the seminars can include a behind-the-scenes tour of the facilities. Volunteers meet staff members with whom they interact during the year in areas such as marketing and public relations, security, grounds and maintenance, and historical interpretation and education.

Seminars are valuable in setting the context for the nineteenth-century base ball matches. Information on the political, social, and economic issues of the day provides answers to likely questions from spectators. It also gives the volunteers the knowledge and confidence to initiate conversations with visitors on topics ranging from base ball rules to women's suffrage. A museum professional from the sponsoring organization can clarify expectations and responsibilities at a seminar and discuss museum standards and educational goals. Volunteers are also updated on other administrative items, such as the current operating hours for the museum, any construction or renovation projects, staff changes, modifications of traffic patterns, parking issues, or any upcoming special events that, on a specific day, may have an impact on the presentation of the base ball game.

Players, umpires, scorekeepers, and interpreters are strongly encouraged to attend the seminars since all interact with the public. Vintage base ball program participants need to be able to field all kinds of questions, including how to join the museum. Volunteers can not know everything but should be able to make a quick and accurate referral to someone who can respond to the inquiry.

A seminar on the history of the local community during the era portrayed is popular with club members. They learn about landmarks built during the period, retail establishments of the time, and big issues for the locale. Team members who have genealogy information can be asked to share what their ancestors were doing at that time. This information helps connect volunteers to the time period. Other seminar topics could include getting in shape to play (an athletic trainer shows specific exercises for base ball), a history of baseball cards, or an update on recently published books on nineteenth-century base ball history.

To build camaraderie and acquaintance, team members can be asked to share their baseball experiences with the group. At one Muffin seminar, a veteran member shared memories of the old League Park in the Cleveland of his boyhood. On another occasion, having spent 18 months in Japan in connection with his work, a member shared pictures and stories of his travels to each of the major league parks in Japan. These presentations, while not nineteenth-century specific, spark interest in the topics and strengthen team bonds.

The goal of the seminars is to prepare volunteers to represent the base ball program and the museum knowledgeably and effectively, not just on the ball diamond, but whenever they are on the museum grounds in period dress before and after games. These Saturday morning seminars can do an excellent job of preparing the volunteer players, umpires, scorekeepers, and interpreters for a successful season of vintage base ball games once spring finally arrives. They offer a platform for player interaction and build loyalty to the club. Clubs are encouraged to use the seminar model as a way to get the year off to a good start.

The Rules

A valuable part of the orientation and training for everyone who is participating in vintage base ball of any era in the nineteenth century is reading the Knickerbocker Rules of 1845 and the National Association Rules of 1860. These rules form the basis and context for all later sets of rules and provide insight and perspective as to what the writers of the rules had in mind and what they were trying to accomplish. In addition to providing a listing of the 1860 rules, *Beadle's Dime Base-Ball Player* also contains the valuable commentary by Henry Chadwick on these rules. In these comments, the great base ball pioneer and expert on the game (widely considered in his time to be the "Father of Base Ball") endeavored to provide explanatory and interpretive observations on the rules. Chadwick's comments provide many helpful insights that enable the vintage base ball community to re-create the game as it was played in its early years. The rules are readily available on the Vintage Base Ball Association website.

A thoughtful understanding of the 1845 and 1860 rules is especially important for museum professionals who are overseeing or coordinating an institution's vintage base ball program. This will inform decisions made regarding which rules to use and what standards of historical accuracy will be followed in keeping with the institution's educational and interpretive mission. Also, since the rules are not always clear, museum professionals can contribute both their historical knowledge and their administrative expertise to decide how the rules will be interpreted by an individual program. The way the rules are implemented has an impact on the recruitment and retention of volunteer players, safety of the players and spectators, cost of operating the program, and the general atmosphere and tone of the game — all areas of importance for the museum professional who has responsibility for the program.

Safety First

One important seminar topic is the need to put safety first. The website of the American Association of Museums provides the following direct and helpful statement (intentionally framed "in plain English") in its section on Facilities and Risk Management: "Make it safe to visit your museum — or work there." Museums and historical societies, understandably, must be vigilant regarding safety. For both liability reasons and the simple desire not to have anyone hurt while on museum property, safety is an important priority.

As vintage clubs compete on the diamond, safety should always be on the players' minds, whether at a match on the team's home grounds, as guests on another club's playing field, or at a community event. Presentations in training sessions should remind players of their responsibility to see that no spectator gets hurt while watching a game. This sometimes means "unlearning" behaviors that players may have developed from many years of playing and watching modern baseball. An infielder should not be so intent on retiring a runner that he unleashes a hard, wild throw into the crowd behind first base, third base, or home plate where there may be children and senior citizens seated. A batter should be careful not to "pull" a hard line drive into a group of spectators seated in lawn chairs near the foul lines or to chop a "fair-foul" hit into the crowd. A player should be careful when chasing a foul ball near the foul line where spectators are seated. Unlike most other forms of modern baseball and softball, vintage base ball is an educational endeavor, and a player should not get so caught up in the winning and losing part of the contest that he engages in any actions that would put spectators at risk. The old adage "safety first" was never more true than when applied to a vintage base ball.

The second part of the American Association of Museums policy statement, "Make it safe to visit your museum — or work there," also applies to vintage base ball. The phrase "or work there" applies to the staff members and the volunteers participating in the games. The spectators' enjoyment of a vintage game is seriously diminished if one of the players is injured during the match. Therefore, players need to be careful to avoid collisions and to always protect themselves and each other. In a seminar setting, players can share strategies they employ to minimize risk during a match.

Background Checks

In recent times, it has become standard operating procedure for museums and historical societies — along with virtually all organizations whose staff members and volunteers interact with children at schools, day care centers, summer camps, sports programs, and church youth groups — to require criminal background checks for all staff members and volunteers. Since players, umpires, scorekeepers, and interpreters have direct contact with the public, including the children in the audience, vintage base ball participants who represent a museum should expect to undergo a background check. The process for a background check usually requires the volunteer to fill out a form that asks for standard demographic information and to have a fingerprint taken. The information is then matched with a national data base that identifies anyone with a criminal record who should not have any contact with children. While many workplaces require the employee to pay for the background check, volunteer programs should attempt to cover the cost or keep it quite low.

From the museum's point of view, now that computer technology makes this process accessible, instituting a policy whereby all staff members and volunteers undergo a background check is a "no-brainer." First, museum professionals are genuinely concerned about the safety and welfare of visitors and would not want any guest to have any type of harmful or negative experience while making a museum visit. Second, the museum would be leaving itself open to serious criticism, unfavorable publicity, and litigation if any kind of incident did occur on museum grounds or at a museum-sponsored program (such as a vintage base ball game) and it became known that the museum had not utilized all available means to protect its visitors (especially children) from a person with a criminal record. Regrettably, frequent stories appear in the media regarding a teacher, coach, clergyman, health care professional, or other person in a position of trust who has engaged in inappropriate and even criminal conduct with a minor.

While the museum may believe that it has no choice but to require background checks as a standard practice, announcing and implementing a new policy of background checks should be done with care and sensitivity. Many school teachers and others who work with young people have already undergone background checks and are accustomed to the process, but others who have never been asked to have a background check done may be surprised and upset by the new policy. Some, especially those who have been volunteering at the museum for many years, may view a background check as an unnecessary and overly bureaucratic annoyance. They may believe that, having served as a dedicated volunteer for many years and contributed hundreds of hours of volunteer service, no background check should be necessary. Museum professionals should be aware that some of their most loyal and reputable volunteers may be offended and feel their integrity is being questioned by the new requirement of a criminal background check that includes being fingerprinted.

Some long-time volunteers with 15 or 20 years of experience have made the point that their track record should put them above reproach and make them exempt from what they view as the indignity of a background check. Yet, all too often, news accounts inform us of teachers, school administrators, clergy, and others with 15 or 20 of years of experience being involved in child pornography and other inappropriate and illegal activities. These cases make it difficult for the museum to craft a policy that exempts even the most experienced and dedicated volunteers.

Just as everyone wants to be assured of the trustworthiness of the teachers, coaches, camp counselors, and others who have contact with the children in their own family, museum visitors deserve to have similar assurances that their children will be safe and secure among the staff and volunteers at a vintage base ball game. Background checks can be completed in conjunction with the seminars so that everyone can have this piece of business out of the way before taking the field for the first game.

Practice Sessions

With the first signs of spring, club members are eager get together for outdoor practice sessions or games — often referred to as "field exercise" in bygone days — before taking the field for the opening match of the season. Veterans shake off the rust and mentor new members on the basics and finer points of play. The need for pre-season practice is somewhat dependent on the experience level of the players. Veteran teams can probably get along with one or two field exercise days before the season starts, while new teams will need several outdoor practices to get ready to play a match where spectators will be present. Clubs located in the colder climates may find it advisable to rent an indoor facility with a batting cage and an area for playing catch, fielding grounders, and doing some calisthenics and stretching. Ideally, there will be led by a team member who is an experienced high school or college player or a coach familiar with baseball-specific exercises. A local recreation center or college fieldhouse are possibilities for indoor workouts.

Practice sessions after the season begins are a matter for each club to decide, depending on its schedule of games. Clubs that play a full schedule of forty or fifty games a year will seldom have time to practice once the season begins. Clubs with a more limited schedule of a half-dozen games or so may want to hold practice sessions throughout the season, especially if there are new players who are just learning the game or if the schedule contains a gap of three or four weeks between games.

If the museum grounds are open to the public, field exercise should be conducted in uniform, as it would be inappropriate and confusing for the public to see a vintage team playing ball in modern clothing. If the museum grounds where games are to be played are closed to the public for the season, it may not be necessary to be in period dress for all practice sessions. However, it is advisable to have at least one practice in uniform. To make sure everyone has all the uniform parts they need, and to get everyone comfortable playing ball while wearing their old-style uniforms, a "dress rehearsal" will be beneficial. If the public is passing by the practice site, the club should be prepared to distribute brochures and schedules and encourage visitors to see a match once the season starts. The field exercise sessions might even draw the attention of a visitor who is interested in joining the program.

Practice sessions can include stretching exercises, playing catch to get re-accustomed to barehanded play, and an informal game. Rather than drills and batting practice, an intra-squad match is the most common and enjoyable way to organize a practice session. Practicing game situations will let players work on their physical skills while practicing the mental aspects of the game, such as when to run and when to hold on a one-bound out to an infielder or on a fly ball to an outfielder.

If the number of players present for field exercise is not precisely eighteen to form two opposing teams, it would be authentic to have teams of twelve against twelve or eight against eight. Since the early clubs were playing for exercise and recreation, the box scores of their intra-squad games often show various combinations of players on a side other than the standard nine versus nine that was the norm for official matches with other clubs. It is best to divide the players into two sides and get the game going quickly with everyone participating. When a nineteenth-century club had extra players, the box scores show that they put everyone in the striking order and used the extra player or two as an additional outfielder or as a "right shortstop" between first and second. The key is to get everyone present involved in striking, fielding, and running the bases, with no extra players standing around (especially on a cold day) waiting for a chance to play.

Retention and More Recruitment

Retention of players and the recruitment of new members are ongoing activities for a vintage base ball club. Careful roster management can help a club maintain a consistent, successful program. Participants are donating many volunteer hours and spending their money for their uniforms, travel, and other expenses on behalf of the museum. It is important to make volunteers feel that their efforts are valued. Program leaders should examine the reasons for any departures so that they can remedy shortcomings and anticipate the departures over which the program has no control. It is also important to attract new players to maintain a steady flow of new blood into the program. Ideally, the ages of club members reflect a balance across the decades. Younger team members may be more likely to relocate. As children get older, demands on parent time change. And the senior members may be less available due to retirement travel or the aches and pains of age. Target recruitment according to club needs; once balance is achieved, it is easier to maintain as players recruit their peers for the team.

Over time, some of a program's most dedicated and reliable players may reduce their participation. Some may want to spend more time coaching the teams on which their sons and daughters play. Some experience changes in their employment that require them to work on weekends or move out of the area. Some will have minor but nagging injuries, such as a hamstring or quad pull, and others may develop health problems unrelated to base ball that force them to stop playing. The inexorable passage of time may cause some veteran club members to "retire" as active players. But this need not end their participation as umpires, scorekeepers, interpreters, or administrators for the team. For a program to remain viable, vital, and active, its members should never be satisfied with the status quo in regard to its roster of active players. Continuing efforts to attract new players through the word-of-mouth reputation of the team, referrals from current players, newspapers ads, responding to inquiries from spectators, and other means must always be a high priority. Program leaders should nurture the loyalty of current volunteers, never taking for granted their contributions of time, talent, and personal funds for out-of-pocket expenses.

Building Camaraderie

When asked about the positive aspects of vintage base ball, many participants immediately speak of the spirit of camaraderie that exists within their clubs and among other teams throughout the vintage base ball community. As much as playing the games, club members enjoy the fun and fellowship of being part of a lively, active group of people who share a common interest in playing and promoting the national pastime. Volunteers take pride and satisfaction in representing the museum or sponsoring organization and being part of the institution's mission to educate the public about American history through base ball. While playing on a typical softball team can be fun and provide exercise, vintage base ball participants perceive that re-creating a historical era gives their interest in playing ball an added sense of purpose.

Being Part of a Team

The sentiments of many vintage base ball participants were eloquently expressed in an open letter written by Andy Shuman, published in the program distributed at the 2004

Ohio Cup Vintage Base Ball Festival. Shuman was serving as president of the Vintage Base Ball Association at the time. In recounting how he became involved in vintage base ball and the enjoyment he found in being part of the team over the years since, his story is representative of the thoughts and experience of many vintage ballists.

> Ladies and Gentlemen, and Guests of the Thirteenth Ohio Cup Base Ball Festival:
> On behalf of the Vintage Base Ball Association and vintage base ball everywhere, welcome! I am uniquely honored to be addressing you both as a volunteer of the Ohio Historical Society and the President of the Vintage Base Ball Association, a national organization intent on preserving the game of base ball, recreation and education. I hope that my experiences will be your experience this year.
> I saw my first vintage base ball game Labor Day weekend, 1994. It was at the Ohio Cup. I had read about 19th-century base ball, and my brother had played [on an opposing community team in a match with] the Ohio Village Muffins in an effort to start a team back home. I had been to the Ohio Historical Society museum and archives, yet I had no idea what I was about to experience as I walked through the gates at Ohio Village. What an idyllic setting located just beyond the boundaries of a major interstate highway. The place was alive with staff and visitors. Most museums show how Americans worked and lived, but now I was able to actually see how Americans played!
> The players were unpaid volunteers who loved history and the game of base ball. I felt their passion because they involved me in the game. I was not permitted to simply watch the game; they engaged me in conversation. That was part of the fun for them, sharing the game. Without hesitation the Muffins even invited my brother and me to join them for dinner that night. We did, but unbeknownst to the team, we arrived before team members, so we waited and watched as they gathered and shared in the camaraderie of one another. We chose not to interrupt; it seemed like we would have been intruding on a family gathering. I know now that it was my loss.
> A year later, I was drawn back to the Ohio Cup, but this time as a team member. Without knowing my abilities or me, the Muffins welcomed me to the team. For the first time since my youth, I was part of a base ball team! The game that I gave up because I didn't have the skills to make the next level, I was playing once again. Each summer since, I have been back and privileged to stay as a participant and no longer as an observer.
> Ohio Village, home of the Ohio Cup, has come to represent all the towns in the many states where vintage base ball is played. Small towns and big towns, western states and eastern states. People call and we come to play. New teams form wanting to play "the Muffin way." They see the same spirit that drew me to the Muffins. It looks like so much fun, and perhaps it will attract visitors to their towns the way it did Oho Village. Searching for this "holy grail," other clubs emulate the Ohio Cup and show that imitation truly is the sincerest form of flattery. As one of the oldest vintage base ball programs in the country, the Ohio Historical Society and Ohio Village remains a Mecca for all players and fans. The Ohio Cup has become, as I observed that first year, "a family reunion." It just happens that the family is a little larger today than it was thirteen years ago.
> When I am asked what prize is given at the Ohio Cup, I tell people that this is a festival, not a tournament. Scores are kept and victories gained, but there is no single winner at the Ohio Cup. The winners are the participants who make new friendships, the spectators who see a simpler time in American history, and the great game of base ball which lives on in spite of us.
> "For the Glory of the Game of Base Ball!"
> Andrew Shuman
> Ohio Village Muffins

Family Atmosphere

The fact that vintage base ball is often a family affair adds to the sense of camaraderie on the team. Players know the names of the family members of their teammates — wives,

Club members share special family occasions. The Muffins drove more than 350 miles round-trip to form a bat arch after the wedding of teammate Dennis Thompson and his bride Barb.

children, grandchildren, parents, siblings, friends, and girlfriends — who regularly attend the games. A player can bring his young children to the game and know they will have a good time playing with the children of the other players and will be looked after on the sidelines by the trusted family members of his teammates while he is busy playing in the game. Attendees at a vintage game may include the grandparents of a young player in his twenties and the grandchildren of a veteran player in his fifties.

Travel

Team trips are valuable opportunities to build camaraderie. Members enjoy taking road trips together and visiting other venues where vintage base ball is played. The club's traveling party often stays at the same motel and enjoys going out together in a large group for dinner and refreshments after the game. These outings are typically lively affairs with a substantial amount of merriment and good fun, reliving the humorous events of the day: a ball that disappeared into a woodchuck hole in the outfield; a ball caught for an out after bounding off the roof of a barn; or a base runner's miraculous escape after being caught in a rundown play. Every match seems to have its share of odd and memorable plays, and whatever happened at the day's match adds to the team's lore. The common experience of traveling to away games enables everyone to get better acquainted and share common experiences that engender a feeling of camaraderie among the club members.

On several occasions, the Muffins have chartered a bus for trips to matches at a variety of locations, including Deep River State Park in Hobart, Indiana; the Parade Ground at the Virginia Military Institute in Lexington, Virginia; the Civil War reenactment of the Battle of Pea Ridge at Keokuk, Iowa; the Museum of the Civil War Soldier at Pamplin Park in Petersburg, Virginia; and Levee Park on the banks of the Mississippi in Winona, Minnesota, with a stop along the way to step out of the cornfield in full uniform and play nine innings on the Field of Dreams in Dyersville, Iowa.

At other times, the Muffins have traveled by automobile (independently and by carpool) for games at such diverse locations as Richmond, Virginia; Manistee, Michigan; Addison, Pennsylvania; Bethpage, New York; Natchez, Mississippi; and the National Mall in Washington, D.C. In April 1994, the Muffins accepted an invitation to travel to Cleveland to take part in the ceremonies associated with the grand opening of the Indians' new ballpark, Jacobs Field. Prior to the Indians meeting the Seattle Mariners in the new park's inaugural game, the Muffins and the Forest City Club played a two-inning demonstration game featuring 1860-style base ball before the large crowd in attendance on Opening Day.

One especially memorable travel experience came on June 19, 1996, when the Muffins were invited to travel to Hoboken, New Jersey, to play at the celebration of the 150th anniversary of the game that has often been cited as the first base ball match played by New York rules between two clubs — the contest between the Knickerbocker Club and the New York Club at Hoboken's Elysian Fields on June 19, 1846. While some researchers have shared findings regarding other early games that may predate this legendary contest, it was an unforgettable experience to travel to Hoboken to celebrate the sesquicentennial of the national pastime by marching in the parade (with a number of former major league players and other dignitaries) and playing nine innings before a large and appreciative crowd near the historic spot where the Knickerbockers and their contemporaries played countless matches in the game's early days. The view of the Manhattan skyline directly across the river had changed considerably since the Knickerbockers started playing at the Elysian Fields a century and a half earlier, but several players reported they could sense the ethereal presence of the ghosts of the Knickerbockers as they took the field in Hoboken on that historic summer evening. It was a shared team experience that will never been forgotten by all who made the trip.

Many other vintage clubs have similar memories of enjoyable road trips, invitations to participate in special events, and opportunities to play in minor and major league parks. When teammates and their families share the experience of travel — whether it is a pleasant day trip to a familiar site for a game with old friends, a once-in-a-lifetime excursion to help christen a new major league park, or the opportunity to walk in the footsteps of the original Knickerbockers — a strong and enduring feeling of camaraderie is established among the members of the program.

Sportsmanship

The sportsmanlike nature of vintage base ball contributes to the camaraderie on the ball club. Members enjoy being part of a group that takes its base ball seriously in the sense of enthusiastically playing to win and providing an accurate representation of the game's early years. At the same time, it never sinks into disappointment, despair, or petty behavior if the team happens to comes out on the short end of the score on a particular day. Bickering and disputes, too often a part of modern baseball and softball, are a rarity in the vintage game. The gentlemanly tone of the matches carries over to all activities of the club, creating an atmosphere that causes members to be proud of their association with the team.

Attracting and Retaining Players

An environment of camaraderie is an important part of recruitment and retention. A potential member is always attracted to a group that looks like it genuinely enjoys what it is doing and one in which the members seem to get along well and enjoy each other's company. Similarly, current members will want to continue to be part of a group that is characterized by an unmistakable feeling of *esprit de corps* and congeniality.

Staying Informed and Connected: Internal Communications

It is important to keep all program participants well informed regarding upcoming games and other activities. In the 1980s and 1990s, many vintage clubs had some type of newsletter to report on the outcome of recent matches and promote the next scheduled games. These newsletters kept club members informed and connected, sharing news of the club's activities with other programs. From 1991 to 2006, editors John and Mardi Wells published *The Muffin Tin*, using fonts and layout styles reminiscent of nineteenth-century newspapers. *The Muffin Tin* (consisted of four to ten pages) and contained articles on base ball history; discussions of rules and practices; suggestions and ideas on historical interpretation; examples of period language, manners, and customs; accounts and tintypes (photos) of road trips; features on players; book reviews; and news of other clubs and events throughout the vintage base ball community. With a circulation of approximately 200, this fine publication kept the OHS program members connected and well informed and was a valuable resource for many other programs.

In recent years, the popularity and economy of electronic communications have led clubs to use websites, social media, and email newsletters. Setting up a website or Facebook page is essential for a club to establish a presence and identity in the vintage base ball community. For examples, club organizers are encouraged to visit the website of the Vintage Base Ball Association at www.vbba.org. The section "Member Clubs" contains a list of the organizations that belong to the VBBA arranged by state. This roster includes a link to the website of each member club.

Email is an effective way, of course, to communicate with all program members on such day-to-day matters as the schedule of matches and other events. Email has the great advantage over paper newsletters and phone trees to inform members instantaneously regarding time-sensitive matters, such as the cancellation of a game due to weather, a change in starting time for a match, or other announcements. Accommodations may need to be made for those who have limited access to e-mail or rely on work email. Others are regulars on social networks and can carry the club to new audiences on Facebook and other modern channels available for communications.

Another effective communication tool is a club handbook for members. This could be an actual paper publication or an electronic resource available on the club website. John and Mardi Wells, long-time leaders in the Muffin program, wrote, complied, and published such a handbook for the Ohio Historical Society's program that did an excellent job of providing all the basic information a volunteer would need to know in one convenient booklet. The 27-page publication contained informative text and more than 40 photos that illustrated various facets of the game. The handbook included: a list of contact people for the program (team manager, advisory board members, etc.); mission statements for the vintage base ball program and the historical society; responsibilities and benefits of being a museum volunteer; expectations for participating in the program; a description of the seminars and practice sessions; instructions on effective historical interpretation in the museum setting; maps and information on the physical configuration for the Ohio Historical Center (indoor museum) and Ohio Village (outdoor museum); how to acquire uniforms and period clothing; a history of the Muffins and Diamonds program; a description of the Ohio Cup Vintage Base Ball Festival; a brief history of early base ball in America and the evolution of base ball through the years; the rules of 1860, including the original interpretive comments by nineteenth-century rules expert Henry Chadwick and further interpretations by chief Muffin umpire Richard Schuricht; a brief history of the founding of the VBBA with a list of known vintage clubs; and a list of related publications of interest to members.

A handbook of this type is of great value to a program. A printed handbook represents a major writing and editing task and can become dated as policies are modified and the names of staff members change. However, an electronic version of a handbook could be updated and edited much more easily, and no publication cost is involved. Clubs may wish to consider compiling a handbook that would communicate the program's policies, procedures, customs, practices, standards, history, and expectations to all of its members. The time spent on this project will be saved in orientation and answering questions from newcomers. The handbook can be shared with family members, drawing them into the program as well.

Social Events and Activities

Post-Game Hospitality

In the era of the 1850s and 1860s portrayed by most vintage clubs, matches with other clubs were special events with a social as well as an athletic component. This included the host club providing a post-game meal and entertainment for their guests. Vintage clubs often follow the custom of the amateur clubs of the nineteenth century by providing cold drinks, sandwiches, box lunches, or a potluck meal. This is an opportunity for the members of the two teams to mingle and chat about the unusual plays in the day's game or share ideas about operating a vintage team. Veteran players enjoy sitting down with their acquaintances on the other club. New players are introduced and made to feel at home. Once a club becomes established, it should plan to have some post-game gatherings and try to set aside some funds for hospitality.

At a club match played between nines of the same club during the middle of the season, a post-game picnic is a good idea to make sure everyone in the program has become acquainted and stays connected to the club. Family members of the players are always included in these social situations and may be asked to bring some food items to share.

At festivals and tournaments there is often a supper or picnic for the participating clubs and their family members. The two-day Ohio Cup Vintage Base Ball Festival includes a picnic on the evening of the first day with more than 200 enjoying a supper of homemade covered dishes, salads, and desserts. Such an occasion provides an opportunity for a short program, including a speaker, awards, or base ball-themed entertainment. Old-time social activities like contra dancing (an activity similar to square dancing featuring period music and a caller) can add to the nineteenth-century flavor of the event. Many vintage programs host picnics and social gatherings reminiscent of the post-game get-togethers of 150 years ago.

Post-Season Events

A common social event for a vintage base ball club is a year-end picnic or banquet that celebrates the season and sends everyone into the off season with an eagerness to return next year. This is an excellent opportunity for the director, CEO, or other appropriate representative of the sponsoring institution to recognize and thank the volunteers for their service. Typically, volunteers in a vintage base ball program have had some out-of-pocket expense over the season for historic clothing, equipment, and travel and have often rearranged family and work commitments to participate in vintage base ball activities. While the volunteers undoubtedly have had some very enjoyable times over the season, it is always good to hear that their efforts in behalf of the institution are noticed and appreciated.

Awards and Recognitions

An end-of-the-season celebration is a good occasion to give thanks to those whose efforts made a great year possible for all involved. To be consistent with the goals of the program, leaders should consider what type of contributions should be honored and what type of award items should be presented.

Award Categories

It is strongly recommended that vintage clubs create awards based on participation and other contributions to the program rather than performance on the field. It is easy to slip into the modern format followed by many amateur and professional teams and give the usual trophies for the leaders in various offensive categories or a team MVP. But this approach is not consistent with the culture of vintage base ball and is not the best model for most vintage base ball clubs.

Over the course of the season, everyone connected with the team already knows who the most skilled players are, and they, being team-oriented gentlemen, do not need individual accolades to validate their fine play on the field. Also, there are likely several players on any club who play the game with considerable skill, and it is a difficult task to single out one from the others without slighting someone. Authenticity is an important consideration. Since familiar modern statistics such as batting average and RBIs were unknown and not kept in the 1860 era, it would not be historically accurate to give awards based on impressive statistics in these nonexistent categories.

In an effort to find alternatives to performance-based awards, program leaders are encouraged to find creative and meaningful ways to recognize the truly important contributions to the success of the program. A certificate of participation recognizes each person who served the program as a player, umpire, scorekeeper, or sideline interpreter or who supported the program in other off-the-field activities, such as making uniforms or equipment, creating a club banner, raising funds, assisting with publicity, or doing research. Everyone leaves the awards event with something tangible that marks his or her association with the base ball club. Certificates are an inexpensive way to show appreciation while serving a valuable public relations function. Volunteers hang the certificates in offices or at home where colleagues and friends will see them and ask about the vintage base ball program. These inquiries should increase the program's visibility in the community, attract more volunteers, and boost attendance at future games.

Retention can be enhanced by recognizing years of service to the club. Recognition pins can be presented to volunteers as they reach the benchmarks of five, ten, fifteen, and twenty years of service to the vintage base ball club. This honor underscores the longevity of membership. A player who consistently plays with enthusiasm may be recognized for always doing his best to hustle throughout the long season. An "Interpretation Award" can recognize the individual who furthers the educational goals of the program by interacting with spectators and answering questions about rules, customs, and the history of the game.

It is consistent with the congenial nature of vintage clubs to present several humorous awards for a variety of remarkable achievements (of both legitimate and dubious merit) during the season, and these add to the fun of the evening. Such exploits as forgetting to ask permission before retrieving a foul ball from under the hem of a vintage lady's long skirt, chasing after a dog that ran off with the ball during the middle of a match, or getting wildly lost on the way to a game are ripe for "special" honors.

In 1996, the Henry Chadwick Award was established by the Ohio Historical Society's vintage base ball program. Chadwick's entry in *The Biographical Dictionary of American Sports: Baseball* reads: "Early promoter, shaper, chronicler, and conscience of baseball, was known as the 'Father of Baseball' and later 'Father Chadwick.'" Inducted into the National Baseball Hall of Fame in 1938 (the year before the museum's doors opened), Chadwick's contributions are summarized in the following passage on the Hall of Fame website:

> A pioneer of early baseball, Henry Chadwick influenced the game by wielding a pen, not a bat. A renowned journalist, he developed the modern box score, introduced statistics such as batting average and ERA, wrote numerous instructional manuals on the game, and edited multiple baseball guides. He was an influential member of baseball's early rules committees. His tireless work and devoted love for the game greatly aided in popularizing baseball during its infancy.

In the spirit of his magnificent and enduring contributions to the game, the Henry Chadwick Award is presented annually "for outstanding service" to the Muffins/Diamonds program and to the sport of vintage base ball. Three or four Chadwick Awards are given each year to volunteers who have made significant contributions to the program in a non-playing capacity. Past recipients have included umpires, scorers, interpreters, and those who have worked behind the scenes in the areas of editing and publishing newsletters, scheduling matches, organizing special events and hospitality efforts, conducting research, raising funds, and promoting the club and the game through public relations efforts. Active players are eligible to be recipients but only for their off-the-field contributions, not their playing skills. The award has also been presented to museum professionals and sponsors for their support of the program. On occasion, a Chadwick Award has been presented to a worthy individual outside of the OHS program or to another vintage base ball program for outstanding work in spreading and promoting the sport.

A report on a banquet held by the Eclipse Club of Elkton, Maryland, that appeared on the vintage base ball listserv in the fall of 2006 provides additional creative ideas for year-end recognitions by a vintage program. At their event, this vintage club officially recognized its scorekeepers and mascots. In addition to awards to their players, the club presented the McFarland Award (named after the club's first treasurer in 1866) "to the player who raises the most money for the club" and the Maxwell Award (named after the club's first president) "to the player who excels both on and off the field (in research or other areas)." Awards of this type reflect the excellent job the Elkton program has done in two areas: researching and honoring its own early history and moving beyond the modern MVP-type award to let their members know how much their off-field contributions are valued. The club also recognized its sponsors — the area's travel and tourism council and three local businesses (a bank, a home builder, and a hardware store). This is a fine example of a club remembering to recognize those members and supporters who have made truly important contributions to the long-term success of a relatively young vintage program.

If a club wants to recognize its most effective and productive player or players on the basis of batting statistics, the most historically accurate measure to use is the concept of "average and over." A valuable resource on nineteenth base ball, *The National Association of Base Ball Players, 1857–1870* by Marshall Wright contains an excellent discussion of this calculation, which involves dividing the number of runs scored by the number of games played. Further information on keeping track of records and statistics is provided in Chapter 13, which discusses the role of the scorer.

Trophies and Keepsakes

To extend the re-creation effort from the playing field to the post-season recognition event, modern trophies should be avoided since they often include a figure of a baseball player in modern attire, complete with a glove or a batting helmet. A more authentic item would be a better choice.

A certificate with the proper design, paper, type face, and language can have a nineteenth-century appearance. Since early clubs followed the practice of presenting a trophy ball to the winner of a match, an inscribed vintage ball is a good choice for an award. If the recipient displays the ball at his workplace or home, the ball's distinctive old-style design is sure to elicit questions and comments about vintage base ball from colleagues and friends.

For a special award, a vintage-style bat is another option. Vintage bats can be inscribed with an appropriate message of congratulations or appreciation. Because of the craftsmanship that goes into making a vintage wooden bat, such an award would be a handsome addition to the recipient's home or office. The Henry Ford Museum, home of the Lah-De-Dah vintage club, acquired a gold-mounted rosewood bat in 2005 that was originally awarded to the Unknown Club of Jackson, Michigan, for winning the World's Tournament of Base Ball in Detroit in 1867. This fine example of an 1860s award serves as a reminder that a re-creation of a nineteenth-century trophy bat would be an excellent and historically accurate award to a outstanding program member.

Participation Points

It is wise to keep track of participation at matches throughout the season so that those who have made a consistent and significant effort to take part in the club's events can be recognized at the end of the year. Some clubs simply tally the number of matches in which a member appeared. Others use points to reward attendance at home and away matches, special events, and fulfilling support roles. By giving bonus points for road trips or awarding points for school visits, researching and writing an article, or marching in a parade, participation is encouraged. Ribbons, buttons, or even plaques can be presented to those at the top of the list of participation points at the end of the season. Recognizing a club's top participation point earners is much more in keeping with the spirit and values of vintage base ball than presenting an award to the club's batting average or RBI leader.

To encourage players to take on other roles, the Muffins established a policy that for every four games a volunteer earns participation points as a player, he is expected to earn points by serving one game in a non-playing capacity (umpire, scorekeeper, or interpreter). This policy reinforces the value of the non-playing roles by reminding everyone that the real purpose of the program is education and historical interpretation rather than merely playing to win the games. Taking a turn in these other roles also helps players appreciate the contributions of the non-playing volunteers. A player who is called upon to umpire occasionally gains an appreciation for the difficulty and complexity of the job.

Keeping track of participation points has another advantage when special occasions arise to play in particularly desirable games or events. A vintage club may be invited to play in a major league or minor league ballpark, appear on television, or take a trip to an attractive location. In such instances, participation may be limited to a specific number of players. The Ohio Village Muffins encountered this situation when they were invited by the Forest City Club of Greater Cleveland to take part in the pre-game festivities at Jacobs Field on the occasion of the grand opening of that ballpark on April 4, 1994. Since the game was a sellout, each vintage team was allotted only twelve tickets. How can program leaders make a fair decision on the composition of its "traveling squad" when a team has more than thirty players but only twelve open spots to participate in such a memorable event? It is difficult to make these decisions without having some people feel slighted and excluded.

Awarding a limited number of coveted spots on the basis of points earned for participation in previous games is one answer. There is an undeniable logic and fairness in rewarding those who have contributed the most to the growth and development of the program that everyone involved tends to understand and accept. Keeping track of participation points provides a quantitative basis for the club to make these kinds of decisions without hurting the feelings and alienating fine volunteers who did not quite qualify for the final list of those taking part in a special event. An invitation to play before a big crowd at a major league ballpark should be a wonderful and memorable day in the annals of any vintage club.

But care must be taken not to generate negative feelings of unfairness or favoritism in the selection process. If all volunteers know participation points are being counted and that decisions regarding participation in special events will be made accordingly, they should have no hard feelings if their total falls short. If a club keeps track of participation, players can be recognized for their total contributions to the program instead of just their batting prowess.

8

Women in Vintage Base Ball: A History of Involvement

Women have been an important part of base ball since the earliest days of the game in the mid-nineteenth century. Women are also an important part of vintage base ball. They have made significant contributions to the game from its beginning and continue to assume a variety of key roles.

Women Setting the Tone for the Game as Spectators

Since base ball's formative years, the presence of women at matches has been highly valued. In the introduction to Haney's *The Base Ball Player's Book and Reference* for 1867, Henry Chadwick enthusiastically observed that "one of the strongest aids to the popularity of Base Ball lays in the fact that it is a game — and about the only one, by-the-way — which can be countenanced and patronized by the fair sex." While women had been "shut out" from attending other games and contests "by the low character of the surroundings of most of the sports and pastimes men indulge in," Chadwick was clearly proud of the fact that base ball represents "an exception in favor of the ladies," noting "the presence of the fair sex by hundreds at a time at the leading contests of the past five or six seasons." The attendance of women in large numbers at games caused Chadwick to conclude that "if our National Pastime had no other recommendation than this, this alone would suffice to give it a popularity no other recreation could reach or compete with, in the estimation of Americans" (p.viii).

In an article in the Winter 2004 issue of *Memories and Dreams*, a publication of the National Baseball Hall of Fame and Museum, Tim Wiles wrote of the historical role of women in baseball. Wiles reports that in the 1860s, the Knickerbocker Club "encouraged its players to invite women — wives or girlfriends, mothers and daughters — to the games."

Wiles observes that "one of the leading publications of the day, *The Ball Players' Chronicle*, approved of the Knickerbockers' idea, and editorialized, 'The presence of Ladies at games purifies the moral atmosphere of a base ball gathering, repressing...all outbursts of intemperate language which the excitement of a contest so frequently induces.'" Wiles writes that women "were invited to ball parks in hopes that they would civilize the environment. If women were present, gentlemen might behave better, or so the thinking went."

And so it continues today. As in Knickerbocker days, wives, girlfriends, mothers, and daughters (along with female friends and family members of all ages) enrich the vintage

In Salisbury, North Carolina, ladies in the Ohio Village Muffins traveling party contribute to the success of a Civil War base ball re-creation: (left to right) Jackie Forquer, Oulanje Regan, Marilyn Andersen, Dulcy Francis, Julie Large.

games by their frequent attendance (in period dress or not) and help create the wholesome, festive, family environment that has contributed so much to the success of the game. The tone and atmosphere of a vintage match are definitely enhanced by the female presence. Women who attend games in period dress, portraying the spectators of the game's early days, are a splendid asset to any program. Some bring children in period dress as well, making club involvement truly a family affair.

Women as Club Leaders and Organizers

Important as their presence was at early matches and is at vintage games, women are not restricted only to the role of spectator mentioned by Chadwick and assigned to them by the customs of the nineteenth century. In a posting to the SABR Women in Baseball Committee, Debra A. Shattuck shares a note on a June 2, 1859, article in the *Brooklyn Daily Eagle* that reports on the officers of the new Neptune Base Ball Club. The list of the club committee includes Celia Brower, whom Shattuck identifies from 1860 census records as a 30-year-old Swiss-born resident of Brooklyn. While further research may indicate whether this example of a woman taking a leadership role in a men's club was rare or common in the 1850s and 1860s, there is no doubt of the pivotal role of women in vintage base ball.

Off the field, women have played an important part in the growth and development of vintage base ball, as both museum professionals and volunteers. They have filled important leadership roles with great enthusiasm, judgment, and distinction by creating new teams and providing wise leadership while overseeing the numerous organizational and administrative activities that make an established program successful.

Vintage base ball would not be the growing sport it is today without the contributions of energetic and capable women who have provided dedicated leadership to both men's and women's clubs over the years. One of the originators of the Muffins at the Ohio Historical Society, Vicky Tabor Branson, conducted research on early base ball and did much of the organizational work that resulted in the formation of the men's team in 1981. The late Sharon Antle of OHS had administrative responsibility for reorganizing and upgrading the Muffins in the 1990s and added the women's team, the Diamonds.

Joanna Shearer is the founder and administrator of the Deep River Grinders vintage program at Hobart, Indiana. In addition to overseeing the team's scheduling and other administrative operations, she is a familiar sight in period dress while serving as the scorer at the Grinders' games, both home and away. A recognized leader in the vintage base ball movement, Shearer was elected the first treasurer of the Vintage Base Ball Association upon its founding in 1996, and continues to be one of the game's admired and respected leaders. Helen DeGeatano has been the inspirational founder and driving force behind the Douglas Dutchers team in western Michigan and has served as a director of the VBBA. Dr. Connie Bodner emerged as a leader in the vintage base ball community when she helped create and organize the vintage base ball program at the Genesee Country Village and Museum in Mumford, New York, in 2001. In 2007, she joined the Ohio Historical Society in Columbus as director of museums (later director of interpretation and education), where overseeing the Muffins and Diamonds became part of her extensive portfolio of responsibilities. Mary Jane Schmitt of the Olmsted County Historical Society has provided leadership for the vintage program in Rochester, Minnesota. Her team's home grounds have been named Schmitt Field in recognition of her superb contributions to vintage base ball.

Women Researchers and Writers

In addition to those in key administrative roles, the sport of vintage base ball also benefits from the contributions of many women in the community of scholars and researchers doing valuable work on nineteenth-century base ball history. Some are affiliated with vintage programs and others are teachers or independent scholars. Those turning their attention to women in the early years of the sport include Jean Hastings Ardell and Gai Berlage. Dorothy Seymour Mills, included in the inaugural class of recipients of SABR's Henry Chadwick Award in 2010, has been given belated credit and joint recognition for her work on the landmark three-volume study *Baseball: The Early Years*, *Baseball: The Golden Age*, and *Baseball: The People's Game*, the authorship of which had been previously attributed solely to her late husband, Harold Seymour. Monica Nucciarone's 2009 biography of Alexander Cartwright is a significant addition to the literature on this pioneer and on the era of the Knickerbockers. Priscilla Astifan and Debra Shattuck continue to be generous in sharing their valuable research findings on the early years of the game. The research and writing of these women increases our knowledge of the historical period when base ball was in its formative years.

Women as Interpreters

Women are valuable members of vintage base ball programs in the role of interpreters. Some "sideline interpreters" are historical society staff members while others are volunteers, often family members of the gentlemen who play on the team. Attired in the manner of the

1860s, they walk in parades and participate in on-field activities and ceremonies. Their colorful period dress adds greatly to the general atmosphere at a vintage game. They remind onlookers immediately that they are in a different time period and engage their interest in the customs and culture of the day. Some are familiar with game rules and practices and can describe the action, while others are skilled in discussing women's suffrage or the life of a teacher or shop worker of that time. As they greet visitors, answer questions, and help spectators enjoy attending a vintage game, they make a contribution to the success of any program.

Women and Scorekeeping

In vintage base ball, the role of scorer is sometimes filled by a woman associated with a men's vintage club. A number of ladies who attend matches in nineteenth-century dress as volunteers or museum staff members enjoy performing scorekeeping duties. The practice of having a woman serve as scorekeeper at a men's match may not be strictly authentic, but by acting in this capacity, women provide a valuable service since every club should keep a box score of each of its games. The practice of having a woman serve as the scorer has become so widely accepted in vintage base ball that no one gives it a second thought on authenticity grounds.

In addition to the outstanding scorekeeping work done by women museum professionals like Joanna Shearer of the Deep River Grinders, several spouses who attend the matches in period dress as program volunteers have fulfilled the role of scorer with dedication and distinction. Linda Hunkele, the wife of veteran player, team organizer, and rules expert Paul Hunkele (of the Regular Club of Mt. Clemens, Michigan) has scored many games and, as a result of her research on the topic, is especially knowledgeable regarding early scorekeeping methods. When not on the field as an excellent player for the Lady Clodbusters, Melissa Wilson, the wife of Clodbusters Base Ball Club captain Jim Wilson, has often staffed the scorer's table for the men's team in her 1860s dress, keeping a neat and accurate record of each game. At the Ohio Village, the late Toby Bennett, wife of veteran player Pat Bennett, handled the scorer's duties for the Muffins in an excellent manner over many seasons.

Women who are knowledgeable about the rules and practices of the game and have kept score at vintage matches have enhanced, advanced, and enriched the sport of vintage base ball by their dedicated work. While not yet known to have any historical basis, having women as scorers is an intelligent accommodation that helps vintage base ball continue to grow.

Hospitality

Post-game hospitality is one of the traditions that has been handed down from the earliest clubs to today's vintage teams. Women have often provided organizational leadership in this area, as well as providing homemade food for these gatherings. Marilyn Andersen, wife of veteran player Don Andersen, is well known among vintage base ball clubs for her work in organizing a hospitality room, which is open during both days of the Ohio Cup Festival. Players and their families stop by whenever they have a break between games for baked goods, sandwiches, fruit, kid-friendly snacks, coffee, and cold drinks at no charge. In addition to building camaraderie, hospitality efforts by the home club reduce costs for the visiting players and their families who have traveled to the site for the game. The women

Joanna Shearer of the Deep River Park Grinders of Hobart, Indiana, scores her club's match as a member of the Clodbusters of Dayton, Ohio, checks the progress of the game.

associated with vintage programs who lead these hospitality efforts deserve everyone's sincere appreciation for all they do to keep a nineteenth-century tradition alive by graciously hosting visiting teams and their families.

Women Players on Men's Teams

On the playing field, women have occasionally appeared on men's vintage teams dressed in the standard men's uniform of the club. Women players on men's teams usually have some background in high school or college athletics or women's softball. Women players who have chosen to wear the regular uniform of the men's team have been accepted, without significant discussion or controversy.

A woman likely would never have played on a men's club in the mid-nineteenth century. On the basis of historical accuracy, a strong case can be made against participation of women on men's vintage teams. However, rather than getting into acrimonious discussions over the issue of on-field participation by an occasional female player, vintage base ball clubs have had a history of avoiding the type of gender-based squabbles that have plagued amateur baseball at various levels. While women would not have played on men's teams in the nineteenth century, any club inclined to bar women from playing should consult an attorney familiar with precedents set by cases involving Civil War re-enactor groups where attempts were made to exclude women on grounds of historical authenticity. In regard to authenticity issues, if a female player is wearing the standard men's uniform, she probably will not be a distraction from the presentation of the game.

Women's Teams

Where there are sufficient numbers and interest, a handful of programs with a men's team have created a women's team. Historical evidence regarding the existence of women's teams in the 1850s and early 1860s has been slow in coming. Women were playing base ball in college in the mid–1860s, but other examples have been difficult to find. This puts historical societies and museums in a bit of dilemma. With so little evidence of women playing base ball in its early days, and since vigorous physical activity for women was often discouraged in that era, questions have emerged regarding the historical accuracy of sponsoring a women's team and presenting it to the public as something that would have actually existed in the 1850s or 1860s. On the other hand, the vintage base ball community is very welcoming to anyone who wants to get involved in playing the game. In that spirit of inclusiveness, opportunities have been made available for women to play vintage base ball. Women's teams typically put on an entertaining game that is enjoyable for participants and spectators alike.

In regard to the question of historical authenticity, the best hope for the formation of more women's teams is that recent research shows that women may have been more involved in athletic pursuits than previously believed. Author Gai Ingham Berlage in *Women in Baseball: The Forgotten History* points out that according to the standards of the time, women were "envisioned as the weaker sex" and "seen as biologically frail and in need of protection." Women "were expected be to be passive, gentle, soft spoken, delicate, and unobtrusive." Berlage writes that "strenuous activity of any kind was to be avoided. Sports and outdoor activities were male preserves." However, times were beginning to change. "The second half of the 1800s set the stage for an unlikely convergence. A small group of Victorian ladies left their parlor couches, their smelling salts and their feminine frailty behind to participate in the new national pastime of baseball, both as spectators and as players" (pp 1–2).

Vassar College in Poughkeepsie, New York, had women's teams soon after its founding in 1865. *Baseball: An Illustrated History* by Ken Burns and Geoffrey C. Ward includes a special section titled "An Assemblage of Ladies," which states that "in 1866, at Vassar College, freshmen women formed the Laurel and Abenakis baseball clubs, with the support of a female physician who thought exercise for women essential to good health." Commenting on the general relationship between women and base ball in this era, Burns and Ward note, "At first women were meant to watch, rather than play, putting male spectators and male players alike on their best behavior through their refined presence. But some women, like Annie Glidden of Vassar College, insisted on playing all along. 'They are getting up various clubs now for out-of-door exercise,' she wrote home in 1866. 'They have a floral society, boat clubs and base-ball clubs. I belong to one of the latter, and enjoy it highly, I can assure you.'" In addition to the reference to the base ball clubs, the existence of a boat club is further evidence of women being involved in outdoor exercise (p. 18).

Historian Debra A. Shattuck sheds more light on the Vassar clubs in her *Journal of Sport History* article (Summer 1992) "Bats, Balls and Books: Baseball and Higher Education for Women at Three Eastern Women's Colleges, 1866–1891."

> The tone of Annie's often-quoted comment seems innocuous, but the rest of the letter, which isn't often quoted, suggests some attitude: "We think after we have practiced a little, we will let the Atlantic Club play a match with us. Or, it may be, we will consent to play a match with the students from College Hill [a local boys' preparatory school], but we have not decided yet."

Recent work on the relationship of women and athletics in the 1840s and 1850s points to women becoming increasingly involved in exercise and outdoor activities. Jean Hastings

The Lady Clodbusters of Dayton, Ohio, and the Diamonds of Ohio Village pose for a "tintype" after a well-played match.

Ardell's *Breaking into Baseball: Women and the National Pastime* takes us back to the 1840s to remind us that "just as the women's emancipation movement was quickening, Alexander Cartwright's 'new' game made its appearance in Hoboken. Two hundred miles to the northwest and two years later, in July 1848, the Convention for Women's Rights took place in Seneca Falls, New York. The delegates spoke up for the freedom to be educated, to earn a living on equal basis with men, to vote, and to maintain a separate identity and existence." Ardell contends that "the right to enjoy baseball went hand in mitt with those aspirations. Feminist leaders understood that physical fitness exhilarates and empowers a woman and made it a part of their agenda." (p.18)

According to Ardell's analysis of the period, "base ball held a powerful attraction for Victorian era women. Having learned of the possibilities of gaining suffrage, an education, and equal pay — in short the right to fully partake in America life — the weaker sex would not be dissuaded from the diamond" (p. 18). Ardell's work supports the view that women were becoming involved in base ball and other athletic activities.

In vintage base ball, the formation of a women's team has worked well for a few museums. The creation of these teams provides opportunities for significant numbers of women players to take the field. Women's games are popular with the public, and adding a women's team adds to the strength and vitality of any vintage program. There is also an the educational component in that women's games tend to initiate discussions about the limited opportunities for exercise and athletic activity available to women and girls in the nineteenth century, as compared to the abundant opportunities that exist today.

As a companion program to its successful men's club, the Ohio Village Muffins, the Ohio Historical Society broke new ground by forming the first women's team, the Ohio Village Diamonds, in 1994. This action was the product of OHS staff member and Muffins team manager Doug Smith and volunteers Dianna Frias and Pam Koons, who became the founding team captains. With no other women's vintage teams to play, the Diamonds held practice sessions, played intra-squad games, and had occasional matches against area women's softball teams using 1860 rules.

After the creation of the Diamonds, other women's teams began to form. The Colorado Vintage Base Ball Association organized a women's team, the Columbines. Several Ohio vintage programs embraced the concept. In the Dayton area, the Carriage Hill Farm Clodbusters added the Lady Clodbusters in 1997. The Akron Black Stockings program at Stan Hywet Hall in Akron added the Lady Locks in 1998. These three women's teams in Ohio have been able to get together a few times a year for spirited matches. A game involving any combination of these fine ladies teams at any of their home grounds is enjoyable to watch, and women's games are a highlight of the Ohio Cup Vintage Base Ball Festival. Spectators who attend the Ohio Cup Festival, including the many women and girls, are especially interested in seeing the women's teams play according to the 1860 rules and customs.

The Genesee Country Village and Museum near Rochester, New York, in addition to creating a successful four-team men's program also formed two women's teams. The GCVM reports that "the first is inspired by the barnstorming tradition of ladies' base ball — brought to life here by Priscilla Porter's Astonishing Ladies Base Ball Club. The second is a group of village residents who come together for love of the game, and it is named the Brooks Grove Belles, after the town that was home to three of the buildings now found in the museum's historic village." The History Center of Olmsted County, Minnesota, vintage base ball program formed the Rochester Roosters men's team in 1997 and a women's team, the Hens, in 2004.

Unfortunately, women's vintage teams have turned out to be difficult to create and fragile to maintain. The museums that sponsor them and the men's teams that play at the same sites have been supportive and would like to see them succeed. Embryonic programs at Cincinnati and Canal Fulton, Ohio, have had difficulty getting off the ground; the Akron program, after considerable early success, has struggled to continue.

One factor limiting success is the lack of other teams to play, resulting in an abbreviated schedule. This makes the recruitment of players difficult. Also, women and girls who enjoy baseball and softball have other outlets for their interests and talents, and it is has proved difficult to recruit women who are already busy playing on two or three softball teams or who are involved in coaching girls softball.

The lack of hard evidence regarding the existence of organized women's teams in the pre–Civil War period continues, to be an issue for museums. Women may have participated in informal games at family and community gatherings from time to time. Since local and national evidence is sparse regarding "formal" women's clubs that would be analogous to the many well-documented men's base ball clubs of that era (that have left behind their constitutions, club minutes, scorebooks, and other written evidence of their games), it is difficult to get people motivated to "re-create" something that may not have existed. Museum professionals and other researchers have sought to uncover more examples of women and girls playing base ball in the 1850s and 1860s. Such findings could support the creation of more women's teams, a welcome development that would strengthen the existing women's teams.

Proper Attire: Uniforms or Dresses?

If a museum decides to form and maintain a women's team, the issue of appropriate attire for the players arises. This is an important question for the growth and success of women's vintage teams and perhaps one that has been underestimated as a reason more clubs have not formed. Just as uniforms are vital to the success of men's teams, they may be a key element in the success of women's teams.

An item found in 2007 by researcher Craig B. Waff in the September 4, 1849, issue of the *Milwaukee Sentinel and Gazette* references women wearing a type of uniform while playing sports. "Nine married ladies beat nine single ones at a game of wicket in England recently. The gamesters were all dressed in white — the married party with blue trimmings and the others with pink." Waff speculates that the reference might have been to cricket rather than wicket and to New England rather than England, but "whatever the case, the account is interesting as an early report of women playing bat-and-ball games." It is also interesting to note that they were wearing colors to designate the two sides.

One early photograph of a women's team that has appeared in a number of published histories of early base ball is an image of Vassar College Resolute Club of 1866. Fortunately, the photograph is of high quality and provides a head-to-toe view of nine young women posing before the door of what appears to be one of the college buildings. One holds a bat and one holds a dark-colored base ball. The composition of the photograph is very similar to photographs of men's team from this era. They project an aura of pride and accomplishment in being photographed as members of the base ball club. They are not wearing matching base ball uniforms, but rather very stylish, full length, long-sleeved daytime dresses of various shades and patterns. However, uniform elements are present as they are wearing matching billed caps and dark belts with the club name "Resolute" in bold white capital letters across the front.

This interesting image of an early women's team raises as many questions as it answers. The written reference that the women of Vassar formed two base ball teams in 1866 — the Laurel and Abenakis — along with the photo of a third club, the Resolutes, raises the question of how many clubs and players were engaged in base ball at the college. Were the Resolutes an existing club that served as the model for the freshmen when the Abenakis and Laurels were formed? Are the dresses in the photo the ones the Resolutes actually wore to play base ball, or did they get dressed up to pose for their formal group portrait, as people often do for a picture taken by a professional photographer? Given that it may have been considered inappropriate for women to be photographed in exercise clothing, could they have worn something entirely different while playing base ball, and then donned their team caps and belts when posing in dresses with their bat and ball for the club picture?

Commenting on the growing women's emancipation movement as expressed at the Seneca Falls Convention of 1848, Jean Hastings Ardell in *Breaking into Baseball* writes:

> This more active lifestyle recommended the shedding of restrictive corsets and unwieldy skirts of the day in favor of more comfortable dress.... Whether it was bicycling or baseball, women who exercised were hampered by their heavy garments. The solution to this dilemma — the bloomer — appeared in 1851, but the sight of a woman appearing in public in a short skirt over full trousers scandalized traditionalists and delayed widespread acceptance of the bloomer for decades. Not until the late in the 1800s do we find accounts of women "baseballists" wearing the controversial costume" [p. 18].

Ardell's reference to the bloomer calls for an explanation of this type of women's clothing.

Bloomers were invented by Elizabeth Smith Miller of Peterboro, New York. They began to be referred to as "bloomers" when Amelia Bloomer, an advocate for dress reform, called for women to dress more functionally and comfortably. In the early 1850s, a few women began wearing a knee-length dress worn over loose trousers gathered at the ankle. According to the National Women's Hall of Fame, after Bloomer wrote favorably about the attire in her newspaper, *The Lily*, others picked up the story and attached her name to the fashion. The Women's Rights National Historic Park reports that when she began wearing the new dress, she was inundated with requests for patterns, which, she wrote, showed "how ready and anxious women were to throw off the burden of long heavy skirts." This would be especially true for women engaging in athletic activity. Many of the dress reform advocates were also involved in other reform causes, such as temperance, women's voting rights, and the abolition of slavery.

In the collection of the National Baseball Hall of Fame and Museum in Cooperstown, there is an image of two women's teams dressed in bloomers playing a spirited game of base ball at Peterboro, New York, in 1868. The story behind this interesting image, and the details in the image itself are important evidence in the study of women in base ball in the 1860s. This is not a "pick-up" game. The women in the picture are wearing matching uniforms and playing in a well-organized, formal setting before a large crowd of male and female spectators. Therefore, women's base ball appears to be have been fairly well established in upstate New York by 1868.

Peterboro is only about 200 miles from Poughkeepsie, New York, the home of the Vassar College clubs that are known to have existed in 1866. It seems no coincidence that this well-organized and well-attended women's game took place only about 75 miles from Seneca Falls, the site of the historic Convention for Women's Rights held 20 years earlier. In addition to being the home of the originator of bloomers for women, Peterboro was a community known for its strong support of the social reform movements of the time, including women's suffrage, temperance, and abolition. With the area's heritage of support for women's rights, the emergence of both bloomers and women's base ball in Peterboro was not a random occurrence.

There were, of course, reform-minded young women in many communities throughout the country. Were they also starting to wear bloomers for athletic activities that included base ball? It may have been the case that in the environment of Peterboro, which was friendly to women's rights and social reform, women were able to play ball in public while other areas were less accepting of the practice. Perhaps games were being played in more out-of-the-way locations such as the grounds of a school for girls or college for women where the female players could enjoy a game of base ball without drawing attention or criticism.

Although the Peterboro image is dated 1868, the fact that the women are wearing uniforms in an organized game with a large crowd on hand suggests that this was not the first time women played base ball in that area. Women's participation as players may date back to a few years earlier. Eric Enders reported on his website that the illustration of women playing base ball in 1868 in Peterboro "appeared soon after the game in a New York newspaper called *It's the Day's Doings*." Along with the illustration, the newspaper published an article on the game, "The Last Illustration of Woman's Rights — A Female Base-Ball Club at Peterboro, N.Y." that contains several interesting and favorable comments about the propriety of exercise for women. As "a player of base ball...she deserves our unqualified attention and commendation. Physical exercise is one of the needs of American men, especially of American women." Instead of various other forms of exercise, the article hopes that the

Interpreters at Ohio Village encourage the crowd to support women's rights during the Glorious Fourth Independence Day Celebration.

attention of women "is being directed to physical sports of a bracing and healthy character." The article continues with a ringing endorsement of base ball for women: "Every well-wisher of women — (and what man with a wife, sweetheart, sister or daughter is not such a well-wisher) — will wish our female base ball clubs, and similar organizations, all success, and only wish that there were more of them."

This newspaper account supports the view that the game in Peterboro was not a one-time-only informal gathering. The article refers to the fact that women have followed the men's model of forming formal base ball *clubs*, and it speaks of clubs in the plural, indicating the existence of more than one group of women playing base ball at this time.

Having provided the important information that by 1868 women had formed their own base ball clubs, the article goes on to state that "the last success in female base-ball, occurred in Peterboro, a thriving little village in New York State." In this context, the term "last success" means "latest success," meaning there were previous successful instances of women playing base ball. This point is supported by a quote from "the local [Peterboro] paper":

> The young women of Peterboro, N.Y., jealous of the popular sports enjoyed by the more muscular portion of mankind, have organized a baseball club, and have already arrived at a creditable degree of proficiency in play. There are about fifty members belonging to it, from which a playing nine has been chosen, headed by Miss Ninnie Miller as captain. The nine have played several games outside the town and away from the gaze of the curious. Having thus perfected themselves, this nine lately played a public game in the town of Peterboro, as may well be supposed, before a multitude of spectators.

Historical societies and museums with women's vintage teams have wrestled with the proper attire dilemma for several years. While supportive of the idea of women's vintage teams, a lack of evidence of uniforms for women has led some museums to the conclusion that women, if they played base ball at all, would have done so only on an informal basis and would have worn the full-length housedresses they usually wore to do their daily household chores. The issue of bloomer-style uniforms versus housedresses may be important to the recruitment and retention of players. Some athletically inclined women who might be interested in playing vintage base ball are reluctant to play clumsily while wearing cumbersome 1860-style women's clothing. Active women who enjoy playing ball are accustomed to the freedom of wearing shorts and short-sleeved shirts, typical of modern softball uniforms. The bloomer-style uniform would be period-appropriate and player-friendly. Furthermore, having matching uniforms instills a sense of team pride.

Since evidence of women wearing base ball uniforms is scarce, players on women's vintage teams, such as Ohio Village Diamond Dianna Frias, often play in housedresses and aprons.

The illustration of women playing in an athletic costume and the accompanying article's references to a club structure and the existence of multiple clubs enables the vintage base ball community to take a fresh look at vintage base ball for women. Based on the analysis by authors Jean Hastings Ardell and Gai Ingham Berlage regarding women's interest in playing base ball and other sports in the nineteenth century, it is likely that women were more involved in exercise and forming sports-based clubs than previously thought.

Future Directions

The following proposals are suggested to revitalize and strengthen women's vintage base ball.

1. Based on the advent of bloomers in 1851 and the pictorial evidence in the illustration of the 1868 Peterboro game, museums should rethink the idea of uniforms for women and, if team members prefer them over housedresses, adopt bloomer-type apparel for women's teams. Uniforms can contribute to a sense of pride in being a member of a formal club and the feeling of satisfaction and accomplishment that goes along with being part of a "real" base ball team.

2. Based on the recent research on the formation of women's clubs, museums can be comfortable with supporting a vintage team for women. It is suggested that women's programs recruit enough members to field two teams so that they can conduct a game among their own members, just as the women in Peterboro did in the 1860s. All program members would have the same basic uniform. A ribbon or rosette of some distinctive color would

then be attached to distinguish the two sides. This would reflect the pattern of both the early women's and men's clubs, which played mostly intra-squad games and attached a ribbon to their shirt to denote which side they were on. One clear example of this appears in the illustration *Union Soldiers at Salisbury N.C.*, which shows members of one team wearing red ribbons and the other wearing blue ribbons, perhaps a carryover from the way they distinguished the two sides in pre-war games back home. Women's clubs can continue to schedule games with other women's clubs as opportunities arise, but given the scarcity of clubs, it might be a wise policy to concentrate on intra-squad matches to demonstrate the sport to the public and help grow the sport in the manner that men's clubs proliferated in the 1990s.

3. Some consideration may be given to adjusting the size of the diamond used by women's teams. While men's teams play on a field with bases placed 90 feet apart, 60 feet is the distance on a softball diamond. Women should not necessarily be held to the standard men's dimensions and, if they wish, should be permitted to reduce the size of the diamond. The distance between bases was originally based on the concept of "pace" with a distance of 42 paces from home plate to second base. In "The Evolution of the Baseball Diamond" in the 1994 edition of *The Baseball Research Journal*, Tom Shieber points out that while a pace is often defined as either 3 feet or 2½ feet, "Other historians take the view that a pace, being a unit of measurement defined solely by the individual doing the pacing, allowed for a scalable diamond dependent on the size of the players." Therefore, since the pace of a woman or child would be shorter, a smaller, scaled-down diamond would be the result. Based on this interpretation, women should have the option of pacing off their own playing field, which would probably result in the base lines approximating the 60-foot distance of modern softball. Shieber points out that due to the continuing debate over the definition of a pace, "the exact size of the Knickerbocker infield square remains uncertain." Since there is a degree of ambiguity in this matter, if a smaller infield would be more workable and enjoyable for women's teams, museum professionals and club leaders should have the latitude to lay out their playing field accordingly.

These proposals are offered for consideration in the spirit of that reporter for *It's the Daily Doings* in 1868 who wrote that we "wish our female base ball clubs, and similar organizations, all success, and only wish that there were more of them."

9

Period Uniforms

The Knickerbocker Base Ball Club of New York City, formed in 1845, is credited by numerous sources as being the first base ball club to create and wear uniforms. According to the informative "Dressed to the Nines: A History of the Baseball Uniform" exhibit on the website of the National Baseball Hall of Fame and Museum, "Four years later, at a meeting on April 24, 1849, the club adopted an official uniform: blue woolen pantaloons, white flannel shirts and chip (straw) hats. Though the straw hats were abandoned a few years later, the Knickerbockers retained the blue and white team colors for decades to come." Other base ball clubs followed the Knickerbockers' example and started wearing uniforms in the pre–Civil War era. Club members took great pride in their uniforms, endeavoring to "present themselves as respectable, gentlemanly organizations." The "Dressed to the Nines" exhibit points out that "as late as the 1860s, baseball clubs were more than happy to associate themselves with well-established, manly organizations such as fire departments and volunteer military companies. Indeed, early uniforms often looked identical to those worn by these other longstanding fraternal clubs."

The Importance of Uniforms

Historically accurate uniforms contribute significantly to making vintage base ball an interesting and colorful game. Playing by old-time rules while wearing modern workout clothing, such as T-shirts, nylon gym shorts, and sweat pants, would have virtually no appeal for players or spectators. Playing the game in authentic-looking nineteenth-century uniforms, using period equipment, and adopting the language and behavioral norms of the period are among the key elements for a successful vintage base ball program.

To enable the spectators at a vintage base ball match to step back in time, every player on the field should be in a complete uniform worn correctly. Dr. Connie Bodner, then director of education and interpretation at the Ohio Historical Society, created a humorous but effective power point presentation for the Muffin/Diamond seminar held on March 15, 2008. "The Good, the Bad, and the Ugly of Uniforms in Vintage Base Ball" emphasized the reasons uniforms are so important. The topic was introduced with the question "Why Care What You Wear?" which was followed by a discussion of these points:

> Your most effective interpretive tools are what you say and what you wear.
> You can draw attention to what's different about base ball through your uniform.
> Your uniform can help visitors suspend disbelief.

Suspension of disbelief is an essential concept for any living history activity. In the case of a vintage base ball program, spectators need to feel as if they have traveled through

Period Uniforms 125

The uniforms worn by the clubs that make up the Colorado Vintage Base Ball Association are based on uniform styles worn by nineteenth-century Colorado teams. These various designs are represented by players from CVBBA clubs who traveled to the Ohio Cup Festival to play as the "Territorial All-Stars" since Colorado was still a territory in the 1860s.

time and are watching a game from a bygone era. Anachronisms disrupt the visitor's belief that they have left the modern era. An anachronism was defined in Bodner's presentation as

> An error in chronology; especially a chronological misplacing of persons, events, objects, or customs in regard to each other.
> A person or a thing that is chronologically out of place; especially one from a former age that is incongruous with the present.
> The state of being chronologically out of place.

Staged photos of a vintage player displaying examples of anachronisms in his uniform were shown to the group. Both veteran members and newcomers to the program were asked to study the photos and identify the common errors to be avoided. The photos included such mistakes as wearing shirt sleeves rolled up, a vintage cap worn backward or with the bill turned up, an untied tie, an unbuttoned shield, a shirt-tail out. The point was made that a gentlemanly 1860-era player would not have appeared in public in a disheveled state and always would have worn his uniform correctly.

After the audience members had discussed these errors, additional photos were shown and the group was asked to identify various other anachronisms that were "chronologically out of place." These photos showed a player wearing a complete uniform but damaging the overall effect by wearing a wristwatch, wrist bands, modern sneakers, and sunglasses; holding a plastic sports drink bottle and vinyl bat bag; and bringing to the bench such modern items as an iPod, cell phone, and car keys. Again the audience had fun identifying the various examples of anachronisms, all of which had been observed at vintage matches. The conclusion of Bodner's presentation offered the following points to keep in mind throughout the season:

> What you wear IS important.
> Draw attention to yourself and be sure what people see is consistent with mid-19th-century style.
> Your uniform can help visitors suspend disbelief and be more receptive to understanding what you're trying to teach about base ball.

The points made in the seminar presentation and discussions are reinforced in *From Clueless to Class Act: Manners for the Modern Man* by Jodi R. R. Smith, an etiquette consultant on matters of behavior and dress. The chapter "Personal Appearance" opens with the following observation:

> Marketing executives know that it's all about packaging when it comes to selling a product. Similarly, when you get dressed, you are selling yourself to the world. What is it you are saying about yourself? Is it the message you want to send? Like it or not, the way you appear to others sets the tone for your interactions and the way in which others treat you. The key is to think about the people you are going to come in contact with and use your image to your advantage by making the best impression possible [p. 97].

While this statement was written with job interviews and business situations in mind, the points apply directly to vintage base ball. One product the program is trying to market and sell is "the suspension of disbelief"—providing the experience of attending a base ball game as it would have been played in the nineteenth century. To use the business example, if a player's uniform is incomplete, if it is not being worn correctly, or if anachronisms are in public view, the museum visitors will not be "buying," and it will be very difficult to make a sale of the product.

Players accustomed to not giving much thought to what to wear while playing in a softball game should remember that a vintage base ball match is different. The player is not just representing himself but the vintage base ball program and the organization that sponsors the team. In *From Clueless to Class Act*, the author cautions, "You are the company: Any time you make contact with someone outside the office, you represent the company for which you work." She then reminds the reader that in all interactions "you should be as polished as possible" (p. 168). To the public attending a game, the players are the museum and the attention paid to appearance—striving to be as "polished as possible" by always wearing a complete uniform that is clean and in good repair with no anachronisms—will reflect positively on the entire program.

In addition to the impact uniforms have on spectators, wearing nineteenth-century attire seems to have an immediate and almost magical effect on the behavior of players. Being dressed in the manner of the 1860s, 1880s, or whatever period is being portrayed encourages players to speak and act like people from that era. For this reason, clubs may want to consider having players dress in their uniforms at practice sessions so that they feel comfortable wearing them and adopt the behavioral patterns and language of the period.

Choosing a Uniform Style and Club Colors

Before making an investment in team uniforms, it is wise to consult with an apparel expert at the museum or local historical society regarding the appropriateness of various fabrics, styles, colors and patterns. Understandably, many museums have very specific standards regarding the authenticity of the period dress to be worn by its representatives while engaged in public programming. A vintage team would not want to spend money on uniforms only to find out too late that the uniforms that have been ordered do not meet the museum's standards or are inappropriate for the time period represented by the village or historic farm where the team's home grounds are located.

Vintage clubs that are considering the style of uniform they want to wear should spend time studying photographs, engravings, paintings, and other visual images to get an idea of typical uniform elements of the period being re-created. "Dressed to the Nines: A History of the Baseball Uniform," on the National Baseball Hall of Fame and Museum website is a very helpful resource on early uniforms. Both the text and the illustrations of this well-researched and attractively presented electronic exhibit will provide the vintage club with guidance in the area of uniforms. Another excellent source of photographs of nineteenth century uniforms is *Base Ball Cartes: The First Baseball Cards* by Mark Rucker, a book that contains many photographs of nineteenth-century players and clubs. There are a number of books on the history of the national pastime that include images of nineteenth-century uniforms illustrating the game's early years. Auction catalogs (both print and online) and magazines for baseball collectors may also contain informative period photographs.

Many vintage clubs have taken various elements from period illustrations to create a uniform that is representative of the general style of uniforms commonly worn in the 1850s and 1860s. The drawing (made from a photograph) of "The Champion Nine of the Union Club of Morrisania, New York" that appeared in the October 26, 1866, issue of *Harper's Weekly* is often studied as a resource since it shows full-length images of all the players, thus providing various views of the uniforms being worn. The 1866 Currier and Ives illustration "The American National Game of Base Ball: Grand Match for the Championship at the Elysian Fields, Hoboken, N.J." also shows the uniform styles of the era.

If taking the identity of an actual club that played in the community in the nineteenth century, program leaders will want to research local newspapers and other sources to find an image or description of the uniform worn by the team being re-created. Pictures of the uniform worn by such famous teams as the 1869 Cincinnati Red Stockings or 1884 Providence Grays are relatively easy to find. Others may take some digging, but local research can be very rewarding. The diligent researcher may be fortunate enough to find an old photograph, a passage in a newspaper article, a letter, a diary written by a player or spectator, or the minutes of a club meeting that include a description. Such a discovery will provide inspiration and direction in coming up with a historically accurate club uniform. The newspaper reporting of the day often included passages that are very helpful in providing descriptions of uniforms and in determining uniform colors from black-and-white images. In the September 16, 1867, edition of the *Columbus Morning Journal*, an account of a game played at the Franklin County Fair included this detailed description of the uniform worn by the Capital Club of Columbus:

> The appearance of the Capital nine was very fine. The boys appeared for the first time in their new uniform, which is the prettiest one we have ever seen. It consists of dark blue pants, a checked white and blue woolen shirt, and a checked white and blue cap. The bosom of the shirt consists of a shield, in the center of which is a red letter "C." The Eureka B.B Club of New Jersey has a similar uniform. In their new uniform the boys are favorites more than ever before.

Programs fortunate enough to find such accounts can use this information to put a

Dressed in authentic uniforms based on period illustrations of their forebearers, the Cincinnati Red Stockings present the game as played by the acclaimed 1869 team of the same name.

vintage team on the field that captures the look of the original team and the history of the community.

Vintage teams typically get many questions from spectators regarding their attire since the uniforms are the first thing observers notice when arriving at a match. The club might include in its brochure a description or illustration of the club uniform on which the vintage club's uniform is based. Spectators will appreciate the research and respect the effort that has been made by the club members to be authentic in their appearance.

Team colors should be selected from among the colors seen commonly in the time period. Clubs might choose colors that represent or complement those of the sponsoring organization or that are important to the community. The colors should lend themselves to use on banners, flags, in print, and online. The uniform shirt, shield, hat, and tie provide opportunities to show the colors. The uniform colors must stand up to repeated washings and sun exposure. A team starting out with rich, red fireman-style shirts may find themselves wearing pink after repeated washings. Dark shirts absorb the heat on sunny summer days.

When selecting a uniform, club leaders should try to choose uniform components that will continue to be available in future seasons. It is important that new players who join a program are able to obtain uniforms that are identical to the ones worn by the original players. As shirts and pants wear out, players will need to have a convenient source from which to obtain replacements.

Shirts

From the study of period photographs and illustrations, it is evident that most 1860-era base ball teams wore long-sleeved, collared shirts that featured a shield with the monogram, initials, or symbol of the club. The shield, attached with buttons, may be bound on the edges in a contrasting color. According to "Dressed to the Nines," "the shield-front jersey style first gained popularity as the baseball craze boomed in the late 1850s. Many of the leading clubs of the 1860s and 1870s wore the style that was reminiscent of volunteer fire company uniforms. Though sporting goods supplier A. G. Spalding & Bros. advertised the 'Fancy Shield Shirt' as late as 1893, few baseball clubs wore the style after the mid–1870s when lace-front shirts became popular."

Shirts should fit loosely to allow for the athletic movements required for a strenuous base ball game, but sleeves should not be too billowy, since that style would be more suited to the colonial or Revolutionary War period. Some vintage teams wear flannel or woolen shirts and others wear shirts of heavy cotton. Like many 1860s clubs, many vintage teams choose white shirts, but some opt for a dark color or even a check or plaid design, especially if research indicates such would be historically accurate.

In choosing the fabric and color of uniform shirts, keep in mind that shirts will need frequent washing or cleaning. Players will perspire heavily on hot summer days and will get dirt, mud, and grass stains on elbows and shoulders from diving for balls on defense and taking occasional spills running the bases.

In regard to fabrics used in making uniform shirts, the text of "Dressed to the Nines" comments on the type of material specified by the Knickerbockers for their original uniforms. "The choice of wool is also telling. While cotton would have made for less expensive and more comfortable uniforms, the fabric was at the time associated with work clothing, not fashionable and respectable dress. By donning wool uniforms, early clubs distanced themselves from the working class and aligned themselves with organizations of a higher status."

Programs will need to weigh the qualities of wool versus cotton, considering both initial cost and cleaning. Some vintage clubs play many more games over the course of a typical season than their 1860s counterparts and, therefore, frequent laundering can become an important consideration. White cotton shirts require the least effort and expense to keep clean since they can be machine-washed and dried after each wearing. They are the most frequent choice of programs throughout the vintage base ball community. However, some vintage clubs do wear handsome woolen uniforms. This is a matter for discussion by team leaders and museum professionals before making any purchases.

If wearing a white uniform shirt, it is advisable for a player to wear a plain white T-shirt underneath with no printing or designs. A white T-shirt worn under the uniform shirt will save wear and tear on the uniform shirt, enhance player comfort, and keep a more crisp look. Any type of lettering, cartoon, or advertising design may show through a white shirt and detract from the nineteenth-century look that the player is trying to achieve.

Suppliers of uniform shirts can be found on the website maintained by the Vintage Base Ball Association (www.vbba.org). New teams may want to consult with established clubs regarding reliable vendors that have a good reputation for providing quality uniforms on schedule. Vintage teams can sometimes acquire uniform shirts locally, as some historical societies and museums have a wardrobe expert on hand who supervises the making of period clothing for volunteers and staff members of the institution.

Ties

Many period illustrations show a necktie being worn with the uniform shirt. While the custom of wearing a tie while playing an active sport may seem hard to believe today, it was once standard practice. "Dressed to the Nines" reports that "ties were a popular accessory to the baseball uniform through much of the 19th century. Ballplayers of the 1860s and '70s often wore bow ties with their shield-front jerseys. Later in the century they donned short ties, often tucked into their jersey's placket, as was the fashion of the day."

The 1850s and 1860s were definitely a more formal time in manners, language, and dress. In business or social situations, a gentleman would not have rolled up his sleeves or discarded his tie, especially while in mixed company. The gentlemanly members of a base ball club, especially with ladies present at the match, would have preferred the proper formality of a shirt with long sleeves worn with a tie while engaging in sports. This practice endured well into the twentieth century. As photographs from the 1920s and 1930s indicate, Bobby Jones, Walter Hagen, and their contemporaries wore a necktie (often with a sports jacket) while playing golf. Movies made in the 1920s, 1930s, and 1940s often depict gentlemen involved in outdoor activities such as golf, fly fishing, hunting, and target shooting wearing neckties and jackets.

Photographs from the late nineteenth century and the first half or so of the twentieth century show men wearing collared shirts, ties, and jackets with long trousers when engaged in such everyday leisure activities as going on a picnic, attending a family birthday party, or sitting down to Thanksgiving dinner. College students wore suits and ties to class, not sweatshirts, jeans, and sneakers. Photos from the 1950s and 1960s (a hundred years after the era most vintage clubs represent) show that many men were still wearing ties with suits or sports jackets and long trousers when attending baseball games (not T-shirts and shorts, as might be the norm today).

It should be remembered that the current highly casual standard of dress is a recent development. It was not too long ago that men wore business suits with ties and hats, and women wore dresses with hats and gloves when they went to work at an office, shopped at a downtown department store, or traveled by train or plane. Wearing a tie with a vintage base ball uniform is authentic to the period and serves as a good conversation starter when players and interpreters are talking with spectators about nineteenth-century social norms and customs.

Hats

Early base ball club uniforms consistently included hats, but there were variations in regard to style. An informative discussion of hat styles, complete with illustrations, appears in "Dressed to the Nines." As noted above, the first uniform of the Knickerbocker Club in 1849 included a straw hat with a circular brim. It is easy to imagine that a hat of this type would blow off the players' heads while running. Therefore, it is not surprising that the exhibit text points out that "a few years later, the club switched to a cap made of merino (a soft, fine wool) that featured the two main characteristics of the modern-day baseball cap: a crown and a bill (or visor)." The Baseball Hall of Fame website also mentions that there was great variety in hat styles in the nineteenth century, pointing out that the 1888 edition of the *Spalding Guide* included advertisements for ten different types of caps. It includes illustrations of all ten, accompanied by a sidebar full of explanatory notes.

A cap with a full crown and a short bill was one of the most popular styles of the early years, according to the "Dressed to the Nines" text. It was known in the Peck and Snyder catalog as the "No. 1." Period photographs often show versions of this cap (similar to what later became known as a "newsboy cap") being worn by noted clubs of the 1850s and 1860s, and today this style is worn by a number of vintage teams. This hat style appears in the October 26, 1866, *Harper's Weekly* illustration of the Union Club of Morrisania.

Another type of hat that is commonly worn by vintage teams is the "Chicago" style, which is characterized by a short bill, straight sides, and a flat crown (often with horizontal stripes on the side of the cap). Some vintage base ball participants contend that this style was not worn in the 1850s and 1860s and is more appropriate for the 1870s and later years. Interpretations vary, and the Chicago style cap is in widespread use throughout vintage base ball. Caps of this shape (but without the horizontal stripes) are pictured as being worn by the Knickerbocker players in 1858 when the members of the Knickerbocker and Excelsior clubs lined up for a photograph that often appears in baseball histories.

A third style popular among vintage teams is the "jockey" cap, which has a long bill and a crown that fits close to the head. This type of cap was worn by the Excelsiors in the 1858 Knickerbocker-Excelsior photograph. Of the three, this style most closely resembles a modern baseball cap.

It should be noted that 1860-era clubs did not put an initial or symbol of their club on the front of the hat above the bill, as became common practice in the twentieth century. The club's initials monogram or symbol was usually on the shirt's shield (although some clubs did put a symbol centered on the crown of the cap). While a letter or logo was not commonly used on the hat, team colors were certainly a big part of the hat's design. Vintage teams have chosen many combinations and varieties of colors, usually something that matches or complements the necktie and the lettering on the shield. Period photographs indicate that white hats and various dark colored hats were worn. White hats (often with horizontal stripes in the club colors) are often worn by vintage teams. They look excellent when new, but after being worn through a season or two, they can become discolored by dust, dirt, rain, and perspiration. Consequently, they need be replaced more often than darker caps. With that in mind, programs may want to choose a cap design and color that that will not easily show the soil. It is also important to choose a style that is easily obtained so that a new player can acquire a cap that is identical to those of his teammates.

Every player in a vintage game should have a hat. No player or other adult male who is on the field in period clothing at a vintage game, such as an umpire or scorer, should be without a hat. The hats of all the players on the team should match. Hats should be worn at all times on the field and worn properly (never backwards, sideways, or with the bill turned up). Wearing a cap requires attention to hat etiquette. A player should remove his hat if any kind of prayer is offered at a game. The cap should be removed, of course, and held in the right hand over the heart if the National Anthem is played before a match or if a color guard passes by.

If a player draws cheers or applause from the crowd after making a good fielding play or striking the ball well, he may acknowledge this positive reaction to his performance by modestly tipping his hat to the audience. A player should not ignore the spectators when he makes a good play, as modern professional players often do. When the spectators applaud and cheer, they are, in effect, trying to communicate with the player on the field by saying, "Nice play, and thank you for giving such a good effort." When the player modestly tips his hat in their direction, he is politely responding, "Thank you for the applause and you are most welcome." This interaction helps keep the spectators interested and engaged. Hat tipping should not, of course, be accompanied by any grandiose gestures that could be interpreted as calling undue attention to one's achievements or boastfully showing up the other club.

The Mules of Canal Fulton (Ohio) doff their authentic caps. This style with a star on the crown and short bill, known as the "No. 1," was popular with many clubs in the 1860s.

When vintage clubs exchange three cheers at the end of the match, the players should remove their hats in unison and hold them aloft with each cheer. As the members of the teams exchange congratulatory handshakes at the conclusion of the match, removing one's hat would be in keeping with the manners of the time. It is noteworthy that this custom carries over today in golf. After the last putt on the eighteenth hole, PGA players and their caddies customarily remove their hats or visors as they shake hands with the other players and caddies in their group. This modern yet traditional display of respect and good sportsmanship is an excellent model for vintage base ball.

If a gentlemanly player has occasion to greet or speak to a lady in period dress on the sidelines, he should tip his hat to her. If, when walking to or from the playing field on museum grounds, a player in uniform should pass a lady in period dress going in the opposite direction, he should tip his hat to her. If he is acquainted with her, he may offer a greeting. If he is not acquainted with her, he should wait for her to initiate any conversation. In all of these instances, tipping the hat means removing it briefly from the head, not merely touching the bill. Ladies in modern dress who are on the museum grounds as visitors also seem to enjoy it if a gentlemen in an old-fashioned base ball uniform or other period dress displays good manners by greeting them with a tip of his hat, wishing them a pleasant afternoon, and thanking them for coming.

Even when not participating in a game, players should observe nineteenth-century customs while in uniform. In *How to Be a Gentleman*, author John Bridges advises that although a gentleman may own "a stack of baseball caps...he should never forget that it is still a *hat* and that common courtesy demands that it be treated as such. A gentleman does not wear his cap inside most public buildings, especially houses of worship. Traditionally, a gentlemen would remove his hat if he were greeting a woman or being introduced to a new acquaintance of either sex" (p. 28). In her "Practical Advice" column in the May 24, 2007, edition of *The Columbus Dispatch*, Thelma Domenici's response to a question from a high school teacher regarding the appropriateness of students wearing baseball caps in class included this comment on hats worn indoors: "Taking it off shows your level of respect for the society you live in and its tradition of civility."

This is good advice to keep in mind before or after a match on museum grounds when a player in period uniforms often has the opportunity to enter various buildings, including a general store, historic home, exhibit area, a building where food is served, or other period or modern structures. A gentleman does not wear a hat (even a base ball cap) when sitting down with others at the table to have a meal. In these instances, the player should always remove his hat and not put it back on until he goes outside again, just as a gentlemanly ballplayer would have done in the nineteenth century.

Pants

Period illustrations show that in the early years of the game players wore long trousers, not the knicker-style pants usually associated with the term "baseball pants." A close examination of illustrations shows that players sometimes used a band or strap around the ankle to prevent pants cuffs from getting caught in shoe cleats while running (just as a bicycle rider might put a clip around his pant leg to keep the cuff from getting caught in the chain). In addition to ankle straps, photographs included in "Dressed to the Nines" show that some pants had several buttons at the cuff area and that the player could button his cuff close to his ankle.

As is the case with uniform shirts, references suggest that early baseball trousers were made of wool. However, for reasons of expense and ease of laundering, many vintage teams wear heavy cotton trousers instead. Woolen trousers are much more expensive to purchase and replace, hotter to wear on summer days, and much more difficult (and expensive) to keep clean. In keeping with the highest standards of historical accuracy in regard to nineteenth-century clothing, some museums may choose to require woolen pants and shirts. This is an admirable position, and players should cooperate if the museum's policies require woolen clothing. However, due to financial considerations, heavy cotton trousers are very common throughout vintage base ball.

Sturdy cotton trousers are easily obtained in either in the work clothing section of department and discount stores or online through manufacturers that sell clothing to companies that require their employees to wear uniforms on the job. These durable work pants come in several colors (usually black, gray, navy, dark green, brown, and tan) and hold up well through frequent laundering.

Work pants have simple pockets and no ornamentation, unlike some casual slacks sold at fashion retailers. Vintage base ball pants have no pleats or cuffs. All visible modern labels, of course, need to be removed before these pants are worn in a vintage game. Because of all the washing, some shrinkage is to be expected from these cotton pants and, in order to retain freedom of movement while running and bending, the player will want to purchase pants one waist size larger than he usually wears.

Some vintage teams have chosen white pants as part of their uniform and have been successful with them. Both white pants and dark pants appear in period photographs. When

Cleveland Blues Ken Schutz (left) and Tom Inch wear knicker-style base ball pants which were popularized by the 1869 Cincinnati Red Stockings. They were widely adopted by clubs in the latter part of the nineteenth century. Long trousers were the norm prior to the late 1860s.

choosing a uniform style, club leaders need to think about the problem of keeping white uniform pants clean. Dark-colored pants are a more practical choice for most teams.

Period illustrations show that long trousers were in style through the decade of the 1860s. Harry Wright's Cincinnati Red Stockings are usually cited as the first team to wear knicker-style pants with long stockings when they adopted that fashion in 1868. The bright color of the long stockings worn by the Cincinnati club members resulted in the team's nickname. In the section on stockings in "Dressed to the Nines," the following passage is cited on the advent of knicker-style pants with tall stockings in Cincinnati:

> As club president Aaron Champion later recalled, "The showing of the manly leg in varied-colored hose ... [was] unheard of, and when [team captain] Harry Wright occasionally appeared with the scarlet stockings, young ladies' faces blushed as red, and many high-toned members of the club denounced the innovation as immoral and indecent." While some may have objected to the new look, ballplayers quickly embraced the style, and the bold change in baseball pants resulted in an important new element of the uniform: stockings.

While knickers caught on throughout the base ball fraternity and long trousers fell out of fashion, it is recommended that teams playing by any set of rules prior to the late 1860s should adopt a uniform that includes long trousers.

After laundering, heavy cotton trousers worn as part of a nineteenth-century base ball uniform should be pressed flat to get the wrinkles out. It would not be authentic to put a sharp crease down the center of each pants leg, as would be done when ironing a pair of modern slacks. If a professional laundry is preparing the uniforms, make it clear that they are not to crease the pants.

For those clubs portraying a later period, wool knicker-style baseball pants are available through suppliers of uniforms and period clothing listed on the VBBA website. Players who are members of clubs that wear knicker-style pants with tall stockings should put on the pants and stockings correctly in order to attain the proper look and fit. Knicker-style base ball pants should not be pulled on like sweat pants or pajamas. The proper procedure, followed by amateur and professional ballplayers for many decades (until the recent fad of wearing baseball pants so long that the bottoms are down around the shoe-tops or even dragging on the ground), is something of a lost art. Following the traditional method will result in a more authentic look and fit.

When putting on a pair of knicker-style pants, the player should first put on everything he plans to wear under his base ball pants, including stockings. He should turn his baseball pants inside-out, and place them flat on the floor (still inside-out) straight out in front of him. The knee openings should be at his toes and the waistband farthest away from him. The front of the pants (the fly area) should be facing up with the seat of the pants on the floor. He should next put one foot in the knee opening of one pant leg, and then the other foot in the knee opening of the other pant leg. He should then slide the elastic or string-tie bottoms of the pant legs up over the calf to the bottom of the knee joint. If the pants have string ties, this is the time to tie them securely around the bottom of each knee so that the strings will be out of sight. The player then leans over and grasps the waist band, pulls the pants up, and fastens them. As he pulls them up, the pants will automatically turn themselves right-side-out and will blouse correctly, comfortably, and authentically over the knee (with elastic bands or string ties out of sight).

Pants with string ties at the knees must have the strings tied before they are pulled up, not afterward. This practice keeps the strings hidden inside the pants legs and tied snugly so that they are less likely to come untied during the game. If pants with string ties at the knees are put on improperly, with the strings tied in a bow on the outside of the knee, the strings tend to come untied during the game, causing the bottom of the pants to come loose at the knee with white strings dangling at the calf. This "coming apart at the seams" look is not a good one for vintage players but can easily be prevented by putting on baseball knickers in the traditional manner. The process of putting on knicker-style pants correctly is not complicated. It takes only an extra moment, but it is one of those details that will add to the overall presentation of the uniform.

Belts

Many period photographs show that belts worn with base ball pants in the early years of the game were wide and made of leather, a heavy woven cloth material, or a combination of the two. These images also show that teams often buckled their belts in the back in order to display their team name on the front. On the Baseball Hall of Fame website "Dressed to the Nines," states that "the earliest known team to display a club nickname on their uniforms was the 1860 Excelsiors of Brooklyn. Surprisingly, however, the name was not found on the cap or jersey, but on the team belt. The word 'EXCELSIOR' in an Old English font was embossed on the belt so that the club's name was displayed across the front of the player's waist. Other clubs in the 1860s followed this style, but by the mid–1870s the fad had passed."

While some teams have leather belts with their club name on the front, vintage clubs are not expected or required to have belts emblazoned with the club name if the expense of having belts specially made would be a financial burden. Plain belts (with plain buckles) are very acceptable and can be buckled in the front in the regular manner. The important point to keep in mind is that everyone on the team should have a belt and the belts of every player should be of the same color and width. When lining up for a tintype after a match, it would not do for one player to have a wide brown belt, the next a modern narrow dress black belt, and the next no belt at all. The belt gives the uniform a finished look and, since it is part of a *uniform,* the belts worn by all the players on a team (like their pants, shirts, and hats) should match. A specialty belt with the club name does add to the uniform's appearance and might be ordered through a local leather craftsman or a purveyor of western wear.

Period illustrations do not show players wearing braces or suspenders. In photographs and drawings, belts seem to be standard and are recommended for new clubs. Over the years, braces have been worn by some vintage clubs and individual players for comfort or because they believe that braces are an item of men's apparel commonly associated with the nineteenth century, giving the club an old-fashioned look. If braces are worn, they should have leather tabs that are fastened by buttons to the waistband of the player's trousers. Suspenders should not be of the modern metal clip-on type. Club organizers and players should note that while they may convey a nineteenth-century look, both button-style braces and clip-on suspenders can become unfastened and pop off when the player runs, jumps, and dives in the course of playing a strenuous game of base ball. This may also be the reason that, judging by the pictorial evidence we have, braces do not seem to have been worn by nineteenth-century players. Wearing braces instead of belts is probably an issue best discussed by club leaders and museum professionals when deciding on the club uniform. Perhaps future research will uncover photographic evidence that braces were more commonly worn than present evidence indicates, but based on available images, belts are recommended.

Shoes

"Dressed to the Nines" states that "little is known about the very earliest baseball shoes. Most likely they were identical to athletic shoes of the day: high-tops, with simple canvas uppers and no spikes." Some base ball shoes pictured in photographs from the 1860s and

1870s and in nineteenth-century sporting goods catalogs seem to be of high-top design and constructed of a combination of canvas and leather. Early photographs show that players wore both smooth-soled and cleated shoes. According to the Baseball Hall of Fame exhibit text, "by the late 1860s, spikes similar to those found on modern golf shoes were used by top-flight players."

Shoes are the most difficult part of the vintage base ball uniform to authentically re-create. The leading athletic shoe companies do not make an affordable product that resembles an 1860s-style base ball shoe. Reproduction canvas and leather shoes similar to the ones seen in 1860s photographs are sometimes offered through companies that sell shoes and boots to Civil War reenactors, but they are difficult to find and relatively expensive. Safety and comfort are also important considerations for vintage programs. Due to the lack of availability of serviceable authentic-looking shoes, and the need for players to do a lot of running without slipping and falling, this is an area in which necessity calls for accommodation and compromise.

Players need a functional shoe that will provide good footing while they are batting, fielding, and running the bases (sometimes on wet grass, muddy areas, or sun-baked hard ground that can feel almost like concrete under foot). Modern athletic shoes answer these needs in terms of comfort, performance, and traction. But the appearance of modern baseball shoes is a major obstacle to overcome since modern shoes bear little resemblance to the shoes worn while playing the game in the nineteenth century. Despite these problems, this is an area where creativity, common sense, and reasonable compromise can overcome challenges and produce some very workable and economical solutions.

Some players prefer smooth-soled shoes. Acceptable high-top leather models can be found in stores that carry work shoes and boots or stores that stock footwear suitable for hunting and similar outdoor activities. Shoes can usually be found that are plain in their design, solid black or dark brown in color, and with the uppers and soles not made of obviously synthetic materials. A perusal of Civil War reenactor suppliers may provide a suitable shoe. Theatrical costume shoes are generally not sturdy enough to stand up to hard use.

In order to avoid slipping and falling, most vintage players prefer shoes with cleats. There are, of course, many brands of modern baseball shoes on the market that have some type of cleats. But, if cleated shoes are worn, most safety-conscious programs wisely require rubber cleats and prohibit metal spikes. Keeping metal spikes off the vintage base ball field is strongly recommended. This is one of those areas where a reasonable accommodation needs to be made. While it is true from an authenticity standpoint that shoes with rubber cleats were not worn in the nineteenth century, metal spikes can cause injuries to the wearer, his teammates, and players on the opposing team. Concerns over institutional liability would also suggest that museums and historical societies prohibit shoes with metal spikes. Shoes with metal spikes may also damage canvas bases.

Since replicas of early base ball shoes are not available, the general solution that has been worked out by most vintage programs is to allow modern footwear (with rubber cleats) as long as all modern logos have been removed or obliterated and the shoes appear to the spectator to be all black or all brown. Wearing white basketball or running shoes is not acceptable. Similarly, a dark-colored athletic shoe with a prominent advertising logo in white or some bright color is an obvious anachronism and detracts from the nineteenth-century look that vintage clubs try so hard to create. It should not be obvious to the spectators that the shoes worn by the players are of modern manufacture. Since shoes should give the appearance of being made of plain leather, three-dimensional logos should be avoided. Players should make modern shoes as inconspicuous as possible and draw the spectator's eye to the parts of the uniform that are more authentic.

It is best to select a shoe that is all black or nearly all black to begin with, but black athletic shoes can be difficult to find. An all-black officials shoe made for umpires and referees can be an excellent choice. Soles and cleats should also be all black since it is very difficult to retain paint on soles and sole edges. If the player finds a desirable modern rubber-cleated baseball shoe that has any white or colors in the design of the trim or logos, it should be remembered that all these markings must be totally blackened before the player takes the field in a vintage game. The common black liquid shoe polish brands are usually not adequate to obliterate modern logos. A product called Quality Super Black is used by some vintage players and does a good job of covering most logos and labels. Black spray paint, applied in several even coats over the logo, is another alternative. High-gloss plastic or resin logos are very difficult to paint. Shoes take a beating over the course of a season and will need to be touched up with additional spray paint from time to time. Normal use will cause the black paint to wear off, re-exposing the modern logos. Therefore, the fewer white or brightly colored markings the shoe has when new, the easier it will be for the player to achieve and maintain the necessary all-black leather appearance.

A vintage player may want to have two pairs of all-black shoes to wear with his uniform — a pair with cleats for playing in games and a smooth-soled pair to wear when walking in parades, touring historic homes and museums before and after games, and giving presentations on vintage base ball to school groups or civic organizations. Cleats should not be worn indoors, and a vintage base ball player should not wear sneakers, shower shoes, or any other modern footwear with his nineteenth-century uniform when in public view.

If a community team has been formed for a "one time only" vintage game, it is understandable that the players would not be required to paint their shoes black. However, any individual who is going to play vintage base ball on a regular basis needs to make the commitment to either purchase a pair of all-black shoes or take an existing pair and paint the logos and trim black for game wear. An established vintage team should not take the field with players who are wearing modern-looking shoes with visible brand logos.

A study of mid-nineteenth century baseball shoes would be a worthy area for further research. Sharp-eyed researchers poring over old sporting goods catalogs and newspaper advertisements may provide some additional insight into the products that were available in the nineteenth century and help the vintage community learn more about the shoes (and other forms of wearing apparel and equipment) associated with the era being re-created.

On the subject of footwear and the related issues of safety and liability, club organizers should be aware that occasionally a vintage player may attempt to play in his bare feet. Some players who prefer the barefoot approach may try to make a case for this practice on the grounds that some nineteenth-century players, especially in small towns and rural areas, may not have worn shoes. This may have been true for individuals playing informal pick-up games. On a gentleman's club, however, it would seem highly unlikely and out of character for any player wearing a full uniform to be playing without shoes. From an authenticity standpoint, photographs of nineteenth-century players and clubs show all players wearing shoes.

From a safety standpoint, it is not a wise policy for team captains, museum professionals, event organizers, and tournament directors to promote or permit playing in bare feet. Barefoot players who pitch, catch, or play any of the infield positions run the risk of getting stepped on by teammates or opponents while trying to field balls or cover bases. All players anywhere on the field could get hurt by stepping on stones or sharp pieces of metal or glass that may lurk unnoticed in the grass. While some players have gone barefoot in many games with no injuries, an incident could occur at any time. Therefore, in the interest of reducing the possibility of injury, it is a good idea for clubs and institutions hosting games to have a policy requiring players to wear shoes while playing vintage base ball on museum grounds.

Socks and Stockings

Players who are members of teams that wear long trousers rather than knicker-style pants still need to think about socks. With long pants, socks should be inconspicuous. Therefore, it is best not to wear white socks because, even if the pants legs completely cover the socks when the player is standing still, flashes of white will often show when the player is running the bases or chasing a ball. Dark athletic socks (with the same comfort and cushioning characteristics of white athletic socks) are easily obtained at sporting goods, discount, and department stores and look much better than white socks when worn with long dark trousers and black shoes.

Teams that wear knicker-style pants, of course, always wear long stockings. Stockings of this type are similar to those worn by modern baseball and softball teams and are available in a variety of colors at sporting goods stores. According to "Dressed to the Nines," the practice of wearing stirrup-style stockings in the team color over white sanitary hose did not begin until the early twentieth century. Therefore, nineteenth-century teams wearing knicker-style pants should wear tall, solid-colored stockings rather than the stirrup-style stockings.

Uniform Adaptations and Accessories
Cool Weather Attire

In order to keep warm on chilly days in the spring and fall, players may need another layer or two for warmth. It is always a good practice to wear a plain T-shirt under the uniform shirt. On cool days, a long-sleeve plain T-shirt can provide extra warmth. For that reason, players may want to order uniform shirts a size larger so that extra layers can be worn under the shirt in colder weather. Many vintage players, in an effort to keep their leg muscles warm to prevent pulled quads and hamstrings, routinely wear compression shorts under their uniform pants. On cold days, some players wear running tights under uniform pants for a layer of warmth. Although made of modern synthetic materials, compression shorts and running tights are fine for vintage play since they are out of sight.

No matter how unpleasant the weather may be, a player, umpire, or scorer should never wear a modern jacket or sweatshirt over his uniform shirt while on the playing field at a vintage match. Extra layers should always be worn under uniforms or other period clothing. Any outerwear should be authentic to the period. Items such as a woolen vest or sack coat can be obtained from clothing suppliers that specialize in Civil War-era clothing.

Glasses, Watches, and Jewelry

While wearing an authentic uniform and portraying a nineteenth-century ballist, a vintage player should remember not to spoil the uniform's effect by wearing any items that immediately give him away as a person from the twenty-first century. Therefore, some items should be left at home or in the car.

Players who need eyeglasses may wear them in games. Ohio Village Muffin Chip Moore's glasses with wire frames look best with an 1860s uniform. No modern sunglasses are worn by vintage players.

If a player needs eyeglasses to play the game, it is the custom in vintage base ball to allow modern glasses. However, vintage participants who play or umpire regularly might consider obtaining a pair of prescription lenses in nineteenth-century style frames. Modern sunglasses, of course, should not be worn during games or at any time the player is in uniform (such as pre-game practice or walking across museum grounds on his way to the ball field).

Wristwatches were not worn in the nineteenth century and therefore should not be worn with a vintage uniform. A pocket watch is an excellent accessory for a person in period dress who is engaged in umpiring, scorekeeping, or interpreting.

Players should keep in mind that earrings and necklaces for men are a modern fad and would not have been worn by the gentlemen who played on mid-nineteenth century clubs. In the spirit of maintaining historical authenticity, program participants should remove these anachronistic items while on museum grounds and portraying members of a nineteenth-century base ball club. In addition to the authenticity issues, players have a responsibility to minimize risk of injury. It is advisable not to wear jewelry, especially rings, for safety reasons since nineteenth-century base ball is played barehanded or with very thin, primitive gloves. After making several gloveless catches, hands can get puffy, causing rings to become uncomfortable and difficult to remove. While fractures and dislocations (accompanied by considerable swelling) are relatively rare, they can occur. If a player takes a hit on a finger from a line drive or a hard throw while wearing a ring, the injury could turn out to be much more serious than if he were not wearing a ring. All the discomfort and expense associated with an injury of this type (in addition to the damage to a ring that may have considerable monetary and sentimental value) can be avoided by simply removing jewelry before the game.

Accessories

To carry valuables and keep modern items out of sight, many vintage players own a haversack, a square or rectangular bag worn over the shoulder. Since they were commonly carried by Civil War soldiers as a place to keep their rations and personal items, haversacks are available through companies that sell clothing and supplies to Civil War reenactors. Haversacks are made of leather, canvas, or other materials of the period. A haversack is an excellent place for a player to keep his wallet, wristwatch, keys, electronic devices, sunscreen, and other items out of sight while participating in the game (and while walking back and forth from the parking lot to the ball field). It can hold the items he may need for the game, such as a bandana or tin cup. He can also use it to store any brochures, schedules, cards, and anything else he may want to have close at hand to pass out to the spectators. In addition to the important consideration of keeping non-period items out of sight while on the playing grounds, a haversack is good for security reasons. Since it is of period design and construction, a player can take it with him to the bench and keep an eye on his valuables throughout the game. He can wear it over his shoulder in parades and while posing for photographs.

Modern equipment bags and bat bags should never be brought to the playing field since they are not constructed of materials authentic to the period being re-created. Such bags should be made of cloth, canvas, or leather — never plastic or vinyl with modern logos.

Extra Uniform Parts

Players who belong to clubs that play home games on both Saturday and Sunday on a given weekend or clubs that take road trips to multi-day tournaments might want to consider obtaining at least two shirts and two pairs of pants. Gentlemanly vintage players will want to wear a clean uniform each time they step out on the field to begin a game. Having two shirts and two pairs of pants enables a player to avoid spending the evening of the first day of the event at the local laundromat getting his uniform washed and dried so that it can be worn again the second day. I learned this lesson the hard way. During my first year as a vintage base ball player on a trip to Cooperstown, I spent a couple of hours at a coin laundry when I could have been enjoying the magnificent exhibits a block or two away at the Baseball Hall of Fame. I resolved them that it would not happen again.

Along with their uniform, vintage players often own a vest and broad-brimmed straw hat. These items can be worn with the player's uniform shirt and pants on those occasions when he may be called upon to act as umpire, scorer, or interpreter.

Summary: Basic Principles

To reinforce the point made at the beginning of this chapter, vintage uniforms and accessories make the game. No one would be interested in watching a vintage game if the players or officials were wearing modern clothing. Everyone on the field should be in complete period dress and maintain an authentic nineteenth-century look while participating in a vintage match. The player's uniform and the bench area should not exhibit any anachronisms. A player should never be seen changing into or out of his uniform before or after the game by the public.

Providing Uniforms for the Opposing Team

Vintage teams are often invited to participate in community festivals and celebrations. Some of these invitations involve a match between two established vintage teams. Demonstrating the game of vintage base ball before a large crowd assembled for the local event invariably provides a very positive experience for all participants and spectators.

On other occasions, the match calls for a vintage team to play a local team, typically a one-time-only group formed for the special occasion. The team might be composed of the local school teachers and coaches, the mayor and other city officials, a local softball team, the people who are on the festival's organizing committee, or the members of the sponsoring civic organization. The Ohio Village Muffins have approached these opportunities with special enthusiasm and are always ready to assist the local organizers in putting on a successful day of enjoyable, educational, family-oriented activities.

For many years the Muffins have maintained an extra set of uniform shirts, ties, and caps for the local team to wear for the game. The regular Muffin uniforms consist of gray pants, white shirts with red trim on the shield, red ties, and white hats with red trim. The local team is provided with white shield-front shirts, blue ties, and white hats with blue stripes. The hats are paper caps (painter's hats) that are printed with stripes and resemble the Muffins' Chicago-style caps. These are low-cost mementos for each participant. Those participating in the game are asked to wear long pants, preferably blue jeans, since denim jeans date to the mid-nineteenth century and go well with the blue and white colors of the shirts, ties, and hats. Players on the community team are reminded not to wear shorts, nylon warm-up pants, or modern baseball pants, as these would be obvious anachronisms that would detract from the look of the game.

The Muffins supply a knowledgeable umpire to provide structure for the game, the scorer's table and scorer, and several interpreters in period dress to mingle with the crowd, distribute brochures, chat about the 1860s, and explain the game as it unfolds. The Muffins also provide the bats, balls, and bases, including a round home plate and pitcher's point. Several Muffins arrive early to set up the field for play.

The key to success in these community events is having members of the local team dress as 1860s base ball players for the game with the Muffins. Their friends and families attend the game and enjoy taking photos of the local players in their old-style uniforms. By providing uniforms for the local players and taking care of all the field set-up and interpreting, the Muffin program is usually able to arrange for a donation for appearing at the festival and putting on an educational and entertaining game. Playing six to ten of these matches each season generates funds for sustaining the program. Vintage clubs may want to consider this approach as a way of scheduling games at interesting community events while simultaneously raising funds to help with program expenses.

10
Vintage Equipment

Vintage base ball is played using bats, balls, and other equipment that represent the era being portrayed on the field. Period equipment and period uniforms are essential components that contribute significantly to the successful presentation of the vintage game to the public. In addition to giving the game a historically accurate visual appearance, period equipment also connects players and spectators to the game through the senses of touch, smell, and hearing.

Bats

In his poem "Game Called" published in the August 17, 1948 edition of the *New York Sun* to mark the passing of Babe Ruth, sportswriter Grantland Rice observes that one of the classic sounds of the game has been forever silenced—"the crash of ash against the sphere," produced by Ruth's mighty hitting. In an article on the acoustics of baseball in the June 26, 2001 edition of the *New York Times*, James Glanz, writes that the sounds of the game are "one of the most evocative aspects of the national pastime." Vintage base ball restores one of the traditional sounds to the game—the crack of the wooden bat hitting the leather ball, the "crash of the ash against the sphere" in Rice's words. Veteran baseball fans who have never become accustomed to the metallic "ping" of a metal bat hitting the ball appreciate the distinctive sound produced by a wooden bat. Hearing that sound and holding a vintage wooden bat brings back recollections of games played in their youth. At a time when museums want to be more interactive, vintage equipment engages visitors young and old alike.

Nineteenth-century bats had thicker handles and less taper between the knob and the barrel than modern bats. Some had a knob in the shape of an acorn or mushroom. Some were made with two "knobs," one at the end of the bat and one about six to eight inches up the handle to facilitate the spread grip that was used by some batters in earlier times. Examples of these interesting bats of the past can be accessed on the website of the Phoenix Bat Company, a supplier of nineteenth-century bats for the vintage base ball community, at www. phoenixbats.com.

Spectators often ask about the bats being used and are eager to see them up close. It is a good idea to have several typical bats as well as a few of the more unusual styles of the past available for them to examine. For younger spectators who have grown up in the era of aluminum bats, vintage base ball introduces them to traditional baseball equipment. Players and interpreters who often carry a bat and ball with them as they interact with the crowd during the game report that school-age spectators frequently say that this is the first time they have ever held a wood bat. Bats are also good conversation starters. Upon taking a bat in their hands parents and grandparents will often begin sharing their memories of playing baseball when they were the age of the younger family members in the group.

The bats used in vintage games are replicas of bats used in the nineteenth century. Some spectators ask if these bats are actually from the nineteenth century, but such bats are very rare and too valuable to risk being broken. Fortunately, nineteenth century-style bats that are ideal for use in vintage games are readily available through vintage bat makers listed on the VBBA website.

Most craftsmen who make bats for use in vintage base ball games are very research-oriented and conscientious. To create authentic-looking bats for game use, these craftsmen study the specifications that appear in nineteenth-century rule books, descriptions of bats in nineteenth-century club records and purchase orders, actual nineteenth-century bats owned by private collectors or museums, and images of bats that appear in nineteenth-century photographs and sporting goods catalogs. These sources enable the vintage bat maker to become knowledgeable about the length and weight of bats, the various types of wood that were used, their design, and any forms of trim or decoration such as knobs, rings, and bands created by staining and painting, or grooves and patterns made by carving.

A wooden nail keg is a convenient way to store vintage bats during the game.

No mention was made of any specifications for the bat in the original Knickerbocker Rules of 1845. Section 2 of the "Rules and Regulations, as Adopted by the Convention of Base Ball Clubs, Held February 25th, 1857" reads as follows: "The bat must be round, and must not exceed 2½ inches in diameter at the thickest part; it must be made of wood, and may be of any length, to suit the striker." The specifications in Section 2 in the 1857 rules were repeated in the 1860 rules.

In the 1860 edition of *Beadle's Dime Base-Ball Player*, Henry Chadwick advises that "bats are from thirty to forty inches in length, and from two to three pounds in weight, the former weight being most desirable." To put this in perspective, present-day major leaguers, according MLB-licensed bat maker Charley Trudeau of the Phoenix Bat Company, typically use bats that are about 32 to 34½ inches long and weigh approximately 32 to 33 ounces. Modern bats have noticeably thinner handles and larger barrels than bats that were used in the nineteenth century and well into the twentieth century. In regard to length, the phrase "of any length, to suit the striker" is imprecise, and the length of bats can vary. Period photographs seem to show that the old-style bats were slightly longer and had thicker handles.

The weight of the bat, a point not mentioned in the rules, depends not only on the length and circumference of the bat but on the type of wood used. Chadwick reports that "the description of wood most in use is ash, but maple, white and pitch pine, and also hickory bats are in common use, weight for the size governing the selection." He recommends that "for a bat of medium weight, ash is preferable, as its fiber is tough and elastic." Ash, of course, is the wood that has been most closely associated with bat making throughout the nineteenth and twentieth centuries. Using hickory, oak, maple, and other hardwoods that have greater density than ash results in a heavier bat than one of the same dimensions made of ash. For a lighter bat, Chadwick states that "English willow has recently been used, and is favorably regarded by many" (p.19). Using willow would produce a bat that is slightly lighter than an ash bat of the same length and noticeably lighter than hickory, maple, or other hardwoods. Interestingly, maple bats have enjoyed a rebirth in the last decade or so. Many recent major leaguers known for their home-run hitting have come to believe that the denser grain of a maple bat propels the ball slightly farther than an ash bat.

It is very important for vintage base ball players to use bats that are specifically made to resemble those used in the nineteenth century. Modern thin-handled bats, even if made of traditional ash, should not be on the vintage playing field. It is not acceptable to take a modern wood bat and try to make it look old by obliterating the logos and trademarks of well-known present-day manufacturing companies by sanding or painting. The shape of a vintage bat should be true to bats used in the early years of the game.

While it may seem like a minor point, the preference of some players for the thinner-handled modern bats can be an area of potential problems in a vintage program. Because they believe they can hit the ball farther with a thin-handled bat than with a thick-handled bat, some players may attempt to use a modern wooden bat in a vintage game. Sponsoring museums and team captains should make sure that all players are using bats appropriate to the time period being represented on the field. This should be made clear in a team's orientation and training sessions. An attempt to increase one's hitting performance by using a modern bat in a game in which all the other players are using authentic old-style bats is both unsportsmanlike and not in keeping with the goal of the vintage base ball community to present a base ball game as it was played in earlier times.

Requiring vintage bats will sort out players who are more interested in personal statistics than re-creating the historical aspects of the game. If a modern bat makes its way onto the field, the opposing team, the umpire, or the batter's own captain is put in the awkward position of confronting a player about not using it. Incidents of this type can spoil the spirit of good sportsmanship that is one of the hallmarks of vintage base ball.

As often happens, should someone in the crowd asks to see a bat, a player or interpreter should be able to hand that spectator *any bat that is being used in the game* as an authentic example of nineteenth-century equipment. The player or interpreter should not have to worry about the spectator observing any modern logos and brand names or evidence of attempts to disguise these markings. Also, if a spectator should pick up a bat to take a closer look and find that it has the modern thin handle and big barrel configuration, it will be immediately apparent it is a "camouflaged" modern bat.

Programs can insist on players using vintage bats because they are readily available and affordable. Their initial affordability is enhanced by the fact that well-made vintage bats with thicker handles rarely break. If used against the slower pitching associated with the 1860 rules and practices followed by most clubs, a bat should last many seasons. Although a modern major league player may break several bats in a single game, it is common for a veteran vintage player to use the same wooden bat for ten or fifteen years. This also enhances safety for players and onlookers.

When forming a vintage club, the organizers should obtain three or four vintage bats of various sizes and weights and make them available to the players for use in practice sessions and games. Sources for obtaining vintage bats are listed on the website maintained by the Vintage Base Ball Association. After trying out different sizes and styles and deciding on a model that seems comfortable and has an authentic look and feel, a player may acquire his own bat. Owning a bat is an enjoyable part of being a vintage player. Working with a bat maker on the specifications and characteristics of the bat — length, weight, wood type, thickness of handle and barrel, degree of taper, knob style, stain color, and the addition of any stripes or other period designs — can be a learning experience that adds to the player's knowledge of the nineteenth-century game. Many players consider these attractive vintage bats to be works of art and appreciate them for their handsome appearance as well as their utility.

Many vintage clubs make wooden bat boxes that add to the appearance of the bench area.

While some of today's professional players are careless about their bats, others such as Ichiro Suzuki display a respectful relationship with their bats that is more in keeping with the approach taken by many vintage players. In an interview with Jim Caple of ESPN in 2002, Ichiro observed through his translator, "To become a better player, you have to take care of your equipment." Ichiro went on to comment, "The same thing applies to a chef and his knives. You're a professional. You earn money with a profession, therefore you respect the tools you use to earn the money." While amateur vintage players do not earn a living with their bats, many can relate to Ichiro's philosophy of respect for the tools of the game.

When ordering a bat, a player should not, on grounds of authenticity, demand that the finished product not bear the trademark of a twenty-first century bat maker. Charley "Lefty" Trudeau of the Phoenix Bat Company once related the story of a potential customer who called to order a vintage bat and insisted that the bat have no trademark. The customer felt, for purposes of authenticity, that an 1860-era bat would not have had one. Trudeau explained to the customer that any reputable and ethical vintage bat maker will put a trademark on any bat. It can be small and unobtrusive, but it should be there. This insistence is not based on advertising or promotional benefits. Rather, the maker always places his trademark on each vintage bat in order to prevent the replica from being passed off as a genuine antique. Vintage bats are the product of considerable research, attention to detail, and handcrafted care on the part of the bat maker. The finished products are so similar to antique museum pieces that confusion could occur. The reputable bat maker would not want to risk giving even the slightest appearance, intentionally or unintentionally, of being a party to any deception. The bat maker's trademark, which is usually so discreet as to be invisible from the spectator area, prevents any future misrepresentation or misunderstanding as to the antiquity and provenance of the bat.

In regard to bat etiquette, a vintage player should always ask if he can use another player's personal bat before grabbing it and taking it to home plate to hit. Vintage players are usually very generous in allowing others to use their bats. However, veteran players who grew up using wooden bats may be surprised to learn that a younger borrower who has always used aluminum bats might not be aware that there is a right and wrong way to hold a wooden bat. The trademark, small in the case of vintage bats, is not placed on a wooden bat randomly. The trademark is stamped in a specific spot on the bat according to the grain pattern of the wood. Most older players learned to always hold the trademark up when they first started playing the game in the backyard as kids. Some younger players who have grown up using aluminum bats may be unfamiliar with this important point and may need to be cautioned before stepping to the plate. Even if the pitching is relatively slow, a borrowed wooden bat can be broken if held incorrectly.

Another point of bat etiquette and gentlemanly conduct is that a vintage player should never slam the bat down in anger when making an out. Such a display of temper represents poor sportsmanship, and such an outburst would not be in keeping with the tone and spirit of a game set in the 1860 era. Gentlemanly golfers are expected to maintain their composure and seldom slam and throw their clubs after an unsuccessful shot. In the same spirit, vintage base ball players do not slam and throw their bats after an unsuccessful turn at bat (a practice ones sees too often on television or at a modern game).

Players in any era should always keep in mind that they are not the first person in the history of the game to make an out at an inopportune time. Strikeouts, pop-ups, foul tips to the catcher, and other unsuccessful outcomes of a turn at bat should not be viewed as unacceptable and ignominious failures, but rather as "all part of the game." Even the most talented players who ever played have had these things happen, sometimes in crucial situations. Undoubtedly there were times when Babe Ruth struck out with the game on the line, Henry Aaron popped up to make the last out of an inning, or Ted Williams hit into a double play. The mature player understands that it is not the bat's fault if he makes an out and carries himself accordingly when his turn at bat is over.

Slamming the bat down upon making an out can break the bat, a particular problem if the bat does not belong to the striker. An incident of this type occurred when the Muffins were playing a game at the home field of another Ohio team several years ago. Since the opposing team was a new group in the process of forming, the Muffins had furnished the bats and balls for the match. After being retired on hitting a foul tip to the catcher, one of the opposing players turned from the plate in disgust. He was a strong and athletic young fellow who looked like he had played a lot of baseball and softball and probably expected to drive the ball far into the outfield. Frustrated at being put out on a weak foul ball, he slammed the handsome, handmade wooden bat against the hard ground and cracked it at the handle. To his credit, the player who broke the bat instantly realized his mistake. It was apparent that he wanted to crawl into a hole. Not only had he impetuously slammed a bat and broken it (and thus set a poor example for the many youngsters watching the game), the bat in question was not his to break. Contrite, he was full of sincere apologies for his actions, instantly offering to pay for the damages caused by his inappropriate behavior. From his expressions of profound regret, it appeared to be a watershed moment for him in his approach to proper conduct on the ball diamond. Although he may not have thought much about field behavior before playing vintage base ball for the first time, judging by his heartfelt apologies, he probably never forgot what happened that day and likely went on to be a more even-tempered and mature player in the future.

Taking out one's anger on the bat can cause injury to the player involved. In the 2008 season, two key major league players had to go on the disabled list for a significant length of time following temper tantrums with their bats. On July 5, Troy Tulowitzki, the outstanding shortstop of the Colorado Rockies, suffered a cut on his hand that required 16 stitches and missed more than two weeks. "I was a little bit frustrated," commented Tulowitzki. "I came in the hallway, grabbed a bat, hit it on the ground and the bat exploded in my hand and cut open my palm running up to my index finger." Carlos Quentin, the power-hitting outfielder of the Chicago White Sox who was a leading candidate for MVP honors at the time, broke a bone in his wrist on September 5 by striking his bat with his fist in frustration after hitting a foul ball and missed the rest of the season. The September 6, 2008, edition of the *Chicago Tribune* observed of the Quentin incident, "His approach looks silly and stupid and more that a little selfish." Both key players were lost to their teams for several weeks when their talents could not be spared. These players not only hurt themselves physically, but harmed their teams' chances of winning.

A finely crafted wooden bat is a treasured possession that deserves to be treated well by its owner out of respect for the time, effort, and care the bat maker put into creating it. This point was expressed in the ESPN interview with Ichiro Suzuki about the great respect the Seattle Mariners outfielder shows toward his equipment. Reporter Jim Caple commented, "He cannot believe the way many major leaguers treat their bats—flinging them in disgust, smashing them against a wall in frustration, snapping them in half, and not storing them [properly]." Ichiro is quoted as saying, "Think about it. Those bats and gloves are not machine-made—they are hand-made. If someone who makes a glove or a bat sees their product thrown away, they will be very sad about it. They feel invested in it. Hopefully, the players will think of the people who made the equipment."

Both the bat and the behavior of the player swinging it should be authentic to the period being portrayed in the game. Handsome wooden bats representative of the mid-nineteenth century are available at reasonable prices and should be used in the respectful and mature manner that is also representative of that time.

Batting Gloves

Batting gloves should not be worn in vintage matches. While almost all present-day professional players wear batting gloves, this practice is a fairly recent development. Photos of players in the 1950s and 1960s show that wearing batting gloves was rare, even in that more recent era. Younger vintage players have grown up using batting gloves since their Little League days and may not be aware that batting gloves have been part of the game for only a short time. Orientation programs should inform new players of the history of all equipment. Pine-tar rags also were not part of base ball in the nineteenth century.

Balls

According to the 1860 rules, "The ball must weigh not less the five and three-fourths, nor more than six ounces" and "must measure not less than nine and three-fourths nor more than ten inches in circumference." As a reference point, the specification on the ball's size means that it is larger than a modern baseball (9 to 9¼ inches in circumference) and smaller than a modern softball (either 11 or 12 inches in circumference).

The 1860 rules regarding the ball state that "it must be composed of India-rubber and yarn, and covered with leather...." To create a mid-nineteenth century-style base ball, the ball maker starts with a rubber core (solid rubber or rubber bands), then carefully winds layer after layer of yarn, keeping it perfectly round, which is the tricky part of the process. Several styles of covers were used in the 1860 era. The most common style used in vintage base ball is the one-piece cover known as the "lemon peel" design, because the pattern of the seams resembles the peel of a lemon or an orange that has been scored with a knife into four equal sections. The cover of a modern baseball or softball consists of two pieces of leather cut into the familiar figure-eight shape and sewn together. Spectators often enjoy comparing the two styles of covers. The color of the cover of a vintage base ball (which was not specified in the rules) can range from off-white to tan to dark brown. The suppliers listed on the VBBA website have wide offerings of nineteenth century-style base balls.

The lemon peel design with a one-piece leather cover was common in the early days of base ball.

The base balls used in vintage games always kindle considerable spectator interest. For the sake of authenticity, old-style balls should always be used in vintage games. There was a time in the 1980s and early 1990s when balls that were true to the nineteenth-century specifications and appearance were very hard to come by and quite expensive ($40 to $50 each). Consequently, the Muffins and other early teams sometimes had to use various substitutes in practices and some games, saving the rare authentic-looking balls for special occasions. The commercially produced "Incrediball" by Easton made an acceptable substitute in terms of performance but did not have the appearance of a nineteenth-century base ball.

The best source for authentically crafted balls in those days was J. R. Ferguson, a splendid artisan in Louisville, Kentucky, who made each ball by hand with great attention to detail. On several occasions, Ferguson came to Ohio Village and, dressed in period clothing, set up his workbench near the diamond while a game was in progress and demonstrated his winding and sewing techniques to the players and spectators. These demonstrations were educational and fascinating to watch. Every finished product was a masterpiece. Ferguson was a main supplier for the vintage teams at that time. Eventually, with the advent of more vintage teams, Ferguson was unable to keep up with the increasing demand for his product and, although a relatively young man, decided to "retire" from ball making. Ferguson's reputation lives on among veteran vintage players and the surviving balls he made several years ago are highly prized. A classic Ferguson ball that has never been hit with a bat is always in my haversack to use for demonstration purposes when talking to spectators, school groups, civic groups and other audiences about 1860-style equipment. It is a handsome example of the ball maker's art and many people have enjoyed seeing and handling it over the years. An authentically constructed 1860-style ball is always a good conversation starter.

While Ferguson was phasing out of the ball-making business, several members of the vintage community studied the art of ball making and began practicing the difficult process of fashioning a ball by hand. Some became very adept and served as small suppliers for their own clubs and other clubs. One individual who has developed considerable expertise in the art of ball making is Ed Shuman, founder and captain of the vintage club in Canal Fulton,

Ohio. In a 2009 posting on the VBBA listserv, Shuman shared the valuable insights of an experienced ball maker regarding the mysteries of the composition and construction of an 1860-style ball. Shuman reported that he has made "probably over two hundred base balls of different sizes, styles, (lemon peel, figure eight, gusset/ band ball, town ball) and materials for my team as well as other teams." In his posting, he humorously observed that "not all were as good as the machine-wound balls that most use today, but there have been shades of greatness. I provide the information below for your entertainment only. Follow at your own risk. (It can become addicting, trying to make that perfect ball)."

While most vintage base ball participants may not plan to take up ball making, Shuman's instructions will enable players to develop an appreciation for the work that goes into making a ball and will help them respond to questions from spectators who ask how a vintage ball is made.

1. My best suggestion for the amounts of yarn, rubber center, etc., is to get a scale, or use one.
2. To make a "pill" buy a bag of rubber bands (probably not the thick ones). Weigh out around 1 oz. of them. I like to add another half oz. because of the yarn usually being a bit light (more on that later).
3. Tie the rubber bands together into a chain and wind them like string into a ball. This may seem a little time consuming but you have the most control of the material doing it this way. I have also tried molding my own rubber balls to the weight that I want but it was even more work. "Super Balls" just didn't seem to come in the right size.
4. Lay your cover and the "Pill" on your scale and see how much they weigh. Do the math to figure out how much yarn you need. Example: If the cover weighs 1.2 oz. and the pill weighs 1.5 oz. for a total of 2.7 oz., you need 3.1 oz. of yarn to make a finished ball right between 5¾ and 6 oz. with a 9¾" to 10" in circumference, as stated in 1860 rules.
5. You can buy yarn at any local craft store. They usually have a leather-working section, too, so you ought to be able to find needles and a spool of stitching thread (waxed cotton is the ideal). The secret to the yarn is get as high of wool content as possible. Some are 80% wool-20% acrylic blends.
6. If you have 100% acrylic, just remember that you will need more because the fibers are lighter than real wool. More yarn means wrapping it tighter with the possibility of the ball finishing a little large. Acrylic makes a harder ball but it is lighter; wool makes a slightly softer ball but is heavier.

Additional information on constructing a ball can be found on the VBBA website under "Links of Interest" by following the link under "Making Your Own Equipment" to the section "Homemade Lemon Peel," in which Billy Pollifrone, an experienced vintage player, explains his method of making a lemon peel baseball. The text and photos show how to make the rubber core and the pattern for the one-piece lemon peel leather cover. As Pollifrone thoughtfully points out, being able to explain how a ball is made "does make for good interaction with spectators. Describing what is in the ball certainly works, but having them be able to see the inside of the ball, or having 4 at the various stages or having them do a couple stitches goes much more than the former. Another interesting activity is to have a workshop where kids get to make their own lemon peel ball and then later get to use it in a game."

Several of the companies that provide bats and other equipment to the vintage community have hired people to make nineteenth century-style base balls, replicating the old-style designs and materials. Some vintage balls are now machine-wound, which tends to make them more firm than a hand-made ball. Now that nineteenth century-style base balls are much more affordable and readily available, vintage teams have an adequate supply for practices and games.

As the ball-making process suggests, the degree of firmness of a vintage base ball can vary, as was the case in the 1860s. Most balls that are firm when new tend to soften gradually the more times they are hit. While not quite as hard as a modern baseball, catching a hard-hit or swiftly thrown 1860-style vintage ball barehanded can be a challenge. Fortunately, catching the ball is a skill that improves with experience. Some knowledgeable vintage base ball participants have thoughtfully proposed that the balls used in the 1860s may have been less firm than some machine-wound balls used in vintage base ball today, speculating that modern players have gravitated toward a firmer ball because some prefer hitting a ball that will go a greater distance when struck. In 2005, researcher Paul Hunkele contributed a posting to the VBBA listserv that speaks to this issue:

> I'm an advocate of less-hard base balls for vintage play. I do not believe that in the 1860s they were using the machine-wound "rocks" that we sometimes use in vintage base ball. I believe they were using balls that were much more resilient — a.k.a. "bouncy." It is actually the weight and mass of the ball that seems to cause injury as much as the surface hardness.

This is an area deserving further discussion and research. Programs should give serious consideration to sacrificing a little distance in hitting for greater authenticity in the degree of firmness of the ball. In addition to replicating the characteristics of balls used in the 1860s, adopting a slightly softer ball would also be safer for both the fielders playing barehanded and for any spectators who might be struck accidentally by a foul ball or an overthrow. Also, if the playing field is a bit undersized, a softer ball will stay in play and reduce the time spent hopping over a fence to retrieve the game ball. Since issues of historical authenticity and safety are involved, selecting the proper ball for a vintage program is another matter that should be discussed by team leaders and museum professionals and not left up solely to the players, who might simply choose a ball they can hit the farthest.

In the nineteenth century, it was the custom that one ball was used for the entire game. The rules specify that "in all match games, the ball shall be furnished by the challenging club, and become the property of the winning club as a trophy of victory." The common practice was for the ball to be presented to the winning club at the end of the game and then the date and score would be neatly lettered on the cover and kept by the winners at their club room as a treasured memento of the contest. Some of these old "trophy balls" from the 1850s and 1860s still survive in museums and private collections. These intriguing relics from 150 years ago (with the date, score and club names still legible) are wonderful to behold as tangible artifacts from the nineteenth-century matches that the vintage community attempts to re-create.

Bases

The 1860 rules state that "the bases shall be four in number, placed at equal distances from each other, and securely fastened upon the four corners of a square, whose sides are respectively thirty yards. They must be so constructed as to be distinctly seen by the umpire, and must cover a space equal to one square foot of surface. The first, second, and third bases shall be canvas bags, painted white, and filled with sand or sawdust."

For years, vintage programs have struggled with the problem of finding an adequate base to use in games. Some bases filled with padding are only about an inch thick and are therefore very difficult for runners, umpires, and spectators to see, especially if the game is being played (as it was in the mid-nineteenth century) on an all-grass field and the grass is a little long. These thin bases are usually fastened to the ground by spikes through grommets on the corners. Unfortunately, grommets tend to tear out of the corners over time, making it difficult to anchor the bases to the ground. Thicker bases that stand two or three inches high are easier to see, but if stuffed with sand can be very heavy and messy to handle if they get wet. Both the thin and thick bases get dirty quickly and it has been almost impossible to keep them clean. After being stepped on repeatedly by players with muddy shoes, the bases retain their soiled appearance and never regain their original white color.

In recent times, a base-making technique has emerged that has proved to be much more satisfactory. A white canvas cover is put over a heavy plastic bag that contains sawdust or straw stuffing. Since the white canvas cover can be unbuttoned and the plastic bag of stuffing removed, the canvas can be laundered and kept reasonably clean. The plastic bag keeps the stuffing dry. Since the inner plastic bag containing the stuffing is completely out of sight during the game, the authentic appearance of the base is not compromised.

The 1860 rules specify that home plate (and the pitcher's point 45 feet from home) be marked with "a flat circular iron plate, painted or enameled white." Experience has shown that an iron home plate works well if it is permanently installed on the team's home grounds, but it is rather heavy to transport. Therefore, a round wooden home plate, painted white, works well. If the team does not have permanent home grounds or if home plate needs to be taken along for away games, the plate should have two quarter-inch holes through which two long spikes can be driven to attach it firmly to the ground. Notice that there is no width for home plate specified in the rules. If no balls and strikes are going to be called, the width is not important. Most round home plates used by vintage clubs are about 12 to 16 inches in diameter. The disk marking the pitcher's point can be the same size or slightly smaller.

The shape of home plate changed over time. In the 1873 Rules, home plate is no longer round. Rather, it is "a one square foot hard rubber base, placed so that the lines which form the corner of the diamond and extend to the first and third bases meet in the center of the base with the front corner of the base pointing to the pitcher's position." According to Tom Shieber's "The Evolution of the Baseball Diamond" in the 1994 issue of the *Baseball Research Journal*, "this had been implied in diagrams of the baseball infield since 1869<in> (p. 7).

Several rule changes governing the placement of home plate and the other bases occurred during the latter part of the nineteenth century. Teams that play by the rules of the 1870s through the 1890s will want to consult Shieber's article in order to have bases (including home) that match the placement relative to the foul lines that was specified in the later rules.

In regard to home plate, Shieber points out that a one-foot square base gives the pitcher a target with a width of almost exactly 17 inches across. The hypotenuse of a right triangle 12 inches on a side is 16.97 inches. That figure was rounded to 17 inches, and later adopted as the standard width of the modern home plate (pp. 10–11). Therefore, the width of the modern five-sided plate, which was adopted in 1900, can be traced to the one-foot square home plate of the late 1860s.

Gloves

If a vintage game represents the period of the 1860s or earlier, no gloves are worn. The baseball glove has become so much a part of the modern game that it is one of the principle

As in this match between the Dayton, Ohio, Clodbusters (left) and the North Canton, Ohio, Hoover Sweepers, bases should be light in color and of sufficient thickness to be seen by the umpire, players, and spectators.

symbols of the national pastime. Newcomers to vintage base ball, players and spectators alike, find it difficult to believe that base ball was ever played without gloves, and their absence triggers a lot of discussion among spectators and players. On one occasion when two vintage teams played a demonstration game prior to a minor league game, the professional players watching the match from the dugout remarked that they could not imagine giving up their gloves.

The absence of gloves forces players to go back to the fundamentals of fielding — get in front of the ball, keep your eye on the ball, and use both hands. The fact that the players are not wearing gloves creates opportunities for more muffs but also for some truly spectacular barehanded fielding plays. An occasional barehanded fielding play in a major league game is shown again and again on ESPN's "web gems." Each vintage game yields many barehanded catches, several of which are truly amazing.

Spectators often ask about the introduction of gloves. As with so many things about the history of the game, the origins of the glove are a bit murky. The story of the development of the glove is one of evolution, not a magic day or year when all players suddenly began to wear gloves in the field. In "Glove Story," an article in the Fall 1996 issue of *Beckett Vintage Sports* magazine, author Joe Phillips states, "The player generally given credit for wearing the first baseball glove was catcher Doug Allison of the first all-professional baseball team, those immortal Cincinnati Red Stockings of 1969–70." According to Phillips, Allison had "seriously injured his hand in a June 1870 exhibition" and "decided that his sore hand required some protection from wicked fouls and the hard throws from his pitcher, Asa Brainard." Consequently, "on June 27, 1870, in Washington, D.C., before a game against the local Olympic Club, Allison persuaded a saddle maker to fashion a padded buckskin glove for him. Allison used it that day as his team beat the Olympic Club 35–24."

In "The Evolution of the Baseball Glove" in the July-August 1998 issue of *The Vintage & Classic Baseball Collector* magazine, author Mike Egner also attributes the advent of the glove to Allison. Egner gives the year as 1869 and says, "he had a saddle maker make him a pair of buckskin mittens to protect his sore hands. One mitten was for catching, the other for [his] throwing hand had less padding" (p. 40). It is not clear if Allison only wore the glove for a short time while his hand healed or if he began to wear it regularly. As pitching became faster, catchers needed protection for their hands and adopted the practice of wearing small gloves. Phillips points out that "the catcher's gloves were often worn in pairs, cut off at the fingers of both hands" (p. 64).

Peter Morris, in *A Game of Inches: The Game on the Field*, also cites Allison's use of a glove, acknowledging a referral from Darryl Brock, researcher, author, and expert on the 1869–70 Cincinnati Red Stockings, who "alerted me to the note in the *Cincinnati Commercial* the next day [June 29, 1870] that 'Allison caught ... in a pair of buckskin mittens, to protect his hands.'" Morris also offers earlier examples and states that the first baseball player to wear gloves regularly may have been a catcher [for the Knickerbocker Club of Albany, New York] named Ben Delavergne, around 1860." Morris also cites a reference to gloves in the *Detroit Free Press* in describing a local tournament held in August 1867: "The use of gloves by the players was to some degree a customary practice." However, this reference was followed by the editorial comment that the use of gloves was a practice "which, we think, cannot be too highly condemned" (p. 419).

While Phillips observes that "Allison's device led to a glove evolution that would transform the game forever," the change was slow in coming, and players at other positions did not adopt gloves immediately (p. 64). Many sources quote a passage from Albert G. Spalding's 1911 book *America's National Game* in which he remembers the coming of gloves. "The first glove I ever saw on the hand of a ball player in a game was worn by Charles C. Waite, in Boston, in 1875. He had come from New Haven and was playing at first base. The glove worn by him was of flesh color, with a large round opening in the back." A right-handed pitcher in his playing days, Spalding reports that he had "for a good while felt the need of some sort of hand protection for myself" since he had "developed severe bruises on the inside of my left hand. When it is recalled that every ball pitched had to be returned, and that every swift one coming my way, from infielders, outfielders or hot from the bat, must be caught or stopped, some idea may be gained of the punishment received." When Spalding inquired about the glove, Waite "confessed he was a bit ashamed to wear it, but had it on to save his hand." Peer pressure against wearing protective gloves was apparently quite strong. Spalding states he waited two more years until "I overcame my scruples against joining 'the kid-glove aristocracy' by donning a glove" and reports he was relieved that "the presence a glove did not call out the ridicule that had greeted Waite" (pp. 311–312).

Even after gloves came into more general use in the 1880s and 1890s, not every player wore one, as some of those who had played all their lives barehanded thought they could continue to play well without one. In *The Bill James Historical Baseball Abstract*, under the headline "1894: The Last Real Man Retires," the author reports that "the last position player who did not wear a glove in the field was Jerry Denny, the ambidextrous third baseman who retired from the Louisville team following the 1894 season." James adds that "pitcher Gus Weying, who lasted until 1901, also did not wear a glove" (p. 51). Hall of Fame second baseman Bid McPhee, who played his entire career (1882–1899) in Cincinnati, was another notable holdout who did not start wearing a glove until very late in his career. The National Baseball Hall of Fame website states that McPhee was a "superior second baseman, despite playing barehanded for the majority of his 18-year big league career. The last second baseman to play gloveless in the field, he regularly led the league in double plays, fielding average, assists and putouts."

Identifying the "last gloveless player" in *A Game of Inches: The Game on the Field*, Peter Morris states, "The last prominent nonpitchers to reject gloves were Bid McPhee and Jerry Denny. Denny's career ended in 1894, and Bill James described him as 'the last position player who did not wear a glove.' This, however, can't be true since, as James himself noted [in the "New" edition of his *Abstract*], Bid McPhee did not start wearing a glove until 1896." Morris suggests that "perhaps James meant that Denny was the last player to retire without ever wearing a glove." Morris goes on to point out that "there were gloveless players in the minor leagues well into the twentieth century" (pp. 428–429). While there is a fascination with various firsts and lasts in baseball history (perhaps yet an even later gloveless player will be identified by another researcher), these descriptions of Denny and McPhee support the point that gloves came in gradually and were not accepted for a number of years.

Evidence of this lingering sentiment against the use of gloves is cited in "Charlton's Baseball Chronology," a reference section found on the BaseballLibrary.com website, which includes this entry for December 15, 1894:

> Veteran manager Jack Chapman expresses his support of a proposed rule change forbidding all but catchers and 1B from wearing gloves. Citing Cincinnati's Bid McPhee as an example of one of the few remaining outstanding gloveless fielders, Chapman remarks that "as it is now, inferior players with big gloves can get into the game and force good men out."

As barehanded play faded out in the 1880s, Egner points out that "most fielders gloves of this period were open fingered, resembling a modern handball glove" (p. 40). In the 1890s, "padding was added around the base of the palm that extended to the thumb." Gloves continued to evolve but it was not until the early 1900s that "all fielders gloves [were] made with a web between the thumb and forefinger." Egner describes the web design that came in around 1910 as "a modified triangular web" that was "a flat piece of leather usually measuring from 1" to 1½" wide." It was not until the 1940s that "leather was added to connect all the fingers and strengthen the glove altogether" (pp. 41, 43).

For clubs that play by the rules and customs of the latter part of the nineteenth century, gloves are appropriate, but they should be of the small, "primitive" type with characteristics consistent with those actually used in the time period being depicted on the field. Illustrations show that gloves were very flat and were intended to protect the hands, rather than large, leather basket-shaped devices with a deep pocket and huge web designed to snare the ball one-handed, as is the case with modern gloves. The subtle differences and gradual changes in the development of gloves should be kept in mind by clubs portraying base ball as it was played in the 1880s, 1890s, or the early twentieth century. As in the case of bats and balls, reproduction nineteenth century style—leather base ball gloves are available through the suppliers listed on the website of the Vintage Base Ball Association.

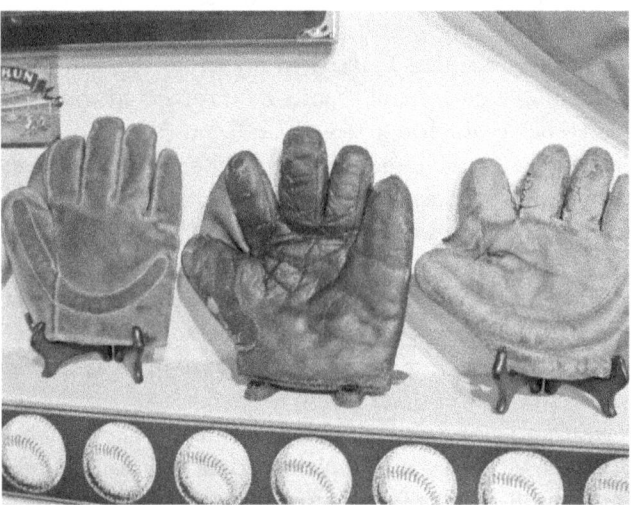

These examples from the Tracy Martin Collection show the evolution of the glove in the late nineteenth and early twentieth centuries.

Catcher's Equipment

In the 1860s, masks and the other pieces of equipment commonly worn by the modern catcher had not been invented and therefore are not worn by a vintage base ball catcher recreating a game from that era. When following the rules and practices of 1860 and earlier periods, catchers need no protective equipment. The catcher plays well behind the plate, usually receiving the pitch on the first bounce. As long as the pitching is relatively slow (similar to modern slow-pitch softball), the catcher can receive the pitches without getting bruised hands and is in little danger of being struck by a foul tip in such a way as to sustain an injury. A discussion of the evolution of catcher's equipment is included in the section on the vintage catcher in Chapter 16.

Summary

For programs portraying later eras, the VBBA website lists vendors for period gloves and catching gear in addition to bats and balls. Since base ball equipment evolved throughout the nineteenth century, it is important for program leaders to make sure that the equipment being used on the field is consistent with the time period being represented. Just as authenticity in uniforms inspires the player and engages the spectator, authenticity in reproduction equipment is also an important part of the vintage game.

11

The Field of Play

Selecting a Location to Play: The Home Grounds

Having a regular place to play, a "home grounds" as it was often called in the nineteenth century, will contribute to the success of a vintage base ball program. One great advantage of being affiliated with a historical society or museum is the opportunity to establish a playing field on the property of the institution where history-minded visitors can watch a game. Having a playing field adjacent to or surrounded by nineteenth-century buildings, farm fields, and wooded areas — with perhaps a steam-powered railroad train, a horse-drawn wagon, or a passing canal boat — is especially beneficial in that it helps create the feeling that the participants and spectators have stepped back in time. Vintage base ball at its best is played in an "old-time" setting where modern sights and sounds are blocked out and forgotten, at least for the afternoon.

Games played at the same place on a regular basis can build what is referred to in modern terminology as a "fan base" for the vintage club. Spectators who attend once and have a good time may get in the habit of coming back. A vintage game also draws baseball-minded people to the historical society for other types of programming, exhibits, and activities, and those who have come for the museum's other attractions have the opportunity to discover a vintage base ball game in progress. This mutually beneficial connection is good for the base ball program as well as the institution.

Many programs have capitalized on this symbiotic relationship between the nineteenth-century environment and the placement of the ball field. The home field of the Lah-de-Dahs is at the meadow adjacent to the stately trees and historical houses and shops of Greenfield Village at the Henry Ford Museum in Dearborn, Michigan. The ambiance is enhanced when, several times during a match, a steam-powered locomotive passes, pulling a passenger train on the tracks that border right field. This diamond has the advantage of a natural embankment along the left-field line that provides a shaded seating area for hundreds of spectators.

At Deep River Park at Hobart, Indiana, spectators walk by a working grist mill and adjoining millpond to reach the scenic playing field of the Grinders, where fly balls to the outfield can bound off the side of a wooden barn or the roof of a picturesque old sawmill. In Fremont, Ohio, the Spiegel Grove Squires play on the lawn of the home of President Rutherford B. Hayes. The field is bordered by the historic residence and a grove of large trees, some of which date to the days when the Hayes family lived there.

The Mules of Canal Fulton play in that northeast Ohio town's Village Park, which has a mature woods on one side and the towpath of the old Ohio and Erie Canal on the other. The local attraction is the *St. Helena III*, an accurate replica of a canal boat that carried passengers and cargo on this important waterway in the nineteenth century. Drawn by a team of draft animals, the *St. Helena III* traverses this beautifully restored mile-and-a-quarter section of the canal and visits the nearby dock several times during a match. The passengers often stop and watch the ball game before or after their boat ride, and visitors who come for the vintage game look forward to a trip on the canal boat before or after the match.

The Genesee Country Village and Museum near Rochester, New York, "Where 19th Century America Comes to Life," includes a historic village of 68 period buildings, a carriage museum, the John L. Wehle Art Gallery, the Genesee Country Nature Center, and an Heirloom Garden. In 2001, it added a nineteenth-century base ball program with four men's teams and two women's teams to complement its other programming. The GCVM has enhanced its vintage base ball program by constructing the Silver Base Ball Park, a dedicated playing field billed as "the first replica 19th century base ball park in America." The ball park consists of "bleachers; an outfield fence sporting period-style advertising; a manual scoreboard operated by two young lads on scaffolding; a press box; a tower for the scorekeeper and announcer; special seating for unattended young ladies; and a refreshment tent serving peanuts, birch beer and other period-appropriate food." Visitors are promised the opportunity to "meet and interact with players as well as the members of the press, the umpire" and others.

The home grounds of the St. Louis Perfectos are in Lafayette Park, a graceful and elegant thirty-acre expanse of green grass and mature trees on land set aside for use as a city park in 1836. Although near the busy downtown area in St. Louis, the traffic and modern buildings of the city are blocked out and spectators see only the green playing field, the large old trees that surround it, and the beautifully restored nineteenth-century homes that border all four sides of the park.

These examples are representative of the way vintage base ball can be integrated into the physical location and programming activities of a museum, historical society, or community organization. It is always a pleasure for visiting clubs and their traveling parties to come to grounds like these for a match. Each location has its own look and ambiance based on the geographic setting, the local heritage of the area, and the character and mission of the sponsoring organization.

If a suitable outdoor historic site is not available, other settings can be found in partnership with recreation and parks departments, local corporations, or schools with ample grounds. Since base ball was played on all-grass fields in the early days, planners should think in terms of a lawn rather than the more familiar configuration of a modern softball or baseball diamond with a skin infield and chain-link fences. A vintage game requires only an open lawn or meadow; team organizers can be creative in selecting a club's home grounds.

What makes a good home site for the vintage game? In choosing a field, it is a good idea for program leaders to visit the home grounds of several established programs to take notes and photos and talk to the local program leaders. It is also instructive to study the details of playing fields portrayed in period illustrations, such as the well-known Currier and Ives image of base ball being played at the Elysian Fields in Hoboken in 1866.

In "Baseball the Way It Should Be," an article in the August 1997 issue of the of the US Airways magazine *Attaché*, Ron Fimrite writes that "it took Major League Baseball almost three decades, or until the Orioles' new home was built at Camden Yards, to realize that a ballpark is not a stadium. The Baltimore park, along with its slightly younger cousins in Cleveland, Denver, and Arlington, Texas, has its own unique characteristics, its asymmetrical delights, its nooks and crannies" in the tradition of Fenway Park and Wrigley Field, both built in the second decade of the twentieth century. Many vintage base ball grounds take the concept of idiosyncratic characteristics back to an even earlier time, re-creating the quaint and authentic look of the grounds where the early clubs held their games.

In the 1860 *Beadle's Dime Base-Ball Player,* Henry Chadwick provides the following advice regarding the playing field:

> In selecting a suitable ground, there are many points to be taken into consideration. The ground should be level, and the surface free from all irregularities, and, if possible, covered with fine turf; if the latter can not be done, and the soil is gravelly, a loamy soil should be laid down around the bases, and all the gravel removed therefrom, because, at the bases frequent falls occur, and on gravelly soil injury, in such cases, will surely result to both the clothes and body of the player, in the shape of scraped hands, arms, knees, etc. The ground should be well rolled, as it adds greatly to the pleasure of playing to have the whole field smooth and in good order; it will be found that such a course will fully compensate for the trouble and expense attending it [p. 27].

It should be kept in mind that Chadwick is describing the ideal field and that terms such as "level" and "smooth" are relative. Note that the phrase "if possible" is used as a qualifier. Many clubs of that time did not have the financial resources to bring in "loamy soil" or to have the field rolled. In reality, the site chosen for a playing field for a vintage base ball club need not be perfect, and it is probably more true to the nature of many mid-nineteenth-century fields if it contains a few irregularities. Fields that are used regularly for vintage base ball sometimes have a tree or two in the outfield, some shrubbery in fair territory, or perhaps a building or fence that may come into play. These features create some interesting plays, especially if the game is being played according to the bound rule in which the striker is out if the ball is caught before it hits the ground the second time. If a drive to the outfield hits the ground, bounds against a fence and is then caught by an outfielder before it hits the ground again, the striker is out. If a fly ball goes into a tree, trickles down through the limbs, strikes the ground, takes a bounce, and is caught before it hits the ground for the second time, the striker is out. A fly ball that lands on the sloping roof of a barn or shed and is caught by the outfielder as it rolls off before it hits the ground counts as a fly catch and any runners are in jeopardy of being put out if they do not return to their bases and tag up.

A good historical example of a building being in the field of play appears in the July 1, 1865, issue of *Frank Leslie's Illustrated Newspaper.* The image accompanying an article on "The Grand Match Between the Athletic Ball Club, of Philadelphia, and the Resolute Club of Brooklyn," which was played at the Union Grounds in Brooklyn, shows a substantial gazebo-like wooden structure squarely in left-center field. A tall pole decorated with pennants appears to be in fair territory in right field. Vintage base ball fields are seldom uniformly level. Fields often have slopes, swales, dips, hills, and depressions. A runner may find himself sprinting up a steady incline or down through a shallow valley when advancing from one base to the next. Part of the outfield might be lower or higher than the infield.

One humorous example of playing on an irregular field occurred while on a road trip to Natchez, Mississippi, a few seasons back. The Muffins were playing a local nine on a unique field on the grounds of the Jefferson College Historic Site, where base ball was actually played in the nineteenth century. The drop-off behind the shortstop's area of the infield was so steep that the left fielder, playing in his normal position, could not see the batter and had no idea when a fly ball might be headed his way. If the left fielder moved up the hill and played closer to the shortstop in order to see the batter, he risked having a routine fly ball go over his head and roll down the hill for extra bases. The left fielder's predicament was the subject of a great deal of laughter among players and spectators. This minor problem was resolved by putting our tallest player (normally the first baseman) in left field since he was the only one who could see over the top of the hill and view the striker as he swung at the pitch. After this adjustment, the game went on and a wonderful time was had by all despite this topographic irregularity.

Everyone accepted the fact that the field was full of irregular challenges — even when fly balls to right field rattled off the trunks of a copse of majestic live oaks festooned with Spanish moss or a foul ball came down among the several large magnolia trees around the perimeter of the home plate area. Everyone recognized that it was the largest open space in the area, the playing field was the same for both nines, it was a beautiful summer-like day in late October, and our hosts were a most hospitable group, serving a tasty Southern-style luncheon of red beans and rice with sweet tea between the games of the doubleheader. It was a great day for vintage base ball, made all the more memorable by the idiosyncrasies of the field.

In an era when games were held on grassy fields, lawns, parks, pastures, and village greens, there were no professional groundskeepers with modern rollers and precision mowing equipment. A club's home grounds would not have had the manicured look of a modern professional diamond (which is closer to a golf course green than a mid–nineteenth-century base ball field). The uneven nature of the playing fields in the early days of the game is described by baseball historian Peter Morris in A *Game of Inches: The Game Behind the Scenes*. Morris includes a humorous passage from an 1863 newspaper account of a game held on the playing field at Princeton that calls to mind many of the irregularities of vintage baseball fields in use today. "No one but a topographical engineer could describe that ground. To get to first base you ran uphill, ran down to get to second base, up to third base and home base. The right field played at the top of a hill, the center field at the bottom and the left field in a gully" (p. 57). Morris also includes an 1875 description of a playing field in Ionia, Michigan, that featured "a series of hills and valleys, in the midst of which the ground is laid out, and a score or two of stumps and stone heaps in the outfield, separated here and there by rail and board fences" (p. 58). Irregular and uneven playing fields with trees, shrubs, fences, and buildings, all influencing the action from time to time, are part of the game, then and now.

It should be noted that no outfield fences are needed if playing by 1860 or earlier rules and practices. The Elysian Fields in Hoboken and other grounds where base ball was played in this era usually had no fences. In *Baseball (1845–1881) from the Newspaper Accounts*, Preston Orem states that "the first park to be enclosed solely for baseball purposes was the Union Park, Brooklyn" in 1862 (p. 38). The image in the July 1, 1865, issue of *Frank Leslie's Illustrated Newspaper* cited above shows there was a fence behind the outfielders. Most historians agree that the concept of a fence around the park came in with the practice of charging admission for the games. Owner William Cammeyer constructed a fence around the Union Grounds in order to charge admission for ice skating in winter and base ball in summer. Because of the fence, patrons of the park would have to pass through a gate where the admission fee could be collected. The absence of a fence does not mean, of course, that there are no home runs in vintage base ball. It only means that home runs in the vintage game are more exciting plays than in modern baseball. Instead of jogging around the bases, the striker is racing around the bases in an effort to circle them as quickly as possible before the outfielders can run the ball down and get it back to home plate.

General Field Placement and Spectator Areas

The orientation of the field is determined by topography, the architecture and landscape of the area, and spectator considerations. It is best if home plate is near the spectators so they can be close to the action. Placing home plate near the natural pedestrian traffic flow of the site will help draw spectators once the game begins. Program leaders should keep in mind any natural embankment that would provide good seating and notice the location of shade trees for spectators on hot summer afternoons.

Home plate should be located far enough from the spectators and any fences or other obstacles so that the catcher has a reasonable amount of room to chase after foul tips (a frequent and important play in vintage base ball since a foul ball caught on the fly or first bound is an out). The catcher should have enough room to catch foul balls without stepping on anyone or running into a fence or building. In the 1860 era and before, playing fields did not have permanent backstops or other fences and screens around the playing area to protect spectators.

In placing the field, program leaders should consider the possibility of errant throws from infielders or outfielders with strong arms. The area behind home plate is a place where the ball could strike an inattentive spectator or a breakable window should a fielder make a hurried throw to the plate to retire a runner attempting to score. Program leaders may need to block off some areas to discourage or prohibit spectators. Using straw bales for seating helps define the playing area and keeps visitors from getting too close to the plate. If playing by the rules of a later era that involve faster pitching, a backstop and other protective fences or screens may need to be constructed. In the 1860-style game, any pitches that get past the catcher will be bouncing or rolling on the ground and will probably not have the velocity to do any personal or property damage. Also, with slow pitching, there are seldom any hard, line-drive type foul balls going directly into the spectator areas around the plate.

Thought should be given to the spectator areas behind first base and third base, spots where observers often like to sit. Once again, keep safety in mind, balancing the desire of the audience to get a close view of the game with the need to prevent anyone from getting hit by a batted or thrown ball. The potential for injury to spectators occurs mainly from overthrows that sail into the crowd. Most vintage teams (like most modern professional teams) have some of their best athletes with the strongest arms playing shortstop and third base because they have the agility to field grounders and the arm strength to make the long throw across the infield to first base to retire the striker. Sooner or later one of these athletic young players may send a hard throw to first base that gets through or over the first baseman, who is, of course, not wearing a glove. Since vintage base ball is popular with senior citizens and families with small children, the audience will likely include people who are not always watching the ball and/or not able to get out of the way quickly if an off-target throw comes their way. The area directly behind third base does not come into play as often as the areas behind first and home, but it is another place where spectators should not be seated too close.

Most fields are oriented so that home plate is located close to the spectators and balls are hit away from the crowd. Vintage clubs should ensure that that there are no areas in the farther reaches of the outfield where long hits could cause any damage to property (e.g. the windows of a historic buildings) or people (e.g. visitors watching a blacksmith demonstration or visiting a refreshment stand with their backs to the playing field). If adequate space in the deeper parts of the outfield is a cause for concern, programs may wish to use a softer ball which does not carry as far as some of the more resilient, firmer vintage base balls.

Each field is unique and the location of houses, barns, and fences may help define the spectator areas. Since it is important to take some wise precautions to reduce the possibility of injuries. The following points need to be considered.

1. Vintage program organizers should identify safe and comfortable seating areas and encourage spectators to sit there by placing benches, straw bales, or simple wooden bleachers. Portable metal bleachers may be available but detract significantly from the historical ambience. Guests can be encouraged to bring lawn chairs and blankets.

2. Program leaders should configure areas behind first, third, and home in such a way as to prevent spectators from being in the line of overthrows or batted balls. Roping off the field is historically authentic. When the Washington Nationals visited Columbus, Ohio, in July 1867 on their tour of the West, Henry Chadwick, who was accompanying the Nationals on their journey, commented: "The arrangements for the match were excellent, a roped boundary enclosing the field, and all the base lines laid down properly." The tone of these remarks, which appeared in the July 18, 1867, edition of *The Ball Players' Chronicle*, indicates that roping off the field was a common practice. Therefore, it is certainly acceptable as an authentic crowd-control measure in vintage base ball.

3. Vintage program leaders should remind and caution their players about the danger of overthrows and players should play responsibly. In the excitement of a close game, an infielder should stop and think before firing a bullet to first base to try to nip a runner by a step. An outfielder should be careful about attempting to throw the ball all the way to home on the fly to try to retire a runner at the plate if the throw might sail into the crowd. Players should heed the advice against overthrows that Henry Chadwick passed along in Haney's *Base Ball Book of Reference for 1867*: "In throwing from base to base hastily, take care that you throw low rather than high, as a low ball can be stopped if not handled, whereas a ball overhead gives a run on bases in nearly every instance. In fact, in the long run it is safer to allow a player to make one base than to run the risk of helping him to two or three bases by an overthrow" (p. 131). In other words, sometimes the best throw is the one that the player decides not to make. Smart defensive play and spectator safety are two reasons to avoid overthrows, making Chadwick's advice as relevant today as it was when it was written long ago.

4. Batters need to be mindful of the location of spectators, and avoid hitting hard line drives directly down the foul lines if spectators are seated in these areas. In order to get a good view of the home plate area, spectators will sometimes edge their lawn chairs and blankets into fair territory in left and right field. While on deck, all batters, but especially those who tend to pull the ball, should look down the foul lines to see if any spectators would be endangered by a well-hit ball and adjust their swing accordingly.

5. Fielders and bench players should remain cognizant of spectator issues throughout the game. Perhaps a group of senior citizens has just arrived and taken seats under a tree behind first base. Perhaps a couple with a baby in a stroller has stopped behind home plate to watch the game. If especially vulnerable visitors are seated in an area, a bench player can position himself near them to field anything coming their way while interpreting the action for all who are in the vicinity.

Marking the Field

The 1860 Rules called for "the home base and pitcher's point to be each marked by a flat circular iron plate, painted or enameled white." Once the general location of the playing field has been determined, the specifics of marking off the diamond can begin in order to place home plate and the pitcher's point in their correct locations on the field. If the area selected is to be the regular playing field for the club, the four bases and pitcher's point can be marked permanently with small identifying stakes (level with the ground) so that the somewhat complex task of marking off the field described below does not have to be repeated every time a match is to be played.

Having determined the orientation of the playing field, home plate is the starting point in laying out the diamond. Section 1 of the Knickerbocker Rules of 1845 states that "the bases shall be from 'Home' to second base 42 paces; from first to third base 42 paces equidistant." This approach of first establishing the axis that runs from home plate to second base is the best way to begin when establishing either a permanent or temporary playing field.

If a pace is understood to be three feet, the distance from home to second would be 126 feet, and the distance between the bases is 89.1 feet. This works out to a configuration that is very close to the modern dimensions of 127.281 feet from home to second, 127 feet and approximately three inches being the hypotenuse of a right triangle, which has sides of 90 feet.

In analyzing the term "pace," some baseball historians have pointed out that military marching manuals and other sources from the period specify that a pace is 2.5 feet. Using 2.5 feet as the definition of a pace, 42 paces (home to second or first to third) would translate to 105 feet. This would make the distance between the bases about 75 feet (74.246).

The 1857 Rules are very clear about the distance between the bases, stating that "the bases must be four in number, placed at equal distances from each other, and securely fastened upon the four corners of a square whose sides are respectively thirty yards." The 1860 Rules repeat this language. Since the 1857 and 1860 Rules established the base paths at 30 yards, most programs have accepted that distance as the original intention of the 1845 Rules and have adopted the standard length of 90 feet that has been used in most forms of baseball played by adult men up to the present.

To set up the field, measure a length of rope 130 feet in length. Mark with paint or a ribbon a zero point and then the distances of 45 feet, 90 feet, and 127 feet 3 inches. Once the location of home plate has been established, it should be affixed to the ground. Have one person stand on the plate and hold the zero point of the pre-marked rope at the center of home plate. A second person should take the coiled rope and walk toward the area where second base will be located. He should be carrying the pitcher's point, second base, and a hammer with several large spikes. At the 45-foot mark on the rope, the pitcher's point can be placed on the ground and attached with spikes. Continuing to walk toward center field, stop when the 127-foot 3-inch mark is reached on the rope. At this point, the second base bag should be affixed to the ground with spikes.

Return to home plate, re-coiling the rope, and, maintaining the zero point at the center of home plate, walk at a 90-degree angle from home plate toward the location of first base. When the 90-foot mark on the rope is reached, first base can be dropped at that location and affixed to the ground with spikes. Once first base is established, the person who has remained at home base should take the end of the rope he has been holding and walk in the direction where third base will be located. The person on first base lets the rope unwind until it reaches the 127-foot 3-inch mark used to measure the distance from home to second base. With the zero end of the rope at third and the 127-foot 3-inch mark at first, the rope should be stretched taut, perpendicular to the axis previously established between home and second. The person who has now reached third base can mark the spot where third base should be located and affix the bag to the ground. The 90-foot distance between third and home can be checked by the person on third holding his end of the rope on the base and the person on first walking back to home while coiling the rope. When the person on first reaches home, he should have also reached the 90-foot mark on the rope.

Henry Chadwick describes a similar way to lay out the playing field in his commentary in the 1860 *Beadle's Dime Base-Ball Player*:

> There are several methods by which the ground may be correctly measured; the following is as simple as any. Having determined on the point of the home base, measure from that point, down the field, *one hundred and twenty-seven feet four inches*, and the end will indicate the position of the second base; then take a cord *one hundred and eighty feet long*, fasten one end at the home base, and the other at the second, and then grasp it in the center and extend it first to the right side, which will give the point of the first base, and then to the left, which will indicate the position of the third; this will give the exact measurement, as the string will thus form the sides of a square whose side is ninety feet. On a line from the home to the second base, and distant from the former *forty-five feet*, is the pitcher's point [pp. 17–18].

After laying out a base ball diamond several times with the rope method and participating in a number of games, veteran players and umpires develop a good intuitive feel for the 45-foot pitching distance and the 90-foot base path distance. With practice, experienced club members can do a very adequate job of laying out a diamond by simply pacing off the 90-foot distance from home to first and home to third, then placing second base on a line with home and the pitcher's point at its proper location where the imaginary lines from first to second and third to second would intersect.

Rather than beginning the process by starting at home and locating second base, the approach of beginning at home and then locating first or third base (either by walking 30 paces or using a pre-measure rope to establish the 90-foot distance) may be preferable in some instances. If the club wishes to orient its field so that the right-field or left-field foul line corresponds to some prominent feature of the local landscape, such as a distant tree or a telegraph pole that can be used to help the umpire judge fair and foul hits, a club may choose to begin by laying out the first-base or third-base line (directly toward the tree or pole) and then proceed with locating the other bases and the pitcher's point.

Foul Lines and Foul Poles

Foul lines marked by chalk are considered optional and are not always used in 1860-era vintage games. However, if they are used, they can be a very effective tool that defines the field for the spectators and helps the umpire make correct decisions as to whether a struck ball hits fair or foul. In "The Evolution of the Baseball Diamond" in the 1994 edition of *The Baseball Research Journal*, Tom Shieber writes that the practice of marking the foul lines with chalk was first set forth in *Beadle's Dime Base Ball Player* in 1861: "And in all match games, a line connecting the home and first base and the home and third base, shall be marked by the use of chalk, or other suitable material, so as to be distinctly seen by the umpire." The 1874 Rules called for the extension of the foul lines beyond the bases by stating that "the foul lines shall be unlimited in length." It seems reasonable to assume that some clubs had adopted the practice of using chalk or other substances to mark the foul lines before 1861. It is unlikely that Chadwick suddenly invented the idea of chalk lines. Rather, he probably adopted it as one of those "best practices" that some clubs had already been using to enable players and umpires to assess if a ball was fair or foul. Similarly, as games were most likely played with chalk lines before 1861, games were undoubtedly played without chalk lines after that date.

If the decision is made to mark foul lines from home to first and home to third, club leaders should make sure to use a substance that will not damage the grass. This is especially true if playing a game at a public park or on the lawn of a historic home. If a modern device is used to put down the white foul lines, the lines should be marked prior to the arrival of any spectators.

Once the field has been laid out and the exact location of the bases has been determined (but before any chalk lines are marked), the appearance of the diamond can be enhanced by mowing the base paths so that the grass is considerably shorter than the rest of the field. This practice helps define the field for spectators and players and gives the field an authentic appearance similar to that depicted in the Currier and Ives 1866 illustration *The American National Game of Base Ball*.

Poles can also be used to mark the foul lines. In addition to being functional, foul poles add to the festive appearance of the playing field, especially if streamers or pennants representing the home club's colors are attached. In his commentary on the 1860 Rules, Henry Chadwick states:

> The foul ball posts are placed on a line with the home and first base, and home and third, and should be at least one hundred feet from the bases. As these posts are intended solely to assist the umpire in his decisions in reference to foul balls, they should be high enough from the ground and painted, so as to be distinctly seen from the umpire's position [p. 18].

In the course of a discussion of foul poles on the 1860 vintage base ball listserv in 2005, veteran vintage player Paul Hunkele shared an informative note from Dean Thilgen, another expert on rules and practices, who had written: "Game accounts in Minnesota during the post-war years (1865–1869) mention the club 'silks' flying from the foul poles. On occasion, the account will mention the local ladies who created the team colors for the pole, and the formal presentation ceremony. These foul pole flags were an important part of the amateur game in those days." In 2006, correspondent Jon Burpee pointed out another advantage of the foul poles based on his experiences at Fort Vancouver National Historic Site in Vancouver, Washington. "At our better-attended games (1,000+ visitors) these poles ... helped provide visitors with an unmarked line that demarcated the field and kept them from sitting [in fair territory] upon the field." Not all programs employ foul poles. If they are used, Hunkele recommends dowels about six-feet tall. They are usually painted white with flags attached so that they can be plainly seen by the umpire and by outfielders chasing fly balls near the foul line.

Marking the Pitcher's Point and Home Plate

After all warm-up activities have been concluded and the match is about to begin, the umpire should place by hand two additional and important white lines on the field. Home base and the pitcher's point having been established, it is now time to follow the provision of Section 5 in the 1860 Rules that states, "The pitcher's position shall be designated by a line four yards in length, drawn at right angles to a line from home to the second base, having its center upon that line, at a fixed iron plate, placed at a point fifteen yards distant from home base." Follow those instructions by marking a twelve-foot line that runs through the pitcher's point. In *Beadle's Dime Base-Ball Player*, Chadwick writes that "the line of the pitcher's position should be marked by the insertion in the ground of a piece of hard wood, six feet long, about two inches wide, and from six to eight deep. It should be inserted so as the umpire can see it" (p. 18). This practice of installing a permanent wooden marker in the ground is not generally followed in vintage base ball, as it would require a significant amount of work and would not be appropriate on fields used for other purposes. Therefore, vintage programs use a white line to designate the pitcher's position. The next step is to mark a line directly through the middle of home plate in order to comply with Section 17, which states, "The striker must stand on a line drawn through the center of the home base, not exceeding in length three feet either side thereof and parallel to the line occupied by the pitcher."

In the vintage base ball community, the line at the pitcher's point and the line through home plate are often marked with white flour (poured from a period container), rather than chalk, lime, paint or any other substances that might damage the grass. White flour does no damage to the field and disappears quickly and naturally into the grass and dirt at the conclusion of the game. If the white line through the plate becomes partially obliterated during the game by the foot traffic of the players, the umpire may need to keep the can of white flour handy to touch up the striker's line between innings.

Backstop

1860 Rules call for a line through the middle of home plate extending three feet on each side to mark the batter's position. Chalk lines from home to first and home to third were specified in the 1861 Rules, but may have been used earlier.

If a program chooses to portray an era after the advent of faster pitching, a backstop will need to be constructed, unless, of course, the club plays its games on a modern baseball field that already has a backstop in place. If a backstop is needed, club leaders

Straw bales form an effective, inexpensive, temporary backstop that helps define the playing area.

will want to consult with similar programs on matters of period design and materials. If playing according to the era of slower pitching, no backstop is needed. However, a program may wish to orient the playing field so that there is some kind of barrier, such as a fence or wall that will keep the occasional errant pitch or foul ball that eludes the catcher from rolling into the spectator area. A backstop made of a wall of straw bales stacked about six or seven wide at the base and three or four high and placed about 20 or 30 feet behind home plate makes an effective backstop that can be easily dismantled after the game. A backstop made of straw bales helps define the field, prevents spectators from wandering too close to home plate, and adds to the nineteenth-century look of the playing area. Banners and flags can be easily attached to the straw bales that form the backstop.

Scoreboard

It is not clear when the scoreboard first came into general use. The scoreboard is defined in the *New Dickson Baseball Dictionary* as "a signboard erected for the benefit of the spectators that at a minimum, shows each team's inning-by-inning scoring, as well as the number of hits, runs, and errors credited to each team" (p. 432). Peter Morris, in *A Game of Inches: The Game Behind the Scenes*, reminds us that "the limited size of early baseball crowds ensured that the scoreboard was also a gradual development. Early spectators could sit close enough to the scorer's table that there was no need for an enlarged tote board" (p. 93). This is the case at many vintage games where the spectators are kept informed by announcements from the umpire or scorer.

A scoreboard keeps the spectators informed of the progress of the game (courtesy Joel Moore).

In studying period illustrations of early games, vintage program leaders and other researchers have had difficulty finding examples of scoreboards. As Morris points out, "As crowd sizes grew, the need for a board that was distinct from the scorer's table slowly became evident. For instance, at a game in Columbus, Ohio, in 1875, mention was made [in the July 17 edition of the *New York Clipper*] of the 'bulletin board near the scorers' table'" (p. 93).

Although evidence of early scoreboards is sparse, many programs do find it beneficial to have some type of scoreboard to keep spectators informed and involved. It is often the case in vintage base ball that spectators will walk up to the field while the match is in progress to see what is going on and ask, "What's the score?" Since many vintage games are high-scoring affairs, even spectators who have been playing close attention from the beginning have trouble keeping track of the score and the inning. A scoreboard can be a sturdy permanent installation at the home grounds or a folding wooden device that can be placed wherever it can be seen best by the crowd at home and away games. Some programs use wooden squares with pre-painted numbers that are then hung on hooks on the scoreboard. Others keep score on a chalk board.

Ground Rules

One of the most interesting features of the vintage game is the idiosyncratic nature of the grounds. Each field is unique. Various obstacles, both natural (such as rivers, ponds, and wooded areas) and man-made (such as barns, fences, and roads), may come into play, requiring a set of ground rules. Ground rules have been part of the game from the beginning. Section 14 of the Knickerbocker Rules of 1845 states that "but one base allowed when the ball bounds out of the field when struck." This statement was expanded to read as follows in Section 32 of the 1860 Rules: "Clubs may adopt such rules respecting balls knocked beyond or outside of bounds of the field, as circumstances of the ground may demand; and these rules shall govern all matches played upon the ground, provided that they are distinctly made known to every player and umpire, previous to the commencement of the game."

The standard procedure in vintage base ball is that every ball is in play, with players hopping over a rail fence, diving into shrubbery, or crawling under a farm wagon to chase after balls as the runners dash around the bases. However, many vintage clubs follow the practice of having ground rules to cover specific situations unique to the field where the game is being played. The safety of the players is one consideration that may cause the home club to adopt a ground rule. For example, it is wise to set a ground rule calling for the ball to be dead and only one base awarded to the runners on a ball that rolls onto a busy roadway adjacent to the field. Similarly, it is a good idea to limit the runner's advance to one base if the ball goes into an area where farm equipment is kept. Antique farm machinery and hand tools may have hidden implement points and sharp metal edges that could result in an injury to a fielder racing into the area in pursuit of a ball. Fielders should be advised that they can retrieve balls from potentially dangerous areas in a deliberate and careful manner with no need to hurry in order to prevent runners from advancing.

If a field has an outfield fence that is judged to be too close to home and therefore too easy to reach, a ground rule may be established to prevent the scoring of "cheap" runs by allowing for only one base for the striker and any base runners on a hit that goes over the fence. In a similar attempt to prevent tainted runs, a ground rule might specify that the runners may take only one base on an overthrow that goes into a wooded, watery, or weedy area near the field.

To keep games moving briskly and to prevent the loss of expensive vintage base balls, a ground rule might specify that the batter is limited to one base (or perhaps even called out) if the ball is struck over a fence or into a river, pond, swamp, or any area of heavy vegetation bordering the field where the ball might become lost or difficult to retrieve. Spectators should not be subjected to waiting several minutes as players poke around in the underbrush while looking for a lost ball. The home club should always have a second game ball ready and resume play quickly. Extra players who are not in the game at the moment, the club mascot, or perhaps some youngsters among the spectators can search for the lost ball while the game continues. One way to prevent balls from being hit into areas where they will be difficult to retrieve is to establish a ground rule that specifies a penalty for hitting the ball into certain restricted areas, thereby encouraging strikers to avoid these problem areas during the match.

Also, in the case of a game played on the grounds of a historic farm or a nineteenth-century home with a garden, a ground rule may be necessary to prevent balls from being struck into areas where young plants are growing. Morris confirms that such ground rules are not new, citing a rule for an 1870 match played in Calumet, Michigan. "Before the game a rule was made that balls struck into a certain potato patch in the right field should only count as one base" (p. 58). Faced with the prospect of having their long hits reduced to singles if the ball goes into plowed or planted areas where the feet of the pursuing outfielder might damage crops or flowers, thoughtful strikers will try to direct their blows into the more open areas of the field where their strength can be rewarded with an extra-base hit that will do more to help the team than a hit of equal length that lands in an area that is off-limits.

All strikers should be gentlemanly and cooperative in regard to the intent and purpose of any ground rules that are agreed upon by the captains or any restrictions that are announced by the host club. Players should always respect the wishes of the home team and the organization it represents in regard to ground rules put in place to protect flower beds, vegetable gardens, freshly cultivated fields, and newly seeded lawns.

The Bench

Some of the very early base ball illustrations do not show benches for the teams. Players are depicted standing or sitting in the grass in foul territory as they watch the action, waiting to take their turn at bat. For example, the familiar Currier and Ives 1866 illustration *The American National Game of Base Ball* shows the six players other than the batter and two base runners standing, kneeling, and sitting off to the right of the plate while watching the action. Similarly, an illustration in the July 1, 1865, issue of *Frank Leslie's Illustrated Newspaper* portraying a game at Brooklyn's Union Grounds shows the players on the club that is up to bat standing, sitting, and kneeling in foul territory between home and first base. However, in describing the playing field for the game between the touring National Club of Washington and Capital Club in Columbus, Ohio, in 1867, Henry Chadwick states, "Tables were provided for the scorers and members of the press [and] seats for the players." The frequently published image of the 1870 match between the Red Stockings and the Atlantics provides a good view of a team bench on the third-base line. The fact that there is no bench on the first-base line suggests that both teams used the same bench. This model of having the two teams share a bench is fairly common in vintage base ball.

While it is not clear exactly when they came into common use, benches are strongly recommended in vintage base ball. First, it is a good idea to provide a place for players to sit, especially on days when the grass is too damp to sit on the ground. Second, players need to be seated so that they do not block the view of the spectators. Players (except for the striker and the person on deck) may need to be reminded throughout the game to stay seated so that they do not obstruct the spectators' line of sight.

To provide a place for the players to sit, some programs use simple wooden benches. Museums and historical societies often have benches on hand to provide seating for other types of programming, and they can be placed along the foul lines at base ball games. But even if none are available, plain wooden benches can be constructed fairly easily and inexpensively. Another seating option is to place a row of several rectangular bales of straw in foul territory parallel to the base lines. Straw bales have a natural, old-fashioned look, and the straw can be used later for maintenance and upkeep of the grounds. Straw bales are an excellent way to provide extra seating for special events like tournaments or festivals, where additional temporary seating may be required for teams and spectators.

Water

There should be a supply of drinking water on or near the bench. To preserve the period appearance, many clubs provide drinking water in a crock or other period container rather than in plastic bottles and jugs. Large ceramic crocks with a capacity of several gallons (some with a spigot at the bottom) are available through antique dealers, museum gift shops, Civil War reenactor suppliers, suttlers, kitchen and cookware catalogs, and other sources. Water and ice can be placed in the crock well in advance of the match and the crock can be placed in the bench area before spectators arrive. If the teams have separate benches on opposite sides of the field, it is best to have a crock placed on each bench.

Another source of water at the field may be the large round plastic containers that are a familiar sight at modern baseball, soccer, and football games (the kind of container that gets dumped over the coach's head at the end of an important win). If used, this type of container should be placed in a wooden box or under an easy-to-make burlap or canvas cover. A cover made of some period material will hide the bright colors and modern logos characteristic of these containers while still making water readily available to the game participants. Depending on the location of the field, the container might be placed near the bench but out of public view behind a clump of shrubbery or inside a barn or canvas tent.

Some clubs use tin cups so that each participant can have his or her own cup to use for that game. Cups can be washed afterward. Better yet, in the interests of hygiene, each participant can be encouraged to bring his or her own tin cup for personal use. The cup should be marked with a name or initials. Tin cups (actually stainless steel cups or enameled camp-style cups that have an old-fashioned look but won't rust) can be found at a very reasonable price at many stores that handle housewares or camping gear.

The appearance of the bench and the ambience of the match are improved by the use of period containers for drinking water. A player and mascot from the Fulton Mules (Canal Fulton, Ohio) get a drink from a stoneware crock.

If plastic bottles of water are provided, attempt to shield them from view with a blanket or place them in a basket. Sitting on the bench while drinking water from a tin cup (with the plastic bottle having been stowed away out of sight) would be infinitely preferable to standing in the bench area chugging water from a plastic bottle in full view of the spectators.

Participants should avoid being photographed drinking from or holding a plastic bottle or aluminum can (or engaged in any other anachronistic activity). Members of the media covering a vintage game will often spot these historical anomalies and, thinking it humorous, will intentionally try to snap a picture of a person in an old-fashioned base ball uniform or period dress drinking from a Disani water bottle, a Starbucks cup, or a Gatorade container. It would be unfortunate if, after all the effort expended to present an authentic-looking nineteenth-century tableau for the game, the one picture that appears in the newspaper the next day turns out to be a photo of a vintage player holding a modern plastic bottle showing the label of a twenty-first-century product. This kind of picture, intended to be light-hearted rather than mean-spirited, nonetheless reflects poorly on the player, the program, the organization sponsoring the team, and the site hosting the game. Such a photo also gives an inaccurate image to the public of what vintage base ball is all about.

If a program or an individual has to make a choice between health and authenticity — drinking water from a non-period container or going without water on a hot day — the decision should always be to encourage participants to consume all the water they need through whatever source is available, period or not. Historical authenticity is an important consideration, but never compromise health and safety. However, with a little planning, a club can usually provide water in a period container so that plenty is available with no need to spoil the spectators' view by having plastic bottles and jugs in plain sight.

The bench area is considered part of the playing field and should be kept free of any modern items, such as plastic bottles, Styrofoam cups, gym bags, coolers, vinyl jackets, electronic gadgets, and the like. Personal items like car keys and cell phones should not be placed on the bench in view of the spectators. A large market basket can be placed at the end of the bench to hold all personal items out of sight. As a very visible part of the vintage base ball playing field and an important component of the presentation of a vintage game, the bench should be constructed of period materials and kept free of any modern items. It should also be occupied by only those in base ball uniforms or other period dress, never by friends, family members, or spectators in modern clothing.

Remember the invisible line at the ball field in *Field of Dreams*? When Doc Graham crossed the line to treat Ray's daughter, he was no longer part of the group of old-time players on the field. There is a similar "invisible line" around the field at a vintage game inside which the club members are in the nineteenth century. Outside of the line, it is the current twenty-first century, but everything (people, equipment, etc.) inside the line should be of the year being represented in the game.

First Aid

Every club should have a well-equipped first-aid kit in the bench area to treat any minor scrapes, cuts, and bruises that may occur during the game. First-aid kits are often packaged in plastic boxes. If so, the first-aid kit and any other medical supplies in modern packaging can be kept on or near the bench or scorer's table in a wooden box, canvas or leather bag, woven basket, or other period container. It is a good idea to have some ice handy (somewhere in the vicinity of the playing field, but not necessarily on the bench) in case an injury occurs that involves swelling. Participants should be aware of how to summon emergency assistance if a player suffers a more serious injury that requires the attention of a medical professional. Participants also should be familiar with the protocol for notifying the proper museum staff member if someone is injured during the game.

Taking the Game on the Road

Vintage base ball is an extremely portable game that can be played at a variety of venues. In addition to attracting crowds of visitors to the home grounds at the museum, it can also be a good idea to take the museum's vintage base ball team to places where crowds of people are already gathered and play games at festivals, fairs, and celebrations. These games are beneficial for the historical organization that sponsors the team in that they represent a very positive form of outreach.

The Field of Play

When making arrangements to play at a community festival, county fair, sesquicentennial, or similar event, the vintage team representative should discuss the playing area with the host organization well ahead of time. Since the organizers may not have seen a vintage game, they often assume that the visiting vintage team requires a modern baseball or softball diamond. If not told otherwise, they may go out of their way to arrange for the use of a modern diamond and possibly even pay a rental fee to obtain it. The vintage club representative making the arrangements for the game should make it clear that a plain grassy field is perfectly acceptable, even preferable, and that any open space at the city park, school yard, fair grounds, or town square where the event is being held is quite suitable for a vintage game.

At times, however, event organizers (even if they know an open, grassy field is preferable to replicate the look of the 1860s) want to stage the game on a conventional baseball diamond because of the availability of grandstand seating, proximity to concession stands and restrooms, traffic flow of the event, or other considerations. If the organizers are inclined to hold the match on a modern diamond, the vintage team should readily agree and not insist on playing on a grassy field on the grounds of historical authenticity. In the interests of promoting the game of vintage base ball and connecting with the public, it is better to play before a big crowd on a modern diamond than to insist on playing on a grassy field in a more remote area where few will come to watch. If the game is to be held on a modern diamond, the vintage team manager should let the host organization know that they need not go to the trouble of chalking in the batter's boxes or pitcher's area (as their grounds crew might do as standard procedure whenever any baseball game is scheduled to be held on that field). The vintage atmosphere can be enhanced on a modern diamond by displaying the club banner, distributing an informative brochure, and taking advantage of a public address system to provide game announcements and play-by-play using period language.

Advance planning always helps make a special event a success. If laying out the ball diamond on an open grassy field where base ball is not usually played, it is necessary to come prepared with a measuring rope and bases. If two vintage teams are meeting for a match at a neutral site that is not the home field of either club, they should confer in advance as to which team will be responsible for bringing the bases and laying out the field before the game.

Home or away, the playing field, including the bench area, is an important part of the presentation of a vintage base ball game. Although the field for a community game may be in a more modern environment than the club's home field, care and thought should be given to making it look like a base ball field from the early years of the game, thereby fulfilling its function as an authentic setting for a nineteenth-century match.

12

The Umpire

Re-Creating the Historic Character

From the earliest days of base ball, the umpire has been an important part of the game. Two of the original Knickerbocker Rules of 1845 mention the role of the umpire. Immediately after the first rule gets everyone on the field at the appropriate time and place for a game ("Members must strictly observe the time agreed upon for exercise, and be punctual in their attendance."), the second rule establishes the role of the umpire: "When assembled for exercise, the President, or in his absence, the Vice-President, shall appoint an Umpire, who shall keep the game in a book provided for that purpose, and note all violations of the By-Laws and Rules during the time of exercise."

Rule 17 gives the umpire the authority to make decisions when needed throughout the game by stating, "All disputes and differences relative to the game, to be decided by the Umpire, from which there is no appeal." Both rules indicate that from the beginning, the umpire was part of the game. Reading between the lines, it is apparent that the umpire was an experienced and respected member of the club who could be counted upon to know the rules and make good decisions.

The 1860 Rules provide information and insight as to how the role of the umpire had evolved. Section 28 states: "The umpire shall take care that the regulations respecting balls, bats, bases, and the pitcher's and striker's positions, are strictly observed. He shall keep record of the game, in a book prepared for the purpose; he shall be the judge of fair and unfair play, and shall determine all disputes and differences which may occur during the game; he shall take especial care to declare all foul balls and baulks, immediately upon their occurrence, unasked, and in a distinct and audible manner."

Section 29 of the 1860 Rules goes on to state that "in all matches [meaning matches with other clubs rather than intra-squad games involving members of the same club], the umpire shall be selected by the captains of the respective sides, and shall perform all the duties enumerated in Section 28, except recording the game, which shall be done by two scorers, one of whom shall be appointed by each of the contending clubs."

Section 30 includes a prohibition against wagering: "No person engaged in a match, either as umpire, scorer, or player, shall be, either directly or indirectly, interested in any bet upon the game." Section 30 also upholds his authority by stating that "neither umpire, scorer, nor player shall be changed during a match, unless with the consent of both parties." Section 31 provides the umpire with the authority to decide "when play should be suspended" due to darkness or rain. The level of knowledge implied in Sections 28 though 31 is further supported by Section 34, which states, "No person shall be permitted to act as umpire or scorer in any match, unless he shall be a member of a Base-Ball Club governed by these

Dressed as a gentleman from the 1860s, umpire Richard Schuricht addresses the spectators in the opening ceremonies at an Ohio Village Muffins match at Schiller Park, Columbus, Ohio.

rules." Taken together, these sections do much to define the role and function of the umpire in 1860. They also establish a set of guidelines for the umpire in a vintage base ball game.

Period Clothing

Period clothing is essential in re-creating the umpire's role. The umpire for a vintage game should never be in modern clothing. Illustrations show the umpire dressed as a gentleman of the day in business attire, not a base ball uniform. Vintage participants who umpire matches on a regular basis enjoy putting together a gentleman's suit of period clothing consisting of a shirt and tie, trousers, vest, coat, hat, and perhaps other accessories, such as a pocket watch and walking stick. The hat can be a top hat, straw hat, or other style authentic to the period. A hat with a brim wide enough to provide some protection from the sun is often preferred. A pair of period leather shoes (or boots) makes a superb complement for the outfit, but since the umpire will be on his feet throughout most of the game, he will want to make sure his footwear is comfortable.

A member of a club who is called upon occasionally to umpire a match can do so in his playing uniform, but it is best to modify it to show his neutrality. He can easily assemble an adequate outfit for service as an umpire (or scorer) by starting with his uniform shirt and pants and adding a vest, tie of a color different from his uniform tie, and a straw hat. These simple and inexpensive modifications to his regular playing uniform will help the spectators identify him as a game official rather than a player. Having a vest and hat (and perhaps a walking stick) close at hand helps a vintage base ball participant make a quick

At a match at the Ohio Cup, the umpire takes a position on the field in accordance with 1860 rules and practices.

change from player to umpire and back to a player again in a matter of minutes. This is advantageous during a tournament or festival where many games are played and some individuals are called upon to assume multiple roles.

Position on the Field

The familiar Currier and Ives image, *The American National Game of Base Ball*, and other illustrations of the period clearly show a gentleman in civilian clothes stationed off to the side of home plate who is serving as the umpire for the game. To the untrained eye, the presence of the umpire may not be readily apparent since these illustrations do not show a person in a blue uniform wearing a mask crouched directly behind home plate, as in today's game. However, although he was dressed in civilian clothes and stood to the side of the plate, the umpire was there from the beginning.

"The Evolution of the Baseball Diamond" by baseball historian Tom Shieber in the 1994 SABR publication *The Baseball Research Journal* provides information on the umpire's location on the field. The article includes a diagram published in the December 13, 1856, issue of the *New York Clipper* showing the umpire's position in foul territory on the first-base side of the diamond, perhaps 15 to 20 feet from home plate. This is consistent with Henry Chadwick's description of the umpire's location in the 1860 *Beadle's Dime Base Ball Player*. "His position is to the right of, and between, the striker and the catcher, in a line with the home and third base; in the case of a left-handed striker, he should stand on the left of the striker" (p. 30). From this vantage point the umpire has a good view of whether a ball chopped in front of the plate or struck anywhere along the third-base or left-field line should be declared fair or foul and whether a batter's swing had resulted in a clean miss or a foul tip. From this position, he also has a good view of first base to judge whether a striker is safe or out on a close play. In addition, he can judge whether the pitcher has made a balk by committing some infraction of the rules in his delivery of the ball. In order to successfully re-create the character of the umpire, the vintage base ball umpire should station himself in this location.

Rather than standing, some period illustrations show the umpire seated in a chair, sometimes shielding himself from the sun with an umbrella. In the section on umpires in *A Game of Inches: The Game on the Field*, Peter Morris provides a highly informative picture of the 1860-era umpire's role and stature by sharing the following recollections of an 1860s base ball player named Jimmy Wood that appeared in an interview in the *Marion* (Ohio) *Star* in 1916. Looking back more than a half-century, the veteran player reported that in those bygone days "an umpire was highly honored. After each game the players would give three cheers for each other and then, as a grand finale, they would bellow forth with three more — and sometimes nine — for the umpire" (p. 31). Going back to the game's early days, Wood recalled, "The old time umpires were accorded the utmost courtesy by the players. They were given easy chairs, placed near the home plate, provided with fans on hot days and their absolute comfort was uppermost in the minds of the players." Morris quotes another observer, Charles Deming, who remembered that the umpire was "an imposing figure" whose position was "even with home plate and about twenty feet away. There an arm chair was set for him and, on sunny days, he was entitled to an umbrella ... fastened to the chair" (p. 32).

Providing a chair for the umpire at a vintage game is done by some programs, although once the game begins the umpire usually spends most of the game on his feet as he moves around quickly to get a clear view of the action in case he needs to make a judgment on a ball struck near the foul line or a close play at one of the bases. Also, the umpire frequently moves around the home plate area to interact with the crowd. The presence of a wooden chair is authentic, but it should not be placed too close to the plate where the catcher might collide with it while chasing a foul tip. Whether he is seated or standing, the umpire is treated with great respect in vintage base ball as he was in the mid-nineteenth century. "The position of an Umpire is an honorable one," wrote Henry Chadwick in his 1860 commentary in *Beadle's Dime Base Ball Player*, and it remains so today in the presentation of an 1860-style game (p. 28).

The Rules of 1860 speak of having only one umpire, and in most vintage games this pattern is followed. Occasionally, two umpires are available for a vintage game. In such cases, it is customary for one to take his place near home plate and the other to position himself in the vicinity of second base in order to be able to make calls on plays at second and on balls hit to the outfield. If two umpires are present, they may switch potions at the midpoint of the game. The rules call for only one umpire, but if two are present, dressed appropriately and ready to officiate the game, it is good to get both involved by sharing the duties.

Knowledge of the Game

Standing in the right place on the field and wearing period clothing, of course, is only the beginning. In the early days of the game, the umpire was a person of good judgment and fairness with a thorough knowledge of the rules, and this remains true in vintage base ball. In games played in any era under any rules, the umpire in a vintage match should be a very knowledgeable and experienced member of the vintage community. As Henry Chadwick advised the 1860 edition of *Beadle's Dime Base-Ball Player:* "The Umpire should be ... familiar with every point of the game." Chadwick also states, "He should also be as prompt as possible in rendering his decisions, as promptitude, in this respect, implies good judgment, whereas hesitancy gives rise to dissatisfaction, even where the decision is a correct one" (pp. 28–29). Even in the sportsmanlike environment of the vintage game, players can become perplexed and agitated and spectators can be confused if the rules are interpreted or applied inappropriately and inconsistently or if calls are slow in coming.

The umpire's important duties begin before the game starts. The umpire should go over the rules and practices under which the game will be conducted with the captains and perhaps all the members of both teams. Since the Rules of 1860 and other historic eras are vague on certain points, programs may have adopted different interpretations of some rules. Therefore, it is important for the umpire to make sure everyone understands the way the game will be officiated before the match begins, anticipating any areas that could lead to misunderstandings.

Included in this meeting should be a review of any ground rules associated with the playing site. The proximity of a wooded area, stream, fence, barn or other natural feature or man-made structure sometimes necessitates the creation of unique ground rules, which need to be communicated to all parties before the game begins. The umpire should be clear himself about the local rule interpretations and ground rules and should explain them clearly to others.

If an experienced vintage team is playing a community team new to nineteenth-century rules, the umpire's role is even more important. In these situations he will need to hold a more extensive pre-match meeting with the novice team to go over the rules and explain the major differences, such as the one-bound rule, the fair-foul rule, the need to return to base quickly on a foul ball, and other basics so that the community team members will have an understanding of what to do upon taking the field.

Making Calls

The umpire should make calls in the way they were made in the 1860 era. Some calls were made only after the players asked for a judgment, such as on a close play at one of the bases where the ball and the runner arrive simultaneously. Other calls need to be made immediately without being asked. For example, Chadwick advised that "he should give all his decisions in a loud tone of voice, especially in cases of foul balls, keeping silent when a fair ball is struck" (p. 29). An immediate decision was needed in this case because the 1860 Rules specified that when the striker hits a foul ball, "the players running bases shall return to them, and may be put out in so returning [provided the ball had first 'settled in the hands of the pitcher'] in the same manner as the striker when running to first base."

The situation covered in this rather complicated-sounding rule is not as difficult to grasp as it first appears. Consider the following situation. With a runner on first, the striker hits a ground ball down the third-base line. From the runner's perspective, he may not be able to tell if the ball is fair or foul, but he must quickly decide if he should run to second or hold at first base. If he runs to second and the ball is foul, the third baseman can pick up the ball and throw it to the pitcher, who will throw it to first base. If the runner has not returned to first by the time the ball gets there, he is out ("in the same manner of the striker when running to first base," which means that he does not need to be tagged). Conversely, if he does not run and the ball is fair, the third baseman can pick up the ball and throw it to second base and the runner will be forced out. Therefore, the umpire must make the "foul" call immediately and unasked so that the runner knows if he should run or hold. If no call is made, everyone should assume that it is a fair ball, and the batter and runner should both start running while the defensive players try to field the ball and throw to first or second.

Another situation in which the call should be made immediately and unasked is covered in Section 7, which specifies that "when a baulk is made by the pitcher, every player running the bases is entitled to one base without being put out." Therefore, the umpire should loudly announce "baulk" as soon as he detects it and award any runner his next base.

Most calls, such as on a close play at one of the bases, were not made unasked. If the ball arrived at the base ahead of the runner, the runner would, as a gentleman, walk off the field and return to the bench without being told to do so. The atmosphere in which the mid-nineteenth-century players approached the game was permeated with a sense of honesty and fair play. This significantly reduced the number of times the umpire was required to get directly involved in the game. While the umpire was an important figure in early base ball, his role was less intrusive than it is in the modern game. Because of the sportsmanlike nature of the proceedings, the players were expected to arrive at most decisions themselves, calling upon the umpire for a decision only when the play was truly too close to call and the fair judgment of an unbiased third party was needed.

Section 33 of the 1860 Rules states that "no person shall be permitted to approach or to speak with the umpire, scorers, or players, or in any manner to interrupt or interfere during the progress of the game, unless by special request of the umpire." Some in vintage base ball have construed the wording of this rule to mean that no player (except possibly the captain) should be allowed to speak to the umpire during the match. A more careful reading, however, indicates that this rule is aimed at protecting the individuals on the field from inappropriate interference from spectators not directly involved in the game. Players on the field should not be prohibited from routinely asking the scorer or the umpire about the score or inning of the game or how many outs there are. Players and officials could talk to each other throughout the game and polite exchange should not be discouraged in an 1860-style vintage game.

In an April 2004 post to the vintage base ball listserv, Paul Hunkele, a knowledgeable researcher and experienced vintage player, provides a logical and sensible explanation of how the umpire made calls and how the umpire and the players interacted. His observations provide a fine template for how a vintage umpire approaches his duties.

> I believe that not only were 1860 players allowed to address an umpire, they were required to, in "requesting judgment" for outs on the bases including all tags and forces "if the runner did not walk [off the field voluntarily when he knew he was out]." The umpire did not call base outs unasked. It was an appeal play by the players. In 1860, if runners were out, they were expected to walk off [the field]. To know you were out and to remain on the base hoping the umpire would miscall the play was considered dishonest, even if it was only you who knew. Hard to believe? Consider if you were watching a golf tournament today and, as the golfer was lining up his shot, he happened to inadvertently tap the ball a couple of inches. Would it be an accepted professional practice to kick it back hoping nobody saw? Only he knew. This ethic that still exists in golf existed in early base ball. If you believed that you were "not out" and remained on the base and the fielder also knew you were "not out," play resumed with no call. If the fielder

believed you were out, yet you believed you were "'not out," the fielder would call to the umpire "judgment" or a holdover from cricket, "how's that?" Only then would the umpire pass judgment.

Having addressed the way that most decisions were made, Hunkele goes on to observe that there are two meanings for the term "appeals" as used in the rules of the game. "These appeals for judgment are not to be confused with arguing an umpire's decision on a call that has already been made. This 'kicking and chaffing' was well documented as poor form." While some 1860-era programs have a policy against anyone but the captain making an appeal of a call by the umpire, Hunkele points out that it was not until 1868 that the rules stated that "the captains of each nine shall alone be allowed to appeal for the reversal of a decision of an umpire." Prior to that, gentlemanly communication between the players and the umpire was the norm.

Members of the early clubs were playing with, against, and in front of people they knew from previous matches and with whom they had business and social interaction away from the ball diamond. Consequently, with his personal reputation on the line when he stepped upon the ball field, a player would not have acted in a way that would show him to be anything but an honest, upright, well-mannered person who would not do anything to sully his standing in the community. But even among fair-minded base ball players who are trying to conduct themselves in a gentlemanly manner, sometimes a play is very close and a ruling from an impartial arbiter is needed. Did the runner beat the throw to the base on a close play? Did the fielder, diving on the grass, catch the ball on the first or second bounce? Sometimes the participants in the play honestly cannot tell. In such cases the players would ask for a judgment from the umpire and he would make the call.

The vintage base ball umpire, when asked to make a decision on a close play, should not make the calls in a dramatic, flamboyant manner (with accompanying emphatic gestures), as is often the case with modern professional baseball umpire. He should not shout, "Yer out!" while raising his thumb in the air or "Safe! Safe! Safe!" while rapidly spreading his arms wide with palms down. Umpires announced their decisions in a restrained and dignified manner, and hand signals were not yet commonly used.

In addition to knowing the existing rules inside and out and understanding how to interpret them, the vintage umpire must also know which rules were not on the books yet and must be able to react quickly and correctly to situations not covered in the rules. For example, the 1860 Rules do not specifically address what should happen when a base runner is struck by a batted ball from the striker. The umpire needs to know how to handle this situation should it arise. The thoughtful, well-informed, umpire usually makes rulings based on the intent of the player and the gentlemanly context of the times and endeavors to determine how an 1860-era umpire would have made the call. In this case, as "the judge of fair and unfair play," he would probably let play continue if he believes the runner was struck accidentally by the ball. If he believes the runner let the ball hit him to prevent a fielder from getting to it or if the runner intentionally kicked the ball, he may call him out for conduct that seems to be contrary to the rules on interference and therefore unsportsmanlike for the period.

Despite his reserved and understated role during the match (consistent with the historic figure he represents), the umpire is the glue that holds the vintage game together, and it would be difficult to overemphasize the importance of his role. As Chadwick observed in *Beadle's Dime Base-Ball Player*, "The Umpire should constantly bear in mind that upon his manly, fearless, and impartial conduct in a match mainly depends the pleasure that all, more or less, will derive from it" (p. 30). Chadwick's words ring true today. If planning a special game before a large audience, the first person who should be lined up to be present at the match is the vintage club's most experienced and most competent umpire.

The umpire's conduct and demeanor will set the tone of the day for the players and the spectators. His ability to make quick decisions that are accurate and fair will enable the game to move smoothly without confusion or misunderstandings. By paying close attention to the action on the field and making the correct calls in a confident manner, he can quietly and effectively establish a pleasant environment and orderly structure for the game. By earning the confidence, respect, and good will of all participants, a first-rate umpire can ensure the game will be a success, regardless of the final score.

Appeals of Decisions

The umpire at a vintage base ball match is always treated with courtesy and respect. Therefore, once he makes a call, appeals of his decisions should be rare and not result in any serious "rhubarbs" of the type that are common in modern professional baseball or amateur softball. If there is a question about a rule, the issue should be raised in a gentlemanly, respectful tone. If the umpire affirms his original decision, the matter is closed and play should proceed without further discussion. There comes a time in any ball game when everyone must agree that the matter has been settled and play needs to proceed. In a vintage game this moment should come quickly, with no protracted arguments to mar the day. Spectators come to a vintage match to watch a base ball game being played and learn about the history of the national pastime. They did not come to watch arguments (that they probably cannot hear) over the finer points of a set of nineteenth-century rules (that they probably do not completely understand). As Henry Chadwick advised a century and a half ago, when a call goes against a player, he should "silently acquiesce" to the decision of the umpire rather than argue about it, and that philosophy continues today in vintage base ball.

Interpreting the Action on the Field

The umpire of the 1860s did not intervene in the game unless called upon and did not make loud and showy calls with hand signals. While the umpire's role at a vintage game is unobtrusive and restrained, he is an extremely vital part of the ongoing effort to keep the spectators informed as the game progresses. His dignified bearing, eye-catching period clothing, and unusual position off to the side of home plate capture the attention of the spectators. Once they figure out that he is the umpire, they sense that he is the person in charge and that his decisions are both fair and binding. Consequently, spectators will be interested in listening to his comments.

If called upon to make a decision, the umpire should make sure the spectators understand the issue involved. For example, if giving a ruling on a questionable catch, instead of merely saying, "The striker is out," he might announce, "Had the fielder caught the ball on the second bound, the striker would have made his first base. But since the catch was made on the first bound, the striker therefore is out."

Period Language

In the above example, note that the umpire used the period phrase "would have made his first base," not the modern terminology "would have gotten a hit." Any time the umpire is called upon to speak, period language adds to the ambiance of the game. Even if the play does not demand that he make a decision, such as an obvious catch of a hard-hit line drive on the first bound, the umpire can help the crowd follow the game and understand what just happened by turning to the spectators seated behind him and remarking in a conversational way, "What a splendid manly catch on the first bound by the left fielder for the first out of the fourth inning!" Comments of this type reinforce the rules for those who have not read the program or have walked up after the match has begun and are trying to figure out what is going on. An umpire who can skillfully employ a bit of period language and the more formal speaking style of the time adds a great deal to the spectators' enjoyment of the match. The umpire can provide an explanation that helps spectators understand what occurred while also transporting them back to the era being portrayed.

For examples of period language, note the vocabulary and phrasing of the rule books, newspaper accounts of games, and the writings of such contemporary observers as Henry Chadwick. For example, if explaining a rule, it is sometimes good to quote the rule in its original language (before providing an explanation in modern terminology if any clarification is still needed). Examples such as a striker "making his first base" or a fielder making a "manly catch" can be assimilated into one's conversation when serving as the umpire at a vintage game. When announcing the score at the end of each inning, if one team has not scored, use of the old-fashioned sounding "aught" (instead of "zero" or "nothing") is encouraged: "At the conclusion of two innings of play, the Forest City Club has scored three runs and the Buckeye Club aught."

Engaging the Spectators

If spectators have difficulty understanding what is going on, they drift away from an activity or demonstration at a museum, historical society, community festival, or other event. In addition to his official duty to make calls on close plays, the umpire is a key figure at a vintage game because of his role as a communicator with the audience.

The umpire's opportunities to get the spectators involved in the match begin before the first pitch. He can approach the spectator area while the players are warming up and chat with them about the weather, the names of the teams that will be playing, other activities going on that day at the grounds, or topics of a period nature if the umpire is knowledgeable and feels comfortable discussing them. Imagine how much audience members at a concert would enjoy it if the conductor or one of the musicians would mingle with them before the performance, chatting about what was on the program of the day and telling them what to watch and listen for when the performance starts. Spectators at a vintage game will be pleasantly surprised to have the opportunity to step back in time and be part of a conversation with a person in period dress, especially when they learn he is the umpire for the game.

As the game progresses, the umpire should call attention to the interesting differences between the 1860 game and the modern game. For example, if the umpire cannot see a play clearly, he may ask the fielder to state if he caught the ball on the first or second bounce, if he tagged the runner with the ball, or if he had his foot on the base when he caught the ball. Similarly, the umpire may ask a runner if he was on or off base when tagged or if he arrived at a base before or after the ball. Although norms have changed dramatically over the decades, players in the game's early days would have answered these questions truthfully, and vintage players do the same. When such incidents occur in a match, the umpire should make it clear to the audience that he is asking the players, on their honor as gentlemen, to provide him with the correct information so that he can make the proper call. Spectators are intrigued by the concept of a fielder acknowledging that the ball hit the ground twice before he caught it and, therefore, the striker should be not be declared out, or a runner admitting he was tagged while off base and, therefore, should be called out. Because this practice is so different from the way close calls are decided in the modern game, the crowd may not immediately realize what is happening unless the umpire explains why there is a brief pause in the match while he steps into the infield area and asks the players what occurred. Such incidents offer a wonderful lesson in the norms of nineteenth-century sportsmanship, but audience members may miss what has transpired in the umpire's short conference with the players if no explanation is provided.

There is evidence that umpires occasionally asked spectators for their advice on making a call. In Haney's *Base Ball Book of Reference for 1867*, Henry Chadwick strongly encourages the umpire to rely on his own judgment in making calls in most cases. However, if the umpire does not have a clear view of the play, he does allow that "there are cases when the testimony of hundreds can be accepted, as in the instance of a foul ball catch outside the circle of spectators, or a fly catch taken close to the ground in the outer field near the circle of spectators, when the testimony of those in the vicinity of the catch may be fully relied on. But unless such overwhelming proof be afforded, the umpire should only decide on points of play actually seen by himself" (p. 51). Asking for input from the spectators might not be a wise course of action in a close match between two vintage clubs in a tournament since the crowd will likely act on its modern-day bias toward the home team and invariably rule accordingly. However, it is an interesting ploy to introduce in a one-sided game where the outcome is not in doubt and the result of one call will not spell the difference between a win and a loss. Regardless of the score, asking for the opinion and assistance of the crowd in making a call on a close play does have historical precedent and obviously gets the spectators involved in the game.

Announcing the Status of the Game

In order to keep the spectators apprised of the progress of the game, it is a good practice for the umpire to announce the score and the inning every time the two clubs change sides, especially if there is no scoreboard to provide this information. Even if there is a scoreboard near the field, verbal interaction with the umpire is appreciated by the spectators and helps the crowd follow the flow of the match.

Amplification

Members of the vintage base ball community have engaged in some interesting discussions over the years regarding the use of electronic amplification at nineteenth-century games. Obviously, microphones and loudspeakers did not exist and would not have been used in the early days of base ball. On the other hand, an important part of the mission of vintage base ball is education and, if the game has drawn several hundred spectators, everyone in attendance will not be able to hear the calls and comments of the umpire as he endeavors to educate the crowd about the game.

At games where the umpire has been provided with a microphone to make announcements and keep the spectators informed, the spectators seem not to notice the microphone or quickly forget about it after the first few minutes it is in use. Veteran vintage base ball umpire Richard Schuricht, who has worn a microphone on numerous occasions when a large crowd is in attendance, endorses this practice. He points out that when a vintage game is fortunate enough to have drawn a large crowd, clubs should make the most of the opportunity to educate and inform the spectators about the game.

When it has been used, electronic amplification seems to add significantly to the spectators' understanding and enjoyment of the game. If the umpire is to be provided with a microphone, it is best if it is a small clip-on or lavaliere type that is not noticeable from a distance. Even if the microphone is a large hand-held model, it is almost always a good compromise to use it for a large crowd. If the game site has announcing facilities (such as a press box), a player or other knowledgeable member of the club may sit in this area and make announcements and share points of play instead of the umpire taking on this role.

As microphones have become increasingly small in recent years, their presence has become less obvious. Nineteenth-century teams did use megaphones to address the crowd. One effective way to downplay the fact that a microphone is being used is to conceal it in a megaphone. This technique can keep the crowd engaged while minimizing the intrusion of modern electronic equipment.

The policies of the museum that provides the setting for the match may govern whether or not any kind of electronic amplification is appropriate. The question of whether or not to use a microphone raises the issue of balancing historical authenticity with the importance of educating the crowd and communicating effectively. Each program should decide this matter according to its own policies and preferences. If the museum hosting the program uses electronic amplification in presenting other demonstrations and programs, it may have no problem using this technology for vintage base ball. If its policies prohibit non-period electronic equipment on the museum grounds, it may want to remain consistent in regard to its base ball games.

If playing at a community event, clubs should always cooperate with whatever arrangements the local organizers have made. If those putting on the program want to have an announcer or umpire use a microphone to keep the crowd informed, the vintage team should readily agree to do so, even if the team, on the basis of historical authenticity, does not use a microphone for games at its home grounds. Each program will need to discuss this point and arrive at an arrangement that fits its situation and institutional policies.

Fines

The constitution of the Knickerbocker Club included a schedule of fines for various transgressions during games. *Baseball: An Illustrated History* by Geoffrey C. Ward and Ken Burns (the companion book to the notable television series) includes a facsimile of a page from the 1848 version of the Knickerbocker Base ball Club's constitution that provides valuable information about proscribed offenses, the magnitude of the fines, and the method of collection.

Section 1 states, "Members when assembled for field exercise, who shall use profane or improper language, shall be fined 6¼ cents for each offense." Subsequent sections called for a fine of 12½ cents for any member "disputing the decision of an Umpire" or "who shall audibly express his opinion on a doubtful play, before the decision of the Umpire is given (unless called upon by him to do so)." Further, "Any member refusing obedience to his Captain, in the exercise of his lawful authority" was subject to a fine of 50 cents. The constitution provided that the fines resulting from these violations "must be paid to the Umpire before leaving the field; and any Member refusing to pay such fines shall be suspended from field exercise until such fines are paid." This last policy is in keeping with the second section of the original Knickerbocker Rules of 1845, which specifies that the umpire "shall keep the game in a book provided for that purpose and note all violations of the By-Laws and Rules during the time of exercise" (p. 7).

Drawing on these precedents, some vintage teams follow the custom of assessing fines for various lapses in decorum and behavior during matches. The player or his captain is asked to pay the fine to the umpire on the spot. The assessment of the fine informs the spectators that early clubs did, in fact, have such a schedule of fines and that there was an expectation of gentlemanly behavior on the part of the players. It also provides an interesting bit of conversation between the umpire and the player that entertains the crowd while providing a quick lesson regarding rules. Other clubs in vintage base ball have questioned whether the match should be temporarily stopped to actually collect the fine on the spot or if it would be more accurate to collect it at the end of the game.

Ed Shuman, founder and captain of the Fulton Mules Base Ball Club in Canal Fulton, Ohio, and a recognized leader in the vintage base ball community, has suggested a procedure for those uncomfortable with interrupting the game to collect the fine. In a posting on the VBBA listserv, he proposed having the umpire publicly announce the fine to the player when the offense occurs, then state that the fine is being recorded in the club book and is to be paid at the conclusion of the match. Shuman observes that this action "does not stop play" yet "it allows a quick example of the fine system," which the club's interpreters can discuss as they chat with the crowd during the match. Some clubs enjoy weaving a few theatrics into the presentation of the game more than others, sometimes even intentionally creating a situation where a fine is assessed in order to convey the point that such fines existed. This is one of those issues best left to each club to discuss and determine what approach it wishes to take in regard to representing fines as part of the early game. Shuman's suggestion is a worthy model. If fines are announced, it would be authentic to state the amount — 6¼ cents or 12½ cents, for example — as specified in the Knickerbocker Club's constitution. Interpreters could explain that these amounts were not trifling sums in 1860. In acknowledging the assessment of the fine, the player involved might issue a brief public apology for his transgression.

Umpiring Advice

There are many excellent umpires throughout vintage base ball who do an outstanding job of officiating at the matches. Among these dedicated and capable arbiters is Richard Schuricht, who umpired in competitive softball leagues for more than 20 years before becoming involved in the vintage base ball program at the Ohio Historical Society in 1991. Since then, he has officiated more than 500 vintage matches as the principal umpire for the Ohio Village Muffins. He has traveled widely to serve as an umpire at numerous tournaments and festivals involving other clubs, and has also umpired a number of special vintage games before large crowds at minor league and major league parks. Schuricht has shared his umpiring acumen and experience through presentations at a number of meetings, seminars, and training sessions. He is known throughout the vintage base ball community for his knowledge of the playing rules, his authentic period clothing and accessories, and his skill at communicating with the spectators while employing period language.

From his earlier training as a softball umpire and his twenty seasons of experience officiating vintage games, Schuricht's most important piece of advice for the new umpire is that he must know where the ball is at all times. "There can not be a play without the ball being involved," he reminds us. Therefore, it follows that the umpire should direct his attention to the ball at all times. "There are a few interference plays that come up now and then that occur away from the ball, but an umpire can't call them correctly unless he first knows what happened to the ball." While this principle may sound easy to observe, Schuricht points out that failure to watch the ball is the most frequent source of missed calls.

When making a call on an on extremely close play involving the runner and the ball arriving at the base at about the same time, Schuricht suggests following the directions of Henry Chadwick in the 1860 edition of *Beadle's Dime Base-Ball Player*: "When the point, on which the judgment is required, is a doubtful one, the rule is to give the decision in favor of the ball" (p. 29). When making a call on whether a ball is fair or foul, Schuricht again looks to the instructions of Chadwick. If the ball is foul, the umpire should make the "foul" call loud and clear, but he should not say anything if the ball is fair (p. 29). A runner may have difficulty distinguishing the difference between the words "fair" and "foul," but if he hears the umpire shout any word, he knows the ball is foul and therefore needs to get back to his base.

In those rare instances when a player in a vintage game may become upset over a close call that goes against him, Schuricht advises that the umpire should not confront the player directly. The best strategy to diffuse any hostility is to walk away from the player and resume the game. If he senses any lingering undercurrent of anger, the umpire should speak to the team captain between innings and ask his cooperation in calming the unhappy player. This advice from Schuricht is in keeping with Chadwick's thoughts on how to handle an instance in which a player forgets himself and complains inappropriately about a call. Acknowledging that "it is next to an impossibility to give entire satisfaction to all parties concerned in a match," Chadwick advised that "the Umpire should ... turn a deaf ear to all outside comments on his decisions, remembering that no gentleman, especially a player, will be guilty of such rudeness and none others are worthy of notice" (p. 29).

Throughout the decade of the 1860s, as the game of base ball became more rough and tumble and players increasingly began arguing with umpires over calls, the position of the umpire became more difficult. The fact that Chadwick had to advise the umpire to turn "a deaf ear" to criticism means that by 1860 such criticism had begun to creep into the game. As the years went on and winning became increasingly important, umpires were subjected to abusive comments and threats. Ernest Thayer's 1888 poem "Casey at the Bat" contains a passage that shows how much things had changed in a fairly short span of time since the days when umpires were "given easy chairs," "provided with fans on hot days," and honored with three cheers by the players in appreciation for their service:

"Kill him! Kill the Umpire!" shouted some one from the stand;
And it's likely they'd have killed him had not Casey raised his hand.

Vintage programs portraying the antebellum era represent the antithesis of the "kill the umpire" mentality that became part of the game as time went on. These programs endeavor to preserve the gentlemanly behavioral norms of the early years of the game when the umpire was treated with great respect. However, while 1860-style vintage base ball is played for recreation and exercise and is conducted in a sportsmanlike atmosphere, it is still important, in fairness to the players on the two clubs who are giving their top effort, to get the calls right. The skilled umpire who maintains the dignity and decorum of the game, applies the nineteenth-century rules appropriately, makes the proper calls in the correct manner, keeps the game moving at a brisk pace, and effectively interacts with the spectators throughout the course of the match is a valuable asset to any program and a splendid ambassador for the sport of vintage base ball.

13

The Scorer

Re-Creating the Historic Character

The scorer was an important figure at a mid-nineteenth-century match. The scorer is often pictured in nineteenth-century illustrations sitting at a table near the playing field while recording the action. In order to portray the game authentically, the scorer should be represented at a vintage base ball match. Box scores of matches from the 1850s and 1860s typically include the names of the umpires and scorers. Like the umpire, the scorer was a respected official of the game.

In the early days of the game, the scorer was a member of one of the clubs playing in the match (rather than an official provided by the association). In vintage base ball, as in the nineteenth century, the scorer may be a club member who enjoys serving as the club's scorekeeper on a regular basis and prefers this role to playing on the field. The scorer sometimes is a player who is injured or (especially if the vintage club has a policy that calls for a rotation of duties) a member who usually plays but is taking the day off in order to take his turn at keeping the score of the game. The important point is that in addition to at least nine players in uniform, a vintage base ball club should always have a person in period dress seated at a table keeping score at every game.

Section 28 of the 1860 Rules lists four responsibilities for the umpire, some of which relate to record keeping. The second of these responsibilities is the stipulation that (for intra-squad games) "he shall keep a record of the game in a book prepared for the purpose." For matches between two different clubs, Section 29 of the 1860 Rules transfers this record-keeping responsibility to others by stating that the umpire "shall perform all the duties enumerated in Section 28, except recording the game, which shall be done by two scorers, one of whom shall be appointed by each of the contending clubs."

It could be inferred that the practice of having two scorers, one from each club, may have been adopted so that they could keep an eye on each other and make sure all runs and outs were being credited as they should be. However, due to the emphasis placed on sportsmanship and fair play in the 1860s, honesty would not have been a concern. Two more probable explanations come to mind.

First, it is likely that (in that long-ago time before photocopiers) each team wanted to keep and preserve a record of the game. Since keeping a box score of each match is specified in the early rules and is one of the oldest traditions of the game, vintage clubs should definitely follow this practice of maintaining a written record of all their matches.

Second, due to the fast pace of a high-scoring vintage game, it is sometimes difficult for one person to observe and record all the action as quickly as it happens. Vintage games tend to move along briskly with many base runners, batters often hitting the first pitch, and an abundance of scoring. Therefore, it can be difficult for one person to keep track of the action. Just as one runner has crossed the plate and his run is being recorded, the next batter may have stepped in and struck the first pitch, scoring another runner or two. As the scorekeeper looks down to tally those runs on the score sheet, another batter may have come to bat and hit the first pitch, either making an out that needs to be recorded or perhaps making his base and sending more runners scurrying around the bases.

While all this is going on, a spectator may choose that moment to approach the scorer with a question about the rules or something that happened on the field, distracting the scorer from his job of keeping track of the game. Consequently, it is helpful to have more than one pair of eyes watching the game to make sure everything gets recorded correctly and to double-check the total number of runs and outs.

This practice of having two scorers is followed whenever possible in a vintage match. It is sometimes the case that there is only one scorekeeper available to keep the box score for both teams. Two scorers are preferable since that practice would be more historically authentic.

The captains should submit the lineups for the match in writing to the scorer in advance of the game so that the scorer has time to enter the striking order on the score sheet before the game starts. The scorer should not be handed a scrap of paper containing the lineup moments before the match begins and then be expected to record the names of the batters correctly as they go through the batting order for the first time. The striking order should contain the last name of each player (as was the custom of the day), not just first names or nicknames.

In the 1860 Rules for the Massachusetts Game, as published in Preston Orem's *Baseball (1845–1881) from the Newspaper Accounts,* runs are referred to as tallies, and the person keeping the score of the game is referred to as the tallyman. The terms "tallyman" and "tallies" were also used in cricket. Although the Massachusetts Game and cricket declined in popularity in America after the Civil War, use of the term "tally" in reference to scoring a run seems to have remained part of the language of the game. The popular 1877 base ball song written by John T. Rutledge "Tally One for Me" includes the lyric:

> I always make a clean base hit,
> And go around you see,
> And that's the reason why I say
> Just tally one for me, Oh!

The rules for the New York Game published in the 1860 edition of *Beadle's Dime Base Ball Player* and the box scores from the era consistently refer to the person keeping the score of the game by the term "scorer." However, some vintage programs also use the terms "scorekeeper" or "tallyman." Since games were being played under both Massachusetts Rules and the New York Rules in the 1840s, 1850s, and early 1860s, and since cricket was played in this period, it seems likely that, in addition to referring to the person keeping the score of the game as the scorer, the terms tallyman and tallies may well have been used informally and interchangeably by practitioners of the New York Game as synonyms for scorer and runs.

Period Clothing

The scorer at a vintage match should always be in period dress. As in the case of vintage base ball umpires, those who serve as scorers on a regular basis enjoy assembling a set of period gentleman's clothing (shirt and tie, trousers, vest, coat, shoes, and hat) to wear at games. Unlike the players and the umpire, who may be able to move in and out of the shade during the game on a hot sunny day, the scorer typically remains seated at his table throughout the match. If the table is in the direct sun, the scorer is trapped in that location for the duration of the match. From his years of experience in scoring hundreds of vintage games, John Wells offers the following thoughts on staying comfortable while sitting in the sun for several hours on a hot day:

> 1. The most important part of a scorer's vintage clothing is a straw hat with a wide brim to keep the wearer cool and prevent sunburn.
> 2. A light-colored or white suit of clothes is much more comfortable on hot sunny days than a dark suit.
> 3. If wearing woolen trousers, it is wise to wear a pair of light-weight cotton pajama bottoms under them. This extra layer keeps the wearer cooler and more comfortable than having the hot, scratchy woolen fabric next to the skin. Also, the pajama bottoms can be easily laundered, and the woolen trousers will not need to be dry-cleaned as often.
> 4. Sunscreen should be kept on hand. While his arms and legs are covered by period clothing, the scorer should be careful about the backs of his hands, since his hands are resting on the table for several hours, exposed to the sun's rays. This can be a serious problem at a festival or tournament where the same person may be assigned to serve as the scorer for three or four consecutive matches, spending most of the day in the sun. Since the nineteenth-century scorekeeper did not have sunscreen, it should be applied before arriving at the field. If any further application of sunscreen is needed, it should be done discreetly (out of the view of the spectators, if at all possible).

Like the players and the umpire, the scorer strives to accurately portray his nineteenth-century counterpart, particularly in matters of language, attire, scorekeeping materials, and equipment.

Position on the Field: The Scorer's Table

In modern professional baseball, the official scorer is out of sight in the press box. Most fans never see him and are unaware of his existence during the game. In the mid-nineteenth century, however, the scorer was seated near the playing field, where he could observe and record all the action.

The two scorers, one for each team, can share a wooden table and should be provided with wooden chairs. Modern lawn chairs and folding metal card table chairs seriously detract from the look of a vintage game and should not be used. The first thing a spectator sees when looking upon the field should definitely not be the back of a modern-looking vinyl or aluminum lawn chair. While a vintage club is not expected to use authentic antique furniture in an outdoor setting where it might get damaged by rain and sun, every effort should be made to use wooden furniture that does not have a modern appearance. Old wooden dining room chairs, kitchen chairs, or school room chairs obtained at a yard sale or flea market work well for this purpose.

The table should be made of wood and be large enough to accommodate two scorers. Many clubs use a wooden folding table of nineteenth-century design. These are available through companies that make equipment and camp furniture for Civil War reenactors. Sometimes referred to as a campaign table, one of these tables is ideal for use by the scorer in that it can be collapsed and easily transported to games.

Period illustrations indicate that the scorer's table was situated near the infield in foul territory, sometimes off the first-base line and sometimes off the third-base line. The "Evolution of the Baseball Diamond" by Tom Shieber in the 1994 edition of *The Baseball Research Journal* includes a diagram published in the *New York Clipper* in December 1856. This drawing indicates that the position for the scorer is in the foul territory on the first-base side of home plate. The location in this diagram is on a line that is an approximate extension of the third-base line through home plate. In other words, if a runner proceeding from third base to home would cross the plate and continue jogging or walking in a straight line for several more yards, he would arrive at the scorer's table.

An often-reproduced illustration of an 1866 game in progress at Athletics Park in Philadelphia also shows the scorer's table in foul territory on the first base side of the diamond. Unlike the 1856 diagram, the table is quite close to the base line and much closer to first base than home plate. In this illustration, distances appear to have been foreshortened and some elements in the picture are not to scale, apparently due to the artist's attempt to capture a large scene on a relatively small surface. Even allowing for these inaccuracies, it is apparent that the scorer at this game was positioned not behind the plate as in the 1856 diagram, but fairly close to the first-base line and the first-base bag.

Other illustrations place the scorer on the third-base side of the diamond. Two fine books on early baseball history, *The Old Ball Game* by Mark Alvarez and *Diamond: The Evolution of the Ballpark* by Michael Gershman, include an illustration of a June 15, 1865, game in progress between the Philadelphia Athletics and the Brooklyn Resolutes at the Union Grounds in Brooklyn. The scorer's table is shown in foul territory down the third-base line, a few feet outside the base line and much closer to third than home. *The Old Ball Game* also contains a woodcut depicting an 1857 game at the Elysian Fields between the Gotham Club and the Eagle Club that shows the scorer's table (occupied by two scorers) in foul territory off the third-base line, about halfway between home and third.

Since the evidence from the period provides several locations for the scorer's table, there is no fixed pattern in vintage base ball. As long as the scorer has an unobstructed view of the game so that he can record it correctly, other factors, such as the location of shade trees and the placement of the spectator areas, may be taken into account. Placing the scorer's table in the shade (if there is any near the field) is a good idea. Cool shade on a hot and sunny summer day is no small consideration, especially if the scorer is wearing woolen trousers, vest, and coat.

Some common sense and safety considerations also enter into the decision. For instance, the scorer's table should be placed sufficiently far from home plate so that it would be unlikely that the catcher would run into it while chasing after a foul ball or trying to catch it on the fly or first bound — a common play in vintage base ball. For safety's sake, the table should be far enough in foul territory so that the scorer is not likely to be struck by a foul line drive hit by a pull hitter who gets a little out front of the pitch. The table should not be so close to the third-base line that it would be a hazard to a runner making a wide turn around the base as he heads for home. To reduce the chance of injuries, this possibility should be anticipated and all care taken to protect the base runner and the scorer.

No matter where the table is located (unless it is under a tree or canopy), it is always possible that a foul pop fly may come down near or directly on the table. The catcher, first baseman, or third baseman in hot pursuit of the ball could collide with the table, especially if they are looking up while following the flight of the ball. For this reason the scorer's table should not have any sharp edges, protruding nails, a glass top, or other unnecessary hazards that could lead to injuries to the players. If a foul pop-up does appear to be coming down in the vicinity of the scorer's table, the scorer needs to be alert and ready to move immediately to avoid being struck by the descending ball or a fielder sprinting after it. The ball bounding off the table is still very much in play since it has not hit the ground.

Spectator proximity is another important consideration in table placement. Ideally, the person keeping score should be seated close enough to the spectators to be able to talk to them during the game and help them understand and follow the game. Some commentary from the scorer can be very helpful, especially in the case of the rules relating to unfamiliar plays, such as first-bound catches, fair-foul hits, and foul-tip putouts by the catcher. These plays, which occur frequently in vintage games, differ from the modern game and may need some explanation. If located close to the spectators, the scorer can have a stack of handouts and programs to distribute and can field questions from the audience. Interacting with the spectators may tip the scales in favor of placing the scorer's table on the third-base line. Since the umpire usually stands along the first-base line, having the scorer's table on the third-base line places one official on each side of the field. With these considerations in mind, the ideal location for the scorer's table would be a spot close enough to the diamond to afford a clear view of the action, yet far enough from the foul line to stay out of harm's way and in a shady spot close to the spectators.

The Well-Equipped Scorer's Table

Period illustrations and other references to cricket indicate the score was sometimes kept by a tallyman using a knife to cut notches on a stick. This practice may have carried over to early forms of base ball. However, the 1845 Knickerbocker Rules specify that the record of the game shall be kept "in a book provided for that purpose." Therefore, the experienced scorer brings all the proper supplies needed to fulfill his duties. These supplies should be carried in a woven basket, wooden box, canvas or carpet-style bag, or other container made of natural materials and of a design and color consistent with the period being re-created.

Through both formal presentations and informal conversations, long-time scorer John Wells has provided many clubs with instructions and suggestions on effective scorekeeping. From his own experiences and information shared by veteran scorers for other clubs, he recommends taking a large wicker basket to the game that contains the following items:

1. A supply of score sheets. A club should devise and print an authentic-looking score sheet for use at matches and have an ample supply printed in advance. The scorer should keep score on an official score sheet, not on the back of an envelope or a piece of notebook paper. White paper is fine, but various shades of ivory or light tan are widely available and printing the score sheets on off-white paper gives an old-time look. The score sheet should contain spaces for the information the club retains in its records, such as the lineup for the game, the names of the participating clubs, date, location of the match, time of day the match began, the name of the umpire, the name of the scorer, and a place to keep a running tabulation of the score and the final score of the match.

The score sheet should have a grid similar to a modern scorecard or scorebook in which the striking order is listed and each turn at bat is recorded, inning by inning. Vintage games are often high-scoring affairs, and it is not uncommon for a team to bat completely through the order, with some players getting more than one turn at bat in an inning. Therefore, it is wise to have a double column for each inning. A place for a tenth and eleventh inning is a good idea for tie matches extending to extra innings.

2. A dozen sharpened pencils. These pencils should have both the erasers and paint removed (an Exacto Knife is recommended for this purpose). In the Civil War era, pencils did not have erasers and were of natural wood color. The task of preparing the pencils only takes a few minutes but should occur well in advance of the game — not at the game site with spectators watching. If natural wood pencils can be obtained at an office supply store, that saves much of the work of stripping off the paint; even so, any manufacturer's logos should be removed. A modern pencil sharpener can be kept in the basket for preparing pencils ahead of time but should be kept out of sight when spectators are present. A scorer adept at whittling a sharp pencil point with an antique pocket knife would be an amusing detail for the crowd.

3. Eraser. With no erasers on the pencils, a block-style eraser in an unobtrusive color should be kept on hand.

4. Weights to hold the score sheet down on windy days. Clean flat stones are adequate for this purpose, and a few should be carried in the basket. Nothing of modern manufacture (such as car keys or a cell phone) should ever be used as a weight to hold down the score sheets.

5. Eyeglasses. If the person who performs scorekeeping duties on a regular basis wears glasses, he might consider obtaining a pair of eyeglasses of period design or a modern style of wire-frames with a near-period look.

6. Tin cup. A scorer should remember to drink water during the game when sitting out in the sun on a hot day. He should drink from a period container such as a tin cup and never have a plastic water bottle, Styrofoam cup, or aluminum beverage can sitting on the scorer's table. The scorer can refill the tin cup from the water supply available to the players or carry more water in his basket, discreetly refilling the cup.

7. Clean white handkerchief. Perspiration can be a nuisance on a hot day, especially when wearing woolen clothing (coat, trousers, vest, and tie). As a well-dressed gentleman wearing period clothing, the scorer carries a white handkerchief rather than a red bandana.

8. Several period base balls. With spectators frequently approaching the scorer's table to ask about the ball being used in the game, it wise to be prepared for this inquiry. Also, the scorer should always be ready to promptly replace a game ball that is temporarily lost. If the game ball goes into woods or underbrush bordering the playing field, the scorer can quickly provide the umpire with another game ball and the match can continue without any delay. Vintage base balls are relatively expensive and need to be found, but teams should never keep spectators waiting while players stop the game and rummage around in dense foliage looking for a lost ball.

9. Ink well and pen (optional). Using pen and ink to keep score is usually not practical since the ink in the pen point tends to dry out too quickly on hot days. However, an old-fashioned ink well and a pen are a nice touch on the scorer's table. The scorer might want to use pen and ink to fill in some of the information on the score sheet (date, clubs, location) before the game, use a pencil to keep score during the game, and then use the pen again to record the final score and sign the score sheet at the end of the match.

10. Handouts. If the club has a brochure or program that is given to spectators, the scorer should have a supply close at hand for distribution.

11. Coin. In case the umpire forgets to bring a coin to toss at the beginning of the match, the scorer should be ready to provide one.

12. Patriotic bunting and thumb tacks (optional). A small piece of red, white, and

blue cotton bunting provides a colorful touch when installed on the front edge of the scorer's table.

13. Period calling cards (optional). In the mid-nineteenth century, a gentleman sometimes carried a card advertising his business or profession with a photograph on one side. Known as a Carte-de-Visite (or "CdV"), the card is an interesting item for the scorer to hand to a spectator. In addition to the photograph on the front, the card can include facts about scorekeeping or general information about the program.

The well-prepared scorer may also have several non-period items out of sight in the basket, such as sunscreen, a first-aid kit (since minor injuries can occur among the players), and a club fact sheet since spectators may ask questions that call for follow-up, such as how to schedule the vintage club to appear at an event, how to start a vintage team, or how to become a team participant or a volunteer at the historical society.

Knowledge of the Game

The scorer must be familiar with the rules by which the game is being conducted and watch the game action closely in order to compile an accurate record of what happened. It is especially important for the scorer to help the team captains and the umpire determine that the batters are striking in the proper order. The rules of base ball published in *Porter's Spirit of the Times* in December 1856 state that "players must take their strikes in regular rotation; and after the first inning is played, the turn commences with the player who stands next to the one on the list who lost the third hand." The rules adopted by the February 25, 1857, convention of base ball clubs and the 1860 Rules in *Beadle's Dime Base-Ball Player* contain this same language regarding the batting order.

Wood chairs and scorer's table set the scene, as do details like Ohio Village Muffin Mark Large's pewter inkwell and tankard.

At first glance, this rule appears to be the same as the modern rule, but, in fact, it operates quite differently because it includes outs made on the bases as well as by batting. If the last out of an inning is made by a base runner, that runner (not the striker who hit the ball) was considered to be the player who "lost the third hand." Under these rules, it is easy for the players to lose track of whose turn it is to go to the plate when the next inning starts. The scorer has the correct information on the score sheet and, in order to keep the game moving along smoothly and avoid any mix-ups, should remind the umpire and the captains of the name of the player who should lead off the inning. More detail on this rule is presented in Chapter 21.

Scoring the Game: Scorekeeping Methods

In *The Joy of Keeping Score: How Scoring the Game Has Influenced and Enhanced the History of Baseball*, Paul Dickson observes that "the world is divided into two kinds of baseball fans: those who keep score at a ball game ... and those who have never made the leap" (p. 1). Dickson includes a passage from "The Pleasure of Keeping Score," an article by C.P. Stack in the May 1914 issue of *Baseball Magazine* that suggests, "The fan who fails to do it misses half the game. Most spectators ... leave the grounds with a hazy idea of a rather enjoyable afternoon," but will need to read the newspaper account of the game later to recall the details of what happened. "Keeping score remedies all this," writes Stack. "It burns the play into memory. It greatly increases the spectator's knowledge of the game. It increases ... his pleasure in watching a contest."

In a similar spirit, every vintage club that aspires to any degree of historical accuracy should make sure that a score sheet is kept of every game. To paraphrase Stack, the club that fails to do it misses half the fun and a good part of the experience of playing vintage matches. Memories fade. Box scores preserve memories and attach an aura of purpose and accomplishment to the games. Without a box score of each game, the members of a club will have difficulty recalling what happened in past games and will have no record of who played in the game, the date, the location, or the outcome. Fortunate is the club that has several members who enjoy the non-playing pursuits of umpiring and scorekeeping. These members elevate the club and the sport of vintage base ball by their service as game officials. A skilled and dedicated scorer—a club member who knows that keeping an accurate box score "increases his pleasure in watching a contest" and takes satisfaction in preserving a record of the club's activities on the field of play—is a valuable asset to a vintage base ball program. That person's contributions should be not be overlooked.

Dickson points out that from the game's early days "many different systems emerged—some of which were so informal as to be lost to the twentieth century." Dickson reports that in 1874, Henry Chadwick, usually credited in his lifetime with being the "Father of Base Ball" and the person who brought the box score to the game, called for one uniform scoring system to be adopted. "Then as now," Dickson writes, "there is no single system of scoring, and Chadwick's call for unity has gone unheeded. However, the urge to keep score and keep track of the game remains keen, for baseball begs to be recorded and recalled in shorthand" (pp. 7–9).

While it is true there are many systems for keeping score, one way to get started in basic scorekeeping would be to use the a grid with space for the players' names and positions down the left side, with two columns allotted for each inning. If a player makes an out, either while batting or running the bases, simply put a 1, 2, or 3 after his name, indicating whether it was the first, second, or third out of the inning. This provides a handy reference if anyone asks how many outs there are or what batter should lead off the next inning. If the striker reaches base, the scorer begins to draw the four sides of a diamond to track the runner's progress around the bases, and fill in the diamond if he scores a run.

The scorer should keep a tally of the runs scored each inning and a running total of runs scored in the game at the bottom of the page. This will enable the scorer to answer quickly and correctly if the umpire, players, or spectators inquire about how many runs have been scored in the inning or the score of the game. At the end of the match, the scorer can add up the total runs scored by each player and enter that number in the far right column of the score sheet. The basic system of recording runs scored and outs made (sometimes designated as "O" for outs or "H.L." for hands lost in box scores) is recommended for those getting started in vintage base ball and for those who wish to keep an authentic box score in a way that everyone can read and understand.

Examples of nineteenth-century score sheets appear in a number of books, including Dickson's *The Joy of Keeping Score* (pp. 8, 15) and *The Barry Halper Collection of Baseball Memorabilia, Vol. I: The Early Years*, the auction catalog published by Sotheby's in 1999 (pp. 86, 93, 100, 105). *The Old Ball Game* by Mark Alvarez contains a very legible page of an 1847 game recorded in the Knickerbocker Club score book, which shows the system of marking 1, 2, and 3 for the outs as they occurred each inning and placing tally marks for each run scored. In addition to providing insight regarding scoring methods, these images of score sheets from the nineteenth century furnish excellent examples of the layout and fonts that were used so that a vintage club can create a score sheet that has an authentic appearance.

Some vintage base ball participants who enjoy keeping score have done considerable research on the history of scorekeeping and scoring methods used by specific clubs in various eras. Some of these historic systems capture not only information on whether the striker reached base and scored, but also the fielding record of which defensive player made the putout and how he did it (fly catch or bound, fair or foul). This can work if each of the nine players plays the same position throughout the game, but it is difficult for the scorer to keep defensive records if the players change positions frequently, as is often the case in a vintage game. These more advanced and complex scoring systems from the game's early days were often based on a set of scoring symbols that is considerably different from those in use today. They can be complicated to use and decipher unless one is an expert on period scoring methods. Those interested in the scoring system used and recommended by Henry Chadwick are encouraged to consult "How to Score in Base Ball" in Haney's *Base Ball Book of Reference for 1867* (pp. 61- 71). This section contains Chadwick's scoring symbols, including "K" for "struck out," a notation that remains in use today. Chadwick provides a narrative of a sample game along with his explanation of how to score each play as it occurs. While interesting to examine, many find his system difficult to master, and choose to use the more basic method of recording runs and outs. Keeping records of runs scored and outs made is the usual pattern followed by most vintage clubs.

Interpreting the Action and Involving the Spectators

In vintage base ball, the scorer plays an important role in keeping the crowd informed and engaged in the game. If the table is located near the spectators, the scorer can converse with them throughout the match, anticipating their possible confusion over novel and complicated plays and offering helpful explanations of rules and practices. The scorer can also respond directly to their questions and comments.

Some conversation between the umpire and the scorer between innings is also a good way to keep the spectators engaged while the nines change sides on the field. The umpire can ask the scorer how many runs were scored during the half inning just completed. He may know the answer to his own question, but by asking it in a loud voice and receiving an answer from the scorer's table, the spectators are kept informed. Similarly, the umpire can ask for the total number of runs scored by each club so far in the match and announce it to the crowd every half inning. This is especially important if there is no scoreboard or if the placement of the scoreboard makes it difficult for some of the spectators to see it. The umpire and scorer may conduct a ongoing "conversation" (loud enough for the spectators to hear) to provide comments on unusual plays in order to make sure that everyone understands why a batter was called out or why a run was either permitted to count or disallowed.

This exchange has some practical value in making sure the scorer and umpire truly are in agreement on the score of the game, but usually the conversation is more of a semiscripted short theatrical performance — a device to keep the crowd entertained and informed. In addition to discussing the game, the scorer and umpire may wish to make a few comments on some of the political and social issues that would have been a topic of conversation in the period represented on the field, such as women's suffrage, the temperance movement, or which candidate they plan to vote for in an upcoming election. They may also evoke the realities of nineteenth-century travel by commenting on the visiting team having made a long "carriage ride" to the game. They can keep visitors informed of other activities that are scheduled after the game (a concert or picnic) and the next scheduled matches for the clubs.

Even if simply making small talk about the weather or the size of the crowd, any period conversation between the umpire and the scorer's table is well received by the spectators. An experienced umpire and scorer who can conduct these conversations in period language form an interpreting team that is exceptionally valuable for the success of a vintage base ball program. Their conversations (some extemporaneous and some rehearsed) add immeasurably to the total experience of the spectators.

Keeping Statistics

In the game's early years, the scorer kept track of two statistics for strikers: runs scored (sometimes called "aces") and outs made (sometimes called "hands lost"). Marshall Wright, in *The National Association of Base Ball Players, 1857–1870*, explains that in the early days of the game scorers recorded the number of games each player participated in, the number of runs he scored, and the number of outs he made.

The "average and over" system was then applied to evaluate his performance. Using the statistical records that Wright has meticulously compiled for the NABBP era, consider the 1860 statistics for Asa Brainard, a member of the Excelsior Club of Brooklyn who gained great fame later in his career as a pitcher on the undefeated 1869 Cincinnati Red Stockings. In 1860 Brainard played in 19 games at second base and the outfield and scored 48 runs. Dividing the runs scored by the games played (48 divided by 19) gives 2 whole runs per game plus 10 left over. His average and over statistics for runs scored would be listed with a decimal point as 2.10 (also listed sometimes with a comma, as 2, 10). He also was charged with 58 hands lost, or outs. Dividing outs by games played (58 divided by 19) we get an average and over of 3.1 (or 3, 1). Teammate Joe Leggett, one of the great catchers of the era, scored 70 runs in 20 games, giving him an average and over of 3.10 (3, 10). He had 46 hands lost for an average and over of 2.6 (2, 6). One could conclude from this comparison that Leggett was the better offensive player since he scored more runs per game (3.1 to 2.10) than Brainard and made fewer outs (2.6 to 3.1) per game.

Batting averages (hits divided by times at bat) were not calculated at this time. Scorers did not even keep track of hits. The practice of recording what we think of today as "hits" did not begin until after the Civil War in the late 1860s. In his history of the NABBP,

Wright provides this interesting account of the origin of the new custom of counting hits. "In the report of the September 10, 1867, game between the Eureka and Union clubs, a new wrinkle was added to the box score. As well as the usual hands lost and runs reported, a new category was added. This was explained in a brief addendum in the *New York Clipper*: 'In addition to the usual columns of outs and runs we have added ... bases on hits, designated 'B' ...We shall pursue this course in all first class games hereafter.'" Wright comments that "with this new statistic, baseball was endeavoring to find a new yardstick to measure a player's worth" (p. 186).

Although the number of runs scored had been the principal offensive statistic up to that time, Wright concludes, "Base ball scribes were rightly reasoning that to score runs, a player had to reach base. It followed then that the surest way to reach base was on a safe hit, beyond the reach of any fielder." In 1868, a new format for the box score debuted that "contained the number of hits garnered by each player in addition to his total bases" (p. 187). As with many changes in the rules and practices of the game, not everyone accepted the new scoring conventions immediately. "Unfortunately," observes Wright, "most teams clung to the old ways as they still only kept track of outs and runs" (p. 187).

Examining the statistics and scorekeeping practices of 1870, Wright points out that a player's success was measured by his number of hits and total bases, his average number of hits per game, and his average number of bases per game. George Wright of Cincinnati, considered by many to be the best player of this era, led the NABBP in both of the categories where averages were computed with 4.27 hits per game and 7.08 bases per game (248 hits and 411 total bases divided by 58 games played).

If scorers for a vintage club are going to keep any individual statistics over the course of the season, they should be kept in the manner consistent with the era the team represents, not according to modern statistical categories. For 1860-era clubs, the average and over method (rather than the modern and more familiar statistics, such as batting average and runs batted in) should be used. All club members, including players, should have some knowledge of early record-keeping in order to answer questions from the crowd and to know that it would be anachronistic for an 1860-era vintage player to speak of his batting averages or RBIs since those terms were not yet in use.

Knowing how statistics were kept is an interesting part of the game, but program leaders should think carefully about how widely the numbers are shared. This discussion of early statistical methods is intended as a caution against keeping the modern statistics that did not exist in the 1860s. It should not be taken as an endorsement of keeping these individual statistics or making "average and over" statistics public. Publishing any individual statistics in a club newsletter, website, or game program has a definite downside and should be approached with great sensitivity. The average and over statistics can carry some sting for some players, which is needless in the context of a vintage base ball club. Those players near the bottom of the list may be embarrassed if their statistics are significantly lower than those at the top. They may conclude they are not doing their part for the team and even drop out of the program. One of the last things a vintage club should want to do is embarrass a member, especially if that individual is a good contributor to the program in other ways.

While the statistics of modern professional players are published in the paper every day, all vintage players are amateurs playing for fun and do not need to have any weaknesses in their play exposed by a public printing of their statistics. In the interest of building camaraderie and retaining players, great care and restraint should be taken in this area. The best individual statistics to publish are the number of games played or volunteer hours contributed to the program. Participation is to be rewarded and recognized.

Information on nineteenth-century statistics might be covered in a club newsletter or on the website. A club might publish the names of the top three or so run scorers on the team since runs scored is not a statistic that is as emotionally charged as batting average. But any statistical list of all the players on the team, arranged top to bottom in descending order of performance, is likely to lead to problems. A player can always calculate his own "average and over" or modern batting average privately if such numbers are important to him. Every club has its own personality and values in matters of this type and can set its policies on statistics. But copying the way the modern media calculates and publishes individual statistics for major leaguers is not a good model for vintage base ball clubs. Vintage base ball is a team game. Therefore, team statistics are more appropriate to publish.

The Value of Club Records

An accurate score sheet for every match should be kept in a book or folder in a central location. If the club has one primary scorer, he may be the logical one to keep the records. Depending on the organizational structure of the team, score sheets may be turned in to the team manager or someone who has been designated as the secretary, historian, or archivist for the club.

These records should be retained in order to keep everyone informed of how the season is going. It is also important to keep a season-by-season record of the number of games played and the participation by each member. If the club has a weekly or monthly newsletter or maintains a website, some team scores and statistics can be included from time to time to keep members informed. At the end of the season, the club will undoubtedly want to announce or publish a summary of the club's accomplishments. If the club has a year-end picnic or banquet, the information available through the score sheets can be summarized and presented. Participants will be interested in the number of games played, how many people participated in the program, and perhaps other statistics, such as how many runs per game the team averaged or the number of miles traveled as ambassadors for the club's sponsoring organization. If the club or the historical society with which the club is affiliated recognizes participation and volunteer hours, some member of the club needs to keep track of this information.

The members of a successful vintage team, with their interest in the history of base ball, should keep in mind that they are also creating their own history as an organization. In lean financial times, as museum and historical society professionals have to make decisions on financial allocations and apply for appropriations, grants, and subsidies, they need reliable information on team activity, including games played, number of appearances, number of volunteers in the program, and how many volunteer hours were contributed by the program participants. Therefore, it is wise to keep those kinds of records.

Financial issues aside, statistical records will be increasingly important in forming the backbone of the club's history as the seasons go by. Box scores and other statistics bring back memories of enjoyable road trips and special games. Like a personal journal or family scrapbook, the club's record book provides program members with a feeling of continuity and a sense of pride in all the club has accomplished over time. And, of course, all this starts with having a capable, dedicated, and properly dressed scorer keeping an accurate record of each game.

While the male pronoun has been used for the scorer throughout this chapter, there are a number of women who regularly do the score keeping for vintage clubs. As mentioned in the discussion of women in vintage base ball, they make an excellent contribution to the sport of vintage base ball in that capacity. A female scorer should be in appropriate daytime wear authentic to a lady of the period being depicted in the game. In all other respects, her role is the same as a gentleman recording the match at the scorer's table.

14

Interpreters: Enhancing the Game Experience

A vintage game is enhanced by the presence of interpreters in period dress. Historical interpreters typically include museum staff members and/or volunteers. Their presence adds to the effectiveness of re-creating a time period, extends the educational impact of the event, and makes game day fun for everyone.

Re-Creating the Historic Characters

In the terminology used by museum professionals, those who interact with the public to enable them to understand what is going on at a vintage base ball game are classified as either first-person or third-person interpreters. The Association for Living History, Farm and Agricultural Museums (ALHFAM) website includes a glossary of terms, originally published in *Past into Present: Effective Techniques for First-Person Historical Interpretation* by Stacy F. Roth. First-person interpretation is defined as "the act of portraying a person from the past (real or composite).... The standard form is one in which the interpreters refer to the past in the present tense." To accomplish this, interpreters "employ a combination of techniques including storytelling, demonstration, question and answer, and discussion; encourage verbal interaction with the audience; and avoid breaking character." First-person interpreters at a vintage game portray those who would have been in attendance at a ball game in the nineteenth century. Third-person interpretation is provided by "informative, often interactive talks and demonstrations by interpreters who may be dressed in period attire but do not assume character roles." Third-person interpreters do not assume the identity of a character from the past or speak in period language. Rather, in the manner of a traditional museum guide or docent, they describe to the visitor what is happening at the game from the perspective of a person living in the present.

In *Exploring Museum Theatre*, Tessa Bridal, a museum professional in the field of public history, shares Freeman Tilden's Principles of Interpretation from his classic work, *Interpreting Our Heritage*. Writing in the 1950s, Tilden defined interpretation as "an educational activity that aims to reveal meanings and relationships rather than simply communicate factual information" (p. 13). The vintage base ball community uses the term "interpreters" in a general way to refer to those ladies and gentlemen in period dress who mingle with spectators during the game. Interpreters welcome visitors to the match (using period language, if possible), distribute brochures or programs, engage the visitors in conversation, and answer questions about the game. Interpreters at a vintage base ball game can be either first-person or third-person, or a combination of the two. They may present themselves as the town

Acting as interpreters, Jim Kimnach (center) and other club members in period clothing explain the 1860s rules and customs to spectators at Ohio Village Muffin games.

mayor, a teacher, or seamstress. Club members who are ministers, physicians, carpenters, or farmers can present those occupations in the 1860s. A skilled first-person interpreter can carry on a substantial conversation representing a person from the 1860s and, dressed in period clothing and using period language, will consistently "refer to the past in the present tense" in conveying information to the visitor.

However, at times it is necessary to break character to answer questions from spectators about changes in the game over time, such as, "When did they start using gloves?" or "When did they stop playing by the one-bound rule?" An actual person living in 1860 would not know the answers because these developments are in the future and haven't happened yet. If the interpreters pretend they never heard of baseball gloves or requiring the ball to be caught on the fly, it might be humorous for a while, but it can also be frustrating for the museum visitor expecting an answer to a valid question about base ball history. Therefore, an interpreter sometimes will need to step out of his or her 1860 persona and become a third-person interpreter for a few minutes to provide the information the guest is seeking. A skilled and experienced interpreter is more able, of course, to remain in character and find creative ways to respond to inquiries while maintaining his or her nineteenth-century persona. For example, in regard to a question about the bound rule, the interpreter might answer, "I have read that some of the clubs in New York City have been experimenting with requiring the ball to be caught on the fly in order to be declared an out. I predict that within five years or so fly catches will be required. I'll wager that by the time the 1865 rule book is published, there will be no more bound outs on fair balls." This reply provides the information while the interpreter remains in character.

A vintage club is very fortunate to have several ladies and gentlemen who enjoy attending the matches in period dress and performing the educational role of talking with spectators before, during, and after the game. Some interpreters spend considerable effort assembling authentic period clothing and researching the language and customs of the day so that they can interact effectively with the spectators. They model the language players will want to use in their conversations as well. Ballplayers know that interpreters in period dress are an important component of the total experience of attending a match, and their good work adds significantly to the visitors' enjoyment of an afternoon of vintage base ball.

Period Clothing

Men, women, and children in period dress are valuable assets to a program even if they do not interact verbally with the crowd. Just being at the game in period dress adds to the look of the occasion and helps create an interesting tableau at the game site. Some visitors who have only a casual interest in watching a base ball game often enjoy stopping by the match to see people in period dress. Interested in the clothing and accessories being worn by the interpreters or drawn in by a discussion of the political and social issues of the day, they may join the crowd to see what is taking place.

As in the case of properly interpreting the base ball rules and practices of a given era, it is important to be historically accurate in the matters of clothing and accessories. It is helpful to remember that the interpreter's attire is not a costume assembled hastily for a theme party or for Halloween. The interpreter needs to be dressed in the appropriate clothing of the day. A person may own a fringed umbrella, or always wanted to have a Vivian Leigh ball gown, but would the wife of a member of a base ball club wear either to a daytime 1860s game? No. Period dress needs to be authentic.

Many museums and historic sites have high professional standards regarding the period dress worn by their staff members and volunteers while at the museum site. Some prohibit anyone from entering the site in period dress that has not been approved. A volunteer who is interested in putting together a period outfit to wear at vintage games should be aware that this worthy project needs to be approached with a good deal of thought and care, and should be undertaken in consultation with the museum associated with the base ball team rather than independently.

With careful planning, volunteers can avoid the mistake of going to the trouble and expense of obtaining a gentleman's suit or a lady's dress only to find out too late that the clothing they have purchased is inappropriate for the period being re-created by the team. Obviously, it would not be appropriate to wear an 1890s-style dress or hat at an 1860s-style game, but mistakes like this happen if the volunteer does not have knowledge of the attire that would be proper for each era. To the untrained eye, various eras of nineteenth-century clothing may look alike, but there are both substantial and subtle differences in such elements as collar styles, pleats, designs used in fabrics (plaids, checks, etc.), width of hat brims, and other considerations that clearly mark an item as being from a specific time frame.

There are a number of books on fashion history that provide good starting places for information. Picture books on the era being interpreted show images of individuals that can provide clues to dressing authentically. Having done some reading to come up with a few general ideas, it is a good practice for the volunteer to talk to an expert. Museums often have professionals on the staff who have devoted many years to the study of clothing styles and related matters. They may have official responsibilities for costuming staff interpreters, ensuring that everyone in period dress is accurately portraying the correct period. These professionals are eager to share their knowledge and assist volunteers in assembling authentic attire.

These experts know which fabrics, colors, patterns, and styles were worn at various times, and which styles of accessories, such as shoes, hats, bags, and jewelry, are authentic to a historical period. These specialists are great sources of interesting details, such as when it would have been proper for a lady or gentleman to wear gloves and the color and style the gloves. They know what items a lady of 1860 might have carried in her sewing basket or reticule (purse). They are well informed as to when a lady would wear a hoop skirt and the hoop size appropriate to the date and occasion. They know when zippers started replacing buttons and what kind of underclothing is an appropriate accompaniment for various clothing styles. They are knowledgeable about umbrellas and hair nets (snoods, in the terminology of the day) for ladies. They know about pocket watches, walking sticks, and neckties for gentlemen. They can provide good advice about hair styles and eyeglass frames for men and women. Volunteers enjoy learning about these nuances and distinctions and will take pride and satisfaction in knowing that their period attire is truly representative of the era they are attempting to re-create. This background will also be useful when answering questions from spectators.

In addition to their knowledge of what styles are appropriate for a given era, museum professionals and experienced volunteers know where and how to obtain the proper clothing and accessories. They can refer volunteers to websites and catalogs published by companies that sell period clothing, accessories, and other merchandise. They can help with estimating sizes and placing orders. They may know local individuals who sew period clothing and sources for historically accurate sewing patterns if the volunteer wants to take on the project of making his or her own clothing. Those presenting 1860s-era base ball have the advantage of resources developed for the sizeable Civil War reenacting community.

Obtaining a period outfit is highly encouraged and will be a source of great enjoyment. However, for ladies, it takes more than grabbing a modern blouse from the closet and a long skirt from a holiday outfit. For gentlemen, it requires more than attaching clip-on suspenders to a pair of Dockers. Many items from a contemporary wardrobe can be adapted, but attention to detail is required for success. With all the expertise that is often available through a museum or historical society, assembling period attire to wear to the games is a project that need not be undertaken alone.

Gentlemen

In the nineteenth century, not all of the gentlemen who belonged to the club actually played in the game. Men joined the clubs because they enjoyed the social aspects of membership and supported the club's activities by paying dues, serving as club officers, and attending matches. They formed what we might think of in modern terms as a booster group for the nine players who were selected to take the field that day. They may also have served on the field as umpires or scorekeepers.

The American Game of Base Ball, the often-published 1866 Currier and Ives depiction of a game played at the Elysian Fields in Hoboken, New Jersey, shows a group of well-dressed gentlemen standing in foul territory between home and first base. These were probably the members of the club who were not playing in the game. Historians have noted how these gentlemen are turned toward the artist (rather than the game) so that their faces

Vintage base ball is a family activity for many players including this Ohio Village Muffin. Having the whole family wear period clothing to the game is fun for the children and helps spectators identify with the historic period.

are visible and recognizable. This positioning indicates that they are probably members of the club who were fully aware that an artist had been commissioned to do an illustration of the game that would include images of all the club members — the ones participating directly in the game on the field and those supporting the first nine from the sidelines.

In vintage base ball, interpreters may be club members who enjoy coming to the games but do not choose to play, or they may be members who normally do play on the field but are taking the day off from game action (perhaps due to a minor injury or the fact that the club has an abundance of other players available for the day's game). Since they will not be playing that day, they have come in period dress to support their colleagues who are in uniform. Gentlemen in period dress who interact with the spectators are a very valuable part of any vintage club and their presence adds greatly to the overall presentation of the game.

Ladies

Dressing in period clothing is an excellent way for ladies and children to share the enjoyment and excitement of being an active part of a gentlemen's base ball club. Friends and family members of players who enjoy attending vintage games in period dress and chatting with the audience make outstanding interpreters. Vintage teams often have opportunities to walk in pre-game parades; appear on field at minor league and major league ballparks; put on programs for schools, libraries, and civic groups; and visit local community festivals and celebrations. If family members are in period dress, they are usually invited to join in the fun and can march in the parade, go on the field at the professional ballpark, or appear at the community event along with the ball players. Having ladies and children in period dress adds considerably to the look and charm of a vintage game, whether on the playing field or at special events with the team.

In addition to the fun of being a participant in a special event, wearing period clothing and taking part in these activities can be valuable learning experiences. Many wives, girlfriends, siblings, children, and grandchildren enjoy learning more about the period represented by the base ball team and then sharing their knowledge with others. Instead of being a "stag" activity, as is the case with many recreational softball teams, basketball teams, golf leagues, and other sporting activities, women are an important part of vintage base ball. The presence and participation of ladies, especially their willingness to contribute to the overall success of an event by wearing a nineteenth-century dress on a hot summer day, is sincerely appreciated by the gentlemen of the club and the historical organization hosting the match. Having ladies and children in period clothing enables many couples and families to enjoy the vintage base ball experience together.

Vintage teams often have several well-informed ladies present at matches who do a superb job of interpreting the game for the spectators. It should not be assumed that the ladies in period dress are only knowledgeable about clothing styles, food preparation, and similar topics. Many of these women are very knowledgeable about nineteenth-century base ball rules and practices. They are prepared to field base ball-related questions as well as inquiries about their dresses and hats. Many ladies have witnessed dozens of vintage games and have an excellent working knowledge of the finer points of nineteenth-century base ball rules and customs. Some are well-informed fans of major league baseball and understand how the modern game developed from the Knickerbocker Rules to the present.

Children

Putting on the clothes of another era is of special value to children as it gives them a first-hand perspective on life in America 150 years ago. It can stimulate their interest in and their curiosity about history and inspire them to want to learn more. While they would not be expected to interact verbally with the spectators, their presence shows what kind of clothing children wore in the nineteenth century. Having them in the bench area or accompanying adult interpreters adds to the appeal and ambiance of the game.

Being associated with vintage base ball can be a valuable and enjoyable experience for school-age children. These younger members of the families involved in vintage base ball get a magnificent education in sportsmanship by watching at close range as vintage players handle the successes and failures associated with playing base ball — getting a hit or popping up, making a great catch or making an error, winning or losing. They see how vintage players handle both positive and negative outcomes with grace and maturity. Since gentlemanly vintage players do not argue with the umpire, get into tiffs with the opposition, use bad language, engage in showboating, or taunt opponents, these young people observe countless good examples of how to compete and have fun playing sports while maintaining a sense of dignity, decorum, and respect for others.

Hopefully, these lessons carry over to their participation in youth sports or other activities. Children may be exposed to a constant stream of arrogant, inconsiderate, and boorish behavior by some modern professional athletes when they attend games or watch them on television. By re-creating the behavioral norms and standards of another time, vintage base ball sends the message that there is another way to approach athletic competition, one that emphasizes sportsmanship, fair play, appropriate language, civility, respect for officials, and good manners.

Younger children enjoy wearing period outfits on the level of "playing dress-up" and getting a lot of attention from visitors, who often pay them compliments on their period clothing. A nice touch, of course, is to have them looking through a copy of *McGuffey's Reader* or playing with period toys and dolls while at the vintage game (rather than sitting on a blanket and amusing themselves with transformers, video games, and Barbie dolls).

Older children often become genuinely interested in American history as they see connections between topics they are learning in school, the clothes they are wearing, and what is being portrayed on the vintage base ball field. Dressed in period clothing at a vintage game, they may even have the educational experience of being in the right place at the right time to meet an Abraham Lincoln or Mark Twain reenactor. Since vintage teams often play matches at museums and historic sites, road trips to other venues can be quite broadening for a youngster who is part of the team's traveling party. When the Muffins play at various historic sites around Ohio, players whose families include school-age youngsters make it a point to arrive early in order to have time to tour the museum, fort, author's home, or historic farm before the game starts.

Youngsters in period dress may also serve as team mascots and experience the fun of going onto the field and sitting on the bench, often accompanying parents and older siblings who are playing on the team. Mascots (who perform the role of "batboys" in modern terminology) need to be supervised so that there are no incidents like one in the 2002 World Series between the Angels and the Giants in which the oblivious three-year-old son of the San Francisco manager scampered onto the field to retrieve a bat while the ball was still in play and was nearly run over by a player dashing down the third-base line toward home plate.

Properly managed, however, this role can be a lot of fun for a youngster, provide a fine family experience, and teach first-hand lessons about the history of the country and the national pastime. In addition to retrieving bats, youngsters enjoy being assigned jobs, such as chasing after foul balls, putting the numbers on the scoreboard, or taking the umpire or scorer a drink of water between innings. Being on the bench in period clothing and chatting with the players can inspire a youngster to learn more about American history and to think about being a member of the team a few years down the road.

It is critically important that anyone on the bench be in period dress, including children. The entire look and ambiance of the nineteenth-century match is compromised by a youngster sitting on the bench in nylon shorts, a Lebron James jersey, and a pair of sneakers with neon trim. This might be appropriate attire to wear while going to a softball game with dad on Friday evening, but not to sit with him on the bench at the vintage game on Saturday afternoon.

A youngster may not grasp the difference in the two very different types of ball teams, so parents need to inform their children in advance and consider dressing their children in vintage clothing so they can sit on the bench or go on the field before, during, or immediately after the game. Period clothing is also a requirement for being included in team photos. Children look great in vintage outfits and enjoy wearing them. They are very welcome to participate if properly dressed and are encouraged to take part, but they should not be on the playing field or on the bench in modern attire.

Sutlers

Historically, sutlers were nineteenth-century civilian purveyors of merchandise who set up their tents or wagons near the army camps to sell clothing and other items to soldiers. Sutlers do the same today at Civil War reenactments and encampments. One great advantage of a vintage base ball club taking part in a Civil War reenactment is that these events attract sutlers, who are great sources of 1860-style clothing and other wares. Knowing that vintage base ball enthusiasts, like Civil War reenactors, are interested purchasing these items, sutlers sometimes attend vintage base ball gatherings and add to the general ambiance of the day.

A trip to the sutler's tent may yield such useful period items as a coat, vest, or straw hat to wear while umpiring or scorekeeping, or perhaps an authentically made haversack in which to store valuables. Ladies associated with a vintage base ball program always enjoy browsing through the sutler's wares for period clothing, such as dresses, blouses, shawls, capes, aprons, bonnets and various accessories like jewelry, gloves, snoods, combs, and mirrors. Sutlers often carry personal items, such as sewing kits, tooth brushes, soap, picture frames, tin cups, walking sticks, and cooking utensils. These reproduction items are interesting to examine as examples of what people wore and used in their daily lives in the 1860s, and vintage base ball participants often find items to purchase that contribute to their efforts to effectively re-create life in the 1860s. Sutlers are business people who are understandably interested in selling their goods, but they are also usually very well informed about their merchandise. By sharing their knowledge with participants and spectators who visit their tents and wagons, they take on the role of de facto interpreters and add to everyone's understanding of the clothing and customs of the period.

Programs and Printed Information

The work of interpreters is complemented and enhanced by the existence of a printed program. Distributing a program or brochure helps spectators establish the time period of the game they are watching, learn about the early history of base ball, understand the rules and equipment of the period being re-created, and discover the sport of vintage base ball. It extends the vintage base ball experience beyond the game itself. It is best if the printed program is handed directly to the visitor by an interpreter in period dress, rather than just putting out a stack to be picked up by spectators. Having received the program directly from an interpreter upon arrival, the visitor will know who to approach with questions.

The sponsoring museum or historical society may want to use the vintage base ball publication to provide information about some of its other activities and events. If the crowd is large and the interpreters do not get to talk to everyone during the game, the program will provide the basic information about what is going on.

The material in the printed program provides openings for conversation with visitors. The interpreter might approach a visitor and comment on a one-bound catch and point out that this rule is explained in the program. The interpreter can call attention to the team's schedule of upcoming games, especially if the team is about to embark on an out-of-state trip or has a festival or other special event coming up.

Some clubs publish the names of their players in the program. An interpreter can provide some interesting information about a player as he comes to bat or makes a play in the field. Spectators enjoy learning the names and backgrounds of the participants in the game. At a Muffin match, spectators (especially the youngsters) are always interested to know that

Mr. Nightwine, the third baseman, has had a long career as a railroad engineer (an occupation that existed in the 1860s as well as the present day). An interpreter might point out that the first baseman is the father of both the shortstop and the right fielder, or that Professor Kimnach at the scorer's table teaches mathematics at the local college, or that the wife of Mr. Wertz, the center fielder, is one of the ladies in period dress at the match, pointing her out as "the young lady in the yellow dress and bonnet sitting under the apple tree tending the children." If someone asks a question about bats, they enjoy finding out that the pitcher, Mr. Trudeau, and his associate, the left fielder, Mr. Armbruster, make the handsome wooden bats being used in the game. Using the names of some of the players and telling something about them helps engage the interest of spectators. They are more likely to approach a player to ask questions, and it may pique their interest in joining the program.

To attract the eye and the interest of the visitor, the printed program may include a few photos and contain enough content to introduce the spectator to the basics of nineteenth-century base ball. In addition to serving as a reference, it also should function as a nice "takeaway" or souvenir of the visit to the game. Visitors who do not take the time to read it while at the field may look it over more thoroughly later. It should also provide contact information in case a visitor has further questions or is thinking about getting involved in vintage base ball.

No matter how good printed pamphlets and other educational materials might be, some people will simply wander up to see what is going on. During the game, interpreters should repeatedly comment on those practices that are different from today's game (without specifically mentioning contemporary practices) and call attention to the gentlemanly behavior and good sportsmanship that convey the basic character of the game. Comments addressed to the audience can also include frequent references to the year being portrayed on the field when base ball was a fairly new sport, rapidly gaining in popularity as the "national game." Remarks of this type will help establish a general tone for the game, provide the historical context, and encourage spectators to learn more by reading the information in the printed program.

Players as Interpreters

Uniformed players, along with the umpire and the scorekeeper, can also serve as interpreters by striking up conversations with the spectators between innings. If a player's turn at bat is not coming up for a while or if he is sitting out for an inning on defense, he can take a seat among the crowd during the game and explain the action as it unfolds. Rather than sitting on the bench alone while his teammates are in the field, it is common for a player to go over to the spectator seating area, talk with them about the game as it progresses, and point out any unique 1860 rules that come into play.

Spectators react very positively to the opportunity to chat with people in period dress — especially players — during the game and value these interactions. At many professional games, players often ignore spectators. The official policies of professional baseball leagues prohibit players from talking to fans for a specified time before the game until it is concluded. Even during batting practice, an hour or so before a game when players are permitted to talk to the fans, they often walk right past, preferring not to make any eye contact or acknowledge their presence. Vintage base ball players take the opposite approach. Players are glad to talk with spectators before and during the game, using period language whenever possible and trying to stay in first-person character. Spectators, especially families with children, truly appreciate the willingness of players to stop and speak with them before and during the match.

The astronomical salaries of current professional athletes represent quite a contrast to the old-time values of the amateur era being portrayed on the field. This is an interesting topic to introduce with the spectators during a vintage game. The dialogue can begin when a vintage player approaches a spectator wearing a major league baseball cap and casually remarks, "I see you are wearing the insignia of the Cincinnati Red Stockings on your hat. I was shocked recently to hear rumors that they may be paying their players to play on their base ball club. The gentlemen in this game before you are, of course, all amateur players, playing solely for recreation, exercise, and their enjoyment of the national game. Do you think this business of having paid professional players on a club will ever catch on?" A lively discussion is sure to ensue, raising important issues in a light-hearted way and pointing out differences between the 1860s and the present.

Another natural opportunity for a player to slide gracefully into the role of interpreter comes when, as a striker, he is retired without reaching first base safely for the first out of an inning. Knowing he will have a few minutes while his teammates continue batting during the rest of the inning, the player can stop by the first-base seating area on his way back to the bench. An effective opener for a chat with the spectators is, "Thunderation! I was hoping to make my base. Drat!" This is all said with a snap of the fingers and a good-natured smile rather than a scowl, an indication that the player is disappointed about making an out but is able to accept it as part of the game and is not blaming anyone else for his lack of success.

"Thunderation" and "drat" are two good, socially acceptable words that were used in the nineteenth century when things did go not well. The fact that they are words that are seldom if ever used in modern conversation gives them a quaint sound that will usually get a reaction from the spectators. Players and spectators did not speak in terms of getting a hit. The phrase "make my base" was common in the 1860s. Newspaper accounts of games from that era say that a player "made his base" if he hit the ball and reached first safely or "made his second base" if he got a two-base hit. By making these brief remarks (only nine words in this case), the player-interpreter is able to convey two period words to express disappointment, acquaint the audience with a period base ball phrase, and demonstrate the predisposition of a ball player from this era to try his best to do well but accept the fact (in a gentlemanly and sportsmanlike way) that he has made an out. He has also opened the door for further conversation if the spectators have any questions or observations about the game.

Thoughtful comments on the importance of period language appeared in an interview with author M. T. Anderson conducted by Cecelia Goodnow in the November 3, 2008, edition of the *Seattle Post-Intelligencer*. In discussing the research for his book *The Astonishing Life of Octavian Nothing: Traitor to the Nation — Volume II: The Kingdom on the Waves*, which is set in the Revolutionary War era, Anderson reported: "I tried to read only 18th-century texts or books about the 18th century or books they would have read in the 18th century." This approach was based on his belief that "in order to get inside the mind-set of a period, I feel like you also have to enter into its language." While vintage base ball participants are not expected to undergo the total immersion experience adopted by Anderson, reading a few secondary and primary sources related to the mid-nineteenth century provides the opportunity to pick up a few old-fashioned vocabulary words and phrases the player

Players engage the crowd with game programs and by answering questions during the match.

can use in his interaction with the crowd. Period language helps the spectators feel as if they have stepped back in time.

Whether using period language or not, there are many points that a player can talk about when chatting with spectators. When a striker has been put out, a teammate visiting with the crowd might comment on how the out was made and praise the player on the other team who made the play. He could say, "The third baseman certainly made a good catch on the first bound." This reminds the spectators of the rule that the batter is out if the ball is fielded on the first bounce. Or, he could say, "That was an outstanding barehanded catch on the fly by the left fielder." This reinforces the fact that the game is being played without gloves and reminds the audience that an outfielder catching a well-hit ball barehanded constitutes a very fine play. Comments of this type also demonstrate the good sportsmanship and manners of the time by complimenting the skill of an opponent rather than grumbling and grousing about an out being made.

Especially for a family with children or senior citizens in their group, having a ball player in uniform stop by and chat briefly (even if he just gives them a wave or tip of the cap and says "thank you for coming") is an experience that is appreciated more than many vintage players realize. Vintage players know they are amateurs whose playing skills are relatively modest compared to the talents of professional players. Team members know they are all regular people with regular jobs through the week who play vintage base ball on the weekends for fun, exercise, recreation, and to provide a living history lesson on the early days of the American institution of base ball. Generally unassuming in their deportment, many vintage players do not think of themselves as "real" ball players. But to many in the audience, especially the youngsters who have never had a uniformed ball player come over during a game and talk to them, a brief exchange about a play or even about the weather

("What a splendid day for the match!") can be a highlight of the day and a moment they will remember long after they have forgotten the score of the contest or which team won. Players should not underestimate the impact of an opportunity to interact with the crowd or let it pass by.

Some players, of course, may not be as comfortable as others with interacting with the public as interpreters. Especially if relatively new to vintage base ball, some may not feel sufficiently confident of their knowledge of the rules and the history of the game to field questions. Veteran members of the program who know the game well may be naturally on the quiet side and a bit reserved about striking up conversations. This is to be expected. Not everyone will be a skilled interpreter. A player can make a valuable contribution to the presentation of a vintage game as an interpreter without verbally interacting with the crowd just by doing a good job of portraying a nineteenth-century ball player on the bench and on the playing field. The conscientious player who is dependable about showing up on time; wears a complete uniform that is clean and in good repair; wears his full uniform correctly at all times when he is in public view; helps maintain the period look of the bench by not bringing with him a bat bag, cell phone, or plastic bottle; gives his best effort on every play; knows the rules; and conducts himself in a mature and sportsmanlike manner throughout the game is a superb asset to any program. He may be "a man of few words," but such a vintage club member serves as a very effective interpreter by accurately representing, though his appearance, actions, and the way he carries himself, a gentlemanly player of the 1860 era.

Root, Root, Root for the Home Team — and the Visitors

In addition to answering questions about rules and equipment, interpreters can, as the game rolls along, teach important lessons about the norms of sportsmanship at a time when it was common for spectators to applaud good plays by both teams. Unfortunately, the opposite situation often exists at collegiate and professional sporting events today, where it is the norm to routinely and loudly boo the visiting team's players when they first appear on the field or court before the game even begins. At a vintage game, interpreters can reintroduce the nineteenth-century standard of giving the visiting team a warm welcome and cheering good plays by both sides.

The quaint sounding word "Huzzah!" is generally accepted throughout the vintage base ball community as the 1860 equivalent of the familiar terms "Hurrah!" and "Hoo-Ray!" Interpreters can teach the audience this term and encourage the spectators to shout "Huzzah!" when a player gets a long hit, scores a run, or makes an excellent fielding play. At most games the teams will exchange three cheers — "Hip, Hip, Huzzah! Hip, Hip, Huzzah! Hip, Hip, Huzzah!"— at the conclusion of the contest. They will also extend three cheers to the umpire, with another round for the spectators for attending the game.

When the National Base Ball Club of Washington, D.C., made its notable tour of several western cities in the summer of 1867, rules authority and journalist Henry Chadwick accompanied the Washington club, serving as the scorer for the games and writing newspaper articles about the matches. In the July 18, 1867, issue of *The Ball Players' Chronicle*, Chadwick gave a detailed account of the game played between the Nationals and the Capital Club of Columbus, Ohio, the first stop on the tour. He closed his report on the game with the following comments on the sportsmanlike crowd behavior at the match:

We take pleasure in according to the Columbus players and the assemblage present the palm of superiority for their deportment on the ground. We have never seen more creditable conduct at a ball match than was shown on this occasion by the citizens present. The applause was given with thorough impartiality, and none of that narrow-minded, ignorant prejudice which, in its partiality for the local organization, forgets the courtesy due to strangers, was shown on this occasion.

Sportsmanlike conduct at base ball games was not always the case in the 1860s, as the increased emphasis on winning was beginning to have a negative influence on the manners and "deportment" of the crowd. In praising the "assemblage" at Columbus, Chadwick's article mentions that "the conduct of the Columbus people was in striking contrast to that of the Bostonians with the Athletics, the Richmond crowd with the University students, and with that of other cities of the North, South, and East on similar occasions." These comments indicate that the visiting team was not always being given a hospitable reception by the local populace. However, the admirable and impartial behavior of the Columbus spectators in welcoming the visiting National Club from Washington and cheering for both teams represents the high ideals with which the game was associated in its earlier days.

Walter Camp, known as the "Father of Football" in his lifetime (just as Henry Chadwick was known as the "Father of Baseball"), offered advice reminiscent of Chadwick's writings in his 1893 publication, *Walter Camp's Book of College Sports*: "Now about the treatment of your rivals. A gentleman is courteous. It is not courtesy upon a ball-field to cheer an error of the opponents. If it is upon your grounds, it is the worst kind of boorishness. Moreover, if there are remarkable plays by your rivals you yourselves should cheer; conceal any chagrin you may feel at the loss it may be to your side, but be courteous to appreciate and applaud an exceptional play by the opponents." By pointing out that this is the way things should be done, the writings of Chadwick and Camp provide a model for the atmosphere that vintage programs strive to create at their matches.

While rudeness and hostility toward the members of the opposing team is common at many major league parks, the custom of cheering opposing players continues to exist in modern times and is one of the reasons St. Louis is considered "one of the top baseball cities in the country," according to a *USA Today Sports Weekly* informal survey of current and former major league players. In "St. Louis: Baseball's Diamond of a City" in the publication's July 8–15, 2009, issue, Bob Nightengale echoes Chadwick's praise of the Columbus spectators in the 1860s by pointing out the present-day "Midwestern hospitality" shown by St. Louis fans toward opposing players. "It was just last week when the Cardinals were losing badly in a lackluster game against the San Francisco Giants. Randy Johnson, who got his 300th win earlier in the season, was pulled from the game. He walked off the mound and was momentarily startled by the rising noise. It was Cardinal fans giving him a standing ovation. 'That was great,' Johnson says. 'They really appreciate their base ball here, even when it's not by their own players. That shows how much they appreciate and respect the game. I was surprised (at the ovation) but knowing these fans coming here, I shouldn't have been."

Cardinal pitcher Adam Wainwright commented on the applause for Johnson's career accomplishments. "Our fans were awesome acknowledging that. They have appreciation for good baseball and the history of baseball. They realized it might be the last time they see him. Our fans are never ruthless. They just have an appreciation of good baseball." Veteran outfielder Andruw Jones expressed similar sentiments regarding the intelligent and fair-minded St. Louis fans. "The Cardinals have the nicest fans in baseball," Jones is quoted in

Musicians Barry Chern (left) and Michael Allen entertain the crowd at Ohio Village (Columbus) before the game and between innings with lively period tunes.

the article as saying. "I remember once I ran a ball down against [popular Cardinal player] Jim Edmonds, crashed into wall, and they gave me a standing ovation when I walked off the field. I'll never forget that" (pp. 4–7).

The custom of cheering opposing players was very much a part of the matches of the 1850s and 1860s. Interpreters can involve the spectators in creating a more authentic atmosphere at vintage games by teaching the crowd to direct their cheers and applause to both teams. Encouraging the crowd to cheer for good plays by both clubs will undoubtedly be a new concept for many modern spectators at a vintage game. It provides insight into the customs of the past and, by offering an alternative to "the narrow-minded, ignorant prejudice which, in its partiality for the local organization, forgets the courtesy due to strangers," it also generates some thoughtful reflection on twenty-first century crowd conduct.

Period Music

Some sites that have vintage teams have vocal and instrumental music groups play period music on days when vintage base ball games are scheduled. Everything from entire brass bands to individuals, duos, or trios playing period songs on banjos, guitars, and fiddles has worked well.

The Ohio Historical Society has an excellent vocal musical group, the Ohio Village Singers. This mixed ensemble, under the direction of OHS staff member Priscilla Hewetson, is known for researching songs that were popular in a given historical period, preparing and rehearsing authentic arrangements of the music, and performing the songs while wearing period dress. They chat with the spectators in period language and provide background information about the songs they are performing. An appearance by this clever and capable

At the annual Glorious Fourth Celebration, the Ohio Village Singers lead the crowd in patriotic songs of the period.

vocal group at a vintage game adds a superb musical component to the afternoon. Visitors who hear the singers perform a number between innings of a vintage game can make it a point to take in the ensemble's concert later that day in the Town Hall or on the Village Green.

In August 2009, the Freetown Village Singers visited Ohio Village as part of a special day of "Celebrating African American Base Ball Heritage." day. Following a vintage base ball double-header, this talented vocal group from Freetown Village in Indianapolis, "a living history museum without walls" where "the lives of African Americans are presented through theater, story telling, folk crafts, heritage workshops, day camp, and special events," performed an enjoyable and educational concert in period dress.

On various occasions when playing games on the road, the Muffins have enjoyed performances by Civil War-era concert bands that play antique instruments and wear historic band uniforms. These performances before or after the game are a wonderful accompaniment to a base ball game set in the same time period of American history as the music. Any type of musical entertainment involving period songs played by people in period dress is recommended and encouraged as part of interpreting the era being portrayed in the ball game.

Informal Theatrical Performances

A museum may also have a group of staff members or experienced volunteers who visit the vintage games and, in period dress, circulate among the spectators as actors, discussing

The Freetown Singers from Freetown Village, Indianapolis, present a concert of period songs after a match in Ohio Village.

the social and political issues of the day. This way of presenting information to visitors is known as "museum theatre," a concept defined by the International Museum Theatre Alliance as "engaging visitors in the willing suspension of disbelief—in pretend or imagination—to enhance the educational experience that happens within a museum." It is a "successful medium for educating visitors and evaluation studies have confirmed its effectiveness." Museum theatre is presented in the first-person format in which interpreters "interact with one another and the audience members as if actually living in the past." In *Exploring Museum Theatre*, Tessa Bridal quotes International Museum Theater Alliance board member Paul Taylor, who said, "While theatre can be enlightening, it is not generally bound to the idea that it must teach something. In museum theatre, the genesis usually has contained within its seed the understanding that the piece will relay some educational idea to the audience" (p. 3).

At a vintage base ball game, a group of ladies representing the local temperance society (in period clothing, of course) may visit the field to ask the players (and even some of the spectators) to "sign the pledge" not to consume alcohol. Between innings, their brief speeches against the evils of "demon rum" are representative of the debate over an important social issue of the era when base ball was in its formative years. Ohio Village has had success with groups of placard-carrying ladies demonstrating in favor of women's suffrage, another controversial topic of the time. Interaction with the spectators on this issue can produce some exchanges that are both humorous and thought-provoking. These skits and conversations between actors and spectators during the game provide a good—and entertaining—history lesson. There are undoubtedly young people in the audience who have no idea there was a time when women did not have the right to vote, and that there were women's groups in the mid-nineteenth century who were actively campaigning to be enfranchised.

On another occasion, a very spirited woman (played by an actor/interpreter in period dress) interrupted the game to let everyone know that she considered it to be outrageous that an activity such as base ball was being played on a Sunday. This presented another opportunity for interpreters to engage the public in comparing the customs of the 1860s to the present. Another glimpse of nineteenth-century life at Ohio Village is provided by Mike Follin, a talented actor/interpreter portraying a "snake oil salesman" known as Dr. Balthazar, who hawks the curative powers of his "magic elixir" (a tonic of dubious medicinal value) to the amusement of the audience.

An actor doing a first-person portrayal of Abraham Lincoln is a popular addition to an 1860s vintage game. On their travels through Ohio and beyond, the Muffins have encountered "President Lincoln" several times at various festivals. On the lawn of Stan Hywet Hall, the home grounds of the Akron Black Stockings, he threw out the ceremonial first pitch. In Keokuk, Iowa, another President Lincoln stopped by the ball field just before the game was to begin, doffed his black coat, and took a turn at bat. These encounters with Mr. Lincoln provide an opportunity for the players to find out if there is any truth in the legend that Lincoln was playing base ball in Springfield when he learned that a delegation from the Republican Convention in Chicago had just arrived by train to inform him that he had been selected as the party's nominee for the office of president in the election of 1860. Did Lincoln actually say (as has often been reported), "I am glad to hear of their coming, but they will have to wait a few minutes till I get my turn at bat"? Vintage players are encouraged to ask him when he visits one of your matches.

Civil War History

Civil War activities and programs often fit well with vintage base ball. At the annual "Glorious Fourth" celebration of Independence Day at Ohio Village, the town mayor (portrayed by the versatile Mr. Follin) and other dignitaries (portrayed by other staff members and volunteers) deliver a series of patriotic speeches in period language. Between the speeches urging that the Union be preserved, visitors are led in the singing of period patriotic songs, such as "The Battle Cry of Freedom" and the "Battle Hymn of the Republic" by the Ohio Village Singers. There is a parade around the town square, which includes the dignitaries, the base ball team, the musical group, and other museum staff members and volunteers in period dress. The afternoon's activities feature a ball game played by the rules of the time. Combining the colorful presentation of an 1860s base ball game with other activities conducted by volunteers and museum staff members in period dress creates an educational experience that is enjoyable for participants and visitors and takes them back to another time. The observance of the sesquicentennial of the Civil War presents an opportunity for 1860-era vintage base ball programs to partner with other organizations in a variety of special events associated with the re-creation and interpretation of this critical period in American history.

Other Sporting and Leisure Activities

Playing the game in the setting of a historic village or farm creates the possibility for horse-drawn wagons and carriages to pass by the base ball field during the game, adding to

Mid-nineteenth century diversions for youngsters at Ohio Village (Columbus) include attempting to walk on stilts, rolling a hoop with a stick, and a spirited tug-of-war. Activities are led by period interpreters, including Ellen Ford (above).

the nineteenth-century ambiance of the afternoon. On a Muffin Club road trip to Winona, Minnesota, several years ago, a local bicycle club was present at the game. Members of the club brought their nineteenth-century bicycles (or "wheels," as they were sometimes known in those days) to the park where the game was held and, in appropriate period dress, gave riding demonstrations before the game.

At some outdoor museums and historical society properties, characters in period dress may put on craft and cooking demonstrations near the ball field. At various festivals or Civil War reenactment events, there may be bean soup, corn bread, and pies being prepared according to nineteenth-century recipes and methods. A photographer with an antique camera on a tripod may be on hand. Any nineteenth-century activities of this type going

An itinerant photographer in period dress adds to the ambiance of a vintage base ball event by using a nineteenth-century camera and old-time plates to create tintypes of players and interpreters.

on in the vicinity of the game always help set a general tone for the day that enables visitors to get a sampling of daily life in the period represented on the ball field.

Various nineteenth-century toys and games can be made available in an area near the ball diamond. Having stepped back in time to watch the 1860s base ball game, the children in the audience might want to try playing other games of that era. With the assistance of an interpreter in period dress, youngsters can attempt to walk on wooden stilts or roll a hoop, activities popular with children in the nineteenth century. An old-fashioned wooden croquet set is available for youngsters and adults to use. The youngsters can also try out a wooden seesaw or rope swing. If enough youngsters are present to form two sides, a tug-of-war can be organized. These activities enable them to expend some energy while keeping their minds in the historical period represented by the ball game and the surrounding village.

Horseshoe pitching is a popular hobby in some communities. Like base ball, the sport's popularity grew during the Civil War era. If a group of local participants would be willing to wear period clothing while playing, or if several members of the base ball club are reasonably proficient at the game, the construction of a nineteenth-century-style horseshoe court near the ball field can provide another period-appropriate competitive sport.

Food and Refreshments

Many programs make food and drink available to spectators at vintage games. Even if the museum does not have any food preparation facilities, the base ball program might want to sell soft drinks with an old-time look. Root beer and cream soda date to the mid-nineteenth century and several brands are available in old-fashioned glass bottles. Peanuts are another popular snack to enjoy while watching the game. They should be sold in a plain brown paper sack (not pre-packaged in plastic bags). A popcorn wagon will be frequented by visitors. Cookies and soft pretzels sell well. Some sites have a grill area near the field for cooking hot dogs, brats, and burgers. Others make box lunches available, and this is a good adjunct to the game, especially if the base ball field is near a picnic area. An old-fashioned ice cream social is an enjoyable complementary activity for a vintage base ball match.

Depending on facilities and other considerations, programs can decide if they want to sell refreshments as a fund-raiser for the ball club or if they want to want to use food as a "friend-raiser" by giving away bags of popcorn or peanuts or asking a surprisingly low fee (e.g., five or ten cents), thereby connecting with their spectators in a positive way that will encourage them to return for more games.

Programs will need to check into any local licensing restrictions and food handling laws before providing any food or drink for sale or free to visitors. However, if these requirements can be met, the atmosphere of a vintage game is enhanced by making sandwiches, snacks, and cold drinks available. With a wooden cart and vendor in period dress, the food serving area can be made to look more in keeping with the era and the vendor can become another de facto interpreter, adding to the ambiance of the occasion. Actor Humphrey Bogart once remarked, "A hot dog at the ball park is better than steak at the Ritz." While his observation was made in reference to taking in a mid-twentieth century major league game, it is equally applicable to a visit to a mid-nineteenth century vintage match.

Visiting the Past

Thanks to interpreters, visitors coming to the vintage base ball game can have a memorable experience. While watching the match and learning about the rules, customs, uniforms, and equipment of the national pastime, they can also have conversations with interpreters in period dress, interact with the players and umpire, listen to period music, take part in a discussion of the issues of the day, find out about the clothing styles and language of the period, learn to cheer for both teams, and even sample the same refreshments that spectators at a ball game might have enjoyed in 1860. Interpreters — both professional staff members and volunteers — play important roles in making all these things happen, providing a complete 1860s experience that enhances the visitors' pleasant (and educational) afternoon at the ballpark.

15

Points of Play: Infield and Outfield

The Infield

In vintage base ball, the infield positions are similar to modern baseball and softball. Like today's infielders, vintage players stationed at first base, second base, third base, and shortstop need to be proficient in fielding ground balls. An accurate throwing arm is an asset. Most vintage base ball fields are, like nineteenth-century playing fields, rougher and bumpier than modern diamonds, with irregular patches of grass, bare dirt, and various dips, hills, slopes, and swales that make fielding more difficult. If playing by rules of the 1860 era, players do not wear gloves. If playing by the rules of a later period, the gloves worn are very primitive. Even if the game is being played on a modern well-groomed infield, every ground ball is a fielding challenge. There will be few ground balls during the course of a game that can be safely labeled as "routine plays." Barehanded infield play requires a return to the fundamentals taught by parents and youth league coaches: get in front of the ball; bend your knees; get down on the ball; keep your eye on the ball all the way in to your hands; use both hands when catching the ball. Since the field is relatively uneven and players are fielding without gloves, it is important to back up teammates whenever possible while expecting an errant bounce or throw.

In addition to handling ground balls, infielders should be proficient in catching pop-ups, including running back to catch a ball in the outfield and racing in toward home plate to catch a ball hit just over the pitcher's head. There are typically a number of pop-ups to the infield area in a game. Some are hit high in the air and have considerable backspin. Therefore, infielders not only have to judge the trajectory of the ball but catch a rapidly spinning ball barehanded. Catching a high, spinning pop-up barehanded is much tougher than it looks, and the infielder who can turn a high pop fly into an out is a valuable player on defense. Since even the best fielders will drop a pop-up occasionally, it is a good idea for teammates to surround the spot where the ball is coming down. Should the ball pop out of the hands of the one who initially tried to catch it, the others should be alert to grab it on the first bounce for an out.

First Base

While modern professional teams consider first base to be one of the easier positions to play, in vintage base ball it is one of the most difficult. An old saying in modern baseball states "You put the donkeys on the corners." This colorful expression translates into the conventional wisdom that to have a winning team, it is best to have the most skilled defensive players "up the middle"—catcher, second base, shortstop, and center field. The less adept are assigned to the corners of the infield and outfield—first base, third base, left field, and right field. First base is often the place where modern teams try to "hide" a mediocre fielder.

In vintage base ball, first base is one of the most challenging positions to play and requires one of the team's best players. Catching hard throws from the other infielders bare-handed requires strong, sure hands and a significant amount of skill, courage, and determination. As Henry Chadwick observed in the 1860 *Beadle's Dime Base-Ball Player*, the position of first base "requires the player filling it to be the very best of catchers, as he will be required to hold very swift thrown balls."

As in modern baseball, a tall player makes a good target for throws, but there is more to playing first base than above-average height. Because of the uneven playing surface, infielders often bobble a grounder, then (sometimes unwisely) try to recover by sending a hard throw across the diamond to nip the runner. If the throw is on target, catching a "swift thrown ball" from an infielder with a strong arm is a difficult play. If the throw is low, it becomes even trickier because the first baseman must have the reactions and coordination to dig the throw out of the grass on the short hop with his bare hands. If the throw is high or wide, he must be able to stretch and reach the throw with one hand while keeping his foot on the base. He may even have to leap in the air, catch the errant throw, and come back down on the base. Like the other infielders, the first baseman should also be a competent fielder of both grounders and pop-ups (including catching them on the fly or first bounce in foul territory). He will be called upon to make a significant number of plays in a typical game. First base is a demanding position to play and is not the best place for an inexperienced newcomer.

Period illustrations show that the first baseman played in the vicinity of his base. This is in keeping with Henry Chadwick's advice in *Beadle's Dime Base-Ball Player* that the first baseman "should play a little below his base and inside the line of the foul ball post." Chadwick points out that playing close to the base is important for the first baseman because "the moment the ball is struck, and he finds that it does not come near him, he should promptly return to his base, and stand in readiness, with one foot on the base, to receive the ball from any player that may have fielded it" (p. 23). Another reason for playing close to the baseline is that since any foul ball caught on the fly or first bound is an out, the first baseman is responsible for covering the foul territory outside the baseline. Also, he needs to guard against the smash down the line that can initially strike the ground in fair territory and then veer into foul territory—a likely extra-base hit for the striker unless the first baseman is playing close to the bag and can stop the ball before it passes first base. A good-fielding first baseman is a vital component of a good defense.

Second Base

In *Beadle's Dime Base-Ball Player,* Henry Chadwick says that the position of second base "is considered by many to be the key of the field and therefore requires an excellent player to occupy it. He should be an accurate and swift thrower, a sure catcher, and a thorough fielder" (p. 24). As in modern baseball, he needs to be a quick thinker who can understand various situations as they unfold. Because of his place in the middle of the field, he should be continually reminding the other infielders and outfielders of the number of outs, where force plays can be made, and where to throw the ball.

Vintage games of the 1860s often feature a number of "manly" barehanded catches by infielders, as seen in this play by a member of the Deep River Grinders (Hobart, Indiana) (courtesy Joel Moore).

In regard to throwing, the second baseman must be able to throw accurately to first. Since 1860-era second basemen seemed to play much closer to the base than their modern counterparts, the throw to first base is often longer than in modern times. On an extra-base hit to deep right or right-center, the second baseman needs to go into the outfield for the relay, receiving the outfielder's throw and then making an accurate throw to second, third, or home.

A common play in vintage base ball is the force out a second base when, with a runner on first, the infielder who fields a ground ball elects to throw to second base to retire the runner (no tag needed) rather than to first base to retire the striker. Since the force play at second base (and the chance for a double play involving the second baseman as the middle man) comes up fairly often, the second baseman needs to be a very steady, dependable, and alert fielder who can get to the base and catch a teammate's throw to complete the force out. Just making the plays that should be made (and not giving the opposition four or five outs in an inning) is especially important in vintage base ball, and second base is a good place for a reliable player. He doesn't need to be flashy or spectacular, but he does need to be a person who rarely makes mental errors and is sure-handed while taking a throw from the shortstop, third baseman, pitcher, or perhaps even an outfielder to complete the force play at his base.

On hard grounders and line drives, the second baseman will often be called upon to stop smashes up the middle. He needs to have the range to go to his left in case a right-handed striker who is adept at place-hitting tries to reach base safely or advance the runners by directing the ball to the right side of the field.

The issue of where the second baseman should be positioned in a vintage game is the source of lively ongoing debate. Most programs require or at least encourage the second baseman to play no more than a step or two from the base. The reasoning for this is that period illustrations and diagrams consistently show the basemen stationed on or very near their bases. Also, we have the commentary of Henry Chadwick in the 1860 edition of *Beadle's Dime Base-Ball Player* to shed light on how second base was played at that time. Chadwick advises that the second baseman "should play a little back of his base, and to the right or left of it, according to the habitual play of the striker, but generally to the left, as most balls pass in that direction" (p. 25).

Taking another view, some members of the vintage community have pointed out that if the first baseman and the second baseman both play within a step or two of their bases, a large gap is created on the right side of the infield, which produces an inviting target for right-handed batters adept at hitting the ball to right field. To counteract this situation, and citing Chadwick's reference to the second baseman positioning himself "according to the habitual play of the striker," they advocate that he should be permitted to position himself wherever he wants to play in the area between first and second.

Perhaps influenced by the modern practice of the second baseman playing 30 or 40 feet to the right of the bag, some vintage players cite the fact that there is no written rule that requires the second baseman to play near the bag. While it was not a "rule," it seems to have been common practice for the second baseman to play in the immediate vicinity of his base. Not only does Chadwick's commentary place the second baseman near the bag, he even advises that he usually play on the *left* (or shortstop) side of the base, "as most balls pass in that direction." While not the same as official rules, Chadwick's instructions do indicate that it was the standard practice at that time for the second baseman to play close to the base. On those areas not specifically covered in the rules (such as player placement), Chadwick's views are extremely valuable as they represent the most well-informed and widely respected contemporary opinion on how the game was to be played.

While strategy on the positioning of the second baseman has changed significantly over the past 150 years, there were some sound reasons for playing near the bag in the earlier era. It is much more difficult to catch a throw from a teammate barehanded while running toward the base than to catch the ball with both hands when already standing on the base. The second baseman did not stray very far from the bag because he wanted to get to the base quickly in order to give his teammate a good target, get his body squared to the direction of the throw was coming from, and (while stationary) take the throw with both hands. He would not want to arrive at the base just barely ahead of the runner and try to take a throw from a teammate barehanded while on the dead run. Also, moving very far off the bag toward first base (in the manner of the modern second baseman) is a trade-off in that it opens up the center of the diamond for balls hit up the middle.

It is true that when the second baseman played close to the base there was a gap in the right side of the infield, and it continued to be there until the mid–1870s. Chadwick discusses this gap in the 1876 edition of *Beadle's* in the course of describing an interesting experiment undertaken in 1875 to add a tenth man (and tenth inning) to the game. Chadwick states that the idea of a tenth man was first proposed ten years earlier when several experimental

The first baseman of the Douglas (Michigan) Dutchers prepares to make a barehanded catch of a teammate's throw (courtesy Joel Moore).

games were played in Brooklyn "for the purpose of practically illustrating the then new rule of the 'fly game.' In these games we had ten men on each side, the tenth man playing at 'short right.' The result of the experiment was fine displays of fielding, shorter games and smaller scores than had previously been known in the history of the game. At the next convention, the fly game was adopted. We did not present the ten man improvement at that time as we were content with getting the fly rule passed."

The tenth man, sometimes referred to as a "short right" or "right shortstop," was needed, Chadwick said, because "the base-ball field, as at present placed, is what sailors would call lopsided; the position of short stop giving one man more of the left side of the field than the right side has." The shortstop evolved into "one of the most important in the infield" because "in the early years of the game, before anything like scientific batting came into vogue, the hitting was more to the left field than the right." This is consistent with Chadwick's 1860 instructions calling for the second baseman to play near the base (and even "generally to the left, as most balls pass in that direction"). But, Chadwick pointed out in 1876, "since skill and judgment have been brought to bear on the batting, those handling the ash skillfully have not been slow in discovering the open space between first and second bases and the result has been a decided increase in the average of hits to the right field until now the hitting in that direction in first class matches is equal to that to the left."

Chadwick observed that various defenses had apparently been tried by team captains to combat "this weak point of late seasons ... [to] cover 'short right' more than was previously done," but the realignments had proved unsuccessful, resulting in "an increase in chances for hits to the left, and especially over second base." This was probably a result of trying to place the second baseman farther from the bag. The answer to covering the gap between first and second was not moving the second baseman. Instead, Chadwick was convinced that "with a 'short right' added to the infield," the second baseman could continue to play on the base and protect the middle while the shortstop could "play up nearer to third," allowing the third baseman to guard against fair-foul hitting.

While the proposal to add a tenth man did not catch on, Chadwick's advocacy of the creation of a second shortstop on the right side of the infield shows that there was a gap in the area between first and second and it was being exploited by "scientific" hitting (right-handed batters intentionally hitting to right field). The gap was not being covered by the second baseman for fear of leaving the middle of the diamond exposed. The importance of this for 1860-era vintage base ball is that Chadwick's 1876 comments show that the second baseman likely did play close to the base, leaving a gap on the right side for those hitters who developed the skill of hitting the ball through the gap and into right field. The practice of positioning the second baseman no more than a step or two from the bag appears historically sound and is recommended.

Club leaders should remember that having the second baseman play on or very near his base should not be referred to as a "rule." It does appear to have been a common practice, however, and if a program elects to include it as an established practice for vintage games on that club's home grounds, a visiting club should be informed of it and should respect that policy.

Third Base

Chadwick's discussion of the position of third base is a little puzzling since he characterizes third base as "not quite as important a position as the others, but it nevertheless requires its occupant to be a good player as some very pretty play is frequently shown on this base." While the term "hot corner" did not come into use until later (1889, according to the *New Dickson Baseball Dictionary*), the phrase is apt for understanding and describing the position of third base in any era. Right-handed hitters often send hard grounders and line drives down the third-base line that the third baseman must try to stop. When he is able to catch one of these line drives barehanded, the spectators (and his teammates, who always appreciate a good play on a hard-hit ball) are often in awe since they sense the nerve and skill it takes to stand firm and make the play. High pop-ups are frequent since right-handed hitters sometimes get a little under the pitch and lift towering flies toward third base that are tough chances. The third baseman should, of course, have a strong arm since, after fielding a ground ball, he will need to make an accurate throw across the diamond to first base, a distance of about forty yards on a diamond with 90-foot base paths. Similar to the first baseman and second baseman, the third baseman should play about a step or two from the base.

Other talents associated with the position of third base include the agility to race to the right into foul territory to pick off a foul ball on the fly or first bound. The third baseman needs to be alert for the occasional fair-foul hit, a chopper down the line that strikes the ground in fair territory in front of the plate and then shoots off into foul territory. For a period in the nineteenth century (about 1864, when the practice began, until 1877, when the rule was changed to require the ball to pass third or first base in fair territory to be judged a fair ball), some batters were adept at this tactic. A fair-foul hit requires the third baseman to charge the ball and make an extra-long throw from foul territory to first base in time to retire the runner. It is exceptionally difficult to retire a speedy striker who makes a well-executed fair-foul hit. Therefore, it is often best to hold the ball and not attempt a throw that has no chance of beating the runner. In such instances, the third baseman needs to have good judgment, knowing that sometimes the best throws are the ones that are not made.

The third baseman may receive throws from all over the field during the course of a game as runners try to advance to third. If the runner cannot be put out, it is important that the third baseman at least block these throws with his body and not let the ball skip though him into foul territory behind third base. If the ball gets through, the runner arriving at third will probably be able to score and any others runners will continue to advance around the bases while the ball is being retrieved.

Shortstop

As is the case in modern baseball, the shortstop position requires a vintage player with exceptional defensive abilities. He will be called upon to handle a large number of fielding chances in a typical vintage game and must be adept at scooping up grounders, grabbing hard-hit drives on the fly or on the bound, and catching pop-ups (sometimes going out into shallow left field to make the play). He must have an accurate arm, giving the first baseman and other teammates throws they can catch without leaving their bases. In addition to a good arm, he must have the good judgment not to make unnecessary throws. He must possess valuable intangibles: the self-confidence to want the ball hit to him with the game on the line; the eagerness to take charge on pop flies in the infield; and, the alertness to always know the score of the game, the inning, and number of outs and to remind his teammates what play to make given those circumstances. Shortstop requires a player with both good athletic ability and "base ball sense," the knack for anticipating what needs to be done, thinking quickly, and being in position to make the correct play.

"This position on the field is a very important one," wrote Henry Chadwick in 1860, "for on the activity and judgment of the Short Stop depends the greater part of the in-fielding." In addition to fielding ground balls and making accurate throws to first base, Chadwick points out that the shortstop must be ready to back up second and cover third, depending on the situation.

In regard to his position on the diamond, Chadwick places the shortstop "generally in the center of a triangle formed by the second and third bases and the pitcher's position but he should change it according to his knowledge of the striker's style of batting" (p. 23). The proper interpretation of this passage has been widely discussed and debated in vintage base ball circles.

It seems odd to many that the shortstop would play so close to the batter by taking a position inside the base line between second and third. One theory is that placing the shortstop inside the baseline may be the result of many playing fields having long grass in earlier times. In vintage base ball, the shortstop tends to move inside the baseline only if the grass is long and damp, slowing the progress of even a hard-hit grounder. Such balls can die before reaching the infielders. However, if the grass is relatively short and the field is dry, the shortstop in vintage base ball plays a little behind the baseline, similar to the modern shortstop.

In the case of a left-handed batter, the usual custom in vintage base ball is to have the shortstop move over to the right side of the infield, taking a position between first base and second base, with the second baseman remaining a step or two from the second base bag. While Chadwick instructs the umpire to move to the other side of the field when a left-handed batter comes to the plate, he provides no specific directions on what the infielders should do. Chadwick does say, however, in instructing the shortstop to "generally" take his position between second and third, "he should change it according to his knowledge of the striker's style of batting." This statement has led to the conclusion among most vintage programs that, while the other infielders should play close to their bases, the shortstop can move around the infield according to where he thinks the ball will be hit, which would logically include the right side of the infield in the case of a left-handed batter. This was likely the common practice of the day, which is followed in vintage base ball.

As demonstrated by shortstop Bill Dieckmann of the Cincinnati Red Stockings, catching a bounding ball on a bumpy field calls for a return to fundamentals: Get in front of the ball, keep your eye on the ball, and use both hands (courtesy Joel Moore).

Knowing the Rules

In order to present the game on the field as an authentic example of how base ball was played when the bound rule was in effect, it is especially important that all infielders (including the pitcher and catcher) know the rules and react accordingly so that each player thinks and acts like a player from that bygone time. Consider this situation: With a runner on second and no outs, the striker hits a ball directly at an infielder who fields it cleanly on one bound. The infielder needs to immediately realize that the striker is out the instant the ball is caught on the bound, and there is no need to throw to first base to retire him. The proper play is to simply hold the ball and make the runner hold at second base.

If the infielder who caught the one-bounder forgets how the rules work and throws to first base to complete the out on the batter (as would be the case in modern baseball), he has made two mistakes — one that hurts his team's chances of winning the game and another that damages the game's credibility as an authentic presentation of how base ball was played in former times. First, by throwing to first base, he allows the runner on second base to have an opportunity to advance to third while the ball is heading unnecessarily to the wrong base. Second, by throwing to first base when there is no need to make a play there, he has confused the spectators who have been told that a batter is out immediately if the ball he hits is caught on the first bound. A spectator might understandably ask the umpire or an interpreter, "If the rules say a batter is out when the ball was caught on the first bound, why did the infielder throw to first base?" There would be no logical period-specific explanation that the umpire or interpreter could provide that would explain why an infielder would have made the throw.

As is the case with baseball in any era, it is important for all players — especially infielders — to think ahead as to what play to make if the ball is hit to them. Throwing to first base to retire a batter who is already out is never a wise play, but it is a fairly common mistake that detracts from the presentation of a vintage game.

The Infield Fly Rule

In understanding how the infield was played in the game's early period, it should be kept in mind that the infield fly rule was not adopted until 1895. In *The Official Rules of Baseball: An Anecdotal Look at the Rules of Baseball and How They Came to Be*, David Nemec comments that before the rule was passed, "infielders, including pitchers and catchers, were free to drop infield pops and line drives on the gamble that they could force out runners who had been frozen to their bases on the assumption the ball would be caught." While dropping a ball on purpose in order to get a double play may have been legal, most vintage base ball players consider an intentionally dropped ball to be a gamble. Infielders are usually unwilling to take the risk of trading an out by catching the ball for an attempt at the risky maneuver of dropping it and then trying to retire two runners on force outs. Too many things can go wrong. An attempt at getting two outs requires two accurate throws and two barehanded catches of those throws in order for the defensive team to come out ahead. Citing the unpredictability of catching the pop fly, Nemec notes, "Part of the reason it took so long for an infield fly rule to be adopted was that until the 1890s, when gloves become a fielding tool as well as a protective device, there was little assurance that a pop fly would be caught, and it seemed absurd for an umpire to rule a batter automatically out and then sheepishly watch as the ball falls safely" (pp. 29–30). When playing barehanded, most vintage players are satisfied to catch the ball and get the batter out and rarely, if ever, plan to drop the ball in order to try for two outs.

The Outfield

The ability to judge a fly ball is a key skill for outfielders in any era. Outfielders were urged by Chadwick "to start the moment the ball is hit and try their utmost to take it on the fly." Chadwick observed that a ball caught "on the fly, or even on the bound after a good run for it" was cause for those present to "applaud the skill that has been so successfully displayed." On the other hand, Chadwick thought the tactic of intentionally waiting to let the ball drop and then taking it on the bound "disappoints the spectator" and "dissatisfies the batsman." He therefore characterized the practice as "boy-like" and "childish." Most vintage players follow Chadwick's advice that "a fielder has two chances in attempting a catch on the fly, for should he fail in the first instance, he has the resource of the catch on the bound afterward" (pp. 26–27).

Another reason for attempting fly catches whenever possible is that on the imperfect fields where most vintage games are played, the outfielder cannot rely on getting a true bounce. Intentionally allowing the ball to drop with the idea of playing it on the bound often results in the ball hitting an uneven spot, taking a bad hop, and bouncing erratically away from the fielder. At times while running to catch the ball, the outfielder will see that the ball is going to strike the ground just at the limit of his reach and must decide whether to attempt a fly catch or play it on the bound. Making good decisions in such cases is the mark of a good outfielder. The one-bound rule does provide the opportunity for some remarkable and entertaining outfield catches. On a drive deep into the gap, a fleet-footed outfielder will sometimes have no possibility of catching the ball on the fly but can make a bound catch if the ball takes a high bounce. This situation leads to some miraculous catches that bring great excitement to the game.

Then as now, getting the ball to the proper location quickly was deemed important.

All three outfielders, Chadwick declared, "should be able to throw the ball from long field [his phrase for the deep part of the outfield] to home base, and after they have either caught or stopped the ball, they should promptly return it, either to the base requiring it, or to the pitcher, but they should never hold the ball a moment longer than necessary to throw it" (p. 26).

In modern professional baseball, left field is often considered the easiest field to play, so a team's slowest and least-skilled defensive outfielder is usually placed there. Center field is almost always the position with the most ground to cover, so a team usually assigns an exceptionally fast runner with excellent fly-judging skills to that area. Right field is considered very difficult to play because a ball struck off a right-handed hitter's bat often possesses a wicked spin that resembles the slice on a golf ball. This spin causes the ball to curve away from the outfielder while it is in the air and, when it strikes the ground, to bounce sharply away from the fielder toward the foul line, often ending up in foul territory or in the right-field corner. The distance from the right-field corner to third base is the longest throwing distance on the diamond. Therefore, a professional team usually assigns a player to right field who knows how to play the difficult spins and caroms that may come his way and has an outstanding throwing arm.

Chadwick advises a different strategy for 1860-style base ball by suggesting the placement of the club's best outfielder in left. He recommends a player who is "a good runner, a fine thrower, and an excellent and sure catcher" for that position since, by Chadwick's estimate "probably three out of every six balls hit are sent toward the left field." In regard to center field, he states, "The same qualities are requisite also in this position, as necessary in the left field, but not to the extent required by the latter fielder (presumably since fewer balls are hit to center)." Chadwick points out that right field is the position that "the poorest player of the nine — if there be any such — should occupy" because "it is only occasionally, in comparison to the other portions of the field, that balls are sent in this direction" (pp. 25–26). Vintage clubs usually follow Chadwick's recommendations in making outfield assignments. This approach can be modified, of course, if the opposing team has several accomplished left-handed hitters and perhaps several right-handed place hitters who are adept at hitting to right field. In the course of a typical vintage game, all outfielders will have a number of balls hit their way and, while an outstanding left fielder is a definite asset to any club, no one should feel slighted if asked to play right field. The clubs that are the best at preventing their opponents from scoring are those that can field a nine composed of three equally competent outfielders, all of whom can run, catch, and throw.

In regard to the positioning of the three outfielders, Chadwick mentions that the center fielder "should always be in readiness to back up the second base, and should only go to long field in cases where a hard-hitter is at the bat." These words advise the center fielder to play shallow. There was nothing in the rules of the day that prevented the outfielders from moving in and out (closer or farther from home), depending on the hitting strength of the striker.

Whether or not 1860-era outfielders had adopted the modern tactic of shading batters to the left or right has been the subject of considerable debate in vintage base ball circles. A woodcut of a game published in the *New York Clipper* in 1857 seems to show the outfielders playing in the middle of their fields. The famous painting of Union prisoners playing base ball at the Salisbury, North Carolina, prison camp has the outfielders playing in the middle of their fields but unusually close to the infield, indicating considerable artistic license may have been taken (or else they were playing on a very compact playing field with short base paths and were using a very soft ball). Some other illustrations are inconclusive since different perspectives can make the positioning of the outfielders difficult to judge.

The 1866 Currier and Ives image, *The America National Game of Base Ball*, which depicts a game at the Elysian Fields, shows the outfielders playing straight away in the middle of their respective fields. However, another well-known 1870 illustration, *Base-Ball—The Match Between the "Red Stockings" and the "Atlantics,"* depicts a scene from that game in which, with a right-handed batter at the plate, right field appears to be unoccupied. The right fielder is shown to be almost directly behind second base, the center fielder is in left-center, and the left fielder is playing near the left-field line. In determining the customs of the 1850s and 1860s, it should be remembered that this image is from a slightly later era. Also, one wonders if this alignment is actually akin to a modern shift designed to defense a right-handed pull hitter or if the artist's perspective has misrepresented the outfielders' positions.

Making a running barehanded catch is a challenging play for outfielders such as Brad Graley of the Ohio Village Muffins, especially when taking the ball on the fly (courtesy Joel Moore).

Since most period illustrations and diagrams show the outfielders stationed in the approximate center of their areas, many vintage programs follow the custom of asking outfielders to play in the middle of their fields. Outfielders should feel free to play shallower or deeper depending on their knowledge of the striker's batting tendencies. In maintaining the character of an early game, it would probably be best if the outfielders in a vintage game did not engage in extreme shifts to the left or right, like the ones employed in modern baseball against some pull hitters.

In an attempt to demonstrate how the game was played in the early years, some programs have encouraged the umpire to stop the game momentarily and motion an outfielder to move back to the middle of his field. In these situations, an umpire or an interpreter might even erroneously explain the stoppage of play by saying that it was "a rule" that each outfielder had to play in the middle of his field. Such an explanation would be inaccurate since there is nothing in the rules about outfielders being required to play in the middle of their fields.

Accordingly, some experienced program leaders have advised against the practice of stopping the game to direct an outfielder to move several steps one way of the other, and they have made a good point. Since there was no rule specifying that an outfielder must play in the center of his field, it is recommended that the umpire should not stop the game to direct an outfielder to move or fine an outfielder for being "out of position." If a program wishes to follow the practice of having each outfielder play in the center of his field, the umpire should tell the captains before the match and, if there are any problems during the game, quietly remind the captains between innings to have their outfielders play in the middle of their fields in order to maintain the look of a typical nineteenth-century match. This approach would be preferable to the umpire interrupting the game to reposition the outfielders (an act that probably would not have happened in a nineteenth-century match). As in the case of differences of opinion regarding the second baseman playing near the bag rather than roaming in the gap between first and second, all captains and players should respect the established practices of the home club and cheerfully comply with whatever instructions they receive from the umpire or the game hosts in regard to positioning of the players on defense.

In the course of a vintage game, all the infielders and outfielders will likely have many opportunities to demonstrate their skill "in taking difficult fly balls, and in making beautiful stops, and accurate throws to bases," which Chadwick, in Haney's *Base Ball Players Book of Reference for 1867* called "the most attractive features of the game." In a match characterized by pitchers delivering hittable pitches and strikers consistently putting the ball in play, Chadwick reminds us "it is on the excellence of the fielding" that the outcome of the game will be determined (pp. 107–108).

16

Points of Play: Catching and Pitching

Catcher

In comparing base ball as it was played in its early days to the way it is played today, a good case can be made that the position of catcher has changed the most. Whether playing by rules of the nineteenth, twentieth, or twenty-first century, infielders have always had to field grounders, outfielders have had to catch fly balls, and pitchers have had to pitch the ball over the plate (the underhand motion of the 1860-era being similar to the modern slow-pitch softball delivery). Under the 1860 Rules, however, the role of the catcher is much different than either the modern baseball catcher or the modern slow-pitch softball catcher.

The key rule that makes the catcher's role different is Section 11 of the 1860 Rules, which states, "The striker is out if a foul ball is caught, either before touching the ground, or upon the first bound." This rule makes it possible for the catcher (along with the first and third basemen, the left and right fielders, and occasionally the pitcher) to retire the batter by catching a foul ball on the first bound (unlike modern baseball and softball). This adds a different dimension to the game, creating interesting and exciting opportunities for the defense to put batters out in a way that is not possible under modern rules.

Accordingly, in his 1860 commentary on the catcher's position in *Beadle's Dime Base-Ball Player*, Henry Chadwick states that in addition to being "expected to catch or stop all balls pitched or thrown to the home base," the catcher "must be fully prepared to catch all foul balls, especially tips." Chadwick adds that he should also "be able to throw the ball swiftly and accurately to the bases, and also keep a bright look-out over the whole field" (p. 21). These extensive duties and opportunities to make plays make catcher an interesting position to play in the vintage game.

Equipment

The Era Before Equipment

Spectators will notice that the catcher, when playing by any set of rules before the late 1870s, not only wears no glove, but also wears none of the other protective equipment — mask, chest protector, shin guards — usually associated with the position. If the speed of the pitch is relatively slow, the catcher does not need any protective equipment because he will very seldom be struck by any sharply hit foul balls, a regular occupational hazard for a modern catcher. The vintage catcher plays far enough behind home plate to take the pitch

In games using slower pitching, the catcher positions himself several steps behind the plate and takes the pitch on the first bounce. Since the catcher is not close to the plate, he does not wear a mask or other protective equipment.

on the first bound. Since beginning to play vintage base ball in 1991, including hundreds of games playing behind the plate, I have never been hit or seen any catcher hit by a foul tip in such a way as to cause an injury in a game involving slow pitching. However, if a vintage program adopts rules and practices that include faster pitching, and the catcher is expected to move closer to the plate to receive the pitch before it bounces, the potential for injuries on foul tips becomes an issue. When faster pitching came into the game, catchers started to use gloves and other protective equipment. If a program decides to re-create a later era when catcher's equipment was used, this equipment will need to be provided.

The Catcher's Mask and Other Protective Equipment

Protective catching equipment evolved slowly and accompanied the development of faster pitching and base stealing. These changes required the catcher to wear a glove and move closer to the plate, be in position to catch the swift pitch before it hit the ground, and make a quick throw to second or third base in an attempt to put out the runner.

The practice of playing close to the batter put the catcher at risk of getting hit in the face, body, or fingers by a hard-hit foul tip. An informative resource on the development of the protective gear worn by the catcher is the website "Encyclopedia of Baseball Catchers," created and maintained by Chuck Rosciam at www.baseballcatchers.com. The section "Catcher's Equipment — Tools of Ignorance" reports that "Red Stockings founder Harry Wright preceded the mask with a 'mouth protector.' His invention was a fifty-cent rubber mouth guard similar to the mouthpiece a boxer wears." The website attributes the invention of the catcher's mask to "an Ivy League man, Fred Thayer, who in 1876 adapted a fencing mask for Alexander Tyng, for the Harvard Nine." The Rosicam website states that Thayer's mask was first worn by Tyng on April 12, 1877, and "caught on quickly among pros and amateurs alike."

Peter Morris, in *A Game of Inches: The Game on the Field*, also attributes the invention of the mask to Thayer, the captain of the Harvard team, but has found evidence that a mask constructed by Thayer may have been worn in 1876 by Howard Thatcher, Tyng's predecessor as the Harvard catcher. Analyzing the evidence supporting the claims of Thatcher and Tyng and the statements of various contemporary witnesses, Morris points out that "the identity of the first catcher to don a mask was a subject of a lively controversy in the nineteenth century and may never be definitively resolved." Agreeing with Rosciam's observations on the mask's rapid acceptance, Morris adds, "What is beyond question is that Tyng's use of the mask caused it to become popular, and this happened surprisingly quickly" (pp. 432–433). Professional catchers, fearing ridicule from spectators for wearing a mask, were at first reluctant to adopt the practice. Morris reports that "the first professional to wear the mask may have been Pete Hotaling, the catcher for the Syracuse Stars who was still recovering from the effects of being struck in the eye with a foul tip" in July 1877 (p. 434).

In regard to the other pieces of a catcher's equipment, Rosciam's "Encyclopedia of Catchers" reports that the chest protector was introduced by Detroit's Charley Bennett, who wore a chest pad "outside his jersey in 1886." Earlier experiments with chest protectors could have occurred, but the catchers involved may have "tried hiding the devices beneath their uniforms to avoid razzing." Shin guards did not come into use until the early part of the twentieth century and, as in the case with masks and chest protectors, catchers faced ridicule for wearing them, as evidenced by this passage from the Encyclopedia of Catchers:

> Catchers are expected to take their lumps without grumbling. But the early efforts of catchers to protect themselves met with a lot of flak. A typical reaction came from the crowd at the Polo Grounds when baseball's New York Giants opened the 1907 season against the Philadelphia Phillies. As the Giants took the field, star catcher Roger Bresnahan looked more like a goaltender than a backstop when he squatted behind the plate in a pair of thickly upholstered shin guards.

After masks, chest protectors, and shin guards became available, the catcher was in the difficult position of having to choose between wearing protective equipment and being ridiculed as unmanly. In his discussion of the catcher's physical vulnerability, Morris includes an important statement in favor of the catcher's mask from Henry Chadwick, which appeared in the May 19, 1877, edition of the *Brooklyn Eagle*: "Thayer's invention to protect the catcher from dangerous hits in the face when playing close up behind the bat attracted considerable attention. In fact the wire mask is something all catchers who face swift pitching should have." As the 1877 season went on and professional catchers were slow to adopt the mask as quickly as the amateurs had "wisely" done, Chadwick wrote that they should have the "moral courage" not to "tremble before the remarks of the small boys of the crowd of spectators." Rather than "run the risk of broken cheek bones, dislocated jaws, a smashed nose, or blackened eyes," catchers were advised to disregard "the chaff of the fools in the assemblage" and adopt Thayer's "valuable invention," the catcher's mask (p. 434).

The catcher's increased exposure to injury from sharply hit foul tips is a pivotal consideration when a new team is deciding what era they will present. If playing by the more safety-friendly pre–1860 or 1860 rules with slow pitching, the catcher is in little or no danger of being struck by a foul tip and no equipment is necessary. However, if the decision is made to emulate the style of play of a later era, which includes faster pitching and stealing, vintage base ball becomes more complicated and involves greater risk of injury to the catcher (and to spectators) from sharply hit foul tips. Under the later rules and customs, the vintage catcher, for the purposes of authenticity, will need to move closer to the plate, in the manner of the modern catcher who plays directly behind the batter. If wearing no mask or other protective equipment, the catcher is more vulnerable to potential injury by swift foul tips. While catchers in the fifteen years between the introduction of swift pitching around 1860 and the development of the catcher's mask in the mid–1870s might have been expected to play without protective equipment and "take their lumps without grumbling," this is not a situation that is appropriate for a vintage base ball program, where one of the chief goals of any program should be to make sure no one gets hurt while playing or watching. Programs should not expect catchers to move "close up behind the bat" without protective equipment. Nineteenth-century catchers, especially professionals on the elite clubs, might have been willing to take these risks and endure the "smashed nose or blackened eyes" mentioned by Chadwick, but the peer pressure and misplaced machismo of the nineteenth century that forced catchers to face the prospect of injury should not be allowed to resurface in vintage base ball today.

If playing according to the rules and practices of the 1880s or 1890s — the era after masks and other equipment came into use — and the catcher is provided with protective equipment, additional decisions must be made regarding the nature of the equipment. If the equipment used has been made to resemble nineteenth-century equipment, it may not provide the same type of protection for the catcher as modern catcher's masks and other gear. If modern masks, chest protectors, and shin guards are used, the safety factor goes up considerably, but the authenticity of its appearance decreases. Perhaps starting with a modern mask or chest protector and covering any synthetic materials and logos with canvas or other appropriate cloth would prove successful. Some vendors offer nineteenth-century catcher's equipment. Programs opting to portray the 1880s or 1890s may want to consult with existing programs from this era to learn what success they have had in purchasing or fashioning equipment that provides adequate protection while preserving an authentic look.

Programs should be aware of the marked changes in the game that occurred after 1860 or so, especially the advent of "swift pitching" and its immediate effects on the role of the catcher. Both the gentlemanly antebellum style of play and the rougher post–Civil War style have their strong suits and their passionate adherents. Both are valid forms of vintage base ball. They are quite different, however, and may not mix well, as the need for protective equipment for the catcher indicates.

Playing the Position

In a vintage game in which slow pitching is used, the catcher receives the pitch on the bound. Under the 1860 rules and practices, the exact distance the catcher plays behind the plate will vary from game to game and field to field, depending on the resiliency of the ball being used and the firmness of the soil or grass around home plate. If the soil is loose and sandy or if the ground has been softened by recent rains, the catcher needs to play relatively close — perhaps only six or eight feet behind the plate. If playing on a field (especially a modern skin infield) that has been baked in the sun until the surface resembles concrete, the catcher may play 15 to 20 feet behind the plate.

The correct place for the catcher to stand is determined by the natural path of a pitch after it bounces the first time. The catcher should be in a position to catch the pitch on the first bound, just after it reaches its peak from the first bound and starts to descend. To be prepared to receive the pitch, the catcher does not go into the deep crouch or squat associated with the modern catcher. Instead, he should go into a slight crouch with knees bent, ready to move up or down, left or right to catch the pitch or a foul tip. The pitch should be caught before it hits the ground the second time. If the ball is tipped by the batter, it can be caught for an out by either grabbing it in the air or after its first bounce. This sounds easier than it is. Unlike the perfectly groomed playing fields of modern baseball, the ground around home plate and the catcher's area is often quiet irregular, with all kinds of small hillocks and depressions, tufts of grass, stones, sticks, ruts, and other abnormalities that can cause the ball to bounce erratically once it hits the ground. The catcher must be alert for all of these bumps, holes, pebbles, and soft spots, and anticipate a bad hop.

Foul Tips

Standing ready to catch the pitch just as it starts to descend after the first bounce puts the catcher in the ideal position to retire the striker on a routine foul tip. The catcher should always be alert for the situation in which the striker swings at the pitch and barely nicks it, thereby hardly disturbing the trajectory of the ball. The ball continues on its original path, strikes the ground, and often bounds right into the catcher's hands if he has positioned himself correctly and is alert. If the catcher catches the foul tip before the ball hits the ground the second time, the batter is out. If the ball hits the ground twice (because the catcher is playing too deep) or if the catcher muffs the catch and drops it on the ground (for the second bound), the striker is not out and continues with his turn at bat. Retiring the striker on a foul tip is a very valuable out. Like a strikeout in modern baseball, the striker is out and has not advanced the runners.

The key to success for the catcher is alertness and concentration. He should assume that every pitch is going to result in a foul tip, keep his eye on the ball, keep his hands ready, and shift his feet to get in front of the ball as the pitch approaches the plate. This play — the routine foul tip right into the catcher's hands — usually occurs several times in a game, and it is incumbent upon the catcher to be poised to make this catch. When the striker starts to swing, there is a tendency for the catcher to relax momentarily and start following the expected flight of the ball into fair territory. Like the golfer who must remind himself to keep his head down and keep his eye on the ball as he hits it rather than glancing up too soon to follow the flight of the ball, the catcher must keep his eye on the pitch in order to follow it right into his hands if it is tipped. There will be plenty of time to watch where the ball goes if, in fact, it is hit into fair territory. If the pitch is tipped and the catcher has taken his eye off the ball, he will probably not catch it since the foul ball will quickly go past him before he can recover. Anticipating the foul tip on every pitch is the key to success in recording these valuable outs.

As is the case with any version or baseball or softball, one important factor in winning games is having a good defense that consistently avoids giving the other team four or five outs per inning. If an opportunity to make a fairly easy out presents itself in the form of a routine foul tip, it is important to make sure that the out is made. Of all the pitches that are thrown in a game, relatively few will result in a foul tip. But if the catcher gets only three tips during the course of a game, that is the equivalent of one entire inning's worth of outs. It is not unusual for the catcher to make six to eight outs per game on foul tips, and occasionally more — some on the fly and some on the bound, some routine and some difficult. These outs are rally-killers of the first magnitude and they take the burden off the other defensive players to make difficult barehanded catches of hard-hit flies, line drives, and grounders.

A foul tip caught on the first bounce does *not* result in an out in the modern game, which confuses spectators when a striker is put out in this manner. Consequently, the umpire should announce what has happened. Since, by the rules, the umpire should call all foul balls immediately and unasked, he can easily work an explanation into this announcement. "Foul! And caught on the first bound by the catcher. The striker is out."

The foul tip that just grazes (or just misses) the bat is a difficult call for all concerned. If the path of the ball is virtually unaltered, it is not easy for the umpire to know for sure if it is a foul tip or not. Often, the sound of the bat nicking the ball is the giveaway, and the umpire may make this call by ear rather than by eye. These borderline decisions present an opportunity for sportsmanship to come to the forefront. If the striker has tipped the ball, he usually knows it, and should not argue with the umpire's call that he is out. Although such outs can be frustrating for the striker, he should simply acknowledge that he is out by carrying his bat back to the bench (not slamming it to the ground) and taking a seat on the bench without any display of body language or bad language to express his distaste for the tip or the call. These things happen. The mature player realizes even the most talented players are retired on a foul tip now and then. Foul tips are part of the vintage game and players learn to take them in stride when they occur.

In cases in which the striker swings and the catcher thinks the bat tipped the ball but the umpire makes no call (indicating the swing was, in his judgment, a clean miss), the catcher should remain silent. He should not shout, "Hey, that was a foul tip! The striker should be out!" The umpire has made his decision and the catcher should abide by it, even if he is relatively certain a foul tip occurred. It is not the catcher's place to question the umpire's ruling on the play.

In rare cases, if the striker is called out but is very sure that he did *not* tick the ball, he may make a brief comment to the umpire to that effect. The umpire may simply say, "No, I am certain that I saw (or heard) the tick." If so, that is the end of the matter and the striker should not pursue it further. In some instances, the umpire may look to the catcher for corroboration. If invited by the umpire, the catcher may offer his view of what happened. On his honor as a gentleman, the catcher should be truthful and should not allow a striker to be declared out if he is reasonably sure that there was no tick. He might say, "I did not hear or see a tick, so I believe the striker is correct that no contact was made," in which case the umpire could reverse his original call. Another alternative is that the catcher might say, "I could not honestly tell if the bat struck the ball or not." If, on the other hand, the catcher believes that the striker did tip the ball and should be declared out, he should be courteous and diplomatic. He should not address the striker directly and snap, "No way! You were out!" or "No! I got you!" or any similar phrase that could be construed as being impolite or confrontational. If asked, he should respectfully address his comment to the umpire and say, "I believe I did hear the bat strike the ball" or "Yes, I observed the ball's path change just a bit, so I think some contact did occur." Even if the catcher thinks the batter did tip the ball, in the interests of good sportsmanship he might say, "I am sure the striker is an honorable gentleman and if he did not believe his bat touched the ball, he must be correct." The umpire, striker, and catcher should work together in these situations to try to make sure the correct call is made, and the players should be truthful in their comments to the umpire.

These gentlemanly exchanges bring great enjoyment to the spectators. If the striker acknowledges that he did nick the ball (and should be called out) or if the catcher indicates that the striker did not nick the ball (and should not be called out), the umpire and the interpreters can use this as an opportunity to discuss the culture of the game in this early period. Unaccustomed to the rules and gentlemanly norms of vintage base ball, the spectators may not understand why the original call was made and why it was either confirmed or reversed. Having been made aware of what is a happening, they marvel at this exceptional display of good sportsmanship and fairness since it represents an entirely different approach to sport than they are used to seeing. Instances of this type add to the charm and attraction of vintage base ball. Regardless of the score or which club eventually wins the game, the spectators (especially parents, grandparents, and educators) will admire both vintage teams and their high standards of sportsmanship, especially for the message being sent to the young people in the audience about honesty and fair play.

While foul tips that come straight back on a nice, easy bounce are common, the catcher typically has a number of opportunities to earn the appreciation of the crowd and his teammates with some unusual and even spectacular grabs. If a batter tops the ball, it may bounce directly on or in front of the plate and shoot straight up. The catcher must quickly dive forward and try to snare it on the first bound for an out (sometimes before the batter has even taken a step). The catcher should keep in mind that if the ball bounces and hits the striker, it is still a live ball and can be fielded off the striker's arm or shoulder for an out before it hits the ground for the second time.

An especially tough play for the catcher occurs when a batter takes a very hard cut at the ball and hits just enough of the bottom part of the ball to send a swift, low line drive behind the plate. If a sharply hit foul tip comes back around chest or belt high, the catcher needs to be quick to grab it before it deflects off his body or goes over his shoulder. If one of these swift foul tips is hit directly at the catcher's feet (as often happens), the catcher must drop down quickly, hoping to stab at the ball and come up with it on the fly or the short hop. If it is off to one side or the other, the catcher may have to dive laterally for the ball while trying to grab it with one outstretched hand near the ground, usually on the short hop. In addition to catching foul tips on the first bound, the catcher will be called upon to field some foul pop-ups on the fly. Foul balls often have considerable backspin, making these pop-ups difficult to catch barehanded

If playing on a diamond with a backstop, the catcher needs to keep in mind that the ball is in play until it hits the ground for the second time. Therefore, even if a high foul pop or a hard-hit foul ball has gone over his head, it is possible for the catcher to spin around and take it on the rebound off the backstop for the out. On a field with no backstop, the side of a barn or trunk of a tree may serve the same purpose.

Since any ball, fair or foul, caught on the fly or the first bound is an out, the catcher is called upon to range far from his position behind the plate to chase foul balls. The 1860-era rules create some very interesting plays that would not occur in a modern baseball or softball game. These plays call for agility and hustle on the part of the catcher.

Some plays require effective infield teamwork. On a foul pop-up down the third-base line, the catcher, third baseman, and pitcher should converge on the ball, as it will sometimes bounce straight up in the vicinity of the baseline and sometimes kick off into foul territory. By forming a triangle and surrounding the ball, one of the players should be in position to make the play. If a right-hander hits a foul pop-up down the first-base line, it will almost always bounce sharply at a right angle into foul territory. Therefore, instead of running directly down the line to the spot where the ball is going to hit the ground, the catcher should anticipate the direction of the bound and dash over by the bench in foul territory to try to catch the ball on the bound before it hits the ground for the second time. All this takes some experience in reading the speed and spin of the ball and developing a sense for knowing the direction it will bounce.

When chasing a foul ball, the catcher should remember that everything is in play unless specifically mentioned in the ground rules peculiar to that field. A foul ball may bounce off a tree, fence, barn, shed, the players' bench, scorer's table, or similar object and still be caught for an out. Over the years, many unusual and even humorous outs have been recorded on foul balls that have bounced off a variety of objects. At a Muffin game at a community festival several years ago, a high pop foul came down on the roof of a portable outhouse located in a parking lot about 50 feet from the plate, took a high bounce in the air before coming down onto the top of a historic carriage and, as it trickled off the front of the vehicle, was caught by the catcher before it hit the ground. Constituting one of those "truth is stranger than fiction" incidents that can occur under the bound rule, it was dubbed "the privy play" and has never been forgotten by those who were in attendance. The catcher needs to be ready for anything.

Fair Balls

A ball that hits the ground in fair territory is judged to be a fair ball even if kicks back into foul territory. If the catcher can move forward quickly and catch the ball on the first bound as it reverses direction, the batter is out. The ball is in play, however, and runners can advance at their own risk. If the catcher dives for a fair ball in the vicinity of the plate, he must recover quickly and be ready to make a throw to second or third base to retire a runner trying to advance. If the ball could not be caught on the first bound, the catcher needs to be alert and make the appropriate play. He may be able to grab the ball after it has bounced for the second time and make an accurate throw to the first baseman to retire the striker, or (depending on the number of outs, number of runners, and the score of the game) he may elect to try to put a runner out at another base.

On this play the catcher must be careful not to charge out so quickly that he overruns the ball. If he does, it may, due to its backspin, bounce past him into foul territory, where it may roll a considerable distance behind the plate. Since this is a fair ball, the striker will likely end up making first base and the runners will advance while the catcher chases the ball. Basically, on a pop-up hit out in front of the plate, the catcher needs to watch where the ball is going to hit on the first bound and then move to where he thinks the ball will bounce again, prepared to make the catch before it hits the ground for the second time.

The Play at the Plate

A play that has potential for being far from humorous occurs when a runner is trying to score on a close play at the plate. In modern baseball, a collision can result if the ball and the runner reach home plate at the same time. In vintage base ball, players should try to make sure this does not happen. In order to avoid a collision at the plate, the catcher should not block the plate as a modern catcher would do, but position himself about three feet in front of the plate where he can take the throw and then make a swipe tag on the runner as he goes by. He should allow the runner a clear path to the plate. This is in keeping with Section 21 of the 1860 Rules, which says that "if the player is prevented from making a base, by the intentional obstruction of an adversary, he shall be entitled to the base, and not put out." Perhaps the catcher does not mean to obstruct. Maybe an errant throw has pulled him into the runner's path or, due to inexperience or forgetfulness, the catcher may just happen to be standing on the plate directly in the path of the incoming runner.

In this case, the umpire should not require the runner to step directly on the plate if the catcher, waiting for the throw, is blocking the runner's path. If the runner passes directly behind the catcher while the catcher is standing or kneeling on the plate, the runner may be declared safe and his run counts. It is a common (and wise) practice in vintage base ball not to split hairs over whether the obstruction was intentional or not. Whatever the circumstances, if the runner appears to have beaten the throw, is acting in a sportsmanlike manner by trying to avoid colliding with the catcher, and passes near the plate, the umpire should not call him out for not touching the plate and should declare that his run counts. If the catcher has received the ball and is ready to make the tag as the runner approaches home, the runner should never crash into the catcher in order to try to make him drop the ball. The proper course of action in this scenario would be for the runner to either stop and try to get back to third or to acknowledge that the throw has beaten him to the plate and submit to being tagged out.

The Catcher's Role

Vintage base ball catchers come in all sizes and ages. In *A Game of Inches: The Game on the Field,* Peter Morris includes a section on "Catcher's Size," in which he discusses the requirements for the position. One school of thought felt it was best to have a tall player with a long reach at catcher. "As a rule, however, early clubs put one of their best athletes behind the plate, which more often meant a small, athletic man." But change was coming. "Once catchers began to play directly behind the plate, the focus shifted away from agility and toward size" (p. 201). In vintage base ball, the possibility of making outs on foul tips throughout the game makes the position of catcher more like an extra infielder stationed behind the plate than the modern baseball catcher who is usually a sturdily built but less-agile player.

In the 1860 *Beadle's Dime Base-Ball Player,* Henry Chadwick advised, "As the position occupied by the Catcher affords him the best view of the field, the person filling it is generally chosen captain." In vintage base ball the catcher is not always the captain. However, whether he is the official captain or not, because he has the entire field in front of him, he should assume some leadership throughout the game by reminding the pitcher and the infielders of situations as they develop — how many outs there are, where force plays can be made, whether to try to put out a runner scoring from third or make the play on the striker at first base. Chadwick also directs the catcher to make the call on which player should handle a pop-up in the infield. "The Catcher, whenever he sees several fielders running to catch a ball, should designate the one he deems most sure of taking it, by name, in which case the others should refrain from the attempt to catch the ball on the fly, and strive only to take it on the bound in case of its being otherwise missed" (p. 21).

Because his location on the field is close to the spectator areas, the vintage catcher will have the opportunity to do considerable interpreting while the game is in progress. He can move toward the audience between batters and offer a comment or two regarding what just happened on the field while explaining plays that differ from modern baseball rules. For example, he might turn to the crowd and, anticipating their questions, comment that a batter was out immediately on a sharp one-bounder to the pitcher and therefore the runner on first was not forced to run and wisely elected to hold his base. Or he might explain that a grounder struck down the third-base line and passed third in foul territory is considered fair because it first hit the ground in fair territory. The catcher can also comment on superb defensive plays by teammates so that the audience is reminded of the skill the fielder has shown in making a running catch on a high fly ball, a play that might be fairly routine with a modern glove but one that takes extraordinary skill without one. If the catcher can sprinkle his remarks with the names of some of the players and a few period phrases, all the better. "The left fielder, Mr. Graley, certainly made a very manly barehanded catch on that well-struck ball to prevent the striker from making his base. Extraordinary catch, Mr. Graley! Well done!" Remarks of this type keep the spectators informed and engaged in the game.

One duty of the vintage catcher that is usually taken for granted but is still important is returning the ball to the pitcher. The catcher should take care to give his pitcher a good chest-high throw on every return toss so that the pitcher does not have any difficulty catching it. If an errant throw gets through the pitcher, a runner may be able to advance to the next base while the ball is being retrieved. Also, on a hot day, it is always a good idea to make it easy for the pitcher by not making him repeatedly jump in the air, go down on one knee, or run laterally to catch erratic return throws.

The vintage catcher faces many challenges and is fully engaged in the match. He may be standing far behind the plate by modern standards, but onlookers quickly learn that he is in the center of the action and in the course of a typical game, a number of unusual and interesting plays are made by the catcher.

Terminology

In vintage base ball circles, the catcher has sometimes been referred to as the "behind." Recent research has shown that this is probably an incorrect term for the catcher and one that was not used in the nineteenth century. In all the rule books, guidebooks, and box scores, the term "catcher" or the abbreviation "c" is consistently used. The confusion began in the 1980s when some of the early vintage base ball researchers read game accounts that used such phrases as "Smith was the pitcher, Jones behind." In these cases, "behind" is shorthand for "Jones was behind the plate at the position of catcher." The term "behind" was not the official name of the position being manned by one of the players but simply a description of the catcher's location in reference to home plate. Although the misunderstanding had endured, most agree that "behind" is not an authentic term and "catcher" is the correct name of the position.

Pitcher

In a vintage base ball game played according to the rules and practices of the 1860 period or earlier, the first duty of the pitcher is to consistently deliver the ball over the plate.

Playing the Position

The Delivery

According to the original Knickerbocker Rules of 1845, "The ball must be pitched, and not thrown, for the bat," a phrase repeated verbatim in the 1854 Rules. This means that the pitcher was expected to deliver the ball with an underhand motion so that the striker could hit it and put it in play.

In a *Game of Inches: The Game on the Field*, Peter Morris states, "In many of the bat and ball games that were popular in the first half of the nineteenth century, the action was initiated by a 'feeder' who tossed the ball to the batter without any thought of making it difficult to hit. Under the Knickerbockers Rules, the pitcher was initially still expected to toss hittable balls to the batter" (p. 25). This style of slow pitching was also used in early cricket. In an article published in the May 11, 1888, edition of the *Brooklyn Eagle*, Henry Chadwick, describing the various sports and pastimes he enjoyed as a boy growing up in Brooklyn a half-century earlier, recalled, "In those days they played old fashioned cricket, with a slow underhand twisting bowling, the swift round arm bowling of the present day being then unknown."

This original style of slow pitching (similar to modern slow-pitch softball) makes perfect sense if the purpose of having a base ball club is to provide exercise for the members. The Knickerbockers wanted a fast-paced game marked by a lot of action (and few lulls in activity) that would provide exercise — hitting and baserunning for the side at bat and catching, throwing, and running for the side in the field.

Henry Chadwick's commentary on the 1860 Rules says of the pitcher: "He must pitch the ball, not jerk or throw it; and he must deliver the ball as near as possible over the home base, and for the striker, and sufficiently high to prevent its bounding before it passes the base." To keep the game moving along briskly — a very important consideration for a vintage game played before a crowd of spectators — it is important to select a player who possesses excellent control for the role of the pitcher. Nothing kills spectator interest faster than a pitcher who has trouble getting the ball over the plate or is trying too hard to make his pitches difficult to hit. A good rule of thumb is that the striker should be able to put the ball in play on the first pitch and certainly within the first three pitches he sees. If a batter has to let four or more pitches go by without getting a good one to hit, the spectators will get restless and, thinking of other ways to spend a summer afternoon, will drift away from the game.

One effective way to identify players who have the muscle memory skills to be effective pitchers is to set up the following exercise at a practice session. Place a small towel (approximately 18 inches by 24 inches) on the ground, with the front edge of the towel about two feet directly behind the back edge of the plate so that the towel marks the location where a good pitch (one that has passed directly over the plate about waist high) would hit the ground. After some warm-up pitches to find the range from the standard pitching distance of 45 feet, those who aspire to be pitchers should be able to hit the towel about three tosses out of four attempts. This exercise identifies those who can consistently deliver the ball over the plate and "for the striker." If a pitcher experiences problems putting the ball over the plate in a match, the captain should be prompt in replacing the pitcher to keep the game moving at an interesting pace.

An illustration of a pitcher about to deliver the ball appears in Haney's *Book of Base*

Ball Reference for 1867 and serves as an excellent model of the proper stance and form for a pitcher in vintage base ball. The pitcher is standing in an upright pose, facing the plate, with his arm drawn back. The caption above the drawing reads: "The following is the attitude of the pitcher when about to make the last swing of his arm in delivery." The caption below the illustration reads, "In delivering the ball, the arm can be bent at an angle, but not outward from the body; when so bent, it must hang perpendicularly."

Further evidence that slower pitching was the standard through the late 1850s and early 1860s comes from an article published in the April 5, 1879, issue of the *Brooklyn Eagle*. The article appeared under the headline "Old Games / Base Ball Matches of Twenty Years Ago/ Putnam vs. Eckford in 1859 — General Dakin's Old Record." In recapping the 1859 lineups of Brooklyn's four clubs, the following observation is offered regarding the "very strong battery" of the Putnam Club: "Masten was one of the most graceful catchers that ever handled a ball, and Dakin was quite a strategist in pitching. The swift — Creighton style — pitching had not then come into vogue, THE SQUARE PITCH of the ball being then the rule."

Using the underhand motion of the 1860s is Dave Brooks of the Cincinnati Red Stockings. Overhand pitching was not permitted until the mid–1880s (courtesy Joel Moore).

According to the illustration in Haney's *Book of Base Ball Reference for 1867* and the accompanying instructions, Chadwick's use of the term "the square pitch" likely refers to the pitcher squarely facing the batter and, as he takes a step toward home plate, simultaneously swinging his arm and delivering the ball with a smooth underhand motion, keeping his arm close to his body and perpendicular to the ground. The palm of his hand should be open and facing the batter throughout the delivery. This style of pitching would be in contrast to the style that developed later in which the pitcher would turn his body away from the batter in a wind-up and then lift his arm away from his body, creating a sidearm delivery in order to get more velocity on the ball (and perhaps snapping his wrist in the process). The illustration and the captions show that even after swift pitching had entered the game, Chadwick tried to preserve the original underhand motion and limit the pitcher's ability to put too much speed on the ball.

The Pitcher's Point

In the 1860 Rules, the pitcher's location on the field was called the "pitcher's point" and was marked by a white disk. As Chadwick's 1860 commentary states, "The player's position is behind a line four yards in length, drawn at right angles to a line from home to second base, and having its center upon that line at a point distant forty-five feet from the former base." The pitcher could move laterally along the twelve-foot white line, but was required to deliver the ball from behind the line.

In referring to the pitcher's location on the field, vintage players will sometimes slip and refer to the pitcher being "on the mound," since that is such a common phrase in modern baseball. However, especially when talking to spectators, vintage base ball participants should keep in mind that the pitcher's mound did not exist in the 1860s. In *A Game of Inches: The Game Behind the Scenes*, Peter Morris states, "The pitcher's mound originated sometime in the late 1880s or early 1890s" (p. 71). Prior to the advent of the mound, Morris points out that "the pitcher's box was introduced as two parallel lines; the pitcher had to be standing between them to deliver the ball. It was modified repeatedly and finally eliminated after the 1892 season" (p. 69). After providing a history of the evolution of the pitcher's place on the field through the nineteenth century, Morris describes the origin of the modern-day pitching rubber. "In 1893, the pitcher's box was eliminated entirely and replaced with a single plate with which the pitcher's foot had to remain in contact until the ball left his hand." To prevent the pitcher's foot from slipping (as had been the case when marble was used in earlier years), the plate "was made of rubber and became known as the rubber" (p. 71). Therefore, it was not until the 1890s that the rubber and the mound became part of the playing field.

Vintage programs that play according to the rules of the period from 1863 to 1892 will want to research the dimensions of the pitcher's box during the year being portrayed on the field and mark it off accordingly. The presence of the pitcher's box should provide an interesting conversational topic when interpreting the game to spectators. As Morris points out, while its existence in the nineteenth century lingers on in present-day references to a pitcher being "knocked out of the box" or the ball being hit "back through the box," the actual pitcher's box has not been part of the playing field for more than a hundred years.

In the 1860-era game, many vintage teams follow the custom of having the pitcher hold the ball in his pitching hand out in front of his head or chest area as he stands at the pitcher's point. This is done in order to show the ball to the batter and indicate that he is about to deliver the ball, allowing the batter to be ready to swing. There does not seem to be any specific statement in the rules that requires the pitcher to show the ball to the batter and make sure he is ready for the pitch. But this custom does seem to be in keeping with the sportsmanlike nature of the game. As he holds the ball where the batter can see it and prepares to deliver the ball, the pitcher should stand about three feet behind the line so that when he takes a normal step toward the plate, he will still be in compliance with the rules.

Chadwick's commentary is clear: "When in the act of delivering the ball, the Pitcher must avoid having either foot in advance of the line of his position, or otherwise a baulk will be declared; this penalty is also inflicted when he moves his arm with the apparent purpose of delivering the ball, and fails so to do" (p. 22). In addition to not stepping over the line, the pitcher needs to remember that once he draws his arm back, he may not stop in the middle of his delivery and is required to complete the pitch to the batter. In keeping with the gentlemanly nature of the game, he could not fake a pitch in order to deceive the

The following is the attitude of the pitcher when about to make the last swing of the arm in delivery.

In delivering the ball the arm can be bent at angle, but not outward from the body; when so bent in delivery it must hang perpendicularly.

Drawing on the illustration and captions in Haney's *Base Ball Book of Reference for 1867*, Ohio Village Muffin Frank Thompson practices the proper delivery.

batter or the base runners as to when the pitch was coming, nor should he deliver a "quick pitch" before the striker is ready.

The Pitcher as Fielder

In addition to re-creating the act of pitching the ball as was done in the mid-nineteenth century, it is important to consider the pitcher's key role as fielder in the game's early days. Chadwick recommends, "He should be a good player at all points, but it is especially requisite that he should be an excellent fielder, and a swift and accurate thrower." The phrase "swift and accurate thrower" in this case refers not to delivering the ball to the plate but to making good throws to the bases to retire the striker or the base runners.

Chadwick's statement regarding the attributes of a good-fielding pitcher applies to vintage base ball. In the course of a typical game, the pitcher will have the opportunity to make a significant number of fielding plays. Strikers will send pop flies, hard-hit grounders, one-bounders, and line drives in the direction of the pitcher's position on the field and, since he is delivering the ball from only 45 feet from the plate, he needs to be an alert and agile fielder with quick hands and a good sense of what to do with the ball when it is hit to him. It is especially advantageous if he is skilled at grabbing a hard-hit ball on the first bound for an instant out. The pitcher can improve his chances of being in the right place to field a ball by anticipating where the striker is likely to hit the ball and positioning himself accordingly. He can deliver the pitch from anywhere behind the twelve-foot line that runs through the pitcher's point. Therefore, he can move from side to side along that line, depending on whether the batter is right-handed or left-handed, and what direction he thinks the striker will attempt to hit the ball.

Chadwick notes, "The Pitcher will frequently have to occupy the bases on occasions when the proper guardian has left it to field the ball" (p. 22). A common example of this situation occurs when the first baseman goes far to his right to field a ball, then throws back to first base where the pitcher, hustling over from the pitcher's point, should be in position to take the throw and cover the base ahead of the arrival of the striker.

Under 1860-era rules, Ohio Village Muffin pitcher Mark Large delivers the ball from behind a 12-foot line through the Pitcher's Point, a disk located 45 feet from home plate.

Chadwick also points out that "in cases where a foul ball has been struck, and the player running a base endeavors to return to the one he has left, he [the pitcher] should be ready to receive the ball at the point nearest the base in question, in order to comply with Section 16 of the rules, wherein, in such cases, it is required that the ball be settled in the hands of the Pitcher before it is in play" (p. 22). This play involving a runner trying to get back to his base on a foul ball usually comes up several times in a vintage game. Take the example of the striker hitting a fly ball hit down the right-field line. The first baseman goes back and the right fielder comes in to field the ball while the runner on first starts for second, thinking the ball might be fair, in which case he can advance. While the ball is in the air, the alert pitcher should be running toward first base. If the ball comes down in foul territory, the runner must get back to his base before the ball does. The wording of the 1860 rule is that on a foul ball, the ball must "settle in the hands of the pitcher" during the play on the runner, but it doesn't say that the pitcher must remain on the pitcher's point. If the right fielder retrieves the ball and can throw it directly to the pitcher who is already covering first base, all provisions of the rule have been satisfied and there is a good chance the runner can be put out. If the right fielder retrieves the ball and must throw it all the way to the pitcher's point, where the pitcher catches it and then throws it to the first baseman who has returned to his base, so much time will have elapsed that the runner will probably have made it back safely.

The pitcher is often called upon to catch high pop flies in the center of the infield during the course of a typical game. Because of the dimensions of the diamond, it is often difficult for one of the infielders to be able to reach the area of the pitcher's point in time to make the play, requiring the pitcher to make the catch. A softball infield with 60-foot baselines contains 3,600 square feet, but a vintage base ball infield (like a modern baseball diamond) with 90-foot baselines contains 8,100 square feet — more than twice as much area. The degree of difficulty of catching a pop fly can be substantial since the ball often has considerable backspin. If the ball is hit over his head, the pitcher will need to make a difficult over-the-shoulder catch with his back to the plate. In a typical game there will also be several dribblers or "swinging bunts" in front of the plate that the pitcher will need to charge quickly and then make an accurate throw to the first baseman to retire the striker. On a passed ball that gets through the catcher, the pitcher must be ready to cover the plate if there is a runner on third. On throws coming to the infield from the outfield, he will need to back up the play at the appropriate base.

In vintage base ball, the pitcher with good control of his pitches is the key to keeping the game moving at a rapid pace that maintains spectator interest. In addition, he often makes a dozen or so defensive plays during a game. The pitcher who fields his position well can make a substantial contribution to his club's defensive strength.

17
Pitching: Slow or Swift?

An earlier discussion of "Choosing an Era" (Chapter 4) describes several periods of vintage base ball and provides basic information on selecting an era to portray. However, from club to club and region to region, there was variation in the rules and in rule interpretation within each era. One of the most important differences was slow and swift styles of pitching.

Until the late 1850s and early 1860s, clubs employed a style of slower pitching similar to that used in modern slow-pitch softball. Around 1860, changes began to occur in the speed of the pitched ball. In Haney's *Base Ball Book of Reference for 1867*, Henry Chadwick reports that "swift pitching came into vogue with the lamented Creighton," a reference to young Jim Creighton (born 1841), who was regarded as the most talented player of his day at the time of his sudden passing at age twenty-one near the end of the 1862 season while playing for the Excelsior Club of Brooklyn. Chadwick acknowledges Creighton's influence on the game through "the host of imitators that followed him," but points out that Creighton's success "led to the introduction of the era of fast pitching and 'waiting games,' an evil which was only put a stop to by the changes made in the rules of the National Association, by which the penalty of calling balls was inflicted for unfair pitching, and more recently the much-needed reformation of describing unfair balls and defining fair pitching was introduced" (p. 107).

Ever the champion of traditional slower pitching, Chadwick, encouraging pitchers to value accuracy over speed, opined that while Creighton's "brilliant success as a pitcher" was usually "attributed entirely to his speed," it was actually "his command of the ball and consummate accuracy of aim" that "had more to do with the effectiveness of his pitching than anything else." Swift pitching made the ball much more difficult to hit. Therefore, if a vintage program decides to play by the 1860 rules and practices, the program leaders will need to further decide which interpretation the 1860 rules and practices in the area of pitching—slow or swift—is the better fit for the games it will present in a museum setting.

The difference between slow and swift pitching is significant. In their landmark work *Baseball: The Early Years*, Seymour and Mills wisely observed, "Baseball revolves around pitching. Change the pitching rules and you change the entire complexion of the game." With Seymour's advice in mind, program leaders need to think carefully about which way they want to present the 1860-style vintage game. It is essential to weigh the implications of preserving the original Knickerbocker practice of slow pitching versus adopting the later practice of faster pitching that would take over the game as the years rolled on.

The decision to use either slow or swift pitching will have a significant impact on the way the game is played. Ohio Village Muffin Andy Shuman pitches to a Dayton, Ohio, Clodbuster.

Co-Existing Pitching Styles

Both pitching styles—slow and swift—are historically accurate. Henry Chadwick's 1868 work, *The Game of Base Ball: How to Learn It, How to Play It, How to Teach It*, provides evidence that slow pitching continued to be widely used after swift pitching had made its way into the game. In discussing the position of catcher, Chadwick states, "If his pitcher has a medium-paced or slow delivery he must be a very active player, a sure catch, a swift and accurate thrower, more than ordinarily skillful in judging and catching foul balls, and expert in watching the bases. If, however, his pitcher be one swift in his delivery, the catcher must pay more attention to stopping the ball and to catching sharp tips from the bat" (Chapter III). This passage indicates that both slow and swift pitching styles are historically accurate for the 1860s era. If a program wishes to adopt the use of swift pitching, it may certainly take that step. However, those adopting swift pitching should not consider those who choose slow pitching to be less authentic in their presentation of the game. Both styles are authentic.

Nineteenth-Century Communications

In the late 1850s and the 1860s there was no standardized set of rules being used everywhere at the same time, largely due to the state of mid-nineteenth-century communications. This is a principal reason that both slow and swift pitching were used concurrently. Given the state of communications at the time, it would be unrealistic to assume that all the clubs conducted their games in accordance with the latest edition of the National Association of Base Ball Players Rules. Some clubs outside of the greater New York City area may have never seen a copy of *Beadle's Dime Base Ball-Player,* Haney's *Base Ball Book of Reference,* or any other guide or rule book. They would have continued playing the game according to the rules with which they were most comfortable, learned perhaps by word-of-mouth or from an older rule book. Some clubs were undoubtedly unaware of the rule changes voted on at the annual NABBP meetings, and those that were aware of them may have ignored them.

In the vintage base ball community today — even with e-mail, websites, social networks, and other modern methods of instant communication — clubs have arrived at different interpretations regarding rules and their implementation. Even when vintage clubs are communicating effectively about what various program are doing, they sometimes have honest differences of opinion as to how certain rules should be interpreted and how the game was played. Weighing various alternative rule interpretations, individual clubs may develop a set of rules, practices, and customs that is suitable for their players and compatible with the mission and environment of their host institution. In fact, such variations are true to the state of the game they are re-creating. It is easy to imagine how difficult it would have been for all the nineteenth-century clubs to play by exactly the same rules at the same time, even if they were inclined to do so, which they probably were not. The differing interpretations and applications of the rules provide a museum with a vintage base ball team (or a museum thinking of starting one) with the advantage of flexibility in presenting a successful program that is historically accurate and in keeping with the overall goals and mission of the museum.

Pitching Rules, Practices, and Styles

At a meeting on February 25, 1857, representatives from sixteen clubs (listed as the Knickerbocker, Gotham, Eagle, Empire, Putnam, Baltic, Excelsior, Atlantic, Harmony, Harlem, Union, Eckford, Bedford, Nassau, Continental, and Olympic) adopted a set of rules for the coming season. Section 6 of the 1857 Rules amends the rule on pitching by stating, "The ball must be pitched, not jerked or thrown to the bat." By adding the term "jerked," the rule makers may have been trying to ban a delivery similar to that used in modern fast-pitch softball to propel the ball more swiftly. The ban on jerking the ball indicates that some pitchers must have been putting more speed on the pitch in this manner. It also suggests that the major clubs of the day were trying to put a stop to it and preserve the status quo of slow pitching.

In "The Art of Pitching a Baseball," an article published in 1886 in *Scientific American,* Henry Chadwick offered several illuminating observations as he compared the game of the 1880s with the earlier days. Chadwick pointed out that "one cannot look back to the early period in the history of baseball without being struck with the great contrast between the work done on the diamond field at Hoboken, in the 'fifties,' and that which marks the play of the leading professional teams of the present era." The major change, according to Chadwick, was in "the great degree of skill now shown in the pitching department," especially the development of *"the horizontal curve of the ball through the air,* something practically unknown in the days of old on the historic Elysian Fields at Hoboken." Since it takes some speed to throw a curveball (either underhand or overhand), the absence of curves supports the case that the pitching of the 1850s was relatively slow.

A *Brooklyn Eagle* article of April 5, 1879, characterized the year 1859 as representative of an earlier time when the rules and practices of base ball and the general atmosphere surrounding the game were far different. "That was in the days of legitimate amateur playing, when professionalism had not been thought of, and pool selling, with its sequel of 'crooked' play, was something unknown." The professionalism and the fast pitching of Creighton and the others who quickly followed changed the character of the elite clubs of the East. Winning became more important than the old goals of playing for recreation and exercise in a sportsmanlike manner.

Before things changed, Chadwick reminds his readers that "the old pitchers of the period in question [the late 1850s] literally *pitched* the ball to the bat, they not being allowed the advantage of throwing the ball [overhand] as our modern pitchers are." Writing in the 1880s after the overhand delivery had been legalized, Chadwick points out that since the term "pitcher" originally referred to one who delivers the ball underhand, applying that term to the "occupant of the box in our professional teams of today is a misnomer." These comments indicate that the underhand pitching of the 1850s was considerably slower than the overhand pitching of the 1880s. He also says that the pitcher delivered the ball to the bat, which supports the point of view that in the original way base ball was played, the pitcher was a feeder for the striker and delivered his pitches over the plate at a slow speed. This style of pitching continues to be the preferred custom among many of the vintage clubs that play by the rules and practices of the late 1850s and early 1860s, especially those emphasizing the gentlemanly character and sportsmanlike nature of the early game.

Increased emphasis on winning matches led to the recruitment of more highly skilled players than might be found among the general membership of the club. Players who were more skilled further contributed to the pressure to win since bets were increasingly being placed on the games. Placing bets created an environment for gamblers that Henry Chadwick strongly opposed throughout his long career. Since some players were now taking money or other rewards for their services rather than playing strictly for the honor of their club, they could be bribed and bought by gamblers, leading to the "crooked" play that Chadwick found so objectionable and contemptible.

Considerations for Program Leaders

As programs weigh the pros and cons of slow pitching and swift pitching, there are a number of factors that should be kept in mind. The following areas should be considered in structuring the club and interpreting the rules and practices.

Length of Games and Spectator Appeal

In vintage games that are played with slow pitching, the match moves along at a brisk pace, with nine innings usually being played in about ninety minutes (often less), and almost always in less than two hours. The pace and length of the game are ideal for the spectators at a museum or historic site. Commenting on the practice of slow pitching that was characteristic of early bat and ball games in *A Game of Inches: The Game on the Field* Peter Morris correctly points out that in these games, including the "New York Game" of the Knickerbockers, "the premise was that each batter got to strike the ball once and that the pitch was the prelude to the fundamental conflict: The batter's effort to make his way home before the fielders could put him out" (p. 25).

The length of the game changed, however, when some pitchers began using "speedy pitching and spinning their pitches," while others "hit upon the simpler and maddeningly effective approach of deliberately throwing wide pitches to tempt batters to swing at pitches that were difficult to hit squarely." Morris believes that some pitchers began using these new tactics as early as 1856 (p. 25).

Swift pitching emerged despite the fact that the rules of the period tried to require the pitcher to deliver a pitch that could be hit. In 1854, Rule 3 stated, "The ball must be pitched, not thrown, for the bat," which refers to an underhand toss delivered to the area where the batter can reach it and at a speed that is hittable. Section 6 of the 1857 Rules specified, "The pitcher must deliver the ball as near as possible, over the centre of the home base." Section 5 of the 1858 Rules contains similar wording. After defining the pitcher's position as "a point fifteen yards distant from the home base," it was specified that "the pitcher must deliver the ball as near as possible over the center of said base, and for the striker." Section 5 of the 1860 Rules is almost identical: "The pitcher must deliver the ball as near as possible over the home base, and for the striker." Despite the consistency of the rules requiring the pitcher to do his best to deliver hittable pitches, pitchers could get away with deviating from the letter or the spirit of the rules because there was no penalty for throwing any number of pitches that were outside the area the batter could reach with his bat. In his commentary in the 1860 *Beadle's Dime Base-Ball Player*, Henry Chadwick clearly states that "it will be seen that the rule requires the ball to be pitched as near as possible over the home base, *and for the striker*; the pitcher, therefore, has no right to pitch the ball to the catcher ... and umpires should see that the rule is enforced" (p. 12).

In regard to the practice of pitchers intentionally delivering unhittable pitches, Morris points out, "Batters retaliated by playing what was known as the 'waiting game' and not swinging at all" (p. 25). In his 1860 commentary, Chadwick admonishes the batter to keep the game moving and play in an upright way by swinging at hittable pitches:

> A good Batsman strikes at the first good ball pitched to him, and this is decidedly the fairest and best method to be adopted, as it is the most likely to lead to a successful result, and keeps the game lively and interesting. It is exceedingly annoying to the spectators, and creates a bad impression of the merits of the game on those not familiar with it, to see good balls repeatedly sent to the Batsman without being hit, or the ball passed to and from the pitcher and catcher, while the Batsman stands still, awaiting the movements of the player on the first base.

To address this problem, the 1858 Rules introduced the important new concept of the called strike. Section 37, labeled "Calling Strikes," states, "Should a striker stand at the bat without striking at good balls repeatedly pitched to him, for the purpose of delaying the game, or of giving advantage to a player, the umpire, after warning him, shall call one strike, and if he persists in such action, two, and three strikes. When three strikes [are] called, he shall be subject to the same rules as if he had struck at the balls." The text of the rule is repeated nearly verbatim in the 1860 Rules.

In his commentary on the 1860 Rules, Chadwick notes that "Section 37 is a rule that should be strictly enforced, as it refers to a point of the game that is oft times a very tedious and annoying feature" (p. 16). Chadwick was especially critical of the growing practice of the batter letting good pitches go by, hoping that sooner or later a pitch would be mishandled by the catcher, allowing runners to advance to the next base. "How often do we see the striker — the moment his predecessor has made his first base — stand still at the home base, and await the moment when the player on the first base can avail himself of the first failure of the pitcher and catcher to hold the ball, while tossing it backward and forward to each other." Even when the pitcher and catcher "are inclined to do their duty" by putting the ball over the plate, the batter should not be allowed to "stop the progress and interest of the game, by his refusal to strike at good balls, under the plea that they do not suit him, when it is apparent to all that he simply wants to allow his partner to get to his second base."

Gridlock

In trying to get pitchers to toss hittable pitches and batters to strike at hittable pitches, Chadwick points out the defects of the style of play in which many pitches were being made and few swings were taken. "In every respect it is preferable to play the game manfully and without resorting to any such trickery—for it is little else—as this, which not only tires the spectator, but detracts from the merit of the game itself." Morris quotes similar passages from the *New York Clipper*. In 1861, one player's "habit of waiting at the bat" was criticized as being "tedious and useless." In 1863 the *Clipper* admonished a club known for playing the "waiting game" to "repudiate it altogether" and to do "'the fair and square thing' with their opponents." Morris makes the key observation that Chadwick's efforts were not always successful because "these were appeals to the gentlemanly spirit, and that spirit was giving way to competitive fervor." While the rules allowed the umpire to call strikes, Morris reports that "few did so" and players were "increasingly taking the view that any tactic they could get away with was acceptable" (pp. 25–26).

For a period in the late 1850s and early 1860s when swift pitching entered the game, some pitchers began to ignore their traditional role as a feeder. Instead of keeping the game moving by consistently getting hittable pitches over the plate, a pitcher could repeatedly send balls that were out of reach in an attempt to get the batter to swing at a bad pitch. There was no rule to force him to throw the ball over the plate. This caused the number of pitches thrown in a game to get out of hand. The game of base ball was at a crossroads around 1860, and Morris makes the important observation that "the result was gridlock" (p. 26).

Morris cites an 1884 interview in the *St. Louis Post-Dispatch* with the knowledgeable Bob Ferguson, a leading player of the Enterprise and Atlantic clubs of Brooklyn in the 1860s. Since he had a long career as a manager, executive (president of the National Association), and umpire, his statements can be considered expert testimony on the state of the game in the 1860s. Looking back on his playing days, he remembered, "In an ordinary game, forty, fifty, and sixty balls were considered nothing for a pitcher before the batsman got suited" (p.26).

Ferguson's' recollections are no exaggeration. Similar examples have been reported in discussions among members of the vintage base ball community. In October, 2005 Dean Thilgen, a member of the St. Croix Club and a museum professional at the Minnesota Historical Society, noted that the recently published *Smithsonian Baseball: Inside the World's Finest Private Collections* included a box score dated November 8, 1859, of a game between the Portland Club of Maine and the Tri-Mountain Club of Boston, played on Boston Common. Under "Balls Pitched," the totals were 421 for the former and 259 for the latter—a total of 680 pitches for nine innings (p. 7). In December 2006, historian John Thorn shared his findings that in one of the early "all-star" benefit games played at the Fashion Race Course on Long Island in 1858, the totals were 297 by the New York pitcher and 436 by the Brooklyn pitcher, or 733 for the game. In January 2009, researcher Priscilla Astifan shared her discovery of a box score of a game played in Rochester, New York, in September 1860 that provides evidence of base stealing. The box score also shows what was beginning to happen when stealing and swift pitching came into the game: pitch totals of 407 for the Live Oak Club and 331 for the Olympic Club, adding up to 738 for the match, which had to be called after seven innings due to darkness. In an April 2009 post, veteran player and researcher Bob Tholkes of the Minnesota Quicksteps pointed out that in the August 23, 1860, match between the Excelsiors and Atlantics, 638 pitches were thrown before the game was called in the sixth inning (when the Excelsiors left the field due to the unsportsmanlike behavior of the supporters of the Atlantics).

These numbers have important consequences for a vintage base ball program that is considering adopting the practice of swift pitching as part of its presentation of an 1860-era game. The evidence shows that faster pitching created a situation marked by 700-pitch games that lasted for hours and sometimes had to be called due to darkness. The *New York Clipper* of August 15, 1863, reported on a game between the Union and Eckford clubs that "began at 3:30, and so irregular was the pitching, or so particular the batsmen … that it was 6:30 P.M. before the 5th inning was terminated, an average of nearly half an hour to an inning, or four hours and a half to a game. This, of course, made the contest a wearisome one for the on-lookers." Interpreting the 1860 Rules and practices to include swift pitching (and base stealing, which promotes the batter taking many hittable pitches to give the runners the chance to advance) is probably not something that most visitors to vintage base ball programs would find appealing to watch. Criticism is often leveled at the length and pace of modern major league games with "only" 200 to 300 pitches per game. Imagine if there were 600 to 700! For those clubs of the late 1850s and early 1860s that started to use swift pitching, the state of "gridlock" seems to have remained in effect for several seasons, presenting what Morris called "a grave dilemma for the game's rules makers." Instead of a contest between the batter and the fielders as it was originally conceived, the game had evolved into a contest between the batter and the pitcher, with the role of the fielders diminished. To resolve the impasse, Morris writes, "In 1864 the concept of called balls and called strikes was added to the rule book, along with a warning system by which the count began only when the umpire decided that either the pitcher or the batter was deliberately stalling." Since warnings continued to be required for several years, the gridlock was not resolved immediately. For several decades, the rule makers experimented with establishing the point in the striker's turn at bat when the warning should be issued to the pitcher and how many subsequent "unfair" pitches should constitute grounds for awarding the batter his base (a "walk" in modern terminology). Although imperfect, the 1864 rule empowered the umpire to start calling balls as well as strikes, providing a way to keep the game moving.

Program leaders should keep in mind that if the pitching is accurate and slow ("over the center of the home base, and for the striker"), there is no gridlock. The 1858 and 1860 rules allow the umpire to call strikes, but in vintage games with slow pitching it virtually never happens. If the pitcher is able to put the ball over the plate, the batters will usually swing at the first good pitch they see, and the game will advance at a lively pace.

In noticing the differences between 1860 base ball and modern baseball, spectators will observe that the umpire stands off to the side of home plate and does not usually call any balls and strikes. They may ask if not calling balls and strikes will mean that the game will last an unusually long time. If the pitcher follows the spirit and intent of the rules by acting in the traditional role of a feeder, they can be assured that the opposite is true and that the game will proceed at a much more rapid pace than when balls and strikes are called.

Even after the gridlock situation had been addressed by rule changes that allowed for the calling of both balls and strikes, Henry Chadwick continued to advance the fact that slower pitching made the game more interesting for players and spectators. Swift pitching, Chadwick observed, over-emphasized the role of the pitcher and de-emphasized the role of the other players on defense. In Haney's *Base Ball Book of Reference for 1867*, he remarked, "In swift pitching the work in the field lays chiefly between the pitcher and catcher, the infielders only occasionally getting a little employment, the main dependence for success being on the swift pitching." With slower pitching, however, "the reverse is the case, for it is on excellence in fielding" that success in the game is determined. With slower pitching, "instead of the tedium of listening to the cry of 'foul' or 'three strikes out' from the Umpire, in a game marked by swift pitching, ... we have ... a display in the field of the most attractive features of the game, ... affording ample opportunities for a development of fine fielding in the way of taking difficult fly balls, and in making beautiful stops, and accurate throws to bases, while all the attraction of double and treble plays are shown" (pp. 107–108).

These 1868 comments were in keeping with Chadwick's earlier interest in seeing stellar defensive play preserved as a key element of the game. In the September 9, 1863, issue of the *Brooklyn Eagle*, he expressed the view that "lively fielding is the beauty of base ball, ... and the moment anything is done to deprive it of this special attraction, as swift pitching does, that moment it will cease to be the popular game that it will otherwise ever be." The modern reader could take exception to this prediction about the game's future popularity and point to current statistics that show millions of people attending professional baseball games every year as spectators. However, Chadwick was right on target in regard to the popularity of *playing* the game. Very few adults play fast-pitch baseball or softball. The version of base ball that is played by millions today is slow-pitch softball, where the pitching is similar to the rules and practices of the national pastime from 1845 through the 1850s and early 1860s.

Safety of Spectators

One consequence of adopting swift pitching is the increased possibility of injury to spectators. With slow pitching, foul balls usually do not pose much danger to spectators. With fast pitching, however, foul balls have greater velocity and the batter has less control of the direction where foul balls go, resulting in more line drives entering the spectator area. Therefore, if faster pitching is permitted, spectators should be moved farther away from the home plate area of the playing field and/or placed behind a backstop or screens in order to decrease the possibility of being struck by sharply hit foul balls.

Safety of Players

The safety of the catcher is another point that programs should keep in mind when considering the era to be represented. In the 1860s, with the advent of swift pitching and stealing bases, the catcher started to move closer to the plate, playing directly behind the batter. This means that policy decisions will need to be made about the expectations for the catcher in a vintage game — whether he should continue playing far enough behind the plate to take the pitch (safely) on the bound or if he should play directly behind the plate and catch the pitch just after it crosses the plate. When playing well behind the plate, as the catcher does in games involving slower pitching, catchers are not in danger of being injured by foul tips. But in games involving faster pitching and stealing, Chadwick offers this advice in *Beadle's Dime Base-Ball Player*: "When a player has made his first base, the Catcher should take a position nearer the striker, in order to take the ball from the pitcher before it bounds." If these instructions are followed, and the catcher is positioned directly behind the batter, he is much more likely to be struck by sharply hit foul balls, or occasionally by the bat.

Aside from being struck by a foul tip, the speed of the pitch is another consideration for a catcher representing an era before gloves were used. In Haney's *Base Ball Book of Reference for 1867*, Chadwick points out this problem with swift pitching—the potential for injury to the catcher's hands. "A swift pitcher requires his catcher to stand up well and receive his punishment boldly, and especially to stop all balls, even if they happen to be too hot to hold neatly" (p. 106).

Protective equipment is not a viable option from a historical perspective for an 1860-style game involving swift pitching since gloves, masks, and other protective wear were not yet in use. While some catchers in the 1860s, especially those on the elite eastern teams who were perhaps being paid (openly or under the table) to play as professionals, may have been willing to move up and play directly behind the batter and catch swift pitches with no glove and risk being hit by foul tips with no mask, expecting a catcher on a vintage team to assume these risks is neither realistic nor wise.

The Added Expense of Equipment and Playing Field Modifications

Adopting faster pitching can also add to the expense of running a program. Construction of a backstop to protect the spectators from sharply hit foul tips and to contain the increased number of pitches that will inevitably get through the catcher increases costs. Construction of a permanent backstop may make the area of the playing field less versatile for use by the museum in staging other events. A portable backstop may be an option but would still be an expense. The more aggressive style of base running (with stealing and sliding) that is usually adopted by programs based on faster pitching is rougher on uniforms and will require more frequent replacement, especially uniform pants. The cost of maintaining the program is a consideration in choosing an era and style of play and playing by the later rules that involve faster pitching can be more expensive for the sponsoring organization.

Faster pitching also increases the frequency of broken bats, which can have implications regarding the expense of replacing them as well as for the safety of both spectators and players. Against slow pitching, batters will more often strike the ball with the barrel (rather than the handle) of the wooden bat. A player can usually use the same bat for many years if playing by slow-pitch practices. With bats costing in the range of $45 to $65, the expense is very manageable if the bat can be used for ten or fifteen seasons. But if swift pitching causes a player to break several bats per season, the expense becomes a factor.

Playing Matches at Other Venues

Swift pitching seems best suited to a league or tournament setting where all players are familiar with the characteristics of the game and have the talent to hit faster pitching. Slow pitching also works well in a league or tournament setting but is more adaptable to games with community teams. The two versions of the 1860 game require different field set-up and a different skill set for the players. A club that has adopted swift pitching may have difficulty taking their game on the road to another museum. If the host club is a program based on slower pitching, its home field may not be set up properly to accommodate a swift-pitch game (for example, no backstop and spectators seated too close to the plate). Swift pitching may not be a good fit for clubs that intend to play games with community teams for fun and education. Inexperienced newcomers to vintage base ball — from elected officials to teachers to business owners — may not have the skill to hit swift pitching, and could easily be over-matched. Slow pitching produces a game that is enjoyable and playable for everyone involved, including both experienced and novice players. When scheduling matches, it is important to communicate the rules and practices to ensure that the opponent will be able to perform well and enjoy the experience.

Maintaining an Atmosphere of Good Sportsmanship

Swift pitching, along with the aggressive base running practices of stealing and sliding, tends to produce a style of play in a vintage game that may diminish its gentlemanly character and cause it to become marked by overly competitive play. Replicating the faster pitching and more aggressive character of the game that emerged in the 1860s and continued into the later nineteenth century carries the increased likelihood of ill-will between players on opposing teams and between the players and the umpire.

In describing the characteristics of an 1860s vintage game played according to swift pitching and unlimited stealing practices, one veteran vintage base ball pitcher reported that he is able to deliver the ball "between 55 and 60 mph to home plate from 45 feet away," making it difficult to hit. In a posting on the VBBA listserv, he commented that a pitcher who is skilled at swift pitching can make many opposing batters "uncomfortable" when they find that trying to hit underhand pitching turns out to be more difficult than expected. When batters have trouble hitting the ball squarely, they begin to be put out on foul tips to the catcher or pop-ups. When this happens in a game involving swift pitching, batters feel "enormous pressure" to reach base safely and then avoid being thrown out while trying to advance. Strikeouts also occur, and when a skilled batter strikes out against an underhand pitcher, it can cause teammates to become "self-conscious."

These points expressed by a proponent of swift pitching and unrestricted stealing describe succinctly and effectively the difference in the atmosphere at a fast-pitch game and a slow-pitch game. If a program chooses to adopt fast pitching, the result likely will be very competitive games conducted in a stressful atmosphere similar to the one described above. This style of play calls for the club to be composed of talented younger players who prefer the challenges and tension of a hotly contested match.

Those programs that prefer the slow-pitch interpretation of the rules and practices of the 1860 era also play hard to win and many have a reputation for highly skilled players who give a fine performance on the field. However, these clubs typically do not think in terms of trying to make the players on the opposing team "uncomfortable," "self-conscious," or to feel "enormous pressure" during the game. Players on vintage clubs that prefer the slow-pitch style of play are energetic and try their best to win. They also define success more broadly to include the sincere hope that opposing players will feel welcome, that everyone on both clubs will do well in the game, and that visiting players will thoroughly enjoy the experience of playing a game at the host club's home field.

The faster pitching and the more aggressive base running that started to emerge around 1860 continued to grow in the post–Civil War period. Players and clubs that prefer this faster version of vintage base ball are correct in pointing out that adopting swift pitching represents the direction the game took as the decade of the 1860s proceeded. Moving to this style of play should be the result of a careful decision by program leaders and museum professionals and not simply the gradual evolution away from the 1860s slow-pitch game. Some programs field separate teams that present different eras. For some players, however, it may be difficult to move back and forth in eras, especially in maintaining the gentlemanly demeanor and sportsmanlike culture of the earlier periods.

Maintaining the Spirit of the Amateur Era

The advent of swift pitching and aggressive base running coincided with the movement from amateurism to professionalism in the 1860s. Evidence of professionalism shows up in the 1860 Rules that included provisions aimed at curtailing the practice of players jumping from one club to another. Whether players jumped because of some kind of payment or to help one club load up on talented players in order to beat a rival, this practice was not in keeping with the amateur spirit of the game's early days. This problem was addressed in Section 27 of the 1860 Rules: "In playing all matches, nine players from each club shall constitute a full field, and they must have been regular members of the club which they represent, and of no other club, for thirty days prior to the match." A statement prohibiting players from jumping from club to club while owing back dues and outlawing the practice of players being paid to play appears in Section 36 of the 1860 Rules: "No person who shall be in arrears to any other club, or who shall at any time receive compensation for his services as a player, shall be competent to play in any match." It is clear that clubs were prohibited from paying someone to play and could not add skilled players right before a big game as "ringers." The fact that these points had to be addressed in the rules indicates that these practices were apparently becoming an issue.

In the post–Civil War period, these problems seemed to grow worse. The 1868 Rules of the National Association of Base Ball Players continued to try to prohibit players from jumping from club to club. The use of ringers and the payment of players were also addressed. Under the heading "The Game," Rule 5, Section 2 reaffirms the 1860 rule that the players "shall be members of the club which they represent" and not "members of any other club, either in or out of the National Association for thirty days immediately prior to the match." Section 9 repeats some of the language of the 1860 Rules, then goes on to make an even stronger statement against the use of paid professional payers: "No person who shall be in arrears to any other club, or who shall at any time receive compensation for his services as a player, shall be competent to play in any match. No players who play baseball for money shall take part in any match game."

Having confirmed its stance against compensation for players, the rules specified serious penalties for clubs that paid its players by stating, "Any club giving compensation to a player, or having, to their knowledge, a player in their nine playing in a match for compensation, shall be debarred from membership in the National Association, and they shall not be considered by any club belonging to this Association as a proper club to engage in a match with; and should any club so engage with them they shall forfeit membership." This more adamant wording against using paid players suggests that the previous rules were not having the desired effect and the problem was growing.

After taking a harder line in 1868, the corresponding rules for 1869 show significant changes: "In playing all matches, nine players from each club shall constitute a full field; and they shall be members of the club which they represent." This wording sounds familiar, and even the added phrase, "They also must not have been members of any other club — College clubs excepted — for sixty days immediately prior to the match," seems like a minor clarification. However, the strong 1868 statements — "No person who shall at any time receive compensation for his services as a player, shall be competent to play in any match" and "No players who play base-ball for money shall take part in any match game" — are no longer part of the rules in 1869. By 1869, the rule makers had apparently become resigned to the growing trend from amateur to professional players. This acceptance of the changing times appears in Section 7, which merely defines two types of players but does not prohibit professionals from playing: "All players who play base ball for money, or who shall at any time receive compensation for their services as players, shall be considered professional players; and all others shall be regarded as amateur players." In 1869, the NABBP has clearly changed its stance, recognizing and accepting the growing practice of clubs paying players to play and opening the door for the Cincinnati Red Stockings and other elite clubs to become openly professional organizations.

As Marshall Wright points out in *The National Association of Base Ball Players, 1857–1870*, a significant reorganization was the next step. "In March 1871, ten members of the National Association met in New York for the purpose of forming a new group ... dubbed the National Association of Professional Base Ball Players." Wright points out that not everyone was comfortable with the concept of clubs paying players to play and therefore did not welcome this move from amateurism to professionalism. "To counter the professionals, several amateur teams also met in March 1871 to form a group of their own. Calling themselves the National Association of Amateur Base Ball Players, the thirty-three clubs formed a contingent, as the *New York Clipper* said, '...which reminded those present of the good old days of amateur playing which prevailed some ten years ago.'" Wright remarks that "the roster of teams had a familiar feel as three of the oldest New York clubs, the Knickerbocker, Gotham and Eagle, joined the group" (p. 328).

The NAPBBP continued for five seasons, when Wright reports it "evolved into the National League in 1876, the very same National League of professional baseball today." The new amateur organization conducted a championship season in 1871 but held only one more convention, in 1872. On the demise of the amateur association, Wright points out that while a professional league "needs to be run in a logical and organized manner" to survive as a business, amateur sports ("played ostensibly for fun") do not require as much structure. Therefore, the end of the organization "didn't mean that interest in non-professional baseball waned. On the contrary, interest in the game continued to increase though the decades, serviced adequately by a range of state-wide and local entities. To this very day, these groups keep baseball alive in all corners of the country carrying interest in the game far beyond the narrow confines of the professional teams" (pp. 328–329).

This observation will, of course, resonate with vintage programs, especially those playing according to the way the game was played in its early years. Just as the major league teams of today trace their origins to such early professional teams as the 1869 Cincinnati Red Stockings, the formation of the National Association of Professional Base Ball Players in 1871, and the creation of the National League in 1876, many in the vintage base ball community see themselves as the lineal and spiritual descendents of the Knickerbocker, Gotham, and Eagle clubs that opted to maintain the amateur game. These vintage programs, with their emphasis on the gentlemanly, amateur game, are at the front rank of those who "keep baseball alive in all corners of the country."

Compatibility with the Mission of the Organization Sponsoring the Team

The changing nature of the game and the development of fast pitching as the nineteenth century progressed are important considerations for museum professionals when choosing an era to be portrayed and adopting playing rules for the operation of the institution's vintage base ball program. The decline of sportsmanship and increase in the risk of injury are significant issues. Also, the sportsmanlike, slow-pitch version of the game, which emphasizes educational interaction with spectators, may be a better fit for the museum's family-friendly programming than the rougher, less-gentlemanly version of 1860s base ball, where the players' focus is more on winning the game.

Recruitment and Retention of Players

Much of the popularity and growth of vintage base ball has been due to the practice of slow pitching adopted by most 1860-style (and earlier) programs. Slow pitching makes the game very playable. If conducting the game according to slow-pitch practices, almost every batter puts the ball in play. Strikeouts are rare. One consequence of adopting swift pitching for the 1860 era (or any later era, of course) is that batters will begin to strikeout more frequently. This is a situation that museums and historical societies need to keep in mind when selecting an era and style of play.

Being unable to hit swift pitching consistently and striking out repeatedly becomes embarrassing and takes much of the enjoyment out of playing. A player who strikes out three or four times in a game and then does the same thing the next week is not likely to continue playing very long. Discouraged by his failure to hit fast pitching and sensing he is not helping the team, he is more likely to drop out of the program, give up vintage base ball, and go back to slow-pitch softball. Fast pitching may be appropriate for vintage programs composed primarily of younger, athletic and skilled players. But program leaders and museum professionals should keep in mind that there is a reason that millions of men and women across the country play slow-pitch softball every summer and very few adults play fast-pitch softball or fast-pitch baseball — most people can not hit fast pitching.

Whether in the nineteenth or twenty-first century, players generally enjoy playing a game based on slow pitching that produces many opportunities for hitting, running, and fielding. Players who are attracted to the historical and educational aspects of vintage base ball but have trouble hitting a fast pitch will be reluctant to play if a program is based on swift pitching. This is not a good outcome if one of the goals of the program is to attract, retain, and grow a steady core of volunteer players from a wide age group. When vintage base ball is played using slow pitching, the bound game, and less aggressive base running (advancing only on passed balls), it can be enjoyed by players from a wide range of skill levels and ages. With slower pitching, injuries are relatively rare and sportsmanship is a dominant trait of the game.

Is the Future Slow or Swift Pitching?

Those clubs that want to play the more competitive, aggressive style that eventually took over the game can interpret the 1860 Rules in this manner. They can also gravitate toward the latter eras of base ball, when fast pitching and a more combative style of play became the norm. Vintage base ball enthusiasts are attempting to re-create a number of time periods, and some have adopted swift pitching and aggressive base stealing with good results.

However, since fewer people can play the fast-pitch version of the game, a general movement in this direction would likely decrease the number of participants and clubs now playing vintage base ball. Most of the growth and expansion of the vintage game has been in the slow-pitch era. Clubs that prefer playing the more sportsmanlike version of 1860-style vintage base ball characterized by slower pitching, restricted stealing, and no sliding are proliferating, and because it is more accessible to a wide range of players and well received by spectators, it is likely to remain the more common version of vintage base ball.

Since games involving swift pitching in the late 1850s and early 1860s produced a state of "gridlock" (with 700-pitch games lasting five hours and games being called after six or seven innings due to darkness), the result was a version of base ball that would not be much fun to play or watch. Therefore, this is not something that most vintage programs want to emulate. It is impractical to introduce individual elements, such as swift pitching and unlimited stealing, without the later changes in the rules (called strikes and called balls), which eventually restored order and balance to the game.

For those programs that wish to play according to the Rules of 1860 and retain the gentlemanly style of play associated with the earlier era, slow pitching, with limited stealing only on passed balls, is a very workable model that has been successful for many programs over many years. Experience shows that unlimited stealing does not work well with slow pitching and was not likely to have been part of the game until swift pitching also appeared. Most 1860-era programs would be wise to retain slow pitching and allow the runners to advance to the next base only on a passed ball (a pitch that is not fielded cleanly on the fly or on one bounce by the catcher).

For those programs that wish to adopt a more aggressive style of play by incorporating swift pitching and unlimited stealing as components of their games, it would be best to play according to the 1864 or 1865 (or later) rules. Under the 1864 Rules, the umpire could begin to call strikes and balls, thereby preventing the 700-pitch marathons that historically occurred when swift pitching was used in conjunction with the 1858 or 1860 rules. If the 1865 Rules are used, the program can also incorporate the fly game, a feature that some programs that prefer swift pitching may also enjoy.

In his memoir *Let Me Finish*, author and baseball expert Roger Angell points out that when one reaches a certain age, professional baseball "no longer feels feasible. We know everything about the game now, thanks to instant replay and computerized stats, and what we have concluded is that almost none of us are good enough to play it." His observation is right on target. Fast-pitch baseball is playable only by the very few. The game of base ball before the Civil War was based on slow pitching and therefore was a game most people could play. When fast pitching began to creep into the game in the late 1850s and early 1860s, the game changed forever, becoming a game played by, in Angell's words, "the hulking young men we have hired to play baseball for us." The 1860 version of vintage base ball with the slow pitching that characterized the pre–Civil War era thankfully remains a game we can play ourselves.

18

Points of Play: Batting and Base Running

In the 1860 Rules, the batter is referred to as the "striker" until he reaches first base safely, at which point he becomes a runner. In Chadwick's commentary on the 1860 Rules, the striker is also referred to as the "batsman."

The Striker's Position

The spot where the striker is to stand during his turn at bat is described in Section 17 of the 1860 Rules as follows: "The Striker must stand on a line drawn through the center of home base, not exceeding in length three feet from either side thereof, and parallel with the line occupied by the pitcher." This chalk line was used instead of the present-day rectangle on each side of the plate known as the batter's box to define where the striker is to stand when the ball is pitched.

Some programs have adopted a literal interpretation of Section 17 by requiring that one foot must be placed directly on the line. Other vintage programs have interpreted the phrase "on a line" in a less-literal sense and have taken it to mean that the striker should stand so that he is on the line in the same sense that a person might be said to be standing "on line" or "in line" to buy a ticket for a play or concert. These programs interpret the rule to mean that the striker may stand either with one foot directly on the line or can straddle the line with one foot on each side. The literal view seems to be more in keeping with Chadwick's comment in the 1860 edition of *Beadle's Dime Base-Ball Player*, which says, "The striker should keep one foot on this line." Since the line runs through the middle of the round home plate, and the front part of the plate is in fair territory and the back part is in foul territory, it is difficult for the umpire to determine if a ball that strikes the plate is fair or foul. With this in mind, Chadwick is apparently referring to the batter's back foot (the right foot for a right-handed batter) because he explains that keeping the back foot on the line will ensure that "a ball striking the ground perpendicularly from his bat" will be considered a fair ball since it will hit the ground in front of the plate (p. 13).

The fact that Chadwick says the striker's foot *should* be on the line indicates he is recommending what the batter *should* do in order to eliminate any confusion as to whether a ball hit straight down should be judged a fair ball rather than a foul ball, not what he *must* do in order to be in compliance with the rule. Therefore, standing with the back foot on the line seems more like a recommended practice than a formal rule. Placing the front foot on the line would not seem to be against the wording of the rule, but it does mean that a ball hit straight down could strike the plate or the ground behind or in the vicinity of the chalk line, causing uncertainty as to whether the ball should be called fair or foul. Chadwick's comments seem to be intended to reduce the number of difficult decisions made by the umpire on balls that are hit straight down in the area of home plate and the batter's feet. This play is common in vintage base ball and necessitates an immediate and loud call on the part of the umpire so that the batter and base runners know whether they should run or stay where they are. A change in wording occurred in 1868. Instead of saying the striker "must stand on a line drawn through the center of the home base," the rules on batting for 1868 state that "the striker, when in the act of striking the ball, must stand astride of a line drawn through the center of the home base." As in many cases involving the nineteenth-century rules, it is often difficult to determine if the word "astride" represents a clarification and confirmation of the way things have been done all along or if it represents a change from the past.

The important point all programs agree on is that the striker should not stand with both feet either in front of or behind the line. Note that neither the rule nor Chadwick's comments specify what should be done if the striker, in stepping into the pitch, should take his foot off the line or step over it. It is strongly recommended that the umpire not take any action if the striker inadvertently moves his foot as long as he is not attempting to generate extra power by intentionally running up on the ball as he swings at it.

The striker takes his position at the line that extends three feet on each side of the round home plate, as demonstrated by Mike Nightwine of the Ohio Village Muffins.

Batting Stances

The proper batting stance is the subject of much discussion throughout the vintage base ball community. Most period illustrations show the striker standing in an upright position rather than a crouch. Observers have noted that the right-handed batters in the illustrations often seem to be adopting an open stance with their feet spread, moderately apart and the left foot pointed toward third base. Some strikers appear to be almost facing the pitcher. However, due to a lack of consistency in period illustrations, an authentic batting stance is difficult to define. While the rules do not specifically prohibit the batter from bending the knees and going into a deep crouch or placing his feet close together, players should be encouraged to look at these illustrations as examples and take their place at the plate accordingly. As a matter of good practice, the batter should generally stand fairly upright and not use any extreme batting stance that he might have developed playing modern baseball or softball.

Veteran player and researcher Paul Hunkele shared some of his findings on batting stances in a post to the 1860 vintage base ball listserv in April 2005 in which he finds that an open stance seems to have been common in the 1860s. "The 1867 edition of Haney's *Base Ball Book of Reference* (page 112) illustrates the batsman taking his position with his forward foot turned out so that his toe is pointing toward the pitcher and his rear foot is parallel to the batsman's line. Sort of a 'T' stance 'as a backwoodsman does when using his axe in cutting down a tree' (page 115)." Hunkele adds, "There is also an illustration on page 113 that initially seems to be a very closed stance but it is actually a view from the side of the striker looking toward the pitcher and is also a very open stance."

Hunkele cites another source of information on the proper batting stance found in Henry Chadwick's 1868 book, *The Game of Base Ball: How to Learn It, How to Play It, and How to Teach It*, which also recommends the open stance. According to Chadwick, the batter "should place his left foot, with the toe pointed towards the pitcher, just over the line of the base, and about one foot to the left of the base. His right foot should rest firmly on the ground on the other side of the line, with the toe pointing the same way as the line of the base." Hunkele mentions other examples, showing a closed stance with the front toe pointing toward right field to be used for "scientific hitting," a reference to a right-handed batter trying to hit the ball through the gap on the right side of the infield created by both the first and second basemen playing close to their bases. There is debate in the vintage base ball community as when the practice of "scientific hitting" began and when the second baseman began to shift his position accordingly. Hunkele's conclusion is that "through most of the 1860s the open stance (toe toward the pitcher) was the norm." With this in mind, it would be good to see more vintage players experiment with the open stance that seems to have been commonly used in the mid-nineteenth century.

Batting Grips

Just as there was no one stance that was universally used in 1860, there was apparently no one way to grip the bat. In the 1860 *Beadle's Dime Base-Ball Player*, Henry Chadwick comments: "Players have different modes, and adopt different styles of batting; some take the bat with the left hand on the handle, and slide the right from the large end toward the handle; others grasp it nearly one-third of the distance from the small end, so that both hands appear near the middle of the bat; others again take hold with both hands well down on the handle, and swing the bat with a natural and free stroke, while great force is given to the hit: all give good reasons for their several styles."

Note that the first example given by Chadwick refers to a batting style that resembles the stroke a person might use to chop wood with an axe. Some period illustrations seem to show this technique as the batter holds the bat in his left hand at the knob and has his right hand around the middle of the bat, preparing to slide his right hand down toward the knob as he swings at the pitch. Chadwick's second example ("both hands near the middle of the

The scorer and an interpreter chat with spectators about the way base ball was played in the nineteenth century. As Ohio Village Muffin striker Kevin Hartmann connects with the pitch, everyone enjoys the sound of the wood bat meeting the leather ball squarely (courtesy Joel Moore).

bat") describes what would be referred to as a "choke" grip. Chadwick's third example ("both hands well down the handle") describes the grip most commonly used in modern baseball and softball, with the left hand on the knob and the right hand directly on top of the left. Period illustrations also show some players using a spread grip, with the left hand on the knob and the right farther up on the handle with a gap of about three inches or so. While several types of grips appear to be historically accurate, some players may wish to try batting with their hands apart in the spread grip, thereby adding to the historic appearance of vintage games. In addition to giving an old-time look to the game, players might find it quite effective. The spread grip continued to be used into the twentieth century in the major leagues by such luminaries as Ty Cobb, who achieved a lifetime batting average .366, the highest in history.

Chadwick advises each player to develop consistency and, predating the sage counsel given by thousands of coaches through the years, suggests the batter concentrate on meeting the ball squarely rather than trying to kill it. "Practice with one bat, as a player thereby becomes more sure of striking than he would were he constantly to change his bat. In striking the ball, do not try to hit it so hard that you throw yourself off your balance, but plant your feet firmly on the ground, and swing the bat in as natural a manner as possible. The secret of hard-hitting lies in the quick stroke and firm position of the batsman the moment the ball is struck. This will account for some small and light men being hard hitters" (p. 19). Although the terms were not in use in Chadwick's day, his principles of hitting seem to be similar to modern concepts of hitting, which emphasize "bat speed" and a "short stoke," traits widely accepted today as keys to successful hitting.

Keep the Game Moving

In Haney's *Base Ball Book of Reference Book for 1867*, Henry Chadwick offers a number of suggestions on batting. "Being too particular in selecting a ball to strike at is poor policy.

Make up your mind when you take your stand, to hit the first good ball that comes" (p. 118). These remarks are consistent with Chadwick's 1860 commentary in which he says the batsman "can await the coming of a suitable ball for him to strike, but he should not be too fastidious in this respect." Chadwick makes the strong recommendation that "a good Batsman strikes at the first good ball pitched to him, and this is decidedly the fairest and best method to be adopted." Maintaining spectator interest was important in the 1860s just as it is today, and vintage players should follow Chadwick's reminder that swinging at the first good pitch "keeps the game lively and interesting. It is exceedingly annoying to the spectators, and creates a bad impression of the merits of the game on those not familiar with it, to see good balls repeatedly sent to the Batsman without being hit.... No good players resort to this style of play ... and it would therefore be desirable to avoid it as much as possible" (p. 27).

Batting Strategies

Daisy Cutters

If the opposing club has experienced players who are adept at catching pop-ups and taking drives to the outfield on the fly or the first bound, a ball hit into the air often results in an out unless it finds the gap between two outfielders or goes completely over an outfielder's head. Therefore, captains often encourage the members of their nine to try to strike the ball low and hard, producing a sharply hit grounder known as a "daisy cutter," which many batters believe is a good way to reach base. The nineteenth-century base ball song written by John Rutledge, "Tally One for Me," reflects this approach:

> I never knock the ball up high,
> Or even on the bound,
> But always send it whizzing,
> Cutting daisies in the ground.

On the subject of daisy cutters, *The New Dickson Baseball Dictionary* quotes Henry Chadwick as saying, "It is a hit ball very difficult to field, and, consequently, shows good batting" (p. 147).

Fair-Foul Hits

Prior to 1877, a ball was judged fair or foul according to where it first struck the ground. As Tom Shieber explains in "The Evolution of the Baseball Diamond" in the 1994 issue of SABR's *The Baseball Research Journal*, "A ball that initially landed in fair territory, regardless of whether it stayed in fair territory or whether it passed first or third base in fair territory, was a fair ball. A fair-foul hit was one in which the batter deftly hit the ball such that it first touched the ground in fair territory and then bounded into foul territory." A play of this type can occur accidentally when the batter swings in his normal manner but tops the ball, so that it hits in front of the plate and then bounds or rolls into foul territory.

In time, some players became adept at the tactic of deliberately chopping the ball in front of the plate so that it would bounce into the foul area between home and third base, where, as Shieber accurately points out, "fielders would have to run a great distance into foul territory to retrieve such a hit ball." In "The Lost Art of Fair-Foul Hitting" in Volume 20 (2000) of *The National Pastime: A Review of Baseball History,* published by SABR, researcher Robert Schaefer writes that "a select group of clever hitters perfected a technique for deliberately striking the ball in a manner so that a spin — "English" — was imparted to it" (p. 3). In tracing the origins of the tactic, Schaefer adds, "According to nineteenth-century newspaper accounts, the creator of the fair-foul hit was Dickey Pearce, the innovative short fielder of the old Brooklyn Atlantics" (p. 4). Schaefer cites an 1894 article by Henry Chadwick that states the idea for the fair-foul play came out of a discussion between Chadwick and Pearce in 1864.

In *A Game of Inches: The Game on the Field*, Peter Morris agrees with Schaefer's conclusion that Dickey Pearce "invented the fair-foul in the 1860s" (p. 81). Schaefer mentions George Wright and Davey Force as other experts in fair-foul hitting, along with "the Great and Only" Ross Barnes, "who won three batting titles in six years and hit over .400 in four of them" (p. 4). Morris observes, however, that "the play became increasingly controversial" as "spectators perceived the play to be unsporting and often became openly hostile" (p. 82). Morris points out that "the impetus to abolish the fair-foul was the fact that it was very difficult for umpires to determine whether a ball that was hit into the ground first hit fair or foul. Accordingly, the rule makers redefined the concepts of fair and foul in 1877 and, in the process, eliminated the fair-foul" (p. 82).

Since intentional fair-foul hitting apparently did not become part of the game until around 1864, clubs using the 1860 Rules should probably not employ the tactic of intentional fair-foul hitting in their matches. A few unintentional fair-foul hits usually occur during the normal course of the game and will catch the spectators' attention, which provides an opportunity to talk with them about changes in the game over the decades.

While there are no rules limiting the frequency of fair-foul hitting in vintage base ball, clubs playing by later rules are encouraged not to employ the fair-foul tactic excessively in their games. Programs should keep in mind that it was considered by many to be unsportsmanlike, it was a difficult play for the umpire to judge, and it was so unpopular that it was eventually legislated out of the game. It would have been considered both more manly and more gentlemanly for batters to strike the ball in the normal manner rather than resorting to trickery and deception to gain an advantage over the opposing club. Frequent use of the tactic, such as several consecutive strikers employing it in the same inning or the same player using it every time he comes to bat, would probably not be in keeping with the gentlemanly nature of the era of the amateur clubs. Fair-foul hitting seems to be associated more with the post–Civil War period and the professional era of the late 1860s until it was ended by a rule change in 1877.

Leaders of programs representing any era (even those portraying the mid–1860s to 1876, when the fair-foul hit was used) should keep in mind that too many fair-foul attempts in a game can bog down the pace of the match and become a bit "tedious" for the onlookers, to use the word Chadwick often employed to describe practices that become tiresome for spectators. Each team using it once or twice in the course of a game as a surprise maneuver (provided it puts no spectators at risk) would be sufficient to demonstrate the technique and the rules that permitted it. Also, on many fair-foul attempts, the ball goes into the crowd, raising safety issues. At times a batter contemplating a fair-foul hit will fail to notice that there are small children, senior citizens, or perhaps a person in a wheelchair in the spectator area along the base line where he is trying to hit the ball. If there are spectators sitting close to the base lines, it would be best not to do any intentional fair-foul hitting since audience members are not expecting a batter to intentionally strike the ball sharply in their direction. At any vintage game, the fewer times the ball goes into the crowd, the better.

Strikeouts

Strikeouts are very rare in 1860-era vintage base ball if played according to slow-pitch practices. According to Section 12 of the 1860 Rules, a striker is out "if three balls are struck at and missed, and the last is caught, either before touching the ground or upon the first bound." This wording is very similar to Rule 11 in the original Knickerbocker Rules of 1845: "Three balls being struck at and missed and the last one caught, is a hand out; if not caught is considered fair, and the striker bound to run." Note that the rule refers to pitches that are "struck at and missed." Foul balls do not count as strikes, which is one reason strikeouts are infrequent. A striker must swing and miss the ball three times in order to strike out.

While strikeouts are a common occurrence in modern baseball, it should be kept in mind that the 1860 Rules state that "the pitcher must deliver the ball as near as possible over the center of the home base, and for the striker." For most programs that play by the 1860 Rules, the pitching and hitting components of the game are very similar to modern slow-pitch softball. The expectation is that everyone will hit the ball and put it in play. The game moves along at a brisk pace with lots of hitting, fielding, and running of the bases. This style of play is in keeping with the intent and practices of the original Knickerbocker Rules, which created a game that would provide exercise and recreation for the club members.

Note that the rule that allows the batter to run on a dropped third strike has been around since the Knickerbocker days. The striker who misses on three swings has a second chance to reach first if the catcher fails to catch the third strike on the fly or first bound. Apparently, the Knickerbockers wanted everyone, even a batter who swung and missed three times, to have a chance to run the bases. However, since swinging and missing three times is rare and dropped third strikes are infrequent, this provision of the rule seldom comes into play with experienced vintage players. This situation is more likely to occur in games with community teams or school groups with novice players.

Foul Tips

While strikeouts are rare in the vintage game, a batter making an out on a foul tip occurs more frequently. Section 11 of the 1860 Rules, which states, "The striker is out if a foul ball is caught, either before touching the ground, or upon the first bound," comes into play several times during the course in a typical game. A foul ball caught by the catcher (or the other fielders) is important since it constitutes and unproductive out (similar to a strikeout) on which runners are not permitted to advance. Since Section 16 states, "No ace nor base can be made upon a foul ball," no runner may score (make an ace) or advance (make a base) on a ball hit into foul territory. In modern baseball, a runner on third could tag up and score on a long foul fly to left or right field, but under the 1860 Rules the runner must return to his base and hold.

The batter being put out on a foul tip caught on the first bound is an interesting play under the 1860 Rules that, of course, does not exist in modern baseball or softball. While it can be disappointing for a batter to be retired on a foul tip, it is a play that happens occasionally to even the best hitters.

The Fly Game

On December 14, 1864, just as General Sherman's army was about to enter the city of Savannah in the final stages of its march from Atlanta to the sea, the National Association of Base Ball Players met in New York to establish the rules for the 1865 season. An important change was adopted at that meeting. Previously, Section 14 had stated that the batter could be put out "if a fair ball is struck, and the ball is caught either without having touched the ground, or upon the first bound." In establishing the playing rules for 1865, however, Section 14 was modified to read that the batter could be put out "if a fair ball is struck, and the ball is caught ... without having touched the ground." A clarifying note stated that the phrase "upon the first bound" had been deleted from the previous year's rules and that "fair balls can only be caught out on the fly not the bound."

It is noteworthy that the provisions of the fly game, as adopted for the 1865 season, applied only to fair balls. The 1865 Rules continued to specify that "the striker is out if a foul ball is caught, either before touching the ground, or upon the first bound" (Section 12). Also, a player was still out if the third strike was caught on the bound, declaring the striker to be out "if three balls are struck at and missed, and the last is caught, either before touching the ground, or upon the first bound" (Section 13). Chadwick confirmed the status quo regarding one-bound catches in these two areas — foul tips and the missed third strike. "The bound-catch, in this instance — the ball striking the ground back of the home base — is considered in the light of a foul ball, as far as the fly-game is concerned, and consequently when the ball is caught on the bound, on the third strike, the player must be given out, the same as he was last year under the bound rule."

Some vintage base ball programs have chosen to follow the rules of 1865 or later and play all or some of their matches according to the rules of the fly game. Club leaders should remember that adopting the fly game and eliminating the one-bound catch does change the nature of the matches by making outs more difficult to obtain. A barehanded catch of a well-hit fly ball or line drive is anything but routine. The fly game places more importance on having highly skilled players in the outfield. With outs harder to come by, matches played according to the rules of the fly game tend to be higher scoring and take longer to play. Since fly catches are more difficult to make, there will be more strikers reaching base and more scoring.

When in Doubt, Run to First Base

When a batter takes a full swing but tops the ball and hits it into the dirt in the vicinity of home plate, he should be alert and start running immediately — even if he sees the ball rolling away in foul territory. Henry Chadwick's commentary offers very clear directions on what the striker should do in this situation: "The Batsman, when he has hit the ball, should *drop* his bat, not throw it behind him, and run for the first base, not waiting to hear whether the ball has been declared foul or not, as if it be a foul ball, he can easily return to the [home] base, but should it be fair, he will be well on his way to the [first] base. The umpire will call all foul balls immediately [when] they are struck, but will keep silent when the ball is a fair one" (pp. 27–28).

It is a common mistake in vintage base ball for a striker to hit a ball at his feet and then, seeing the ball in foul territory, continue standing at the plate, assuming it is a foul ball. If the umpire has not called the ball "foul," that means he has determined that it first hit the ground in fair territory, which makes it a fair ball. All the catcher needs to do is pick up the ball and tag the striker for an easy out. As Chadwick states, the umpire will make an immediate and loud call on a foul ball but will "keep silent" if it is a fair ball. If no call is made, the ball is in play and the batter should be running toward first base as fast as possible.

Base runners must stop directly on the base (including first base) and can be tagged out if not on the base. On close plays, the umpire may be asked to make a judgment.

The striker also should always run on a pop fly. In his 1868 book, *The Game of Base Ball: How to Learn It, How to Play It, and How to Teach It*, Henry Chadwick provided wise counsel on the importance of always running out every pop fly, even if it appears to be an easy catch for the fielder. "This habit of stopping when running to first base, because the striker happens to think that there is no chance for him to make it, is a very bad one, and frequently loses a man his base. The invariable rule with the striker, when he hits the ball, should be to drop his bat and take a 2.40 gait for the base, and not to stop until he is declared out, or 'foul ball' is called." Chadwick's quaint reference to a 2.40 gait is explained in the 1877 edition of John Russell Bartlett's *Dictionary of Americanisms*, which reports that the phrase "a 2.40 gait" meant "with great speed. A 2.40 gait for a trotting horse was, not long ago, considered to be very fast" (p. 725).

Chadwick's advice was sound in the 1860s and holds true for modern times. Spectators in the nineteenth century or twenty-first century always appreciate a player who runs out every grounder and pop fly at top speed and never quits on a play. Every player should keep in mind that high pop-ups provide a difficult challenge for the barehanded infielder. These plays look much easier than they are. The ball often has considerable backspin on it, making it difficult to catch cleanly. If the leather ball is slightly damp due to wet grass, it will be slippery, making the ball even tougher to catch. The wind can be a factor or the fielder may lose it in the sun. And, of course, even the most talented and experienced vintage players (and even major leaguers playing with gloves) drop one occasionally. Many things can go wrong and, once he hits the ball, the batter should be running to first base at the swift pace of Chadwick's speedy trotter.

Arriving at First Base

According to the 1860 Rules, the striker must stop directly on first base and may not overrun it. If he does, he is at risk of being tagged out, the same as if he had overrun second or third. This interpretation is based on Section 17, which states, "The striker ... shall be considered the striker until he has made the first base," at which point he becomes a player running the bases. Section 15 says, "Any player running the bases is out, if at any time he is touched by the ball while in play in the hands of an adversary, without some part of his person being on a base." The standard interpretation is that once the striker has made his first base by crossing the bag, he becomes a runner and is susceptible to being put out if "touched by the ball" while not in contact with the base.

There is no provision in the 1860 Rules for making first base an exception to this general rule. In A *Game of Inches: The Game on the Field*, Peter Morris sheds further light on this subject by explaining that the question of overrunning bases was "a hot topic for a number of years. Some observers contended that runners should be allowed to overrun any base while others argued for the status quo. Finally, before the 1871 season, a compromise was reached and runners were allowed to overrun first base only" (p. 22).

Since players are accustomed to overrunning first base in modern baseball and softball, overrunning first base is a common mistake made by novices until they get accustomed to the old-time rules. A striker may beat out a close play at first, but if he runs a few steps beyond first base and then turns to go back, there is a good chance the first baseman will have the ball in hand, waiting to tag him for an easy out. Occasionally, clubs suspend the rule against overrunning first base. If the grass is wet, it may be difficult for the striker to come to a sudden and complete stop at first base without slipping and falling. If the footing is slick, the captains and the umpire may agree to permit overrunning first base to prevent injuries.

Rule Interpretations

Nineteenth-century rule books are often difficult to read and understand. Therefore, club leaders should always give careful thought to what the rule makers had in mind and how various interpretations of the convoluted and vague nineteenth-century phrasing will actually work on the field of play.

In regard to batting, an example of the need to thoughtfully consider the outcomes and consequences of overly strict rule interpretations occurred several seasons ago when the Muffins were invited to play in a multi-club tournament at another museum site. It was announced by the host club that the event would be played according to 1867, Rules which everyone knew meant that the games would be conducted according to the rules of the fly game rather than the bound game. The clubs were also informed that another more obscure rule was also to be observed, one that apparently had been enacted in order to prevent a batter from running up on the ball while taking his swing. Section 21 of the 1867 Rules states: "The striker, when in the act of striking, shall not step forward or backward, but must stand on a line drawn through the center of the home base, not exceeding in length three feet from either side thereof, and parallel with the line occupied by the pitcher." At the start of the tournament each striker tried his best to comply with this unfamiliar rule that seemingly prohibited taking a normal stride while swinging the bat. The umpires officiating the games interpreted the rule very literally and, if detecting the slightest movement of a batter's foot while striking, called him back to the plate for a "do-over" if he hit the ball. The result was that both safe hits and outs were nullified and many batters, having been judged to have moved a foot illegally while swinging, were called back to the plate to strike again. At times, the games became the base ball equivalent of the movie *Groundhog Day*, with batters returning to the plate to repeat their turns at bat.

This strict interpretation interrupted the flow of the games and prolonged the contests unnecessarily while many batters were cited for unintentional infractions. Spectators became confused and then annoyed, losing interest in the game. They were disappointed when they cheered a long hit or a great catch and then discovered the play had been nullified because the batter had moved his foot slightly when swinging. It was no surprise that by the second day of the tournament, the umpires began allowing the batters more latitude and became more inclined to permit a normal stride into the ball. It is also no surprise to learn that this rule (probably because it proved as unworkable back in 1867 as it did in this twenty-first century tournament) was quickly modified in the 1868 Rules, which called for a rule violation only if the striker took "any backward step when striking at the ball" and clarified the penalties for any infringement. There are several lessons from this experience that should help all vintage base ball programs steer clear of some of the mistakes that were made when the rules of baseball were being developed in the nineteenth century. Generally speaking, the written rules should be observed in good faith. However, as indicated earlier, not every club had a rule book or knowledge of the details. This provides programs with some flexibility in creating an enjoyable presentation for audiences.

No matter what year's rules and rule interpretations are being observed, it is probably not a good idea to set up any procedures whereby the umpire stops play for a "normal" base ball move, such a stepping into the pitch while batting. The umpire could tell the captains before the game that he does not intend to strictly enforce the rule that requires no foot movement unless it is abused, and could mention that the rule was dropped the following year. Furthermore, if the infraction is so minor that only the umpire can see it, and it is undetectable to the spectators, it is probably wise not to make an issue of it. Vintage base ball should be fun for players and spectators, and enforcing violations on invisible infractions detracts from everyone's enjoyment of the game. Finally, it is unwise for a program to adopt any procedure that requires a player's turn at bat to be nullified and repeated, even if the rules for a given year could be interpreted in such a manner. Rather than call repeated unintentional infractions and "do-overs," the umpire should try to settle any problems quietly with a reminder to the captains and players between innings.

In all cases, program leaders should think about the original intent of the rule rather than the "letter of the law" when trying to wade through the convoluted language of the nineteenth-century rule books. In the above example, if the intent of the rule was to prevent taking several steps back and then running up on the ball, an infraction should be called only when that offense actually happens, not every time a batter takes a normal step into the ball as he swings. It is often a good idea to read the rules of several years before and after the year being portrayed on the field. This helps to put the rules of that year into context and adds to everyone's understanding of how a given rule came into being and whether or not it proved workable. If a new rule governing batting or any other phase of the game was rescinded or substantially modified the following year, that could mean it proved unworkable in the past and, therefore, will likely be a source of problems for a vintage program trying to follow it in the present.

The Basics of Base Running

In a vintage match that includes the bound game that was part of the 1860 Rules, it is base running that differs most from the modern game. Accordingly, base running is one of the most interesting and challenging aspects of the game to master. Since there were no base coaches until the 1870s, the runner must remember how many outs there are and decide for himself when to run and when to hold. He must run the bases with an intelligent mixture of daring and caution. Speed is always an asset in base running, but a slower player can still be a good base runner by knowing the rules, keeping the game situation in mind (inning, number of outs, score), and making good decisions while running the bases.

A Bound Catch in the Infield

Runners must remain focused on the nineteenth-century rules being used in the game so as not to follow habits developed over years of playing modern baseball and softball. Under the rules of the bound game, the striker is out the instant the ball is caught on the first bounce by the fielder, and runners need to react accordingly. To take a common situation, when the striker hits a ball that an infielder catches on the first bound, a runner on first is *not* forced at second (as he would be under modern rules). Unless there are already two outs, on a ball hit sharply on one bound to the pitcher or one of the infielders, the runner will almost always want to hold at first base rather than immediately start running toward second base. The rules permit a runner to advance at his own risk on any fair ball caught on the first bounce. However, such an attempt on a one-bound catch by the pitcher or an infielder will almost always result in his being tagged out when he arrives at second base, resulting in a double play. This is a common base running faux pas often committed by novice players whose first instincts are still shaped by modern rules.

A Bound Catch in the Outfield

If a runner is on base and a fly ball is hit to the outfield, he needs to quickly assess whether the ball is going to be caught on the fly or the first bound. If the runner sees that the outfielder is not going to catch the ball on the fly, he should start running immediately and advance as many bases as possible. He does not have to wait until the outfielder catches the ball on the bound to tag up and start running (as on a fly ball under modern rules). For example, if a runner is on second with fewer than two outs and a fly ball is hit into the left-center field gap, the runner may be able to determine at once that neither the left fielder nor the center fielder will be able to catch the ball on the fly, although one of them may be able to make a bound catch for an out. In this case he should start to run while the ball is still in the air. By running immediately, he can probably round third and score before the ball is caught on the bound and returned to the infield. But, if he mistakenly waits until the bound catch is made before starting to run, he may be able to advance only one base and would not score on the play.

A Fly Catch in the Outfield: Tagging Up, Advancing, and Returning

The 1860 Rules are similar to modern baseball in that when the batter hits a fair ball that is caught on the fly, a runner may tag up after the catch and try to advance to the next base if he thinks he can make it. However, Section 16 of the 1860 Rules speaks to the procedures governing the fly catch by disallowing any advancement on a foul ball and establishing the need for the runner to return to his base promptly.

Lively vintage matches provide many opportunities for quick thinking at bat, in the field, and while running the bases (courtesy Joel Moore).

No ace nor base can be made upon a foul ball, nor when a fair ball has been caught without having touched the ground, and the ball shall, in the former instance, be considered dead, and not in play until it shall first have been settled in the hands of the pitcher; in either case [whether the ball is fair or foul] the players running the bases shall return to them, and may be put out in so returning in the same manner as the striker when running to the first base.

Although the rule does not say anything specifically about tagging up and advancing on a fair ball caught on the fly, Chadwick's commentary adds that important point and explains the runner's options more fully. Chadwick states that the runner can advance to the next base after the catch if he returns to his base before trying to move on to the next base. "If, however, he should succeed in this case in reaching the [original] base before the ball, he can immediately re-endeavor to make the base he was running to without being obliged to return to the base he has left" (p. 28). Simply put, the runner can advance if he tags up after the catch, just as in the modern game.

Consider the typical situation of a runner on second base with fewer than two outs. The striker hits a fly ball to right field. The runner on second base should look to see if the outfielder has a chance to catch it on the fly. If he sees the right fielder is going to take the ball on the first bound, he can start running immediately. But, if it appears the ball will be caught on the fly, he should return to second and tag up by touching the bag. This would satisfy the requirement of "reaching the base before the ball." He can then "re-endeavor" to move on to third base if he thinks he can reach third before the ball can be thrown there.

It should be noted that tagging up and advancing on a fly ball was not permitted until 1859, making it relatively new in 1860. The 1858 Rules do not allow for any advancement after tagging up on a fly ball. Under the heading "Running on fair and foul balls," Section 16 states that "no ace nor base can be made upon a foul ball, nor when a fair ball has been caught without having touched the ground." This means that runners are not eligible to try to advance after the catch. Section 16 also states, "In either case [fair or foul ball] the players running the bases shall return to them, and shall not be put out in so returning unless the ball has been first pitched to the striker." Therefore, runners are not subject to being put out if they get back to their bases before the first pitch to the next batter.

Returning to Base on a Foul Ball

In 1860-era vintage base ball, the runner does not get a free way back to his base on a foul ball, as is the case in modern baseball. If he starts running to the next base on the belief the batter has hit a fair ball but the ball is declared foul, the runner must hurry back to his base or risk being put out. Section 16 of the 1860 Rules is interpreted to mean that when a foul ball is hit, the runners can not advance. Furthermore, a runner can be put out if he does not return to his base before the ball arrives (similar to the runner getting back to base on a fair ball caught on the fly). However, in the process of throwing the ball to the base ahead of the runner, the ball must have "settled in the hands of the pitcher" at some point during the play.

For example, with a man on first, the batter hits a ball down the left-field line and the runner takes off for second. The ball hits in foul territory and the umpire calls the ball "foul." As the left fielder retrieves the ball, the runner reverses his course, trying to get back to first before the ball. The left fielder throws the ball to the pitcher, who flips it to the first baseman. If the ball gets there first, the runner is out (in the manner of a play at first with no tag needed). If the runner gets back to the base ahead of the ball, he is not out. If the left fielder throws the ball directly to the first baseman and neglects to have the pitcher handle the ball, the runner would not be out (even if the ball arrives before he does). The runner must make sure the ball will be judged fair before he gets too far off his base. It is also important for the runner to listen for the umpire's call, and if he hears "foul," he should get back to his base as quickly as possible. If the umpire makes no call, the ball is fair.

In modern baseball, if a batter hits a ball that strikes the ground in foul territory, the runner (who may have started to run to the next base) gets a free way back to his base. In cases in which the foul ball is not caught on the fly, the ball is dead and the runner can walk or jog back to the base at a leisurely pace. In 1860 vintage base ball, things are much different and he must get back to his original base quickly.

Force Outs

The 1860 Rules contain a provision for the force play. The language of the rule is a bit convoluted, but reads as follows:

> SEC. 18. Players must make their bases in the order of striking; and when a fair ball is struck, and not caught flying (or on the first bound), the first base must be vacated, as also the second and third bases, if they are occupied at the same time. Players may be put out on any base, under these circumstances, in the same manner as the striker when running to the first base.

This statement seems to indicate that on a grounder (a struck ball that takes two or more bounces before being caught by the fielder), the 1860 Rules are the same as for a grounder in modern baseball, and base runners should react accordingly. As soon as the ball strikes the ground the second time, the runner is subject to being forced and, therefore, must run as quickly as possible to the next base. The defensive players can put him out by throwing the ball to the base the runner is trying to reach. If the ball arrives at the base ahead of the runner, he is out. The phrase "in the same manner as the striker when running to first base" means that the ball needs to be caught by the baseman, who simply touches the base before the runner arrives. The point is, like a play at first base, the runner does not need to be tagged out.

Pop flies to the infield also require alertness, keen judgment, and quick decision-making since three things can happen: the ball can be caught on the fly; the ball can be caught on the first bound; or the ball can hit the ground and bounce more than once. If it looks like the ball will be caught on the fly, the runner will want to stay close to first base. As in modern baseball, if the runner starts for second and the ball is caught on the fly, the fielder catching the ball can throw it to first base and the runner is out if the ball beats him to the base.

If the pop fly is dropped but the fielder recovers and re-catches the ball on the first bounce, the batter is still out. In this case the force is not on and the runner is not obligated to run. Since it would probably be unwise to try to run 90 feet to second base at this point, the runner usually holds at first base. However, if the ball falls to the ground and is not caught on the first bounce, the runner is forced and must run as fast as possible for second before the fielders can recover and throw to someone covering second base. Meanwhile, the batter should, of course, be running as speedily as possible for first base, even if it looks like an easy catch for the infielder. As is the case with baseball in any era — but especially in the barehanded game — the batter should never assume that the ball will be caught. If the ball does fall between the fielders or is dropped and hits the ground twice, both the runner and the striker (if they are alert and hustling) might be safe.

Is the Force Play Always On?

Differing interpretations of the rules can lead to lively and interesting discussions within the vintage base ball community. One such area of controversy involves force plays, with some knowledgeable vintage base ball veterans making the case that under the terms of Section 18 of the 1860 Rules, the force play remains in effect no matter which offensive player — the striker or the runner — is retired first. While this may appear to be a case of splitting hairs, this play does come up in games, making it a good idea to have an understanding of how it should be called before the game starts. The rule states that "when a fair ball is struck, and not caught flying (or on the first bound), the first base must be vacated, as also the second and third bases if they are occupied at the same time. Players may be put out at any base, under these circumstances, in the same manner as the striker when running to the first base." The rule does not say anything about the order in which the outs need to be made.

Those taking the view that it does not matter which offensive player is put out first sum up their position with the phrase, "The force is always on." They base their case on the passage that says, "Players may be put out on any base, under these circumstances, in the same manner as the striker when running to the first base," meaning that all the defense has to do is throw the ball to the base to which the runner headed, "in the same manner" as a play at first base where no tag is needed.

In his section on playing first base in the 1860 *Beadle's Dime Base-Ball Player*, Chadwick seems to support "the force is always on" school of thought. Chadwick presents a situation where the bases are loaded with no outs, and the striker hits a grounder to the shortstop, who throws to first to get the striker out. Chadwick says that the "proper play" for the shortstop should be to throw to home, but even if he makes the play at first base, the alert first baseman can still get a double or triple play if "the First Baseman seeing the player on the third base running home, immediately sends the ball to the catcher, who, in turn, sends it to the third base; and if this be done rapidly in each case, all three players will be put out, as it is only requisite, under such circumstances, for the ball to be held — not the player to be touched with it — for each player to be put out." While no tag is needed in this case, Chadwick points out that "should, however, there only be players on the second and third bases when the striker is put out at the first, and the ball is sent to the catcher as above, and by him to the third baseman, it will be requisite that each player be touched with the ball, as in the first case they are *forced* from their bases, but in the latter they are not. We give this as an illustration of a very pretty point of the game." This example from Chadwick seems to indicate that the outs can be made in any order. Vintage programs that wish to interpret the force play in this manner have good grounds to do so.

In modern baseball, the order in which the plays are made does matter, with the force no longer being in effect the moment the batter is retired at first base. If the batter is retired first, any other runner is not obligated to run, and if he does try to advance, he must be put out by a tag, not by merely throwing the ball to the base ahead of him.

In sorting out the confusion over how the force play should be interpreted, it is helpful to look at the 1854 Rules, agreed to at a meeting that included the Knickerbocker, Gotham, and Eagle clubs. The 1854 Rules support defining the force play the same way the play is called in modern baseball and softball (that is, the force is *not* always on). Rule 8 from 1854 states: "Players must make the bases in the order of striking, and when a fair ball is struck and the striker not put out, the first base must be vacated as well as the next base or bases if similarly occupied; players may be put out, under these circumstances, in the same manner as when running to the first base." The key phrase is "when the striker is not put out." This would seem to mean that when the striker is the first out made on the play, the force is no longer in effect, the same as in the modern game. Familiar with the 1854 Rules, players in 1860 may have understood that the force is not in effect if the striker is retired first.

Chadwick's commentary on this topic in Haney's *Base Ball Reference Book for 1867* is also helpful. His 1867 comments would seem to apply to 1860, since the wording of the provision on force plays is basically the same in the rules for 1860 and 1867. Chadwick says, "Players running bases can only be forced to leave their bases when each base is occupied, and the striker hits a fair ball." His explanation makes the point that if the striker is retired first, the base to which he is entitled — first base — is no longer occupied. This, in turn, means that it still belongs to the runner who was on first when the play began. Therefore, if the striker has been put out, the runner on first is not forced at second, a runner on second is not forced at third, and a runner on third is not forced at home. Once the striker is put out, any other runner must be tagged out.

In summary, interpreting the 1860 rule to mean that the force is no longer in effect if the batter is retired first (in keeping with the modern rule) has historical support (the 1854 Rules and Chadwick's 1867 commentary). It also seems more logical that if there is no player occupying first base because the striker has been put out, the other runners are not forced at the next base. This interpretation would also have the advantage of causing less confusion for players and spectators when this situation arises. Also, Chadwick's attempt to clear up the matter in his commentary may indicate that some clubs were interpreting the rule one way and some were interpreting it the other way. This gives vintage clubs flexibility in determining how they want to handle force plays.

Experienced vintage teams that are familiar with the subtleties of the 1860 Rules may prefer playing "the force is always on" and the order in which the batter and any runners are put out does not matter. However, interpreting the rules to mean the force is still on even if the striker is put out first may be a bit too complicated for matches with community teams, school groups, and other novice players. Either interpretation is workable for experienced clubs, but this point should be reviewed by both clubs before the match.

Courtesy Runners

In keeping with the sportsmanlike nature of vintage base ball, clubs usually allow a courtesy runner for a striker who reaches base safely but would have trouble continuing around the bases due to some injury, medical condition, or equipment problem. A courtesy runner is different than a pinch-runner in that (a) the runner being replaced may return to the game when his team takes the field and (b) the new runner is usually someone who is already in the game at another position, not a new player who is permanently replacing the original player in the lineup.

The need for a courtesy runner usually arises when a striker has a permanent or temporary disability, such as an ankle sprain, pulled muscle, or has been shaken up in a fall or collision. On these occasions, a player might be able to return to the game after taking time to recover while his team completes its turn at bat. Similarly, a player might have a minor equipment problem, such as a broken shoelace that could be repaired or replaced by the time his team has finished batting and is ready to take the field.

Using a courtesy runner is a wise practice in that it keeps the game moving. Removing the runner from the game temporarily means that the spectators will not have to wait patiently while a player tries to walk off an injury or tries to make some type of on-the-spot equipment repair. Using a courtesy runner also protects the health and well-being of the player involved by not forcing him to aggravate his injury by continuing to run the bases (or possibly tripping and falling due to a loose shoe).

To utilize a courtesy runner, the captain of the team at bat should approach the umpire and indicate the runner is injured and has asked to be replaced temporarily by a teammate. The umpire then asks the captain of the team in the field if he will grant permission for the use of the courtesy runner. The captain routinely agrees, but in the spirit of good sportsmanship, he should definitely be consulted for permission before the substitution is made. These questions should be asked and answered in a loud voice by all parties so that the spectators (unaccustomed to the use of courtesy runners in modern baseball) will understand the nature of the delay on the field. One very workable practice is to have the player who made the last out serve as the courtesy runner since his turn at bat will not be coming up again for a while. This also provides for a random selection of the courtesy runner that avoids the impression of any attempt to seek an advantage by inserting a faster runner and prevents any unseemly haggling over the selection of the new runner. This situation does not arise often but frequently enough to have a policy in place to cover it. When it does come up, asking and granting permission to use a courtesy runner provides an instructive illustration of the gentlemanly nature of base ball in 1860 and the vintage game.

In the interests of fair play and good sportsmanship, the team at bat should never abuse this practice by falsely claiming an injury or equipment problem simply to replace a slower runner with a faster one (especially in the late innings of a close game). The purpose of permitting the use of a courtesy runner is to allow a player with a minor injury or equipment problem to be able to take a few minutes to attend to his situation so that he can continue in the game. It should never be used to gain a competitive advantage over the other team, especially a club that has been kind enough to agree to the temporary substitution.

Interestingly, the practice of allowing courtesy runners continued into the professional era when games became much rougher and more competitive. Retrosheet.org, the informative baseball reference website, lists several dozen known instances of courtesy runners being used in the major leagues between 1877 and 1949. In these instances, the injured runner typically was hit by a pitch, shaken up in a collision, or suffered a cut, sprain, or strain while running or sliding. The injured player was replaced by a courtesy runner who was a player already in the game. The batter then returned to play in the field the next inning if he had recovered. Employing a courtesy runner should not be overused or abused, but it seems appropriate for vintage games where it would have been a good fit with the social norms of the era being portrayed.

Even as the base-running rules described in this chapter are sometimes confusing and often open to interpretation, so too are the rules and practices regarding the additional base running topics of leading off, sliding, and stealing, which are discussed in the next chapter.

19

Base Running Interpretations: Leadoffs, Sliding, and Stealing

Leadoffs, sliding, and stealing are base-running issues that are the source of many questions, controversies, and honest differences of opinion among the members of the vintage base ball community. Interpretations of these base running issues are intertwined with the discussion regarding slow pitching versus fast pitching, and have a major impact on the way in which vintage base ball is played and presented to the public.

Since the wording and meaning of the 1860 Rules are not always clear, different interpretations and practices have been developed by vintage programs in different parts of the country. Through research and experimentation, vintage clubs have tried to piece together how the game was played in the 1860s and how vintage base ball should be played today. Noting that even today baseball is played differently in Japan, Cuba, and the United States (and even, due to the designated hitter rule, in the two major leagues in the United States), the VBBA website's section on rules offers the following observation:

> In vintage base ball, where the game from a time and place in the past is re-created, it [uniformity of rules] becomes even more complex, for depending on the time and place, the game could be quite different. If you watch an 1860 game in Columbus, Ohio, the emphasis is on the spirited, amateur gentlemen clubs of the day, whereas in an 1873 rules game played in New Jersey, depicting a time when the best players were sought and professionalism of the game was taking root, the emphasis is on how well the game is played.

With no absolute right or wrong way to portray leadoffs, sliding, and stealing, it is wise for program leaders to consider both the historical basis for these base-running practices and what works best in vintage games. The historical basis of base running is reflected not only in the wording of the rules but also in the base-running customs of other bat-and-ball games and in the prevailing culture of adult conduct on the base ball field in the period being portrayed. Safety and spectator appeal are other factors to keep firmly in mind, especially if the games are being played at a museum, historic site, or another public setting.

This chapter examines the rules, summarizes the varying viewpoints, and offers suggestions on the application of these rules and practices to 1860-era vintage base ball. As in the case of selecting an era to portray, making informed decisions on how a program will interpret the rules on base running (and the related subject of pitching style) will have long-range consequences for the operation of that program.

Leading Off

The 1860 Rules are silent on the question of leadoffs, so we have no definite information as to whether runners took a few steps off the base as the pitcher was preparing to deliver the ball to the plate. Originally, it was believed by many vintage teams (especially those in the Midwest) that leadoffs were not permitted under 1860 Rules, and as a consequence, most did not allow leading off in vintage games. This approach (no leadoffs) has its roots in the base-running rules of other games.

When the Knickerbockers and the other early clubs formed, the players would have known the basics of existing games like town ball, cricket, and rounders. The Knickerbocker Rules for what became known as the New York Game may have assumed a general understanding of which carryover practices from the other bat-and-ball games were to be continued and therefore do not specifically address those points. One general understanding that may have come from town ball, cricket, and rounders was that the runner did not advance on his own between pitches, but had to hold his base until the next batter hit the ball.

In rounders, the basic method of scoring is the same as in base ball — to hit the ball and then run around a series of bases until returning home, thereby scoring a run for your team. A player can make it as far as he can around the bases on his own hit and then stop at one of the bases, where he is safe as long as he is in contact with the base. He must wait at that base until the next batter hits the ball, when he can again try to advance. The bases are stakes (instead of bags) and are called sanctuaries. As in base ball, a runner cannot be put out while touching his base or sanctuary.

Information presented in "Description and Rules of Rounders" on the website Chaos media.com shows how similar many of the fundamental rules are in rounders, town ball, and baseball. In both rounders and the Knickerbocker Rules, the striker is out if the hit is caught in the air or on one bounce. In rounders and town ball, the runner is out if he is hit with a thrown ball while running between bases, but he is not out if he is hit with the ball while he is grasping a base (sanctuary). The rounders rules on base running specify, "If the runners have all stopped running and are hovering near a Sanctuary, and if the Feeder [pitcher] has the ball in his control back by his stone [pitcher's point], the play shall be deemed ended and the Runners shall grasp the Sanctuaries and the next Defender [striker] is up." There is a specific prohibition of any leading off or advancing (stealing) until the next batter hits the ball. "If a Runner mistakenly lets go of a Sanctuary after the play has ended but before the Striker has hit the ball, that Runner is automatically Out." This means that the runner must remain in contact with his base until the next batter hits the ball and puts the ball in play. He may not lead off or try to run toward the next base while the ball is being pitched. If he leaves the base too soon, which is defined as before the next batter hits the ball, the penalty is that he is called out. These rules suggest that leading off was not part of early bat-and-ball games. The 1860 edition of *Beadle's Dime Base-Ball Player* includes both the rules for the New York Game and "The Rules and Regulations of the Game of Base Ball, adopted by the 'Massachusetts Association of Base-Ball Players' held in Dedham, May 13, 1858." Neither set of rules contains any references to leadoffs.

Since the Knickerbocker Rules do not mention any change in procedures that would allow the runner to start moving toward the next base before the next batter hits the ball, there is reason to believe there may have been no leadoffs or stealing in the early years of the New York Game. As with many characteristics of the New York Game that were not specifically mentioned in the short list of rules drawn up by the Knickerbockers, it may have been the general understanding of the club members (based on their experience with playing other bat-and-ball games) that a runner did not try to advance to the next base until the ball was hit by the batter.

Some vintage programs have favored a less restrictive leadoff policy and have pointed to several illustrations from the 1850s and 1860s showing base runners a few steps off the bag while the pitcher is delivering the ball. The 1866 Currier and Ives image *The American National Game of Ball Base* is a good example of this, as the runners on first and third are taking a lead of about two steps off the base. (This illustration is from 1866, not 1860, and rules and practices changed from year to year.) Examination of the pictorial evidence showing runners taking leads has caused most of the teams to relax their rules against leading off and allow the runner to take a few steps off the base (at his own risk, of course) while the pitcher is holding the ball or as he delivers it to the plate.

The longer the runner's lead, however, the more he puts himself in jeopardy of being caught off base and put out. This could happen in three ways. First, (as in modern baseball) he can be picked off if the pitcher throws the ball to the baseman and the baseman tags the runner before he returns to the base. Second, (as is also the case in modern baseball) if the runner is very far off base and the batter hits a line drive to the pitcher or one of the infielders, the player catching the ball on the fly can throw to first base and the runner is out if he does not get back before the ball arrives in the hands of the baseman. Third, if the batter hits a foul ball, the runner must get back to his base before the ball arrives or he will be put out (provided the ball has first "settled in the hands of the pitcher" during the play).

In this third example, if a runner starts toward second base and the batter hits a foul tip to the catcher, the catcher could throw the ball quickly back to the pitcher, who would in turn throw quickly to the first baseman. If the ball (having been handled by the pitcher) reaches first base before the runner can get back, he is out. If the catcher fields the foul ball and throws directly to first base, the runner is not out, even if the throw beats him back to the bag. On a foul ball, the throw must go from the player fielding the ball to the pitcher and then to the base.

Since the rule book is not instructive on the question of leadoffs, some programs believe it is authentic to permit unlimited leadoffs. Other programs have raised concerns that, without any guidelines or restrictions, some vintage players seem to be taking leads much larger than the leads pictured in the nineteenth-century illustrations. Therefore, to preserve the general look of the 1860 game (which seems to point to the practice of taking only modest leads), they have developed two alternative approaches: adopting the practice of limiting leads to two steps from the bag; or, allowing runners to take whatever lead they wish, but requiring them to be stationary when the ball is pitched.

Those favoring unlimited leads have pointed out that some period illustrations (such as *Union Soldiers at Salisbury, N.C.*) show the base runner has not only taken a lead but is moving toward second as the ball is being pitched. In analyzing nineteenth-century pictorial depictions of games, it should be kept in mind that an illustration showing a runner leading off his base could be an indication that taking a lead was a common practice of the time. It also could be the case of an artist who was unfamiliar with the nuances of the game not recording the sequence of events correctly. Returning to his studio and painting from memory several days, weeks, or months after observing a game (as was the case with Otto Boetticher, who did the Salisbury painting), an artist might capture the general look of the game but might depict some of the details incorrectly. In this instance, he might have painted the base runner moving as the pitch was being delivered when, under the rules and practices of the time, the runner would not have started to move until after the pitch was on its way or even until after the ball had been hit. Paintings and drawings are helpful in understanding how the game was played, but they are not always entirely accurate, depending on such variables as the artist's knowledge of the subject matter and any artistic license (such as shortening the base paths) employed in rendering the scene.

The evidence on leading off is inconclusive, which reflects the general circumstance of the game being played under slightly different rules by different clubs in different communities. If leading off is permitted in a vintage game, it would be best to have the runner take a few steps off the bag and then stop and stand in an alert manner as he watches the pitcher deliver the ball. Any excessive dancing and jockeying back and forth (as might be observed in a modern base runner) should be discouraged since such behavior would have been considered childish and not in keeping with period views on gentlemanly decorum.

The important point is that whatever leadoff policy is adopted by a program, it should be made clear to the players and inquiring spectators that it is a practice that has been established to present a vintage game, not an official "rule" of base ball circa 1860. When the participating clubs and the umpire meet before the game to discuss ground rules and local rule interpretations, policies on leadoffs are reviewed and the visiting club abides by the local customs of the host club. If the club has printed the rules and practices it uses, this document can be shared in advance with the visiting club, giving them a chance to become familiar with the manner in which the game will be conducted.

Long leadoffs are more appropriate for programs that portray later eras, when faster pitching, aggressive base running, and stealing were the norm. Some programs prefer to prevent or discourage the aggressive base-running style of later times so that it does not become a dominant feature of the match. If a program's goal is to preserve and present the gentlemanly tone of an 1860-era game, it may want to adopt the policy of no leadoffs or limited leadoffs of about two steps (in the manner portrayed in the 1866 Currier and Ives illustration) that has worked well for many established clubs.

Sliding

A question that has sparked considerable debate in vintage base ball circles is the issue of sliding into bases. Some clubs have favored including the practice of sliding and have adopted it as part of an 1860s-style game. The rationale used is that since sliding was not specifically prohibited by the 1860 Rules, it should be permissible in a vintage game. Others programs, while acknowledging that sliding is not specifically "against the rules," are convinced that it was not done in the early days of base ball and continue to maintain that it should not be done in 1860-era vintage base ball. Once again, the 1860 Rules do not address the issue, and the absence of a rule has left it to the vintage programs to come up with answers to this question that work well for them. Factors for program leaders to consider include historical evidence, safety, expense, the general tone of the game, and the gentlemanly spirit of the times.

Historical Considerations

While sliding did eventually become a common practice in nineteenth-century base ball, it does not seem to have been introduced until the mid–1860s. As part of an ongoing discussion on the origins of sliding on the nineteenth century base ball listserv, historian

When playing according to slow-pitch practices, base runners are asked to either take no lead or a relatively short lead off the base.

John Thorn shared a passage he found on page 25 of Connie Mack's autobiography, *My 66 Years in the Big Leagues*, in which Mack reports, "The first slide to base is supposed to have been developed by a player named Studley of Washington, in the late 1860s. This was considered a circus stunt and created considerable excitement." In *A Game of Inches: The Game on the Field*, Peter Morris discusses several players as candidates for the distinction of making the first slide, including Eddie Cuthbert of the Keystone Club in a game at the Capitoline Grounds in Brooklyn in 1865. Morris concludes that "sliding does appear to have been uncommon in the early days of baseball, and generally inadvertent" and observes "it was not until the early 1880s that sliding became at all customary" (pp. 265–266).

Chadwick's Commentary: Preparing the Field

In *Beadle's Dime Base-Ball Player* for 1860, Henry Chadwick provides information that speaks to the question of sliding. Evidence against sliding as a common practice comes from the section "Selection of a Ground" on how to prepare a field for playing base ball. "The ground should be level, and the surface free from all irregularities, and, if possible, covered with fine turf; if the latter can not be done, and the soil is gravelly, a loamy soil should be laid down around the bases, and all the gravel removed therefrom, because, at the bases frequent falls occur, and on gravelly soil injury, in such cases, will surely result to both clothes and body of the player, in the shape of scraped hands, arms, knees, etc." (p. 17).

Chadwick's stated reason for playing on a turf (grass-covered) field or putting a softer, "loamy" soil around the bases is to provide a cushion for "frequent falls," not slides. If players were sliding on a regular basis, it seems reasonable that Chadwick would have mentioned sliding as a reason for recommending a bed of softer, less-abrasive loamy soil around the bases. Chadwick is correct in pointing out that there are frequent falls around the bases in games played by 1860 Rules. In vintage games, runners who are approaching a base and then endeavor to stop without overrunning the bag sometimes lose their footing and can end up falling down in the area around the base. Runners sometimes lose their footing rounding a bag as they make the 90-degree turn toward the next base. Runners sometimes round the base too far and then, to avoid being tagged out, end up falling, stumbling, diving, and lunging to get back to the base safely. On pick-off attempts runners can slip and fall while getting back to the base ahead of the ball. On rundown plays, the base runner and one or more fielders can end up on the ground in the vicinity of one of the bases as the runner darts and dodges to escape the "pickle" he is in. Basemen also end up falling as they lunge to catch a low throw from a teammate or dive to tag a runner. There are usually several plays in which players end up on the ground in every game, which would prompt Chadwick's advice in favor of loamy soil.

Protecting Uniforms

Chadwick's statement also points out concern for clothing, which is another reason to believe the early clubs did not practice sliding. Modern professional players think nothing of tearing the knee out of their pants while sliding. They can always get another pair of pants from the clubhouse man at no cost to the player. But Chadwick specifically cites potential damage "to both the clothes and body of the player" as a concern. Club members of the 1860 era probably owned only one uniform, which they may have paid for out of their own pocket or club funds. They were very proud to wear the uniform and would not want to rip the knee out of their good woolen uniform pants or the elbow out of a uniform shirt.

If it was cost-effective to consider going to the trouble of replacing gravel with loam, the concern over the damage to uniforms must have been significant. Uniforms were made for active wear, like the volunteer firemen's uniform from which they were derived, and appear to have been similar to band, police, and military uniforms of that day. Uniform pants were made for fairly strenuous physical activity, but they would not have held up well if subjected to sliding into bases on a regular basis. In addition to becoming ripped and torn, they could become stained by grass and mud. The 1860 base ball uniform was simply too valuable (expensive to replace) and valued (cherished by the owner as a symbol of his membership on one of the leading gentlemen's clubs) to subject it to the harsh treatment of sliding. Chadwick's concern over the protection of uniforms supports the case against sliding.

Safety for Amateur Players

Chadwick's concern for the possibility of personal injury is another reason to believe sliding was not commonly practiced. The members of the base ball clubs of the 1850s and early 1860s were amateurs in the truest sense. With the exception of the few paid professionals beginning to creep into the game around 1860, players received no salary for playing. In fact, as is the case with vintage players today, they likely incurred some out-of-pocket costs in the form of membership dues, uniform purchases, and travel expenses as part of belonging to the club.

Since they earned no money playing base ball, they all had regular jobs. Studies of the Knickerbocker membership reveal they worked through the week in such areas as banking, insurance, retail, skilled crafts, and the professions. In this way they were probably not far demographically from the composition of a typical vintage club of today — men with regular jobs through the week who are not wealthy, just sufficiently comfortable to be able to afford the expenses of belonging to the club and to have the leisure time to play base ball once or twice a week. They would not have risked an injury that would have kept them out of off. The Knickerbockers and their contemporaries would not have had a financial safety net in the form of workers' compensation, disability benefits, and company health insurance, as is available to most employees today. If these amateur players were injured and missed work, they likely would have had no income.

Chadwick's reference to possible harm "to the clothes and body of a player" also raises the safety issue for vintage base ball programs. Sliding is not permitted in many adult recreational softball leagues today because of the general view that it increases the chance of injury. Vintage clubs that oppose sliding on grounds that nineteenth-century clubs would not have wanted to damage their uniforms also oppose sliding because it can result in injuries to players.

Every year, several major league players, who presumably know how to slide and are playing on exceptionally level, well-groomed fields, sustain significant ankle, knee, shoulder and hand injuries while sliding. Just as many modern softball leagues prohibit sliding to reduce the likelihood of collisions and injuries, it would seem reasonable that the early base ball club members would have wanted to enjoy their exercise and recreation time without the risk of personal injury and would have disdained the practice of sliding.

Gentlemanly Decorum: Sliding as Unmanly and Unsportsmanlike

The general deportment of gentlemen in the 1860 era also strengthens the case against sliding. Amateur players of that era tended to conduct themselves with a degree of dignity that would be inconsistent with the practice of sliding. They were eager to portray base ball as a manly enterprise for mature adults rather than a childish game. Since there does not seem to have been sliding in other bat-and-ball games, it seems doubtful that the gentlemanly members of the early clubs would have started sliding as part of the new national game.

A post from frequent contributor Richard Hershberger on the nineteenth century base ball listserv on November 14, 2008, contained the text of an article in the June 24, 1865, edition of the *Philadelphia Inquirer* that speaks to contemporary views on sliding. The article's author is not named, but the style and tone are similar to Henry Chadwick's writings. The author begins by "calling the attention of first-class players of Base Ball, to a notorious custom" that had entered the game. "The system of which I disapprove, and I am confident I will be upheld by the majority of players is, that on the field we notice the 'slide game,' ... when a player in an effort to gain his base will throw himself on the ground, feet foremost, sliding for fully a distance of twenty feet." The author then raises several objections to the practice:

> It is not only the unmanliness of such a proceeding, but the danger encountered by a basekeeper from his opponent dashing at the base, feet first, convincing you that in the attempt to "put him out" half a dozen steel spikes may enter your hands or body, hence the necessity of

abolishing such an unfair practice, benefiting only the party in play, and angering and intimidating the base players.

It is almost impossible to put out a player who is determined to enforce this manner of avoiding the ball, unless you are willing to risk the severe injury of your hands. It is not only an improper play, but destroys the spirit of the game.

The practice of sliding does seem to change the gentlemanly tone of the vintage game. It may seem innocuous enough to permit sliding as a means of stopping at a base without overrunning it. Once sliding is permitted, however, it opens the door to "hard" sliding — the practice of a runner sliding aggressively into a fielder in an effort to disrupt him from catching the ball, or to cause him to drop it so that he is not able to tag the runner.

The view expressed in the 1865 *Philadelphia Inquirer* article that sliding is responsible for "angering and intimidating the base players" and that it "destroys the spirit of the game" represents a valid concern for a vintage program. Once a fielder is knocked over by a runner's slide, the game takes on a different character as the fielder or his teammates begin looking for opportunities to retaliate when they are on the base paths. Museums and historical societies put a high priority on presenting a game that is suitable for family viewing, and that objective could be compromised by players exchanging words or getting into any kind of a tussle over a hard slide (as often happens in modern baseball).

Preserving and promoting the sportsmanlike atmosphere under which the early clubs competed is definitely a point to consider in regard to sliding. Playing the game in a combative, edgy environment moves the game away from the gentlemanly behavioral norms of its early days. Historically, this is what actually happened as the game got rougher through the decade of the 1860s and beyond, and sliding in vintage base ball is sometimes defended on grounds of authenticity. However, this is not the kind of atmosphere most teams and certainly most museums and historical societies want to foster. Therefore, programs need to decide the direction they want to go—preserve the sportsmanlike, gentlemanly version of the early amateur era of the game or adopt the newer practices that led to faster, rougher style of play that accompanied the coming of the professional era. A program should exercise great care before authorizing sliding since a strong case can also be made on historical accuracy that the practice of intentionally sliding into a base did not exist until the mid–1860s, and even then it was viewed as a "notorious custom."

While sliding can be restricted or barred by a vintage program on grounds of authenticity, player safety, or other considerations, spectators should not be told that sliding was "against the rules" of 1860. In the past, the umpires in some programs have called a runner out for sliding into a base in the belief that sliding was prohibited by the rules. In some cases, a runner has been called out for sliding even when the "sliding" was unintentional and was more a matter of the runner diving, lunging, or losing his footing. Calling a runner out for such inadvertent sliding misinforms the public. If a program prefers to prohibit the practice of sliding (as many successful programs have done), the umpire should simply tell the captains in the pre-game meeting that there should be no sliding in the match. All players should then comply and refrain from sliding during the game.

The Knickerbockers and their contemporaries were not the type to be continually looking for loopholes and gray areas in the rules. It would have been out of character for them to adopt a practice such as sliding—just because it was not expressly prohibited in the rules—if it ran counter to the way they conducted themselves on and off the field.

Sliding is not a good fit for the 1860-style game based on slow pitching, limited stealing, and a gentlemanly atmosphere. If sliding is to be permitted, it is best suited to programs that portray the rules, practices, and customs of a later era that would include faster pitching, the fly game, and stealing.

Stealing

There is no mention of advancing from one base to the next by stealing in the original Knickerbockers Rules of 1845 and nothing in the rule changes in subsequent years through the 1840s and 1850s that mentions stealing. The Rules of 1860 make no mention of either permitting or prohibiting stealing as a way for a runner to advance from one base to the next.

Since stealing bases is not specifically mentioned anywhere in the early rules, baseball historians and vintage players are divided on the advent of the practice of a runner attempting to advance to the next base while the ball is being passed between the pitcher and the catcher. Some contend it was part of the game from the beginning. In contrast, others believe that while the 1860 Rules do not prohibit advancing before the ball is struck, they also do not authorize leadoffs or stealing before the ball was struck. They point out that no mention is made of "stealing" bases or any means for the runner to advance except by the hitting of his teammates that follow him in the batting order. It seems logical that if players were allowed to advance from one base to the next by their own running, that is, by some means other than the next striker hitting the ball, there would be some mention of it in the rules. They believe there was no base stealing in the game's early years and that it was not a part of the game until the 1860 era and after. As in the case of leadoffs, stealing may not have been mentioned in the Knickerbocker Rules because it was generally understood, based on previous experience playing other bat-and-ball games, that the runner had to remain at his base until the next batter hit the ball.

Most vintage clubs playing by the rules of 1860 have taken a conservative view on allowing base stealing. Some prohibit stealing entirely, but the most common approach is to limit stealing to situations in which the catcher misplays the pitch, such as a passed ball. A passed ball is defined as a pitch not fielded cleanly by the catcher on the fly or first bounce.

Section 10 of the 1860 Rules states: "If three balls are struck at, and missed, and the last one is not caught, either flying or upon the first bound, it shall be considered fair, and the striker must attempt to make his run." This rule establishes the principle that the offensive player who strikes out can advance on a mishandled pitch but may not advance if the pitch is caught by the catcher on the fly or first bounce. Applying that principle to the base runner, it seems logical to permit him to advance only on a passed ball but not on a pitch fielded cleanly by the catcher on the fly or first bounce. On the third strike, catching the pitch on the first bounce ends the play and prevents advancement by the striker. In the interests of consistency, catching the pitch cleanly on the first bound could also exclude any advancement by the runners. Considerations for programs weighing whether to prohibit, limit, or permit stealing are discussed below.

Searching the Rules for Clues

Proponents of open stealing point to the existence of the balk rule in the original Knickerbocker Rules of 1845 as evidence of early stealing: "A runner cannot be put out in making one base, when a balk is made by the pitcher." These proponents point out that if there was no stealing, there would be no reason for a balk rule. They maintain that the basic reason for having the modern balk rule is that it is intended to prevent the pitcher from stopping in the middle of his delivery in order to try to catch a runner attempting to steal the next base.

However, there may be another purpose for the balk rule in the game's early years. One reason the rules of what came to be known as the New York Game are so few and brief is that they speak mainly to the elements of the new game that were different from what the players were already accustomed to from their experience with other bat-and-ball games. If several practices were present in early games (e.g., underhand pitching in rounders and early cricket versus overhand throwing in town ball and later cricket), they specified which method was to be used in the new game.

In writing the 1845 Rules to cover exceptions and clarify established practices, the Knickerbockers were acting in a way similar to the customary organizational methods of a modern softball league, where it is assumed that everyone already knows the basics of the game. When the "league rules" are distributed at the beginning of the softball season, each player is not handed a thick rule book, but only a one- or two-page handout clarifying how the rules are going to be interpreted, modified, and applied in that specific league. The rules do not cover everything, just the new or unique rules that may not be understood by all.

While rounders and town ball were played differently in various communities, the basic rules of these games do not seem to provide for the runner leaving his base and advancing to the next until the ball is struck by the next batter. As noted in the discussion of leadoffs, the rules of rounders state that when one batter's turn is concluded, "the Runners shall grasp the Sanctuaries [bases] and the next Defender is up." The accompanying explanation contains a provision against trying to advance until the next batter hits the ball, even declaring the runner to be "automatically out" if he "mistakenly lets go of a Sanctuary after the play has ended but before the Striker has hit the ball."

This prohibition against leaving the base too soon brings the discussion back to the Knickerbockers' balk rule. In order to prevent the pitcher from faking a delivery to the plate that might cause the eager runner to leave the base too soon, the pitcher is prohibited by the balk rule from stopping in the middle of his delivery. It is unlikely that the gentlemanly Knickerbockers would have wanted to create a game in which a runner could be put out on the technicality of leaving the base a moment too soon because he was tricked by the pitcher into thinking the pitch was on its way to the striker. Any attempt by the pitcher to get an out through deception (faking a pitch) would have been out of place, and was therefore prohibited by the balk rule.

While some have made a case that the balk rule of the Knickerbockers can be construed as evidence that stealing was part of the early game, this alternate view is also a possibility — that there was general understanding from other bat-and-ball games that a runner had to remain at his base until the next striker hit the ball, and it would be an unsportsmanlike and tedious practice to try to mislead him into leaving his base too soon. The Knickerbockers were playing for exercise. Therefore, to keep the game moving, they would not have wanted the pitcher to make repeated feints toward home plate in the hope of getting the runner to step away from his base too soon.

Chadwick's Commentary

Some programs have adopted unrestricted or "open" stealing and enjoy playing by these rules. They see stealing as authentic to the period. To support their position that stealing was allowed, they cite the 1860 *Beadle's Dime Base-Ball Player* where Chadwick's section on "The Pitcher" calls for the pitcher to be "exceedingly cautious and on the alert in watching the bases when the players are attempting to run, and in such cases should endeavor his utmost to throw a swift and true ball to the baseman" (p. 22). They see this statement as a reference to runners about to steal. Chadwick's section on "The Catcher" states that "when a player has made his first base, the Catcher should take a position nearer the striker, in order to take the ball from the pitcher before it bounds; and the moment the ball is delivered by the pitcher, and the player runs from the first to the second base, the Catcher should take the ball before bounding, and send it to the second base as swiftly as possible, in time to cut off the player before he can touch the base; in the latter case it would be as well, in the majority of cases, to send the ball a little to the right of the base" (p. 21). This description of how to best defense a runner trying to advance from first to second would seem to be an indication that stealing was occurring. Further reading of Chadwick's commentary is in order, however, for there is more to the story.

Later in the section on "The Catcher," Chadwick advises, "We would suggest to the Catcher the avoidance of the boyish practice of passing the ball to and from the pitcher when a player is on first base," adding, "it is a feature of the game that is a tiresome one." Chadwick is describing a state of affairs that he finds seriously flawed. With a man on first base, the pitcher and catcher, afraid that the runner will attempt to advance to second, are apparently throwing pitchout after pitchout, "passing the ball to and from the pitcher" wide of home plate out of the batter's reach. This allows the catcher to take a swift pitch on the fly, ready to throw it to second if the runner tries to advance. The runner may be reluctant to run on one of these pitchouts and will instead wait for a pitch to get away from the catcher so he can advance to second. Meanwhile, the batter is taking many pitches, good and bad, in the hope that one will be dropped by the catcher and allow his teammate to run to second. This scenario would constitute a very "tiresome" feature of the game.

What is Chadwick's remedy? In "The Pitcher" section he emphasizes the need for the pitcher to throw hittable pitches by admonishing, "We would remind him that in cases where a player has reached his first base after striking, it is the Pitcher's duty to pitch the ball to the bat, and not to the catcher [the practice of throwing repeated pitchouts described above]; and should the batsman refuse to strike at good balls repeatedly pitched at him, it will be the umpire's duty to call one strike, etc., according to section 37 of the rules" (p. 22). Chadwick is adamant in his desire to make the catcher go behind the plate and insists also that the pitcher deliver the ball over the plate, a sure sign that pitchouts were a common practice. Pitchers and catchers were preventing the runners from advancing by repeatedly throwing wide of the plate so that the runner would be hesitant to run and the catcher would have a decent chance of throwing him out.

Reading the entire commentary in the 1860 *Beadle's Dime Base-Ball Player* shows that Chadwick is urging the pitcher and catcher to play the game in a more traditional way by pitching to the batter and forcing the umpire to call strikes on the batter if he fails to hit good pitches. Chadwick's suggestions work if the pitches are over the plate and slow enough to hit. But, if the pitches are swift, the batter may still be reluctant to swing. If the umpire resorts to calling strikes, it still takes quite a while under the rules to strike the batter out. According to the wording of Section 37, "should a striker stand at the bat without striking at good balls repeatedly pitched to him, for the apparent purpose of delaying the game, or of giving advantage to a player, the umpire, after warning him, shall call one strike, and if he persists in such action, two and three strikes. When three strikes are called, he shall be subject to the same rules as if he had struck at three fair balls." No specific number is given, but "repeatedly" would indicate that a pattern of taking good pitches must be established — at least three or four good pitches. The batter then gets a warning. Following the warning he still gets three more strikes. Some have suggested that if the batter swings at a pitch, the original warning is voided and he again has to establish a pattern of taking hittable pitches before again being warned. A combination of good pitches, bad pitches, a warning or two, and several foul balls easily extends a typical turn at bat to at least ten or fifteen pitches.

By allowing stealing, games between the elite teams of the New York area, as observed by Chadwick, had been reduced to a stalemate, with the batter taking many pitches (even if they are hittable over the plate) while waiting for his teammate to try to advance to the next base. This provides the vintage community with a dilemma. The 1860 *Beadle's Dime Base-Ball Player* is the best source we have for re-creating the game. However, since recent developments, including swift pitching and stealing, had transformed a base ball game into a long, drawn out affair that was often not much fun to play or watch, is this "gridlock" version of the game the one that vintage clubs should try to emulate and present, especially in a museum setting with spectators on hand?

There is an alternative method of conducting a game that is authentic to the period and is one Chadwick clearly advocates — going back to the time just past, when pitchers delivered slower, hittable pitches and strikers swung at the first pitch that was over the plate, putting the ball in play. This approach creates continuous action and results in the game moving along briskly.

Game Accounts and Box Scores

Game accounts and box scores can provide insight as to how the game was played. The old box scores and game accounts generally mention passed balls but not stealing. Including the category of passed balls indicates that runners could advance when the pitch was not fielded cleanly by the catcher. For example, Section 7 of Preston Orem's *Baseball (1845–1881) from the Newspaper Accounts* includes game accounts and detailed box scores from a series of three notable games played in 1858 at the Fashion Race Course in Queens between teams of "all-stars" from the prominent New York and Brooklyn clubs. The box score for the first game includes the category "passed balls on which bases were run." It records that Leggett of the Excelsiors, the starting catcher for the Brooklyn nine, had eleven while Masten of the Putnams, who started at third base and "exchanged places" with Leggett after Leggett "lost two balls in succession," had one. DeBost of the Knickerbockers, the catcher for the New York nine, was charged with two passed balls. The box score for the second game of the series is incomplete, giving no listing of "passed balls on which bases were run," but the box score for the third game lists Boerum, the Brooklyn catcher, having eight passed balls and DeBost of New York with three. These 1858 box scores account for bases gained through passed balls, but not for bases gained by stealing, an indication that advancing was permitted only on passed balls (pitches not handled cleanly on one bound by the catcher).

Evaluating the Evidence: Terminology and Geographic Differences

As the question of whether stealing was part of the game in the early days is examined, it is important to remember that while references to stealing bases sometimes turn up in nineteenth-century publications, caution should be exercised in assuming that these references always describe the modern definition of stealing—a runner advancing to the next base while the pitcher is delivering the ball to the plate, without the pitch being struck by the batter. Some of these nineteenth-century references to stealing a base may refer to a runner doing what would now be called taking an "extra" base. For example, an alert and speedy base runner might advance from first to third on a single, stretch a double into a triple, take an additional base when a throw from the outfield is mishandled by an infielder, or run from first base to second on a passed ball. While none of these plays would be a "steal" in modern terms, they may have been considered a form of stealing a base in nineteenth-century accounts.

As was the case involving many rules and practices associated with early base ball, there were likely significant differences in the way the game was played from region to region. This would be especially true for the elite clubs of the East Coast, which seem to have adopted such changes as using professional players, swift pitching, and stealing well before these concepts became more widespread. Even within the same region, some clubs embraced certain changes in the game while other clubs resisted these changes and tried to maintain the status quo.

Experiments in Vintage Games

Experimenting with the rules by playing vintage games with either restricted stealing (advancing only on a passed ball) or unrestricted stealing (running as soon as the pitcher goes into his delivery motion) provides insight on how the game was played in the nineteenth century. An example occurred in June 2009 when a team from the East Coast accustomed to playing according to practices that permit unrestricted stealing came to Dayton, Ohio, for a multi-club tournament on Saturday and a double-header with the host team on Sunday. The Easterners suggested the Dayton club try playing the two Sunday games using unlimited stealing and unlimited leadoffs. Experienced umpire and scorer Jim Kimnach of the Muffin program in Columbus was invited to umpire the Sunday matches. Kimnach observed that numerous attempts were made to steal both second and third during the two nine-inning games. "It is interesting to note that not one single runner was thrown out by the catcher," he observed, noting that slow runners as well as speedy runners were successful in their steals, and batters repeatedly did not swing at good pitches until their teammates had advanced by stealing.

The fact that no runners were thrown out trying to steal points to one reason for making the assumption that stealing was not part of the game in its formative years. It is the general consensus among historians that slow pitching was the norm at that time, and stealing does not work with rules and practices that call for slow pitching. In *Baseball: The Early Years*, Seymour and Mills remind us that the pitcher "was not allowed to jerk or throw the ball to the batter. Instead, he had to toss it gently underhand as near the plate as possible so than the batter would have the fullest opportunity to hit it" (p. 19). With slow pitching, it is too easy for almost any player who reaches first base to steal second and third while the next batter lets several pitches go by. And, having waited for the slow pitch to arrive, the catcher finds it almost impossible to throw out an average runner attempting to steal. Once the pitcher starts to draw back his arm to deliver the ball, he can not interrupt his pitching motion without balking. By the time the ball gets to the plate, the runner is well on his way to second and even a catcher with an excellent arm has little chance of throwing him out.

The fact that it is too easy to steal a base when the pitcher is pitching the ball slowly is the reason modern slow-pitch softball leagues (and many youth baseball leagues) do not allow stealing or permit it only after the pitch has crossed home plate. Allowing unrestricted stealing in combination with slow pitching slows down the game since many runners reach base and subsequent batters almost always take several pitches to allow their teammates to steal any open base before swinging. This increases the number of pitches delivered, prolongs the game, and makes it less interesting for players and spectators.

Experiments indicate that stealing can be contained only by adopting swift pitching. If the ball reaches the catcher more quickly, it inhibits runners from trying to steal and provides a reasonable opportunity for the catcher to throw out a runner who does attempt to advance.

A Research Discovery of Note

In January 2009, researcher Priscilla Astifan reported an important discovery — a Rochester, New York, newspaper account and box score of a game that seemed to verify the existence of stealing in an area far from the elite clubs of New York City. The game was played between the Olympic Club and Live Oak Club on September 6, 1860. The account mentions passed balls but also includes references to stealing. For example, in the first inning, Stanton of the Olympic "made 2nd base on a ball passing the catcher and stole third." In the sixth, Andrews of the Olympic Club "stole second and third and made his tally on a ball passed [sic] catcher."

Vintage base ball players who are of the opinion that stealing was occurring in the 1850s and early 1860s felt their position was supported by this piece of evidence that seemed to indicate base stealing (as that term would be understood today) was taking place in this game. This find was circulated among the vintage base ball community, and those who had supported unlimited stealing in the past expressed the view that since the account mentioned stolen bases in this 1860 game played some distance from New York City, stealing bases may have been more widespread than had been thought. They suggested, therefore, that perhaps stealing bases should be more widely accepted in the vintage game.

Before heading down that road, two factors need to be considered. First, the game in question may have been experimental rather than typical. As described by James Terry in *Long Before the Dodgers: Baseball in Brooklyn 1855–1884*, the Excelsior Club of Brooklyn made "a barnstorming trip to upstate New York in July [1860]. Traveling by rail, the club embarked on the first intercity road trip playing against clubs in Albany, Buffalo, Rochester, Troy, and Newburgh. The Excelsiors drubbed all opponents" (p. 31). Interestingly, one of those opponents was the Live Oak Club. In *Baseball 1845–1881*, Preston Orem reports that while in Rochester, the Excelsiors first "won from Flour City 21-1<in> and then "over Live Oak 27-9<in> (p. 30). From the experience of playing the Excelsiors, an elite club from the New York City area, in July and being involved in a game employing more aggressive base running, the Live Oak and the Olympic clubs may have decided to experiment with this style of play (stealing and perhaps swift pitching) for their September game.

Second, the box score of the game between the Olympics and the Live Oak clubs that includes several references to stealing bases also shows that 739 pitches were thrown in seven innings before the game had to be called due to darkness. While this 1860 game in Rochester provides an example that some teams outside of the elite clubs of the New York City area may have been doing some base stealing in 1860, it also points out the problems with that style of play. Vintage programs need to think about all the factors before deciding if it would be wise to emulate this example and present games to the public that involves an average of more than 100 pitches per inning.

Considerations for Program Leaders

Whether the practice of stealing has been part of the game since the early days or was a new development around 1860, it did become an important part of the game. Along with swift pitching, stealing led to the introduction of called strikes and called balls. Vintage base ball programs need to weigh the implications of playing by the rules of the various eras and make further choices on how they will interpret the rules of the era chosen.

If the rules and practices of the 1860s are interpreted to include swift pitching, unlimited leadoffs, unrestricted stealing, sliding, and the fly game, the players tend to be young, skilled, and athletic. Games take longer, and are often characterized by an atmosphere that places a high priority on aggressive play and winning the match.

When the rules and practices of the 1860s are interpreted to include slow pitching, the bound game, limited leadoffs, no sliding, and stealing only on a passed ball, vintage base ball is playable by those with a wide range of ages and talents. Games move along at a brisk pace (nine innings in about 90 minutes), and are usually characterized by energetic play in an atmosphere that puts a high priority on good sportsmanship and gentlemanly behavior.

20

Game Day: Preparation and Pre-Game Activities

The Setting

Many baseball fans have warm and vivid memories of attending their first big league game. Years later they can recall walking through the portal at a major league park and looking out upon a vast expanse of spectacular green grass with white lines and bases defining the playing field. Recollections probably include the noise and electricity of an enthusiastic crowd. They retain memories of pennants flying over the field; the color and design of the uniforms; the sights and sounds of batting practice; the smells of peanuts, popcorn, and hot dogs; the starting pitcher warming up with his catcher; the announcement of the lineups; and the managers and umpires meeting at the plate to exchange lineup cards and go over the ground rules. For many fans, these first impressions are as much a part of their memories as the actual game and the final score.

In August 1868, when Harry Wright's Cincinnati Red Stockings made a visit to Columbus to play matches with two local teams, the Railroad Club and the Capital Club, *The Ohio State Journal* published the following description of the setting at Olentangy Park:

> The circling rows of carriages with the inner rows of spectators seated or standing; the members of the clubs in their uniforms; the stars and stripes and the colors of the two clubs flying from the staff—all these made a pretty picture, call it a base ball scene or what you will.

This paragraph from the 1860s represents the kind of impression a vintage program should strive to make when guests arrive at a game site. The field may not be circled by horse-drawn carriages, but the appearance of the ball grounds, the look of the players, game officials, and interpreters in period dress, and the atmosphere created by the pre-game activities should create the feeling of stepping back in time and set the stage for a memorable day of base ball as it once was played.

This interest in re-creating a nineteenth-century game goes beyond the first things the spectator might notice — players dressed in old-fashioned uniforms and using wooden bats. On a hot day, players drink water from a crock using a tin cup (with no plastic bottles, aluminum cans, or Styrofoam cups anywhere near the bench), even during warm-up activities. No modern logos are visible on shoes or equipment. No vinyl gym bags, bat bags, or coolers are in sight. No fast-food containers or wrappers are in the bench area. Players do not arrive at the field wearing sunglasses, wristwatches, or shower shoes with their uniforms. Players shake hands in the conventional gentlemanly way when greeting each other (with no high-fiving or fist-bumping). The scorer uses a pencil to enter the lineups on the score sheet.

Teams sometimes make a parade entrance, building interest in the match.

Details are important and none should be overlooked in creating the authentic look and tone of a nineteenth-century game. The details help participants and spectators develop a stronger sense of history. The vintage base ball experience encourages awareness and understanding of the beginnings of the national pastime and of the times that saw the advent and early development of the game. Attention to detail in the presentation of the game makes a vintage match more entertaining and educational. And the details of the pre-game sights and sounds are often remembered long after the outcome of the match is forgotten.

Club Banners and Flags

Many vintage base ball programs have some type of team banner or flag that carries the name of the club and its hometown or museum sponsor, along with its monogram or insignia. These can be hung on a fence or a suitable pole or rod. The existence of club banners is well documented. The reporter who witnessed the Cincinnati Red Stockings visit to Columbus in 1868 took note of "the colors of the two clubs flying from the staff" along with the U.S. flag. Period illustrations of early base ball matches often show club flags flying from poles near the playing field.

The club flags of the 1860s appear to have been rectangular or pennant-shaped and included the same colors as the players' uniforms. Flags of this type, with grommets on the vertical edge, look great flying from a flag staff with the lettering and design visible if the wind is blowing. However, since most vintage fields do not have flag poles, many vintage clubs have made their banners with the grommets (and/or a sleeve to accommodate a pole) across the top edge. A rectangular banner of this type can be displayed between a pair of free-standing iron stakes, hung between two trees, or affixed to a fence adjacent to the ball grounds. It can also be fastened to the backstop if the game is being playing on a modern diamond. This type of horizontally banner can also be carried in parades and held in front of the club members when photographs are taken before or after the match.

Whatever shape and design is chosen, it is beneficial for a club to own a banner. Spectators often walk up to a game after the opening announcements have been made and have no idea what teams are playing. A pair of club banners hanging nearby will identify the participants and perhaps encourage the newcomers to stop and watch the game. A flag or banner is especially worthwhile when playing away games to inform the viewing public where the teams are from. By putting the club's hometown and sponsoring institution on the banner, spectators learn that vintage teams travel considerable distances for matches. As was the case in base ball's early years, flags and banners add considerably to the overall appearance and ambiance of the playing area. In the case of a tournament involving a number of teams, the display of several colorful club banners around the perimeter of the ball grounds is festive, eye-catching, and reminiscent of an earlier time.

Placing streamers representing the colors of the home club on the foul poles is an inexpensive touch that adds to the setting for the game. In addition to providing a splash of color on the boundaries of the playing field, streamers make the poles more visible so that the umpire will be assisted in making the correct call on a ball hit close to the line and outfielders will be able see the foul poles more easily and therefore be less likely to run into them when chasing a fly ball.

U.S. Flags and Bunting

Displaying a U.S. flag at the game site adds to the color and pageantry of the occasion and is also highly recommended. Once a vintage program has decided on what era it will represent, a reproduction American flag can be purchased that has the authentic design and number of stars that would be appropriate for 1857, 1860, 1884, or whatever year is being portrayed on the field. Reproduction period flags are widely used by military reenactment groups and, therefore, are readily available on-line and through stores that specialize in flags and banners. A club banner and the appropriate American flag greatly enhance the team's visual presentation in parades and photographs.

Red, white, and blue cotton bunting is another nice touch that adds to the appearance and atmosphere of the playing field. Bunting can be hung on the front of the scorer's table or placed on any convenient structure, such as a rail fence, an entry gate, or a bandstand adjacent to the ball diamond. Bunting is relatively inexpensive and readily available at many home improvement and party stores (especially around Memorial Day and the Fourth of July).

The Re-Creation Begins Before the Game

Warm-Ups

In *A Game of Inches: The Game on the Field*, Peter Morris observes, "From time immemorial, batters have engaged in some form of pregame practice. In the early days, it consisted largely of 'fungo hitting,' and its development into a more formal process was slow and uneven" (p. 96). Since baseballs "represented a major expense for early baseball clubs, and they could ill afford to lose or deface them for the sake of a little practice, ... the gentler

A club banner identifies the base ball team and its sponsoring museum or historical society in parades and at the ball field at both home and road games.

and more controlled practice of fungo hitting was generally used." Morris provides several examples of pre-game batting practice occurring in the 1880s and 1890s, but points out that "it does not seem to have been until the twentieth century that batting practices became highly structured" (pp. 96–98). The vintage base ball community is generally unaware of any specific organized exercises or drills that preceded the matches. However, with all we know today about injury prevention, vintage clubs are encouraged to engage in warm-up exercises.

In all the pre-game activities, it is important to create the illusion that everyone on the playing field and surrounding area, by their appearance and by their actions, looks like part of a living tableau from the past. Therefore, warm-up activities are always conducted in full uniform. No player is ever out on the field before a game playing catch or taking batting practice in a T-shirt and shorts, making cell phone calls, or wearing ear buds. Any children on the bench or the field should be in period dress.

Warming up is a wise practice for all baseball players, whether on chilly days in the spring and fall or hot mid-summer days. Players should engage in some pre-game stretching activities to loosen up for the match. Since players are usually present well ahead of the match, they typically start by playing catch, "the exercise of throwing and catching being as necessary for the expert as the tyro," according to Henry Chadwick in Haney's *Base Ball Book of Reference for 1867* (p. 120). This standard activity serves two purposes. First, it reduces the risk of injury. It is never a good idea for a player (in any season or any century) to attempt to make the long throws required in a game without getting his arm stretched out and warmed up ahead of time. To avoid injuries, a pair of players should begin throwing easily at a short distance, then gradually increase the distance and put a little more force behind the throws. The cooler the weather, the more time should be spent playing catch before the match. Second, playing catch will reacclimate the player to catching the ball barehanded as he practices the basics of getting in front of the ball, following the ball all the way to his hands, using both hands to catch it, and letting his hands "give" a little on impact in order to hold onto the ball.

While the clubs of the 1850s and 1860s may not have engaged in a formal batting practice, many vintage teams enjoy a casual round of striking if there is time before the match. As in the case of playing catch, taking five or ten swings is a good warm-up exercise for shoulder, leg, and back muscles. In the friendly, sportsmanlike atmosphere of vintage base ball, it is customary for both clubs to take the field simultaneously for these pre-game exercises. The teams alternate sending a striker to the plate, with a mixture of players from both clubs in the infield and outfield making plays on the balls that are struck.

It is a good idea for players to take the opportunity to do some jogging around the farther reaches of the outfield. Some stretching exercises are also a good idea. To avoid injury, a player should not go to bat for the first time in the match, hit the ball, and then to sprint down the baseline to first without having done some running and stretching before the game.

Safety is an important consideration during batting practice since there are often several balls in play at the same time. There is a tendency for an infielder or the player retrieving balls for the pitcher to turn his back to the plate to take a throw from the outfield, then turn around to toss the ball to the pitcher. However, while the fielder is taking the ball from the outfield, the pitcher may have delivered another pitch to the batter. If the batter hits a line drive, it could strike the fielder just as he turns around. Every player in the field should know when the next ball is being pitched and always keep an eye on the batter.

In addition to providing an opportunity for strikers to take some swings before the game, this session also provides fielding practice. Practicing the skills needed to catch a grounder, pop-up, or outfield fly will usually pay off in the game. Fielding practice can be especially valuable if playing on an unfamiliar diamond with some irregularities and idiosyncrasies. Having both teams on the field at the same time also creates an environment for players to chat and become better acquainted. In addition, the sights and sounds of batting practice may draw spectators to the field for the upcoming game.

The Captain

To present the vintage game effectively, the participating clubs should be prepared and organized. On the day of the match, the responsibility of running the ball club falls to the captain. The leadership of the players is in his hands.

The captain functions in the role of the present-day field manager. In the game's early period, the captain was one of the players, usually one of the more able and experienced members of the club. The custom of the captain being an active player remained common practice, with professional teams commonly having player-managers in the latter part of the nineteenth century and well into the twentieth. The rules published in the December 6, 1856, issue of Porter's *Spirit of the Times* specify that "the captains shall have absolute direction of the games, and shall designate the position each player shall occupy in the field" (p. 229).

On some vintage base ball teams, one player serves as team captain on a permanent basis; on others, the captain's role is rotated. The arrangement of having one permanent captain works well in many cases, especially with newer teams composed of inexperienced players. In such circumstances, one player who is a good organizer, is knowledgeable about the vintage game, and has the respect of his team can be very valuable (even indispensable) in a leadership role in the club's first few years.

The programs that choose to rotate the captaincy among players on a game-by-game basis are typically the more established clubs composed of veteran players, many of whom have the necessary experience to guide the

The captain of the Blue Ashlars Base Ball Club (Worthington, Ohio), Chad Simpson (right), and Michael Braatz make out the lineup and turn it in to the scorer's table well in advance of the start of the game.

club. This approach has the advantage of providing many different players with the experience of directing the team for a day and making all the pre-game and post-game ceremonial announcements. This gives everyone a greater appreciation for the captain's administrative responsibilities of making sure the field is laid out properly and all equipment is at hand, making out the lineup so that players share equally in the playing time, making any strategic decisions, offering encouragement or reminders, and representing the club in any conferences with the umpire and the other captain, such as establishing the ground rules for the day or deciding whether to call the game or continue playing in case of rain.

Once a player has served as captain for a game or two, he better understands the responsibilities and challenges of running the club. As on any base ball team in any era, players occasionally may want more playing time or a chance to play certain positions. Serving as the captain for a day will help teach the lesson that it is difficult to please everyone and accommodate everyone's preferences. Consequently, allowing various players to be captain for a day can improve team morale and spirit and eliminate any petty grievances from building up over time. Sharing the leadership responsibilities by giving several players the opportunity to be captain can enhance their loyalty to the program. It also ensures a smooth succession when a veteran captain leaves the program.

If the rotating system is used for designating the captain, it is helpful for the captain to know in advance that he will be performing these responsibilities on a given day. This will enable him to give some thought to how he will construct the lineup and what he will say when called upon to address the spectators. The captain needs to be prepared and organized in order to get the game started on time and keep it moving along briskly, thus holding the interest of the spectators. A knowledgeable, well-prepared captain (whether he serves on a permanent or rotating basis) contributes significantly to the smooth operation of a vintage game.

Before the game begins, the captain should make out the batting order and assign the defensive positions before he arrives at the field. In regard to making out the lineup, Section 27 of the rules of 1860 required that "no substitution or change shall be made after the game has been commenced, unless for reason of illness or injury." This means the same nine players would play the entire game for each club and that these nine would play the same positions throughout the game. A base ball team was commonly referred to as a "nine" because it was composed of nine players who were expected to play the entire match.

While vintage clubs place a high value on historical authenticity, the prohibition on substitutions in Section 27 is difficult and impractical to follow. If exactly nine players are present, they can each be assigned by the captain to play a position for the entire game and the historical rules and customs can be maintained. However, as is more often the case, if the vintage club has ten or twelve (or more) players present, dressed in their uniforms, and eager to play, it would be unrealistic and unwise to use just nine players for the entire game and leave several extra players sitting on the bench.

Accordingly, instead of adhering to the letter of the law and playing only nine in the game, it is customary among vintage clubs to get all available players involved by including all players in the striking order and arranging for everyone to play about the same number of innings in the field. Unlike the mid-nineteenth-century rules and customs, most players will also shift positions several times to accommodate everyone.

The practice of free substitutions on defense and batting more than nine players in the striking order is one of those areas where some practical accommodation needs to be made between the original rules and the realities of creating a viable vintage team. In the interest of retaining players and maintaining team morale, everyone needs to have an opportunity to play approximately the same amount of time. Extra players not in the starting lineup would quickly lose their enthusiasm for being part of a vintage team if they had no opportunity to play.

Arranging the Defensive Alignment

Getting all the players into the game means that defensive substitution practices in vintage base ball resemble those used in modern recreational softball leagues. The lineup often consists of more than nine players, and the players change positions and move in and out of the defensive alignment. The integrity of the striking order should be maintained, with no player batting out of turn. On the defensive side, it is common practice to allow players to sit out an inning and then re-enter the game, either at the same position or a different one.

The nineteenth-century captain did not have to think much about the lineup because, especially on the club's first nine, the same players consistently played the same position. Conversely, one of the vintage captain's toughest challenges is to skillfully construct a lineup that provides nearly equal playing time for everyone when there are more than nine players on hand. One approach is to multiply the number of innings scheduled to be played (usually nine, but perhaps fewer in a tournament situation) by the number of positions (nine) to get the number of available innings (usually 81), then dividing by the number of players who are on hand for the game. For example, with twelve players available, the equation would be $9 \times 9 = 81$, divided by 12, or an average of 6.75 innings for each player. In this situation, each player should expect to play six or seven innings in the field. While the captain obviously can only have nine players on the field for the first inning, a good rule of thumb is to start making the defensive changes as soon as possible in order to get everyone in the game on defense by the second inning.

It is helpful for the flow of the game and for team morale if the captain makes out an inning-by-inning grid showing each player's defensive assignment for each inning. Such a grid makes it clear to all that playing time is equitable and enables everyone to take his defensive position immediately at the start of an inning. Where fractions of an inning are involved, a player recovering from an injury or an older player (especially on a hot, humid day) might not mind sitting out and resting an extra inning or two. A new player just learning the game or a player who arrives late might be one of the players with fewer innings. If a good throng of spectators is on hand, a player who is an effective interpreter might volunteer to "work the crowd" for a couple of innings. Also, players who get to handle the ball a lot, such as pitchers and catchers, might be assigned fewer innings. Another effective lineup strategy, especially with 10 players, is to assign two players to the pitcher's spot, allowing them to work alternate innings. This provides both with plenty of action while reducing the need to switch the other players in and out of their positions in the defensive lineup.

Minor injuries can also change the defensive playing assignments as the game goes on. Someone who sustains a sprained ankle or is shaken up diving for a ball may want to take an inning or two off to recover before going back in the game.

Skill level can also play a part in constructing the lineup. A captain may want to play his more capable and experienced players an extra inning here and there at key defensive positions, such as shortstop and left field, and may want to allocate the playing time so as to have a strong defensive nine on the field for the ninth inning in case the game is close. However, for purposes of club morale and the long-term health of the program, the captain's goal should be to assign every available able-bodied player about the same amount of playing time. It is important that all players who come to the match prepared to play feel their contributions are valued. They may have family and friends in the audience that have come to see them play. Therefore, everyone should receive approximately the same amount of playing time, barring such circumstances as an injury or arriving after the lineup has been made out.

It often happens that a club will have an ample number of players for the games in May and June and then experience a drop-off at mid-season when players may be unavailable for July and August matches due to vacations, minor injuries, employment conflicts, or family commitments. A club would be unwise, in the interests of historical authenticity, to limit the lineup to nine players (unless only nine are available on a given day) early in the season. A literal interpretation of Section 27 would undoubtedly cause any "extra" players who are not used in a game to drift away from the team, leaving the club shorthanded later in the season.

If a "carriage" breakdown or other emergency causes a player to arrive after the lineup has been turned in, the usual custom is to work him into the game. The scorer's table should be notified of his arrival and his name should be placed last in the striking order. He may then bat in that spot the next time it comes up. The captain can try to work him into the defensive alignment as best he can for an inning here or there, but the player who arrives late (for whatever reason) should understand that he may not get to play as many innings as if he had arrived before the lineup was made out.

Arranging the Striking Order

There is little historical information on constructing the striking order. In intra-club matches, evidence from the old box scores shows that the two sides would sometimes bat in order according to their positions in the field (pitcher, catcher, first base, second base,

At Spiegel Grove in Fremont, Ohio, home of President Rutherford B. Hayes, the historic grounds serve as the home field of the Spiegel Grove Squires BBC. The Squires line up for the opening ceremonies of a match with the Columbus (Ohio) Capitals.

etc.). In games with other clubs, the striking order is decided by the captain, and he tries to construct a striking order he thinks will produce the most runs. Most vintage teams seem to follow the modern approach of beginning with a couple of hitters at the top of the order who get on base frequently and run well. The third, fourth, and fifth batters tend to be the hitters who best combine consistent hitting with the ability to get extra-base hits that will score the runners who are on base ahead of them. The terms "lead-off" hitter for the first striker in the order and "clean-up" hitter for the fourth striker were not in use yet and, therefore, should be avoided by vintage players.

Players should not attach too much importance to the alleged "prestige" of batting in a certain spot in the order. Since vintage games are usually fairly high-scoring affairs, everyone receives numerous chances to begin a rally by getting on base or to keep one going by driving runners home. Therefore, no player should feel slighted if asked to bat near the end of the order.

The striking order should be submitted to the scorer's table well in advance of the start of the match so that the scorer has time to enter the names on the score sheets before the game begins. Players should be encouraged to arrive early (at least 30 minutes before game time) in order to allow time to warm up properly and to make it easier for the captain to construct the lineup. The captain is understandably reluctant to turn in his lineup to the scorer's table without actually seeing that everyone in the lineup is on hand and ready to play.

The captain has a taxing job in trying to make out the striking order and the defensive alignment. For that reason, no player should make his task more difficult by arriving late, showing up unexpectedly, or making any negative comments about his spot in the striking order or his position on defense. Most vintage players understand these matters, and are glad to bat anywhere in the order and play anywhere in the field.

When submitting the lineup to the scorer's table, the captain should, in the manner of the era being re-created, use the last names of the players, not their first names or nicknames. A striking order should not read: Andy, John, Bob, Dale, Mike, etc. While vintage players often refer to each other informally by nicknames, the official lineup submitted to the scorer's table should not read: Freight Train, Scrap Iron, Doc, Dew Drop, Choo-Choo, etc. Using the players' last names is historically authentic. It also builds a better team archive of participants so that it is possible to look at the club's scorebook a year or two after the game and know who played in the match.

Announcements and Introductions

Bringing a picturesque, historic scene to life does not happen automatically. Careful planning, knowledge of nineteenth-century base ball, and organizational skills are essential. Our understanding of how clubs opened their nineteenth-century matches is incomplete. While research continues into the details of actual contests in the 1860s, vintage programs have tried to come up with informative and entertaining combinations of procedures for beginning the game. These "opening ceremonies" are based on what we know about the 1860 rules and practices; what seems likely, logical, and reasonable given the customs of the period; and what needs to occur in order for the spectators at a vintage match to understand what is about to take place.

Opening Remarks

Constructing a model for the opening of the game calls for program planners to draw upon nineteenth-century manners, formal introductions, and oratory. Clubs should try to capture the culture of the nineteenth century, a time when oratory played an important part in public life and good manners were expected of gentlemanly players. The courteous nature of the times, along with an appreciation for the rigors of travel experienced by the visiting club (when a trip of even five or ten miles would have been a major undertaking), suggests that some type of pre-game welcoming ceremony is likely to have been held.

In vintage base ball, a brief presentation at the start of the game creates an opportunity for the umpire and the captains to announce to the crowd what is happening so that they can follow the action and learn something about the earlier days of base ball. The introductory part of the match is of critical importance in that it establishes the tone of the day's activities and helps the spectators, especially those who have not witnessed a vintage game, take that giant step back in time and imagine that it really is a different era. Procedures vary somewhat geographically, but most vintage clubs observe a fairly similar series of steps to begin a match.

To illustrate the manner in which a vintage game can be presented, let us look at the example of a typical match. The Arcadia Club and the Franklin Club, two fictional teams representative of the many veteran clubs who share a commitment to an educational and enjoyable presentation of vintage base ball, have traveled to one of the birthplaces of vintage base ball, Ohio Village at the Ohio Historical Center, to play in the Ohio Cup Vintage Base Ball Festival hosted by the Ohio Village Muffins. While many variations are seen at other venues — sometimes with a colorful local flair — the following case study will provide an example of how a game can be effectively staged and presented.

At precisely the time that the game has been announced to start (care should be taken not to keep the spectators waiting), the well-dressed umpire welcomes spectators and motions

Nick Herold, a first-person interpreter in period dress, uses period language to welcome the audience to Ohio Village.

for the players to step onto the playing field along the baselines. In making the opening remarks, the umpire captures the style of speaking that was common in the days when rhetorical skill was highly prized, sentences were long and full of flourishes, and speeches were expected at any public event. Formal posture, a loud and distinct voice, and period phrasing add to the presentation.

If he has not already been introduced by a museum professional or someone playing the role of the town mayor or president of the base ball club, the umpire begins the proceedings by introducing himself. Without an introduction, the spectators may not comprehend that the gentleman before them in a frock coat and top hat is the umpire.

The opening remarks include welcoming the spectators, identifying the participants, establishing the time period, telling spectators something about the match, and setting the tone for the vintage game. The umpire assumes the first-person role of an actual nineteenth-century official when addressing the spectators. A sample announcement to the crowd might be as follows:

> Ladies and gentlemen, it is my great pleasure to welcome you to the playing field here at the Ohio Historical Society's Ohio Village. [always use the name of playing field or museum hosting the event]. We are gathered here today to enjoy a game of base ball as played by the rules of 1860. I am James Kimnach [give name, whether real or the name of the character the person is portraying] and, as a member of the Ohio Village Muffins, I have the honor to have been chosen to serve as the impartial umpire for today's base ball match between the Arcadia Club of Clintonville, Ohio, and the Franklin Club of Port Dominion, Ohio.
>
> Thank you for attending today's festivities on this glorious and sunny day, a perfect day for healthy outdoor exercise played in the fresh Ohio air. Recently, various groups of gentlemen — in our fair city and beyond — have organized themselves into clubs for the purpose of playing this noble game, the manly sport of base ball that is fast emerging as our national pastime.

It is with great pleasure that we welcome the two fine clubs you see before you, the Arcadia Base Ball Club, a local organization, resplendent in their white uniforms with maroon and gold trim, and the Franklin Base Ball Club in their handsome dark blue and cream uniforms, who have traveled the great distance of over one hundred miles, all the way from northern Ohio, to be with us today. These two distinguished clubs will endeavor to provide us with a magnificent exhibition of this wonderful American game. I encourage you to acknowledge good play by both clubs. I am confident that you will witness a match today conducted according to the highest standards of base ball playing skill and good sportsmanship. Both of these clubs are composed of fine gentlemen who enjoy playing our great national game the way it was meant to be played.

The first paragraph of the opening remarks gets everyone's attention and gives them a general idea of what is about to happen. While some spectators have come for the purpose of seeing an 1860s base ball game, others may have just wandered by the ball diamond with no idea of what is about to take place. Also, by providing his name, the umpire has helped the audience establish a personal connection with him so that they will know how to address him should they have questions during the match (as it is hoped they will as the game progresses).

The second paragraph provides some historical information regarding base ball's rapid growth in this period and its emerging status as a national institution. In addition to being quaint, the word "manly" is historically accurate. It appears often in the writing of the period to indicate that members of base ball clubs were participating in a recreational endeavor suitable for adults rather than engaging in a childish activity. Also, the term "manly" hints that some degree of athletic ability and courage is needed to play this game. Repeating the year 1860 reinforces the message of what era is being portrayed.

The third paragraph identifies the clubs (their uniform colors should be mentioned to distinguish one from the other) and tells where they are from. Any reference to one club being the home team, however, should be done carefully so as not to cast the visiting team in the role of an enemy. The adversarial nature of the contest should be downplayed. The visiting team should be introduced as honored and welcome guests to be treated with respect and courtesy, thus establishing the friendly, sportsmanlike nature of the upcoming contest. Even before the game starts, it is important to establish an atmosphere that will encourage the audience to cheer for good plays by both sides. There was no booing or jeering at the amateur club matches being re-created. There should be nothing in the tone or language of the introductions that would make it sound like the spectators should treat the visiting club as a reviled opponent.

Introducing the Scorers

The umpire next introduces his colleagues, the scorers for the match. This calls the attention of the crowd to the scorer's table and clears up any confusion about the purpose of the table and chairs located near the diamond and the person or persons seated there. In making his introductions of the scorers, the umpire might indicate something about each scorer's club membership, standing in the community, and role at the match. This is necessary because in modern baseball, the official scorer is out of sight and out of mind while in the press box. Spectators are not accustomed to seeing the scorer down on the field and will not grasp who he or she is unless they are informed. It is in keeping with the good manners associated with the time to make a formal introduction of anyone serving as an official for the match. The scorers, like the umpire, are in period dress. The umpire could introduce those who have taken their place at the scorer's table as follows:

> The scorers for today's match will be Mr. Large for the Arcadia Club and Mr. Lehr for the Franklin Club. Both of these individuals are upstanding citizens of their communities who are well known for their integrity, honesty, and knowledge of the game.

As their names are called, the scorers should stand and tip their hats to the crowd, gestures that will elicit polite applause from both the players and the spectators in recognition of their valuable service.

Research has revealed that for several years in the 1850s the scorers were referred to as the "umpires" and the official stationed near home plate was known as the "referee." If portraying a pre–1860 era, clubs may want to use these older terms to refer to the game officials, but this may prove confusing for the spectators. "Umpire" and "scorer" are the terms most frequently used in vintage base ball.

Introducing the Clubs

Having introduced the scorers, the umpire proceeds with the introduction of the ball clubs. When the umpire first steps to the home plate area, the club members take their places on the field for the introductions. The two clubs usually line up on the third- and first-base lines to be presented to the crowd. If, due to the configuration of the field the spectator area is primarily on one side, both teams should line up on the same baseline to face the majority of the crowd. The objective is to enable everyone to see their uniforms and to hear the pre-game proceedings. The two captains are on either side of the umpire, who is usually stationed near home plate in front of the crowd.

Having welcomed the spectators, the umpire calls on the captains to introduce their clubs:

"And now, may I present the captain of Arcadia Club, Mr. Andersen."

The captain takes a step or two toward the crowd, removes his cap as a sign of respect, and says:

> Ladies and gentlemen, we thank you for coming out to witness the match today, as we present an exhibition of the great game of base ball. As captain, it is my honor to extend a word of welcome to the distinguished members of the Franklin Base Ball Club, and we thank this fine group of gentlemen for making the long journey all the way from their home grounds far to the north for today's contest. It is also my honor to present, from nearby Clintonville, the gentlemen of the Arcadia Base Ball Club.

Having been introduced, the Arcadia Club members tip their hats to the crowd. The Franklin Club members lead the applause. As the Arcadia captain remains standing next to the umpire, the umpire then calls upon the Franklin Club's captain. The umpire states, "We will now hear from the captain of the Franklin Club, Mr. Moore."

The captain of the Franklin Club takes a step or two toward the crowd, joining the umpire and the other captain. He acknowledges the spectators with a tip of the cap, and addresses them:

> Ladies and Gentlemen, it is with great anticipation and pleasure that the members of our club have been looking forward to this opportunity to travel from our home on the shores of beautiful Lake Erie for today's match. We are pleased to be with you this afternoon to take part in this splendid event. We thank our hosts, the Ohio Village Muffins, for the invitation to play today

In 1858, the Knickerbockers and Excelsiors lined up for a photograph that is often published in books on baseball history. In 2004, the Champion City Reapers (Springfield, Ohio) and Ohio Village Muffins re-created the scene with each player assuming the pose of his counterpart in the famous photo. The 1858 photograph provides evidence that early clubs lined up together before the game, as is the custom in vintage base ball.

in the Ohio Cup Festival upon their well-kept grounds, and we look forward to the prospect of a spirited and sportsmanlike game of base ball with of the fine gentlemen of the Arcadia Club. I present to you, the Franklin Base Ball Club of Port Dominion, Ohio.

The Arcadia Club leads the spectators in applause as the Franklin Club players tip their hats to the crowd in acknowledgement. Some clubs introduce the individual members of the team. Either the captain announces each name or each player steps forward, tips his cap, and says his full name. It should be kept in mind that the crowd may be unable to hear the individual names if the players are some distance from the seating area, there is a large noisy crowd on hand, or if the wind is blowing in the wrong direction. If the players' voices can be heard, it can add to the overall presentation to have their names spoken, especially if it is a community team playing at a special event. This practice also shows respect for each player and delights his family and friends in the audience. Most clubs prefer to introduce the club (with an oratorical flourish or two, of course) as a group since this speeds up the process of getting the game under way. Either way, the spectators are drawn into the festivities.

In performing the duties of the captain, a club member should speak in the more formal manner of the nineteenth century, which takes a little preparation and practice. Some are self-conscious at first in attempting to make a presentation of this type. However, using the language of the 1860s adds considerably to the occasion, alerting the spectators to the fact that they have come upon a match that promises to be far different than just another baseball or softball game. The period dress of the participants and the period language employed by the umpire and captains helps them understand that they are in for a unique base ball experience, even before the first pitch is tossed and the game commences. If the captain wishes, he may write out his remarks in advance.

To add to the entertainment and educational value of this opening ceremony, the umpire might compliment a visiting club for traveling a long distance "by carriage" to take part in the contest. Depending on where the visiting club is from, the umpire might indicate that the visiting team has arrived by railroad, canal boat, or omnibus, a reference to the method of travel that a team from that area would have used in the nineteenth century. This reminds spectators that the visiting team would have had to make quite an effort in 1860 to travel to play a game at another club's grounds. The umpire or opposing club's captain can emphasize this point by saying a visiting club has come "all the way" from whatever town they are from, even if it is a short distance away. A relatively short trip of only 10 or 20 miles, easily made in a few minutes in a car today, sounds like the significant journey of several hours that it would have been in 1860.

Even with automobiles and the interstate highway system, traveling to an away game takes energy, time, and expense, and everyone truly appreciates the visiting club members making the trip. Acknowledging their effort with period language and oratorical flair is historically accurate and represents the true feelings of gratitude on the part of the museum or historical society hosting the game.

The umpire can use this occasion to make any other specific announcements associated with the game or other events going on that day at the historical site. Distinguished guests, from "Abraham Lincoln" to a local congressman, may be acknowledged along with any sponsors or benefactors. Doing so in period language adds to the enjoyment for all. The conclusion of these opening comments provides a segue to the actual opening of the game.

The Coin Toss

After both clubs have been introduced, the umpire conducts a coin toss at home plate to decide which club will bat first and which will take the field. In the 1860 time period, even in cases in which one club visited another at the latter's home grounds, the visiting team did not automatically bat first and the home team last, as is the practice today. Instead, the teams tossed a coin for the choice of batting first or taking the field.

Through the years, several different systems have been used for determining which team would bat first. David Nemec, noted authority on nineteenth-century base ball, explains these various arrangements in *The Official Rules of Baseball: An Anecdotal Look at the Rules of Baseball and How They Came to Be*. Describing the proper method for beginning a modern game, Nemec presents the text of the current Rule 4.02: "The players of the home team shall take their defensive positions, the first batter of the visiting team shall take his position in the batter's box, the umpire shall call 'Play,' and the game shall start." While this process sounds automatic and unremarkable to the modern observer, Nemec offers the following informed commentary on how this practice evolved, which may be of interest to clubs portraying various eras:

> Rule 4.02 says in effect that the home team must bat last, but such has not always been the case. In fact, the opposite was true in 1877, when a new rule required the home club to take the bat first. The following season the National League reverted to the pre–1877 custom, which called for the two captains to determine which club first took the bat. The usual method was to flip a coin, with the visitors accorded the honor of making the call and the winner of the flip then given the option of batting first or last.

In 1885 the American Association [a major league from 1882 to 1891] allowed the home captain to choose which club batted first, and the National League adopted the same policy in 1887, when the two circuits agreed to be governed by one rulebook. It remained more of an ingrained tradition than a rule that the home team would bat last until 1950, when Rule 4.02 was added to the manual [pp. 62–63].

Nemec states that it was not until the early part of the twentieth century that "having your last at bats was viewed as an advantage." In the nineteenth century, "teams had often preferred to bat first, largely because it gave them first crack at the game ball, which was likely to be the only new ball put in play that day" (p. 63). With that historical background in mind, the umpire and the captains determine which club will bat first in an 1860-era game by a coin toss. It adds a touch of authenticity to have an old coin on hand for this purpose if possible, but this is not a necessity since most spectators are not close enough to notice.

To inform the crowd of what is happening, the umpire announces the coin toss procedure. Despite a natural tendency to turn his back to the crowd and speak to the captains standing on either side of him, it is important for the umpire to face the crowd and look directly at them while conducting the coin toss so that they can see and hear what is going on. As he pulls a coin from his vest pocket, the umpire motions for the two captains to join him at home plate where they cordially shake hands.

Umpire (addressing the audience): "In order to determine which club will bat first and which shall take the field, we will now toss a coin. Captain Moore, since your club has traveled the farthest for today's match, will you please call 'heads' or 'tails' while this gold piece is in the air?"

Captain Moore: "Thank you. I shall call 'heads.'"

The coin is flipped and the outcome is determined. The umpire announces the result to the spectators and the teams.

Umpire: "Captain Moore, you have called 'heads' and, indeed, 'heads' it is. Since you have won the toss, you may select to strike first or take the field."

Captain Moore: "The Franklin Club will take the field and offer the first strike to the Arcadia nine."

After the captain makes his choice, the umpire announces the result to the crowd.

Umpire: "Ladies and gentlemen, the Franklin Club has won the toss and has elected to take the field; the Arcadia Club will strike first."

When he announces the outcome of the toss, it is important that the umpire does not say "The Franklin Club has won the toss and elected to be the home team." As Nemec explains, being the home team and batting in the bottom half of the first inning were not synonymous terms in the 1860s as they are today.

Just after the coin toss, a statement by the umpire to the players and the audience regarding good sportsmanship is beneficial in setting the tone for the contest. The vintage program at the Genesee Country Village and Museum in Mumford, New York, has used the following quote from Henry Chadwick at the beginning of the championship match of the Silver Ball Tournament as a reminder to all about the nature of the game. These eloquent words seemed perfect for that occasion.

Umpire: "Gentlemen of both clubs, as you take the field for the match today please be reminded of the noble words of that renowned writer and esteemed expert on the national game, Henry Chadwick:

Lest you come to see only the blinding sight of winning, keep in mind that whether you leave this field with victory as your companion or defeat by your side, you must always leave this ground with both your reputation and your integrity firmly in your grasp.

At this point the captains shake hands with the umpire and with each other and wish each other well. The clubs take their positions to start the match, the Arcadia players on the bench and the Franklin players in the field.

The Franklins should already know their defensive positions and the Arcadias their striking order before the introductions and coin toss. With the spectators looking on in anticipation of the game beginning, this is no time for the players to be milling around trying to decide who will play where. The Franklins hustle to their positions in the field, demonstrating their enthusiasm for the game. As the first Arcadia batter gets his bat and approaches the plate, the game is now set to begin.

21

Game Day: Playing the Match

Taking the Field

With the two nines taking their appropriate places following the coin toss, the pitcher for the Franklin Club promptly goes to the pitcher's point. Arriving at the round iron disk 45 feet from home plate and standing behind the 12-foot-long white line drawn through the pitcher's point, the pitcher receives the game ball from the umpire and takes a few warm-up pitches to gauge the distance to home plate. The pitcher keeps his warm-up tosses over the plate, where they can be hit, rather than thinking about ways to make his pitches difficult to hit as a modern pitcher would. Knowing that the crowd will quickly become frustrated and impatient if the pitcher does not put the ball over the plate, he delivers the ball with an easy, continuous, underhand motion.

The catcher, while receiving the warm-up pitches, notes how high the ball is bouncing in order to judge how far he should stand behind the plate to catch pitches comfortably on the first bound. This distance varies from day to day and field to field, depending on the resilience of the ball being used and the firmness of the ground around home plate. A few warm-up pitches enable the catcher to determine where he should position himself in order to catch any foul tips that occur during the game.

As the pitcher and catcher for the Franklins get ready, Captain Andersen of the Arcadias calls out the names of the first three batters and makes sure everyone is aware of the striking order. A copy of the lineup showing the striking order and the defensive alignment is on the bench. Since any materials on the bench often can be seen by the spectators, the captain has the names listed on a single sheet of paper, anchored by a stone (since no brightly colored spiral notebook or a plastic ballpoint pen should be brought to the bench).

The rules do not specify exactly what phrase (if any) the umpire used as the equivalent of the modern "Play ball!" to begin play at the start of a game or the start of an inning. According to the *New Dickson Baseball Dictionary*, the first use of "Play ball!" (sometimes shortened to "Play!") as "the command issued by the plate umpire to start a game or resume action" dates to 1901. However, the fact that the 1901 citation refers to a work of popular fiction, one of Burt Standish's Frank Merriwell novels, indicates the phrase was likely in common use before that year. Some appropriate phrase is needed to alert players and spectators that action is about to commence. The phrase "Striker to the line" has become common in vintage base ball. It calls attention to the period term "striker" for the batter and to the existence of a single white line (rather than a box) as the designated place for the hitter to stand. If program leaders prefer, the umpire can use "play" or any other similar phrase to indicate everyone is in place and ready for the first pitch. After asking the Franklins' pitcher and catcher if they have had a sufficient number of warm-up pitches, the umpire gestures

Before they take the field, the captain again reviews the striking order and defensive assignments so that everyone can take their positions quickly when the game begins.

for the first Arcadia batter to approach the plate and calls, "Striker to the line!" Since the first batter is right-handed, the umpire places himself approximately 15 feet up the first-base line and several steps in foul territory, where he has a good view of the batter and can also see directly down the third-base line.

A Sample Game

Now that the opening ceremonies have been concluded and the first batter has stepped to the line, it might be helpful to "play" a few innings to get the feel and flavor of a vintage game and to try out some of the rules and practices based on the information in the 1860 edition of *Beadle's Dime Base-Ball Player*. With Mr. Andersen of the Arcadia Club and Mr. Moore of the Franklin Club serving as the captains, the following lineups will be used with hypothetical players arranged in alphabetical order (A-I for the Arcadias and J-R for the Franklins) so that the progress of the game and the application of the rules will be easier to follow. The lineups are as follows:

Arcadia Club	*Franklin Club*
Andersen 1B	Johnson CF
Brandon P	Koons RF
Craig SS	Lawrence 1B
Douglas LF	Moore SS
Elliot CF	Newman 3B
Friedman 2B	Oliver C
Green 3B	Peters LF
Hartmann C	Quinn 2B
Irving RF	Rogers P

The Arcadia Club's First Inning

As the first striker steps to the plate, the catcher and striker pause to shake hands. Andersen extends his hand to the catcher and loud enough for nearby spectators to hear says, "Mr. Oliver, good to see you and the Franklins again. What a fine day for the match." The catcher replies, "Thank you. We have been looking forward to the festival and this match with the Arcadia Club." As the spectators note this gentlemanly exchange, the striker focuses on the pitcher.

The pitch is delivered over the plate and Andersen hits a line drive to left field that the outfielder catches on the second bound. Andersen runs to first and makes a turn toward second. When he sees the left fielder has come up with the ball and is throwing it to the second baseman, Andersen returns to first and holds there, having made his first base.

Brandon is up with no outs and Andersen on first. Brandon hits a sharp line drive that the shortstop fields on the first bound. Andersen takes a few steps toward second but sees the shortstop catch the ball on the first bound. Since Brandon is out the moment the shortstop catches the ball, Andersen knows he is not forced to run and, if he tried, the shortstop would toss the ball to the second baseman and he would be tagged out. Andersen returns to first and holds there.

With one out and Andersen on first, Craig is up. As he takes his short lead, Andersen exchanges a few pleasantries with the Franklin first baseman with whom he is acquainted with from previous games. Although cordial toward the members of the opposing team, Andersen is watching the pitcher closely and is prepared to advance if he gets the opportunity. The first pitch comes in too low to hit, strikes a bump in the uneven ground around home plate, takes an erratic bounce away from the catcher, and rolls to the right of the plate near the umpire. Andersen breaks for second on the passed ball. The catcher retrieves the ball and makes a throw to second, but the throw arrives too late. By alert base running, Andersen is now on second base with one out.

Craig hits a pop-up that come down in foul territory, just outside the third-base line. The umpire shouts "foul" when the ball hits the ground as the third baseman charges toward home plate, trying to catch the ball for an out before it hits the ground for a second time. He dives, but as he reaches for it, his momentum causes him to roll over on top of the ball, making it difficult for the umpire to tell whether or not he made the catch on the bound before it hit the ground for the second time. The third baseman rolls over with the ball in his hands. Sensing the umpire did not have a clear view, he shakes his head and tells the umpire, "No, I did not catch it until the second bound." Seeing the runner did not start to run for third and is still at second base, the third baseman flips the ball to the pitcher, returns to his position, and Craig's turn at bat continues. Andersen knows he needed to hold at second when the umpire shouted "foul" since Section 16 specifies that "no ace nor base can be made upon a foul ball." Even if the third baseman had caught the ball on the fly or first bounce or if the foul ball had rolled away some distance from the fielder, the runner can not advance on a foul ball.

Craig hits a long fly ball into the gap in left-center field. Andersen, on second base, sees both outfielders pursuing the fly ball and judges that while one or the other might catch it on the bound, neither will be able to get to it on the fly. Andersen starts running as fast as he can, knowing that on a bound catch (unlike a fly catch) he does not have to wait until the ball is caught to tag up and begin running. Andersen hopes that it may fall in for a safe hit good for two or three bases, but knows that even if the ball is caught on the bound for an out, he is free to advance as far as he can while the outfielders are playing the ball and getting it back to the infield. Andersen, running hard, nears third just as the ball is coming down and is caught on the first bound on a spectacular running catch by the left fielder to retire Craig. Andersen continues around third and on to home before the left fielder, whose momentum was carrying him away from the plate when he caught the ball, can stop and throw the ball all the way back to the infield. Because Andersen alertly started running the second he saw that the ball Craig hit would not be caught on the fly, he was able to advance two bases and score a run on the long bound-out to the outfield.

It is the custom of many vintage clubs to have the runner, immediately after crossing home plate, visit the scorer's table to confirm that his run has been duly recorded. If the program follows the custom of having a tally bell at the scorer's table, the runner rings the bell at this time. After visiting the scorer's table, Andersen returns to the bench. The Arcadia players rise and (with conventional handshakes) congratulate Andersen for scoring and Craig for his long drive to the outfield that brought Andersen around to score a run. They quickly resume their seats on the bench so as not to block the view of the spectators. They do not engage in any excessive celebratory demonstrations that could be construed as "showing up" the other team.

Now there are two outs with nobody on. The Arcadias lead, 1–0, with Douglas coming up. Douglas hits a hard grounder up the middle. The pitcher reacts quickly, fields the ball, and throws to the first baseman for the third out.

At the scorer's table, the notation is made that since Douglas made the last out on the good fielding play by the pitcher, Elliot will lead off the next inning. The two nines change sides. The umpire reinforces the identity of the teams by using their full names as he announces the score to the crowd: "The Arcadia Club has scored one ace after striking in the first inning. The score is one to aught in the Arcadia Club's favor with the Franklin Club coming to bat."

The Franklin Club's First Inning

Johnson comes to bat for the Franklins and hits the ball solidly to center field, where the outfielder makes a nice running catch on the fly. Johnson is aware he hit the ball well and is disappointed to see it caught, but knowing the center fielder has made a fine barehanded catch on a well-struck ball, he tips his hat to the center fielder as he jogs back to the bench. The gentlemanly Franklins applaud both their teammate's good hit and the Arcadia center fielder's fine catch, even though their player was put out.

With one out and nobody on, Koons swings at the first pitch and hits a ground ball down the third-base line. He starts for first base. From his spot in foul ground on the right side of the plate, the umpire is looking directly down the line and sees that the ball first hit the ground a few inches in foul territory. Immediately and unasked, the umpire loudly shouts, "Foul." The third baseman retrieves the ball and tosses it to the pitcher. Had it hit just inside the line, it would have been a fair ball (even if it quickly went foul before passing third base) and the umpire would have made no call. Koons would have sprinted for first base. Since it is a foul ball, Koons returns to the plate.

The next pitch is right over the middle of the plate, but Koons takes his eye off the ball when he swings and misses it completely. "Strike one," the umpire reminds the striker and the catcher (since the foul ball did not count as a strike). Koons then hits a pop-up to the vicinity of the shortstop, who gets set to make the catch. Koons is disappointed at hitting a pop-up but wisely drops his bat and hustles to first base in the event the ball might fall in safely. As is the case with many pop-ups, the ball has a lot of backspin on it, making it difficult to catch barehanded. The shortstop is in good position to make the catch, but when the ball comes down, it pops out of his hands and hits the ground. Fortunately, both the second baseman and third baseman have converged on the spot where the shortstop is waiting for the ball, surrounding the spot. Although both know the shortstop is one of the most reliable fielders on the team, they also realize there are no routine plays in vintage base ball and hustle over to back him up in case of a muff. After hitting the shortstop's hands and then striking the ground, the ball bounces a foot or two. The second baseman dives and catches it with one hand just before it hits the ground for the second time. Koons, nearing first base, sees the play has been made on the bound and returns to the bench.

Lawrence comes up with two out and nobody on base. He is a left-handed striker, so the umpire moves over to the third-base side of home where he can get a good view of balls hit down the first-base line. The shortstop moves from his usual position midway between second and third to the other side of the infield, where he positions himself midway between first and second. The second baseman stays near his bag. Lawrence strikes a hard line drive over first base that quickly gets past the right fielder. The umpire, who is in good position to view the play, sees that it has hit in fair territory, so he makes no call. The well-hit ball rolls into deep right field where it disappears into a patch of shrubbery. The right fielder races after the ball (which is in play), locates it quickly in the foliage, and throws it back to the infield, but Lawrence has made his second base.

The umpire returns to the first-base side of home and the shortstop returns to his position between second and third as Moore, a right-handed batter, steps to the plate with two out and Lawrence on second. Moore hits a ball that looks like it may go over the center fielder's head. With two outs, Lawrence does not wait to see if the ball will be caught and starts running for third as Moore runs for first. The ball does go over the center fielder's head, and by the time he reaches it and throws it back to the infield, Lawrence has scored and Moore has gained his second base.

With two outs, Moore at second and one run in, Newman comes to the plate. Newman hits a chopper that strikes the ground in fair territory in front of the plate and then takes several more bounces down the line in foul territory in the general direction of the third baseman. The umpire makes no call since he determines it is a fair ball on the basis of where it struck the ground first. The grounder is headed toward the vicinity of the third-base bag, so Moore holds at second rather than running into a tag at third. Moore is alert, ready to break for third if the third baseman throws the ball all the way across the diamond to first base to try to retire Newman. When the third baseman fields the slowly hit ball, however, he sees that Newman, a fast runner, is already nearing first base. Therefore, the third baseman, instead of making a desperate throw to first that is unlikely to arrive in time to get Newman and will allow Moore to advance to third, wisely decides to hold the ball. This is a good decision because, thinking ahead, he realized it set up a force play at both third and second.

Oliver is up next with runners on first and second and two outs. Oliver hits a hard grounder between short and third that looks like it might go through to left field. However, the shortstop dives to his right and knocks it down. He then recovers the ball and flips it to third base in time for a force out on Moore. Three outs and the Franklins' first inning is over.

At the scorer's table the notation is made that since Moore made the last out when he was forced at third, Newman is the batter who will lead off the next inning for the Franklins. This is in keeping with Section 17 of the 1860 Rules that states, "Players must strike in regular rotation, and, after the first inning is played, the turn commences with the player who stands on the list next to the one who lost the third hand." Moore made the last out (the third hand) and Newman stands next on the list. Peters, who was on deck when Oliver was up, would be the next batter under modern rules. As the Arcadias come to the bench, they all commend the third baseman for his smart play by not making the throw to first, a decision that set up the inning-ending force out at third. The Arcadia Club gave up one run but stayed out of a big inning by not throwing the ball around unnecessarily, an important lesson in the vintage game.

Since there was a lot of action and several base runners during the inning, the umpire verifies the score of the game at the scorer's table and then announces it to the crowd: "After one full inning of play, the score is tied. Arcadia one, Franklin one.

The Arcadia Club's Second Inning

Elliot leads off the second for Arcadia and makes his first base by hitting a line drive to center field that is fielded on the second bound.

Freidman steps to the plate with no outs and Elliot on first. Freidman, a right-handed batter who is a good place hitter, hits a ground ball through the space between first and second into right field. By the time the right fielder retrieves the ball, Friedman has made his first base and Elliot has moved to second.

Green, a lefty, is now at bat. The umpire and shortstop again shift their positions accordingly. With Elliot on second, Friedman on first, and nobody out, Green hits a ground ball toward right field but directly at the shortstop, who is positioned between first and second. The shortstop fields the grounder and throws to the second baseman, who is standing on the base. The second baseman catches the ball to retire Friedman on the force play, then throws quickly to first to try to get a double play. The swift throw is taken barehanded by the first baseman but it is a bit late. The hustling Green, who has stopped directly on the base, is safe at first. Elliot advances to third on the throw.

Hartmann is up with one out. Elliot is on third and Green on first. Hartmann hits a high fly ball that the left fielder prepares to catch on the fly. Elliot tags up, ready to try to score after the catch. Green goes part of the way toward second to see if the catch will be made. If the left fielder drops the ball, he might be forced at second, so he needs to be ready to advance. If the left fielder catches it and throws the ball to home, Green might be able to return to first, tag up, and advance to second. The left fielder is successful in making a barehanded catch, retiring Hartmann. Elliot, having tagged up at third, breaks for home, and Green quickly returns to first and tags up. After catching the ball, the left fielder throws the ball to home. Elliot beats the throw to score a run while Green alertly tags up at first and moves on to second on the throw to the plate.

With two out and Green on second, Irving is up. Irving swings and tops the ball in front of the plate in fair territory. The pitcher breaks toward home and the catcher charges out from behind the plate as the batter takes off for first. The catcher gets to the ball first, picks it up, and throws to first base, just in time to get the batter by a step. Irving is out, making three outs and ending the inning.

Since Irving, the last striker in the order, made the last out, Andersen, first in the Arcadia striking order, will lead off the next inning. Noticing several new spectators have arrived, the umpire re-identifies the participants for the benefit of the latecomers by using the full names of the teams when he announces the score. "In the middle of the second inning, the score is two runs for the Arcadia Club from nearby Clintonville, Ohio, and one run for the gentlemen of the Franklin Club, who have traveled all the way from Port Dominion, Ohio, for today's match."

The Franklin Club's Second Inning

The scorer reminds the captains and the umpire that Newman is the first striker (although he batted in the previous inning and was on first base, running toward second base, when the inning ended with Oliver striking the ball, resulting in Moore being forced at third). Although Peters was on deck, Newman is the striker. Newman hits a ball over second base. The second baseman goes back as the center fielder comes in. The ball falls in safely in short center field, bouncing several times before the center fielder can reach it. Newman has made his first base.

Oliver steps to the line and on the second pitch hits a hard line drive at the third baseman. The third baseman is stationed in his customary spot a step — from third base inside the foul line. He puts his hands up to his chest to catch the ball, but it is too hot to handle. It hits his hands and glances off, hitting the ground in foul territory. The umpire loudly calls, "Foul." The umpire's call is based on the interpretation that although the ball hit a player while he was standing in fair territory, the ball itself first hit the ground in foul territory, making it a foul ball. Newman, thinking at first that the ball has fallen to the ground in fair territory, which would mean he is forced at second, starts to run for second. When he hears the umpire shout foul, he puts on the brakes and hurries back to first, knowing he can be put out if he does not beat the throw to his base. Meanwhile, the third baseman, seeing Newman has begun to run to second, picks up the foul ball and throws it to the pitcher, who pivots and quickly relays it to the first baseman, who is standing on the bag.

Fortunately for Newman, he gets back to first, a step ahead of the throw. Section 16 states that a foul ball is "considered dead, and not in play until it shall first have been settled in the hands of the pitcher; … the players running the bases shall return to them, and may be put out in so returning in the same manner as the striker when running to the first base." Since the foul ball was recovered by the Arcadia third baseman and relayed to the pitcher (where it met the requirement of having "settled in the hands of the pitcher") before being thrown on to first base, Newman would have been out had he not beaten the throw to the base. Newman would not have been out if the third baseman had thrown the ball directly to first (even if had arrived ahead of Newman) since it would not have "settled into the hands of the pitcher" at any time during the play. The umpire and interpreters provide the spectators with an explanation of the previous play as Oliver gets ready for the next pitch.

Oliver hits a liner between short and third into left field and makes his first base with Newman moving up to second. The left fielder comes in quickly to field the ball and throws to third to hold Newman at second.

Peters is now up with no outs and runners on first and second. He hits a drive into left-center field, where the ball bounces several times before the left fielder can get to it. Newman races around third and scores, but Oliver stops at second as the throw comes into the third baseman and Peters holds at first.

Quinn is up with one run in, Oliver on second, and Peters on first with no outs. Quinn hits a ball sharply back to the pitcher on one bound, but the pitcher drops the ball and it hits the ground for the second time. The runners must react quickly on a play of this type. If the pitcher had caught it cleanly, Quinn would have been out immediately and Oliver would hold at second while Peters would hold at first. Since neither runner is forced on a bound out, an attempt to advance would almost certainly result in being put out. However, since the pitcher dropped the ball and it hit the ground for the second time, the situation changes in an instant and the ball is suddenly in play. Both runners are now forced to run to the next base and the striker, Quinn, must try to make his first base.

The pitcher recovers the ball and throws quickly to third to retire the lead runner, Oliver, on the force play. The third baseman throws to second but Peters beats the throw because he diagnosed what had happened and reacted immediately by running to second when he saw the pitcher drop the one-bounder. Had he hesitated, he might have been out and the Arcadia Club would have had a double play. Quinn makes his first base while the throws were being made to third and second.

Rogers is up next with one out. Peters is on second and Quinn on first. Rogers hits a slow ground ball toward first base. The first baseman goes to his right and fields the ball. Because the ball was hit slowly, he sees he has little chance of forcing Quinn out at second. The pitcher has hustled over to cover first and the first baseman tosses the ball to the pitcher, who steps on the first base to retire the striker. Rogers is out at first but his grounder has advanced the runners, with Peters moving to third base and Quinn advancing to second while the play was made at first.

Johnson is up with two outs and runners at second and third. He hits a high pop-up between home and third about 15 feet outside the line in foul territory. As the third baseman, pitcher, and catcher hustle after the ball, it comes down and hits directly on the scorer's table, bounces in the air several feet on a trajectory that takes it toward the infield, then comes down and hits the ground in foul territory. The umpire shouts, "Foul" when it hits the ground (not when it hits the table, since if it had hit the table and bounced back into fair territory without hitting the ground in foul territory it would be a fair ball). At this point the three defensive players converge on the ball and the catcher makes a nice sliding catch near the table just before the ball hits the ground for the second time. The striker is out because the ball has struck the ground only once before being caught.

The ball hitting the table, which is in play, does not count as a bound. According to Henry Chadwick's commentary, "Whenever the ball is caught after rebounding from the side of a building, a fence, or a tree, provided it has touched the ground but once, it should be considered a fair catch, unless a special agreement to the contrary be made previous to the commencement of the match." Section 32 of the 1860 Rules empowers the clubs to agree on any ground rules that could cover a situation like this. "Clubs may adopt such rules respecting balls knocked beyond or outside of bounds of the field, as the circumstances of the ground may demand; and these rules shall govern all matches played upon the ground, provided that they are distinctly made known to every player and umpire, previous to the commencement of the game." Therefore, if the clubs had agreed before the game that a ball striking the scorer's table or any other object, such as a bandstand, barn, "side of a building, a fence, or a tree," is out of play, Johnson would not be out and he would continue his turn at bat. In this case of the ball hitting the scorer's table, however, the ball is in play all the time and, since it was caught on the first bound, Johnson is out. Spectators and players find these occasional oddities result in remarkable and entertaining plays.

The inning is over and the teams change sides. The umpire announces the score: "Two full innings have been concluded and we have a tie score in the match. The Arcadia Club has scored two runs and the Franklin Club has also scored two."

A Review of the Action

These two innings of a sample game included plays that frequently occur in a vintage match. The spectators saw a lot of action, and yet these two innings would probably have taken only about fifteen to twenty minutes to play. A modern professional game usually requires about fifteen to twenty minutes for one inning.

Because the clubs are employing the slower underhand pitching style that many programs believe was the standard practice in the earlier days of the game, this vintage game played by 1860 Rules is moving along quickly. Since the umpire is not calling balls and strikes, there is little to be gained by letting hittable pitches go by. The striker tries to hit the first good pitch that comes over the plate. Similarly, there is no advantage to the pitcher to deliver a ball that is difficult to hit. If the striker perceives the pitch not to his liking, he will simply let it go by and wait for one he likes better. The pitcher's goal is to consistently put the ball over the plate, and the striker's goal is to hit the first good pitch.

A fast-moving game with the pitcher serving as a "feeder" is in keeping with the intent of the early rules of base ball when players gathered for recreation and exercise. The gentlemen of the Knickerbockers and the other early clubs that adopted the Knickerbocker Rules wanted a game that provided a fast-paced afternoon of physical activity. They created a game that would produce a lot of action: hitting, running, and fielding. Rule 6 of the original Knickerbocker Rules of 1845 reads: "The game to consist of twenty-one counts, or aces; but at the conclusion an equal number of hands must be played." Instead of playing nine innings, the first team to score 21 runs was the winner (provided each team batted in an equal number of innings). In crafting this rule that specified 21 runs were needed to win the game, it is clear that the Knickerbockers fully expected that one of the nines would score 21 runs in the relatively short time allotted for the game (probably two hours or less). Expecting a high number of runs to be scored in a timely way suggests the pitching was slow and fairly easy to hit.

Under these rules, virtually every batter would put the ball in play and take off running, which meant defensive players had to react quickly to every ball that was struck, attempting to catch it on the fly or the first bound, or to field a ground ball and throw it to a base ahead of the runner. Historically, the early games were fairly high-scoring affairs. The game began to change around 1860 with faster pitching coming into play with the elite clubs in the East, but the rules continued to encourage pitching the ball with an underhand motion, putting the ball over the plate "for the striker," and keeping the game moving along at a lively pace.

The spectators at the sample game saw the strikers provide some good hitting, including several long hits to the outfield. The defense turned in a number of excellent fielding plays with a few muffs along the way, which are also part of the barehanded game. The base runners played with intelligence as they were called upon to make quick decisions (on their own and without any base coaches). The fielders also displayed quick thinking and good judgment in deciding what plays to make. There were some plays that would be the same as in modern baseball (such as a fine running fly catch by an outfielder on a well-hit ball) but others (such as fair and foul balls being caught on the bound for an out) that are a product of the 1860 Rules. There were several examples of good sportsmanship. In these two innings, every player in the striking order got to bat at least once and every defensive player had the opportunity to handle the ball at least once. The action was continuous and fast-paced, and very representative of an actual vintage game.

The game action demonstrates that both teams have come to play hard and are trying their best to win. Strikers are hitting the ball well and running as fast they can to make as many bases as possible. Defensive players are running just as hard to catch a ball and throw runners out. The ceremonies before the game have established the tone for the day and the spectators are seeing a base ball game not only played by the published rules of 1860, but also by the nineteenth-century code of sportsmanship and fair play.

Encouraging Spectator Involvement

As the game progresses, it is important to ensure that spectators are involved and engaged in the match. Interpreters are distributing informative printed materials and chatting with spectators. Vendors are hawking refreshments. On occasion, musicians may be playing lively period tunes between innings. In addition to these and other enhancements, the players have opportunities (beyond fielding, striking, and running the bases) to interact with the audience.

Each striker, like Ohio Village Muffin Beau Bevens, is intent on hitting the ball and helping his team win. However, vintage players also exhibit good sportsmanship and gentlemanly decorum throughout the match.

As play unfolds, it is a good practice for the players to exchange comments with the umpire, the scorers, the interpreters, and the spectators about what is happening on the field. For example, if a batter hits a ball to the outfield that is caught on the first bounce, it is helpful to remind the crowd that the batter is out. The umpire might simply state, "Ball caught on the first bound; the striker is out. One hand down." Similarly, the catcher, first baseman, third baseman, and any other players who are close to the spectators can make similar statements so that the onlookers begin to learn the rules. The comments of the players can be phrased in terms of compliments to their teammates for making a good play. For example, since the umpire is positioned along the first-base line and can be heard by the spectators in that area, the catcher might take a couple of steps toward the third-base line and shout to the outfielder making the play, "Splendid catch, Mr. Koons! Caught on the bound for an out! Well done!"

Shouting congratulations to a teammate for making a good play is often for the spectators' benefit. The outfielder is likely too far away to hear the catcher's words, but the catcher's remarks help spectators follow the progress of the game, become familiar with the rules, and hear the period language. If the defensive play is a fielding gem, such as a fly ball taken on the run by the outfielder, any player who is close to the spectators might turn to the crowd and ask, "Was that not a fine, manly barehanded catch by Mr. Elliot in center field?" This technique also gets the crowd interested and involved. They start to think about how difficult it is to catch a fly ball without a modern fielder's glove and begin to appreciate what a good play they have witnessed. Also, they begin to learn some of the players' names, and, since a uniformed player has spoken with them, they understand they can ask the players questions.

Period Language and Behavior

Whenever players and other participants converse on the field, they should try to use words and phrases common to the time. An outstanding hit or catch will elicit the hearty cheer of "Huzzah!" A hard-hit ground ball skimming over the grassy infield area is referred to as a "daisy cutter." A runner trying to advance to the next base will be urged by his teammates to "leg it, leg it!" Rather than the word "team," the players on the field should be referred to as the "club" or the "nine." From reading Darryl Brock's *If I Never Get Back*, many in the vintage base ball community have adopted the phrase "Let's show them our ginger!" which can be used by the captain to encourage the players to act in a spirited and enthusiastic manner. The spectators will quickly pick up the nineteenth-century terminology, adding to their enjoyment of the game and readily joining the cheering by shouting "Huzzah" after an outstanding play.

Using the term "Mister" when addressing any participant, especially the umpire, captain, or players on the opposing club, emphasizes the general attitude of respect accorded each other by members of the ball-playing "fraternity" as it was frequently called in the game's early days. Gentlemen did not call each other by their first names in the nineteenth century as frequently as in more modern times. The common form of address would have been "Mr. Elliot, that was an excellent catch when you took that ball on the fly," or simply, "Moore, outstanding play on that daisy cutter last inning." In the banter among players during the game, this form of address reinforces that we are in another era.

While being encouraged to employ period language, players are reminded to adopt period behavior as well. The 2006 edition of the National Baseball Hall of Fame and Museum *Yearbook* contains an interview with 1973 inductee Monte Irvin, titled "The Complete Hall of Famer," which speaks directly and thoughtfully to this point. Asked about playing on the Newark Eagles of the Negro National League in 1939 for owner Effa Manley (who was inducted into the Hall of Fame in 2006 as the first woman honoree), Irvin recalled, "She did a lot of good things she didn't get credit for. She would tell us, 'Whether you guys know it or not, you're role models. Conduct yourselves properly and dress well. Mind your P's and Q's.'"

These timeless words of advice to Monte Irvin and his teammates from Effa Manley hold true for vintage players, who should remember that anyone who is wearing a base ball uniform is, in fact, a role model for the youngsters in the audience. In their eyes, vintage players are "real" ball players — just as real to them as the professional players they may have seen on television or when attending a minor or major league game. A vintage player should "show his ginger" on every play. He should not argue with the umpire, slam his bat down after making an out, or use offensive language. In vintage base ball, Effa Manley's injunction to "dress well" means that every player should appear on the field in a complete uniform that is clean, in good repair, and worn correctly. And he should "mind his Ps and Qs" regarding gentlemanly decorum.

One way to help new players understand what is meant by gentlemanly conduct is to remind them that in the 1860s the general approach to the game and the atmosphere at a base ball match was closer to modern golf than modern base ball. In vintage base ball, as in golf, opposing players compliment each other on good plays, police themselves in matters regarding rules and scoring, and shake hands when the match has been completed. Vintage players show courtesy and respect toward teammates, opponents, spectators, the umpire, and the scorers. Complaining about an umpire's decision ("kicking" in the language of the day) was strongly discouraged in the 1860s and should not occur in a vintage game. Grumbling in defeat or gloating in victory, all too commonly seen in sports today, were viewed as unseemly in the 1860s and therefore should not occur in vintage base ball.

Complementary Activities and Entertainment

In the nineteenth century, it was not customary to have a vocal or instrumental performance of the national anthem prior to the game. But, in *A Game of Inches: The Game Behind the Scenes*, Peter Morris cites an early precedent for including it at vintage match. "A band performed 'The Star- Spangled Banner' at the opening of Brooklyn's Union Grounds on May 15, 1862. The song, however, was not yet the national anthem, and other patriotic songs were sometimes substituted in the early years of baseball." Expense was a factor since "in the days before public address systems [and recorded music] it was necessary to hire a band to perform music." Morris points out that "The Star-Spangled Banner" was played "at the opening game of the 1918 World Series, when the nation's entry into the world war was on every mind," but that it did not become the official national anthem until 1931 and "it was not until World War II that it became customary for the national anthem to be played before every game."

Since "The Star Spangled Banner" was not performed at ball games on a regular basis in the nineteenth century, and since a band is not often present, vintage programs usually do not include it in the pre-game ceremonies. However, if a vintage club is playing a game at a community festival or other setting, the event organizers may arrange for the national anthem to be performed at the game. Often this is done by playing a recording or having it played or sung by a local music group. On special occasions the national anthem might be performed at a vintage game by a Civil War-era brass band wearing period uniforms, playing antique instruments, and using musical arrangements authentic to the nineteenth-century (calling to mind the look and sound of that 1862 performance at the Union Grounds). If the national anthem is part of the pre-game activities, a vintage player should observe traditional protocol by standing at attention while facing the flag. A player should remove his cap with his right hand and hold it at the left shoulder, with his hand over the heart. He should sing along, with no chatting with teammates during the anthem.

Since the well-known base ball song "Take Me Out to the Ball Game" was not written until 1908, most vintage teams representing an era in the nineteenth century do not pause in the middle of the seventh inning while the crowd stands up and sings. If playing at a community event, however, the well-meaning organizers, unaware that the song was not composed until considerably after the era being portrayed on the field, may ask everyone to sing "Take Me Out to the Ball Game" at some point during the festivities. If this happens, the vintage team should join in the singing and not make an issue of it on authenticity grounds. At the conclusion of the singing, one of the players or the umpire might make a light-hearted comment such as, "What a brilliant new song about the national pastime! Our players have never heard it before, but we think it is sure to catch on and become quite a popular tune. Perhaps some day it will be sung at every base ball game."

Music and singing are natural complements for vintage base ball. With no recorded music available, Americans did more singing in the nineteenth century, and many people played a musical instrument. In his historical novel *If I Never Get Back*, Darryl Brock describes how the 1869 Cincinnati Red Stockings sang their team song with a verse for each team member. Some vintage teams have followed this custom and have written their own words to the tune of a popular nineteenth-century piece, such as "Bonnie Blue Flag" or "Wait for the Wagon." Vocal and instrumental renditions of nineteenth-century songs can be found on several websites. The club song, of course, may also be an original composition.

The Rochester Grangers, who play their home matches at the Rochester Hills Museum at Van Hoosen Farm in Rochester Hills, Michigan, have been very successful at enlivening their matches with the singing of a team song. It is their custom to gather on the infield once during each game as the teams change sides and perform their team song for the crowd. This is an entertaining and enjoyable feature of their matches, and they are to be commended for their willingness to rehearse the song to the point where they are comfortable and confident about performing it before an audience at their games.

For those interested in creating a team song, an excellent model, "'Ball Days' in the Year A.D. 1858," appears in James Terry's *Long Before the Dodgers: Baseball in Brooklyn 1855–1884*. The song was sung "at a postgame banquet following a Knickerbocker and Excelsior match in August 1858," when "players and club members joined in the singing of a tune composed for the occasion by Atlantics player Peter O'Brien." Just as "Ball Days" contained the names of the leading players and clubs of 1858, a vintage program could devise a song with a verse that mentions each player or a verse in honor of each club that it plays. This template was followed by the organizers of the VBBA Convention in 2006, with a quartet of soloists singing the verses that mentioned each club attending the tenth anniversary banquet and everyone present at the dinner joining in on the chorus. As Terry observed of "Ball Days," the song of the type sung at the VBBA banquet "captures the spirit of camaraderie and fraternity" of the early amateur clubs. Team songs can be sung at a variety of settings and make an excellent accompaniment for a vintage game.

Programs are encouraged to make the experience of attending a vintage game enjoyable through the match itself and creative complementary activities. Period music, period language, traditional refreshments, and interaction with the umpire and players all add to the nineteenth-century ambiance and contribute the spectators' appreciation of a vintage game. As they take their turns at bat, run the bases, and make the fielding plays, players are encouraged to play with enthusiasm and maintain their nineteenth-century personae while always keeping in mind the educational goals of the program. As the spectators enjoy the total experience of their afternoon at the ballpark, the sample game is now in the late innings and it is time to see how the match turns out.

22

Game Day: The Ninth Inning and Post-Game Activities

Sample Game: The Ninth Inning

When we left the sample match between the Arcadia Club and the Franklin Club in the previous chapter, the score was tied 2–2 after two innings of play. As we rejoin the action, the lead has changed hands throughout the match, and the score is still close. With the score 9–7 in favor if the Franklins after eight innings, the Arcadias have scored three runs to take a 10–9 lead after their turn at bat in the top of ninth inning. The Franklins are now coming to bat in the last half of the ninth with Lawrence, Moore, and Newman due up.

When a vintage game reaches the ninth inning, both teams bat regardless of which team is ahead. The early clubs played for exercise and recreation, and each team wanted to take all of its turns at bat. Therefore, even if the Franklins were ahead after the Arcadias batted in their half of the ninth inning, the Franklins would still take their final turn at bat in the last of the ninth. If the game is running long or rain is approaching, the captains may agree to dispense with playing the bottom of the ninth, but under normal circumstances the ninth inning should be completed, no matter which club is ahead on the score sheet. In this case, since the Arcadia Club took the lead, and the Franklin Club is trailing by one run, they would, of course, take their turn at bat in an effort to tie or win the game.

The Franklin Club's Ninth Inning

Lawrence, the left-hander, steps to the line and the umpire moves to the third-base side of home as the shortstop takes his position between first and second. Lawrence hits a hard grounder between the shortstop and the first baseman. It looks like the ball may go through into right field, but the shortstop (playing about where the modern second baseman would normally play) goes far to his left and blocks the ball. He scrambles after it and recovers the ball in short right field. From his knees, he sends a swift throw to first base. The first baseman juggles the throw and then grabs it securely just as Lawrence reaches the bag and stops directly on it. Lawrence has had to slow down a bit just before reaching first base so that he does not overrun the bag. Section 15 of the 1860 Rules states that "any player running the bases is out, if at any time he is touched by the ball while in play in the hands of an adversary, without some part of his person being on a base." There is no exception in the 1860 Rules for overrunning first base.

On this play, the umpire's view of the ball and of the first baseman's hands is blocked by Lawrence as he nears the base. The umpire is not certain if the ball beat the runner or if first baseman had a good grip on the ball when Lawrence's foot came down on the bag. All eyes turn to the umpire for a judgment on this close play. But, sensing the umpire's view may have been obstructed, Lawrence, who had the best view of the play as he ran down the line toward the base, knows the throw just beat him to the bag. Instead of hoping the umpire might have missed the play, allowing him to remain on first base, Lawrence leaves the base and jogs off the field toward his club's bench. "I was out," he calls to the umpire. "The first baseman had the ball in his grasp just before my foot touched the base." Although his team is behind by one run in the ninth inning and he knows that getting the leadoff batter on base is the often the key to starting a rally, he also knows he was out. He would not feel right about scoring the tying run knowing the ball beat him to the base. Therefore, he makes sure the correct call is made. The umpire thanks Lawrence for his truthfulness, and the interpreters call the attention of the spectators to this fine act of sportsmanship on the part of the gentlemanly striker. Shouts of "Huzzah for Mr. Lawrence" are heard from the players and the supporters of both nines in recognition of his honesty and sportsmanship.

Moore steps to the plate. With one out and nobody on, Moore hits a line drive to left field that is played on the second bounce, giving Moore his first base. With Moore on first and one out, Newman hits a grounder between third and shortstop into left field, reaching first base as Moore moves up to second.

Oliver advances to the plate with one out and runners on first and second. He tries hitting to right field and sends a bouncing ball toward the gap between first and second. The second baseman and first baseman go after the ball. Simultaneously, the pitcher dashes to first to cover the vacated bag. The first baseman comes up with the ball, and seeing that he has no chance to force the runner at second, throws to the pitcher covering first. The throw beats the striker to the base and Oliver is retired for the second out. However, while the play was being made at first, the base runners advanced to second and third on Oliver's grounder to the right side of the field.

With two outs and two on, Peters steps to the plate and drills a solid line drive to left-center. The ball strikes the ground for the second time before either the center fielder or left fielder can get to it. While Moore scores easily from third with the tying run, there is still a chance to get Newman, who is trying to score the winning run from second. The center fielder picks up the ball and throws it to the second baseman, who throws the ball to home, where the catcher has moved a step or two in front of the plate to receive the throw. From this spot, while not blocking the runner's route to the plate (which would be against the rules on obstruction and also might result in a collision), the catcher is in good position to receive the throw and make a sweeping tag of the runner as he nears the plate. The second baseman, knowing there is a group of spectators sitting behind the plate and making sure he does not make a wild throw over the catcher's head into the crowd, makes an accurate throw to home on one bound to the catcher. The catcher gets set to grab the throw, but Newman arrives and touches the plate just before the ball reaches the catcher. Both runners score. This means that, at this point in the flow of the game, the Franklins have scored enough runs to win the match 11–10. However, while the winning club has been determined, the game is not over. In the spirit of the time, the clubs remain on the field and finish out the ninth inning.

While Moore and Newman receive congratulations from their teammates for scoring the tying and winning runs, the game continues. Peters went to second on the throw to the plate. Quinn comes to the plate with two outs and hits a hard ground ball up the middle that gets past the pitcher but is headed right toward the second baseman, playing near the base. He fields the ball and makes the throw to first base to retire Quinn for the third out of the ninth inning.

The provisions governing the end of the game are in Section 26 of the 1860 Rules: "The game shall consist of nine innings to each side, when, should the number of runs be equal, the play shall be continued until a majority of runs, upon an equal number of innings, shall be declared, which shall conclude the game." This rule attempts to address two issues — how to declare the winner of the match, and what to do in case of a tie after nine innings. Regrettably, the phrasing is so convoluted that the modern reader may feel it does not do a good job of addressing either. Fortunately, Henry Chadwick's commentary in *Beadle's Dime Base-ball Player* puts the first issue in plain English by stating that "nine innings are played on each side, and the party making the greatest number of runs wins the match" (p. 20).

The vintage base ball community has carefully noted that Chadwick speaks of "nine innings to each side," not that the game ends when the team that bats last is ahead after 8½ innings or that the game ends the moment the team that bats last scores the run that gives them "a majority of runs" at some point during the last of the ninth inning. Therefore, the reference to a game consisting of "nine innings to each side" is usually interpreted to mean that each team will play nine full innings. In the sample game between the Arcadias and Franklins described above, nine innings have now been completed, with the Franklin Club having scored "a majority of runs" (11 out of 21) in this 11–10 game.

Tie Score

On the matter of ties, had the Franklins scored only one run in the ninth, leaving the score at 10–10 after nine full innings, further consultation of Section 26 and Chadwick's commentary indicates how this situation should be handled. Since Section 26 says that the game "shall be continued until a majority of runs" is scored by one of the clubs, it could be assumed that extra innings might have been mandatory. However, Chadwick informs us that "in case of a tie, at the close of the ninth inning, the game, by mutual consent, can be prolonged innings after innings until one or other of the contesting sides obtain the most runs" (p. 20). Therefore, if the sample match had been tied after nine full innings, the game would not have automatically gone into a tenth inning.

In doing the extensive research on nineteenth-century base ball for *The National Association of Base Ball Payers, 1857–1870*, Marshall Wright found that "each year several tie games were played. The rules stated that it was up to the participating teams whether or not to play extra innings to determine the outcome" (p. xv). In vintage base ball, if the score is tied after nine innings, the umpire calls the captains together and asks if they wish to play another inning. The answer is usually "yes," but occasionally the game does not go to a tenth inning if another game is scheduled on the field, the weather is threatening, or the visiting team needs to get started for home. If the game is still tied after ten innings, the captains will again meet to decide if another inning should be played. Occasionally, the captains will agree at some point to end the game with the score tied due to the shared sentiment that both clubs have played extraordinarily well and, out of mutual admiration and respect, it would not seem fitting for one or the other to finish the day on the losing end of the score.

Concluding the Match

Returning to the conclusion of the sample game, the Franklin Club has won 11–10 by scoring two runs with two outs by an exciting ninth-inning rally. The members of the Arcadia Club have lost a close game but do not slam their equipment to the ground or show that they are angry or upset about the outcome. The members of the winning club, while pleased to have won, are restrained in celebrating their dramatic come-from-behind win. All players remain in complete uniform and do not start removing their ties or pulling their shirttails out the moment the ninth inning is completed (as some modern players do at the end of the game).

The words of nineteenth-century English novelist and poet George Meredith provide a helpful guideline for the club on the short end of the score. As cited by editor Marty Jerome in *The Complete Runner's Day-by-Day Log and Calendar* for 2007, Meredith advises, "Always imitate the behavior of the winners when you lose." Players should join in the postgame ceremonies with their heads up to indicate that they have had a great time playing the national game, played well, and gave a good effort. No team wins every game, and the victors deserve all due credit and congratulations on their triumph. The words of Meredith are especially enlightening since his life (1828–1909) makes him a contemporary of American baseball pioneers Henry Chadwick (1824–1908), Alexander Cartwright (1820–1892), and Harry Wright (1835–1895). Meredith was establishing himself as a leading writer in England in the 1850s and 1860s when base ball was establishing itself as a popular pastime in America. His recommendation represents the prevailing attitude toward proper behavior in that period on both sides of the Atlantic and is in keeping with the sporting code that the Knickerbockers and their contemporaries observed at that time. Accordingly, vintage players on the losing team never complain or try to blame the loss of the game on the umpiring, the condition of the grounds, or any other factors. Every player on the losing nine carries himself with dignity and decorum when the final out is recorded. Some twenty-first-century players and spectators might find the words of Meredith "old-fashioned." That is exactly the point. When re-creating the national pastime of the 1850s and 1860s, it is important for vintage players to put aside modern behavior patterns and take their cues from the customs of an earlier time, as reflected in the inspirational words of Meredith. At the end of the game both teams approach the next phase of the day's activities in a respectful manner.

Congratulatory Exchanges

When the outcome has been determined, it is customary at a vintage base ball game to conduct a short ceremony to bring closure to the activities. The teams line up on the base lines (as they did at the start of the match), with the captains at the ends of the lines nearest to home plate and the umpire in the center. The umpire makes a brief announcement (in period language if possible) regarding the final score.

Umpire: "Ladies and gentlemen, today's fine match involving the gentlemen of the two excellent clubs you see before you has been concluded. After nine full innings of play, the Franklin Club of Port Dominion, Ohio, has scored 11 runs and the Arcadia Club of Clintonville, Ohio, has scored 10."

Holding up the game ball for the spectators to see, the umpire continues: "As is the custom, the game ball is presented to the winning club as a trophy of their excellent play and their victory in the match. Accordingly, it is my honor to present the ball used in today's contest to Captain Moore of the Franklin Club. Congratulations on your nine's fine performance in the match and for your well-deserved victory, won fair and square on the playing field this afternoon" The umpire hands the game ball to Captain Moore, who receives congratulatory handshakes from the umpire and Captain Andersen.

The presentation of the game ball to "the winning club as a trophy of victory" is specified in Section 1 of the 1860 Rules and is a practice that should be continued at vintage games. Most teams that are engaged in vintage base ball today could not afford to actually give away an old-style leather base ball to the winning club at every match. However, it lends an authentic touch to the ceremonies at the conclusion of the match if the game ball is symbolically "presented" to the winning club (with the prior understanding between the teams that the winning club doesn't actually get to keep it).

In accordance with the sportsmanlike nature of vintage base ball, clubs exchange congratulations at the end of the match, an authentic carryover from the game's early days. As Henry Chadwick advised in Haney's *Base Ball Book of Reference for 1867*, "We trust all captains will observe the good old custom of closing the game with mutual cheers for each other's club, and a field cheer for the Umpire, for it is a custom calculated to promote good feeling between the players" (p. 87).

As the players listen attentively, the umpire calls on the captains to speak. If the game is being played at a neutral site during a festival or tournament, it is best if the captain of the losing club speaks first so he can offer congratulations to the winning club. This gives the captain of the winning club the opportunity to accept the congratulations when it is his turn to address the crowd. If the game is played at the home grounds of one of the clubs, it is good for the captain of the host club to speak first, as this will provide the visiting club captain with a model of what he will say when it is his turn to make his comments. In his brief remarks, the captain commends the other club for a well-played match and thanks them for providing a great day of base ball. He congratulates the opposing club on its skill. He acknowledges the work of the umpire and the scorers and thanks the spectators for coming.

Umpire: "We will now have a word from Captain Andersen, on behalf of the Arcadia Club."

Captain Andersen (facing the crowd): "Ladies and gentlemen, the members of the Arcadia Base Ball Club wish to thank the gentlemen of Franklin Club for traveling all the way from their home grounds in northern Ohio for today's match. We congratulate them on their well-deserved victory, which was fairly won as the result of their superior play."

Captain Andersen (still facing the crowd but gesturing toward the umpire and scorer's table): "We wish to acknowledge the fine work of the umpire, Mr. Kimnach, and compliment him on his thorough knowledge of the rules and his flawless judgment throughout the match. [It is best if the losing captain graciously thanks the umpire for his service to show that his club is in no way blaming the umpire for the loss.] Gentlemen of both clubs, three cheers for the umpire, please."

All members of both clubs lift their hats and join the cheering and loudly shout: "Hip, Hip, Huzzah! Hip, Hip, Huzzah! Hip, Hip, Huzzah!"

Captain Andersen (gesturing toward the scorer's table): "We also wish to express our appreciation to the two exemplary gentlemen who served as the scorers for today's match, Mr. Large of the Arcadia Club and Mr. Lehr of the Franklin Club." Players of both clubs applaud the scorers, which the scorers can acknowledge by rising from their chairs and tipping their hats.

Captain Andersen (tipping his cap to the crowd): "It is with special appreciation that we acknowledge the fine citizens of this community for attending the match today. Thank you all for coming out for the game. We hope you have enjoyed this exhibition of base ball as it was meant to be played. Gentlemen, three cheers for the wonderful crowd of spectators that have honored us with their presence to witness this afternoon's exhibition of the national game."

All members of both clubs (lifting their hats and shouting in unison): "Hip, Hip, Huzzah! Hip, Hip, Huzzah! Hip, Hip, Huzzah!"

Captain Andersen (turning slightly to the Arcadia players): "Gentlemen, please join me in giving three cheers to the victorious club in today's match, the fine gentlemen of the Franklin Club."

Arcadia players: "Hip, Hip, Huzzah! Hip, Hip, Huzzah! Hip, Hip, Huzzah!"

Umpire: "Thank you, Captain Andersen. We will now hear from Captain Moore."

Captain Moore (addressing the crowd): "On behalf of both clubs we thank the Ohio Village Muffins for the kind invitation to come to their home grounds to take part in the annual Ohio Cup Vintage Base Ball Festival. [If playing at a neutral site, one of the captains should always acknowledge the host club, museum, or community organization for sponsoring the event]. At this time, we wish to thank the gentlemen of the Arcadia Club for an excellent match today. It is always a pleasure to have a match with your fine club. As always, your club displayed great skill and enthusiasm on the diamond. All who witnessed the contest will agree that it was a well-played game by both clubs, and since the outcome was in doubt until the final inning, either club could have emerged the victor. We would, of course, be honored to have a future match with your club at a date and location that is convenient for both clubs. [He then tips his hat to the crowd.] We trust the marvelous throng that is in attendance today has enjoyed the match, and we join the Arcadia Club in thanking them for their sportsmanlike support of both nines today. Gentleman, three cheers for our worthy opponents, the Arcadia Base Ball Club."

Franklin players: "Hip, Hip, Huzzah! Hip, Hip, Huzzah! Hip, Hip, Huzzah!"

Before the members of the two clubs exchange congratulatory handshakes, the umpire steps forward with announcements for the audience.

Umpire: "Ladies and gentlemen, as we conclude today's match, please know that in a moment the gentlemen of the two clubs will be standing for a group tintype here on the diamond. You will be welcome to step to the home plate area with your cameras. Also, immediately following the photographs, all of the youngsters in attendance are welcome to come onto the playing field and try their skill at striking the ball and running the bases. The players will remain on the field and invite you to join them."

The umpire makes a closing statement, announcing the date of the next vintage game and any other events or exhibits:

Umpire: "We hope you have enjoyed this exhibition of the national game of base ball and we invite you to come again next weekend when the Ohio Village Muffins will meet the Cincinnati Red Stockings here on this field at 2 o'clock on Saturday. Throughout the day today, you are invited to stop by the American House Hotel to see the impressive and informative display of historic base ball uniforms, equipment, photographs, cards, and other items from the memorabilia collection of Mr. Martin, a member of the Ohio Village Muffins. Mr. Martin will be on hand to answer questions. Also, you are invited to attend the concert of music from the 1860s that will be presented by the Ohio Village Singers at three o'clock in the Town Hall. Thank you for coming and good afternoon."

The members of the two clubs then shake hands all around, exchanging congratulations on a game well played. These handshakes should, of course, be done in the traditional manner, with no high fives, fist bumps, or faux hugs that are sometimes seen between players at the conclusion of modern sporting events. Golfers and their caddies observe the tradition of removing their hats when exchanging congratulatory handshakes as they walk off the eighteenth green at the end of a well-played match, providing a good model for vintage base ball players.

Players remain in first-person nineteenth-century character and full uniform throughout the closing remarks. Complete uniforms are required for the photo session and the opportunity for the children to come onto the field. Players remain in their complete uniforms until they exit the public area of the grounds and reach the changing room or the parking lot.

Post-Game Activities

"Tintypes"

When both teams are on the field at the conclusion of the game, this is an opportune time to line up for a photograph (or "tintype" as vintage participants often say) to commemorate the occasion of a well-played match. A good strategy to get everyone organized quickly for the picture is for someone (usually the host club captain or the umpire) to step forward and ask one team to kneel on one knee in the front row and the other club to stand in the back row. Choose a location that has a background that minimizes twenty-first-century intrusions on the setting (modern buildings, fast-food signs, automobiles). Players should pose with their bats and any other equipment (as players often did in days of old). An examination of period images indicates that it was traditional for the pitcher to hold a ball in his hand when photographs were taken. Club banners and flags are often included in these photos. If a vintage team is playing a community team, it is a good idea to have the vintage team kneel in the front row. If the community team stands in the back row, only their shirts, ties, and hats will be visible in the photo, and any modern pants or shoes that would detract from the photo will be out of sight.

Everyone at the game who is in period dress (but only those in period dress) should be invited to be in the photo, with the umpire, scorers, interpreters, and mascots joining the players on the field. In the nineteenth century, exposures took so long that the people in the photo usually did not smile because they could not hold that expression very long. To replicate the look of nineteenth-century photographs, vintage base ball participants maintain a dignified bearing with a neutral expression and generally do not smile broadly in team photos.

Typically, as the clubs line up to have pictures taken, many spectators will take pictures of the two teams and the other participants in period dress. Therefore, anyone who is not in a base ball uniform or other period dress should not be in the photo. While it is tempting to let small children in modern clothing run out onto the field at the end of the game to join parents or other family members, the integrity of the old-style photo will be seriously compromised by a four-year-old in shorts, crocs, and a SpongeBob SquarePants T-shirt. The outdoor summer theater "performance" is not quite over, so children who are not dressed appropriately should not be brought onto the field until the photo opportunity has been concluded.

Top: Observing the customs of 1860, the captain of the St. Louis Perfectos leads the club in three cheers for their opponent at the conclusion of the match. *Bottom:* After exchanging three cheers, the Rochester (Michigan) Grangers and the Indianapolis Blues congratulate each other on a fine game.

Children line up to take a turn at bat and run the bases at the conclusion of the match.

As the players line up for the post-game photo for spectators, it is a good idea for someone associated with the club to take a photo of the two teams for the team records, website, or newsletter. In addition to serving as a memento of the day's match, a photo of this type can be used later as a publicity picture or as part of a press kit to promote future matches.

Involving Young Spectators

When the match and post-game ceremonies have concluded, there are usually several youngsters in the crowd who are eager for the chance to get on the field. One activity that the Ohio Village Muffins have found to be popular is to let each youngster who has been watching the game have a turn at bat. The club keeps a couple of smaller, lighter bats on hand for the young strikers. The pitcher selects a very soft ball from the ball bag and moves to a spot about half the distance between the pitcher's point and home plate. A player moves behind the plate to serve as the catcher (there definitely needs to be a catcher for this activity, as there are numerous swings and misses). If it is convenient to move the bases, they should be placed closer together since the ninety-foot configuration can be quite long for small children. At least five or six players in uniform are needed to take positions around a "drawn in" infield. As the kids line up for their turn to bat, it is best to form the line at the scorer's table and have one of the players, the umpire, or the scorer supervise this line to make sure that the "on-deck" batter, eager for his or her turn at bat, doesn't get too close to the plate where another youngster is swinging the bat. Those waiting in line to bat should be instructed to leave all bats on the ground to prevent anyone from taking any practice swings that might inadvertently strike one of the other children.

The youngsters enjoy having the chance to swing the bat, hit the ball, and run the bases. It is a good experience for them to get a wooden bat in their hands and try to hit an old-fashioned leather ball. When the ball is struck, the vintage players, who have caught the ball so well during the game, typically find that their defensive skills have suddenly deserted them and begin to make an astonishing number of muffs. This results in each child reaching base safely, circling the bases, and "scoring a run." After batting and running the bases, the kids are invited to come to the infield to help with the fielding. On occasion, some of the parents will also come onto the field to play.

Families enjoy taking pictures when their youngster comes to bat to take his or her swings. Parents sometimes ask the Muffin players to pose for a picture with their son or daughter. Providing the opportunity for the younger spectators to come on the field and have a turn at bat is an excellent "hands-on" experience that is very popular with the both the youngsters and their families and sends them home with a special memory of their day at the ball game. Some parents have been known to email such souvenir photos to the Muffins the following day accompanied by a thoughtful note of thanks for taking time to play ball with their children.

Autographs

While mingling with and talking to spectators in the dual role of player/interpreter, a vintage player sometimes is asked by a youngster for an autograph. This can be an awkward situation for a vintage player. Although he knows that he does not have the celebrity standing of a professional player, for that particular youngster at that moment he is a "real" base ball player, and he should by all means sign the autograph as requested.

The player should remember that the youngster is not really requesting *his* autograph, since he probably does not even know the player's name. The youngster is trying to connect with someone he perceives to be a "real" ball player, and since the vintage player is wearing a base ball uniform and is playing in a game that is being watched by a crowd, the amateur vintage ballist fulfills the young person's concept of a genuine base ball player.

While the vintage player may feel self-conscious about signing an autograph, he puts his awkwardness aside and immediately and enthusiastically agrees to sign the program, thanking the youngster for asking and saying it would be a pleasure to sign. The player shakes hands, asks the youngster's name, and uses the name in the inscription. A bit of period language in the inscription is desirable. The player writes his name legibly on the program and includes a nickname if he has one, thereby making the autograph more interesting.

A major leaguer being besieged by hundreds of autograph seekers might be excused for scribbling his name and hurriedly moving on. A vintage player will not be faced with so many requests that he must rush through the signing. Also, good penmanship was more common in the 1860s than today, and a gentleman of that era would have signed his name in a neat hand, forming each letter carefully. Therefore, the vintage player should sign his name legibly and add a message that includes his role on the team and the name of his team, thus providing a nice keepsake of a fun day at the ball game. Here is an example:

To Wyatt,
Best wishes to a fine young player of the Grand Old Game.
Don "Big Bat" Andersen
First Baseman and Captain
Arcadia Base Ball Club
Clintonville, Ohio

The player converses with the youngster while signing, since meeting and talking with a base ball player is really what he or she is probably looking for more than a signature. The player can ask the youngster if he or she plays baseball and, if so, what position he or she likes best. Whatever the answer is, he can say that base ball is a wonderful game that he has enjoyed playing since he was the youngster's age. The player can use these opportunities to encourage children to play ball whenever they get the chance, as it is a lot of fun.

If there are other players in the area, he might call one over, introducing him to the youngster: "Mr. Moore, this is Wyatt. He was here at our match today with his parents and grandparents. Would you sign his program for him? Wyatt says he plays shortstop on his Little League team, the same position you play on your team." The second player should then greet the youngster cordially, talk to him about baseball, perhaps asking him the name of his team or what school he attends. He might then sign as follows:

Wyatt,
Good Luck from one shortstop to another. Huzzah!
Chip "Deerfoot" Moore
Captain, Franklin B.B.C.
Port Dominion, Ohio

When finished writing, the player should thank the youngster for asking for the autograph, thank him for coming to the game, and encourage him to come again with his family. Make the moment a special one for a youngster who has expressed an interest in playing baseball.

As the day winds down, the youngsters who had a chance to watch the game, take a turn at bat, run the bases, and talk to the players will have a heightened interest in playing and watching the game of baseball, and on the way home may ask their parents about coming to the next vintage game. The youngster's family will appreciate a player talking to their son or daughter. Players who take the time to chat with the young spectators and sign a program are fine ambassadors for their vintage club, the museum it represents, the sport of vintage base ball, and the national pastime.

Post-Game Hospitality

Post-game socializing by the members of the contending clubs was very much the norm in early days of base ball. This custom continues in vintage base ball.

The July 30, 1856, edition of the *New York Times* provides an account of the festivities that followed a match between the Knickerbocker Club and the Eagle Club at the Elysian Fields in Hoboken, won by the Eagles 45–18. The congenial and sportsmanlike spirit that characterized the way base ball was played in the 1850s is apparent in this account.

> After the match, refreshments were served up to the members of the two Clubs and their friends and guests at the Pavilion, at which time some pretty complimentary things were said by Mr. Davis, President of the Knickerbockers [listed in the accompanying box score as an outfielder in the game], and Mr. Bixby, of the Eagles [listed as the first baseman], in which the latter, whilst

receiving the trophy of victory — the ball — took occasion to say that the Eagles, whilst playing the match felt that they were simply contending with friends and that the great disparity in the score arose from the absence of some of the Knickerbockers' principal players.

Further evidence of the importance of the socializing between the clubs comes from an article in the Monday, August 23, 1858, edition of the *New York Times*. The article, regarding an important match played the previous Friday between the Knickerbockers and Excelsiors does not begin with news of the winner and the final score but with the following headline that mentioned the events associated with the match:

> Base Ball. Knickerbocker and Excelsior Clubs —
> Splendid Game, Dinner, Speeches, &c.

Even the text of the article under this headline does not carry a lead sentence providing the outcome of Friday's game. Instead, the first paragraph opens with a description of the crowd and the post-game dinner put on by the Excelsiors when the two clubs met earlier in the year. "The return game of the home and home match between these clubs took place at the Elysian Fields, Hoboken, on Friday afternoon [August 20, the day before the first of the Lincoln-Douglas debates in Illinois], in the presence of the largest number of spectators that have been present at any match in that locality for some time." The article reports that at the conclusion of that game, "The Excelsiors had prepared an ovation [the term used here in the sense of a welcoming ceremony, rather than an outburst of applause], in the shape of a most liberal entertainment, which was served up in Montague Hall, in honor of the Knickerbocker Club, and at which a large number of invited guests sat down."

The reader must reach the second paragraph before finding that the Excelsiors won the game. At that point, the article described the August 20 game as "one of the finest and most exciting contests which has occurred in Base-ball annals for some time, and which reflects equal credit on victors and vanquished." Following a detailed account of the key hits and fielding plays, comments on the performance of various players, and the scoring throughout the game, the *Times* story remarks on the good sportsmanship that characterized the day by commenting, "One thing was very apparent throughout the match — it was the gentlemanly and good-humored courtesy which was displayed by both parties to each other; in fact it seemed anything else but a contest for the superiority between two powerful rival clubs." The reader must peruse four long descriptive paragraphs about the game before reaching the box score, where the score is finally given as 15–14 in favor of the Excelsior Club.

Following the news of the score, the article launches into a description of the post-game gathering. "After the conclusion of the match, the members of the Excelsior Club were escorted by the Knickerbockers to Odd Fellows Hall, Hoboken, where they were met by delegations from numerous other base ball clubs, and the whole party, numbering nearly two hundred, sat down to a sumptuous dinner at the club house." A lengthy report follows that mentions the names of those representing the Eagle, Putnam, and Empire clubs, quotes several of the toasts that were proposed to honor those present, and summarizes the entertaining speeches that were made throughout the evening.

But the socializing was not over. "The evening's conviviality wound up with a song and chorus, improvised for the occasion, in honor of the National Game of Base Ball, composed and sung by Mr. Davis, the chorus being sung by the company, to the tune of 'Uncle Sam's Farm.'" The social events surrounding the afternoon's game concluded with a late-night informal parade through lower Manhattan. "The company broke up about 11 o'clock," reported the *Times*, "and, with Dodsworth's band at their head, marched to escort the Excelsior Club, by way of Barclay-street, Park-row, round the *Times* office, through Nassau-street, and down Fulton-street to the Ferry where, on parting, repeated cheers were given on both sides."

What a splendid occasion it must have been on that day (and evening) in the summer of 1858 when a well-played base ball match between two gentlemanly clubs, who had the highest respect for each other, was followed by a dinner party, complete with the singing of original songs honoring the players and the national game. Judging by the parade, apparently nobody wanted to see it come to an end. Only eighteen players appeared in the box score of the game, but the non-playing members of the contending clubs were included in the dinner, along with their friends and representatives from other New York clubs.

These newspaper articles from the 1850s provide evidence of the gentlemanly spirit of good will and good sportsmanship that was present at the games and the post-game activities. This tradition of camaraderie and hospitality has carried over into vintage base ball. While the food and entertainment may not be as lavish as reported in this *Times* article from 1858, it is always enjoyable for the clubs and their families to sit down together after the match and enjoy the pleasant conversation and good fellowship that flows so easily among the members of the vintage base ball fraternity.

Regardless of the final score, vintage games conducted according to the sportsmanlike norms of the mid-nineteenth century always end on a positive note, with the two clubs exchanging three cheers, handshakes, and good wishes, sharing a meal, and looking forward to their next meeting. This convivial atmosphere did not last forever, with the culture of the game changing significantly in the decade of the 1860s. In the introduction to *Long Before the Dodgers: Baseball in Brooklyn, 1855–1884*, James Terry speaks of "the transformation of the game from a recreational pursuit of gentlemen's clubs to a professional spectator sport" (p. 2). In *Baseball's First Inning: A History of the National Pastime Through the Civil War*, William Ryczek writes that "the passing of the baton from the gentlemanly Knickerbockers, Gothams and Excelsiors to the rougher-hewn Atlantics, Eckfords and Mutuals signaled a change in the direction of baseball, one that came much sooner than the post-war boom" (p. 4). As Terry and Ryczek indicate, transformation and change did come and base ball became less gentlemanly as time went on. But, through the magic of vintage base ball, directions can be reversed. By accurately re-creating everything from the opening coin toss, to the style of play that characterized the game, to the congenial post-game gatherings, vintage base ball has been successful in reestablishing the sportsmanlike atmosphere and spirit of the era of the gentlemen's clubs. Vintage base ball provides a unique opportunity for participants and spectators to travel back in time and experience base ball as it was played in its early years.

23

Authenticity, Accuracy, Accommodations, and Opportunities

Vintage base ball clubs take great pride in staging their games so that the national pastime is presented "as it was actually played" in the words of the Vintage Base Ball Association mission statement. However, this commitment to accuracy can be more difficult to maintain than expected since it is not always clear exactly how the game was played in a given year and geographic area. Some aspects of the sport, such as uniforms and equipment, can be difficult to re-create. The games must be fun to play and entertaining to watch, which may call for some adaptations to the rules. Safety issues may require vintage programs to consider necessary accommodations. Within the sport of vintage base ball, there is a continuing effort to find the proper balance between adhering to historical authenticity and presenting a game that is an enjoyable and safe experience for players and spectators.

Interpreting and Communicating the Rules

As the criteria for choosing an era and presenting the game illustrate, the written rules are silent on many points and vague on many others. Rules and practices changed from year to year in the 1850s and 1860s. The game was in an experimental period and various rules were tried and then retained, modified, or dropped. Some of the clubs held meetings in the 1850s to discuss and clarify the rules, indicating that there were variations in rules interpretations at that time. Likewise, the fact that Henry Chadwick felt it necessary to write his commentaries providing advice, direction, and instruction on how the game should be played indicates the rules were being interpreted differently by different clubs. Vintage base ball researchers, players, and club organizers understand that in matters related to rules and practices, there can be several "right" answers to the same question.

Geography is definitely an important consideration. Even if the meaning of each nineteenth-century rule were absolutely clear, we would still not be certain if all the clubs actually observed the rules in the same way. When a rule book from 1860 or any other year was published, it would strain credulity to believe that everyone throughout the country immediately acquired the new book, abandoned the old rules that they had been playing up to that time, and immediately adopted the new rules. In those days of poor communication between cities and regions of the country, change did not occur quickly and uniformly. Clubs may have been quite content to continue playing base ball according to a combination of conventions based on older rule books, word-of-mouth, and local customs.

For example, while some of the more experienced players of the established clubs of the East may have moved to faster pitching and the fly game, the newer clubs of the Midwest may have preferred the more recreational, gentlemanly version of base ball, characterized by slower pitching and the bound game. Since differences would have existed in the way base ball was played in 1860, 1866, or any other year, vintage programs can, within certain reasonable parameters, develop their own interpretations of the rules based on some logical assumptions and their research into any local teams that existed in the period in question.

Reasonable accommodations and thoughtful compromises may need to be made in the interest of other important goals, such as offering an effective educational experience for spectators; promoting the spirit of good sportsmanship that was present in the mid-nineteenth century (and which has traditionally characterized vintage matches); maintaining the morale and interest of the players and other participants; increasing the number of teams and participants in vintage base ball; and, perhaps most important, creating a safe, positive environment for players, game officials, and spectators.

Even in situations in which the rules are clear, there are times they need to be modified or even ignored. Section 27 of the 1860 Rules states that "nine players from each club shall constitute a full field" and "no change or substitution shall be made after the game has been commenced, unless for reason of illness or injury." Vintage clubs generally do not observe this rule. Each vintage team plays nine players at a time on defense, but if there are more than nine players present, everyone is included in the batting order and there is free substitution in the field, with players moving in and out of the game on defense so that all players who are in uniform and ready to play receive a similar amount of playing time.

Members of vintage programs, keeping historical accuracy and authenticity in mind, continue to do valuable research in primary sources. They study nineteenth-century newspaper game accounts, box scores, guide books, period illustrations, and the writings of Henry Chadwick, Charles Peverelly, and others to increase our knowledge of the game's early years. Vintage programs are grateful consumers of the current research of scholars who are not affiliated with any specific club but who share their findings on the nineteenth-century game digitally or in print. But there can be honest differences of opinion among very capable and experienced people in the vintage base ball community as to how the game was played in the nineteenth century and how it should be presented and played by vintage programs today, resulting in the game being played differently by different programs. But even as discoveries are made and shared, and more missing pieces fall into place, each program, informed by the latest research and guided by the best practices of other programs, makes its decisions on how it will play and present the game according to what is in the best interests of the program members, its affiliated institution, and sponsors.

The vintage community needs to be careful not to become divided by hair-splitting over the details of the rules, particularly those applicable to the areas of pitching and base running, where different interpretations legitimately exist and some practices may work better than others in certain environments. This book seeks to provide guidance for good decision making in regard to the presentation of a vintage game. But, as was the case in the nineteenth century, there will continue to be different interpretations, theories, and ideas as to how the game was played.

Accessible and Affordable Uniforms and Equipment

When there is no need to lower our standards of authenticity and there are no good reasons for modifications and compromises, programs should be diligent in maintaining a high level of historical accuracy. As mentioned in the chapter on uniforms, the members of the early clubs wore woolen shirts and pants, and some vintage teams wear woolen uniforms. However, since they are more expensive to purchase and maintain, many vintage program wear cotton shirts and pants. This is a common accommodation based on practicality and cost.

In the area of equipment, authentic reproduction base ball shoes are not readily available at a reasonable price. Also, while research indicates that some 1860s players wore metal cleats, baseball shoes with metal cleats are generally considered too dangerous for vintage base ball (except in leagues where the players have agreed that metal cleats are acceptable and are therefore expecting the other players in the game to be wearing them). The policy of many programs is to permit modern baseball shoes with rubber cleats to help players keep a good footing and avoid falls. But to maintain an authentic look, shoes must polished or painted solid black with no logos or colors other than black visible to the spectators. This reasonable accommodation, based on cost and safety, is widely accepted in vintage base ball.

Bats are another story. At times, the balance between being a competitive team and an educational program can swing too far toward an emphasis on winning games. In short, some players who have become more concerned with their individual performance and statistics may try to use modern bats, believing they can hit the ball farther with a thin-handled bat than with an old-fashioned thick-handled bat. Where accommodation is necessary on shoes, the use of authentic nineteenth-century-style bats deserves no compromise. There is no reason to use modern bats in vintage base ball other than to give the player an advantage. Old-style wooden bats are readily available and affordable, and programs should require players to use them.

There is a lesson here for all vintage clubs. Sometimes there is need for accommodation (as with shoes) and sometimes there is a need to stand firm for historical accuracy (bats). The ongoing task for the vintage base ball community is to find the correct balance and continually try to educate club members on the reasons for these decisions and policies. This is a difficult task at times and one of the true challenges faced by all clubs in the vintage base ball community.

Safety Dictates Accommodation

Seeking advice from established programs, an organizer of a new vintage team sent an email inquiry to the vintage base ball listserv asking when it is appropriate to put safety over authenticity when making decisions on the operation of a program. The answer to that question is that safety is always the highest priority. Program leaders should think carefully about what they are doing and make intelligent accommodations and compromises where necessary.

Section 15 of the 1860 Rules states that a striker can be tagged out if he overruns first base. But if the grass is wet, stopping directly on first base is difficult when running full speed down the line to beat out a grounder. Falls, spills, and injuries can result. To prevent accidents, the captains and the umpire can meet before the game and agree to waive Section 15, thereby allowing runners to overrun first base.

Similarly, clubs should be careful about players slipping and falling at home plate on rainy days. The rules specify that "home base" is to be "marked by a flat circular iron plate, painted or enameled white." If it becomes wet, an iron plate (or even a wooden one) that has been painted with an enamel finish can become extremely slick, similar to a patch of ice. Consequently, the captains and the umpire may agree to caution the players about the slippery nature of the plate and let them know that they need not step directly on the plate when trying to score. It is reasonable to allow the run to be counted if the runner steps in the vicinity of the slippery plate.

To the extent possible, players should always ensure that no fellow members of the base ball fraternity get hurt during a game. An injury could result in serious financial consequences, such as lost work days, lost income, and medical bills. A base runner should never crash into an infielder or catcher in an effort to get to a base. In the same vein, catchers should be careful not to intentionally or inadvertently block the runner's path to the plate. On those occasions when a throw accidentally pulls a baseman or catcher into the path of the runner, both the runner and fielder should try to avoid a collision.

As members of the vintage base ball fraternity, players should remember that, like the members of the early clubs that we seek to emulate, we are amateurs who are playing for enjoyment, recreation, and exercise. Like the players of the 1850s and 1860s, we all need to return to our regular jobs on Monday. While a few pulled hamstrings and sprained ankles are probably inevitable in any type of athletic activity that involves running, and some finger injuries may occur occasionally while trying to catch a ball barehanded, clubs should make every effort to remind players of the importance of safety and avoiding injuries during the game.

This point was made in a very humorous but effective manner at the start of a tournament hosted by the Rochester Roosters Base Ball Club at their home grounds at Schmitt Field at the History Center of Olmsted County, Minnesota. It is often the custom at such gatherings for the players from all participating clubs to be assembled before the first match begins for a meeting to introduce and welcome all the visiting clubs, go over the rules and ground rules, review logistical arrangements, and answer questions. Concluding his opening remarks, the captain of the Roosters commented, "Now remember you are in Rochester, Minnesota, home of the world-famous Mayo Clinic, which is just a short distance away. However, we would prefer not to have to take any of you there for treatment of any injuries sustained while playing in our tournament. So let's all have fun and be careful not have anyone get hurt over the next two days." Vintage players are generally smart about keeping their energy, enthusiasm, and desire to win the game in proper bounds, but it is a good idea to provide regular reminders about safety so that everyone is in the right frame of mind when the game begins.

Lessons from the Civil War Reenacting Community

The large community of Civil War reenactors, another group re-creating life in the mid-nineteenth century, has been dealing with the issue of balancing authenticity and safety for a long time. Civil War reenactors are known for their research and their attention to accuracy in every detail of what they do. Historical authenticity is very important to them — the fabric and cut of their uniforms, the appropriateness of their military insignia, the style of their hats and boots, the accuracy of their weapons and equipment, and the details of camp life, including food, cooking utensils, and tents. Many of these individuals possess an extremely detailed knowledge of the history of the unit they represent and know precisely on what day and at what time that unit made an advance or retreat, what uniforms they were wearing that day, how many casualties were sustained, and how those actions had an effect on the larger context of war. They take "the hobby," as they often call it, seriously and strive for a commendable level of authenticity in what they do.

Yet, for all their high standards in regard to historical accuracy, Civil War reenactments are governed by a set of important accommodations and compromises. These accommodations are, for the most part, not noticed by spectators as the reenactors seek to maintain the essence of life in the 1860s without endangering anyone's health or safety or driving people out of reenacting. *Reliving the Civil War: A Reenactor's Handbook* by R. Lee Hadden provides a helpful list of some of these rules and guidelines.

Vintage base ball participants may be surprised to learn that one basic tenet of Civil War reenacting, as explained in this informative book, is that "there should be no hand-to-hand fighting unless it is prearranged and scripted." Hadden writes:

> It is far too easy to get carried away and someone might get seriously hurt. If another person insists on attacking, ... gently cross your rifle against your opposer's. Ask in an undertone that the opponent go down or volunteer to "take the hit" yourself. Traditionally the more experienced reenactor should take the hit, allowing the less experienced reenactor to continue the fun of the scenario. When agreed upon, both of you swing to the side as though one of you were hit by a bayonet or stroked with the rifle butt. Never do something unannounced or unexpected to the opposer in such a situation [p. 112].

While on the surface these remarks are directed specifically at Civil War reenactors, they represent some underlying principles that apply to all forms of historical re-creation. Whether it is hand-to-hand combat or a collision at home plate, the reenacting or re-creating community should make wise decisions that promote safety and continued goodwill among participants.

"Never try to touch or capture an enemy flag" is another principle of Civil War reenacting, according to Hadden. "Correct behavior is to take the flag bearer prisoner. The flag bearer will furl the flag and retain possession of the flag and staff." While flags were captured in actual battles, Hadden points that "there are a couple of good reasons for taking the flag bearer prisoner rather than grabbing the flag. First, most regimental flags are historically correct, expensive, and easily torn or ripped. Second, there is an emotional attachment to the unit's colors, and other soldiers in the unit are not likely to simply stand by and watch it be taken by someone from the other side. An attempt to grab a flag will too often start a real fight" (p. 114).

Taking a cue from the Civil War reenactment community, responsible vintage base ball leaders need to think ahead in order to recognize and eliminate potential problem situations (hard slides into second base or collisions at home plate, for example) that could lead to people getting hurt or to an altercation between players over a close play (which would be totally unacceptable in a museum environment with families watching the match).

These examples show that there is a certain etiquette to Civil War reenacting that parallels the concept of sportsmanship in vintage base ball. Out of respect for your opponent, the site or organization hosting the event, and especially out of respect for safety, there may be some nineteenth-century base ball rules and practices (such as intentional fair-foul hitting that could send a sharply hit ball into the spectator area) that need to be modified or prohibited. Safety should be kept in mind continually to keep the fun and magic in the vintage game. "Abide by reasonable rules of conduct, especially those relating to safety matters. Do not participate in any reenactment that is dangerous to other reenactors or to the public," Hadden advises, reminding his Civil War audience as well as the vintage base ball community that "safety is everyone's business. When something is unsafe or dangerous, speak up and a say so. Don't let someone get hurt because you were too polite to insist on safety" [p. 110].

The presence of firearms, artillery pieces, and edged weapons at Civil War gatherings heightens the need for safety regulations to protect the participants and spectators from injury. Hadden cautions his Civil War reenactor colleagues: "While on the field, never use the ramrod to ram cartridges home. Often event hosts insist that ramrods be left in camp and not allowed on the field at all." One reason for this is that "the ramrod can mistakenly be fired from the rifle like a steel arrow. This is deadly." The policy of leaving the ramrod back in camp when participating in a battle illustrates the point that reasonable accommodations can and should be made in any kind of reenacting or re-creating activity when there is good reason to do so. As Hadden indicates, there is a clear need in some instances to make some intelligent compromises. While no weapons are present at vintage games, bats, balls, and colliding bodies can also result in injury and appropriate steps need to be taken to make the sport safe and enjoyable for all.

Everything possible should be done to prevent injuries during games. Accordingly, the general custom throughout vintage base ball of not wearing metal cleats is a wise one. As mentioned in Chapter 9, metal spikes may have been worn in the 1860s, but they can lead to injuries, both to the player wearing the spikes (who can suffer serious foot and ankle injuries if the spikes get caught) and to teammates and opponents who might get stepped on. They can also be intimidating to players not expecting opponents to be wearing them. Museum professionals and club leaders should discuss this matter and devise a policy for the program, giving consideration to liability issues. The policy to either allow or disallow metal cleats should then be made clear to team participants and visiting clubs.

In addition to safety, health issues are another area where reasonable accommodations need to be made. In Civil War reenacting, modern earplugs are recommended for those who will be near the firing of rifles and artillery pieces. The use of sun screen is strongly advised for those who will be out on the battlefield on a hot summer day. While ball players are not usually subjected to loud noises that would require earplugs, exposure to the sun is a concern on summer afternoons and modern sunscreen products are certainly appropriate in vintage base ball, even though they may not have existed in the nineteenth century. At the battlefield or the ball field, however, sunscreen should be applied out of the view of the spectators if possible.

Finding a Balance

The Civil War community includes participants that are considered extreme in their insistence on authenticity and others who are perceived as not being serious enough about historical accuracy. The "hardcore" group, as described by Tony Horwitz in *Confederates in the Attic*, includes people who do not consider a reenactment experience valid unless, in order to re-create the experience of portraying the soldiers of the 1860s, they sleep out on the ground the night before the event, even if the weather is uncomfortably rainy and cold. Incredibly, some of these hardcore reenactors even go on harsh diets in order to achieve the gaunt, haggard appearance of a soldier who has been in the army for several years without enough to eat. Many would consider this degree of commitment to a "hobby," all done in the name of historical authenticity, as going too far. On the other hand, other less-committed Civil War reenactors may show up for events carrying a World War I rifle and wearing modern athletic-style footwear and uniforms made of synthetic fabrics. Such a reenactor is referred to as a "farb." According to "A Cross-Disciplinary Glossary of Terms for Historic Hobbyists" (found at www.historicgames.com), the derogatory term "farb" comes from a phrase used by more authentic reenactors "starting with the phrase 'FAR Be it from me to say anything, but...'" and refers to "those, no matter how often they are told, seem oblivious to major errors in their dress and equipment." In the reenacting community, "farbs" are sometimes criticized (and deservedly so) for not paying enough attention to authenticity.

The goal in all this, whether the re-creating activity is military or athletic, is to find the correct middle ground. If the hobby goes to extremes in the name of authenticity, it faces the danger of dwindling to only a few adherents. Most Civil War reenactors would give up the hobby if they had to sleep out in bad weather or starve themselves. Yet, most would agree that it is not unreasonable to establish some standards of authenticity in the area of uniforms and equipment for participants at a reenactment where spectators will be present.

Balance is the key. In order to keep the sport growing with more teams forming and more people playing every year, the vintage base ball community must not go to the extreme of interpreting the popular 1860 Rules in only one way, insisting that the game must be based on fast pitching and "open stealing" to be considered historically authentic. On the contrary, those re-creating the 1860 era would be wise to adopt a set of rules and practices that can be played by people of various ages and skill levels. Otherwise, vintage base ball will come to have approximately the same age distribution as modern professional baseball, which is obviously a game for younger players in their 20s and 30s, with perhaps a smattering in their early 40s. If that happens, the sport will become overly competitive, the number of teams and participants will decline, and the recent growth of vintage base ball will be reversed.

Those who think they may want to build an 1860s program on swift pitching and unrestricted stealing or emulate the fast pitching and rough-and-tumble play of the 1880s and 1890s, are welcome to do so — as long as they do not insist that this is the only authentic way to play and that every club should adopt this style of play. There are many "right" answers to the question of how the game was played in the various eras of the nineteenth century. The vintage base ball community can embrace re-creation of all forms of base ball as it was played in earlier times, supporting local choice in the manner the rules and practices are interpreted, and encouraging those forms of the game that will gain wide appeal and broad participation.

Customs

In addition to rules, rule interpretations, and practices, vintage base ball clubs also have a number of customs that are employed to govern the conduct of the game and enhance the spectator experience. Some of these local customs are unique to one program, and some (perhaps after beginning with one club) have spread widely. They sometimes have their genesis in a kernel of research or an anecdote regarding the early game, and some may have been created based on best guesses and suppositions of what might have occurred at a nineteenth-century game. Since vintage base ball has been played for about thirty years, and since some of the museum professionals and volunteer players who founded early programs are no longer involved in the sport, the origins and provenance of some of these customs have been lost. Do they have some basis in fact and should they be kept? Or are they fictional and, based on more recent research and the quest for historical authenticity, might they best be discontinued?

One example of a custom would be the colorful and interesting way most games are begun with the two clubs standing along the base lines to be introduced to the spectators. We know from newspaper accounts that 1860s games were marked by a "closing ceremony" in which the captains made polite speeches congratulating each other on a fine match and the clubs exchanged three cheers. We know that at the beginning of the match the umpire called the captains together to flip a coin (similar to the beginning of a modern football game), and the winning captain had the choice of batting first or taking the field. We know from the often-published 1858 photograph taken at a match between the Knickerbockers and Excelsiors that most clubs were on friendly terms and would have been happy to stand together (in this case to have their picture taken) while the spectators looked on.

Based on what we know, it seems reasonable to adopt the custom of having a brief ceremony at the beginning of the match in which the two teams line up on the base lines facing the crowd (so the spectators can get a good look at their uniforms and take photos) while the umpire provides a description of what is about to happen, makes appropriate introductions, and conducts the coin toss at home plate with the captains. This custom fits well with the educational goals of many teams and museums as it provides an opportunity for the umpire to welcome the spectators, announce the teams playing and where they are from, and inform the crowd about what rules are being used and what era is being portrayed. If the umpire is proficient in period language, all the better, as this will help the audience feel they have traveled back into another era. This opening ceremony sets the stage for the game, enables everyone to know what is taking place, and gets the audience thinking about going back in time to the period being presented. While not addressed in the official rules of the day, it represents the way things could have been done, is certainly in keeping with the norms of the time, and is a valuable custom worth continuing.

The program at Greenfield Village at the Henry Ford Museum in Dearborn, Michigan, observes a quaint local custom of stopping the game briefly each time the old-fashioned train pulled by a steam engine passes by the outfield, which happens once or twice during a typical match. Players and spectators are encouraged to cheer the train and wave to the passengers. This ritual has considerable value in that it causes everyone to think back to the time when the railroad was seen as the great symbol of the latest advances in technology, economic and social progress, and the march of civilization. Whether or not a town was on a railroad line could mean the difference between economic prosperity or decline. This custom of stopping to watch the train go by also encourages spectators to take a ride during their visit. The pause may also be based on safety considerations since it ensures that no one will hit a ball onto the tracks at that moment. Regardless of whether games were stopped in the 1860s to greet a passing train, this superb local custom observed by the program at Greenfield Village adds to everyone's enjoyment of the game, provides a quick lesson in nineteenth-century history, and is recommended as a model of creativity and interpretation for other programs.

This history lesson involving the railroad is further enhanced when the vintage club from Canal Fulton, Ohio, is visiting Greenfield Village. Canal Fulton in northeast Ohio is located at one of the locks of the old Ohio and Erie Canal. When the locomotive approaches the Greenfield Village field, the players from Canal Fulton, instead of saluting the train, make it a point to turn their backs on the railroad tracks while their team captain, Ed Shuman (who also served for many years as the captain of the canal boat that travels a restored stretch of the old canal back home), implores the spectators to ignore the noisy and dirty "iron beast" passing the ball field and to continue to patronize canal boats for their shipping needs and personal travel. This humorous interaction with the crowd reminds the audience of the changes brought about by the coming of the railroad and the social and economic significance of trains replacing canal boats as the primary method of transporting goods. The spectators may have come to watch a base ball game but receive the bonus of an entertaining history lesson during the brief break in the action on the diamond.

Such variables as differences in rule interpretations, safety considerations, local customs, and the mission of the sponsoring institution lead to vintage base ball being played differently in different settings. This reflects the authentic lack of consistency in how the game has been played, past and present.

The Tally Bell

The Muffins and some other vintage programs follow the custom of having each player who scores a run visit the scorer's table after crossing the plate (similar to a basketball player making a stop at the scorer's table to announce he is entering the game). The usual protocol is for the player to state, "Tally my run, please" or a similar phrase. The scorer then acknowledges that his run has been properly recorded on the score sheet and invites the player to ring the tally bell located at the scorer's table. In training programs, it has been explained that ringing the tally bell at the scorer's table served several purposes. One, it made sure everyone was in agreement that the run counted, which was not always clear if there had been a close play at the plate. Two, it provided clarification as to whether the run counted if a runner crossed the plate at about the same time another runner was tagged for the third out. Three, it helped the scorekeeper keep track of the runs in the high-scoring games typical of the period. And four, it let the spectators know when each run had been scored so that they could follow the progress of the game.

The custom of ringing the tally bell after each run scored originated from a presentation by Joe Santry, the official team historian of the Columbus Clippers (the city's Triple-A club of the International League), at a Muffin training program in 1990. In his presentation, Santry described conversations with John Daley (1887–1988), a recently deceased former professional player from Mansfield, Ohio, in which Daley told Santry an interesting story regarding the custom of players approaching the scorer's table and ringing the tally bell upon scoring a run.

Daley related that as a young man (probably in the decade of the teens or twenties), he had an off-season job working for retired player Cal McVey, who owned a tavern. McVey was an outfielder on the legendary 1869 Cincinnati Red Stockings and had a long playing career in the National Association of Professional Base Ball Players and the National League. One night when young Daley was cleaning up at the tavern after closing time, George Wright, McVey's teammate in Cincinnati and Boston, came to the door. The two former players, then in their sixties, sat down together and had a long conversation with Daley as an attentive listener. In reminiscing about their playing days in the 1860s and 1870s, Daley reported they talked about the custom of reporting to the scorer's table and ringing a bell each time they scored a run.

On the basis of Santry's presentation, the Muffins, in an effort to authentically re-create base ball as it was played in its formative years, adopted the policy of having the player who scored a run stop at the scorer's table to confirm the run and ring the bell. As

Visiting the scorer's table and ringing the tally bell when scoring a run is a custom adopted by the Ohio Village Muffins. (Left to right) Frank Thompson, Jim Kimnach, Mark Large (seated), Dale Brandon, Nick Herold (courtesy Joel Moore).

the Muffins helped many new vintage clubs get started over the years, the story was passed on and the custom of visiting the scorer's table and ringing the tally bell spread in the vintage base ball community.

In recent years, controversy regarding the authenticity of the tally bell has emerged. Vintage players in some programs have questioned the practice of a player going the scorer's table to ring the tally bell. They point out that they have found no references to this procedure in the rules of the 1860s or other sources and have expressed doubts that it was part of the game in the 1860s.

The Muffins and other clubs that have used the tally bell for years were surprised to learn that other programs were not finding evidence that a tally bell was commonly used in 1860-era games. While ringing a bell is not mentioned, the words to the 1877 song "Tally One for Me" do seem to be in keeping with the custom of visiting the scorer's table after scoring to request that the run be properly recorded:

> I always make a clean base hit,
> And go around you see,
> And that's the reason why I say
> Just tally one for me, Oh!

This rhyme could be interpreted as a reference to a player, having circled the bases, visiting the scorer's table and asking the scorer to tally his run. An illustration of an 1866 match between the Athletic Club of Philadelphia and the Atlantic Club of Brooklyn depicts two players at the scorer's table, with the pose of one player (hand on table, apparently addressing the scorer) consistent with visiting the scorer's table and requesting to have his run recorded. As a practical matter, it is very helpful to the scorer at a vintage match (especially in a high-scoring game) if each player who crosses the plate visits the table to confirm his run.

If clubs feel uncomfortable about using the bell, they are welcome not to observe the custom. If clubs prefer to use the bell, they are also welcome to continue to do so. These clubs that use the tally bell do have an anecdotal basis for doing so — Santry's report of Daley's recollection of the Wright-McVey meeting in which they talked about the custom. Perhaps further research will clear up this interesting matter. Clubs using the bell should be careful not refer to visiting the scorer's table and ringing the bell as being part of the official rules of the game. They also should probably not go so far as to say that the player's run does not count if he fails to follow the procedure. If a visit to the scorer's table and ringing the tally bell is used by a club, it should be presented as a custom, not as a rule.

"Real" Baseball

Occasionally, a spectator at a vintage match will ask a question or make a comment comparing a vintage base ball match with "real" baseball, referring to the modern major league game. Participants in the vintage game have fun with such a remark, good-naturedly pointing out that since vintage base ball is based on the original rules and represents the game "as it was meant to be played," shouldn't it be thought of as "real" baseball? The implication is that the modern game may be an aberrant version of the early game, and perhaps the vintage game they are watching should be thought of as the genuine article. Such a light-hearted exchange capitalizes on a teachable moment by encouraging curiosity, thought, and discourse about the game's origins and history. Questions are asked and answers are given about baseball's beginnings, the stages through which it has passed in its development, and the variations it has taken in different times and places on its way to arriving at its present state.

One point emerging from such discussions is that one of baseball's strengths through the decades is that it has been an incredibly adaptable, versatile game that can take many forms to suit all kinds of environments and skill levels. Each season, tens of thousands of players take the field to play various kinds of baseball. In addition to playing catch and Wiffle ball in the backyard or a pick-up game at the school yard, the more organized forms of the game include T-ball, coach pitch, and machine pitch leagues for young players; youth leagues organized by age groups, slow-pitch and fast-pitch softball for youngsters and adults; baseball and softball leagues for middle school and high school students; summer leagues for secondary school players; recreational/intramural and varsity college teams; wooden-bat college summer leagues; company teams and industrial leagues; professional minor leagues (those which are an official part of organized baseball and the independent leagues); and, of course, the major leagues.

Within these many variations of baseball and softball, there are even more differences. Some leagues allow sliding and stealing bases, some do not. To keep the game moving, some leagues start the count at one ball and one strike, thus requiring only two more strikes for a strikeout and three more balls for a walk. Some speed up the process even further by allowing each batter only one pitch, so that the result is always a strikeout, a walk, or a ball that is hit and put in play. Some allow free substitution; others specify that, once removed, a player can not return to the game. Instead of only one first-base bag, some leagues have two adjoining bases — one for the first baseman's foot to touch and one for the runner coming down the line. Some leagues allow pinch-runners for catchers. Many allow designated hitters for pitchers. Some leagues specify that a game be composed of nine innings, but some specify seven or six, and sometimes the game has a time limit. Factor in all the variations and special rules based on gender differences, age groups, adaptations for various disabilities (there is a "beep ball" version of baseball played and enjoyed by the visually impaired) and the vagaries of local customs (the 16" softball identified with Chicago comes quickly to mind) and it is apparent that there are many forms of baseball being played today, each as "real" as the next. As is the case in the twenty-first century, base ball was undoubtedly played in different ways in the nineteenth century.

Historical accuracy and authenticity are important factors in vintage base ball's growth and appeal. Maintaining high standards in nineteenth-century uniforms, equipment, and gentlemanly behavior are the building blocks of a successful program. Great thought and care must also be given to interpreting the rules and practices so that the vintage game remains playable, safe, and enjoyable for participants and spectators.

Vintage base ball is an increasingly popular form of baseball, one that has grown substantially in recent years, attracting the interest and energies of dozens of teams and hundreds of participants. The growth of vintage base ball is the product of its singular ability to combine the old-fashioned fun of playing the game, the delivery of an engaging and colorful lesson in American history, and the presentation of an outdoor summer theatre performance. It is this unique character and appeal that has enabled vintage base ball to grow, expanding across the continent and gaining an increasing number of adherents every summer.

Oh, the Places You Will Go

The rewards are many for establishing a vintage base ball program that strikes a good balance in historical authenticity and reasonable accommodations that make the game enjoyable to play and watch. Among these rewards are invitations and opportunities to play vintage games at interesting and memorable locations. While every team undoubtedly has stories to tell of great road trips, sharing a few highlights from the travels of the Ohio Village Muffins should provide examples of the kinds of opportunities that can arise.

As mentioned in the Introduction, shortly after this author discovered vintage base ball in 1991, the opportunity for an unforgettable experience occurred when the Muffins traveled to Cooperstown, New York, for two matches with the Leatherstocking Base Ball Club. The first game was played by 1860 New York Rules on historic Doubleday Field, where the Muffins had the chance to sit in the same dugout and play on the same field as the countless major league luminaries who have appeared there in exhibition games over the years. The following day at the Farmers' Museum, we learned about the Massachusetts Game during a match played by those rules ("plugging" the runner with the ball, stakes for bases, and a rectangular field). The matches were umpired by the knowledgeable Tom Heitz, then head of the library at the Baseball Hall of Fame, who provided informative comments on the history of base ball throughout the games. The weekend in Cooperstown also gave the Muffin traveling party the opportunity to spend considerable time learning more about the history of the game (especially its nineteenth-century origins) at the National Baseball Hall of Fame and Museum.

One highlight of the following year was an invitation to be part of a special event in the Cincinnati suburb of Blue Ash, where the scoreboard, ticket booths, and other remnants of Crosley Field have been preserved at a ballpark built in the same dimensions as old Crosley, the home of the Reds from 1912 until 1970, when Riverfront Stadium opened. The first game of the day's double-header was an 1860 match involving the Muffins and the Sharon Woods Shamrocks. The vintage teams provided a well-played demonstration game of early base ball for an appreciative and knowledgeable crowd of several thousand fans on hand for the second contest, an "old-timers" game between former major leaguers representing the 1961 World Series opponents, the Reds and Yankees, with a number of former big leaguers from other teams filling out the rosters. In addition to playing before a large crowd, the vintage players had the opportunity between games to meet and mingle with the former major league players (who asked many questions during these conversations about our uniforms, equipment, and the practice of playing barehanded).

"Is this heaven? No, it's Iowa." That familiar exchange from the movie *Field of Dreams* came to life the following year when the Muffins were invited to play at a community festival in Winona, Minnesota. In planning the route the team bus would take, it was noticed that we could pass within a short distance of Dyersville, Iowa, site of the famous baseball diamond carved out of the cornfield where *Field of Dreams* was filmed. When the bus pulled into the parking lot, the setting — the farm house, the corn field, and the ball field — looked as it had in the movie. The only exceptions were souvenir stands on each side of the field, maintained by the two landowners (their property line ran through the middle of the field) to raise the necessary funds to keep the ball diamond intact rather than returning the plot to agricultural purposes. Since visitors were welcome to stop and play ball on the field, and since our traveling party included exactly eighteen Muffin players plus an umpire and a scorer, we quickly changed into our nineteenth-century attire.

Our first order of business was to disappear into the cornfield that ringed the outfield, and then slowly reappear as family members (and other travelers who happened to stop by the farm to see the movie set on that autumn afternoon) took numerous photographs of players from another time emerging from the cornstalks. We then divided into two nines and enjoyed the experience of playing a full nine-inning game. During the game, we were joined by a player from another era, a ghostly member of "Shoeless" Joe Jackson's 1919 Chicago White Sox. As we later learned, the unexpected visitor was a neighbor, a former college player who was one of the extras in the movie. Seeing the game in progress, he had put on his 1919 uniform and surprised everyone by suddenly walking out of the corn stalks in left field. This apparition joined the game, played several innings with the Muffins, and chatted with the players and spectators who had gathered for the impromptu 1860s match. As the ninth inning began, he announced that it was time for him to depart and jogged back to left field. As he reached the edge of the cornfield, he unexpectedly turned to the crowd, waved his cap, and shouted, "Is this heaven?" Players and fans responded on cue, "No, it's Iowa," as he disappeared into the corn.

As mentioned in Chapter 7, the Muffins were part of the festivities associated with the historic grand opening of Cleveland's Jacobs Field in 1994. This opportunity came as the result of an exciting invitation from Bo Burr, the captain of the Forest City Club, based in the Cleveland suburb of Chagrin Falls, Ohio. The Muffins were informed during the winter that arrangements had been made for a vintage game to be part of the Opening Day ceremonies to celebrate the first game ever played at the new home of the Cleveland Indians. The Forest Citys asked the Muffins to partner with them in presenting a two-inning demonstration match prior to the major league game between the Indians and the Seattle Mariners. As the capacity crowd arrived for the festivities, the two vintage clubs took the field and presented an exhibition of how base ball was played in its early days. Following the vintage game, which was held in center field to point out that an 1860 game would have been played

After entering Jacobs Field from out of the past, walking through several rows of corn, the Ohio Village Muffins and the Forest City Base Ball Club (Chagrin Falls, Ohio) played a two-inning demonstration match as part of the grand opening of the new major league ballpark in Cleveland in 1994.

on a grass field (and to allow the grounds crew to prepare the infield for the major league game), we enjoyed the rest of the Opening Day activities, which included ceremonial first pitches by the governor of Ohio, the president of the United States, and legendary Cleveland Indian Hall-of-Famer Bob Feller (who received the loudest ovation of the three). It was a memorable experience to be part of the official program of activities of the day and to witness the historic first game in the new park.

The following year a major "road trip" was made by air. The Muffins had received an invitation from the Colorado Base Ball Association to come to Denver for a tournament, but the cost of such a long trip presented a substantial obstacle. Fortunately, one of the Muffins who is an experienced and frequent business traveler figured out a way to get the ball club from Ohio to Colorado at a very affordable price. He pieced together an itinerary that had the team flying on one airline that had a special low fare from Columbus to Kansas City, then switching to another airline that was offering a bargain fare from Kansas City to Denver. The Muffins enjoyed a weekend of enjoyable vintage games with a half-dozen Denver-area teams that we, of course, rarely have the chance to play. The trip also included attending a major league game in our nineteenth-century uniforms at Coors Field to celebrate "Vintage Base Ball Night," with representatives from the tournament clubs introduced on the field.

All opportunities to participate in special events such as these are memorable, causing veteran Muffin players to reflect after each one that the experience will be hard to match. But an opportunity always seems to come up for yet another one-of-a-kind vintage base ball experience. The year after the trip west to Denver, an invitation arrived to travel east to Hoboken, New Jersey. As mentioned earlier, the occasion was a match with a New York-area club to be played on June 19, 1996, as part of a local celebration marking the 150th anniversary of the first game ever played by two clubs according to the New York Rules. A steady rain fell all day and prospects for playing the game seemed slim. However, the rain subsided in time for the team and costumed interpreters to march in a grand parade down the main street of Hoboken, followed by the vintage game at a local park very close to the actual site at the Elysian Fields where the original game was played. The crowd of several thousand spectators on hand for the game that evening included Alexander J. Cartwright IV, the great-great-grandson of Alexander J. Cartwright, Jr., who is often cited as the principal author of the Knickerbocker Rules of 1845. The event planners and the officials of the City of Hoboken, understandably interested in promoting its reputation as the birthplace of baseball, staged a wonderful event, and being part of this sesquicentennial celebration of the legendary 1846 game will always be remembered by the Muffin traveling party.

One of the most unforgettable experiences of all occurred in 2007 in Salisbury, North Carolina, the location of a major Confederate prison camp during the Civil War. The often-published image *Union Prisoners at Salisbury, N.C.* by Otto Boetticher is familiar to baseball historians and the vintage base ball community. The painting by Captain Boetticher is based on his observations of the daily base ball games at the prison and shows the captured Northern soldiers playing base ball at the prison camp in 1862. Like most of the prisoners at Salisbury during the early years of the war, Captain Boetticher, a professional artist, was exchanged and returned home to his New York studio where he did the painting, which was published in 1863.

Those keenly aware of the community's history as both the site of an important prison camp during the war and the setting for the well-known nineteenth-century base ball painting belong to a group known as the Salisbury Confederate Prison Association, dedicated to "preserving the history of the prison and those who were there." In the 1990s, community leaders active in the SCPA and the local chapter of the United Daughters of the Confederacy began organizing an annual symposium, a venue for notable speakers and scholarly papers on Civil War prison camps and related topics. In making plans for the tenth anniversary of the symposium in April 2007, SCPA and UDC leaders Ed and Sue Curtis and their colleagues explored the idea of presenting a game of base ball as it would have been played at the time Boetticher was at the prison as a special event for symposium attendees. The Curtises contacted Eric Laudenbacher, who they knew was conducting town ball demonstrations at the Duke Homestead in Durham. Laudenbacher, a former Muffin player who had relocated to North Carolina, was in the process of forming a vintage team in Greensboro, but since his team was not ready for such an important undertaking, suggested inviting the Ohio Village Muffins to come to Salisbury to present the 1860s-style game.

The invitation was extended and accepted by the Muffins, who began planning for the trip to North Carolina for the opening game of the 2007 season. As the Muffins researched the history of the prison camp and the painting, the idea emerged of playing the game in the clothing depicted in the painting rather than base ball uniforms. Over the winter, each Muffin who committed to making the trip (400 miles one-way from Columbus to Salisbury) chose a character in the painting that he would represent and put together an outfit (usually a combination of military uniform parts and civilian clothes) worn by that person. Each Muffin practiced assuming the pose of his character in the painting. The Salisbury organizers determined that the location of the original game was on a site that was currently a vacant lot, and plans were made to hold the 2007 event on the same piece of ground as the 1862 game.

Top: The Confederate prison at Salisbury, N.C. was the setting for the notable painting by Otto Boetticher of Union prisoners playing base ball in 1862. *Bottom:* In 2007, Muffin program members prepare to take their positions as they re-create the prison scene for an appreciative audience.

On game day under cloudy April skies, the Muffins arrived at the field and, each dressed exactly like his counterpart in the painting, took their positions on the ball field. A large crowd composed of symposium attendees and Salisbury residents was on hand to witness this re-creation of the 1862 game. A local professional photographer, Sean Meyers, was engaged to take a high-quality photo of the living history tableaux. Planning ahead, he

At the 1998 SABR Convention in San Francisco, a vintage match was held in Candlestick Park prior to the Giants' game. Players from many vintage clubs around the country participated in the match.

brought a ladder in order to take his photo from the same perspective used by Boetticher when he did the painting. At the appropriate signal, everyone struck and held their poses and the professional photo was taken (along with many pictures by symposium participants and local residents who brought their children and their cameras to the event). After the photo opportunity, the Muffins (augmented by Laudenbacher, a few of his Greensboro players, and another former Muffin who drove up from his home in Atlanta to be part of the game) proceeded to play a game under the rules that would have been used by the Union prisoners in the 1862 game. Muffin interpreters (including a number of ladies in period dress) mingled with the crowd before and during the game to pass out a special brochure about what was happening on the field. Although rain came and the game had to be called after five or six innings, the day was a great success. After months of planning and preparation, the Boetticher painting had come to life on its original site.

The photographs taken by Meyers were excellent and the local media coverage of the event was extensive. When the Muffins returned to Columbus, graphic artist Lee Oldfield was engaged to create a composite image of the event, merging the 2007 Meyers photograph with the 1863 Boetticher painting so that each Muffin was shown standing beside the "ghost" of the Union soldier he was portraying in the game. Each person who made the trip and appeared on the field that day received a copy of the composite as a keepsake of this event.

As can be gathered from the list provided in Chapter 7 of some of the places the Muffins have visited over the past twenty years, there is an interesting trip or a memorable game or two just about every season. Members of the Muffins who have been involved with the program since the 1990s have had opportunities to travel from New York to California and from Minnesota to Florida to play vintage base ball. These include matches on the Muffins'

The Ohio Village Muffins represented the Ohio Historical Society at a State of Ohio booth at the MLB 2006 All-Star Game FanFest in Pittsburgh. Designed to promote Ohio travel and tourism, the exhibit featured Ohio's major and minor league teams and the history of the game as represented by its colorful vintage teams. (Left to right) Dennis Thompson, Tracy Martin, Jim Tootle.

extensive schedule and vintage games that are often part of the annual meetings of the Vintage Base Ball Association (VBBA) and the Society for American Base Ball Research (SABR). When asked about their vintage base ball experiences, Muffins tell of the fun playing in four major league ballparks — Candlestick Park in San Francisco, Three Rivers in Pittsburgh, Riverfront in Cincinnati, and Jacobs Field [now Progressive Field] in Cleveland — and the chance to play before substantial crowds in minor league parks, such as Cooper Stadium and Huntington Park in Columbus, Ned Skelton Field in Toledo, The Diamond in Richmond, Virginia, Scottsdale Stadium in Arizona (spring training home of the Giants), and Roger Dean Stadium in Jupiter, Florida (spring training home of the Cardinals, Expos, and Marlins).

Many of these wonderful opportunities have come as a surprise, and it is difficult to predict where and when the next one will come along. But they are not random happenings. The reader will note that the word "invitation" appeared many times in the preceding paragraphs describing the memorable games. A vintage program should think about what it needs to do to create and build a ball club that will be invited to play on special occasions at special venues. Invitations come as a result of a vintage club's positive reputation as a program that maintains a high level of historical accuracy in uniforms and equipment, interacts effectively with spectators, and approaches its games in a congenial, friendly manner that never allows competitiveness to escalate into combativeness. The key to success is establishing a balance between authenticity and practical accommodations that make the game safe, enjoyable, and educational for participants and spectators.

A vintage club needs to build a reputation for having the personnel to fulfill its obligations when invited — at least nine players (preferably ten or eleven in case of a minor injury), an umpire, a scorer, and an interpreter or two to interact with the spectators. The club extending the invitation needs to know that the invited club will come through and provide a good performance on that special day. Equally important is having all players in full authentic uniforms and using authentic period equipment. Clubs with players who show up without a hat or belt or with white swooshes on their shoes are detracting from the overall presentation of the nineteenth-century game and are unlikely to receive invitations. Club members need to have enough base ball playing ability to hold the match together, but playing ability is not at the top of the list of important qualities for a successful vintage program. Every club would rather win than lose, everyone should play to win with enthusiasm throughout the game, and a club should try its best to give a good account of itself when it takes the field. But the club that has its priorities in order — authenticity, education, interacting with the crowd, sportsmanship, playing nine innings in less than 90 minutes — is the club that will receive the invitations to play in special games and events.

Final scores of games are quickly forgotten. Invitations to play at a major league park, on the diamond where *Field of Dreams* was filmed, in Hoboken near the site of the Elysian Fields on the sesquicentennial an 1846 Knickerbocker game, or at the original site of the 1862 Civil War prison camp game depicted in *Union Prisoners at Salisbury, N.C.* create memories that will last forever. Vintage programs are encouraged to think broadly and creatively and to go beyond the familiar modern model of playing the same rival teams several times a season for a league or tournament championship. Other types of vintage games provide variety and inspiration for team members and have great educational value for both participants and spectators.

24

Vintage Base Ball's Relevance on the Contemporary Sports Landscape

Vintage base ball is a colorful living history activity that furthers the educational goals of any museum or historical organization. But it is more than a quaint re-creation of the way base ball was played in its early days. Vintage base ball provides a number of meaningful benefits for the participants. It also has the potential to make genuine contributions to society in such critical areas as fitness, ethical behavior, civility, education, and sportsmanship.

Exercise and Fitness

One benefit for the vintage ballplayer is exercise. Exercise was a goal of base ball from the beginning. First on the list of the Knickerbocker Rules of 1845 is the statement: "Members must strictly observe the time agreed upon for exercise, and be punctual in their attendance." The second rule, begins "When assembled for exercise, the President, or in his absence, the Vice-President, shall appoint an Umpire...." Exercise was clearly on the minds of the game's founding fathers. Modern baseball is built around the duel between the batter and the pitcher. Many pitches result in called balls and strikes, fewer balls are hit to the fielders, and there is a slower pace to the game. Vintage base ball is a contest between the batter and the fielders. Therefore, especially if played according to the slow-pitch practices that were part of the game's early years, vintage base ball provides players with a considerable amount of exercise during a game.

If the pitcher is consistently getting the ball over the plate, there is a lot of running (and very little standing around) for both offensive and defensive players. The 1860 Rules specify that "the bases must be four in number, placed ... upon the four corners of a square, whose sides are respectively thirty yards." Therefore, to score a run, a player will need to run, often at his top speed, a total of 120 yards (the length of a football field, including both end zones). Since many strikers hit the first or second pitch, base runners have little time to rest at one base before the next striker hits the ball, requiring the runners to continue to advance around the bases in rapid fashion. Games are often high-scoring affairs, with both teams reaching double figures. This means that every player often gets to bat six or seven times and will be doing a lot of base running. In the field, players get a corresponding amount of exercise trying to make plays on balls hit to all parts of the infield and outfield.

With such vigorous activity in the field, vintage base ball players are motivated to get

Playing vintage base ball is an activity that requires considerable running throughout the game. Base runners and fielders get a lot of physical exercise over the course of nine innings (courtesy Joel Moore).

involved in exercise programs to stay in shape in the offseason. Many make an effort to develop healthy eating habits and engage in exercise that can include a combination of running, power-walking, stretching, working out on a variety of exercise machines, and "cross-training" activities, such as swimming or biking. Because of the rapid pace of the games and the need to run ninety-foot base paths, vintage base ball encourages players to adopt a year-round healthy lifestyle.

A Family Activity with Family Involvement

Attending a vintage base ball game is fun for people of all ages and is an activity that families can share. A typical audience is composed of pre-schoolers to the most senior of senior citizens. Vintage base ball is an especially good experience for parents with children who are looking for a wholesome, family-friendly activity that has educational value.

Vintage players also enjoy and appreciate the family atmosphere that characterizes a vintage base ball club. Shortly after playing in his first Ohio Cup Vintage Base Ball Festival in September 2008, Jim Johnson (whose wife and three children usually accompany him to the matches, both home and away) conveyed the following thoughts in an email to his teammates as his first season drew to a close: "As a 'rookie,' I had a great time playing, setting up [the field], and [at the post-game potluck] watching the kids square dance (for those that did not attend, you missed a good time) and just enjoyed a family atmosphere. I think my favorite part of being part of this family (the Muffins) is that it feels like a 2nd

At a vintage game, youngsters see many examples of good sportsmanship and gentlemanly behavior by well-mannered clubs such as the Rochester (Michigan) Grangers. Players are glad to answer questions and encourage the young base ball players.

family, not just a baseball team that plays together. My kids really have fun and they talk about the Muffins and when the next time is we get to get together again."

Another member of the vintage base ball community, a player on the Bay City (Michigan) Club, wrote a thoughtful post on the VBBA listserv in November 2008 expressing how he felt about his vintage base ball experience: "Although not the most important thing in my life, vintage base ball has become a large piece of happiness for me and my family, and one of the things I had to be thankful for. Not just the game itself but more the memories and friendships that have been brought about because of my involvement in it."

After returning from a barnstorming weekend through Indiana in August 2009 that included four games in three cities from Friday evening through Sunday afternoon, Muffin player Curt Green recounted highlights of the busy trip in an email to all members of the program. "The three days were fun-filled and the players and families we met were great people." On the family atmosphere present in the traveling party, he remarked how two families with school-age children "brought a crowd with them and their youngsters added to our trip." Noting how much the children enjoyed wearing period clothing at the games, he included a special acknowledgement to Julie Large, wife of Muffin scorekeeper Mark Large, "who made [1860-style] dresses for the little ladies who came with us."

Education

Vintage base ball is a superb history-based educational activity that enables participants and spectators to better understand the development of the national pastime and nineteenth-century American culture. Students from the elementary grades through college with a paper to write for a history or social studies class often attend a vintage base ball game where they can observe a nineteenth-century match. Vintage base ball can be an effective means of helping young students make connections between what they are seeing on the playing field and what they have been learning in the classroom and from their textbooks.

As representatives of the Ohio Historical Society, members of the Muffins have enjoyed making a number of school visits over the years. The typical program involves a group of three or four uniformed players and an umpire in period dress working with a group of students in the fifth, sixth, or seventh grade outdoors on the school grounds. In a brief presentation (ten minutes or so) the students, most of whom have some familiarity with baseball or softball, are acquainted with the playing rules and the sportsmanlike behavioral norms of the 1860s. The youngsters (boys and girls together) are then divided into two sides for a game. Equipment requirements are minimal; no gloves are used and all that is needed is one wooden bat and one ball (a very soft one for these young novice players is best, of course). Any number can play, with extra fielders and everyone in the batting order. It is a good idea for one of the vintage players to do the pitching since children of that age typically have considerable difficulty getting the ball over the plate. The vintage players who have conducted these school visits often comment on how quickly the students adopt the "old-fashioned" spirit of good manners as they play the game, and, having been briefed on the importance of sportsmanship, treat each other with an unusual degree of courtesy while they have fun batting, running, catching, and throwing.

An outdoor activity of this type can be an enjoyable accompaniment to studying the Civil War era in the classroom. In addition to the history lesson, teachers always appreciate the message of fair play and respect for others that goes along with the spirited base ball game. Vintage base ball has a great deal of untapped potential as a complementary physical education activity for students in those grades that are covering nineteenth-century American history. Educational efforts are not limited to school-age children. Those active in vintage base ball are often invited to give presentations on the history of the game for adult audiences at library programs and meetings of civic groups.

Personal Growth and Changes in Attitudes

Putting on a vintage uniform and presenting the national pastime as it was played in the more gentlemanly days of the mid-nineteenth century seem to produce positive changes in the behavior of the players that transcend the time they spend on the ball diamond. The front-page article on the Ohio Village Muffins and vintage base ball in the September 10, 1992, edition of *The Wall Street Journal* noted the changes that can result from participation:

Craig Andersen, a second-generation Muffin and a 27-year-old assistant paint store manager, is postponing his honeymoon in Hawaii by a day so that he can play in the season finale Sept. 20. His fiancée, Melinda Loomis, says she doesn't mind too much because the game has made Craig a nicer person. "When he used to play on softball teams, he used to scream and holler, but he can't use those words in the Muffins' games," she says. "It's almost as if he changes instantly," she says, when he dons his long-sleeved white cotton shirt with a Gothic M on the chest, scarlet scarf and gray twill pants [p. A5].

To update this 1992 *WSJ* article, Craig and Melinda Andersen are the parents of two daughters who are actively involved in team sports. Craig continues to play on the Muffins and also invests many hours coaching his daughters' teams, sharing not only his considerable knowledge of batting and fielding techniques, but also conveying to the youngsters the lessons of sportsmanship that are part of his own makeup as a veteran vintage base ball player.

Vintage base ball continues to have a positive impact on players. At the conclusion of the 2008 season, a number of Muffin players became engaged in an ad hoc e-mail discussion in which they offered their thoughts on their participation in the program. One very valuable member of the club on and off the field commented that after playing modern baseball and softball throughout his life, he has "loved every moment" of his involvement in vintage base ball. Reflecting on his earlier baseball and softball days, he observed that "for many years I got so involved in the game" that it did not always bring out the best in him and perhaps "made me someone that many people did not want to be around." Vintage base ball, however, represented a different approach to playing on a team. "When I joined the Muffin program my thought process changed. I play the game because I just like playing. I wish I had done it like this for my whole life. I took the game way too serious and, although I played aggressive, I could have just played and let the game progress."

Ethics and Values

Vintage base ball can be a vehicle for addressing a number of contemporary societal issues, making a positive contribution and reversing some negative trends. The Josephson Institute's Report Card on American Youth for 2008 reported that a survey of 29,760 high school students "reveals entrenched habits of dishonesty in the workforce of the future." Among the findings reported are these statistics: "30 percent admitted stealing from a store in the past year" and "23 percent said they stole something from a parent or other relative." Further, "More than eight in ten students (83 percent) ... confessed they lied to a parent about some thing significant." In regard to school, "A substantial majority (64 percent) cheated on a test during the past year (38 percent did so two or more times)," and "more than one-third (36 percent) said they used the Internet to plagiarize an assignment."

The article "Bad behavior is cited in youth sports study" in the November 29, 2005, edition of *USA Today* conveyed similarly troubling statistics compiled in a study by researchers at three universities — Missouri–St. Louis, Minnesota, and Notre Dame — that were published in the *Journal of Character Education*. "A study of youth sports found evidence of cheating, taunting, even intentionally trying to hurt an opponent. And the bad behavior wasn't limited to the kids. Some coaches admitted yelling at athletes — even verbally abusing them — and some players said they were struck." The study found that "nearly one in five admitted cheating" and "13 percent had tried to hurt an opponent." Of the 803 athletes ages 9–15 in the study, "31 percent had argued with an official" and "27 percent had acted like 'bad sports.'"

Vintage base ball represents an alternative code of ethical behavior — gaining success through honest effort, preparation, and merit; being respectful toward officials; and placing more importance upon one's long-term reputation than taking shortcuts that might influence something as temporary as the outcome of a ball game. The statistics revealed in the Josephson Institute's Report Card suggest that young people would benefit from being exposed to the values of vintage base ball, which might help them make better decisions when confronted with day-to-day situations, such as whether or not to look on another student's exam sheet or plagiarize a term paper. Similarly, the findings by the university researchers indicate young athletes are frequently not conducting themselves with civility on the playing field and improvement is needed in this area. Witnessing examples of honesty and ethical behavior in a vintage base ball game can be an important experience for the young spectators, and these examples can serve as guideposts for ethical behavior in all their activities.

Promoting Sportsmanship

Closely related to ethics education, sportsmanship is an important contemporary issue at all levels of athletic competition. Players of all ages (and their coaches and spectators) continually are exposed to mixed messages and conflicting schools of thought on the proper way to approach playing a game. On one hand there is the sportsmanlike ideal eloquently stated by Grantland Rice in his poem "Alumnus Football":

> For when the One Great Scorer comes
> To write against your name,
> He marks — not that you won or lost —
> But how you played the game.

On the other hand, there is the familiar slogan variously attributed to football coaches Henry Russell "Red" Sanders of UCLA and Vince Lombardi of the Green Bay Packers: "Winning isn't everything; it's the only thing." Confronted by these two contradictory approaches, a young player of any sport could become understandably confused when weighing the decision of what kind of player he or she aspires to be.

In regard to sportsmanship, the current state of affairs was effectively described in "On or off the field, it's a 'civility war' out there: Good manners left on the sideline as people 'express' themselves" by Sharon Jayson in the November 30, 2004, edition of *USA Today*. The article was written shortly after two highly publicized examples of extraordinarily unsportsmanlike conduct: the notorious NBA game between the Detroit Pistons and Indiana Pacers in which fighting between players escalated into fighting between players and fans in the stands, and a college football melee between players from South Carolina and Clemson. The article is accompanied by a photograph showing state troopers trying to break up the chaotic on-field football fight as a Clemson player delivers a kick to the head of a South Carolina player who is already on the ground. How did things go so wrong at theses two events (and at other games in other sports before and after these two regrettable but hardly unique incidents)?

Jayson points out that professors, psychologists, and manners experts say that these two events "are symptoms of a larger problem that goes beyond sports or athletes' egos." Jayson supports this assessment with quotes from Michigan psychologist and author Carl

Semelroth, who observes, "We for years have been taught that the problem with anger is that people don't express it. Now the problem of anger is that it's expressed too much. We see it everywhere, and we go overboard with sports." According to Semelroth, "Civilization means every urge isn't acted upon."

Jayson cites the work of Professor P. M. Forni, co-founder of the Civility Project (now known as the Civility Initiative) at Johns Hopkins University, which "aims to assess the significance of civility and manners in society." As reported by Jayson, Forni believes "civility is in sharp decline—a danger sign, because research suggests there is a causal connection between incivility and violence." Referencing violence in both school and workplace settings (some of which have resulted in physical confrontations), Forni states: "Teenagers and people in their 20s and 30s have been encouraged to express themselves. They are imbued with a sense of self-esteem. But sometimes we have gone overboard because we have not balanced this enthusiastic embrace of self-esteem education with an education in self-restraint."

Vintage base ball can serve as an effective model for good sportsmanship and self-restraint. A player does not use bad language or throw down his equipment after making an out. Since the 1850s and 1860s were an era of generally good manners and the game was played in a more gentlemanly way, a vintage player conducts himself accordingly. Winning was important then as it is now, but an 1860-era game puts a higher priority on sportsmanship and honorable play. Players do not attempt to take advantage of an opponent or claim any victory that has not been fairly earned. Rather than complain and argue vociferously with an official's call, the culture of vintage base ball calls for a player to accept the decision of the umpire, even when the call goes against his team in a close game. Henry Chadwick's view of the proper player-umpire relationship is presented in his account of a game between the Atlantic Club of Brooklyn and the Eureka Club of Newark that appeared in the *New York Clipper* of September 12, 1863:

> Mr. Culyer ably discharged the duties of Umpire, his decisions in every instance being correct as far as we noticed. We would suggest to the Eurekas that no matter how erroneous they may think any decision of the Umpire to be, they keep their opinion to themselves, and not give their expression in the manner some of them did in the case of the putting out of Pennington at home base.... There is but one rule to abide by in the matter and that rule is, to silently acquiesce in every decision an Umpire may make, be it right or wrong, and a first-class club will in the future not countenance any other line of conduct by its members.

Chadwick's admonition that a player should always "silently acquiesce" to the umpire's call "be it right or wrong" represents quite a departure from the way modern players and managers behave on the field when a call goes against them. It is the norm in the vintage game.

In "Lovers of Honor" in the "Editor's Letter" section of the Fall 2009 issue of *American Heritage*, Edwin S. Grosvenor comments: "We don't hear the word 'honor' used much these days; it may seem a quaint and old-fashioned notion in some circles, gone the way of dueling, cavalry charges, and trench warfare." He mentions the work of James Bowman, who "recently wrote a thoughtful book entitled *Honor: A History*, in which he notes that honor has virtually disappeared 'from the working vocabularies of English and other European languages.' Mr. Bowman laments that we are living in 'a post-honor society,' with no widely accepted notion against which a given person can be measured." Referring to two articles in the magazine that discuss how the honorable actions of Theodore Roosevelt and George Washington had a positive impact on the course of American history, Grosvenor points out that "the term 'honor' has never been easy to define but I think you'll know it when you read about it here in these pages" (p. 4).

Honor is a concept that is very much alive in vintage base ball, and participants and spectators will know it when the see it in a gentlemanly 1860-era match. A runner will act in an honorable way and leave the field immediately if he knows the ball was caught by the baseman an instant before his own foot reached the bag. Similarly, an infielder will immediately inform the umpire that he did not have his foot on the bag on a force play so that the umpire does not erroneously call the runner out. An outfielder will not act as if he caught a ball cleanly on the fly if he knows it touched the ground first, and he will not claim to have caught the ball on the first bound if he knows it hit the ground twice. An honorable player will not try to find loopholes in the wording of the rules that would give him a competitive advantage. Rather than gripe and grumble when things do not break their way, players and spectators applaud a fine catch by a member of the opposing team, even if it snuffs out a rally and prevents their own team from scoring a run. Clubs are cordial and respectful toward each other before, during, and after the game.

This is the kind of environment that museums and historical societies — and the players who represent those institutions — work hard to establish at vintage matches on their home grounds and in their travels. Since this environment is different from what spectators often witness at a professional, college, high school, or even a Little League game, it stimulates thought and discussion among the members of the crowd about the attitudes and behaviors we associate with team sports. Participation in vintage base ball reminds players and spectators of the value of honesty and gentlemanly conduct on the playing field. In contrast to the win-at-all-costs philosophy that is so embedded in the modern game, good sportsmanship is the guiding principle of an 1860 game.

Youth and High School Sports

Regrettably, examples of extremely poor sportsmanship can involve very young players. Even players in youth leagues and on school teams are not exempt from the problems that afflict college, Olympic, and professional sports.

As reported in an Associated Press article appearing on ESPN.com on September 14, 2006, a jury convicted a 29-year-old baseball coach in Uniontown, Pennsylvania, of "corruption of minors and criminal solicitation to commit simple assault." In circumstances that a district attorney called "a serious breach of sportsmanlike conduct," it was charged that the coach (in a league with rules requiring each player to play at least three innings) had "offered to pay one of his T-ball players $25 to hit a 9-year-old autistic teammate with a ball while warming up before a June 2005 playoff game." A subsequent AP article on October 12, 2006, explained, "Prosecutors said the coach wanted the [autistic] 9-year-old out of the game, because he didn't play as well as his teammates." The eight-year-old player who threw the balls that hit his teammate in the groin and the ear testified that he purposely did so on the coach's instructions. The judge, in announcing consecutive six-to-36-month sentences, commented, "These acts are extremely outrageous and extremely reprehensible since the defendant was involved in the coaching of a youth league." The coach was ordered to undergo a mental health examination and to be "barred from coaching any youth league sports while on parole." The article reported that after being sentenced, the coach "told reporters 'I didn't do nothing' as he was led out of the courtroom."

An August 14, 2006, article by Greg Garber on ESPN.com described a coach's decision in a 10-and-under baseball league in Bountiful, Utah, that "sparked an emotional national debate about the importance of winning in youth sports and the lessons we teach our children." In the final inning of a championship game, with two outs and the tying run on third, the coach of one team elected to intentionally walk the best hitter on the opposing team (who had already hit a home run and a triple) in order to bring to the plate "a frail boy whose growth was stunted by a malignant cranial tumor at the age of 4." While "years of chemotherapy and radiation, a steady dose of human growth hormone and a shunt in his brain" prevented him from playing contact sports, he was permitted to play baseball, but "only if he wore a batting helmet in the outfield." There was no storybook ending. "With two strikes, tears already filling his eyes, he swung weakly. His bat hit nothing but air" and the other team won. "But did they really?" asked the reporter who defined the issue at hand. "It was, in baseball's time-honored tradition of strategy, the percentage move. But in a league of 9- and 10-year-olds where everyone gets to bat and there can be only four runs scored per inning, was it right?" The coach who ordered the intentional walk defended his actions by insisting, "It was a baseball move. We played within the rules. We were trying to win."

Parents as well as coaches can be part of the problem. Under the heading "Dad flings son's opponent out of wrestling ring," an AP story from Aurora, Illinois, dated February 15, 2007, reported that, as his son was being pinned, "a father bounded into a youth wrestling match, picked up his son's winning opponent [age 11] and launched him out of the ring, an episode caught on home video." The father in the video, identified as "a part-time wrestling coach," later admitted that he "regrets his behavior and feels embarrassed" and reported he "will no longer be allowed to coach."

An Associated Press story of September 23, 2006, reported, "A 15-year-old high school football player" in Layton, Utah, "faces simple assault charges for putting a thumbtack in his glove before shaking hands and high-fiving players from a rival school" in the post-game handshake line. Several players on the other team "were jabbed with the tack" according to a local police officer who was involved in the case. The offender was "kicked off the team" for his actions and a school district administrator pointed out "there's been a rivalry between the two [schools] for years, but it doesn't justify one student to hurt the other student."

One team running up the score on another has also emerged as a problem in high school sports. "The blowup over blowouts" in the February 4, 2009, issue of *USA Today* described a Virginia girls' basketball game in which Mt. Vernon High School, leading Falls Church by 40 points, continued to press and make "steal after backcourt steal" long after the outcome had been determined. The article cites an even more lopsided girls' game, a 100–0 shutout in Dallas "that resulted in the winning coach's dismissal and placed blowout basketball squarely in the public conversation." Mary Struckhoff, assistant director of the National Federation of State High School Associations, provided results from a recent survey that showed eight states had "mercy rules with varying specifics." Such rules "help to hasten the end of such games," but these are "no substitute for coaches acting responsibly," Struckhoff observed. "You can't legislate ethics."

On the brighter side, "An Elephant Never Forgets Sportsmanship," an April 26, 2006, article by Vincent M. Mallozzi in the *New York Times*, provides encouraging news of the work of Always Play Fair, a public service organization with the goal of reducing the "increasing amount of ill-tempered players and fans." Founder Walter Halas (a St. John's University administrator and grandnephew of football immortal George Halas) states: "What we are trying to do is change the culture, to help children grow up to become more respectful as players and spectators." The organization's strategy is to send an elephant mascot, Packy Playfair, to schools. "We want Packy Playfair to be a spokesman for sportsmanship in much the same way that Smokey the Bear was a spokesman for fire prevention." The photo accompanying the article shows a group of students at a Manhattan public school who made the Packy Pledge: "I agree to follow the rules, always try my best, include everyone, respect my opponent — and have fun."

Another encouraging AP story involving young people, "Students drop differences then ask teams to," appeared on ESPN.com on March 24, 2005. After resolving the negative interaction between Yankee fans and Red Sox fans at their school, but still troubled that "fans and players are getting too worked up about what's just a game," students at the Merriam School in Acton, Massachusetts, wrote a letter to baseball commissioner Bud Selig asking that Red Sox and Yankee players shake hands before their opening game of the coming season. "After children's sports games we shake hands with the team we are playing. If kids show good sportsmanship, then professionals can, too."

The need for more sportsmanship in baseball is not lost on one major leaguer. In the April 9, 2009, edition of *USA Today*, Johnny Damon provided "an interesting explanation as to why he didn't offer up more of an argument after a fan kept him from catching an Orioles home run Monday. 'I don't condone hissy fits,' Damon said. 'I don't want my daughter to see that and think it's OK to do that at home.'"

Damon's thoughtful response about being a good role model resonates with most vintage base ball players. In 1993, NBA player Charles Barkley famously stated in a Nike commercial: "I am not a role model ... parents should be role models." Most vintage players seem to quietly understand that although they do not possess the talent of major leaguers, anyone who is wearing a uniform and is playing before a crowd of spectators has the opportunity to be a role model for the youngsters in the audience. While parents have the ultimate responsibility for developing good qualities in their children, a ballplayer can either make it easier or more difficult for them to do so. The choice is not whether to be a role model or not, but to be a positive one or a poor one. The fact that most vintage players choose the former, genuinely enjoying playing the role of a mid-nineteenth-century gentlemanly player, makes the sport of vintage base ball relevant as a positive influence on young players in the ongoing conversation between those adopting the "winning is everything" attitude and those preferring the "it's how you played the game" approach.

College and Olympic Sports

Over time, intercollegiate sports have been regarded as a bastion of the traditional values of amateur athletics, including good sportsmanship. In more recent years, however, college games have provided a steady stream of examples of poor sportsmanship. Trash talking, taunting opponents, and even fighting on the court and on the field have increasingly become part of college games. One of the most egregious examples was reported in an ESPN.com article of October 15, 2006: "After reviewing a sideline-clearing brawl between players from Miami and Florida International, officials from both schools and their conferences on Sunday announced the suspension of 31 players — 13 from the Hurricanes, and 18 from FIU." The "ugly melee" was characterized as growing out of "heated words being exchanged during — and even before — the game."

The problem is widespread and, it seems, no school is immune. The *USA Today* article of October 20, 2006, "Even in Ivy League, athletes behave badly," pointed out that on the same day as the Miami-FIU brawl, there was a less-violent and less-publicized fight between players from Dartmouth and Holy Cross. Steve Richardson's article "NCAA seeks to curb poor sportsmanship" in the January 12, 2007, issue of *USA Today* recounted two breaches of sportsmanship that occurred during the recently completed bowl season. "Virginia Tech quarterback Marcus Vick was caught on TV stomping on Louisville defensive end Elvis Dumervil's left calf during the Toyota Gator Bowl. There was a fight between LSU and Miami (Fla.) players in the tunnel leading to the dressing rooms after the Chick-fil-A Peach Bowl." Richardson then quotes Fisher DeBerry, Air Force coach and chair of the American College Football Coaches Association ethics committee: "We as coaches have the responsibility to emphasize what is proper behavior, what is proper decorum and realize again we have an expectation by our fans, our students and the institutions we represent and the alumni to conduct ourselves in a very honorable way."

On the heels of these incidents that marred the college football season, the late NCAA president Myles Brand, speaking at the opening of the organization's annual convention in January 2007, declared sportsmanship to be a key issue for the meeting. Commenting on the recent discussions of the Miami-FIU brawl, Brand observed that while the focus had been on "what we are doing to punish the students," it should be on "what we are doing to educate them on sportsmanship." Brand continued, "Their actions were wrong, but we've got to do a better job of educating them on what is expected from them in regard to sportsmanship."

At the opening game of the 2009 football season, an Oregon player, apparently enraged by something said to him by a Boise State player after the game, punched the Boise State player in the jaw, then had to be restrained from going into the stands when he got into an altercation with fans. ESPN.com reported that Oregon coach Chip Kelly commented, "When you go out and get beat in a football game, you go out and shake that guy's hand and you go in the locker room and prepare for your next opponent. That stuff has no place in our program and won't have any place in our program." Grant Teaff, the American Football Coaches Association executive director, said, "This case points out that we still need to have a commitment to sportsmanship and respect."

Problems of this type are not confined to any one sport or gender. Viewers of videos of a collegiate women's soccer game played on November 7, 2009, were stunned to see one of the University of New Mexico players engaging in exceptionally rough play throughout the game, then grabbing the ponytail of a BYU player and throwing her to the ground. Many sportscasters remarked on the fact that this incident occurred in women's intercollegiate soccer.

The motto of the modern Olympic Games comes from the principles articulated by Baron de Coubertin: "The most important thing in the Olympic Games is not to win but to take part, just as the most important thing in life is not the triumph but the struggle. The essential thing is not to have conquered but to have fought well." This lofty statement was forgotten by one Olympian at the Beijing Games in 2008. Wrestler Ara Abrahamian of Sweden won the bronze medal in his event. He remained angry, however, over the assessment of a penalty that he thought had cost him the match against the eventual gold medal winner in the semifinals. During the medal ceremony, he removed the bronze medal from his neck, placed it on the mat, and stalked off. Abrahamian had his medal taken away and was fined and suspended for two years. IOC spokeswoman Giselle Davies said, "It was felt that his behavior on the medal podium and during the medal ceremony was not appropriate. His behavior was not in the Olympic spirit of respect for his fellow athletes. Whatever grievances you may have, this was not the way to go about it." The IOC said Abrahamian violated two rules of the Olympic charter, one which bans any sort of demonstrations and another which demands respect for all Olympic athletes. "The awards ceremony is a highly symbolic ritual, acknowledged as such by all athletes and other participants," the IOC said. "Any disruption by any athlete, in particular a medalist, is in itself an insult to the other athletes and to the Olympic Movement. It is also contrary to the spirit of fair play."

Incidents of poor sportsmanship in college athletics and Olympic competition receive widespread attention in the media, and young people often see these incidents. In keeping with the call from leaders in college athletics for more sportsmanship education, vintage base ball provides examples of fair play and good conduct that can help instill the higher values of sport in young people in their formative years.

Media

The media often sends mixed messages. Poor sportsmanship sometimes seems to be promoted and perpetuated by the media. In an apparent attempt to increase viewership of an upcoming game, television networks, instead of showing highlights of memorable catches or extra-base hits, sometimes run a clip of a brawl between the two teams or a video of a manager ripping a base out of the ground and throwing it into the outfield. When a batter who has hit a home run remains in the batter's box and admires the flight of the ball as it settles into the stands (instead of running as fast as he can toward first base, as every coach he has ever had has told him to do), the camera often remains on him far too long, giving tacit approval to his disrespectful and self-congratulatory conduct that can lead to ill-will between players and teams and set a poor example for young players. When a fan runs onto the playing field during a game to gain attention, network policy is to cut away from this kind of boorish behavior so as not to encourage more of the same. Yet when a football player engages in choreographed stunts in the end zone designed to belittle opponents and call attention to himself after scoring a touchdown, the network often keeps the camera on this unsportsmanlike behavior and even runs it again in promotional ads for future games.

In promoting its fantasy football program for the fall of 2009, the website for CBS Sports made a direct appeal to poor sportsmanship. Instead of encouraging people to register in order to use their knowledge to correctly pick winners in a series of college games, the website urged potential customers to "experience the greatest part of Fantasy Football — trash talking with your buddies!" Players were encouraged to visit the website "and find 3 great ways to stick it to your friends." Participants can "1. Choose your trash talk tool, 2. Razz your buddies with some creative trash talk, 3. Keep the trash talk going by creating a league with your buddies." Another section of the website asks, "Want to humiliate your friends? Pick from our trash talking tools and invite them to play fantasy football." One of the so-called "tools" involves the opportunity to create an electronic cartoon figure by placing a photo of the face of one of "your buddies" on a body dressed in women's clothing, derisively labeled as the "skirt of shame." This invitation to taunt one's competitors both verbally and through visual images hardly encourages the young males in the target audience to adopt sportsmanlike behavior, develop a respectful attitude toward women, or to associate sportsmanship with college football.

Another example of media negativity in regard to good sportsmanship involves coverage of auto racing. In November 2008, NASCAR drivers Carl Edwards and Jimmie Johnson, the two leading contenders for the Sprint Cup Championship, appeared at a news conference in Miami, prior to the final race of the season that would determine the winner. In an ESPN.com article on the event by David Newton, both drivers were described as being polite and respectful to each other as they fielded questions. Instead of finding their mature behavior classy and admirable, Newton was prompted to complain, "Please, somebody, say some thing bad about somebody. Give us some trash talk. Throw a punch. Something. Anything. Please." Disappointed at the gentlemanly conduct of the drivers at the news conference, the reporter described their statements of mutual respect as "way too nice" and "almost nauseating." While Johnson and Edwards were ridiculed, drivers of the past were praised for making "this sport what it is by their dislike for each other on and off the track."

Fortunately, the article also included a thoughtful statement from Johnson that brings balance and wisdom to the discussion and reflects the approach that vintage base ball participants bring to the playing field. "It's good to have people that respect each other and teams that do as well," Johnson said. "We get warped into reality television shows and lose perspective that you need fistfights and all these different types of things. What's wrong with good competition and people that respect each other and teams that respect each other? You'll see it in pro sports, football games or baseball games, where guys are commending the other team on how prepared they are and how good a job they do. It works." Expressing values consistent with those found throughout vintage base ball, Johnson added, "I don't know why we have to be a circus act to make it a good show. Good competition and respect for one another should be plenty."

Driver Edwards was also gracious and mature in his comments. Recalling Johnson's kindness in welcoming Edwards into the NASCAR community when the latter was an unknown rookie, he said of Johnson's place at the top of the standings: "It's neat to see someone like that succeed. To this day when we have a good run, Jimmie is one of the first people to come over and congratulate me, and when he has a good run, as much as it hurts us in the points sometimes or whatever, it's still good to see good people succeed."

As a counterpoint to these examples, the media can also make a conscious effort to promote good sportsmanship. *USA Today* holds an essay contest each March in conjunction with National Sportsmanship Day. Essays "addressing sportsmanship and ethics or reflections on good or poor sportsmanship" are welcomed from elementary, high school, and college students and judged by a panel from the Institute for International Sport at the University of Rhode Island, which administers the project.

Every day, it seems, there are negative headlines in the sports pages and the sports websites announcing a number of unsportsmanlike actions by athletes and coaches. These can include virulent criticism of officials, fines and suspensions for fighting, cursing and obscene gestures directed toward fans, arrogant and disrespectful behavior toward opponents, performance-enhancing drug scandals, and a variety of unsavory and even illegal activities off the field that reflect poorly on the leagues and the sports. But just when it appears that the traditional ideals of sportsmanship may be a thing of the past, other inspirational examples of fair play and ethical behavior emerge.

In October 2008, British triathlete Chrissie Wellington won the women's ironman in Hawaii for the second consecutive year, but only after an exemplary act of sportsmanship by a competitor. An October 13, 2008, article by Howard Swains in *The Guardian* reported that after the 2.4-mile swim, Wellington had a five-minute lead on the field during the 112-mile cycling stage when "a flat tyre allowed the chasing pack to catch up." When Wellington was "unable to re-inflate the tyre with her own air canisters," rival Rebekah Keat of Australia gave her one of her own canisters so that she could make the necessary repairs to get back in the race. After making up the ten minutes spent on fixing the flat, Wellington won the competition. In Steve Wilson's article in the October 14 edition of *The Daily Telegraph*, Wellington expressed her appreciation for Keat's sportsmanship. "I have to say a huge thanks to Rebekah, she's a legend," Wellington said. "To me what she did epitomizes everything that is good about the sport."

This example of good sportsmanship in the ironman competition is similar to an incident that occurred in the 2006 Winter Olympics in Turin, Italy. As reported in "Honorable Move Made in a Snap" by *Washington Post* sports columnist Mike Wise, "Sara Renner was skiing the cross-country race of her life when she looked down at her pole and saw that it had snapped. She flailed and struggled uphill as the field passed her in seconds. And then something happened, maybe the most serendipitous, skin-tingling moment of the 20th Winter Games. Another pole. Out of nowhere. Given to her by a person she would call 'my mystery man.'" It was later revealed that the "mystery man" was Bjornar Hakensmoen, the coach of the Norwegian team, "whose skier had just passed Renner and was now in medal contention" in the country's national sport. When his sportsmanship received considerable media attention, Wise quotes Hakensmoen as responding simply, "Our policy is to help others when they need help." Wise quotes Hakensmoen's observation that "winning is not everything in sport. What win is it if you achieve your goal but don't help somebody when you should have helped them?" The coach expressed surprised that people wanted to talk to him about this. "I was just helping a girl who was in big trouble. If you saw her you would do the same," said Hakensmoen.

Wise asks the question: Should one assist an opponent even if it costs your nation a medal? Commented Hakensmoen: "How can you be proud of a medal if you win when someone else's equipment is not working? You have to help." Using the borrowed pole, Renner recovered and her Canadian team won the silver medal while the Norwegian team finished fourth. Yet, observes Wise, "Not one person in Norway has sent Hakensmoen an angry letter about costing his country a medal. Quite the opposite. Norwegians have applauded his sportsmanship, as have Canadians."

Honor and integrity were on display on April 18, 2010, at the PGA's Verizon Heritage Classic tournament in Hilton Head, South Carolina. According to an account of the incident on ESPN.com the following day, golfer Brian Davis "couldn't deny what he saw and knew he was honor-bound to tell the world." Davis and Jim Furyk were tied for the lead after the final round, necessitating a playoff. A shot by Davis on the first playoff hole went astray and landed in the rough among weeds and reeds. When he tried to hit it out, his club "ticked a loose reed on his back swing." Although the violation was "indiscernible but for slow-motion replays," Davis saw the reed move out of the corner of his eye, called it to the attention of officials, and called a two-stroke penalty on himself that gave Furyk the victory. The difference between winning and second place — more $400,000 — was significant. Praising Davis' honesty, the PGA Tour tournament director said, "What Davis lost on the course will be regained in his reputation for his honorable act," adding, "he's class, first class." Winner Furyk commented that he knew it was "a tough loss for him and I respect and admire what he did."

Davis' decision to call the penalty on himself is reminiscent of a similar act of sportsmanship by golfer J. P. Hayes. As reported on ESPN.com on November 19, 2008, Hayes, while trying to qualify for the PGA Tour, "discovered that on two shots on one hole, he had unwittingly used a prototype ball not approved for competition by the United States Golf Association." The error was not discovered until Hayes was back in his hotel room after the round. "Hayes had a choice: He could have said nothing and kept playing [the next day], with no one aware of his mistake. Or, he could turn himself in and let his mistake cost him a PGA Tour card. He chose the latter." Hayes refused to blame his disqualification from the qualifying tournament on anyone else or to consider his act of sportsmanship especially praiseworthy. "I would say anyone out here [on the PGA Tour] would have done the same thing."

Those involved with vintage base ball share the sense of fair play demonstrated by one ironman competitor helping another fix a flat and a coach providing a competitor with a ski pole to replace a broken one. Grounded in the competitive but sportsmanlike atmosphere of mid-nineteenth-century base ball, most vintage players would act in a similar manner. The actions of golfers who call penalties on themselves are similar to the expectations of most vintage players. In this spirit, vintage base ball players were not surprised (as many sports fans around the country were) by events that transpired in the April 2008 women's college softball game between Central Washington and Western Oregon.

In a game that will forever live in the annals of good sportsmanship, the two college teams were battling for the conference championship and a bid to the NCAA tournament when they met in a double-header. In the second inning of the second game, Western Oregon right fielder Sara Tucholsky was at bat, with a 0–1 count with two runners on base. As reported by Brian Meehan in the April 29, 2008, issue of *The Oregonian*, she "smashed the next pitch over the center field fence for an apparent three-run home run." Tucholsky rounded first as the ball cleared the fence but missed the bag and "stopped abruptly to return and touch it. But something in her right knee gave way and she collapsed on the base path."

The story of what happened next was picked up by the national media far from Central's home field in Ellensburg, Washington. As reported in George Vecsey's account in the April 30, 2008, edition of the *New York Times*, "The umpires ruled that if Tucholsky could not make it around the bases, two runs would score but she would be credited with only a single." As Western coach Pam Knox paused to analyze the unusual situation, Vecsey reports that Mallory Holtman, the Central Washington first baseman "said words that brought a chill to everybody who heard them: 'Excuse me, would it be O.K. if we carried her around and she touched each bag?'" While Tucholsky, unable to continue around the bases under her own power, could not be assisted by members of her own team, "the umpires said nothing in the rule book precluded help from the opposition."

At that point, "Holtman and the Central Washington shortstop, Liz Wallace, lifted Tucholsky, hands crossed under her, and carried her to second base, and gently lowered her so she could touch the base. Then Holtman and Wallace started to giggle, and so did Tucholsky, through her tears, and the three of them continued this odd procession to third base and home to a standing ovation."

Western Oregon won the game 4–2, sweeping the double-header, but this game will be long remembered for the extraordinary act of sportsmanship by the Central Washington players. As in the case of Norway's Coach Hakensmoen, Vecsey reports, "Holtman downplayed her role, which her coach said is typical" for her. "In the end, it is not about winning and losing so much," Holtman said. "It was about this girl. She hit it over the fence and was in pain and she deserved a home run.... This is a huge experience I will take away. We are not going to remember if we won or lost, we are going to remember this kind of stuff that shows the character of our team. It is the best group of girls I've played with. I came up with the idea, but any girl on the team would have done it." Speaking of Holtman, Wallace, and the rest of coach Gary Frederick's Central Washington team, an appreciative Tucholsky said, "Those girls did something awesome.... It makes you look at athletes in a different way. It is not always about winning but rather helping someone in a situation like that." The story was also not forgotten by the national media. In July, Central Washington's Holtman and Wallace, along with Western Oregon's Tucholsky, were honored as winners of the ESPY Award for the year's "Best Moment" in sports. A photo depicting the notable event appeared on a prominent billboard in Times Square. While many sportsmanlike deeds go unnoticed, this one received the national recognition it fully deserved.

Vintage base ball, when represented by the many teams that value the gentlemanly behavior and sportsmanship that were part of the nineteenth-century game, continues to convey a similar message of sportsmanship and respect for opponents. The vintage base ball community is inspired and encouraged by participants in other sports who bring the same values to their competitive events as vintage players bring to the base ball field.

The period that began around 1845, when the Knickerbockers first wrote down the rules for the game, and continued through the tumultuous decade of the 1860s, was an eventful epoch in American history. It was the time when the spirit of Manifest Destiny resulted in the extension of the boundaries of the country all the way to the Pacific. It was also the time when territorial expansion became thoroughly intertwined with all the important social, economic, and political issues that eventually culminated in the Civil War. For many time-traveling spectators, the period when the New York Game emerged as the national pastime and spread throughout the country is a fascinating era to visit. Many vintage base ball participants enjoy learning more about the historical context of the period being re-created on the ball field, including the norms of gentlemanly behavior, good manners, and sportsmanship.

The period from the 1840s through the 1860s was also an interesting time in American literature. As the Knickerbockers and the other early clubs were creating the game that would become a national institution, many of the classics of American literature were also being created—Hawthorne's *The Scarlet Letter* (1850), Melville's *Moby Dick* (1851), Harriet Beecher Stowe's *Uncle Tom's Cabin* (1852), and Longfellow's lyric poems "The Village Blacksmith" (1841) and "Paul Revere's Ride" (1860). James Fenimore Cooper, Washington Irving, and Ralph Waldo Emerson had already established their literary reputations and continued to be prolific writers in this era. Some members of the vintage base ball community find it enjoyable to re-read some of these classics to get a feel for the period represented in the vintage ball games. Walt Whitman is perhaps best remembered for *Leaves of Grass* (1855) but is appreciated in the vintage base ball community for enthusiastically embracing the new game of base ball, as expressed in this exuberant and often-quoted passage: "I see great things in baseball. It's our game—the American game. It will take our people out-of-doors, fill them with oxygen, give them a larger physical stoicism. Tend to relieve us from being a nervous, dyspeptic set. Repair these losses, and be a blessing to us." Whitman's words capture the character and value of the vintage game. Reflecting on base ball in a conversation with Horace Traubel, Whitman said, "It's our game; that's the chief fact in connection with it: America's game; it has the snap, go, fling of the American atmosphere; it belongs as much to our institutions, fits into them as significantly as our Constitution's laws; is just as important in the sum total of our historic life." Whitman's words reinforce the beliefs of many in the vintage base ball community regarding the game's almost magical qualities. His words also continue to inspire them to enjoy the game to the fullest every time they get a chance to be outdoors on the ball diamond on a beautiful day.

In September 1845, when the Knickerbockers were getting organized in lower Manhattan and writing their rules, Henry David Thoreau was about three months into his two-year experiment of living the simple life on Walden Pond near Concord, Massachusetts. Thoreau has left us with an inspirational passage and, although it does not refer directly to baseball, it does speak eloquently to vintage base ball's mission of re-creating the honorable way gentlemen conducted themselves on the athletic field. Thoreau said, "If you would convince a man that he does wrong, do right. Men will believe what they see." The vintage base ball community knows that its audience is, of course, composed of more than "men." People of all ages and genders will "believe what they see" when they watch a game of base ball "as it was meant to be played." Seeing a runner acknowledge he was out, noticing a player "silently acquiesce" when the umpire's call goes against him on as close play, or witnessing the members of one team cheer an exceptional play by a player on the other team, they will perhaps begin to think more deeply about the nature of competitive sports.

Participants in vintage base ball enjoy the pure fun of playing an exhilarating game while simultaneously presenting an authentic, entertaining, and engaging lesson in American history. By modeling the good manners and gentlemanly conduct of nineteenth-century players, they also impart a persuasive and beneficial lesson in civility and sportsmanship that will endure long after the clubs have exchanged the traditional three cheers at the end of the match, respectfully congratulating each other on a well-played game.

25

Huzzah for the National Game!

The vintage base ball community is just that — a community of players, umpires, scorers, interpreters, researchers, museum professionals, and their families who share an interest in base ball history and have a great affection for the national pastime. Whether the match is played in a light spring rain, the hot summer sun, or the crisp fall air, game day is a special occasion. Every match is different, featuring new places to visit, a reunion with old friends on another vintage team, and a few unexpected plays that are retold again and again.

Sometimes a match is particularly memorable for both the participants and the spectators. As I think back on the hundreds of vintage base ball games I have enjoyed, one day stands out as representative of them all. The Ohio Village Muffins pointed their carriages northwest for the annual match with the Great Black Swamp Frogs of Sylvania, Ohio, at picturesque Sauder Village in Archbold, Ohio. With its nineteenth-century appearance and ambiance, Sauder Village, like the Muffins' home grounds at Ohio Village, provides an excellent setting for an 1860 game.

On this particular August day, there was a large and enthusiastic crowd in the stands along the first- and third-base lines. The throng was welcomed by experienced umpire Richard Schuricht of the Muffins, who conducted the opening ceremonies. Because he was "wired for sound," he was able to provide information on the rules, equipment, and early history of the national pastime throughout the match, keeping the audience entertained and engaged with his usual blend of dignity and good humor.

When the game began, the Sylvania nine jumped out to a 4–0 lead in the first inning, and tallied a total of seven aces in the early innings. The Muffins, through a combination of good defense and timely hitting, held the Frogs in check and cut the margin to 7–6 in the eighth. But just as an exciting comeback win by the Muffins seemed possible, the Great Black Swamp Frogs rallied in the top of the ninth for four additional runs and went on to win, 11–6.

The game proceeded at a brisk pace and was marked by good striking and a number of excellent defensive plays by both teams. This kept the crowd interested and involved in the progress of the game. They asked many questions about the way base ball was played in 1860, shared some baseball stories of their own, and appreciated the enthusiasm for the game shown by both clubs. Everyone especially enjoyed an unusual and humorous play that developed when a line drive hit to right field went through the open door of a barn. The right fielder disappeared from view for several seconds, scrambling to locate the ball in the hay while the runners dashed around the bases trying to score before he found it.

In the closing ceremonies, Captain Green of the Muffins graciously acknowledged the spectators for attending and enduring the heat, thanked Sauder Village for the invitation

An interesting feature of the field at Sauder Village is that a ball that bounds off the barn or goes through the barn door is still in play.

to play in such a fine setting, and congratulated our long-time playing partners, the Great Black Swamp Frogs, on their victory, won fair and square. In his remarks, Craig Stough, the captain of the Sylvania Club, eloquently pointed out that the Muffins and Frogs had been meeting in friendly competition for eighteen seasons. In his sincere and heart-felt comments, he thanked the Muffins for introducing the sport of vintage base ball to the Great Black Swamp Frogs in 1991, concluding, "We appreciate it very much and we have enjoyed every minute of it." The clubs then exchanged three cheers with an extra round for the spectators.

Following the match, the players and their families enjoyed exploring the buildings, livestock areas, exhibits, and shops of the village, especially the ice cream parlor. While walking though the village in uniform, my teammates and I were approached by spectators who expressed how much they had enjoyed the experience. From those conversations, I was struck by the fact that each person had seen the game from a slightly different perspective, and would take away different but complementary memories at the end of the day. As vintage players know, a match is a combination of an exciting base ball game, an entertaining history lesson, and a demonstration of sportsmanship and good manners — all components that were noticed by the spectators.

While browsing in the general store, a knowledgeable baseball fan asked about the advent of baseball gloves and expressed great admiration for the barehanded defensive skills evident in the close and well-played game he had just witnessed. "I couldn't believe it when that ball was hit over your outfielder's head and he ran back and caught it one-handed over his shoulder on the first bound," he recalled. "And that barehanded catch the first baseman made when he grabbed that hard throw on the short hop to complete that double play—that was something!" Since he enjoyed the game so much and said he was from Cincinnati, I told him about two clubs in his area, the 1869 Red Stockings and the Buckeyes, and he expressed great interest in checking their schedules and attending more games.

A couple from Crawford County, Ohio, stopped me to say how much they had enjoyed the match as an example of history-oriented family entertainment. They said they were active in their local historical society and were planning a major event for the following summer. They asked if it would be possible for the Muffins to come to their hometown and appear at the local festival. They thought 1860s base ball would be a great fit for their community celebration. I was happy to provide the appropriate contact information and encouraged them to get in touch soon, as the team was already scheduling playing dates for next season.

Near the entrance to the gift shop, a woman stopped me to say how much she and her husband had enjoyed the game and, commenting on the heat, expressed admiration for our willingness to maintain historical accuracy by wearing long-sleeved shirts with ties. We chatted about the uniform styles of the 1860s and the more formal manners and customs of that era. She expressed regret over the apparent decline of gentlemanly behavior in modern society. "I have to keep reminding my grandson not to wear his hat indoors," she commented as she thanked the Muffins for being models of traditional good manners.

As the Muffin traveling party gathered in the parking lot to plan where all would stop for dinner together on the long drive home, a player new to the program remarked how much he and his family enjoyed both the well-played game before a large crowd and the educational experience of visiting the village. He said he would plan to arrive earlier next year to allow more time to visit the exhibits and craft shops before the game. While the Muffins happened to come out on the short end of the score in the match, it was clear from all these positive comments that the game had been a success. Win or lose, it was a great day for vintage base ball.

Huzzah for the national game!

Bibliography

Alvarez, Mark. *The Old Ball Game*. Alexandria, VA: Redefinition, 1990.
American Association of Museums. "Facilities and Risk Management." www.aam-us.org.
Angell, Roger. *Let Me Finish*. Orlando, FL: Harcourt, 2006.
_____. "The Sporting Scene: Dinosaur." *New Yorker*, August, 17, 1992.
Ardell, Jean Hastings. *Breaking into Baseball: Women and the National Pastime*. Carbondale: Southern Illinois University Press, 2005.
Associated Press. "Baseball Coach Convicted of Two Lesser Counts." www.espn.com, September 14, 2006.
_____. "Brand Rips Schools for Lack of Black Coaches." www.espn.com, January 6, 2007.
_____. "Brian Davis' Playoff Penalty Gives Jim Furyk the Verizon Heritage Title." www.espn.com, April 19, 2010.
_____. "Dad Flings Son's Opponent Out of Wrestling Ring." www.espn.com, February 15, 2007.
_____. "IOC Strips Abrahamian's Bronze Medal for Tantrum." www.espn.com, August 16, 2008.
_____. "Students Drop Differences, Then Ask Teams To." www.espn.com, March 24, 2005.
_____. "T-Ball Coach to Stand Trial for $25 Offer to Bean Player." www.espn.com, September 11, 2006.
_____. "Thumbtack Prank Backfires on Prep Football Player." www.espn.com, September 23, 2006.
_____. "Youth Coach Gets Prison in Autistic Player's Beaning." www.espn.com, October 12, 2006.
"Bad Behavior Cited In Youth Sports Study." *USA Today*, November 9, 2005.
Balto's True Story. www.baltostruestory.com.
Bartlett, John Russell. *Dictionary of Americanisms: A Glossary of Words and Phrases Usually Regarded as Peculiar to the United States*. Boston: Little, Brown, 1889.
Base Ball Discovered. MLB.com, 2009.
"Baseball Cards 1877–1914." American Memory, Library of Congress Exhibit. www.memory.loc.gov.
Bay Area Vintage Base Ball. www.eteamz.com/bavb.
Berlage, Gai Ingham. *Women in Baseball: The Forgotten History*. Westport, CT: Praeger, 1994.
Block, David. *Baseball Before We Knew It: A Search for the Roots of the Game*. Lincoln: University of Nebraska Press, 2005.
Brady, Erik, and Jim Halley. "The Blowup Over Blowouts." *USA Today*, February 4, 2009.
_____. "Even in Ivy League, Athletes Behave Badly." *USA Today*, October 20, 2006.
Brand, Myles. "2007 State of the Association." www.ncaa.org.
Bridal, Tessa. *Exploring Museum Theatre*. Walnut Creek, CA: AltaMira Press, 2004.
Bridges, John. *How to Be a Gentleman: A Contemporary Guide to Common Courtesy*. Nashville: Rutledge Hill Press, 1998.
Brock, Darryl. *If I Never Get Back*. Berkeley, CA: Frog Books, 2007.
Camp, Walter. *Walter Camp's Book of College Sports*. 1893. http://books.google.com.
Cannell, Michael. "Return of the Blade Runners." *Sports Illustrated*, March 10, 1997.
Caple, Jim. "Ichiro's Bats More Than Pieces of Wood." www.espn.com, July 1, 2002.
Ceresi, Frank, and Carol McMains. "Early Baseball in Washington, D.C.: How the Washington Nationals Helped Develop America's Game." *National Treasures*. www.fcassociates.com.
Chadwick, Henry. "The Art of Pitching a Baseball." *Scientific American*, 1886.
_____. "Ball Play: An Exciting Contest at Brooklyn, the Atlantic vs. Mutuals, the Mutuals Victorious by One Run." *New York Clipper*, August 15, 1863.

_____. *The Base Ball Player's Book of Reference: The Revised Rules of the Game for 1867.* New York: J.C. Haney. Reprinted by Henry Ford Company, Dearborn, Michigan, 2003.
_____. *Beadle's Dime Base-Ball Player: A Compendium of the Game.* New York: Irwin P. Beadle, 1860. www.vbba.org.
_____. *The Game of Baseball: How to Learn It, How to Play It, and How to Teach It.* New York: George Munro, 1868.
_____. "On Sportsmanship." *New York Clipper*, August 15, 1863.
"The Champion Nine of the Union Club of Morrisania, New York." *Harper's Weekly*, October 26, 1866.
Charlton, James, et al. *Charlton's Baseball Chronology.* www.BaseballLibrary.com.
Colton, C.C. *Lacon or, Many Things in Few Words, Addressed to Those Who Think.* 1826. Kessinger Publishing Legacy Reprint Series, 2004. http://books.google.com.
Commonwealth Vintage Dancers. www.vintagedancers.org.
Coster, Helen. "Revisionist Skiing." *Forbes/Forbes Life*, December 12, 2008.
"The County Fair: Fifth and Last Day." *Columbus Morning Journal*, September 16, 1867.
"A Cross-Disciplinary Glossary of Terms for Historic Hobbyists." www.historicgames.com.
Cullinane, Kevin E. "Batter Up: Muffins of Ohio Are Playing Baseball Like It Used to Be." *The Wall Street Journal*, September 10, 1992.
Cunningham, Bill. "Evening Hours; Memorable Parties of 2009." *New York Times*, January 3, 2010.
_____. "Evening Hours; Newport Nostalgia." *New York Times*, August 9, 2009.
Damon, Johnny. Quoted in "American League Notes," *USA Today*, April 9, 2009.
"Davis Concedes Playoff to Champ Furyk." www.espn.com, April 18, 2010.
della Cava, Marco R. "Old Mountain Men Don't Fade Away." *USA Today*, November 25, 2003.
Dickson, Paul. *The Joy of Keeping Score: How Scoring the Game Has Influenced and Enhanced the History of Baseball.* New York: Walker, 1996.
_____. *The New Dickson Baseball Dictionary.* San Diego: Harcourt Brace, 1999.
Domenici, Thelma. "Practical Advice: Is Removing Hat in Class a Sign of Respect?" *Columbus Dispatch*, May 24, 2007.
Egner, Mike. "The Evolution of the Baseball Glove." *The Vintage & Classic Baseball Collector.* July-August 1998.
Enders, Eric. "Women's Baseball Game, Peterboro, New York (1868)." www.ericenders.com/wib.htm.
Evans, Caitlin. "Replaying History." *USA Weekend*, May 5–7, 2006.
"Evolution of Baseball Equipment." www.19cbaseball.com/equipment.html.
Fesolowich, Tom. "Upon Closer Inspection." *The Base Ball Player's Chronicle: A Quarterly Publication of the Vintage Base Ball Association*, Winter 2005.
Fimrite, Ron. "Baseball the Way It Should Be." US Airways' *Attaché*, August 1997.
Garber, Greg. "Youth Team Plays High Price in Win-At-All-Costs Game." www.espn.com, August 14, 2006.
Gems, Gerald R., Linda Borish, and Gertrud Pfister. *Sports in American History: From Colonization to Globalization.* Champaign, IL: Human Kinetics, 2008.
Gershman, Michael. *Diamond: The Evolution of the Ballpark.* New York: Houghton Mifflin, 1993.
Glanz, James. "The Crack of the Bat: Acoustics Takes on the Sounds of Baseball." *New York Times*, June 26, 2001.
Glass, Keith. *Taking Shots: Tall Tales, Bizarre Battles, and the Incredible Truth About the NBA.* New York: HarperCollins, 2007.
Goldstein, Warren. *Playing for Keeps: A History of Early Baseball.* Ithaca, NY: Cornell University Press, 1989.
Goodnow, Cecelia. "'Octavian Nothing,' Tale for Teens Set in 1700s, Is Timely." *Seattle Post Intelligencer*, November 3, 2008.
"The Grand Match Between the Athletic Ball Club of Philadelphia and the Resolute Club of Brooklyn." *Frank Leslie's Illustrated Newspaper*, July 1, 1865.
Grosvenor, Edwin S. "Lovers of Honor." *American Heritage*, Fall 2009.
Hadden, R. Lee. *Reliving the Civil War: A Reenactor's Handbook.* Mechanicsburg, PA: Stackpole Books, 1999.
Hall, Carol. "How Important Is Accurate Reproduction Clothing?" Association of Living History, Farm and Agricultural Museums. www.alhfam.org.
Henneck, Krista. "Quidditch Team Set to Begin Intercollegiate Action." *The Lantern*, June 8, 2009.
Holzer, Harold. "Election Day 1860." *Smithsonian*, November 2008.
Horwitz, Tony. *Confederates in the Attic: Dispatches from the Unfinished Civil War.* New York: Pantheon Books, 1998.

"Hudson-Fulton-Champlain Quadricentennial." Hudson River Maritime Museum. www.hrmm.org.
Idelson, Jeff. "The Complete Hall of Famer.' *National Baseball Hall of Fame and Museum Yearbook 2006.*
Iditarod, Official Site. www.iditarod.com.
James, Bill. *Historical Baseball Abstract.* New York: Villard, 1988.
Jayson, Sharon. "On or Off the Field, It's a Civility War Out There." *USA Today*, November 30, 2004.
Jerome, Marty. *The Complete Runner's Day-by-Day Log and Calendar 2007.* New York: Random House, 2006.
Josephson Institute. "Report Card on American Youth: There's a Hole in Our Moral Ozone and It's Getting Bigger." www.charactercounts.org, November 20, 2008.
"J.P. Hayes Turns Himself In for Using Wrong Ball, DQ'd from PGA Qualifier." www.espn.com, November 19, 2008.
Kalbacker, Warren. "Golf Collectibles." *Country Living*, August 2006.
Keen, Judy. "Museums Pinched by Higher Costs, Fewer Visitors." *USA Today*, August 11, 2006.
Keillor, Garrison. "Play It for Fun." *Prairie Home Companion*, April 27, 2007. www.newsletter@americanpublicmedia.org.
Kinsella, W.P. *Shoeless Joe.* New York: Ballantine, 1982.
"Knickerbocker Rules of 1845: First Rules of Base Ball." *Beadle's Dime Base-Ball Player.* New York: Beadle, 1860.
"The Last Illustration of Woman's Rights — A Female Base-Ball Club at Peterboro, N.Y." *It's the Day's Doings*, 1868. Reprinted at www.ericenders.com/wib.htm.
Listservs: 1860vintagebaseball@yahoogrouops.com (VBBA site) and 19cBB@yahoogroups.com (SABR 19th Century Committee site).
Lloyd, Marion. "Saving a Mayan Game of Sacrifice." *The Chronicle of Higher Education*, December 10, 2004.
Mack, Connie. *My 66 Years in the Big Leagues.* Mineola, NY: Dover Publications, 2009.
Mallozzi, Vincent. "Cheering Section: An Elephant Never Forgets Sportsmanship." *New York Times*, April 23, 2006.
Martin, Jay. *Live All You Can: Alexander Joy Cartwright and the Invention of Modern Baseball.* New York: Columbia University Press, 2009.
Meehan, Brian. "Softball Opponents Offer Unique Display of Sportsmanship." *The Oregonian*, April 29, 2008. Posted on www.thegloryofbaseball.blogspot.com.
Meredith, George. In *The Complete Runner's Day-By-Day Log and Calendar,* by Marty Jerome, et al.
"Miami, FIU Have 31 Suspended for Role in Brawl." www.espn.com, October 15, 2006.
Miklich, Eric. "Evolution of Baseball Equipment." www.19cbaseball.com/equipment.html.
Millen, Patricia. *From Pastime to Passion: Baseball and the Civil War.* Bowie, MD: Heritage Books, 2001.
Mills, Dorothy Seymour, and Harold Seymour. *Baseball: The People's Game.* New York: Oxford University Press, 1990. *See also* Seymour.
"Mormon Teens Re-enact Migration of the 1850s." *Arizona Republic*, January 3, 2003.
Morris, Peter. *But Didn't We Have Fun? An Informal History of Baseball's Pioneer Era, 1843–1870.* Chicago: Ivan R. Dee, 2008.
_____. *Catcher: How the Man Behind the Plate Became an American Folk Hero.* Chicago: Ivan R. Dee, 2009.
_____. *A Game of Inches: The Game Behind the Scenes.* Chicago: Ivan R. Dee, 2006.
_____. *A Game of Inches: The Game on the Field.* Chicago: Ivan R. Dee, 2006.
National Baseball Hall of Fame and Museum. "Dressed to the Nines: A History of the Baseball Uniform." www.baseballhalloffame.org.
Nemec, David. *The Officials Rules of Baseball: An Anecdotal Look at the Rules of Baseball and How They Came to Be.* Guilford, CT: Lyons, 1999.
New England Vintage Base Ball. www.newenglandvintagebaseball.com.
Newman, Mark. "Documentary Shows Game's Origins." May 2009, www.mlb.com.
Newton, David. "JJ and Carl Put on a Nice Show in Miami on Thursday, Way Too Nice." www.espn.com, November 14, 2008.
"Niagara Festival to Include Largest Kite in the World." *Columbus Dispatch*, September 17, 2006.
Nightengale, Bob. "St. Louis: Baseball's Diamond of a City." *USA Today Sports Weekly*, July 8–15, 2009.
Nucciarone, Monica. *Alexander Cartwright: The Life Behind the Baseball Legend.* Lincoln: University of Nebraska Press, 2009.

Oppegaard, Brett. "Take Me Out to the Ballgame." *The Columbian*, August 19, 2005.
Orem, Preston D. *Baseball (1845–1881) from the Newspaper Accounts*. Altadena, CA: Self published, 1961.
Peverelly, Charles A. *The Book of American Pastimes*. 1866. Reprinted Whitefish, MT: Kessinger, 2008.
Phillips, Joe. "Glove Story." *Beckett Vintage Sports*, Fall 1996.
Plumas Ski Club. www.plumasskiclub.org.
Pollifrone, Billy. "Homemade Lemon Peel." In "Making Your Own Equipment," www.vbba.org.
Porter, David, ed. *The Bibliographic Dictionary of American Sports: Baseball*. Westport, CT: Greenwood, 2000.
Public Broadcasting System. "Frontier Houses: About the Project." www.pbs.org.
Rice, Grantland. "Alumnus Football." In *Only the Brave and Other Poems*. New York: A.S. Barnes, 1941.
_____. "Game Called." Version printed in the *New York Sun*, August 17, 1948. Another version appears in *Base-Ball Ballads*, edited by Gary Mitchem and Mark Durr. Jefferson, NC: McFarland, 2005.
Robson, John, ed. *Baird's Manual of American College Fraternities*. Menasha, WI: George Banta, 1963.
Rosciam, Chuck. "Encyclopedia of Baseball Catchers." www.baseballcatchers.com.
Roth, Stacy F. "Past into Present: Effective Techniques for First-Person Historical Interpretation." Reproduced in part by the Association of Living History, Farm and Agricultural Museums. www.alhfam.org.
Rucker, Mark. *Base Ball Cartes: The First Baseball Cards*. Saratoga Springs, NY: Self published, 1988.
Rutledge, John T. *Tally One for Me: Base Ball Song and Chorus*. Cincinnati: F.W. Helmick, 1877.
Ryczek, William J. *Baseball's First Inning: A History of the National Pastime Through the Civil War*. Jefferson, NC: McFarland, 2009.
Schaefer, Robert. "The Lost Art of Fair-Foul Hitting." *The National Pastime: A Review of Baseball History*. Vol. 20. Society for American Baseball Research, 2000.
Schmidt, Barbara. "Mark Twain and Baseball." www.twainquotes.com/TwainBaseball.html.
"School: Blount's Actions 'Reprehensible.'" www.espn.com, September 4, 2009.
Seymour, Harold, and Dorothy Seymour Mills. *Baseball: The Early Years*. New York: Oxford University Press, 1960. *See also Mills*.
Shaw, Thomas. "How Important Is Accurate Reproduction Clothing?" Association for Living History, Farm and Agricultural Museums (ALHFAM) Historic Clothing Committee, vol. 3, no. 4. Fall 1998. www.alhfam.org.
Shieber, Tom. "The Evolution of the Baseball Diamond." *The Baseball Research Journal*. Number 23. Society for American Baseball Research, 1994.
Smith, Jodi R.R. *From Clueless to Class Act: Manners for the Modern Man*. New York: Sterling, 2006.
Society for American Baseball Research. "Protoball Project." www.retrosheet.org/protoball.
Society of Hickory Golfers. www.hickorygolfers.com.
Sotheby's. *The Barry Halper Collection of Baseball Memorabilia: The Early Years*. New York: Sotheby's, 1999.
Spalding, Albert G. *Base Ball: America's National Game*. 1911. Reprinted Lincoln: University of Nebraska Press, 1992.
Strunsky, Steve. "Hamilton-Burr Duel Re-enactment Stays in the Family: Fatal Match-up's 200th Anniversary Marked in N.J." *USA Today*, July 12, 2004.
Sullivan, Dean A., ed. *Early Innings: A Documentary History of Baseball, 1825–1908*. Lincoln: University of Nebraska Press, 1995.
_____, ed. *Middle Innings: A Documentary History of Baseball, 1900–1946*. Lincoln: University of Nebraska Press, 1998.
Swains, Howard. "Wellington Claims Second Ironman Success in Hawaii." www.Guardian.co.uk, October 13, 2008.
Terry, James L. *Long Before the Dodgers: Baseball in Brooklyn, 1855–1884*. Jefferson, NC: McFarland, 2002.
Thoreau, Henry David. Quoted in Lewis S. Dawes, "The Humanism of Thoreau." Original typescript ca. 1895 with autograph corrections by Samuel Jones. www.walden.org.
Tilden, Freeman. "Interpreting Our Heritage." *Exploring Museum Theatre*.
"Trash Talk Your Friends into Fantasy Football." Newsletters@CBSSports.com, July 30, 2009.
Vecsey, George. "Commentary: CWU Softball Players Show Compassion Beyond Sportsmanship." *New York Times*, April 30, 2008.
Vintage Base Ball Association. www.vbba.org.
Waff, Craig B. "Bat and Ball Among the Ladies." *Milwaukee Sentinel and Gazette*, September 4, 1849.
Ward, Geoffrey C., and Ken Burns. *Baseball: An Illustrated History*. New York: Knopf, 1994.

Whitman, Walt. In *Baseball: An Illustrated History*, by Geoffrey C. Ward and Ken Burns. New York: Alfred Knopf, 1994.

_____. In *With Walt Whitman in Camden,* by Horace Traubel, vol. IV, Sculley Bradley, ed. Philadelphia: University of Pennsylvania Press, 1964.

Wiles, Tom. "Ladies Step Out in Numbers to the Ballpark." *Memories and Dreams*, Winter 2004.

Willoughby, Scott. "Longboard Revival Sign of Good Ol' Days." *Denver Post*, March 17, 2008.

Wise, Mike. "Honorable Move Made in a Snap." *Washington Post*, February 26, 2006.

Wilson, Steve. "How Chrissie Wellington Retained Ironman World Title — With a Little Help from Her Friends." www.telegraph.co.uk, October 14, 2008.

Wright, Marshall D. *The National Association of Base Ball Players, 1857–1870*. Jefferson, NC: McFarland, 2000.

Index

Numbers in ***bold italics*** indicate photographs.

advisory board 16, 94
Akron Black Stockings (Ohio) 45, ***76***, 118, 217
Allen, Michael ***214***
Alvarez, Mark 191, 196
American Association of Museums 97
Andersen, Craig ***85***, 362
Andersen, Don ***85***, 114, ***285***
Andersen, Marilyn ***112***, 114
Andersen, Melinda 362
Andersen, Steve ***85***
Angell, Roger 28, 262
Antle, Sharon 113
Ardell, Jean Hastings 113, 117, 119, 122
Armbruster, Joel ***57***, 209; *see also* Phoenix Bat Company
Association for Living History, Farm and Agricultural Museums (ALHFAM) 69, 201
Astifan, Priscilla 113, 254, 294
awards 106–109

background checks 97–98
backstop ***59***, 166, ***167***
Balcom, Ken 16
balls 148–151, ***149***
Bartlett, John Russell 271
base ball cards 44–45, 194
"base ball fraternity" 69; fraternal groups 70
base coaches 9
base running 270–295, ***271***, ***275***, ***285***, ***359***
bases 151–152, ***153***, 285–286, ***285***
bats ***9***, 143–148, ***144***, ***146***
batting 263–270, ***264***, ***266***
Bay Area Vintage Base Ball (California) 58
Bay City Independents Base Ball Club (Michigan) 360
Bellmore Seminoles (Long Island, New York) 16
bench 170; ***314***; *see also* water
Bennett, Pat 114
Bennett, Toby 114
Berlage, Gai Ingham 113, 116, 122

Bevens, Beau ***322***
Block, David 51
Blue Ashlar Club (Worthington, Ohio) 87, ***301***
Bodner, Connie 113, 124–125
Boetticher, Otto 283, 353, ***354***, 355
Borish, Linda 69
bound catch 274, 320
Bowling, Dave ***40***
Braatz, Michael ***301***
Brandon, Dale ***57***, ***348***
Branson, Vickie Tabor 14, 113
Bridal, Tessa 201, 216
Bridges, John 67–68, 132
Brock, Darryl 4–5, 154, 323, 325
Brooklyn Atlantics (Long Island, New York) 81
Brooklyn Excelsiors (New York, 19th century) 197, 294, ***309***
Brooklyn Excelsiors (New York, vintage club) 16
Brooklyn Stars (New York) 81
Brooks, Dave ***57***, ***244***
Brooks Grove Belles (Mumford, New York) 118; *see also* Genesee Country Village and Museum; women
Burke, Sean ***171***
Burns, Ken (film) 41
Burr, Bo 351
But Didn't We Have Fun? see Morris, Peter

Camp, Walter 71, 213
Candlestick Park (San Francisco) ***355***
Capital Club of Columbus (Ohio, 19th century) 61, 127, 170, 212–213, 296–297
Capital Club of Columbus (Ohio, vintage club) ***304***
captain 300–302
Carey Cayugas (Ohio) ***234***
Cartwright, Alexander 11, 52–53, 70, 329, 353; *see also* Nucciarone
catching 236–242, ***234***; equipment 156, 233–236
Ceresi, Frank 23

Chadwick, Henry 54, 96
Champion City Reapers (Springfield, Ohio) 83, ***309***
Chern, Barry ***214***
children ***29***, ***205***, 206–207, 217, ***218***, 219, ***334***–336, 359–***360***; *see also* mascots
Cincinnati Buckeyes (Ohio) 81, 377
Cincinnati Red Stockings (Ohio, 19th century) 4, 56, 127, 134, 154, 170, 197–198, 231, 234, 260, 296–297, 325, 347
Cincinnati Red Stockings (Ohio, vintage club) ***8***, ***57***, 81, ***128***, ***228***, ***244***, ***275***, ***359***, 377
Civil War reenactors 2, 10, 16, 22, 30, 38, ***43***, 46–47, 49, 65, 87, 103, 115, 137, 139, 140, 170, 190, 204, 208, 215, 217, 342–345, ***354***; *see also* Salisbury, North Carolina
Cleveland Blues Base Ball Club (Ohio) ***134***
Clodbuster Base Ball Club (Dayton, Ohio) 41, 68, ***115***, ***146***, ***153***, ***250***; *see also* Lady Clodbusters
Colorado Vintage Base Ball Association 44, 90, 118, ***125***, 352
communication 104–105; handbook 105; online 104; printed programs 41, 208–209; VBBA 19–20; *see also The Muffin Tin*
Cooperstown, New York 5, 10, 11, 13, 51, 83, 350; *see also* Leatherstocking Club; National Baseball Hall of Fame and Museum
courtesy runners 279–280
"Crosley Field" (Blue Ash, Ohio) 350
Curtis, Ed, and Sue 353

Deep River Grinders (Hobart, Indiana) 45, 83, ***84***, 103, 113, 114, ***115***, 157, ***219***, ***223***
definition of vintage base ball 2, 7
DeGeatano, Helen 113
Della Flora, Evan ***27***

385

Della Flora, Michael 27
Della Flora, Tom 27
Diamonds Base Ball Club (Columbus, Ohio) 16, 105, 113, *117*, 118, *122*; see also Ohio Village Muffins; women
Dickson, Paul 7, 14, 167, 195–196, 226, 267, 313
Dieckmann, Al 16
Dieckmann, Bill *228*
Domenici, Thelma 133
Doubleday myth 11
Douglas Dutchers (Michigan) 113, *225*, *275*, *359*
"Dressed to the Nines: A History of the Baseball Uniform" 124, 127, 129, 130, 133, 135, 136, 139

Eclipse Club (Elkton, Maryland) 108
education 361
Egner, Mike 154, 155
Elysian Fields (New Jersey, 19th century) 53, 62, 70–71, 103, 127, 160, 176, 191, 204, 231, 251, 336–337; see also Hoboken
Enders, Eric 120
equipment 143–156, 341
Everett, John *153*, *176*
exercise and fitness 358–359

fair-foul hits 267–268
Farmers' Museum (Cooperstown, New York) 10, 51, 350
Ferguson, Bob 254
Ferguson, J.R. (ball maker) 149
Fesolowich, Tom 16–17
Field of Dreams (movie) 37, 47, 172; Dyersville, Iowa (locale) 103, 351
field of play 8, *48*, *79*, 157–162, *376*; marking 162–*166*; on the road 172–173; see also backstop; bench; scoreboard; water
Fimrite, Ron 158
flags and banners *42*, *84*, *128*, *167*, *214*, 297–298
fly game 269–270
Follin, Mike 217
Ford, Ellen *218*
Forest City Base Ball Club (Chagrin Falls, Ohio) 103, 109, 351, *352*
Forquer, Jackie *112*
Fort Vancouver National Historic Site (Washington) 39, 45, 165
Francis, Dulcy *112*
Freetown Village Singers (Indianapolis, Indiana) 215, *216*
Frias, Dianna 118, *122*
Fulton Mules Base Ball Club (Canal Fulton, Ohio) 73, 83, 118, *132*, 149, 157–158, *167*, *171*, 185, 346–347

Galloway, Jeff 73–74
A Game of Inches: The Game Behind the Scenes see Morris, Peter

A Game of Inches: The Game on the Field see Morris, Peter
Gems, Gerald, Linda Borish, and Gertrud Pfister 69
Genesee Country Village and Museum (Mumford, New York) 22, 80, 113, 118, 158, *297*, 311; Silver Base Ball Park 158
gentleman 66–69, 146–147, 193, 194, 204–205, 287–288; definition 67, 71; other sports 72–73, 323–324; see also sportsmanship
Gershman, Michael 191
Glenhead Zig Zags (Long Island, New York) 16
gloves 152–*156*
Goldstein, Warren 69, 82
Goodnow, Cecelia 210
Graley, Brad *231*
Great Black Swamp Frogs Base Ball Club (Sylvania, Ohio) 18, 83, 375–376
Green, Curt *42*, 360–361, 375
Greenfield Village (Dearborn, Michigan) 41, 45, 57, 81, 157, 346; see also Lah-De-Dah Base Ball Club
Greensboro Patriot Base Ball Club (North Carolina) *53*, 355
Grosvenor, Edwin 364
ground rules 168–170

Hadden, R. Lee 30, 31, 65, 343–344
Hall, Carol 69
Hartmann, Kevin *42*, *266*
Harwell, Ernie 41
hats 130–133
Hayes Presidential Center (Fremont, Ohio) 25, 157, *304*; see also Spiegel Grove Squires
Heitz, Tom 350
Hempstead Eurekas (Long Island, New York) 10, 16
Heppner, Mark *76*
Herold, Nick 5, *40*, *306*, *348*
Hershberger, Richard 13, 287
Hewetson, Priscilla 214
Hicksville Ozones (Long Island, New York) 16
History Center of Olmsted County (Minnesota) 45, 113, 118, 342; see also Rochester Hens; Rochester Roosters
Hoboken (New Jersey) 103, 352–353; see also Elysian Fields
Holbrook, Mark *43*
Holzer, Harold 66
Hoover Sweepers (North Canton, Ohio) *53*, *153*
Horwitz, Tony 344
Hunkele, Linda 114
Hunkele, Paul 25, 114, 151, 165, 179–180, 265
Husman, John 18–19, 83

If I Never Get Back 4, 323, 325; see also Brock, Darryl

Inch, Tom *134*
Indianapolis Blues (Indiana) *333*
infield play 53, 221–*228*, *225*, 359
Inside Sports magazine 42
interpreters *112*, *121*, 201–220, *202*, *211*, *266*, *306*; see also children; music; sutlers

Jacobs Field (Cleveland) *352*, 356
James, Bill 155
Jayson, Sharon 363–364
Johnson, Jim 359–360

Keen, Judy 38
Kent Base Ball Club (Grand Rapids, Michigan) 81
Kimnach, Jim *168*, *202*, 209, 293, *348*
Knickerbocker Base Ball Club (Long Island, New York, vintage club) 16
Knickerbocker Base Ball Club (19th century) 13, 19, 26–27, 52–53, 62, 66, 70–71, 103, 111–112, 124, 130, 287–288, *309*, 321, 325, 329, 336–338, 346
Knickerbocker Rules (1845) 8, 11–12, 18, 53–54, 80–81, 144, 163, 168, 174, 185, 192, 243, 269, 282, 289–290, 321, 326, 358; see also New York Game Rules; rules
Koons, Duane *15*, *40*
Koons, Pam 118

Lady Clodbusters (Dayton, Ohio) 114, *117*, 118; see also Clodbuster Base Ball Club; women
Lady Locks (Akron, Ohio) 118; see also Akron Black Stockings; women
Lah-de-Dah Base Ball Club (Dearborn, Michigan) 41, 45, 108, *234*; home grounds 157; name 81
Large, Julie *112*, 361
Large, Mark *194*, *247*, 361, *348*
Laudenbacher, Eric "Red" *53*, 353, 355
leagues 22, 58, 80, 89–91
Leatherstocking Base Ball Club (Cooperstown, New York) 5, 10, 51, 83, 350
Library of Congress "American Memory" 44; see also base ball cards
Loveday, Amos 14

major league baseball 28, 41, 103, 213–214, 351–*352*, 355; All-Star FanFest *356*
Mansfield Club (Middletown, Connecticut) 63, 64
Mansfield Independents Base Ball Club (Ohio) *167*
Martin, Tracy v, *156*, *356*
mascots (bat boys) 207

McMains, Carol 23
merchandise 44–45
Meredith, George 329
Meyers, Sean 354–355
Midwest Living magazine 42
Miller, Mark 83
Mills, Dorothy Seymour 51, 66, 71, 113, 249, 293
Mineola Washingtons (Long Island, New York) 10, 16
Moore, Joel v, *40*
Moore, Keith "Chip" *140*
Morris, Peter: *But Didn't We Have Fun?* 49–50, 51, 52, 82; *A Game of Inches: The Game Behind the Scenes* 160, 167, 245, 324; *A Game of Inches: The Game on the Field* 56, 154, 155, 169, 177, 235, 241, 243, 252, 255, 268, 272, 285, 298
Moyer, Thomas *43*
muffin 14, 83; *see also* Ohio Village Muffins
The Muffin Tin newsletter 104
museums and historical societies 37–42, 46–48; forming a team 80–83; museum theater 201, 216; team affiliation 75–79
music *214*–216

names 81–83
National Association of Base Ball Players 19, 56, 60, 70, 251, 259–260, 269–270
National Baseball Hall of Fame and Museum 5, 11, 29, 39, 51, 107, 111, 120, 155, 323, 350; *see also* "Dressed to the Nines"
Nemec, David 229, 310–311
New York Game Rules: (1848) 184–185; (1854) 278; (1857) 144, 183, 251; (1860) 18, 54–55, 96–97, 162, 169, 174, 177, 178, 180, 189, 243, 269, 271, 276–278, 289; (1865) 55–56, 270; *see also* rules
New York Gothams (New York City, 19th century) 62, 63, 191, 338
New York Gothams (New York City, vintage club) 17, 81
New York Mutuals Base Ball Club (Long Island, New York) 16, 44, 81
Nightwine, Mike *40*, 209, *264*
Nucciarone, Monica 52, 113

O'Brien, Conan 16, 17
Ohio Cup Vintage Base Ball Festival 15, 92, 101, 106, 114, 118, *125*, *176*, 359
Ohio Historical Society (OHS) 3–5, 10, 14–16, 17–18, 23, 41, 94–95, 113, 118, *121*, *214*, *215*, *299*, *356*, 361
Ohio Magazine 42
Ohio Village Muffins (Columbus) 3–5, 7, 10, 14, *15*, 16, 23, *27*, *29*, *40*, 41, *42*, *43*, *48*, *57*, *73*, 83–84, *85*, 86, *102*, 103, 109, *112*, 113, 118, *140*, 141, *168*, *175*, *211*, *231*, *246*, *247*, *250*, *264*, *266*, *285*, *299*, *306*, *309*, *314*, *322*, *334*, 347, *348*, 349, *352*, *354*, *356*, 361, *376*; *see also* Diamonds Base Ball Club
Ohio Village Singers 214, *215*, 217
Old Bethpage Village Restoration (Long Island, New York) 7, 10, 16–17, 22, 57, *59*, *79*, 80, 81
Oldfield, Lee v, 355
Olsen, Gordon 81
Oppegaard, Brett 39
Orem, Preston D. 50, 52, 71–72, 160, 189, 292, 294
Osthaus, Carl 89
outfield play *26*, 229–232, *231*

participation points 109
Peverelly, Charles 24–25, 26, 52, 62–63, 66, 70, 340
Pfister, Gertrud 69
Phillips, Joe 154
Phoenix Bat Company 143, 144, 146
photographs (tintypes) *219*, 332, 346
Pingel, Chris *40*
pitching 242–248, *244*, *246*, *247*; slow or swift 249–262, *250*
players 83–86
post-game activities *21*, 326–338, *333*
practice (field exercise) 99, 299
Prasatek, Anthony 25
pre-game ceremonies *304*, 305–312, *306*, *309*
Priscilla Porter's Astonishing Ladies Base Ball Club (Mumford, New York) 118; *see also* Genesee Country Village and Museum; women
Providence Grays (Rhode Island) 59, 81, 127

Rauch, Steve, and family *205*
recruitment 86–88; retention 100–105, 261; *see also* awards; social events
reenacting: historical 31–33, 65; literary 33; sports 33–35; *see also* Civil War reenactors
Regan, Oulanje *112*
Regular Base Ball Club (Mt. Clemens, Michigan) 25, 114
risk management 94, 97, 172, 191, 268, 300, 339, 341–344; fast pitching 55, 58, 256–257; first aid 172; ground rules 169; liability 76; player safety 235–236; shoes 138; sliding 286–287; spectators 151, 161–162; spikes 136–137; *see also* background checks
Rochester Grangers Base Ball Club (Rochester Hills, Michigan) *21*, 25, 44, 89, 325, *333*, *360*
Rochester Hens (Minnesota) 45, 118; *see also* History Center of Olmsted County; women
Rochester Roosters (Minnesota) 44, 45, 118, 342; *see also* History Center of Olmsted County
Rucker, Mark 44, 127; *see also* base ball cards; uniforms
rules *see* Knickerbocker Rules; National Association of Base Ball Players; New York Game Rules; town ball and Massachusetts game
Ryczek, William 13, 63, 338

St. Croix Base Ball Club (Stillwater, Minnesota) 10, 20, 254
St. Louis Perfectos (Missouri) *26*, 158, *176*, *271*, *333*
Salisbury, North Carolina *112*, 353, *354*, 355; *see also* Union Soldiers at Salisbury N.C.
Salisbury Confederate Prison Association (SCPA) 353
sample game 313–325
Santry, Joe 347
Sauder Village (Archbold, Ohio) *375*
Schaefer, Robert 267–268
scheduling games 88
Schmitt, Mary Jane 113
Schuricht, Richard *30*, *43*, 105, *166*, *175*, 184, 185–186, 375
Schutz, Ken *134*
scoreboard 158, 167–*168*, 183, 196
scorer *155*, 188, 194–200, *348*; clothing 189–190; equipment 190–*194*; rules 188–189
Seacliff Idlewilds (Long Island, New York) 16
Seymour, Dorothy 51, 66, 71, 113, 249, 293; *see also* Mills, Dorothy Seymour
Seymour, Harold 51, 66, 71, 113, 249, 293
Sharon Woods Shamrocks (Sharonville, Ohio) 351
Shattuck, Debra 112, 113, 116
Shearer, Joanna 45, *84*, 113, 114, *115*
Shieber, Tom 123, 152, 164, 176, 191, 267
shoes 136–139; *see also* risk management
Shuman, Andy *73*, 100–101, *250*
Shuman, Ed *73*, 83, 149–150, 185, 346
Shuman, Tom *73*
Simpson, Chad *301*
sliding 284–289
Smith, Doug 17, 18, 118, *211*
Smith, Jodi 126
Smithsonian Magazine 16, 42
social events 73–74, 95, 105–106, 114–115, 336–338
Society for American Baseball Research (SABR) 75, 112, 176, 267, *355*, 356

Spiegel Grove Squires (Fremont, Ohio) 25, 157, *304*
The Sporting News 41
Sports Illustrated 15, 41
sportsmanship 9–10, 26–28, 52, 65–69, 72–73, 104, 212–213, 363–373; college and Olympic sports 367–369; competitive championships 90, 92; "friendly" games 62–64; swift pitching 258–259; youth sports 365–366; *see also* gentleman
"Star Spangled Banner" 324
stealing 289–295
Stough, Craig 83, 376
Sullivan, Dean A. 52
sutlers 208
Swains, Howard 370

"Take Me Out to the Ball Game" 40, 324
tally bell *194*, 347, *348*, 349
Terry, James 294, 325, 338
Thayer, Ernest, "Casey at the Bat" 186
Thilgen, Dean 10, 20, 165, 254
Thompson, Barb *102*
Thompson, Dennis *102*, *356*
Thompson, Frank *246*, *348*
Thorn, John 10, 254, 285
Tilden, Freeman 201; *see also* Bridal
tournaments and festivals 22, 91–93, 293, 311, 342, 352; *see also* Ohio Cup
town ball and Massachusetts game 10, 11, 13, 18, 50–52, 54, 189, 282, 290, 353
training seminars 95–96
travel 103–104, 159–160, 172–173, 350–357
Trudeau, Charley "Lefty" 144, 146, 209; *see also* Phoenix Bat Company
Twain, Mark 12, 207

umpire *30*, 90, 174–187, *176*, 364; announcements *175*, 183; clothing 175–176; fines 184–185; *see also* post-game activities; pre-game activities
uniforms *15*, *73*, 124–142, *125*, *134*; accessories 139–141; accommodations 340–341; bloomers 120, 122; choosing 126–128; knickers 133–135; women 119–*122*; *see also* "Dressed to the Nines;" hats; Rucker; shoes
Union Soldiers at Salisbury N.C. (painting) 123, 239, 283, 353, *354*; *see also* Salisbury, North Carolina

Vintage Base Ball Association (VBBA) 7, 17–20, 23, 60, 64, 75, 88, 89, 97, 104, 129, 135, 144, 146, 149, 150, 156, 281, 325, 339, 356; mission statement 19, 72

Waff, Craig 119
The Wall Street Journal 15, 39, 41, 361–362
Ward, Geoffrey, and Ken Burns 116, 184; *see also* women
Wasserman, Jerry 25
water 170, *171*, 172
Wells, John 15, 190, 192–194; *see also The Muffin Tin*
Wells, Mardi 15, 104, 105
Wertz, Chuck "Woody" 209, *334*
Whitt, Jason *40*
Wiles, Tim 111
Wilson, Jim 114, *115*
Wilson, Melissa 114
women 111–123; interpreters *112*, *121*, 216–217; on men's teams 115; scorekeepers 114; teams 115–118, *117*, *122*; *see also* Ardell, Jean Hastings; Berlage, Gai Ingham; uniforms
Woodstock Actives (Ontario, Canada) 18
Wright, Marshall D. 82, 88, 108, 197–198, 260, 328

www.ingramcontent.com/pod-product-compliance
Lightning Source LLC
Chambersburg PA
CBHW081533300426
44116CB00015B/2620